THE WILEY-BLACKWELL COMPANION TO POLITICAL SOCIOLOGY

WILEY-BLACKWELL COMPANIONS TO SOCIOLOGY

The *Wiley-Blackwell Companions to Sociology* provide introductions to emerging topics and theoretical orientations in sociology as well as presenting the scope and quality of the discipline as it is currently configured. Essays in the Companions tackle broad themes or central puzzles within the field and are authored by key scholars who have spent considerable time in research and reflection on the questions and controversies that have activated interest in their area. This authoritative series will interest those studying sociology at advanced undergraduate or graduate level as well as scholars in the social sciences and informed readers in applied disciplines.

The Blackwell Companion to Major Classical Social Theorists
Edited by George Ritzer

The Blackwell Companion to Major Contemporary Social Theorists
Edited by George Ritzer

The Blackwell Companion to Criminology
Edited by Colin Sumner

The Blackwell Companion to Social Movements
Edited by David A. Snow, Sarah A. Soule, and Hanspeter Kriesi

The Blackwell Companion to the Sociology of Families
Edited by Jacqueline Scott, Judith Treas, and Martin Richards

The Blackwell Companion to Law and Society
Edited by Austin Sarat

The Blackwell Companion to the Sociology of Culture
Edited by Mark Jacobs and Nancy Hanrahan

The Blackwell Companion to Social Inequalities
Edited by Mary Romero and Eric Margolis

The New Blackwell Companion to Social Theory
Edited by Bryan S. Turner

The New Blackwell Companion to Medical Sociology
Edited by William C. Cockerham

The New Blackwell Companion to the Sociology of Religion
Edited by Bryan S. Turner

The Wiley-Blackwell Companion to Major Social Theorists
Edited by George Ritzer & Jeffrey Stepnisky

The Wiley-Blackwell Companion to Sociology
Edited by George Ritzer

The Wiley-Blackwell Companion to Political Sociology
Edited by Edwin Amenta, Kate Nash, and Alan Scott

Also available:

The Blackwell Companion to Globalization
Edited by George Ritzer

The New Blackwell Companion to the City
Edited by Gary Bridge and Sophie Watson

THE WILEY-BLACKWELL COMPANION TO

Political Sociology

EDITED BY

**EDWIN AMENTA, KATE NASH,
AND ALAN SCOTT**

A John Wiley & Sons, Ltd., Publication

Registered Office
John Wiley & Sons Ltd, The Atrium, Southern Gate, Chichester, West Sussex, PO19 8SQ, UK

Editorial Offices
350 Main Street, Malden, MA 02148-5020, USA
9600 Garsington Road, Oxford, OX4 2DQ, UK
The Atrium, Southern Gate, Chichester, West Sussex, PO19 8SQ, UK

For details of our global editorial offices, for customer services, and for information about how to
apply for permission to reuse the copyright material in this book please see our website at
www.wiley.com/wiley-blackwell.

Library of Congress Cataloging-in-Publication Data

The Wiley-Blackwell companion to political sociology / edited by Edwin Amenta, Kate Nash,
and Alan Scott.
    p. cm.
  Includes bibliographical references and index.
  ISBN 978-1-4443-3093-9 (cloth)
1. Political sociology. I. Amenta, Edwin, 1957- II. Nash, Kate, 1958- III. Scott, Alan, 1956-
JA76.W483 2012
  306.2–dc23

                                                                      2011036318

A catalogue record for this book is available from the British Library.

Set in 10/12.5pt Sabon by Thomson Digital, Noida, India
Printed and bound in Malaysia by Vivar Printing Sdn Bhd

1 2012

Contents

CONTENTS

B. Structures of Participation

Notes on Contributors

Edwin Amenta is Professor of Sociology, Political Science and History, University of California, Irvine. He has published extensively on political sociology, social movements, historical and comparative sociology, and the news media. He is the author of *When Movements Matter: The Townsend Plan and the Rise of Social Security* (Princeton, 2008), which analyses the political consequences of social movements. He is also co-author of 'All the Movements Fit to Print' (*American Sociological Review*, 2009), which accounts for why social movements receive newspaper coverage.

Valérie Amiraux is on leave from her position as Senior Research Fellow at the CNRS and currently Associate Professor at the Department of Sociology of the University of Montreal where she holds the Canada Research Chair for the study of religious pluralism and ethnicity. Since 1992, she has been working on Muslims in Europe, first by looking at transnational mobilizations of Muslim organizations based in Germany and active in Turkey (*Acteurs de l'islam entre Allemagne et Turquie. Parcours militants et expériences religieuses*, Paris, L'Harmattan, coll. Logiques politiques, 2001), then, when she was a Jean Monnet fellow at the Robert Schuman Centre for Advanced Studies of the European University Institute (Florence), on the state regulation of Muslim minorities in EU member-states and the religious discrimination experienced by Muslims (*Politics of Visibilities. Young Muslims European Public Spaces*, co-edited with Gerdien Jonker, Bielefeld, Transcript Verlag, 2005).

Arnaldo Bagnasco is Professor of Sociology and the University of Turin. A leading economic sociologist, he is well known for his work on economic development and the Third Italy; for example, *La problematica territoriale dello sviluppo Italian* (Il Mulino, 1977). His publications in English include *Small Firms and Economic Development in Europe* (co-edited with C.F. Sabel, Pinter, 1995); *Cities in Contemporary Europe* (co-edited with Patrick Le Galès, CUP, 2000); and 'Social capital in changing capitalism', *Social Epistemology* 17(4) 2003.

David Beetham is Professor Emeritus, University of Leeds, and Associate Director, Democratic Audit. From early work on Max Weber (*Max Weber and the Theory of Modern Politics*, 1974) he moved to the systematic study of Weberian themes (*Bureaucracy*, 1987; *The Legitimation of Power*, 1991). Later work has concentrated on the theory and practice of democracy, and its relation to human rights (*Democracy and Human Rights*, 1999; *Democracy under Blair*, 2002; *Democracy: A Beginner's Guide*, 2005; *Parliament and Democracy in the Twenty-First Century*, 2006; *Assessing the Quality of Democracy*, 2008). A revised and updated edition of *The Legitimation of Power* is to be published in 2012.

Didier Bigo is MCU Research Professor at Sciences-Po, Paris/CERI and Professor in the Department of War Studies, King's College London. He is editor of the journal *International Political Sociology* (ISA and Blackwell), editor of *Cultures et Conflits* (l'Harmattan), and co-editor of *Europe's 21st Century Challenge. Delivering Liberty* (with Sergio Carrera, Elspeth Guild and R.B.J. Walker, Ashgate, 2010). A full curriculum vitae can be found at http://www.didierbigo.com.

Antoine Bousquet is a lecturer in International Relations at Birkbeck College, University of London. His research interests include social and political theory, war and political violence, and the history and philosophy of science and technology. He is the author of *The Scientific Way of Warfare: Order and Chaos on the Battlefields of Modernity* (Hurst & Columbia University Press, 2009) and has contributed articles to *International Affairs, Cold War History, Millennium: Journal of International Studies, Cambridge Review of International Affairs*, and *Journal of International Relations and Development*. He is currently working on a monograph on the logistics of military perception.

Peter Breiner is Associate Professor of Political Science at The University at Albany, State University of New York. He is the author of *Max Weber and Democratic Politics* (Cornell University Press, 1996) as well as numerous articles on Weber and thinkers influenced by Weber such as Karl Mannheim. His present work examines the meaning of political equality when it is set in fields of political conflict.

Colin Crouch is Emeritus Professor of Governance and Public Management at the Warwick Business School and External Scientific Member of the Max Planck Institute for the Study of Societies at Cologne. He previously taught sociology at the LSE, and was fellow and tutor in politics at Trinity College, Oxford, and Professor of Sociology at the University of Oxford. Until December 2004 he was Professor of Sociology at the European University Institute, Florence. He is a Fellow of the British Academy and of the Academy of Social Sciences. He is currently leading a European Union research project on the governance of uncertainty and sustainability in labour markets and social policy in European countries. He is former chair and joint editor of *The Political Quarterly*, a former chair of the Fabian Society, and a founder member of Compass. His most recent books include: *Social Change in Western Europe* (1999); *Post-Democracy* (2004); *Capitalist Diversity and Change* (2005); and *The Strange Non-Death of Neoliberalism* (2011).

Jonathan Dean is Lecturer in Political Theory at the University of Leeds. His research covers feminist politics and contemporary debates in social and political theory. He is author of *Rethinking Contemporary Feminist Politics* (Palgrave Macmillan, 2010) and has published in *Contemporary Political Theory*, *The International Feminist Journal of Politics*, *Political Quarterly* and *Feminist Media Studies*.

Donatella della Porta is Professor of Sociology in the Department of Political and Social Sciences at the European University Institute. Among her recent publications are *Social Movements and Europeanization* (with M. Caiani, Oxford University Press, 2009), *Another Europe* (ed., Routledge, 2009); *Democracy in Social Movements* (Palgrave, 2009); *Approaches and Methodologies in the Social Sciences* (with Michael Keating, Cambridge University Press, 2008); *Voices from the Valley*; *Voices from the Street* (Berghan, 2008); *The Global Justice Movement* (Paradigm, 2007); *Globalization from Below* (with Massimiliano Andretta, Lorenzo Mosca and Herbert Reiter, The University of Minnesota Press); *The Policing Transnational Protest* (with Abby Peterson and Herbert Reiter, Ashgate 2006); *Social Movements: An Introduction*, 2nd edn (with Mario Diani, Blackwell, 2006); and *Transnational Protest and Global Activism* (with Sidney Tarrow, Rowman & Littlefield, 2005).

Marc Edelman is Professor of Anthropology at the Graduate Center of the City University of New York and at Hunter College-CUNY, where he is also Chair of the Anthropology Department. He is the author of *The Logic of the Latifundio* (Stanford 1992; in Spanish, Editorial de la Universidad de Costa Rica, 1996) and *Peasants Against Globalization* (Stanford, 1999; Editorial de la Universidad de Costa Rica, 2005); co-author of *Social Democracy in the Global Periphery* (Cambridge University Press, 2007); and co-editor of *The Anthropology of Development and Globalization* (Blackwell, 2005) and *Transnational Agrarian Movements Confronting Globalization* (Wiley-Blackwell, 2009). His current research is on the campaign of transnational agrarian movements to have the United Nations approve a declaration, and eventually a convention, on the rights of peasants.

Jeff Goodwin is Professor of Sociology at New York University. He earned his baccalaureate and doctorate at Harvard and has taught at NYU since 1991. His writings focus on social movements, revolutions and, more recently, terrorism. He is currently finishing a book titled *Why Terror?* His book *No Other Way Out: States and Revolutionary Movements, 1945–1991* (Cambridge University Press, 2001) won the Outstanding Book Prize of the Collective Behavior and Social Movements Section of the American Sociological Association (ASA). He is the co-editor of *The Social Movements Reader* (Wiley-Blackwell, 2nd edn 2009), *Rethinking Social Movements* (Rowman & Littlefield, 2004), and *Passionate Politics: Emotions and Social Movements* (University of Chicago Press, 2001). His article, 'The Libidinal Constitution of a High-Risk Social Movement', *American Sociological Review* 62 (1999), won the Barrington Moore Prize for the best article in the field of comparative-historical sociology from the Comparative-Historical Section of the ASA.

Alan Finlayson is Professor of Social and Political Theory at the University of East Anglia. He is the author or editor of books such as *Making Sense of New Labour*

(Lawrence & Wishart, 2003); *Contemporary Political Thought: A Reader and Guide* (Edinburgh University Press/New York University Press, 2003); and *Democracy and Pluralism: The Political Thought of William E. Connolly* (Routledge, 2007). He is currently conducting research, supported by The Leverhulme Trust, into the theory of political rhetoric and the historical development of political speech in the UK (see www.britishpoliticalspeech.org).

David John Frank is Professor of Sociology and, by courtesy, Education at the University of California, Irvine. He is interested in the cultural infrastructure of world society, especially as it changes over time and varies across national contexts. In substance, he has studied the global rise and diffusion of environmental protection, the worldwide expansion and transformation of higher education, and the global re-conception and reorganization of criminal laws regulating sexual activity. He has degrees in sociology from Stanford University and the University of Chicago. Before coming to Irvine in 2002, he was on the faculty at Harvard University.

Barry Hindess: After many years as a sociologist in Britain, Barry Hindess moved to the Australian National University in 1987 and then to ANU's Research School of Social Sciences, where he learned to pass as a political scientist. He is now Emeritus Professor in ANU's School of Social Sciences. Like many senior academics he has published more than he cares to remember, including *Discourses of Power: From Hobbes to Foucault*; *Governing Australia: Studies in Contemporary Rationalities of Government* (with Mitchell Dean); *Corruption and Democracy in Australia*; *Us and Them: Elites and Anti-Elitism in Australia* (with Marian Sawer); and papers on neoliberalism, liberalism and empire, and the temporalizing of difference.

Ann Hironaka is Associate Professor in the Department of Sociology at the University of California, Irvine. Her research focuses on civil war and military planning. Her book, *Neverending Wars* (Harvard University Press, 2005), provides a world society account for the persistence of contemporary civil wars. She has also co-authored several articles on the international environmental regime, and is currently working on a book that develops a world society perspective on environmental outcomes.

Brenda Holzinger is a PhD Candidate in the Division of Global Affairs at Rutgers University in Newark, New Jersey. Her dissertation addresses issues of global environmental governance, and focuses on the role of transnational social mobilization in securing new or increased political rights for both the individuals and the environments that are permanently disrupted by large-scale hydropower projects. Ms Holzinger is a graduate of Rutgers University School of Law, Camden (JD 1990) and the Eagleton Institute of Politics at Rutgers University, New Brunswick (MA 1989). She completed her undergraduate work at Pomona College in Claremont, California (BA 1986).

Sven E.O. Hort teaches sociology at Linnaeus University, Kalmar and Växjö, and Södertörn University, metropolitan Stockholm, Sweden. He is the author of *Social Policy, Welfare State and Civil Society in Sweden* (Arkiv, 2011).

Bob Jessop is Distinguished Professor of Sociology and Co-Director of the Cultural Political Economy Research Centre at Lancaster University. He is best known for his contributions to state theory, critical political economy, welfare state restructuring and, most recently, work on governance and governance failure. Recent publications include *The Future of the Welfare State* (2002); *Beyond the Regulation Approach* (2006, co-authored with Ngai-Ling Sum); and *State Theory: The Strategic-Relational Approach* (2007). He currently holds a three-year Research Fellowship to study the cultural political economy of crisis-management in relation to the global financial crisis and its relation to the crisis of the state and governance.

Desmond King is Andrew W. Mellon Professor of American Government at the University of Oxford and Fellow of Nuffield College. His publications on state theory, race and American political development and comparative political economy include *In the Name of Liberalism* (Oxford University Press, 1999); *Making Americans: Immigration, Race and the Origins of the Diverse Democracy* (HUP, 2000); *The Unsustainable American State* (co-edited, Oxford University Press, 2009); and *Still a House Divided: Race and Politics in Obama's America* (co-authored with Rogers M. Smith, PUP, 2011).

Herbert Kitschelt is the George V. Allen Professor of International Relations at Duke University. He has published widely on political parties and party systems in Western Europe, Post-Communist Eastern Europe, and Latin America. His most recent book is *Latin American Party Systems* (Cambridge University Press, 2010), co-authored with Kirk Hawkins, Juan Luna, Guillermo Rosas, and Elizabeth Zechmeister. He currently works on two main projects, one on a global data set to compare patterns of democratic accountability, particularly through programmatic and clientelistic citizen–politician linkages, and the other on comparing the changing strategic appeals and electoral coalitions crystallized around political parties in established Western democracies.

David Knoke (PhD 1972, University of Michigan) is Professor of Sociology at the University of Minnesota. His primary areas of research and teaching are in organizations, networks, and social statistics. He has been a principal investigator on more than a dozen National Science Foundation grants, most recently a project to investigate networks and teamwork of 26 Minnesota Assertive Community Treatment (ACT) teams, a multi-professional mental-health services program. Recent books, some with co-authors, include *Comparing Policy Networks: Labor Politics in the U.S., Germany, and Japan* (1996); *Organizations: Business Networks in the New Political Economy* (2001); *Statistics for Social Data Analysis* 4th edn (2002); and *Social Network Analysis*, 2nd edn (2008). In 2008 Prof. Knoke received the UMN College of Liberal Arts' Arthur 'Red' Motley Exemplary Teaching Award.

Gabriela Kütting is Associate Professor of Political Science and Global Affairs at Rutgers, the State University of New Jersey, Newark. She has published extensively in the field of global environmental politics, including the books *Environment, Society and International Relations* (Routledge, 2000); *Globalization and Environment* (SUNY Press, 2004); and *Environmental Governance: Power and Knowledge in a*

Local-Global World (edited with Ronnie Lipschutz, 2009). Her most recent books are *Global Environmental Politics; Concepts, Theories and Case Studies* (ed., 2010) and *The Global Political Economy of the Environment and Tourism* (Palgrave Macmillan, 2010).

Patrick Le Galès is CNRS Research Professor of Politics and Sociology at the Centre d'études européennes, Sciences Po, Paris and part-time visiting professor at King's College, London. He is the coordinator of Sciences Po's 'Cities and territories' and 'Restructuring the state' research groups and former editor of *The International Journal of Urban and Regional Research*. His publications include *European Cities: Social Conflicts and Governance* (Oxford University Press, 2002); *Changing Governance of Local Economies* (with Colin Crouch, Carlo Trigilia, and Helmut Voetzkow, Oxford University Press, 2004); and *The New Labour Experiment* (with Florence Faucher-King, Stanford University Press, 2010). Homepage: http://www.cee.sciences-po.fr/fr/le-centre/equipe-de-recherche/59-patrick-legales.html.

Ruth Lister is Emeritus Professor of Social Policy at Loughborough University, a Fellow of the British Academy and a member of the House of Lords. She has published widely on topics of citizenship, poverty and gender, including *Citizenship: Feminist Perspectives* (2nd edn, Palgrave, 2003) and *Poverty* (Polity, 2004).

Wesley Longhofer is a PhD Candidate in the Department of Sociology at the University of Minnesota. His work on environmental issues and civic associations has appeared in the *American Sociological Review* and the *International Journal of Comparative Sociology*. His other research interests include comparative political sociology, institutional theory, globalization and development, and philanthropic and non-profit organizations. Currently, he is working on a project examining the origins of global philanthropy and its implications for development-related outcomes. In January 2012, he will join the Goizueta Business School faculty at Emory University as an Assistant Professor of Organization and Management.

Jeff Manza is Professor of Sociology and Department Chair at New York University. His research is in the area of social stratification, political sociology and public policy. He is the co-author (with Christopher Uggen) of *Locked Out: Felon Disenfranchisement and American Democracy* (Oxford University Press, 2006) and (with Clem Brooks) of *Why Welfare States Persist* (University of Chicago Press, 2007). His work has appeared in journals such as *American Sociological Review*, *American Journal of Sociology* and *Journal of Politics*. He is currently working on a study of the impact of policy framings on public opinion.

David S. Meyer is Professor of Sociology, Political Science, and Planning, Policy and Design at the University of California, Irvine. He has published numerous articles on social movements and social change, and is author or co-editor of six books, most recently *The Politics of Protest: Social Movements in America* (Oxford University Press, 2006). He is most interested in the connections among institutional politics, public policy, and social movements, particularly in regard to issues of war and peace.

Valentine M. Moghadam is Professor of Sociology and Director of the International Affairs Program at Northeastern University. Prior to that she was Professor of Sociology and Women's Studies, and Director of the Women's Studies Program at Purdue University. She has also served as Chief of the Section for Gender Equality and Development, in the Social and Human Sciences Sector of UNESCO, in Paris; and was Professor of Sociology and Women's Studies Director at Illinois State University; and coordinator of the research programme on women and development at the United Nations University's WIDER Institute, in Helsinki. Born in Tehran, Iran, Dr Moghadam is author of four books: *Modernizing Women: Gender and Social Change in the Middle East* (2nd edn 2003); *Women, Work and Economic Reform in the Middle East and North Africa* (1998); *Globalizing Women: Transnational Feminist Networks* (2005); and *Globalization and Social Movements: Islamism, Feminism, and the Global Justice Movement* (2009). She has edited seven books, authored numerous journal articles and book chapters, and consulted many international organizations. Her areas of research are globalization, transnational feminist networks, civil society and citizenship, and women's employment in the Middle East and North Africa.

Kate Nash is Professor of Sociology at Goldsmiths, University of London and Faculty Fellow at the Center for Cultural Sociology, Yale University. She has published widely on political sociology and human rights, including *The Cultural Politics of Human Rights: Comparing the US and UK* (Cambridge University Press, 2009) and articles in *Sociology*, *The British Journal of Sociology*, *Economy and Society* and *Citizenship Studies*. She is author of *Contemporary Political Sociology* (Wiley-Blackwell, 2nd edn 2010) (with Alan Scott and Anna Marie Smith) and *New Critical Writings in Political Sociology* (Ashgate, 2009), and she is currently writing *The Political Sociology of Human Rights* (Cambridge University Press, forthcoming).

Aletta J. Norval is Reader in Political Theory and Director of the Doctoral Programme in Ideology and Discourse Analysis in the Department of Government, University of Essex, UK. She is also Co-Director of the Centre for Theoretical Studies in the Humanities and Social Sciences. Her publications include *Aversive Democracy: Inheritance and Originality in the Democratic Tradition* (Cambridge University Press) and *Deconstructing Apartheid Discourse* (Verso). She is co-editor of *South Africa in Transition: New Theoretical Perspectives* (Macmillan) and *Discourse Theory and Political Analysis: Identities, Hegemonies and Social Change* (Manchester University Press). She has written widely on democratic theory; post-structuralism and contemporary political theory; South African politics; theories of ethnicity; feminist theory; and the construction of political identities. She is currently working on a book on Rancière and Cavell.

René Patnode is a PhD Candidate in Sociology at the University of California, San Diego. His research focuses on political education and the construction of national identities among university students within the People's Republic of China as well as the tensions caused within those identities by the effects of cultural globalization. He is further interested in how these processes affect those individuals located on the periphery, that is, Chinese ethnic minorities.

Gianfranco Poggi: After a first degree in Law (Padua, 1956) he took an MA and PhD in Sociology (University of California, Berkeley, 1959, 1963), where he studied with Lipset, Bendix, Lowenthal, Linz, Kornhauser and others. His subsequent teaching and research (chiefly at Florence, 1962–1964; Edinburgh, 1964–1988; Virginia, 1988–1995; European University Institute, Florence, 1996–2001; and Trento, 2001–2005) dealt chiefly with the contributions of major social theorists – especially Tocqueville, Marx, Durkheim, Weber and Simmel – and with modern political institutions, with special regard to the state and other forms of social power. He has taught in many other universities in Canada, Germany and Australia, and held fellowships at the Center for Advanced Studies in the Behavioral Sciences (Stanford), ANU, and at the Wissenschaftskolleg zu Berlin. Book publications include *The State: Its Nature, Development and Prospects* (Polity, 1982) and *Forms of Power* (Polity, 2001).

Charles C. Ragin is Professor of Sociology and Political Science at the University of Arizona. He publishes in the fields of methodology, political sociology and comparative-historical analysis. His books include *The Comparative Method: Moving Beyond Qualitative and Quantitative Strategies* (which won the Stein Rokkan Prize for Comparative Research of the International Social Science Council); *Constructing Social Research*; *What Is a Case? Exploring the Foundations of Social Research* (with Howard S. Becker); *Fuzzy-Set Social Science*; and *Configurational Comparative Methods: Qualitative Comparative Analysis and Related Techniques* (with Benoit Rihoux). In his most recent book, *Redesigning Social Inquiry: Fuzzy Sets and Beyond*, he presents a critique of the 'net-effects thinking' that dominates much of contemporary social science, and proposes alternative analytic strategies grounded in configurational methods. Ragin also has developed two software packages for configurational analysis of social data: Qualitative Comparative Analysis (QCA) and Fuzzy-Set/Qualitative Comparative Analysis (fsQCA).

Larry Ray has been Professor of Sociology at the University of Kent, UK, since 1998 and is Sub-Dean in the Faculty of Social Sciences. His research and publications range across social theory, globalization, post-communism, ethnicity, and the sociology of violence. He has also recently undertaken a project on Yiddish cultural and musical revivals, Holocaust representation, and the politics of memory. Recent publications include *Theorizing Classical Sociology* (Open University Press, 1999); *Key Contemporary Social Theorists* (co-edited with Anthony Elliott, Blackwell, 2002); *Social Theory and Postcommunism* (with William Outhwaite, Blackwell, 2005); *Globalization and Everyday Life* (Routledge, 2007); and *Violence and Society* (Sage, 2011). He is President Elect of the British Association of Jewish Studies.

Dietrich Rueschemeyer is Professor of Sociology and Charles C. Tillinghast Jr. Professor of International Studies, Emeritus, at Brown University. He has taught earlier at the University of Cologne, Dartmouth College, the University of Toronto and, as a guest, at the Free University of Berlin, the Vrije Universiteit Brussel, Bergen University and the Hebrew University of Jerusalem. His publications include *Bringing the State Back In* (co-edited with Peter Evans and Theda Skocpol, 1985); *Power and the Division of Labour* (1986); *Capitalist Development and Democracy* (co-authored with John Stephens and Evelyne Huber Stephens, 1992); *Comparative Historical Analysis in the Social Sciences* (co-edited with James Mahoney, 2003); *Globalization and the Future of Welfare States* (co-edited with Miguel Glatzer, 2005); and *States and Development: Historical Antecedents of Stagnation and Advance* (co-edited with Matthew Lange, 2005). In 2009, Princeton University Press published his *Usable Theory: Analytic Tools for Social Research*.

Roberta Sassatelli is Associate Professor of Cultural Sociology at the University of Milan (Italy). Her research interests include the politics of consumption, the sociology of the body, gender and visual representation, and cultural theory. Among her most recent works in English are *Consumer Culture: History, Theory and Politics* (Sage, 2007) and *Fitness Culture: Gyms and the Commercialisation of Discipline and Fun* (Palgrave, 2010). She is currently working on a book on critical models of consumer practices.

Mike Savage became Professor of Sociology at the University of York in 2010, having previously worked at the University of Manchester for 15 years. He was founding Director of the ESRC Centre for Research on Socio-Cultural Change (CRESC) and is the author of several books on the relationship between class and culture. These include *Culture, Class, Distinction* (with Tony Bennett, Elizabeth Silva, Alan Warde, Modesto Gayo-Cal and David Wright, Routledge, 2009) and *Identities and Social Change in Britain since 1940: The Politics of Method* (Oxford University Press, 2010). He is a Fellow of the British Academy, in both the Sociology and Politics sections.

Garrett Andrew Schneider is a doctoral candidate in the Department of Sociology at the University of Arizona. Garrett has written on the politics of incarceration and comparative methodology and his broader research interests span political economy, qualitative and mixed-methodology, political sociology and organizational theory. His dissertation brings these interests together in a case-based historical study of the restructuring of the American financial sector in the closing decades of the twentieth century.

Evan Schofer is Associate Professor of Sociology at the University of California, Irvine. He seeks to develop world society theory through research on diverse topics in areas including comparative political sociology, sociology of education, environmental sociology and globalization. His work on the origins and global spread of environmentalism, the proliferation of voluntary associations and the expansion of science and educational systems has appeared in the *American Sociological Review, Social Forces*, and in a co-authored book entitled *Science in the Modern World Polity: Globalization and Institutionalization* (Stanford 2003). Professor Schofer received his PhD in sociology from Stanford University.

John Schwarzmantel is Senior Lecturer in Politics, and Director of the Centre for Democratisation Studies, at the University of Leeds. His research and teaching interests are in the fields of political ideologies, nationalism and democracy. His recent publications include *Citizenship and Identity: Towards a New Republic* (Routledge 2003); *Ideology and Politics* (Sage 2008); and *Democracy and Political*

Violence (Edinburgh University Press, 2011). He is also joint editor (along with Mark McNally) of *Gramsci and Global Politics: Hegemony and Resistance* (Routledge 2009) and (with Ricardo Blaug) of *Democracy: A Reader* (Edinburgh University Press 2001).

Alan Scott is professor in the School of Behavioural, Cognitive and Social Science, University of New England, NSW, Australia. He has published widely on political sociology, organizational sociology (particularly higher education governance), and social theory. Recent and forthcoming publications include 'State transformation or regime shift?' (with Paul du Gay, *Sociologica*, 2010); 'A British bureaucratic revolution? Autonomy without control or "freer markets, more rules"' (with Patrick Le Galès, *Revue Française de Sociologie* 51, Supplement, 2010); 'Raymond Aron's political sociology of regime and party' (*Journal of Classical Sociology*, 2011); and 'Development: a Polyanyian view' (*Comparative Sociology*, 2012).

John Scott is Professor of Sociology and Pro Vice-Chancellor (Research) at the University of Plymouth, and has previously taught at the Universities of Strathclyde, Leicester and Essex. He is an Honorary Vice-President of the British Sociological Association, a Fellow of the British Academy and an Academician of the Academy of Social Sciences. His research interests include social stratification and power, social theory, social network analysis and the history of sociology. Recent publications include *Power* (Polity Press, 2001); *Social Theory: Central Issues in Sociology* (Sage, 2006); *Sociology* (with James Fulcher, Oxford University Press, 4rth edn, 2011); and *Conceptualising the Social World: Principles of Sociological Analysis* (Cambridge University Press, 2011).

Sarah Shannon is a PhD student in the Department of Sociology at the University of Minnesota. Her research interests are in law, crime and deviance, especially the intersections between punishment, neighbourhoods and public welfare programmes. Sarah holds a Master of Social Work (MSW) degree from the University of Minnesota (2007). She completed her undergraduate work in sociology at the University of Iowa (BA 1997).

John D. Skrentny is Director of the Center for Comparative Immigration Studies and Professor of Sociology at the University of California, San Diego. His research focuses on the intersection of law, politics and inequality. He is the author of *The Minority Rights Revolution* (Harvard University Press, 2002) and *The Ironies of Affirmative Action: Politics, Culture, and Justice in America* (University of Chicago Press, 1996), as well as the editor of *Color Lines: Affirmative Action, Immigration, and Civil Rights Options for America* (University of Chicago Press). His work has appeared in *American Journal of Sociology*, *Annual Review of Sociology* and *International Migration Review*. He is currently working on a book on the relationship between immigration and civil rights law in America and another book project focusing on regional variations in immigration law in North America, Europe and East Asia.

Christi M. Smith is a doctoral candidate in Sociology at Indiana University. Her research interests include race and ethnicity, culture and politics. Her dissertation examines the reconstitution of the meanings of race after the American Civil War and the mechanisms that brought about segregated education.

Yasemin Nuhoğlu Soysal (University of Essex): Before arriving in Europe Yasemin Soysal studied and worked in the United States. Soysal has published extensively on the historical development and contemporary reconfigurations of the nation-state and citizenship in Europe; cultural and political implications of international migrations; and international discourses and regimes of human rights. Her current research is on the changing concepts of 'good citizen' and 'good society' in Europe and East Asia, comparatively and longitudinally. She has held several research fellowships, grants and guest professorships, including Wissenschaftskolleg, Economic and Social Research Council, British Academy, National Endowment of Humanities, National Academy of Education, German Marshall Fund, Max Planck Institute, European University Institute, Juan March Institute, Hitotsubashi University and the Chinese University of Hong Kong. She is past president of the European Sociological Association.

Judith Squires is Professor of Political Theory at the University of Bristol and is currently Dean of the Faculty of Social Sciences and Law. Her publications include *The New Politics of Gender Equality* (Palgrave, 2007) and *Contesting Citizenship* (co-edited with Birte Siim, Routledge, 2008). She is reviews editor for the journal *Government and Opposition* and is co-editor of the Palgrave Gender and Politics book series. She is currently working on a collaborative project on 'institutionalizing intersectionality'.

Brian Steensland is Associate Professor of Sociology at Indiana University. His interests include politics, culture, religion and inequality. Steensland's first book, *The Failed Welfare Revolution*, won the Clifford Geertz Prize for Best Book on Culture, and the Political Sociology Book Award for Distinguished Contribution to Scholarship, both from the American Sociological Association. He is working on a new project on religious traditionalism, economic libertarianism, and the rise of the conservative movement in postwar America.

Göran Therborn is Professor Emeritus of Sociology at the University of Cambridge, Academician of the Social Sciences UK, dr. h.c.; currently living in Sweden. His latest books are *The World. A Beginner's Guide* (Polity Press, 2011); *Handbook of European Societies* (co-ed., Springer, 2010); *Les sociétés d'Europe du XXe au XXIe siècle* (Armand Colin, 2009); *From Marxism to Postmarxism* (Verso 2008); *Inequalities of the World* (Verso, 2006); and *Between Sex and Power: Family in the World, 1900–2000* (Routledge, 2004). His main current project is *Cities of Power*, on capital cities of the world and their representations of power.

John B. Thompson is Professor of Sociology at the University of Cambridge and Fellow of Jesus College, Cambridge. His publications include *Ideology and Modern Culture* (1990), *The Media and Modernity* (1995), *Political Scandal* (2000), *Books in the Digital Age* (2005), and *Merchants of Culture* (2010). His books have been translated into more than a dozen languages and he was awarded the European Amalfi Prize for Sociology and the Social Sciences in 2001 for *Political Scandal*.

Kenneth Thompson is Emeritus Professor of Sociology at the Open University, UK, and has also taught at Yale, UCLA, Rutgers, Smith College and Bergen University (Norway). He is a former member of the Executive Committee of the International Sociological Association and was Co-president of its Research Committee 16, 'Sociological Theory'; he has served on the Executive Committee of the British Sociological Association and chaired its section on the Sociology of Religion. In addition to sociological theory, his current research interests include issues of moral panics, media regulation, and hate speech. His publications include *Moral Panics*; *Media and Cultural Regulation*; *Beliefs and Ideology*; *Emile Durkheim*; *Sartre: Life and Works*; *Bureaucracy and Church Reform*; and *A Contemporary Introduction to Sociology* (with Jeffrey Alexander).

Christopher Uggen is Distinguished McKnight Professor and Chair of Sociology at the University of Minnesota. He studies crime, law and deviance, believing that good social science can light the way to a more just and safer world. His work appears in journals such as *American Sociological Review, American Journal of Sociology* and *Law & Society Review* and in media such as the *New York Times, The Economist* and *NPR*. With Jeff Manza, he wrote *Locked Out: Felon Disenfranchisement and American Democracy* (2006, Oxford). Chris now serves as chair of his department and editor of *Contexts* magazine, the public outreach publication of the American Sociological Association.

Alberto Vannucci is Assistant Professor in the Faculty of Political Science, University of Pisa. In 1994 he took a PhD in Philosophy of Social Sciences at the Scuola Superiore di Studi Universitari e di Perfezionamento 'S. Anna', Pisa. Since 2010 he has been Director of the Master in 'Analysis, Prevention and Fight against Organized Crime and Corruption' organized by the Department of Political and Social Science, Libera and Avviso Pubblico, University of Pisa. Among his research fields are political and administrative corruption, neo-institutional political theory, organized crime and illegal markets, and public policy (tourism policy, policy against irregular work, anti-corruption policy). Among his latest publications are *The Governance of Corruption* (with Donatella della Porta, Ashgate, 2011); *Nero, grigio, sommerso: attori e politiche per l'emersione del lavoro irregolare* (Felici, 2009); and *Mani impunite. Vecchia e nuova corruzione in Italia* (with Donatella della Porta, Laterza, 2007).

Xi Zhu is an Assistant Professor in the Department of Health Management and Policy at the University of Iowa. His research interests are in organizational behaviour and theory, network analysis and economic sociology. He is a co-author of *The Critical Power of Management Theory* (Renmin University Press, 2007). He received his PhD in Sociology from the University of Minnesota.

Introduction

EDWIN AMENTA, KATE NASH AND ALAN SCOTT

The *Blackwell Companion to Political Sociology* was published in 2000 and established itself as a standard reference within this sub-field. In this follow-up volume the two original editors – Kate Nash and Alan Scott – have been joined by a US-based political sociologist, Edwin Amenta. Rather than simply update the previous volume, we have gone for a substantially new book that both reflects developments over the past decade and will hopefully appeal to an even broader international audience. Thus, of the present volume's 42 chapters only 14 are updated versions of chapters by the same authors; many of these have been very substantially reworked to broaden the topic or include more recent developments while in a couple of cases we have authors from the earlier volume writing on substantially different topics. These changes inevitably mean that there are areas covered by the earlier book that are absent here, even though they remain important to the development of political sociology, and we would still advise anyone who, for example, is interested in rational choice approaches, policy networks or the impact of postmodernism on political sociology to consult the relevant chapters in the earlier volume. New topics covered here, which are in part responses to external events, represent the development of debates within the discipline and/or reflect the interests and expertise of the new editor.

In other respects we have remained faithful to the principles of the earlier volume. Firstly, we have not attempted to impose conceptual order on the area by selecting one of a number of possible paradigms and asserting, or simply tacitly assuming, that the one they have selected is, is becoming, or should be *the* dominant or only legitimate paradigm. Political sociology remains a highly diverse intellectual endeavour. This volume remains a companion rather than a lexicon or dictionary. It does not aspire to be definitive. It does, however, seek to be comprehensive; to cover both the central themes of political sociology and the various perspectives within that sub- or trans-discipline.

Secondly, we shall not attempt in this introduction to offer a gloss on the contributions, but will let these speak for themselves. We shall confine ourselves here to only a few observations about political sociology as a field both distinct from and overlapping with sociology and political science. Given that we have both of these disciplines, why do we need a *political* sociology or a *sociology* of politics? The division of labour between the social sciences is in part a historical accident and, like any system of categorization, both generates and neglects matter at the margins. With respect to the first point, in the French and German traditions political sciences and sociology largely emerged out of legal studies, while in the Anglo-Saxon tradition they tended to emerge out of history and political theory. The contrast is most clearly marked in the German case where what we now consider the social sciences (including economics) were once part of a 'science of the state' (*Staatswissenschaft* or *Staatslehre*), only emerging as separate disciplines in the twentieth century. In this respect, political sociology – like political economy – may be seen as harking back to a 'predisciplinary' past and perhaps, more controversially, as presaging a post-disciplinary future. For now, it provides a space for approaches that exist at the margins or cross the boundaries of sociology or political science, or have not yet established themselves as mainstream within either.

Political sociology seeks to redress the limitations and blind spots of the two disciplines whose borders it crosses. For some working in the area it is superior to both. Raymond Aron, a once-influential figure who is now largely neglected, can be taken as representing political sociology in this campaigning mode. For Aron, political science was focused too narrowly and inclined to disembed political phenomena from their broader social 'environment'. Sociology, on the other hand, tended to deal in abstractions – society, social structure, social systems etc. – at the expense of examining concrete institutions such as parliaments, parties, regimes and constitutions. Furthermore, sociology downplayed, or was simply blind to the importance of, the *event*. It took the current state of affairs to be social facts rather than the outcomes of particular moments, decision and actions. Conversely, political sociology too can be seen as an echo of events precisely because it does not set its own agenda entirely but responds – perhaps in more obvious ways than sociology generally – to external events. Of course, those events are 'worked on' in political sociology in quite specific theoretical terms, which tend to owe more to sociological traditions of thought than to political science. The events of 1989 cast a long shadow over much of the previous volume, as did debates over globalization as 'something new'. In the intervening years we have been living with 9/11 and its aftermath, while perspectives on globalization have become much more thoroughly integrated into all topics and themes. Our coverage of war has changed (though it was also covered in the previous volume), and issues of international terrorism, security, incarceration and human rights have been added as a result, as have chapters on transnational social movements and environmental politics.

Part I of the volume – Approaches to Power and Politics – covers both the central perspectives that have influenced and remain influential within political sociology – Marxist, Weberian, Durkheimian, Foucaultian and institutionalist – and methodologies for studying power and doing comparison. Part II – States and Governance – shifts the focus onto key themes: state formation, governance and violence. Here we have tried to cover issues that have long occupied political sociologists (e.g. state formation, political legitimation, elections and political intermediation) and issues that reflect more recent concerns and events, for example, state failure and corruption, international terrorism and global security. The focus shifts in Part III – The Political and the Social – towards the state–civil society relation, collective action and identity, and citizenship. These debates, which have expanded far beyond a focus on class and nation to include gender, ethnicity and religion, perhaps constitute the most distinctive contribution of political sociology and are located at the point at which the political and the social interact most dynamically. Finally, in Part IV we cover social movements and participation under the heading Democracy and Participation. Here the distinct contribution of political sociology vis-à-vis political science can be seen most clearly: the emphasis is on informal modes of democratic participation and on the social and cultural embeddedness of formal institutions and law (e.g. in the area of human rights).

This edition is an update of the previous one, then, in that the selection of topics represents the best attempt of political sociologists to get to grips with the events of the first decade of the twenty-first century. In this respect, it inevitably looks back. At the same time, however, it is forward looking, in that the frameworks, concepts and themes developed here will surely inform our analysis of events yet to come.

Part I
Approaches to Power and Politics

1

Marxist Approaches to Power

Bob Jessop

Marxist approaches to power focus on its relation to class domination in capitalist societies. Power is linked to class relations in economics, politics and ideology. In capitalist social formations, the state is considered to be particularly important in securing the conditions for economic class domination. Marxists are also interested in why dominated classes seem to accept (or fail to recognize) their oppression; so they address issues of resistance and strategies to bring about radical change. Much recent Marxist analysis also aims to show how class power is dispersed throughout society, in order to avoid economic reductionism. This chapter summarizes the main trends in contemporary Marxism and identifies some significant spatio-temporal aspects of class domination. It also assesses briefly the disadvantages of Marxism as a sociological analysis of power. These include its neglect of forms of social domination that are not directly related to class; a tendency to overemphasize the coherence of class domination; the continuing problem of economic reductionism; and the opposite danger of a voluntaristic account of resistance to capitalism.

Marxists have analyzed power relations in many different ways. But four inter-related themes typify their overall approach. The first of these is a concern with power relations as manifestations of a specific mode or configuration of class domination rather than as a purely interpersonal phenomenon lacking deeper foundations in the social structure. This focus on class domination does not imply that power and resistance are the preserve of social actors with clear class identities and class interests. It means only that Marxists are mainly interested in the causal interconnections between the exercise of social power and the reproduction and/or transformation of class domination. Indeed, Marxists are usually well aware of other types of subject, identity, antagonism and domination. But they consider these phenomena largely in

The Wiley-Blackwell Companion to Political Sociology, First Edition. Edited by Edwin Amenta, Kate Nash, and Alan Scott.
© 2012 Blackwell Publishing Ltd. Published 2012 by Blackwell Publishing Ltd.

terms of their relevance for, and their overdetermination by, class domination. Second, Marxists are concerned with the links – including discontinuities as well as continuities – among economic, political and ideological class domination. Despite or, perhaps, because of the obvious centrality of this issue to Marxist analysis, it continues to prompt widespread theoretical and empirical disagreements. Different Marxist approaches locate the bases of class power primarily in the social relations of production, in control over the state, or in intellectual hegemony over hearts and minds. I will deal with these options below. Third, Marxists note the limitations inherent in any exercise of power that is rooted in one or another form of class domination and try to explain this in terms of structural contradictions and antagonisms inscribed therein. Thus Marxists tend to assume that all forms of social power linked to class domination are inherently fragile, unstable, provisional and temporary and that continuing struggles are needed to secure class domination, to overcome resistance and to naturalize or mystify class power. It follows, fourth, that Marxists also address questions of strategy and tactics. They provide empirical analyses of actual strategies intended to reproduce, resist or overthrow class domination in specific periods and conjunctures; and they often engage in political debates about the most appropriate identities, interests, strategies and tactics for dominated classes and other oppressed groups to adopt in particular periods and conjunctures to challenge their subordination. An important aspect of strategic analysis and calculation is sensitivity to the spatio-temporal dimensions of strategy and this is reflected in growing theoretical interest in questions of temporality and socio-spatiality.

Power as a Social Relation

Marxists are interested in the first instance in power as capacities rather than power as the actualization of such capacities. They see these capacities as *socially structured* rather than as *socially amorphous* (or random). Thus Marxists focus on capacities grounded in structured social relations rather than in the properties of individual agents considered in isolation. Moreover, as these structured social relations entail enduring relations, there are reciprocal, if often asymmetrical, capacities and vulnerabilities. A common paradigm here is Hegel's master–slave dialectic – in which the master depends on the slave and the slave on the master. Marx's equivalent paradigm case is the material interdependence of capital and labour. At stake in both cases are enduring relations of reproduced, reciprocal practices rather than one-off, unilateral impositions of will. This has the interesting implication that power is also involved in securing the continuity of social relations rather than producing radical change. Thus, as Isaac notes, '[r]ather than A getting B to do something B would not otherwise do, social relations of power typically involve both A and B doing what they *ordinarily* do' (1987: 96). The capitalist wage relation illustrates this well. For, in voluntarily selling their labour-power for a wage, workers transfer its control to the capitalist along with the right to any surplus. A formally free exchange thereby becomes the basis of workplace despotism and economic exploitation. Conversely, working-class resistance in labour markets and the labour process indicate that the successful exercise of power is a conjunctural phenomenon rather than being guaranteed by unequal social relations of production. Thus Marxists regard the actualization of capacities to exercise power and its effects, if any, as always and everywhere contingent on specific actions by specific agents in specific circumstances. It follows that there can be no such thing as power in general or general power – only particular powers and the sum of particular exercises of power.

General Remarks on Class Domination

Marxism differs from other analyses of power because of its primary interest in class domination. In contrast, for example, Weberian analyses give equal *analytical* weight to other forms of domination (status, party); or, again, radical feminists prioritize patriarchy, its forms and effects. But its distinctive interest in class domination is not limited to *economic* class domination in the *labour process* (although this is impor-tant) nor even to the economic bases of class domination in the wider economy (such as control over the allocation of capital to alternative productive activities). For Marxists see class powers as dispersed throughout society and therefore also investigate political and ideological class domination. However, whereas some Marxists believe political and/or ideological domination derive more or less directly from economic domination, others emphasize the complexity of relations among these three sites or modes of class domination.

    Even Marxists who stress the economic bases of class domination also acknowledge that politics is primary in practice. For it is only through political revolution that existing patterns of class domination will be overthrown. Other Marxists prioritize the political over the economic not just (if at all) in terms of revolutionary struggles but also in terms of its role in the routine reproduction of class domination. This makes the state central to Marxist analyses not only in regard to political power in narrow terms but also to class power more generally. For the state is seen as responsible for maintaining the overall structural integration and social cohesion of a 'society divided into classes' – a structural integration and social cohesion without which capitalism's contradictions and antagonisms might cause revolutionary crises or even, in the telling phrase of the 1848 *Communist Manifesto*, lead to 'the mutual ruin of the contending classes'.

Economic Class Domination

Marxism is premised on the existence for much of human history of antagonistic modes of production. Production involves the material appropriation and transfor-mation of nature. A mode of production comprises in turn a specific combination of the forces of production and social relations of production. The productive forces comprise raw materials, means of production, the technical division of labour corresponding to these raw materials and the given means of production, and the relations of interdependence and cooperation among the direct producers in setting the means of production to work. The social relations of production comprise social control over the allocation of resources to different productive activities and over the appropriation of any resulting surplus; the social division of labour (or the allocation of workers to different activities across different units of production); and class relations grounded in property relations, ownership of the means of production, and the form of economic exploitation. Some Marxists highlight the role of productive forces in producing social change but the majority view (and current wisdom) is that the social relations of production are primary. Indeed, it is these social relations that shape the choice among available productive forces and how they get deployed in production.

Given the primacy of the relations of production in economic class domination, some Marxists emphasize the power relations rooted in organization of the labour process. This is considered the primary site of the antagonism between capitalists and workers and is the crucial site for securing the valorization of capital through direct control over power-power. Various forms of control are identified (e.g., bureaucratic, technical, and despotic), each with its own implications for forms of class struggle and the distribution of power between capital and labour. Other Marxists study the overall organization of the production process and its articulation to other aspects of the circuit of capital. Thus emphasis is placed on the relative importance of industrial or financial capital, monopoly capital or small and medium enterprises, multinational or national firms, firms interested in domestic growth or exports. Different modes of economic growth are associated with different patterns of power. Atlantic Fordism, for example, based on a virtuous circle of mass production and mass consumption in relatively closed economies, was compatible for a time with an institutionalized compromise between industrial capital and organized labour. This supported the Keynesian welfare national state with its distinctive forms of economic, social and political redistribution. But increasing globalization (or world market integration) combined with capital's attempts to increase labour market flexibility have undermined these conditions and encouraged an assault on this compromise. This is clearest in those economies that underwent neoliberal regime shifts, such as the United States and United Kingdom, associated respectively with Reaganism (sustained under Clinton's Third Way and the George W. Bush administration) and Thatcherism (sustained by New Labour's 'modernization' project). This contributed to a decline in labour's share in income and wealth, to the growing divorce of financial from industrial capital, to the hyper-financialization of everyday life and, in 2007–2009, to the global financial crisis, which has had its own impact on patterns of class domination.

Political Class Domination

Marxist accounts of political class domination typically begin with the state and its direct and indirect roles in securing the conditions for economic class domination. The state is emphasized for various reasons: first, since market forces themselves cannot secure all the conditions needed for capital accumulation and are prone to market failure, there is a need for some mechanism standing outside and above the market to underwrite it and compensate for its failures; second, economic and political competition between capitals necessitates a force able to organize their collective interests and limit any damage that might occur from the one-sided pursuit of one set of capitalist interests; third, the state is needed to manage the many and varied repercussions of economic exploitation within the wider society. Marxists argue that only if the state can secure sufficient institutional integration and social cohesion will the extra-economic conditions for rational economic calculation and, a fortiori, capital accumulation be secured. This requires a sovereign state that is relatively autonomous from particular class interests and can articulate and promote a broader, national-popular interest. Where this project respects the decisive economic nucleus of the society and its capitalist character, then the state helps to secure economic as well as political class domination. This is often held to be more likely in bourgeois democratic political regimes than dictatorial regimes (see Moore 1957; Barrow 1993; Gramsci 1971; Offe 1984; Poulantzas 1978; and Jessop 1990).

There are three main Marxist approaches to the state: instrumentalist, structuralist and 'strategic-relational'. Instrumentalists see the state mainly as a neutral tool for exercising political power: whichever class controls this tool can use it to advance its own interests. Structuralists argue that who controls the state is irrelevant because it embodies a prior bias towards capital and against the subaltern classes. And strategic-relational theorists argue that state power is a form-determined condensation of the balance of class forces in struggle. I now illustrate these three views for the capitalist state. Different examples would be required for states associated with other modes of production.

Instrumentalists regard the contemporary state as a *state in capitalist society*. Ralph Miliband expresses this view in writing that 'the 'ruling class' of capitalist society is that class which owns and controls the means of production and which is able, by virtue of the economic power thus conferred upon it, to use the state as an instrument for the domination of society' (1969: 22). More generally, theorists of the 'state in capitalist society' stress the contingency of state–economy relations. For, despite the dominance of capitalist relations of production in such a society, the state itself has no inherently capitalist form and performs no necessarily capitalist functions. Any functions it does perform for capital occur because pro-capitalist forces *happen* to control the state and/or because securing social order also *happens* to secure key conditions for rational economic calculation. If the same state apparatus were found in another kind of system, however, it might well be controlled by other forces and perform different functions.

Structuralists regard the state as a *capitalist state* because it has an inherently capitalist form and therefore functions on behalf of capital. But what makes a state form capitalist and what guarantees its functionality for capital? Structuralists argue that the very structure of the modern state means that it organizes capital and disorganizes the working class. Claus Offe (1984) developed this view as follows. The state's exclusion from direct control over the means of production (which are held in private hands) makes its revenues depend on a healthy private sector; thus, to secure its own reproduction as a state apparatus, it must ensure the profitability of capital. Subordinate classes can secure material concessions only within this constraint – if profitability is threatened, such concessions must be rolled back. Yet capital cannot press its economic advantages too far without undermining the political legitimacy of the state. For, in contrast to earlier forms of political class domination, the economically dominant class enjoys no formal monopoly of political power. Instead the typical form of bourgeois state is a constitutional state and, later, a national-popular democratic state. This requires respect for the rule of law and the views of its citizens.

The strategic-relational approach was initially proposed by a Greek communist theorist, Nicos Poulantzas, and has subsequently been elaborated by the British state theorist, Bob Jessop. Building on Marx's insight that capital is not a thing but a social relation, Poulantzas argued in his later work that the state is also a social relation. Marx showed how continued reproduction of the material and institutional forms of the capital relation shaped the dynamic of capital accumulation and the economic class struggle – but the dominance of these forms could not in and of itself guarantee capital accumulation. This depended on capital's success in maintaining its domination over the working class in production, politics and the wider society. Likewise, Poulantzas saw the modern form of state as having certain inbuilt biases but argued that these were insufficient in themselves to ensure capitalist rule. Indeed they even served to reproduce class conflict and contradictions within the state itself so that the impact of state power depended heavily on the changing balance of forces and the strategies and tactics pursued by class and non-class forces alike (Poulantzas 1978).

The suggestion that the state is a social relation is important theoretically and politically. Seen as an institutional ensemble or repository of political capacities and resources, the state is by no means class-neutral. It is inevitably class-biased by virtue of the structural selectivity that makes state institutions, capacities and resources more accessible to some political forces and more tractable for some purposes than others. This bias is rooted in the generic form of the capitalist state but varies with its particular institutional matrix. Likewise, since it is not a subject, the capitalist state does not and, indeed, cannot, exercise power. Instead its powers (in the plural) are activated through changing sets of politicians and state officials located in specific parts of the state apparatus in specific conjunctures. If an overall strategic line is ever discernible in the exercise of these powers, it results from strategic coordination enabled by the selectivity of the state system and the organizational role of parallel power networks that cross-cut and unify its formal structures. This is, however, an improbable achievement. For the state system is necessarily shot through with contradictions and class struggles and the political agents operating within it always meet resistances from specific forces beyond the state, which are engaged in struggles to transform it, to determine its policies, or simply to influence it at a distance. It follows that political class struggle never ends. Only through its continual renewal can a capitalist power bloc keep its relative unity in the face of rivalry and fractionalism and maintain its hegemony (or, at least, its dominance) over subaltern groups. And only by disrupting the state's strategic selectivity through mass struggle at a distance from the state, within the state, and to transform the state could a democratic transition to democratic socialism be achieved.

Ideological Class Domination

Ideology (1845–1846) stated that 'the ruling ideas of any age are the ideas of the ruling class' and related this to the latter's control over the means of intellectual production. Their own work developed a number of perspectives on ideological class domination – ranging from the mystifying impact of commodity fetishism, through the individualist attitudes generated by political forms such as citizenship, to the struggles for hearts and minds in civil society. Marxist interest in the forms and modalities of ideological class domination intensified with the rise of democratic government and mass politics in the late nineteenth century and the increased importance of mass media and popular culture in the twentieth century. Various currents in so-called 'Western Marxism' have addressed the mechanisms and effects of ideological class domination – especially whenever a radical socialist or communist revolution has failed to occur despite severe economic crisis or, indeed, during more general periods of working-class passivity. Successive generations of the Frankfurt School have been important here but many other approaches work on similar lines.

An inspirational figure in this area is Antonio Gramsci, an Italian communist politically active in the interwar period until his incarceration by the fascist regime, when he wrote his celebrated prison notebooks. He developed a very distinctive approach to the analysis of class power. His chief concern was to develop an autonomous Marxist science of politics in capitalist societies, to distinguish different types of state and politics, and thereby to establish the most likely conditions under which revolutionary forces might eventually replace capitalism. He was particularly concerned with the specificities of the political situation and revolutionary prospects in the 'West' (Western Europe, United States) as opposed to the 'East' (i.e. Tsarist Russia) – believing that a Leninist vanguard party and a revolutionary coup d'état were inappropriate to the 'West'.

Gramsci identified the state in its narrow sense with the politico-juridical apparatus, the constitutional and institutional features of government, its formal decision-making procedures and its general policies. In contrast, his studies focused more on the ways and means through which *political, intellectual and moral leadership* was mediated through a complex ensemble of institutions, organizations and forces operating within, oriented towards, or located at a distance from the state in its narrow sense. This approach is reflected in his controversial definition of the state as 'political society + civil society' and his related claims that state power in Western capitalist societies rests on 'hegemony armoured by coercion'. Gramsci also defined the state as: 'the entire complex of practical and theoretical activities with which the ruling class not only justifies and maintains its dominance but manages to win the active consent of those over whom it rules' (1971: 244). He argued that states were always based on variable combinations of force and hegemony. For Gramsci, *force* involves the use of a coercive apparatus to bring the mass of the people into conformity and compliance with the requirements of a specific mode of production. In contrast, *hegemony* involves the successful mobilization and reproduction of the 'active consent' of dominated groups by the ruling class through the exercise of political, intellectual and moral leadership. Gramsci did not identify force exclusively with the state (e.g., he referred to private fascist terror squads) nor did he locate hegemony exclusively within civil society (since the state also has important ethico-political functions). Overall, he argued that the capitalist state should not be seen as a basically coercive apparatus but as an institutional ensemble based on a variable mix of coercion, consent, fraud and corruption. Moreover, rather than treating specific institutions and apparatuses as purely technical instruments of government, Gramsci examined their social bases and stressed how state power is shaped by its links to the economic system and civil society.

One of Gramsci's key arguments is the need in advanced capitalist democracies to engage in a long-term war of position in which subordinate class forces would develop a hegemonic 'collective will' that creatively synthesizes a revolutionary project based on the everyday experiences and 'common sense' of popular forces. Although some commentators interpret this stress on politico-ideological struggle to imply that a parliamentary road to socialism would be possible, Gramsci typically stressed the likelihood of an eventual war of manoeuvre with a military-political resolution. But this would be shorter, sharper, and less bloody if hegemony had first been won.

The Articulation of Economic, Political, and Ideological Domination

The relations among economic, political, and ideological domination can be considered in terms of the structurally inscribed selectivity of particular forms of domination and the strategies that help to consolidate (or undermine) these selectivities. The bias inscribed on the terrain of the state as a site of strategic action can only be understood as a bias relative to specific strategies pursued by specific forces to advance specific interests over a given time horizon in terms of a specific set of other forces each advancing their own interests through specific strategies. Particular forms of state privilege some strategies over others, privilege the access of some forces over others, some interests over others, some time horizons over others, some coalition possibilities over others. A given type of state, a given state form, a given form of regime, will be more accessible to some forces than others according to the strategies they adopt to gain state power. And it will be more suited to the pursuit of some types of economic or political strategy than others because of the modes of intervention and resources that characterize that system. All of this indicates the need to examine the differences among types of state (e.g., feudal vs. capitalist), state forms (e.g., absolutist, liberal, interventionist), modes of political representation (e.g., democratic vs. despotic), specific political regimes (e.g., bureaucratic authoritarian, fascist, military or parliamentary, presidential, mass plebiscitary, etc.), particular policy instruments (e.g., Keynesian demand management vs. neoliberal supply-side policies), and so on (see Jessop 1982, 1990).

Whereas Jessop, building on Poulantzas, tends to emphasize the structural moment of 'strategic selectivity', Gramsci focused on its strategic moment. In particular, against the then prevailing orthodox Marxist view that the economic base unilaterally determined the juridico-political superstructure and prevailing forms of social consciousness, Gramsci argued that there was a reciprocal relationship between the economic 'base' and its politico-ideological 'superstructure'. He studied this in terms of how 'the necessary reciprocity between structure and superstructure' is secured through specific intellectual, moral and political practices that translate narrow sectoral, professional or local interests into broader 'ethico-political' ones. Only thus, he wrote, does the economic structure cease to be an external, constraining force and become a source of initiative and subjective freedom (1971: 366–367). This implies that ethico-political practices not only co-constitute economic structures (even where, as he noted, the state assumes a laissez-faire role, which is, itself, a form of state intervention) but also give them their overall rationale and legitimacy (e.g., through bourgeois notions of property rights, freedom of exchange and economic justice).

Where such a reciprocal relationship exists between base and superstructure, Gramsci spoke of an *'historical bloc'*. He also introduced the concepts of *power bloc* and *hegemonic bloc* to analyze respectively the alliances among dominant classes and the broader ensemble of national-popular forces that were mobilized behind a specific hegemonic project. The concept of hegemonic bloc refers to the *historical unity* not of structures (as in the case of the historical bloc) but *of social forces* (which Gramsci analyzed in terms of the ruling classes, supporting classes, mass movements and intellectuals). Thus a hegemonic bloc is a durable alliance of class forces organized by a class (or class fraction) that has proved itself capable of exercising political, intellectual and moral leadership over the dominant classes and the popular masses alike. Gramsci notes a key organizational role here for 'organic intellectuals', that is, persons or organizations that can develop hegemonic projects that give a 'national-popular' expression to the long-term interests of the dominant or, alternatively, the subaltern classes. He also noted how relatively durable hegemony depended on a 'decisive economic nucleus' and criticized efforts to build an 'arbitrary, rationalistic, and willed' hegemony that ignored economic realities.

Spatio-Temporal Moments of Domination

Time and space are closely related and have both structural aspects (the differential temporalities and spatialities of particular institutional and organizational orders and their interrelations) and strategic aspects (such as specific temporal and spatial horizons of action, wars of position and manoeuvre, and efforts to compress and/or extend social relations in time and space). Thus a sound account of specific forms and patterns of domination must include their distinctive spatio-temporal features. This was already evident in Marx's analysis of capital accumulation: this rests on a distinctive political economy of time and also has inherent tendencies to spatial expansion. The *inner* determinations of capital accumulation entail specific ways of organizing time – reflected in the aphorism that 'time is money'. Accordingly Marx developed an array of concepts to reveal the dialectical interplay of concrete and abstract aspects of time during capital accumulation. They include labour time, absolute surplus value, socially necessary labour time, relative surplus value, machine time, circulation time, turnover time, turnover cycle, socially necessary turnover time, interest-bearing capital and expanded reproduction (cf. Grossman 2007). He deploys them to show how the concrete temporalities of particular processes are connected to the constant rebasing of abstract labour time as the driving force behind the never-ending treadmill of competition from which neither capital nor workers can escape (Postone 1993). This driving force becomes ever more powerful as the world market becomes more closely integrated in real time through what is often called globalization but, from a Marxist viewpoint, is better described as changing forms of international economic and political domination. More generally, differential accumulation involves competition to reduce the socially necessary labour time embodied in commodities, the socially necessary turnover time of capital and, increasingly, the [naturally] necessary reproduction time of nature. These pressures exist alongside other forms of competition based on developing new products, new markets, new sources of supply, new organizational forms, new forms of dispossession and so on.

Such pressures generate uneven geographical development, affect the spatial and scalar division of labour, and reorder the spatial aspects of economic domination. There is also a spatial dynamic to capital accumulation. This is reflected in its inherent tendencies to expand, culminating potentially in the formation of a world market but also prompting counter-movements against unbridled market forces. In short, the temporalities of accumulation are crucial aspects of the organization of economic domination and fundamentally affect political and socio-cultural relations, penetrating deeply into everyday life.

These spatio-temporal dynamics also influence forms of political domination. While the development of the world market and its associated space of flows challenge the state's territorial sovereignty, its temporal sovereignty is challenged by the acceleration of time. States increasingly face temporal pressures in their policy-making and implementation due to new forms of time-space distantiation, compression and differentiation. For example, as the temporal rhythms of the economy accelerate relative to those of the state, it has less time to determine and coordinate political responses to economic events, shocks and crises. This reinforces conflicts between the time(s) of the market and the time(s) of the state. One solution to the state's loss of time sovereignty is a *laissez-faire* response that frees up the movement of superfast and/or hypermobile capital – increasing, as we have recently seen, the chances of global crises generated by their unregulated activities.

There are two other options: states can try to compress their own decision-making cycles so that they can make more timely and appropriate interventions; and/or they can attempt to decelerate the activities of 'fast capitalism' to match existing political routines.

A strategy of temporal compression increases pressures to make decisions on the basis of unreliable information, insufficient consultation, lack of participation etc., even as state managers continue to believe that policy is taking too long to negotiate, formulate, enact, adjudicate, determine, and implement. Indeed, the rhetoric of crisis can be invoked, whether justified or not, to create a climate for emergency measures and exceptional rule. This resort to 'fast policy' is reflected in the shortening of policy development cycles, fast-tracking decision making, rapid programme rollout, continuing policy experimentation and the relentless revision of guidelines and benchmarks. This privileges those who can operate within compressed time scales, narrows the range of participants in the policy process, and limits the scope for deliberation, consultation and negotiation. A scholar inspired by the Frankfurt School, Bill Scheuerman, has summarized some of these trends in terms of a general shift to 'economic states of emergency' characterized by executive dominance and constant legal change and dynamism (Scheuerman 2004).

Thus fast policy is antagonistic to corporatism, stakeholding, the rule of law, formal bureaucracy and, indeed, to the routines and cycles of democratic politics more generally. It privileges the executive over the legislature and the judiciary, finance over industrial capital, consumption over long-term investment. In general, resort to fast policy undermines the power of decision-makers who have long decision-taking cycles – because they lose the capacity to make decisions in terms of their own routines and procedures, having to adapt to the speed of fast thinkers and fast policy-makers. This can significantly affect the choice of policies, the initial targets of policy, the sites where policy is implemented and the criteria adopted to demonstrate success. This is especially evident in the recent global financial crisis, where pressure to act forced states to rescue banks that were deemed 'too big to fail' and led to the concentration of decision-making power in the hands of a small financial elite who had played a key role in creating the crisis in the first instance.

An alternative strategy is not to compress absolute political time but to create relative political time by slowing the circuits of capital. A well-known recommendation here is a modest tax on financial transactions (the so-called Tobin tax), which would decelerate the flow of superfast and hypermobile financial capital and limit its distorting impact on the real economy. Another important field of struggle is climate change. Here we see continuing conflicts between national states about the speed and nature of the response along with well-funded and vocal opposition from firms and sectors with vested interests in continued economic expansion that could cost the earth. In this sense, rather than being a purely general problem that affects all equally, there is a strong class aspect to the creation of the environmental crisis and to struggles over appropriate responses and the distribution of costs of adjustment (Burkett 1999).

Another issue raised by changing spatio-temporalities is the increasing complexity of economic, political and ideological relations as they develop in the context of a world market that lacks either a world state or effective global governance. This undermines state capacities to steer the economy, cope with its crisis tendencies and address its effects on inequalities in economic power and resources; but it also generates instability as enterprises exploit global market opportunities without regard to their environmental, political and social consequences. This is reflected in a shift from government to governance, the increased role of networks and partnerships, and resort to multi-level or, better, multi-spatial governance oriented to different spatio-temporal horizons and interactions. These are far from purely technical solutions to new challenges but have their own selectivities on the configuration of class power (Jessop 2002, 2007).

Conclusions

Marxist approaches to power and its exercise address the following themes: (1) power and class domination; (2) the mediations among economic, political and ideological class domination; (3) the limitations and contradictions of power that are grounded in the nature of capitalism as a system of social relations, including their spatio-temporal aspects; and (4) the role of strategy and tactics. These themes indicate the strengths and weaknesses of Marxism. First, in privileging class domination, it marginalizes other forms of social domination – patriarchal, ethnic, 'racial', hegemonic masculinities, interstate, regional or territorial etc. At best these figure as factors that overdetermine the forms of class domination and/or change in response to changes in class relations. Second, Marxist analyses may exaggerate the structural coherence of class domination, neglecting its disjunctures, contradictions, countervailing tendencies etc. Notions of a unified ruling class belie the messiness of actual configurations of class power – the frictions within and across its economic, political and ideological dimensions, the disjunctions between different scales of social organization, the contradictory nature and effects of strategies, tactics and policies, the probability of state as well as market failures and the capacity of subaltern forces to engage in resistance. Many empirical analyses reveal this messiness and complexity but this often goes unremarked in abstract Marxist theorizing. Third, Marxists risk reducing the limits of economic, political and ideological power to the effect of class contradictions and thereby missing other sources of failure. Finally, while an emphasis on strategy and tactics is important to avoid the structuralist fallacy that capital reproduces itself quasi-automatically and without need of human action, there is a risk of voluntarism if strategy and tactics are examined without reference to specific conjunctures and broader structural contexts.

Further Reading

Barrow, C.W. 1993: *Critical Theories of the State: Marxist, neo-Marxist, post-Marxist.* Madison: University of Wisconsin Press.

Jessop, B. 2002: *The Future of the Capitalist State.* Cambridge: Polity Press.

Jessop, B. 2007: *State Power: A Strategic-Relational Approach.* Cambridge: Polity Press.

Marx, K. 1871: The Civil War in France. In D. Fernbach (ed.) *Karl Marx: the First International and After.* Harmondsworth: Penguin, 1973.

Miliband, R. 1969: *The State in Capitalist Society.* London: Weidenfeld & Nicolson.

Poulantzas, N. 1978: *State, Power, Socialism.* London: Verso.

2

Weber and Political Sociology

PETER BREINER

This chapter shows that Weber provides an existential account of political action that is then folded into his political sociology. This existential account does not merely rotate around the rationalization of all social action into routine forms of domination, as so many commentators have claimed, but constitutes a dialectical movement between competition, struggle and selection on the one hand and routine predictability on the other, the former leading to the latter and the latter creating new conditions for the former. This dialectic is operative in Weber's famous definition of power, his typology of legitimate of legitimate domination-rulership (*legitime Herrschaft*) and his application of these concepts to understanding the dynamics of modern politics as business and vocation. An unexpected outcome of reading Weber's political sociology in this way is that his view of direct democracy converges, though quite unintentionally, with those democratic theorists and political sociologists who argue that genuine democracy always appears in resistance to domination.

Though he often claimed this was his intention, Max Weber did not develop a systematic political sociology. But partially because of that, political sociology appears throughout his work. Indeed, from his earliest 'Freiburg Inaugural Lecture' through the many iterations of his sociology of rulership domination to his last lectures on 'Politics as a Vocation' and 'The General Theory of the State', he relentlessly argued for the primacy of politics over economic and social considerations. Moreover, though modernity was characterized by multiple life spheres, it was in politics, he insisted, where the value commitments in every other sphere were

The Wiley-Blackwell Companion to Political Sociology, First Edition. Edited by Edwin Amenta, Kate Nash, and Alan Scott.
© 2012 Blackwell Publishing Ltd. Published 2012 by Blackwell Publishing Ltd.

fought out. But, for Weber, only sociology could reveal to us the various forms this political struggle might take, the social forces impinging on these struggles, the institutional structures though which they would occur and the cost of these struggles to deeply held partisan commitments. And so Weber understood politics and political sociology to be integrally interconnected.

My aim here is to reconstruct Weber's own political sociology based on an unnoticed existential dialectic embedded within it. I would then like to make a brief comment on how contemporary political sociologists have responded to these arguments and concerns. And at the very end I would like to give an ever so brief indication of a vital but undeveloped strand of Weber's political sociology: the testing of political commitments against the sociological and existential conditions of their realization.

Weber's Political Sociology

The dialectic of conflict and selection vs. methodical routine

Typically those who argue for a distinctive Weberian political sociology focus on his definition of power, his typology of legitimate forms of domination (*Herrschaft*) and his definition of the state. And indeed Weber himself saw these ideal-typical concepts as the foundation for his political sociology (Breuer 1991: 25; Hübinger: 2009: 19–20). However, while many commentators root his political sociology in his ideal types of political rule/domination/authority into the routine forms of traditional or rational-legal authority, they neglect a crucial existential assumption behind his dynamic account of political power and domination. Specifically, all social life for Weber oscillates between two modes of social action: between actions that are purposively rational and lead to methodical fitting of means to ends in routine institutions, what he famously calls 'purposive reason' (*Zweckrationalität*) (Weber 1978 [1922]: 24), and actions subject to the process of competition (*Wettbewerb*), conflict (*Kampf*) and eventually selection (*Auslese*) (Weber 1978 [1922]: 38–40). Indeed conflict leading to selection cannot for Weber be extirpated from social life even in the most routine of social relations (Weber 1949a: 26–27; Weber 1978 [1922]: 38).

Once we give Weber's concepts of conflict (*Kampf*) and selection (*Auslese*) equal weight to his more well-known notion of rationalization of social life through the methodical choice of means to given ends, we discover an *existential dialectic deeply embedded in his political sociology*. Viewed through this existential dialectic, Weber's political sociology will be governed by the constant alternation between conflict leading to selection on the one hand and routinization into forms of methodical domination and obedience on the other. Even routine social relations that method-ically seek predictability in the achievement of their goals, such as economic organiza-tions, political parties, states and bureaucracies, select for certain character types at the expense of other types, and this in turn spawns new conflicts from the excluded. This means that for Weber political will and the logic of power struggle are in constant tension with the routine forms of command and obedience in which and by means of which political will is fought for and realized. We might want to call this *a dialectic of selection and institutional routinization*.

This dialectic, I would argue, shapes Weber's political sociology on several levels: his more general ideal-typical concepts of power and legitimate domination, and political action as found in a wide variety of cultural and historical settings; his particular ideal-typical account of the historical developmental tendencies leading to the modern state, the modern political party, the modern parliament and the modern vocational politician as professional and as charismatic actor with a calling; and his assessment of the possibilities for democracy given the crucible of power struggle and routinization of domination suggested both by his general typology of legitimate domination and by his specific sociology of the business of politics. But despite focusing on the rationalizing side of this dialectic, Weber insists, there is no single logic governing the outcomes of political conflicts and their dissipation into routine forms. On the contrary this process takes on many different forms, and it is the job of the political sociologist to map them out.

This dialectic of conflict selection and institutional routinization in Weber's political sociology can be seen first and foremost in the way he maps the political world through his general ideal-type concepts of power (*Macht*), rulership or domination (*Herrschaft*), politics, institution (*Anstalt*) and the state. Famously he defines power as the 'probability' or chance that an actor will be in a position to achieve or impose his or her will over the resistance of others, and it is irrelevant for his definition what kind of situation or resources allow an agent to exercise this capacity (Weber 1978 [1922]: 53). But when power is successfully exercised in a predictable manner and without resistance such that 'a command with a specific content will be obeyed by a given group of persons' (Weber 1978 [1922]: 53), we have a particular routinization of power, namely '*Herrschaft*', which, depending on context, can be translated as rule or rulership in the sense that one rules over subjects, as domination with its emphasis on command and obedience, or as authority in the sense that an agent claims to be obeyed unconditionally due to the validity of his/her rule or entitlement to give commands. Sometimes, Weber emphasizes only one of these meanings, other times all three at once.

Not surprisingly, Weber transfers these two concepts – the first embedded in conflict, the second embedded in day-to-day commands – to his sociological definition of politics. Thus politics becomes the striving 'for a share of power or to influence the distribution of power, whether between states or between the groups of people contained within a state'. And we pursue power either for the prestige of having power or to realize goals separate from it, but in politics we never escape the striving for power (Weber 1919: 33; also 1978 [1922]: 16). But politics is also defined by the achievement of rule or domination in the state, and so rule or domination may serve as the object of politics if we view politics as the striving to impose one's will over resistance and as its consequence when power is successfully achieved, that is, as 'relationship in which people rule over other people' (Weber 1919: 34).

Not surprisingly, then, Weber will place politics as the pursuit of power and rule-domination in the kind of institution that exercises coercion or compulsion on its members (*ein Anstalt*) rather than in the kind of association that rests on voluntary submission based on consent of its participants (*ein Verein*) (1978 [1922]: 52). Thus both political power and political rule or domination are pursued, for Weber, both by means of and within a particular kind of compulsory institution (*politischer Anstalts-betrieb*), the state, which Weber famously defines as 'that human community that (successfully) lays claim to the monopoly of legitimate physical violence within a particular territory . . .' (Weber 1978 [1922]: 54). What is crucial in this definition is not that the state rules over a territory through violence, but that only the administration of the state may use violence as a last resort to impose its commands and to compel obedience to its laws while no other political organization seeking power or the resources of the state may do so.

What might all of these definitions mean for mapping the terrain of politics from a sociological point of view? First off, given Weber's precise though relentlessly instrumental definition of power, politics will always involve a striving to attain the means of imposing one's will on others. But if this is the case, politics will always involve struggle, not just over the means to impose oneself on others, but also against others seeking similar means to impose their will. These means include money, organization, reliable staffs and above all the means of rule or domination possessed by the state such as its revenue, its administration and its coercive power. Most of these means may be possessed by other agents in society, but only the state has the legitimate claim to use force to impose its commands whatever its administrative apparatus (see Mann 1986). So politics – defined as struggle for power – also means seeking domination as obedience to commands both in organizing groups and parties by transforming voluntary into compulsory organizations to mobilize a following in the struggle for power and in gaining control over the state as the ultimate form of 'Herrschaft' – rule over others and obedience to commands – over a territory. This will be true, Weber claims, whatever ends we may pursue through politics – whether nationalism, liberalism, or socialism – for the means of politics, power and domination (rule), are invariant (Weber 1919: 313).

However, if politics defined as the struggle for political power to impose one's will also relies on successfully achieving rule or domination outside of and within the state, then the latter, Weber argues, will not last very long if it happens to be the fortuitous result of an agent finding him/herself to be in the position of coercing another to submit to his/her will out of self-interest. Domination depends on predicable rulership and durable rule, and this in turn depends on the subject of the ruler accepting commands *as if* they were valid, that is in the *belief* that they are valid and hence legitimate (Weber 1978 [1922]: 213–214, 942–943, 946–947). It is on the differing grounds for individuals and for staffs to accept an agent's commands as valid or legitimate that Weber develops his famous three-part typology of legitimate forms of *Herrschaft* (rulership, domination and authority) – though it should be pointed out here that in doing so, he explicitly refuses to draw a distinction between obeying out of legitimate reasons and mere acquiescence to domination because one sees no alternative, claiming instead that from a sociological viewpoint such distinctions are irrelevant (1978 [1922]: 947). In defining legitimacy, Weber claims, only belief in the validity of the commands counts. As we will see, Weber's conflation of this distinction will lead to some surprisingly radical, though unintended, consequences for his theory of democracy.

While it may seem that Weber's typology of legitimate rule and domination describes the routine non-conflictual side of politics, in fact the dialectic between conflict leading to selection and success leading to methodical routine is firmly embedded in his sociology of the three types of *Herrschaft*. Famously, 'charismatic rule or domination' involves obedience-based belief in the unique and extraordinary personality or character of an individual and so for Weber it is the most unstable form of *Herrschaft*. In this sense, in Weber's pithy phrase, it exists 'only in the moment of its inception' (Weber 1978 [1922]: 264), and therefore at the very point it becomes effective as power, it immediately routinizes into one of the two everyday forms of rule and dominance: traditional and rational-legal forms of rule or domination. As is well known, traditional domination is based on belief in the sanctity of time-bound custom and the subject's submission to the commands of 'the chief' whose position requires personal loyalty and the habituation to day-to-day custom based on personal relationships (Weber 1978 [1922]: 228, 1006–1010). Rational-legal rule or domination both imitates and is the opposite of traditional domination as it is based on the validity of formal rules and a hierarchically organized division of labour in which each specialized task is adhered to out of a belief that it is based on procedural correctness. Above all, this form of command and obedience depends on a thoroughgoing separation of administrator from the means of administration (Weber 1978 [1922]: 214,216, 218–219). Interestingly, all three forms of submission 'select' for a particular character type of ruler at the expense of the other: 'the charismatically qualified leader', the patriarchal or patrimonial ruler and the impersonal but order-loving administrator or political office seeker. In turn each type selects a certain claim to obedience and command against the other: personal devotion to the charismatic leader; customary obedience to a chief, though in the patrimonial form of rule this is rendered in exchange for sinecures, tax farming, or personal protection; and subservience to procedural rules rather than persons in the case of rational-legal authority or domination.

But this said, the object of each of these kinds of rule is twofold. They require the obedience to commands by both an organized staff beneath the ruler and the subjects of rule who provide the resources, submit to policies and obey the laws or statutes of the ruler. Hence, charismatic domination depends on disciples emotionally attached to the charismatic leader, traditional domination on the court or clients of the patrimonial ruler and rational-legal authority on the impersonal administrator or office holder. Indeed, if the question arises, which of the two elements within each type of domination are most significant in the constant struggle to stabilize the authority of one's commands and direct them towards a goal, it is the belief of the staff in the legitimacy of the ruler that Weber finds to be most significant: 'For all types of domination the fact of the existence of an administrative staff is vital for the habit of obedience cannot be maintained without organized activity directed to the application and enforcement of order' (Weber 1978 [1922]: 264). For the staff can enforce consistent obedience of the subjects, preventing the form of rule-domination from becoming a mere transitory phenomenon; and yet the following is the source of resources and support for the ruler both in its day-to-day functioning and in its conflicts with other political entities. Hence for the ruler there is a constant tension internal to the three kinds of legitimate rule-domination between retaining the loyalty of the staff and the loyalty of the following. Once applied to politics, this internal problem within each type of rule or domination will become the fundamental external problem of political leadership in organizing to acquire political power within and against the state.

Typically, the conceptual narrative derived from the tension within and between these three types takes on several forms in Weber that are relevant for understanding his sociology of politics. Charismatic authority is portrayed as the rebellion against routine domination and rule either in its traditional form or in the form of impersonal rule. Similarly, charisma represents a revolutionary force mobilizing disciples and a following to recover a lost set of values or reorienting ordinary normative patterns of order from within through the voice of the charismatic leader or prophet who claims that his words trump the accepted or written laws. Or these types describe the process by which charismatic authority routinizes through the staff or disciples into a set of traditional rules, customs and habits, or in turn furthers the process whereby administration imposes formal procedure and rules within a hierarchy of functions and a division of labour based on specialization – for example when Weber claims that charismatic leaders of both revolutionary and parliamentary parties, if successful, will either have to hand out the political spoils to a new set of clients or increase bureaucratic domination over social life or a combination of both (Weber 1919: 350–351, 364–365; see Mommsen 1974: 3–21). Or where charisma plays no role, traditional rule or obedience may contain a dispersion of political and military resources to feudal lords that under rational-legal rule are centralized in the hands of the impersonal state. Or alternatively, Weber's types may be used to describe combinations of all three forms. For example, a charismatic leader may gain leadership over a political association such as a political party or a state but attains obedience to a following through a formal party apparatus and when that leader is successful he or she hands out patronage to clients on the basis of traditional (patrimonial) authority. Or most dramatically, and for Weber most ominously, the typology is used to describe the process whereby bureaucracy under rational-legal rule swallows up all other kinds of rule, leading to subservience to formal rules in all areas of social life and the complete disappearance of politics either as stable political rule or as the struggle for power. But for all these various uses, charisma always ends up on the conflictual side of Weber's dialectic of political power struggle and routinization while the other two forms can end up an either side.

More significantly, if one looks closely at the typology as a whole, one notices that *each of the three kinds of rule/domination mirror one another* so that each contains features of an opposed type – what Weber in his famous *Protestant Ethic and the Spirit of Capitalism* called 'elective affinities'; and this mirroring becomes the basis for Weber's explanations for why one '*Herrschaftsform*' can turn into or give way to one another. For example, both charismatic authority or rulership and traditional authority or rulership represent different kinds of *personal* relations, charisma based on submission of the staff and following to the unique qualities of a person and traditional authority on submission to a person or chief based on custom or habit. Or for example on the other side of the ledger, once administrators follow the formal rules of office regularly and their clients submit to administrative decisions without questioning them, rational-legal rules can become *habitual and customary*, similar to traditional forms of authority, and both administrative officials and their clients come to view bureaucratic rules in a traditional manner, that is as inevitable, existing from time immemorial. Likewise, Weber points out that, similar to the holders of sinecures from a patrimonial ruler, the civil servants may form a status group with its own rules of entry and its own concept of honour using its status to protect intrusion from the political arm of the state as well as from its clients. And even the radically opposed types of rational-legal and charismatic rule may turn into one another through the common logic that they both depend for their sustenance on their organized staffs: in the first case the disciples form a division of labour to continue the cause and solve the problem of succession; in the second case the bureaucratic staff becomes the instrument of the charismatic political leader.

Finally, I would like to point to one last political sociological use of this typology in Weber: namely all three forms both by themselves and in combination at once enable and constrain the process of struggling for power. Specifically, they enable politics by becoming means by which political actors, whether parties, leaders, or movements, engage in competition and struggle to prevent themselves from being selected against. But they also constrain the politics by forming the barriers to that struggle, as every vertical process of conflict between, say status groups or classes, is absorbed at once into a horizontal conflict among types of legitimate domination and a horizontal process by which types settle into routine forms of legitimate rule. And in this way, charismatic, traditional and rational-legal authority/domination – the core of Weber's political sociology – provide a frame within which he draws out his specific sociological account of the dynamics and emergence of modern politics into 'business' and 'vocation'.

Politics as a 'business' and a 'vocation'

In his specific sociology of modern politics, Weber lays out a series of inter-locking developmental tendencies and contingent political conflicts leading to the emergence of politics into an autonomous 'enterprise' or 'business' (*Betrieb*) with its own professional requirements, division of labour and organizations. Once fully formed, this 'organization' of politics selects only for certain types of political actors capable of engaging in the unceasing struggle for power in the modern rational-legal state (Weber 1919: 325). In understanding the origin of politics as business, Weber, I would argue, focuses on the development of five different political entities and their convergence in modernity: the political association as the victory over kinship and clan networks, the modern political party as response to democracy, the modern parliament as an outgrowth of collegial rule, the modern state as the ultimate expropriator of political means and above all, the leading or vocational politician who operates within and against these developments.

First off, a precondition for the development of modern politics for Weber is the process whereby the political community takes over from the warrior communities and clans the task of punishing internal violators of persons and property and defending against external enemies. Simultaneously, a subjective sentiment of 'solidarity against outsiders' develops as membership comes to mean identification with the community's control of force against enemies (Weber 1978 [1922]: 907–908). Viewed this way, the legitimacy of the political community's rule over all other associations follows from its claim to provide protection against internal injury and outside threats. Thus emerges a kind of legitimacy flowing from the political community's definition of the friend–enemy relation through its claim to provide the legitimate monopoly of violence.

But the modern impersonal administrative state based on rational-legal authority and domination emerges from a second development, namely what Weber, transferring

Marx's concept of capitalist expropriation of the independent producers to the political realm, calls 'the political expropriation process' (Weber 1919: 316, 1918b: 281). One should note that it is in traditional forms of rulership and domination – in particular patrimonial forms – that this separation has its origin. Under patrimonial rule the administrative staff, in particular one based on estates, appropriates particular political resources from the ruler in exchange for support (Weber 1978 [1922]: 232–234). The first professional politician, the prince, initiates the expropriation of these political means from the private possessors of financial and military power and centralizes them under his own authority. But he succeeds only to be displaced by his staff which has now become technically specialized in deploying these means; the staff in turn has these means expropriated from it by the central administration that it creates to execute its orders. However, the central administration, though forming a status of its own, is no longer subject to any one individual but to the one institution that can back up its *Herrschaft* (rule or domination) with force, the state (Weber 1919: 315).

The modern political party also develops as part of this political expropriation process in direct response to the struggle for political power in the state. However, it takes its form as response to universal suffrage within mass democracy rather than to the centralization of political means in the state. For with the introduction of mass suffrage, the modern political party has to become an efficient machine to bring in the votes over a vast territory (Weber 1919: 338, 341). To adapt to these conditions, parties must jettison their reliance on traditional notables for whom politics was a part-time job and instead employ officials who permanently live off the party, specializing in organizing local units of the party and deploying the party's finances. In turn the party becomes increasingly bureaucratic in its structure, relying on a division of labour and strict chain of command to organize its following to succeed in the peaceful 'battlefield of elections' (Weber 1919: 331, 341). Any party that fails to submit to this version of rational-legal domination internally will be driven out of the struggle for power to capture the rational-legal state externally.

The expropriation of the means of political struggle by political parties has its parallel in the historical sociology of parliaments for Weber. But the pull is in the opposite direction in that where the monarch or prince, having centralized his domination, developed a collegial form of rule against his dependence on specialists in military force and administration, the collegial body would under certain circumstances separate itself from the executive and declare its own supremacy, as happened in England (Weber: 1919: 323–324 but see Collins 1998: 24–25). Parliament then becomes the arena for the development of political parties and potentially a testing ground for the selection of the new leading politician.

Thus the last development is the emergence of the 'leading politician' or the political leader. This leader is at once a professional politician who lives off politics and a vocational politician who lives for politics as the aim of life (*der Berufspolitiker*). Weber views this development as sociologically tenuous as this figure develops only in the West and only through a remarkably fortuitous combination of political character types: the demagogue of the ancient Greek polis; the prince of the Renaissance who hoards and then deploys the means of power against all enemies; and the charismatic political leader of parties in parliaments who strives for executive power and who uses his oratorical skill to bring the party and the following behind him (Weber 1919: 322–323, 331, 339, 342–343, 349). Ideally for Weber this professional politician with a calling becomes a 'plebiscitary dictator' over both parliament and party, using his or her charisma to win elections and impose substantive aims on the political community in opposition to routine politics. And the routine politics to which the vocational politician is a potential counterweight consists not just of domination by the administration of the state that imposes rules impersonally and dispassionately, as so many commentators have noted, but also the office-seeking professional politicians who use political parties as the instrument of their ambitions and the parliamentary representatives who engage in bargaining and horse trading on behalf of various interest groups – in short, professional politicians without a calling ('*Berufspolitiker ohne Berufung*').

For Weber, there is nothing inevitable about the outcome these five developments. Indeed, it is possible for the modern state to achieve full development in its monopoly of political and administrative means, yet suffer inadequate development of parliaments and parties. In this case, parliaments and parties may be composed of traditional notables and professional politicians who pursue negotiated compromises instead of engaging in political conflict while a strong administrative caste makes all the major decisions in the state, as was the case in pre-World War I Germany (Weber: 1918b). Yet once these five developmental tendencies converge, they produce an internal interlocking set of self-reproducing compulsory institutions that constitute politics as a modern business (*Betrieb*) with its own demands, professional roles and division of labour. And against the combination of rational-legal and traditional forms through which day-to-day politics is conducted Weber now puts the charismatic vocational politician who shares both in the professional routine side of politics and in the non-routine struggle for power; elections, parliamentary debates and ultimately the striving to capture the executive office now constitute a process whereby such politicians are selected. According to Weber – and here we see the existential dialectic at work in matters of political ethics – these 'leading politicians' expect to take responsibility for failing to realize ends that are thwarted by the business side of politics and the logics of legitimate domination, but they also take responsibility for injuring others in using power and domination, backed by force, to achieve their ends (see Weber 1919: 365–367).

This said, one should note that although Weber defines the limits of political action within the 'business' of politics by the extremes of rational-legal and charismatic domination, it is the logic of traditional domination that contains the origin of modern politics. Indeed, within his political sociology the political struggle to expropriate the owners of political means that defines traditional domination is never overcome even under modern conditions. *It is merely internalized within the business of politics itself.* Thus modern political actors are condemned to play out this original struggle against patrimonial rule again and again, resorting at one moment to rational-legal domination, at another to charismatic domination to break the hold of this logic. This is the form, I would argue, in which the dialectic of conflict-selection and routinization plays itself out in modern politics for Weber.

Weber's political sociology and democracy

Where does the conflict between modern liberal democracies and more direct forms of democracy fit into Weber's political sociology so construed? There is much debate on this issue, with some commentators seeing Weber as a resolute defender of liberal democracy who is trying to find the sociological conditions for its sustenance (Beetham 1991b) and others arguing that his theory is in tension with precisely this form (Mommsen 1990; Schroeder 1998: 84–84). If we follow through his account of modern politics, we come to a conclusion that his defence of liberal democracy collides with the sociological conditions of politics that do not necessitate this model. David Beetham has it right when he claims that for Weber political sociology is at once about a problem in liberal democracy and a problem for liberal democracy (Beetham 1989).

Indeed democracy for Weber, even in its minimalist liberal form in which politicians and political parties engage in mass elections for parliamentary and executive office, collides with and must adapt to the logic of political struggle to appropriate the means of power within the business side of politics. And this struggle is itself enabled and constrained by the oscillation between charismatic forms of domination and rational-legal ones, often in combination in the case of leaders and political parties with traditional domination in the form of both residues of patrimonial patronage and the never-ending struggle to appropriate political means from other parties and the state. This struggle in turn must adapt to the impersonal institutions of the 'Anstaltsstaat', the institutional state characterized by rational-legal domination in its administration and its political institutions (see Schroeder 1998: 85). This is why Weber carves out his famous model of plebiscitary democracy from a combination of these conditions, that is, his endorsement of elections as a testing process whereby political leaders with vocational qualities are selected for the executive office of the state.

It should hardly be surprising then that Weber's political sociology would be rather insensitive to movements for popular self-rule or for the extension of political equality into a wide array of social rights. Indeed, precisely because he does not distinguish genuine consent from mere acquiescence in his definition of legitimacy, he cannot accommodate direct forms of popular or citizen participation within his famous typology of domination (see Beetham 1991b: 11). On the contrary, demands for the exercise of a popular will are for Weber simply charismatic revolutionary moments, 'opposed to all forms of domination or rule [Herrschaftsfremd]' (Weber 1978 [1922]: 268–269), and thus extraordinary, occasional and fleeting. When in his first formulations of his sociological concepts and in the opening of Economy and Society Weber does speak of a fourth kind of legitimate domination based on voluntary popular consent (Weber 1978 [1922]: 33, 36–37, 1250), he fails to develop it in relation to his other three types. And when he does discuss it as an institutional form, that is as direct democratic rule, he sees it as inevitably succumbing to the rule of administration (Weber 1978 [1922]: 289–292; see Breuer 1998: 3).

Curiously, despite the fact that he dismisses direct democratic political will as a durable form of legitimate rule in his political sociology, or perhaps as a direct result of it, Weber in effect acknowledges what a significant strand of radical democratic theory has often claimed to be a characteristic of popular democratic involvement: that democratic will cannot be institutionalized in a routine form of command and obedience (Wolin 1996: 54–56; Arendt 1991: 246, 255–257, 268–269). These democratic theorists argue that active citizen-driven democracy does not constitute a form of legitimate command at all, unless, of course, the citizens are also the subjects of their own laws, but the point at which citizens claim to be both rulers and ruled will in the empirical world always appear as a resistance to all three of Weber's forms of domination-rulership – that is, as a constant dissolution of ordinary rule and as constant resistance to it. Indirectly, these theorists acknowledge that demands for democracy beyond its liberal forms are caught in Weber's dialectic of conflict and routinization but draw alternative conclusions to those of Weber regarding the empirical meaning of the acquiescence–consent distinction.

Weberian Political Sociology after Weber

More recent Weberian political sociology has tended to be less concerned with the existential tension in Weber's work between the struggle for political power issuing in selection and its routinization in everyday forms that provide the ground for new struggles. Instead, it has tended in two directions: first, it has expanded upon and revised his concepts of power, state, legitimacy and domination and their application to historical political sociology; and second, it has questioned Weber's application of these terms to modern democracy (see King and Le Galès, Chapter 10, in this volume, for further discussion). A couple of brief examples must suffice to illustrate these shifts of emphasis.

With respect to the first point, Michael Mann in his magisterial *Sources of Social Power* (1986, 1993) dissolves Weber's dualistic concept of power as imposing one's will over resistance and *Herrschaft* (domination-rulership) as imposing a command without resistance into four mobile sources of power – ideological, political, military and economic – each of which enable collectivities to accomplish their goals (1986: 22–28). The emphasis here is on the command rather than the initiatory side of power. Mann sees these four sources of power as fluid between society and the state, so that sometimes the state may exercise ideological or economic power and at other times an actor within society may do so. Following a similar path, Randall Collins (1986) and Charles Tilly (1985) develop in greater depth than Weber the role of military power and coercion in the formation of centralized states. In Tilly's case the state emerges as a protection racket against predators, in Collin's case as a response to geopolitical threats.

With respect to the second point concerning the application of Weber's categories onto modern democracy, Charles Tilly (2004) has sought to identify the various logics and mechanisms that have produced mass protest and contentious mass political initiatives that have furthered democratization. Central to his account is an attempt to point to three mechanisms that develop incrementally over time and that undermine precisely the kinds of domination and rule that frame Weber's account of politics: the slow dissolution of inequalities by category through secret ballots or increased political participation; the dissolution of segregated networks of trust by ending patron–client relations in favour of including excluded groups in receiving benefits; and the increasing equality of relations between citizens and governments. Tilly demonstrates that collective action is not a limiting case of the logic of legitimate forms of domination but follows a counter-logic that Weber's typology of power and domination is unable to register, thus revealing the poverty of Weber's logics of legitimate domination and selection through political conflict for understanding the meaning of protests and democratic initiatives.

In brief, present-day Weberian political sociology does not just expand upon, revise, or criticize some of the central concepts of Weber's political sociology, such as power, domination, or legitimacy; it also, implicitly and at times explicitly, uses political sociology to provide a means of assessing the feasibility and meaning of certain deeply held political commitments. Weber himself saw such testing as one of the central goals of his political sociology (Weber 1989 [1919]: 25–26; Weber 1949a [1917]: 20, 35; Weber 1949b [1904]: 53. See Scott 2000: 33; Brunn 2004; Aron 1964: 67–68, 84) and used his political sociology to draw conclusions about political responsibility, collective action and the fate of democracy, even as he claimed to merely give us a map of political conflict and its routine forms. This use of political sociology to subject the partisan positions to the existential and sociological conditions of politics is still awaiting explicit development (Breiner 2004a).

Further Reading

Beetham, D. 1991: *Max Weber and the Theory of Modern Politics*, 2nd edn. Cambridge: Polity Press.

Breiner, P. 1996: *Max Weber and Democratic Politics*. Ithaca: Cornell University Press.

Breiner, P. 2004: 'Unnatural selection': Max Weber's concept of *Auslese* and his criticism of the reduction of political conflict to economics. *International Relations* 18 (3): 289–307.

Mommsen, W. 1974: *The Age of Bureaucracy: Perspectives on the Political Sociology of Max Weber*. New York: Harper & Row.

3

Durkheim and Durkheimian Political Sociology

KENNETH THOMPSON

The main concepts of Durkheim's sociology are discussed in terms of their relevance for political sociology. Early accounts of his work focused on the somewhat evolutionist description of the changing forms of the division of labour as societies moved from traditional to modern. Subsequently, attention began to be paid to those of his works that dealt more directly with political institutions, including the state. His conceptualization of politics seems particularly relevant to the ongoing discussions of civil society. More recently his work has also proved a rich source of analytic ideas for cultural sociologists inspired by Durkheim's discussions of the symbolic sphere of socio-cultural life, who have used them to explore political processes. Notable examples of this application include Jeffrey Alexander's work on the Watergate crisis and the Obama presidential campaign.

Before discussing some of the more important of Durkheim's contributions to the development of political sociology, it is important to be clear about the relevant and fundamental conceptual building blocks of his sociology. They are as follows: individualism (moral individualism distinguished from egoistic individualism), social solidarity, regulation (social and moral), intermediate associations (such as professional associations, civil society), the state, collective effervescence (as experienced in social movements and gatherings, and collective ritual performances), and symbolic representations of the socially sacred (society itself in an idealized form). Early accounts of Durkheim's sociology were mainly focused on his contrast between the form of the division of labour in traditional society and that in modern society, equating his view with that of others who adopted an evolutionary view of the increasing specialization of the division of labour. It was only later that attention began to be given to his explicit discussions of the

The Wiley-Blackwell Companion to Political Sociology, First Edition. Edited by Edwin Amenta, Kate Nash, and Alan Scott.
© 2012 Blackwell Publishing Ltd. Published 2012 by Blackwell Publishing Ltd.

institutions of politics and the state, and then much later to the political relevance of his ideas about the sphere of culture and the symbolic.

To summarize his view of the main problems facing the modern society of his own day: Durkheim believed that individual liberty was a central value, but it needed to be a moral individualism that respected the needs of society as a whole. Contemporary capitalism tended to encourage individual competitive striving without sufficient regulation and in a system that exacerbated inequalities. The state needed to level the playing field, if necessary by restricting inheritance of wealth and unfair employment contracts, but mainly by encouraging intermediate institutions to practice an ethically based regulation within their own sectors. His personal political position approximated that of the ethical socialists or guild socialism of R.H. Tawney in Britain – although the implications of his theoretical position have been judged by some later commentators to place him potentially much more to the radical left of the political spectrum (Pearce 1989; cf. Laborde 2000 for a discussion of French and Continental pluralism relevant to Durkheim's position). Apart from the state-initiated reforms concerning wealth and contracts, mentioned above, his view of the state rested on a 'communicative theory of politics' which viewed the state as an institution whose task was to elevate and distil the representations and opinions coming from below, so acting as a synthesizing intelligence on behalf of the whole. Its sphere of operations corresponds more to what Habermas and others have termed the 'public sphere of civil society' than it does to the organized state of much state-centred sociology (Emirbayer 1996: 114).

In terms of social philosophy, Durkheim stressed the centrality of the concept of the individual person in modern thought. However, he showed how this could take either negative (socially pathological) or positive (balanced and progressive) forms. The negative form was that of egoistic and anomic individualism, which was characteristic of much of modern economic thought and activity. The positive form was that which fostered social solidarity (Joas 2009: 2–3). A balanced individualism also required an adequate sense of social needs, not least in the economic sphere (Durkheim, 2009 [1917]: 3–6). To put this in disciplinary terms: Durkheim opposed the dominance of economic thinking and sought to stress the need for a sociological perspective that emphasized the priority of the social dimension and its moral basis. Even apparently economic phenomena, such as the market and contracts, could not operate or be understood without regard for their social and cultural dimensions.

It will be argued that the most important methodological and analytical contributions of recent Durkheimian sociology to the study of political processes can be situated within the 'cultural turn' that has occurred in the social sciences and humanities. Sociologists have returned to Durkheim's magnum opus, *The Elementary Forms of the Religious Life* (1995 [1915]), inspired by his discussion of the binary structures of culture, especially the sacred–profane dichotomy. It was this that influenced the subsequent development of structuralism (e.g., the work of Claude Levi-Strauss (1963)), and has recently been drawn on by sociologists attempting to develop a symbolic approach to politics.

Changing Views of Durkheimian Sociology

There is an interesting question that needs to be answered about why it took so long for Durkheim's sociology to gain recognition as an important resource for political sociology. After all, it took very little time for sociologists to appreciate the contribution his works made to the study of subjects such as changes in the forms of the division of labour, suicide, crime, education and religion. But for many years there was little consideration of the relevance of his sociology for the study of political processes and issues.

One reason may be that Durkheim avoided direct involvement in politics, apart from the Dreyfus Affair (1898), and concentrated on developing sociology as a respectable academic discipline. However, another reason for the slow recognition may have been the delay in publishing and translating his most overtly political book, which did not appear until 33 years after his death, and even then it was only as a result of the efforts of a Turkish disciple to have it published by the University of Istanbul. Based on Durkheim's lecture notes, *Lecons de sociologie: physique des meurs et du droit* (1950), the book was translated into English as *Professional Ethics and Civic Morals* (1957). It is not surprising that some of the most influential early commentators on his sociology failed to refer to this work (Alpert 1961 [1939]; Parsons 1937) and consequently minimized the political relevance of his thought. The early American commentators, in particular, were inclined to assimilate Durkheim's thought into a contemporary 'functionalist' or 'voluntarist' approach. Teachers of sociology slipped all too easily into misleading dichotomies, in which Durkheim was identified with a conservative approach preoccupied with 'order' and 'stability', in contrast to Marx and Weber, who could be portrayed as concerned with 'conflict' and 'change' (e.g., Nisbet 1965).

A better acquaintance with his writings on politics in *Professional Ethics and Civic Morals* and lesser works such as *Socialism* (1958 [1928]) and various articles and reviews has led to a greater appreciation of his concern about the need for social change if the ideals of the French Revolution – liberty, equality and fraternity – were to be fulfilled. Unlike Marx, he did not believe that political revolution based on class conflict was the answer. Experience suggested that political revolutions tended to lead to bureaucratic domination: 'It is among the most revolutionary peoples that bureaucratic routine is often most powerful' (Durkheim 1961 [1925]: 137). In Durkheim's view, the problem in France was that the underlying social changes, of which the Revolution of 1789 and the revolutionary movements of 1848 and 1870–1871 were only a symptom, had not yet been accommodated within the structure of modern France. The task of sociology was to analyze the long-term evolutionary character of the changes that had brought about industrialization (the division of labour) and to diagnose the causes of the strains that were present in actually existing society. This was the analytical task taken up in *The Division of Labor in Society* (1984 [1893]) and *Professional Ethics and Civic Morals*.

According to Durkheim's analysis, the differentiation of institutions and functions entailed in the division of labour produced a situation marked by greatly increased individualism. This could be a positive development or it could have pathological results, depending on the type of individualism that prevailed. In fact, as it had developed in France and other capitalist societies, it had taken on pathological characteristics, because egoism rather than moral individualism predominated. Competition and conflict to satisfy individual, unrestrained appetites reigned in place of cooperation to promote the common good. Freedom of contract in the context of inequality simply meant that the strong exploited the weak. The situation could only be changed if the state took a more positive role in securing the conditions under which individuals could develop their potentialities, involving greater equality of opportunity and a drastic reduction in the inequalities perpetuated by the inheritance of wealth. A necessary reform would be the development of intermediate institutions between the individual and the state, so as to cohere the opinions of individuals and communicate them to the state, and to channel the state's leadership down to the grassroots; such institutions would also act as a buffer between the individual and the state, and balance the power of the state. In some respects, Durkheim was anticipating the calls for the strengthening of civil society that have now become topical. However, because he appreciated the importance of the economic sphere in industrial societies, he recognized that the key intermediate institution would need to be one that combined economic and moral functions – something along the lines of occupational associations, analogous to the ancient guilds or corporations. He stressed, however, that the guilds could only perform their function if they modernized and took on a democratic structure.

The analysis developed in *Professional Ethics and Civic Morals* is a direct continuation of that begun in *The Division of Labor in Society*. There could be no going back to the mechanical solidarity of simpler societies, in which the individual was subordinated to the collective conscience, based on uniformity. There was still a 'sacred' quality in society, and it attached to social ideals; in the modern era they were ideals concerning the dignity and worth of the individual. However, the organic solidarity that should characterize modern society would only be realized when society was organized in such a way as to enable the individual to govern his/her self and where moral regulation led to voluntary restraint of the appetites for the benefit of all. For this to occur, solidary groups and group ethics were required. While some critics dismissed this as a conservative hankering for a return to the past or an authoritarian urge to subjugate the individual to society, it eventually became clear that Durkheim was attempting to overcome the dichotomy that opposes individualism to communitarianism (Cladis 1992). His sociological perspective was meant to be a corrective to an overemphasis either on the economy or on the state, focusing instead on the social facts that make up the totality of the social phenomenon, which included a variety of structured layers: morphology (substratum), institutions (normative sphere), collective representations (symbolic sphere) (cf. Thompson 2002: 59–60). According to his definition, the characteristics of social facts were: externality, constraint and generality. A social fact had an existence external to any individual or the mind of any individual. It exercised a constraint over the individual in a number of ways, depending on its position in the continuum of social phenomena ranging from morphological facts that determined the availability of facilities, to the constraining force of norms backed by sanctions, to the constraints imposed by language, the force of myths and symbols, and the pressures of public opinion.

During the period from the 1960s through much of the 1980s the political sociology of leading practitioners of historical-comparative sociology in the English-speaking world paid little attention to Durkheim's general sociology, drawing more on Marx and Weber in focusing attention on the rise and development of capitalism and the formation of national states (see Emirbayer 1996, for a critique of Barrington Moore, Charles Tilly and Theda Skocpol, in this respect). The title of Charles Tilly's essay 'Useless Durkheim' (1981) illustrates this tendency (a rare exception was Robert Bellah 1959). Partly this was due to the tendency to equate Durkheim with the structural-functionalism and social evolutionism of Talcott Parsons, who had selectively appropriated some of Durkheim's ideas. It was only when sociologists began to give more attention to the theoretical juncture in between the modern state and capitalism that they discerned a new relevance for Durkheimian concern with the structures and processes of civil society. It is the intermediate domains of social life – the domestic, associational and public institutions of society – that Durkheim analyzed; not only the domain of political society (or the 'public sphere'), but also 'the intimate sphere' (especially the family), the sphere of associations (especially voluntary associations), social movements and forms of public communication (Cohen and Arato 1992: ix; quoted in Emirbayer 1996: 113).

An example of Durkheim's historical analyses of institutions that play a key role in social and political regulation was his posthumously published *L'Evolution pedagogique en France* (1938; translated into English as *The Evolution of Educational Thought*, 1977). One of the criticisms of Durkheim's sociology before the English translation of that work was that he did not see that ideology, as represented by moral and education doctrines and practices, could be biased and systematically work in favour of the interests of some classes against those of others. Added to this was the charge that he was blind to education's role in restricting the life chances of some classes (cf. Lukes 1975: 133). However, these criticisms are refuted by his analysis of the relations between social classes and educational ideas and practices, as set out in *The Evolution of Educational Thought*. In the example of the educational changes brought about by the Renaissance, he argued that a growth in wealth and consumption led to an increased emulation of aristocratic lifestyles by the aspiring middle class – the educational ideas of humanism, such as those of Erasmus, were aimed at refinement of cultural tastes to fit the 'leisured class' for polite society. Durkheim added that this was at the expense of the educational needs of the masses (Durkheim 1977 [1938]: 205–206). Drawing on Durkheim's ideas, Jeffrey Alexander has pointed out that modern education plays a crucial mediating role connecting 'two kinds of moralities, the affective morality of family life and the more rigorous, impersonal faith that controls civic society' and the state (Alexander 1982: 279–280). It is above all in his later religious sociology, notably *The Elementary Forms of the Religious Life*, that Durkheim links the normative regulation of institutions and the symbolical cultural logics that constrain action in all the institutional sectors of society, including that of modern civil society. He suggests that religious beliefs and, by extension, other cultural formations are organized according to a binary logic, most famously in the contrast between the sacred and the profane, but also in further subdivisions such as the pure and the impure, the divine and the diabolical, and the forces of order and those of chaos. It is through the analysis of these binary codes that cultural sociologists have sought to apply Durkheim's ideas to political processes. In doing so they insist on granting more autonomy to cultural factors in their analyses than did those sociologists of the 1980s who had pointed to the overlap between Althusserian Marxist theories of ideology and Durkheim's ideas on religion (Strawbridge 1982; Thompson 1986; Pearce 1989).

Cultural Sociology and Politics

As disaffection with the structural-functionalism epitomized in Talcott Parsons' work increased during the 1970s, three of his former students and co-workers began to push his framework towards a distinctively Durkheimian emphasis on symbolism, sacred-ness and ritual, which paved the way for the cultural turn in political sociology. Edward Shils argued that secular, differentiated societies have symbolic 'centres' which inspire awe and mystery and that it is proximity to these sources of sacredness that allocates such 'structural' qualities as social status (Shils 1975). Clifford Geertz argued that whether cultural systems are 'religious' has nothing to do with any reference to the supernatural, but rather concerns the degree to which they are sacralized, inspire ritual devotion and mobilize group solidarity (Geertz 1973, chapters 4 and 8). He went on to analyze American political campaigns in similar symbolic and culturalist terms (Geertz 1983). The third member of this group, Robert Bellah, was most explicit in drawing on Durkheim, arguing that secular nations have 'civil religions' – symbolic systems that relate national political structures and events to a transcendent, supra-political framework that defines some ultimate social meaning (Bellah 1970, 1980). Like Durkheim, Bellah calls this framework 'religious' only in order to emphasize the sacredness of its symbols and the ritual power it commands. This cultural turn in political sociology has been described and developed in the work of Alexander, a student of Parsons and Bellah. He traced out the theoretical continuities and innovations in his Introduction to the edited volume *Durkheimian Sociology: Cultural Studies* (Alexander 1988), which also contained his own first attempt to apply this framework to a political process, that of the Watergate crisis that began in 1972. Where Alexander moved beyond his predecessors was in deconstructing the binary sets of good and evil characteristics of the narratives and discourses enshrined in the civil religion that bestowed a sacred character on society. He examines the Watergate crisis and its unfolding as a public drama of ritual cleansing, tracing the transition from one set of binary symbolic classifications to another in the course of the purging process. Subsequently, he and his collaborators have gone beyond the case of American civil religion and drawn up binary codes that they take to be characteristic of all liberal-democratic societies. As Alexander states:

> Democratic discourse, then, posits the following qualities as axiomatic: activism, auton-omy, rationality, reasonableness, calm, control, realism and sanity. The nature of the counter-code, the discourse that justifies the restriction of civil society, is already clearly implied. If actors are passive and dependent, irrational and hysterical, excitable, passion-ate, unrealistic or mad, they cannot be allowed the freedom that democracy allows.
>
> (Alexander 2000: 299)

Alexander's colleague, Philip Smith, also describes the code of liberal democracy in terms of the binary opposites of the sacred and profane. The sacred is said to be characterized by an emphasis on: order, the individual, reason, activism, law, equality, inclusiveness and autonomy; whereas the profane involves: disorder, group emotion, passivity, power, hierarchy, exclusiveness and dependence (Smith 1998: 120). These two sets of binary opposites are particularly prominent where one group is claiming to represent the values of the idealized society and to convince the public that its opponent represents the opposite, negative characteristics. Because of the Western world's shared historical heritage, dating back to Ancient Israel and Classical Greece, Western societies tend to share many of the same forms of discourse and symbols in their idealized civil society. However, as each society also has somewhat different historical components, there are also differences in the forms taken by the binary oppositions and in the way these are summoned up and articulated in public controversies. It is here, in the deconstruction of cultural codes operating through the particularities of discursive narratives, that the neo-Durkheimian approach has most to offer to political sociology.

On the whole, Alexander and his colleagues have tended to stress the similarities in the binary codes operating in liberal-democratic societies or even in an emerging global civil sphere. However, it has been argued that, bearing in mind Weber's distinction between the nation and the state – the nation is a cultural phenomenon, whereas the state is an organized structure (Weber 1978: 922) – it is increasingly the case that in multicultural societies the national element is not always firmly anchored in or supportive of the culture of civil society that is congruent with the liberal-democratic state. This becomes obvious in the light of the different images summoned up by appeals to the spirit of ethnic nationalism or other nationalisms not coterminous with the state (Thompson 2004: 20). The highly charged binary symbolic structures that construct nationalisms are also highly particularistic and often opposed to the more universalistic symbols and values that are typical of civil society in liberal democracies. Of course, ethnic or nationalist groups often seek to broaden political support for their cause by appealing to wider values of civil society. But this is only part of the story. The approach that focuses on liberal-democratic discourses tends to equate civil society with 'normal' political processes and appeals to a consensual set of values. But ethnic nationalisms are culturally significant and of sociological interest precisely because of their totalizing, expressive, emotional, particularisms, rather than because they are similar to all other liberal-democratic processes.

Durkheim was conscious of the power of appeals to nationalism and addressed his wartime pamphlets to countering German nationalist ideology, such as that emanating from Weber's teacher Heinrich von Treitschke, which claimed that state sovereignty is absolute, above morality, and that the state is the realm of unity above and opposed to civil society (the realm of plurality and difference). By contrast, Durkheim maintained that the idealized society underpinning the modern democratic state, such as France, was based upon the moral code whose collective representations derived from values and principles enshrined in the Declaration of the Rights of Man and the Citizen. His vision was of a pluralistic state in which intermediate groups and associations, with their particularistic cultures and interests, would mediate between the state and the individual, while the state would encourage the development of a constitutional patriotism that could supply the organic solidarity compatible with the *conscience collective* of the French nation. Thus, while he recognized the elements of 'mechanical solidarity' in collective nationalistic rituals that would persist, he believed that patriotism would find its ultimate legitimation in the universal rights celebrating the cult of the individual as embedded in the nation and its constitution.

Using Durkheim's own prescriptions, it can be argued that France has found it difficult to develop and accommodate intermediate associations that provide the link between state and individual. The political sociologist, Mabel Berezin (2009), has argued that France is a 'hegemonic' nation-state that combines parliamentary democracy with a strong sense of political community that subsumes ethnic and regional cultures. In this institutional context, citizens rely on the nation to provide them with both cultural identity and social security. When citizens are encouraged by some politicians and the media coverage of socio-economic problems to perceive the nation as endangered by globalization (or Europeanization) and immigration, they react emotionally to both cultural and material threats. These are experienced as threats to personal identity and security and, when politically mobilized, give rise to collective emotions that inspire right-wing populist voting in favour of the National Front. According to Durkheim's political sociology, this should be regarded as an 'abnormal' and 'pathological' condition for a modern society and should prove to be temporary. However, it is a cogent criticism of Durkheim that his ideal type (or model) of modern society was destined never to correspond very closely to actually existing conditions. Nevertheless, it can be argued that it might help to provide a benchmark against which actual political tendencies can be judged in terms of their likely temporary or more permanent character. Jeffrey Alexander pinpoints the gap between Durkheim's appreciation of the importance of moral regulation for the coherence of modern society and his rather empirically vague discussions of how modern morality is connected to institutions, social groups and movements in our complex, fragmented and stratified societies:

> This Durkheim hardly begins to explain. How can moral regulation be squared with the rot and murderousness that have marked so much of modern life? Durkheim died in 1917, in the middle of the first great military conflagration of the twentieth century. Two decades later, as the modern world prepared for a second horrendous war, his closest collaborator remarked that the Durkheimians had never imagined totems as swastikas. They had believed that social morality would be transcendent, universal and abstract, and that social obligations would reinforce sacred good, not sacred evil.
>
> (Alexander 2006: 18–19)

The strategy developed by Alexander and other neo-Durkheimians in seeking to bridge the analytical gap left by Durkheim's political sociology is to use Durkheim's method of analyzing symbolic binary codes and apply it to the symbols and narratives in the wider civil sphere, which contribute to the construction, destruction and reconstruction of the elements of moral community and social solidarity that constitute civil society. This approach follows Durkheim in giving priority to the moral bindings that run across institutions, groups and social movements, leading to either social solidarity or fragmentation, depending on their degree of convergence, coherence and strength. It stresses the notion of moral community as the basis of society, in the same way that Durkheim emphasized the essential moral force of society as exemplified by the 'non-contractual' elements of contract – contracts require a prior, moral framework. In this sense, Durkheimian political sociology stands for a rejection of the new utilitarian theories, including the resurgent rational choice theories and 'realistic' approaches to social and political life (Alexander 2006: 54, 568).

If the fullest statement of the theoretical basis of the neo-Durkheimian political sociology is to be found in Alexander's massive work *The Civil Sphere* (2006), its most compelling empirical exemplification is to be found in the more recent analysis of the Obama presidential campaign (Alexander 2010). Whereas Habermas and others have conceptualized conflict in the public sphere as about truth claims and rational justification, Alexander argues that while truth, honesty and fairness do matter, it is less a matter of *being* these qualities than of *seeming* to be them, of embodying truth, narrating honesty and projecting fairness, and of doing it in a persuasive way. Being truthful, honest and fair are discursive claims, and whether these claims take root and hold is held to be a matter of performative success. Alexander shows that throughout the 2008 presidential campaign, operatives and journalists alike spoke of 'painting' the other side. The campaigners for each candidate sought to project a picture/image of their man as the living embodiment of the 'discourse of liberty', while painting the opposing candidate as embodying the dark and brooding qualities that mark the 'discourse of repression'. Campaigning is then described as an aesthetic activity, not a cognitive or moral one, and it depends on stagecraft rather than ethical worthiness or empirical accuracy. Political struggle achieves clarity and persuasive power by defining the difference between one's own and the other's side, connecting 'us' to the sacred civil qualities that sustain liberty, linking 'them' to the anti-civil qualities that profane political life, undermine liberty and open the door to corruption. Alexander demonstrates, through specific examples from the campaign, how each of the candidates sought to paint the opponent in negative terms and to cast doubt on the authenticity of the other's performance, as in the McCain effort to create a narrative that defined Obama as an arrogant celebrity (Alexander 2010).

While it would be foolish to neglect the contributions of other theoretical schools, especially those concerned with inequalities of power or the institutional mechanisms of politics, it is clear that the approach of Durkheimian cultural sociology could make a significant contribution to political sociology in our media-saturated age. It focuses attention on the ways in which social-political 'facts' are culturally constructed and given meaning through their symbolical representations and the codes that enable us to interpret the narratives or discourses in which they are presented. The particular contribution of Durkheimian cultural sociology has been to analyze the binary nature of those cultural codes, building on the kinds of fundamental dichotomies that Durkheim illustrated with his contrast between the sacred versus profane. Whether the 'facts' at issue are about social inequalities of resources and power in relation to class, gender and race, or about the qualities of politicians themselves, their meaning is constructed (and can be analyzed) in terms of their cultural coding.

Further Reading

Cladis, M. 1992: *A Communitarian Defense of Liberalism: Emile Durkheim and Contemporary Social Theory*. Stanford, CA: Stanford University Press.
Gane, M. (ed.) 1992: *The Radical Sociology of Durkheim and Mauss*. London: Routledge.
Cotterell, R. (ed.) 2010: *Emile Durkheim: Justice, Morality and Politics*. Aldershot: Ashgate.

4

Foucaultian Analysis of Power, Government, Politics

Barry Hindess

Foucault's nominalist understanding of power cautions against reification. It also suggests there is little to say of interest about power as such and in general. Foucault focused on specific, relatively stable configurations of power: domination and the government of a state, seeing the first as a hierarchical relationship in which the margin of liberty of the subordinated is extremely restricted and understanding the second more widely than the conventional view. Where the latter treats government as 'the supreme authority in states' and also, somewhat confusingly, as the legitimate actions of that authority, Foucault sees it as action aimed at influencing the way individuals regulate their own behaviour. This second meaning is the more general one and the other a special case. For Foucault, the modern government of the state aims to conduct the affairs of the population in the interests of the whole. This government is not restricted to the actions of *the* government, but is performed also by agencies in civil society. The two senses of 'government' can also be compared in relation to the notion of individual liberty. Where liberals see liberty as setting limits to government action, Foucault presents it as an instrument of liberal government. Despite the contributions of the Foucaultian approach to our understanding of uses of freedom, however, Hindess argues that it should be extended to encompass: first, the dilemmas posed to liberal government by the politically oriented activity of organized interests; second, government in the international arena; and third, authoritarian aspects of liberal government.

To ask the question 'how do things happen?', Michel Foucault insists, is also 'to suggest that power as such does not exist' (1982: 217). The point of his comment is not to deny the reality of situations in which one individual or group exercises power over others but rather to caution against reification: that is, against the treatment of power as an entity or substance (say, a capacity to impose one's will) of a kind that

---

The Wiley-Blackwell Companion to Political Sociology, First Edition. Edited by Edwin Amenta, Kate Nash, and Alan Scott.
© 2012 Blackwell Publishing Ltd. Published 2012 by Blackwell Publishing Ltd.

some people (the powerful) may possess in greater quantities than others. He goes on to claim that power over others should be seen as a matter of 'the total structure of actions brought to bear' (220) on their behaviour. Thus, to adapt a well-known expression of the reified view of power, what happens when A gets 'B to do something that B would not otherwise do' (Dahl 1957: 204) is that A brings various actions to bear on B's conduct. To say, in Dahl's terms, that 'A has power over B' is simply to claim that there is a causal relation between A's actions and B's response. The reference to A's power is not so much an explanation of the change in B's conduct as a convenient kind of shorthand, an alternative to describing what interactions take place between them.

Since social interaction is always a matter of acting on the actions of others, this nominalistic view of power suggests that power relations will often be relatively unproblematic. It also suggests that power is a ubiquitous component of social life and that there is therefore little of value to be said about the nature of power as such and in general. Nevertheless, in spite of this last point, there are some relatively stable configurations of power that Foucault writes about at length: domination and the government of a state. Domination is a hierarchical relationship in which the margin of liberty of the subordinated parties is severely restricted. This is 'what we ordinarily call power' (1988a: 12) and, in Foucault's view, it is something to be resisted: the problem, he suggests, is to establish conditions in which games of power can be played 'with a minimum of domination' (1988a: 18). There are passages in his discussion of government in which he proposes a closely related politics of resistance, this time directed against the state. When he insists, in the closing section of his Tanner Lectures on Human Values, that liberation 'can only come from attacking . . . political rationality's very roots' (1981: 254) his argument is clearly directed against the political rationality that, in his view, underlies the modern government of the state.

There are striking parallels, and equally striking contrasts, between Foucault's normative critiques of domination and government and the arguments of critical theory (Dalton 2008, Hindess 1996, and Ashenden and Owen (eds) 1999 consider the differences from a Foucaultian perspective, while Fraser 1989a, Jay 1992 and McCarthy 1992 consider them from the perspective of critical theory). Of more interest to the substantive analysis of politics, however, are Foucault's accounts of the emergence of the political rationality of government in the early modern period and the subsequent development of liberalism as a specific form of governmental reason. These accounts have inspired a substantial body of academic work, sometimes called the governmentality school (Donzelot and Gordon 2008 query this label), devoted to the study of government in the modern West (Burchell, Gordon and Miller 1991, Barry, Osborne and Rose 1996, and Dean and Hindess 1998 contain useful samples. Dean 1999 and Rose 1999 offer surveys of the field).

This chapter begins by outlining the Foucaultian treatment of government, and of liberalism as a specific rationality of government, and considers its implications for the study of politics. It then moves on to show how this treatment must be adapted to take account of, first, the significance for government of what Max Weber calls 'politically oriented action', second, government in the international sphere, and third, authoritarian aspects of liberal political reason.

Government

In contemporary political analysis the term 'government' is commonly used, often with a capital G, to denote what Aristotle calls 'the supreme authority in states' (1988 III, 1279a: 27) a usage which suggests that the government of a state should be seen as emanating from a single centre of control – albeit one which may sometimes be divided, for example, between executive, legislature and judiciary, or between national and sub-national levels. However, the term can also be used more broadly, and without the capital letter, to denote a kind of activity. Thus Aristotle discusses 'the government of a wife and children and of a household' (1988 III, 1278b: 37–38), a form of rule which he distinguishes both from the government of a state and from the rule of a master over his slave. In yet another usage it may refer to a rule that one exercises over oneself. Foucault notes that in the early modern period, the term referred to rule over 'a household, souls, children, a province, a convent, a religious order, a family' (1991: 90). He insists that, while they may work on different materials, and accordingly face somewhat different problems, there is nevertheless a certain continuity between these diverse usages: they share an underlying concern to affect the conduct of the governed. Thus, rather than act directly on the actions of individuals, government aims to do so indirectly by influencing the manner in which individuals regulate their own behaviour. In this sense, government is clearly a special case of power: while it is a matter of acting on the actions of others (or of oneself), the fact that it may do so indirectly, through its influence on conduct, means that government involves an element of calculation that is not necessarily present in every exercise of power. Government differs from domination, another special case of power, in allowing the governed a certain margin of liberty in regulating their own behaviour, aiming to work primarily by influencing the manner in which they do so.

However, while he emphasizes the continuity between these various forms of government, Foucault also insists on the distinctive character of the modern art of government – 'the particular form of governing which can be applied to the state as a whole' (1991: 91). We can see what is involved here by turning to another aspect of Aristotle's treatment of government: the claim that each form of government has its own proper purpose or *telos*. Thus, the government of a slave is 'exercised primarily with a view to the interest of the master' while the government of a household is 'exercised in the first instance for the good of the governed' (Aristotle 1988, 39: 34–37). In the case of the state, Aristotle maintains, the only true forms of government are those 'which have a regard to the common interest', the others being 'defective or perverted' (Aristotle 1988 III, 1279a: 17–21).

The modern art of government, as Foucault describes it, takes up a version of this classical perspective by insisting that the state should be 'governed according to rational principles which are intrinsic to it' (1991: 96–97). It is tempting to suggest at this point that the existence and practical significance of such principles are likely to be open to dispute. This raises the issue, to be considered later, of the implications for government of partisan politics. Foucault insists that the normative claims of this art of government should be distinguished from two alternative perspectives: justification of rule in terms of a universal order laid down by God (and thus in no sense intrinsic to the state) and 'the problematic of the Prince', which is primarily concerned with 'the prince's ability to keep his principality' (1991: 90). His point in making these distinctions is not to endorse the classical view of the purpose or *telos* of government – quite the contrary, as we have seen – but rather to present the modern government of the state as a systematic attempt to realize that purpose.

As he describes it, then, the art of government is not concerned primarily with the business of taking over the state, keeping it in one's possession or subordinating it to some external principle of legitimacy, but rather with the work of conducting the affairs of the population in what are thought to be the interests of the whole. Government, in this sense, is not restricted to the work of *the* government and the agencies it controls. Much of it will also be performed by agencies of other kinds, for example, by elements of what is now called civil society: churches, employers, financial institutions, legal and medical professionals, political parties and other voluntary associations. The work of governing the state as a whole, then, extends far beyond the institutions of the state itself.

Perhaps the most influential aspect of Foucault's work on government has been his discussion of liberalism as a rationality of government. His fullest treatment of this theme was in a course of lectures delivered at the College de France in 1979. Since these lectures were not written in the expectation of publication, the published version (2008) is not entirely Foucault's responsibility: it was prepared by others after his death, and we should be careful not to read it as a book completed by Foucault himself. Most readers of this chapter will have attended, or even given, enough lectures to know how difficult it can be for a lecturer to achieve coherence in a single presentation, let alone over a course of lectures. Once we acknowledge this difficulty and that he did not have the opportunity to revise the text for publication, it is no great criticism of Foucault to say that the arguments presented in the published course are less clear than one might wish (Hindess 2009). Thus, the first lecture in the course identifies liberalism with Benthamite radicalism. This, Foucault says, is 'broadly what is called liberalism' (2008: 20). In other lectures, while not explicitly rejecting this first view, he offers a more complex account, insisting that liberalism has confused the view of freedom as matter of principle with that of freedom as pragmatic issue for governments (2008: 28), and even suggesting that the principled and pragmatic perspectives finally came together to focus on a 'new ensemble' ('civil society', which is seen as encompassing individuals as both subjects of right and economic actors) 'that is characteristic of the liberal art of governing' (2008: 295).

Since liberalism is commonly regarded as a normative political theory that treats the maintenance of individual liberty as an end in itself and therefore as setting limits of principle to the objectives and means of action of government, the first of these views can be seen as a challenge to conventional political theory, while the second presents this challenge in a less forceful version. Yet, although the lectures were not published in English until 2008, the first of these Foucaultian views has become familiar indirectly through the work of members of the governmentality school noted earlier.

If individual liberty is central to conventional accounts of liberalism, it is central also to the governmentality account, but in a very different way. We can see what is at issue here by considering the governmental significance of the belief that members of the population to be governed are endowed with a capacity for autonomous, self-directing activity. What does that belief entail for the practical work of government? The governmentality account of liberalism focuses on the implication that government should aim to make use of this capacity, that the maintenance and promotion of suitable forms of individual liberty may be advantageous to the state itself.

A particularly significant illustration of this liberal perspective can be found in Adam Smith's *The Wealth of Nations*. Smith describes the aim of political economy as being 'to enrich both the people and the sovereign' (1976: 428) and he argues that this aim is best served by promoting the free activities of economic agents. This argument turns on a view of economic activity as a system of interaction in which the conduct of participants is regulated by prices for goods and labour that are themselves established by the free decisions of the participants themselves – in effect, by numerous individual decisions to buy or to sell, or to seek a better deal elsewhere. Since these prices are established within the system itself, this view suggests that external interference in economic interaction – by the state setting prices or minimum wages, for example – runs the risk of reducing the efficiency of the system overall. Thus, when he examines the police regulation of economic activity or the workings of the mercantile system, Smith's aim is to show that they detract from the wealth of the nation overall.

Liberalism, as Foucault describes it, treats this image of the self-regulating market as a model for other aspects of society. Accordingly, it regards the populations of modern states as encompassing a variety of domains – the sphere of economic activity, the workings of civil society, the processes of population growth and so on – each one regulated, in large part, by the free decisions of individuals in the course of their interactions with others. This perception suggests that, once they have been securely established, these domains of free interaction will function most effectively if external interference is reduced to a minimum. Thus, rather than subject activity within these domains to detailed regulation by the state, liberal government will aim to establish and to maintain conditions under which the domains themselves will operate with beneficial effects for the well-being of the population and of the state itself. This liberal view, in turn, implies that effective government must be based on reliable knowledge of the processes and conditions that sustain these patterns of free interaction. It suggests, in other words, that liberal government will depend on the abstract and theoretical knowledge of social life provided by economics and the other social sciences.

Governmentality scholars have adapted and elaborated on this account of liberalism in the analysis of neoliberal attempts to govern through the decisions of autonomous individuals. They have focused, in particular, on the governmental uses of individual choice and empowerment and on the more general promotion of market or quasi-market regimes as indirect means of government (for examples, see Cruikshank 1999; Rose 1999; Valverde 1998). To say that individual choice, personal empowerment and markets are widely employed as instruments of government is not to say that the freedom they offer is illusory – although it may sometimes be extremely limited – but it is to insist that individual liberty cannot be seen simply as a limit to the reach of government. In fact, as the market model suggests, the use of individual liberty as a means of governing the population must rely not only on regulation by the state but also on the existence of suitable patterns of individual conduct and on the regulation of that conduct by others. Neoliberal government, on this view, will be particularly dependent on the expertise of psychiatrists, counsellors, financial advisers and the like, all of whom assist, or prompt, their clients to develop appropriate ways of conducting their own affairs, and, at another level, on the efforts of economists and others to extend the model of market interaction to the analysis of all areas of human activity.

Politics and Government

To see what this account of the government of the state contributes to our under-standing of politics we have only to observe that 'politics', 'political' and other such terms frequently refer precisely to the government of the state. Foucault adopts this usage throughout his discussions of government and its rationalities, and it is characteristic also of the governmentality literature. The critique of *political* reason developed in Foucault's Tanner Lectures (Foucault 1981) is in fact directed against the art of government outlined above: against a political reason that concerns itself with the government of the state and with recruiting other forms of government, especially the government of oneself, to its own purposes. He is careful, as we have seen, to distinguish this rationality of the government of a state from understandings of government that are not *political* in this specific sense.

Thus, the Foucaultian analysis of government is itself a contribution to the under-standing of an important kind of politics: one that aims to govern the population of a state in what are thought to be the interests of the whole. Foucaultian accounts of liberal and neoliberal government contribute to the understanding of influential contemporary versions of this politics that aim to govern by promoting certain forms of freedom, and so arranging conditions that the resulting activity furthers the common good. Perhaps the most significant contribution of this literature has been its careful exploration of the ways in which this governmental politics makes use of practices of individual self-government and of diverse elements of civil society (Rose and Miller 1992).

Nevertheless, there are many aspects of politics that this powerful analysis of government simply fails to address. For our purposes, the most important of these concern, first, the politically oriented activity that Max Weber describes in the first section of *Economy and Society*, second, government within the international system of states, and third, authoritarian aspects of liberal government.

Government and Partisan Politics

Weber describes action as being politically oriented if:

> it aims at exerting influence on the government of a political organization; especially at the appropriation, redistribution or allocation of the powers of government.
>
> Weber (1978: 55)

Where the focus of Foucault's 'political reason' is on the overall pursuit of the interests and the welfare of the state and the population ruled by the state, that of Weber's 'politically oriented action' is on the partisan activities of parties, pressure groups and social movements, and, of course, of individuals or factions within them. Politically oriented action could well be motivated by religious doctrine or the problematic of the Prince, both of which Foucault distinguishes from the *political* concerns of the art of government, or by conflicting views as to the practical implications of whatever principles, if any, are intrinsic to the government of the state.

In fact, while politically oriented activity may not be directly governmental, the problem of how to deal with it has always been one of the central concerns of the art of government. Its failure to consider the governmental implications of such activity is one of the more serious limitations of the Foucaultian treatment of government. We can begin our discussion of this point by observing that the scope for a certain kind of partisanship is already inscribed in the classical view of the purpose or *telos* of government – a view that the modern art of government also adopts. Far from preventing partisanship, the identification of this *telos* with the common interest (or some equivalent) serves rather to establish the terms in which partisan dispute will be conducted. Thus, in a pattern that will be familiar to political activists of all persuasions, the common interest and more particular, sectional interests are commonly said to be utterly distinct and yet are frequently confused: invocation of the first becomes a standard means of promoting the second and an opponent's appeal to the common interest is readily seen as just another sectional manoeuvre.

While the conduct of partisan dispute in such terms will be present under any form of government, we should expect it to flourish where the freedom of members of the subject population is promoted by the predominant rationality of government. David Hume notes, for example, that partisan groups are

> plants which grow most plentifully in the richest soil; and though absolute governments be not wholly free from them, it must be confessed, that they rise more easily, and propagate themselves faster in free governments, where they always infect the legislature itself, which alone could be able, by the steady application of rewards and punishments, to eradicate them.
>
> Hume (1987: 55–56)

The most striking feature of this passage is its view of partisan politics as an infection of government. This fear of what partisanship might do to government has been a long-standing feature of political (i.e. governmental) reason but, as Hume's comment indicates, it is has a particular resonance for liberal and neoliberal rationalities of government.

This point suggests that the characterization of liberal and related rationalities of government in terms of their emphasis on governing through the decisions of autonomous individuals is seriously incomplete: they are also substantially concerned to defend the proper purposes of government from the impact of partisan politics. It is partly for this reason that secrecy and deliberate misdirection are so commonly employed by even the most liberal of governments. The neoliberal push of recent decades has taken this defence against partisanship further by corporatizing and privatizing various kinds of state activity, insulating central banks from overt political control, and promoting the use of market or contractual relationships between and within government agencies and between those agencies and citizens.

At one level the aim of such devices is to minimize inducements for citizens to engage in partisan politics – Weber's 'politically oriented action' – by enabling them to pursue their concerns in other ways, notably through contract and the market. The promotion of certain kinds of individual autonomy also serves to inhibit political participation. At another level, the aim is to limit the partisan influence of parties, pressure groups and public officials by removing significant areas of public provision from the realm of political decision, and relying instead on suitably organized forms of market interaction. This, of course, is less a reduction in the overall scope of government than a change in the means by which government is exercised: a form of government that works through the administrative apparatuses of the state is displaced in favour of one that works on individuals and organizations through the disciplines imposed by their interactions with others in market and quasi-market regimes. Since this limited dismantling of the administrative apparatuses of the state is itself conducted by partisan politicians and their chosen advisers, those who are not persuaded by the neoliberal case – and many of those who are – will see in this procedure ample scope for the pursuit of new forms of partisan advantage.

Government in the International Arena

If Foucault's discussions of government depart from the conventional view that government is the 'supreme authority' in a state, they nevertheless follow convention in other respects, most obviously by treating government as something that operates essentially within states. One consequence of this conventional view is that relations between states are often seen as largely ungoverned, that is, as a kind of anarchy which is regulated to some degree by treaties, a variety of less formal accommodations, and the occasional war between them (Bull 1977). Yet, if government in its most general sense is a matter of acting on the actions of others, aiming 'to structure their "possible field of action"', then the modern system of states contains more than enough acting on the actions of others for it to be seen, like civil society and the market, as a regime of government with no controlling centre' (Larner and Walters 2004). Thus, where the Aristotelian view treats the state and the government of the state as 'the highest of all', the modern system of states reflects the emergence of a more complex regime of government. While the state retains its privileged position with regard to its own population, there are also important political contexts in which the 'international community' is now regarded as 'the highest of all'.

Two aspects of this international governmental regime are worth noting here. First, the modern art of government has been concerned with governing not simply the populations of individual states but also the larger population encompassed by the system of states itself. We can see government as addressing this task at two levels: first, by promoting the rule of territorial states over populations, and secondly, by seeking to regulate the conduct both of states themselves and of members of the populations under their control. States are thus expected to pursue their own interests, but to do so in a field of action that has been structured by the overarching system of states to which they belong.

There is an important analytical point behind my insistence that the first of these two levels, the modern partitioning of humanity into citizens of states and a small minority of others, should also be seen as an aspect of government, and thus of power. At this level, government is a form of power with powerful (if I can be forgiven the use of this word) and often destructive effects. For example, it requires each state to assume primary responsibility for looking after its own citizens, and thus to accept a lesser responsibility for others. This in turn suggests to the rest of us that the inhabitants of less fortunate states are ultimately responsible for their own condition and, further, that if their states fail them in a manner which appears to threaten the interests of other states, it may be necessary for the international community to step in and sort them out. There is a disturbing denial of history and, indeed, of responsibility at work in such perceptions (Hindess 2004). Or again, the system of states promotes an exclusive sense of solidarity among the citizens of each individual state. Such commonplace sentiments can thus be seen as products, as much as they are causes, of the institutional arrangements they appear to sustain – in this case of the governmental division of humanity into the discrete populations of individual states. At the international level, just as at the domestic, government helps to make us who we are. It is intentional without being reducible to the pursuit of merely sectional interests.

Second, there are striking parallels between the contemporary international order and the late colonial liberal order in which European states and the United States dominated the rest of the world. Today, there is greater resistance to such domination and many more independent states for it to deal with – a condition that presents Western states with a problem not unlike that faced by the United States in the nineteenth-century Americas and by the East India Company in India in J.S. Mill's time.

If the late colonial order of direct or indirect imperial domination was the form in which the European system of states first became global in scope, the achievement or imposition of independence can be viewed as a later stage in the globalization of the European states system. It was a process of imperial withdrawal, if only in the limited sense that it left behind states with their own governing institutions, but also substantial settler populations, many of whom were able to dominate the newly independent states so that, in these cases, indigenous peoples remained subject to an obvious form of imperial rule (Keal 2003). Moreover, while it dismantled one part of the imperial order, independence left another part firmly in place. It both expanded the membership of the system of states and established a new way of bringing non-Western populations under its rule. As a result, these populations found themselves governed both by modern states of their own and by the regulatory mechanisms of the overarching system of states. This is the latest version of the late imperial practice of indirect rule in which people were governed through their own cultures and structures of authority. The difference, in this case, is that they are governed through markets and by states of their own.

Liberal Authoritarianism

Authoritarian rule has always played a significant part of the government of states, even where liberal political reason has been influential. Nineteenth-century Western states restricted the freedom of important sections of their own populations and some forcibly imposed their rule on substantial populations outside their own national borders. Even now, coercive and oppressive practices continue to play an important part in the government of Western societies: in the criminal justice system, the policing of inner-city areas and the urban poor, the provision of social services, and, of course, the management of large public and private organizations. Elsewhere, in much of Latin America, parts of South-East Asia, Central and Eastern Europe, authoritarian rule has been used as an instrument of economic liberalization.

What do these practices have to do with the liberal government of freedom? With few exceptions (notably Valverde 1996), contributors to the governmentality literature have seen the relationship between them as largely external. Thus, while Nikolas Rose (1999) observes that coercive and oppressive practices must now be justified on the liberal grounds of freedom, these practices play little part in his account of liberal government itself. Or again, Mitchell Dean (1999) insists that any attempt to govern through freedom will have to acknowledge that some people may just have to be governed in other ways. These accounts capture important aspects of liberal political reason, but the government of unfreedom is more central to its concerns than either would suggest.

We can see what is at issue here by returning to the significance for government of the belief that members of the population are naturally endowed with a capacity for autonomous, self-directing activity. One obvious implication seems to be that government should make use of this capacity, and the Foucaultian account of liberal and neoliberal government has therefore focused on its deployment of individual liberty. In fact, the implications are rather more complex: individuals may be naturally endowed with a capacity for autonomous action but this does not mean that the capacity will always be fully realized. Modern political thought has generally taken the contrary view: that there are indeed contexts in which suitable habits of self-government have taken root, but many more in which they have not. Liberals have usually seen the realization of this capacity for autonomous action in historical and developmental terms, suggesting that it will be well established amongst numerous adults only in relatively civilized communities; that extended periods of education and training are required if individuals are to develop the necessary habits of self-regulation; and that, even under favourable conditions, there will be those who cannot be relied on to conduct their affairs in a reasonable manner. They have argued that, where this capacity is not well developed, government simply cannot afford to work through the free decisions of individuals: children must be constrained by parental authority and uncivilized adults subjected to authoritarian rule. John Stuart Mill's comments on the people of India and other colonial dependencies provide a well-known example of this liberal perspective. Since they are not, in his view, 'sufficiently advanced ... to be fitted for representative government', they must be governed by the dominant country or its agents:

> This mode of government is as legitimate as any other, if it is the one which in the existing state of civilization of the subject people, most facilitates their transition to a higher stage of improvement.
>
> (1977 [1865]: 567)

Liberal political reason has been concerned with the subject peoples of imperial possessions as much as with the free inhabitants of Western states, with minors and adults judged to be incompetent as much as with autonomous individuals. Western colonial rule has now been displaced but its developmental perspective remains influential in the programs of economic and political development promoted by independent, post-colonial states and by international agencies.

Authoritarian government in these cases has a paternalistic rationale: its stated aim is to move towards its own eventual abolition. A rationale of a different kind rests on the point, noted earlier, that liberalism is substantially concerned to defend the work of government from the impact of partisan politics. The corporatization and privatization of state agencies might seem to reduce the threat of certain kinds of partisanship, but there will also be cases in which more direct measures seem to be required. These range from limitations on parliamentary and intra-party debate to the direct suppression of political opposition. In societies where paternalistic attitudes towards the bulk of the population are already well entrenched, the supposed imperatives of economic reform have often provided governments and their international supporters with powerful liberal grounds for the restriction of political freedom.

Moving on

The Foucaultian studies of government, and of liberal and neoliberal government in particular, have made substantial contributions to our understanding of the significance of freedom, choice and empowerment in the government of contemporary Western populations. There are, nevertheless, important areas of politics, and indeed of government, which these studies have not addressed. This chapter has commented, all too briefly, on three of these – political partisanship, the contemporary system of states and liberal authoritarianism – and suggested that they are central to the analysis of liberalism and of modern government more generally, both in the West and elsewhere. To insist on the importance of these areas, however, is not to raise an objection to the governmentality perspective. The point, rather, is to show that it has considerably more to offer our understanding of contemporary politics than it has yet been able to deliver.

Further Reading

Dean, M. 1999: *Governmentality: Power and Rule in Modern Society*. London: Sage.

Neuman, I. and Sending, O.J. 2010: *Governing the Global Polity: Practice, Mentality, Rationality*. Ann Arbor: University of Michigan Press.

Rose, N. 1999: *Powers of Freedom: Reframing Political Thought*. Cambridge: Cambridge University Press.

5

Historical Institutionalism

Edwin Amenta

Historical institutionalism is an approach to political analysis that focuses on big outcome-oriented questions about political phenomena and seeks to answer them with historical and conjunctural explanations centring on institutions. Historical institutionalist scholars also intervene in theoretical debates, often making mid-range political institutional arguments, and advance meta-theoretical debates, notably about the importance of path dependence. Historical institutionalist scholarship is catholic in methodology, but identifies historical methods as particularly important. This scholarship should go further in addressing theoretical debates between sociological and political institutionalists, deploy ideas more in its claims and take further conceptual and methodological advantages of its historical approach.

Historical institutionalism had its origins in comparative politics and in the intellectual movements to bring the 'state back in' to the analysis of politics (Evans, Rueschemeyer and Skocpol 1985) and to analyze political outcomes with greater historical sophistication. The pioneering scholars were reacting against pluralism, Marxism, behaviourialism and rational choice modelling in political analysis, as well as work that seemed a-historical (Hall and Taylor 1996; Campbell 2004). Historical institutionalism was named in the late 1980s (Steinmo, Thelen and Longstreth 1992), its initial proponents seeking to unify scholars who shared similar approaches to their work. They also shared some assumptions. Unlike rational choice perspectives in political science, historical institutionalism holds that institutions are not typically created for functional reasons; instead, institutions often are results of large-scale and long-term processes that have little to do with modern political issues, and institutions often have routine if unintended consequences to them. In part for these reasons, historical institutionalists engage in historical research to trace the processes behind

The Wiley-Blackwell Companion to Political Sociology, First Edition. Edited by Edwin Amenta, Kate Nash, and Alan Scott.
© 2012 Blackwell Publishing Ltd. Published 2012 by Blackwell Publishing Ltd.

the persistence of institutions and their influence on policies and other political outcomes. Their standard research product is a book (or long journal article) addressing one or a small number of countries exhibiting a deep knowledge of them and the time period analyzed, and often seeking to explain divergent historical trajectories (see Amenta and Ramsey 2010).

I begin by addressing general issues surrounding institutional theoretical claims and move on to debates within historical institutionalism about how closely to align itself with political institutional explanations, path dependency as mode of argumentation, and the use of historical methods. Despite its origins in state-centred theory and its efforts to be deeply historical, there remain disagreements within the group on its theoretical, meta-theoretical and methodological tenets and practices. Historical institutionalists do not necessarily rely on political institutionalist explanations, nor do their explanations always take a path-dependent or historicist form, nor do all engage in methods similar to historians. Along the way, I discuss some of the main achievements and promise of the perspective, as well as shortcomings, before making some suggestions for the future. To focus the discussion I often address research on comparative public social policy, with which the perspective has been closely associated.

Institutional Arguments and Historical Institutionalism

Like other forms of institutionalism, historical institutionalists define institutions as emergent, higher-order factors above the individual level that influence political processes and outcomes and tend to produce regular patterns or stasis. Institutions constrain or constitute the interests and political participation of actors 'without requiring repeated collective mobilization or authoritative intervention to achieve these regularities' (Jepperson 1991: 145). Political institutionalists see institutions as formal or informal procedures, routines, norms and conventions in the organizational structure of the polity (see Amenta 2005), and often focus on states, electoral procedures, party systems and the like. Sociological institutionalists have a broader view of institutions, adding cognitive scripts, moral templates and symbol systems (Hall and Taylor 1996; Campbell 2004) that may reside at supra-state or supra-organizational levels (Amenta and Ramsey 2010). The influence and durability of institutions is a function of the extent to which they are inculcated in political actors at the individual or organizational level, and involve material resources and networks (Clemens and Cook 1999).

Institutional theories posit two distinct forms of institutions' influence over political action. Institutions can be constraining, superimposing conditions of possibility for mobilization, access and influence and limiting some forms of action, while facilitating others. Theories of 'political mediation' (Amenta *et al.* 2005) and 'political opportunity' (Kriesi 2004) are institutional constraint arguments to the extent that they posit that political institutions limit the conditions under which organized interests mobilize and attain collective goods from the state. Another form of institutional theorizing posits that institutions are constitutive, establishing the available and viable models and heuristics for political action, and evoke an imagery of cultural frameworks or toolkits. Political sociological 'state constructionist' theories of mobilization and identity formation are institutional constitutive arguments, proposing that the actions of states 'help to make cognitively plausible and morally justifiable certain types of collective grievances, emotions, identities, ideologies, associational ties, and actions (but not others)' (Goodwin 2001: 39–40). Sociological institutionalist theories of the influence of 'epistemic communities' on policy paradigms (Haas 1992) or of international non-governmental organizations (INGOs) on a 'world society' (Meyer 1999) similarly propose that normative and cognitive institutions as embedded in networks of expertise constitute the moral and epistemological bases of policy formulation.

Some historical institutionalists, notably Skocpol (1985), previously referred to themselves as 'state-centred' scholars, and many historical institutionalists have a theoretical emphasis involving the constraining role of political institutions. But most have dropped the state-centred label, including Skocpol (1992), as they address political institutions beyond states. Among historical institutionalists, there are political institutionalists in the tradition of Tocqueville, Weber and Polanyi, and others incorporating Marxian ideas regarding institutions in the political economy. In each case these institutions may be treated and understood from both 'calculus' and 'cultural' approaches to action (Hall and Taylor 1996), similar to Weber's classical ideal and material interests. Political institutionalists tend to view political actors as employing a logic of 'self-interest', whereas sociological institutionalists tend see them as working from a logic of 'appropriateness'. Unlike rational choice institutionalists, sociological, historical and political institutionalists are deeply sociological in the sense of rejecting the idea that institutions are simply the result of strategic equilibria (Hall and Taylor 1996; Campbell 2004).

In addition to its eclectic conceptualization of institutions (Hall and Taylor 1996; Pierson and Skocpol 2002; Campbell 2004; Amenta and Ramsey 2010; cf. Immergut 1998), historical institutionalists provide explanations that tend to be multi-causal, thus promoting further theoretical eclecticism. Although historical institutionalists usually put forward theoretical arguments and entertain and appraise alternative explanations, they tend to seek complete explanations, rather than explaining the most variation with the most parsimonious model. As a result the explanations provided are usually configurational and implicate a conjunction of institutions, processes and events (Katznelson 1997). The configurational explanations typically involve the interactions of more than one institution, and different aspects of these institutions, as well as possibly slow-moving processes and contingent factors (Pierson and Skocpol 2002). In these complete explanations, other elements from other theoretical perspectives are added to institutions.

Perhaps more important, because institutions tend toward stasis, explaining institutional change typically requires causal claims that go beyond institutions (Clemens and Cook 1999; Campbell 2004; Béland 2005). Historical institutionalists will often invoke the impetus of crises, the activity of social movements, the rise of new governments and the like in their multi-causal explanations for change (Amenta and Ramsey 2010). This usually involves some theorizing at the meso level of political organization, often involving the interaction of politically active groups with state bureaucrats and other actors, or some combination of theorizing at the macro and meso levels. The causal argumentation sometimes gets quite detailed at the organizational level.

Because historical institutionalists do not form a theoretical school its practitioners do not always identify themselves as such. What is more, historical institutionalism is less significant as an identity among political sociologists than among political scientists, where historical institutionalists seek to differentiate themselves from behaviourists and the rational choice scholars who also deploy the term institutionalism (Hall and Taylor 1996). Historical institutionalists are often located in the subdisciplines of comparative politics and American politics, and within American politics in American political development or the politics and history section of the American Political Science Association. In US sociology, scholars identified or identifying as historical institutionalists are usually connected to the American Sociological Association (ASA) sections on comparative and historical sociology and political sociology.

But because most historical institutionalists rely on political institutional theory, it is worth briefly comparing political and sociological institutionalist arguments. Like political institutionalists, most historical institutionalists tend to see political institutions as being distinctive and extremely influential, and, far more than sociological institutionalists, they are concerned with issues of power. Most historical institutionalists also see political institutions at the country or state level as being constraining and influencing political outcomes; sociological institutionalists mainly see institutions as working at the supra-state level, constraining and influencing all states. For this reason, unlike sociological institutionalists, historical institutionalists rarely emphasize convergence in political processes and outcomes; instead they often argue that country-level political or economic institutions bring enduring differences across countries and over time, often transmuting global processes (see Campbell 2004). Historical institutionalist explanations usually involve showing that some structural and systemic political conditions or circumstances hindered a potential political change in one place and either aided or allowed the development in another, with enduring consequences for differences in political development; thus for historical and political institutionalists 'comparison' usually means 'contrast', such as between successful and failed revolutions (Goldstone 2003), successful and failed transitions to democracy (Mahoney 2003), and policy innovations and failures (Amenta 2003). In path-dependent arguments (see below), initial decisions about the creation of institutions shape all future possibilities for politics.

Path Dependency and Historicism

Among historical institutionalists there has been a turn toward a specific meta-theoretical approach to explanation, involving increased sensitivity to time order and path dependence (Abbott 1992; Griffin 1992; Pierson 2000), and a style of theoretical argument involving 'historicist' causation (Stinchcombe 1968). In narrative causal accounts, as opposed to standard variable-based discussions, when something happens is key to its influence in processes of major change (Griffin 1992; Sewell 2006).

Following the lead of institutional economics, many historical institutionalists argue that time matters by way of path dependence. Some key decision or action at a critical juncture or choice point brings about institutions with mechanisms that provide increasing returns to action and self-reinforcing processes (Mahoney 2000; Pierson 2000). To use the social policy example again, once new policies are adopted and bureaucracies enforcing the policies and corporations adapting employee benefit programmes form around them, politics changes in ways that tend to favour the new policies and disfavour previously plausible alternatives. Path dependence means that causes of the rise of these institutions will have a different influence, possibly none at all, once the institutions are set in place. For example, Pierson (1994) argues that well-established social programmes in the United States and Britain deflected attempts by right-wing regimes to destroy them, whereas right-wing regimes easily prevented or slowed the initial adoption of social programmes (Amenta 1998). Historical institu-tionalists address the issue of institutional change by seeking to identify both the critical juncture and the set of causes that determined the path chosen. Hypotheses about critical junctures are closely tied to conjunctural causal analyses in which several conditions may need to occur simultaneously for a major institutional shift. Thus the meta-theoretical commitment to path-dependent approaches to explanation implies an elective affinity to theoretical eclecticism.

The most extreme versions of path-dependent arguments are ones that produce historical 'lock-in' or 'self-reproducing sequences' (Mahoney and Schenshul 2006); after a specific set of events some political alternatives are removed from the realm of possibility and reversing course may be exceedingly difficult. Lock-in occurs as political actors and the public reorient their lives significantly around the policy and there are increasing returns surrounding the policy (Pierson 1996). While locking in themselves, new policies can sometimes lock out other policies. Skocpol (1992) argues that the adoption in the United State of extensive nineteenth-century military pensions made it very difficult to adopt comprehensive social insurance policy on the European model. Hacker (2002) argues that it was possible for the US government to develop extensive old-age programmes because private benefits were minimal, but more extensive private benefits in health care inhibited national interventions. Fully mature pay-as-you-go old-age programmes, such as US Social Security, are difficult to retrench (Myles and Pierson 2001). From a political economy perspective, it is argued that initial decisions to adopt liberal, conservative, or social-democratic welfare capitalist regimes (Esping-Andersen 1990) shape all future possibilities for social politics (Hicks 1999). The idea of lock-in provides the motivation for historicist explanation. If the enactment or institutionalization of a policy makes it almost impossible to change, inquiry is focused on its period of enactment or institutionalization.

Within the historical institutionalist camp, however, there is disagreement about how central the role of path dependency might be. The strong version, involving lock-in and self-reinforcing patterns, suggests that path-dependent processes are rare and important; the weak version, holding simply that contingency matters, suggests that path dependence is ubiquitous, though less and variably influential (Mahoney and Schensul 2006). From this point of view, the idea of 'layering' (Thelen 2003; Streek and Thelen 2005) suggests that a series of small and incremental changes, rather than a brief disjuncture in a critical period, or a 'punctuated equilibrium', may lead to reinforcing patterns. The layering idea has been claimed to best describe the devel-opment of US Social Security (Béland 2007).

Some of the disagreements among historical institutionalists play out with respect to the concept of 'policy feedbacks', which designates the impact of new policy on politics and the future possibilities of policy. Béland (2010) discusses six different policy feedback mechanisms and research streams. Aside from the lock-in effects noted by Pierson, these include the state-building produced by new policy, the creation or strengthening of interest groups around policy, the influence of private institutions, a policy's promotion of political participation by demographic groups, and the ideational and symbolic legacies of policies. Most of these reinforce policies. But Weaver (2010) finds that the structure of some programmes tends to undermine them, such as underfunded pensions on a non-pay-as-you-go model. US public-employee health and old-age benefits at the state level seem particularly vulnerable to retrenchment. But there still remains the question of the conditions under which aspects of policies will be reinforcing, or undermining, and to what degree.

Difficulties in path-dependent theorizing, whether of the weak or strong forms, go beyond internal disputes about how much history matters, however. Claims about path dependence are typically counterfactual. It seems likely that the reason that a given path is not reversed is not that it cannot be reversed, but because there are no concerted attempts to reverse it. The only way to ascertain an institution's or a policy's true strength would be to subject it to constant and varied challenges, which in practice rarely happens. To return to US Social Security, in its formative years it was challenged significantly only occasionally and thus it is unclear when it was locked in (Amenta 2006; Béland 2007). Also, invoking path dependence may ignore the ways that institutions shape the possibilities for later political contestation.

History as a Methodological Approach

All historical institutionalists employ 'historical' methods, but vary in how they interpret this charge. Almost all historical institutionalists gain extensive knowledge of their cases by mastering the relevant historiography, usually regarding political phenomena in specific countries and time periods; most trace over time the processes by which explanations are claimed to work (George and Bennett 2005). Some address two or a few country-level cases, often gaining the analytical advantages of comparisons (Rueschemeyer 2003). Yet others go in the opposite direction and act more like historians (Sewell 2006), relying mainly on primary sources to appraise and develop arguments and usually addressing just one country. Whether addressing one or a few countries, historical institutionalists have been criticized for having too few cases chasing too many explanations.

Historical institutionalist works, usually monographs or long articles, strategically deploy comparisons or trace historical processes to cast empirical doubt on alternative explanations, especially the mechanisms by which theories are claimed to work, and to provide support for their own explanations. This mode of analysis calls attention to large-scale contexts and processes, which often go unnoticed in approaches to data analysis that focus on events surrounding the specific changes under study and do not examine these events in wider historical or comparative contexts. This sort of work requires detailed historical knowledge of individual countries and time periods. Also, given their wide scope, these analyses often range across different governmental institutions, such as executives, bureaucracies, legislators and courts, unlike much political science research that focuses on one institution. Whether these analyses rely on primary or secondary sources, they usually array in one place a wealth of information scattered among different works, drawing a more analytically coherent picture of what is to be explained. This form contrasts with the modal product of sociological institutionalist analysis, which is a quantitative journal article addressing the diffusion of specific policy innovation across a wide variety of countries or other units (Amenta and Ramsey 2010).

Historical institutionalist questions are motivated by puzzles often with both comparative and theoretical aspects to them. Although not all historical institutionalists engage in cross-national comparisons, their questions usually have comparative motivations and implications. For instance, questions about the failure of national health insurance or the late start of other public social programmes in the United States are at least implicitly comparing these failures to successes elsewhere in similarly situated countries. The puzzling aspect of the big question is also sometimes constructed from the failure of well-known theoretical explanations to provide a satisfactory answer. For instance, US social policy lagged despite being among the richest of countries, and efforts to retrench social policy may fail despite the fact that right-wing parties rule (Pierson 1996), as in Britain and the United States in the 1980s.

Some have noted the similarity between the types of theoretical argumentation of historical institutionalists, which is often configurational and multi-causal (Katznelson 1997), with Boolean analytical techniques and fuzzy set analyses (Ragin 2008). Similarly, sequence analyses can be suited to analyzing path-dependent and historicist theoretical claims. The more successful historical social science research areas, such as on revolutions (Goldstone 2003), democratization (Mahoney 2003), and social policy (Amenta 2003), address quantitative findings and seek to appraise the theories and claims of scholars working with large-scale data sets. However, historical institutionalists only rarely deploy the types of data sets required to carry out either Boolean or sequence analyses and usually do not have the data-analytical inclination or training to do so. Historical institutionalist investigations are usually undertaken in the absence of the possibility of generating the sorts of data sets statistically manipulated in high-profile scholarly articles, such as the modal research products of sociological institutionalists. In addition, historical institutionalist analyses are usually focused on explaining a specific set of outcomes, rather than theorizing about the general impact of individual or joint causes (Mahoney and Terrie 2009), working backward from the outcome, rather than forward from purported causes.

Many historical institutionalists and like-minded historical social scientists now consider it insufficient simply to employ comparative methods and similar approaches, dropping a reliance on secondary sources and working mainly with primary sources like historians. Historical social scientists are warned against biases and gaps in historiography (Lustick 1996), and archival research wards off misunderstandings and reveals what key actors thought about their actions. Being historical in this methodological sense, however, is both time consuming and demands skills, such as interpreting documents, in which social scientists are usually untrained. It is also limiting in that the time required to analyze primary documents about an aspect of politics in a specific country in a short time period makes it more difficult to accrue the analytical advantages of comparing the same phenomena across a few countries or in one country over a long period of time. Process tracings are richer, but deploying comparisons to rule out explanations becomes less easy.

Regardless of whether historical institutionalists act like historians or engage in broader small-N comparisons, their work has been criticized as deploying too few cases or empirical instances to make causal claims stick (Lieberson 1992; Goldthorpe 1999) and as 'selecting on the dependent variable', limiting the value of explanations (King *et al.* 1994). One standard response to the issue of limited observations is through research design, trying to address and hold constant as many possible relevant causal factors, known as a 'most similar systems' design (Przeworski and Teune 1970), notably comparing country cases or historical sequences that were otherwise similar, but differing on key causal elements. Another strategy to increase the analytical leverage of small-N studies is to break down large country cases into various over-time or within-country comparisons (Amenta 2009). However, most strategies rely on the strength of historical research, such as by way of process tracing – which can be done well by historical scholars, but cannot be done by way of statistical analyses (George and Bennett 2005). As for selecting on the dependent variable, examining positive cases is a valid research strategy for explaining unusual occurrences of importance and can be seen as an advantage of historical research (Ragin 2008).

The Future of Historical Institutionalism

As its proponents note, historical institutionalism promotes social scientific research on questions and issues that would otherwise be ignored. Historical institutionalists delve into issues and questions for which it is not easy to generate the sort of data sets required for standard multivariate analyses and thus much of what is known about some subjects is provided by historical social scientists (Pierson and Skocpol 2002). The big picture analyses provided by historical institutionalists will remain relevant in these ways, but there remain ways for historical institutionalists to increase their influence and harness the advantages of their approach to the study of politics.

One way is to pay greater attention to theory. Historical institutionalist theorizing to date has proceeded with an excess of reticence, often failing to theorize beyond the cases and time periods of interest. Historical institutionalist explanations are usually dependent on context, but often aspects of the historical context are set as 'proper name' (Przeworski and Teune 1970) boundaries surrounding the causal claims, by way of specific places and periods, such as 'the United States between the wars'. However, scope conditions are typically understood analytically (George and Bennett 2005), and it would be better for historical institutionalists to make this analytical leap, theorizing, say, about 'rich democratic societies during the period of the rise of welfare states', even if they address closely only a few such examples. Similarly, their configurational causal explanations are not always sorted for prominence or porta-bility. It is worth thinking about the following questions: How influential are various political contexts? Would the combination of variables or conditions likely have implications in many situations or few? If so, what might these situations be?

More specifically, historical institutionalists also would do well to intervene in debates between political and sociological institutionalists. Political institutionalists predominantly address political developments and policies that are consequential in terms of resources and fundamental power arrangements; these issues inevitably attract the attention of the most powerful state and domestic political actors. Sociological institutionalist studies, in contrast, usually address policies for which delegation to an increasingly globally interconnected civil society is unlikely to result in major reallocations of state resources or group interests. Similarly, the need for legitimacy – a key motivator in sociological institutionalist accounts – is typically greater in more newly minted states suffering from power deficits. That may account for the explanatory power of sociological institutionalist analyses, which typically range across a wide variety of states. Positing and evaluating various empirical boundaries to these camps may be useful for historical institutionalist scholarship to explore to ascertain how far the claims of each tradition may go (see Amenta and Ramsey 2010).

Historical institutionalism's theoretical eclecticism leaves roles open for the influence of ideas, but these could use greater attention, especially from a political institutionalist perspective. The roles of ideas can address more fine-grained, change-oriented questions, such as why particular reforms took the forms that they did. Drawing on the policy streams approach of Kingdon (1995) and 'policy learning' theories from political science (Hall 1993; King and Hansen 1999), Béland (2005) notably argues that the content of new policies is heavily dependent upon the national policy domains of state bureaucracies, interest groups, think tanks, academic research institutions and social movements that monitor an issue area and proposes that research engage in careful tracing of the causal influence of policy paradigms and of the diffusion of proposals from policy-producing organizations to decision-making authorities. This suggested integration of norms and schemas presumes relatively autonomous, calculative authorities with agency to adjudicate policy decisions – but operating within the bounds of available and feasible analyses and proposals generated by policy domain actors, which are partly the product of national political structures (see also Campbell 2002). This approach addresses the role of ideas in propelling policy changes over the hurdles of the legislative process, as elected officials and policy advocates must frame policy innovations so as to draw public support or avoid resistance; this contrasts with the standard approach of sociological institutionalist and policy learning theories, which discount domestic political constraints.

Historical institutionalists, like other qualitative researchers, can also address further the sorts of theoretical cases that are discovered or created in the process of research. As they complete their investigations another question that historical institutionalists should ask themselves is this: What is the case a case of (Ragin and Becker 1992)? By the process of 'casing' scholars can make theoretical connections that help to draw new conceptual lines around phenomena previously seen as disparate and not obviously comparable. A study may thus prompt the investigator to identify a new class of phenomena that might have similar causes and consequences or add new instances to existing classes of phenomena. Case studies also provide an opportunity to think more deeply and conceptually about the phenomena revealed during the analysis and aid in placing scope conditions on arguments (George and Bennett 2005). Typically social scientists choose cases on the basis of their being a part of some larger theoretical population, either typical of a larger group or atypical and thus extra worthy of explanation. Historical institutionalist scholars can refine understandings of these more general populations and situate cases more precisely with respect to others deemed as otherwise similar.

Historical work also can harness its deep knowledge of political developments to revitalize standard quantitative scholarship. Scholars with deep understandings of cases often can ascertain which quantitative indicators are truly meaningful and would provide appraisals of more general arguments. For instance, historical scholars are more likely to be able to separate highly conflictual and significant votes in the US Congress from those that are not, or which aspects of policies were at the frontier of political conflict. Although historical research tends to be concerned with explaining specific key outcomes, whereas quantitative research tends to focus on the influence of causal factors (Mahoney and Terrie 2009), having historical institutionalists on the lookout for valid indicators would help advance knowledge.

More generally, great intellectual progress can result from a dialogue between small-N historical studies in large-N quantitative studies. Historical research can appraise the mechanisms in these claims and address variance in larger statistical patterns. If there is contention among theories about these patterns, historical analyses can adjudicate among them (see Amenta 2003). Institutionalist approaches would also benefit from a cross-fertilization of research methods. Historical institutionalist research that applies more rigorous statistical tests to more precisely formulated explanatory claims, analyzing more ambitious sets of data, would shore up explanations whose particularistic scope has consigned them to a frequently marginal status in sociological and political theorizing and research.

Acknowledgement

I thank Daniel Béland, Beth Gardner, Kate Nash and Alan Scott for comments on a previous version.

Further Reading

Amenta, E. and Ramsey, K.M. 2010: Institutional theory. In K.T. Leicht and J.C. Jenkins (eds) *The Handbook of Politics: State and Civil Society in Global Perspective*. New York: Springer.

Campbell, J.L. 2004: *Institutional Change and Globalization*. Princeton, NJ: Princeton University Press.

Hall, P.A. and Taylor, R.C.R. 1996: Political science and the three institutionalisms. *Political Studies 44*: 936–957.

Mahoney, J. and Schensul, D. 2006: Historical context and path dependence. In R.E. Goodin and C. Tilly (eds) *The Oxford Handbook of Contextual Political Analysis*. New York: Oxford University Press.

Pierson, P. and Skocpol, T. 2002: Historical institutionalism in contemporary political science. In I. Katznelson and H.V. Milner (eds) *Political Science: The State of the Discipline*. New York: W.W. Norton.

6

Sociological Institutionalism and World Society

EVAN SCHOFER, ANN HIRONAKA, DAVID JOHN FRANK
AND WESLEY LONGHOFER

Sociological institutionalism, as applied to international issues and global social change, has generated a growing literature on 'world society'. Scholars working in this tradition have sought to understand how international institutions, world culture, global professionals and transnational associations – facets of an increasingly structured world society – shape the identities, structure and behaviour of states, organizations and individuals across the globe. In contrast to theories that focus on interested actors and their resources and military capabilities, the world society perspective sees social action as deriving from culture, knowledge and authority rooted in global institutions and structures. Among other things, the perspective predicts surprising levels of global conformity and distinctive patterns of disorganization or 'loose coupling' in the structure and behaviour of social actors. We discuss key theoretical issues and the empirical literature that has followed, address common misconceptions and chart some promising future directions of the world society perspective.

Introduction

Sociological institutionalism (or 'neo-institutionalism') has had influence across sociology and beyond, but particularly on studies of the transnational sphere and global social change (for general reviews, see Jepperson 2002; Meyer 2010; Meyer et al. 1997; Schneiberg and Clemens 2006). Variously labelled world polity theory, world society theory and simply institutional theory, scholars have drawn on sociological institutionalism to generate an expansive theoretical and empirical agenda

The Wiley-Blackwell Companion to Political Sociology, First Edition. Edited by Edwin Amenta, Kate Nash, and Alan Scott.
© 2012 Blackwell Publishing Ltd. Published 2012 by Blackwell Publishing Ltd.

stressing the importance of global institutions and culture in shaping the structure and behaviour of nation-states, organizations and individuals worldwide.

The world society perspective is historically linked to John W. Meyer and collaborators, working at Stanford University in the 1970s and 1980s. Reacting on one hand to the enduring influence of functionalism in American sociology (e.g., modernization theory) and perspectives stressing economic and military power on the other (e.g., world-system theory, neo-realism), the world society tradition has sought to explain global change – most notably the diffusion of Western-style state policies – as the consequence of emerging global institutions, international organizations and an increasingly common world culture in the period following World War II.

Institutionalisms

Institutional perspectives, generally, shift attention away from individual social actors and toward the social context or environment in which actors are embedded (see Amenta 2005). Institutionalisms vary substantially, however, both in the conceptualization of institutional environments and in the extent to which actor interests and identities are seen as existing a priori versus being fundamentally shaped or even constituted by the external environment. We may think of a continuum with interest-seeking rational actors on one end and 'stage actors' on the other (Meyer 2009). World society theory is on the latter end of the spectrum, characterizing actors as creatures of their context – as enactors of social or cultural rules and scripts provided by their wider environment.

Economic institutionalism (e.g., North 1990) and much work in political science (e.g., Keohane and Nye 1977) begins with the assumption of strong interested actors, and seeks to understand when and why those actors choose to enter into institutional arrangements that may ultimately constrain their behaviour to some degree. Historical institutionalisms focus on the ways that historically emergent features of the institutional environment channel subsequent behaviour (and even interests) in contingent, path-dependent ways (Skocpol 1979). Actors may struggle to pursue their interests, but within a range of possibilities shaped by the past.

Sociological neo-institutionalism goes further in asserting the influence of social context, which shapes or even 'constitutes' social actors – defining their identities and goals (DiMaggio and Powell 1983; Meyer and Rowan 1977). To varying degrees, neo-institutional scholars draw inspiration from the cultural and phenomenological traditions of Berger and Luckmann (1966) and Goffman (1974), which stress the socially constructed nature of reality, and the extent to which social behaviour reflects the enactment of socially appropriate frames in a given context (in contrast to, say, images of rational calculation). The strong emphasis on macro-social dynamics ultimately represents a stark alternative to the methodological individualism that pervades much contemporary (especially American) sociological research (Jepperson and Meyer 2011).

World society and world culture

The initial impulse for the world society tradition came out of comparative research on education and governance in the 1970s. Education systems in sub-Saharan Africa, for instance, seemed surprisingly like those of Western societies despite stark differences in the labour markets they served. Schools and curricula looked like resource-poor imitations of those in the West, rather than functional systems adapted to the educational needs of agricultural economies. It appeared that governments and educators were more attuned to global models of schooling than local needs and realities 'on the ground'.

This similarity across societies, or *isomorphism*, was explained as conformity to dominant, legitimated, or 'taken-for-granted' views. Conventional ideas about governance and education could be seen as *cultural models* – that is, blueprints or recipes that define what a 'normal' or appropriate nation-state looks like (Meyer *et al.* 1997). Cultural models are sometimes referred to as *myths*, emphasizing that they reflect societal ideologies or fads, and are not necessarily functionally optimal. Nevertheless, these cultural models suffuse the international sphere, becoming a key component of the institutional environment surrounding and constituting nation-states. One primary consequence is the global diffusion of ideas and policy models (see Strang and Meyer 1993). The world society tradition thus stresses the historical build-up of international organizations and structures – such as the United Nations and international associations – that serve to *institutionalize* cultural models, effectively embodying and sustaining a *global culture*.

Whereas much work in political sociology stresses both heterogeneity and contestation, the world society tradition focuses on strong commonalities in international discourses on a wide range of topics, from human rights to environmentalism. As with clothing fashions, variability may coexist with clear patterns and trends, such as common assumptions, rules and fads. Ideas and discourses regarding educational policy institutionalized in the international sphere, for example, may vary on specifics yet embody broadly common assumptions that pervade a given historical period – providing common blueprints that generate conformity among countries.

A great deal of empirical research has studied the top-down process through which global models and discourses diffuse to nation-states – particularly those with strong organizational links to the international sphere. As constructed entities of a highly rationalized world society, seemingly disparate nation-states exhibit a great deal of structural similarity in their constitutions (Boli 1987), ministerial structures (Kim, Jang and Hwang 2002), and policies, including those on national security (Jepperson, Wendt and Katzenstein 1996) and women's suffrage (Ramirez, Soysal and Shanahan 1997). Common goals of the modern nation-state are furthermore reflected in such areas as expanded educational systems (Baker and LeTendre 2005; Meyer, Ramirez and Soysal 1992; Schofer and Meyer 2005), environmental protection (Frank, Hironaka and Schofer 2000; Frank, Longhofer and Schofer 2007; Hironaka 2000), and the promotion of science (Drori *et al.* 2003; Schofer 2003).

The content of world culture

World society theory is a theory of modernity. Scholars in this tradition have sought to unpack the institutionalized culture of modern society, and to characterize social actors as products of that culture. Drawing on Weber and other accounts of modernity, world society scholars emphasize rationalization, universalism, belief in progress, and individualism as foundational cultural assumptions that undergird global discourse and organization (Boli and Thomas 1999). This culture supports a very wide array of movements, initiatives and innovations but proscribes many others. It is unthinkable for the United Nations, for instance, to argue for the return of traditional feudal arrangements, which violate cultural norms regarding individual freedom and progress.

World society scholars view global culture as a product of history, not some inevitable or teleological evolution of values. Historically, Christendom and major cultural movements, such as the Enlightenment, formed the basis for an emergent European culture (Meyer 1989). Subsequent European dominance and colonial expansion propagated Western ideas on a global scale. The Allied victory in World War II and the emergence of the United States (rather than Germany) as a dominant power shifted global culture in a more liberal, individualistic and arguably 'American' direction. Yet, world society scholars have resisted the idea that global culture is simply hegemonic ideology, carried by force of arms. Rather, the cultural system evolves substantially autonomously. For instance, the liberal 'American' ideals expressed in the UN Declaration of Human Rights have formed the basis for a much larger international human rights movement than the US state envisioned or (presumably) desired.

More recently, scholars have begun to dig more deeply into the origins and content of world society. Lechner and Boli (2005) suggest that world culture, though riddled with tensions and contradictions, saturates social life through law, organizations, religion, national identity, and even anti-globalization movements. Frank and Gabler (2006), meanwhile, examine world culture as reflected in university curricula worldwide, highlighting striking similarities in substantive emphases in seemingly national institutions. We discuss directions for future research below.

Disorganization and loose coupling

Cultural/phenomenological institutionalisms, in rejecting actor-centrism and functionalism, characterize social life and social actors themselves as rather disorganized and messy. Whereas neo-realist perspectives in political science, for instance, assume that states are coherent and unitary actors, world society theory sees states, organizations and even individuals as loose structures with internal inconsistencies and instabilities over time. Lacking coherent interests or identities, states (and their subunits) draw haphazardly upon cultural models from the institutional environment, moving in multiple (and sometimes inconsistent) directions at the same time. Furthermore, ritualized enactment of global models may be only loosely related to policy implementation – especially in impoverished countries. Disjunctures are the norm. This may seem unsatisfying to those who want a simple answer as to whether world culture 'really matters'. Yet, one of the strengths of the perspective is that it recognizes and helps make sense of the complex forms of loose coupling observed in modern organizations (Orton and Weick 1990).

Both case study and quantitative research support notions of loose coupling as described by world society theory. For example, Boyle (2002) finds that anti-female genital cutting reforms – derived from global principles of human rights and overriding many notions of national sovereignty – did not necessarily diminish the practice, even when individual attitudes aligned with global norms (see also Boyle,

McMorris and Gomez 2002). Similarly, Hafner-Burton and Tsutsui (2005) show that signing human rights accords did not actually improve human rights records in the most abusive countries. Decoupling appears to be especially pervasive in developing countries, where, for example, the pressures of economic globalization produce a variety of science policies in the name of development but rarely a boost in the scientific labour force (Drori *et al.* 2003). Yet, loose coupling does not simply mean the 'absence of real change'. Schofer and Hironaka (2005) seek to identify the conditions under which change is likely to occur 'on the ground'. They argue that institutional forces may push consistently across levels of an organization, generating systematic change even if the organization lacks tight internal coupling.

Related traditions

Complementary perspectives include constructivism in political science, as well as sociological work on transnational civil society and social movements. Constructivism in International Relations is a close cognate of the world society tradition (see Finnemore 1996). Constructivism fundamentally accepts the idea that culture matters – most often conceptualized as 'norms'. State behaviour is, in part, influenced by norms, which are propagated by non-state actors ('norm entrepreneurs') (Sikkink 1998). Within sociology, recent work on transnational social movements also bears much in common with the world society tradition – including an emphasis on international association, and (to varying degrees) an appreciation for 'cultural frames' as a source of mobilization (e.g., Smith 2002). Yet, (despite exceptions) these traditions have retained more of the actor-centrism and emphasis on power that cultural/phenomenological institutionalists seek to reject. Actors are still frequently characterized as prime movers, even if their behaviour is sometimes constrained by 'norms'. Non-state actors or 'norm entrepreneurs' are, themselves, cast as strategic actors rather than agents of a broader culture. And, imageries of interests and incentives, rather than culture, are often more central to arguments. Nonetheless, the broader image – of a thick international environment consisting of non-state actors (organizations) and norms (culture) that influence states – bears much in common with world society theory.

Recent work in science studies on *performativity* is in many ways a cognate of the world society tradition (e.g., MacKenzie 2010). World society scholarship has attended to the role of authoritative knowledge, epistemic communities and policy professionals as the source of global cultural myths and models, which ultimately become recipes or blueprints that diffuse around the globe – transforming how states behave (Drori *et al.* 2003). The world society tradition also shares a surprising amount of common ground with Foucaultian-inspired studies of the state, global institutions and 'governmentality' (e.g., Ferguson 1990; Scott 1998; Goldman 2005). Although the world society research generally de-emphasizes the concept of power (instead stressing 'taken-for-grantedness' and authority), it nevertheless describes a dominant culture of 'high modernity' and driving trends toward rationalization that are reshaping the globe. The authoritative, rationalized models and myths of world culture (embedded in international institutions and regimes) bear similarity to the disciplinary regimes and systems of governmentality described in the Foucaultian tradition.

Myths and Misperceptions

Over time, several interrelated criticisms of world society theory have arisen – and in part grown themselves myth-like and institutionalized. We address them here in hopes of advancing discussion. At the same time, we consider some misperceptions in the literature – to some extent shared by practitioners – that may limit the perspective's contributions to the wider field.

1. World society theory ignores actors, interests and power

It is true that work from the world society perspective – and sociological neo-institutionalism generally – de-emphasizes actors and interests relative to the socio-logical mainstream. It is indeed a core contention of the perspective that 'actors' and 'interests' are best, or at least usefully, conceived as derivative features of the wider institutional environment, and that one gains fundamental insight into their nature and quality by examining the models or blueprints from which they derive.

Related to this, world society theory de-emphasizes the role of coercive power in creating and maintaining institutions, contra the standard American view of a social world comprised of primordial actors – in this case marked not only by interests but by disparities in power. Such views dominate political sociology. The problem they face is that considerable social change occurs without clear assertions of power – that is, coercion by means of violence. Rather, authority – that is, persuasion by status or expertise – is pervasive in social life.

By de-emphasizing actors, interests and power, world society scholars are able to pose questions about phenomena that are unobserved or unremarked upon by more conventional actor-centric and power-based theories. For instance, theorists of actor-centric and power-based theories might note the role of anti-colonial movements in subsequent decolonizations of the 1950s and 1960s. What is striking from a world society perspective is the opposite side of the coin. In the majority of colonies, anti-colonial movements were ostentatiously weak and disorganized – with little control over means of coercion. Nevertheless, decolonizations occurred, even in those colonies that did not mobilize anti-colonial movements. World society scholars have argued that in many cases, the authority and legitimacy conferred by a wider global institutional environment was more effective in generating political independence than armed coercion (Strang 1990). This by no means implies a world without conflict, but even conflict itself is structured by the global 'rules' of the game (Hironaka 2005).

2. World society theory cannot explain the origins of cultural forms or cultural change

This criticism also typically, though not always, arises from conventional actors/interests assumptions. Here, one concedes the importance of cultural 'blueprints' but then asks where they come from or how they change – often assuming that 'real' actors with 'real' interests stand behind the curtain. It is true that much empirical work from the world society perspective focuses on the global diffusion of existing models, and the sheer abundance of this work – and the attention it merits – perhaps tempts the conclusion that world society theorists ignore the origins question. But that conclusion is more caricature than accurate representation. In fact, a growing number of studies attend directly to the origins of cultural forms – articulating the ways in which evolving and intensifying global institutions give rise (and fall) to various blueprints and models. Accounts stress that contemporary world society is replete with individual actorhood and also professionalized expertise, aimed at developing general models of legitimate goals and putative 'best practices'. Models with stronger theories of collective good, with better articulations of the taken-for-granted elements of developing world culture, and with more elaborate international organizational carriers, are more likely to become institutionalized. The origins question in many of these accounts never reverts to actors and interests, as some might hope, but remains in the realm of enactors and culture.

In this vein, for example, one might query the origins of environmental protection. The powerful and interested actors in the story – especially nation-states and corporations – may oppose most forms of protection, insofar as they compromise goals of development and profit. Nevertheless, experts and professionals, authorized by membership in the scientific community, pose models of the human–nature relationship that assert the primacy of collective goods. The victory of the ecosystems model, wherein humans are elaborately and causally connected to wider nature, represents at least as much the triumph of a scientific model, advocated by formally disinterested others, as it does the imposition of a model by interested actors (Frank 1997).

3. World society theory is equivalent to the INGO effect

International non-governmental organizations (INGOs) are a key conduit of world society models and discourses. World society resembles a transnational version of a decentralized Tocquevillian associational landscape, abundant with INGOs in fields ranging from development to human rights to technical standardization (Boli and Thomas 1999; Drori, Meyer and Hwang 2006). INGOs represent the organizational dimension of world society, conveying global models to domestic receptor sites charged with 'unscrambling global signals for local constituencies' (Frank, Hardinge and Wosick-Correa 2009: 277; Frank and McEneaney 1999). Thus, many empirical studies find an important 'INGO effect', or a positive relationship between INGO memberships and policy diffusion. However, the persistent INGO effect is often misinterpreted.

The problem lies in equating the signature INGO effect to the world society effect. The role of INGOs in diffusion is undoubtedly central, and clearly it has been celebrated in the literature. The mistake is to stop there, to collapse the cultural dimensions of world society theory into its organizational dimensions or reify INGOs as causal agents ('norm entrepreneurs'). There is no question that INGOs serve as important organizational expressions of global institutions. But a cultural aspect accompanies the organizational aspect – spurring not only diffusion but diffusion along particular lines, in particular directions.

Thus, for example, world society theory predicts not only the reforms of sex laws – enabled by INGO ties – but also reforms that are consistent with the ascending status of the individual in world models of society. The substantive dimensions of change – the cultural and directional dimensions – too often fade from discussion. Sex-law – and many other – reforms track substantive transformations in world society.

4. World society theory is equivalent to ceremony without substance

As articulated above, conventional sociological accounts privilege actors and interests over enactors and institutions, and thus they prioritize substance over ceremony. This is part and parcel of traditional American sociology. World society accounts, by contrast, stress the extent to which social life bears a ceremonial or 'ritualized' character. Therein, one finds formal adherence to institutionalized blueprints, often only loosely coupled with implementation on the ground (i.e., enactors and scripts). It is mistaken, however, to deduce from the differing emphases that world society theorists envision an enduring state of hypocrisy, with no change at the level of practice. On the contrary, the perspective suggests (a) that the oft-noticed phenomenon of ceremony without substance is accompanied by the less-noticed phenomenon of substance without ceremony, and (b) that a host of processes promote the convergence of the two over time.

It is easiest for world society scholars to counter competing explanations – to show that 'culture matters' – when one observes patterns of global conformity that are (a) obviously dysfunctional, such as copying policies that are ill-suited for local conditions; and (b) do not support, or appear to contradict, the interests of powerful domestic actors. As a result, world society scholars have sometimes presented the 'diffusion of the trivial'. This was, perhaps, a reasonable strategy when world society theory was in its infancy, given the priority of explanations involving power and interests. But it is important to note that even core 'functional' aspects of the modern state – such as economic or military policy – may be analyzed as products of a global cultural system.

Indeed, substance (or, outcomes) without ceremony (adoption) is common in the global system. For example, Frank, Hardinge and Wosick-Correa (2009) find that the global diffusion of rape-law reforms is associated with increased police reporting even in countries without any rape-law reforms. Similarly, human rights practices improve even in countries that fail to ratify human rights accords, given the ascendant legitimacy of the global human-rights movement (Hafner-Burton and Tsutsui 2005). Formal commitments render countries as even more vulnerable than others to pressures for everyday compliance. Global institutionalization involves substance without ceremony – that is, changes in practice without changes in formal commitment – and also vice versa. The two sides of decoupling go together.

5. World society theory predicts that everything will diffuse

The heavy emphasis on diffusion studies in the empirical literature can lead to the misconception that world society theory predicts that everything will diffuse, and some critics take evidence of non-diffusion or resistance (e.g., Vietnam) as disproving the theory. On the contrary, world society is as much a theory of non-diffusion as diffusion (see Strang and Meyer 1993). In particular, it predicts that (a) models that fail to assert collective goods over private interests, (b) models that fail to articulate with prevailing global institutions, and (c) models that lack international organizational carriers will be unlikely to diffuse, regardless of support from powerful and interested actors.

Thus, for example, neoliberal economic policies did not diffuse globally until they were cast as general models promising general benefits, until they embraced the individuated human actorhood that is central to contemporary global institutions (democracy, mass education, etc.), and until they received the authoritative backing of professional economists and intergovernmental organizations (Simmons, Dobbin and Garrett 2006).

The emphasis on global or worldwide effects by no means excludes effects at lower levels of analysis. To find, for example, women's suffrage rights around the world (Ramirez, Soysal and Shanahan 1997) is not the same as finding that such rights are respected to the same extent, in the same way, with the same implications in every country, village and household globally. Of course there are differences and variations, and of course they are important, just as are the global effects to which world society theory calls attention.

6. World society theory is a normative and/or teleological perspective similar to modernization theory

World society scholars study 'modernity' not as an ideal or inevitable trajectory, but as a set of cultural views or ideologies that have become institutionalized components of global culture at a particular point in history. Contemporary world culture can be characterized as 'modernist' in character, involving ideologies of national progress/ development, the expansion of education, science/rationality and so on. World society scholars seek to understand the consequences of this culture. This is different than normatively endorsing this set of cultural views or treating the emergence of these ideas as inevitable.

7. World society theory fails to attend to mechanisms

This criticism has, in part, been addressed in recent empirical work (e.g., Schofer and Hironaka 2005). Scholars have documented a variety of 'carriers' of institutionalized cultural models, including international associations, scientists and professionals, media and telecommunication, modern school systems that convey standardized curricula, and even the legacy of colonial ties. That said, Schofer and Hironaka (2005) point out the limits of searching for concrete mechanisms to explain complex cultural processes. Can one easily enumerate the specific mechanisms through which cultural capital is transferred from parents to children? Countries embedded in global culture are influenced via multiple, often very diffuse, mechanisms operating simultaneously. The more deeply institutionalized a cultural form, the more it becomes 'built in' to many mechanisms, such as law, custom, school curricula and so on. And, dramatic change is often observed even when some specific mechanisms (e.g., a given law or treaty) appear to be ineffective. Those in search of any single 'smoking gun' wholly responsible for diffusion or change are likely to be disappointed.

New Directions in World Society Theory

Research continues apace within the world society paradigm, much of it extending the lines of research outlined above. But distinct new lines of research have also emerged within the past decade. While partaking of the original spirit, these new directions develop theoretical arguments to explain the role of actors in the world polity, theories of institutional change, and theory about the outcomes of world polity processes.

Role of individual actors

As discussed above, one common gloss on world society theory is that it ignores the role of individuals in developing institutions. Recently, however, some scholars have argued that the creation of meaning and interpretation by individuals is an essential aspect of diffusion, particularly in a global context that champions individual human rights and actorhood (Frank and Meyer 2002; Suárez 2008). Such arguments recognize that global institutions continue to influence the perceptions and actions of individuals. Concurrently, however, individuals act as agents, or at times resisters, of global institutions. Such individual actions enable the implementation of the often nebulous influences of global institutions (cf. the old institutionalism represented by Stinchcombe 1997).

Along these lines, Hallett and Ventresca (2006) develop the concepts of an 'inhabited institution'. Instead of conceptualizing bureaucratization as expanding automatically, Hallett and Ventresca find its contours depend upon the particular personalities of the managers, the contingent interpretations of the workers, and the formulation of specific policies. Similarly, Dobbin (2009) argues that the development of equal opportunity practices in the US workplace was not the result of automatons mindlessly carrying out the 1964 Civil Rights Act. Instead, the practice of equal opportunity depended upon the personnel staff that developed policies and standards to construct a definition for equal opportunity.

Thus, a growing line of research links insights from world polity theory to the growing field on transnational movements (e.g., Keck and Sikkink 1998; Smith and Johnston 2002). World polity researchers have expanded on these arguments, finding that global processes also influence the mobilization of social movements. Global political opportunity structures, such as the creation of international organizations, complement and may even supersede the effects of national political opportunity structures (Barrett and Kurzman 2004; Tsutsui 2006; Cole 2006; Longhofer and Schofer 2010). Global cultural frames provide broader legitimacy and meaning to local struggles (Tsutsui 2004; Lounsbury, Ventresca and Hirsch 2003; Ghaziani and Ventresca 2005). And global resources may be available from international organizations or interested players for domestic social movements (Tsutsui and Shin 2008; Berkovitch and Gordon 2008).

Theories of change

One distinctive new line of work explains institutional change as a 'learning' process, in which organizations or states copy newly successful actors. However, 'learning' is in quotes as it does not necessarily connote improvement – but rather the adoption of socially constructed 'lessons' copied from other actors and translated via professionals, experts and other authoritative interpreters. Scholars have studied the rise of business fads such as 'quality circles' (originally a Japanese innovation) in the United States or more enduring shifts in political and military policy (Strang and Macy

2001; Dobbin 1993; Hironaka 2010). These changes occur with the rise of a successful new star, such as the economic success of Japan in the 1980s. Alternately, change may occur during a crisis, when perceived failure creates an opening for policy shifts.

In contrast to realist approaches, world polity theorists maintain scepticism that these processes lead to effective change. Since indicators of success are constructed, the 'successes' that are copied may be misleading. Stories are created to explain the success of particular firms or countries, yet these accounts are often fictive or mythical (Strang and Soule 1998; Strang and Macy 2001). In a sense, states throw out a grab-bag of policies and then ordain those that are followed by economic growth as effective, despite the likelihood of spurious causality (Dobbin 1993). The complexity of economic and military phenomena belies the accuracy of simple cause-and-effect stories (Hironaka 2010). Yet, such stories abound and form the basis for subsequent isomorphic change.

Explaining consequences and outcomes

Scholars in the world polity tradition have increasingly sought to theorize the substantive outcomes that result from global institutional processes – rather than focus solely on formal policies or laws. Early lines of research on loose coupling questioned the link between institutional processes and substantive specified outcomes (Meyer and Rowan 1977; Cole 2005). Yet world polity research has subsequently uncovered a broad set of phenomena in which world polity pressures have led to tidal waves of change 'on the ground' over time. The massive expansion of education, the bureaucratization and rationalization of society, and the broad empowerment of individuals represent fundamental changes to society in the past century (Ramirez and Wotipka 2001; Drori et al. 2006; Dobbin 2009; Frank and Meyer 2002).

In other arenas, most notably in respect for human rights, world polity pressures have failed to produce comprehensive changes (Bradley 2000; Hafner-Burton and Tsutsui 2005; Cole 2005). Such research has shown that discourse alone is insufficient to lead to substantive improvements in outcomes. Yet it is possible that improvements in human rights may have also been confounded by the global legitimacy of authoritarian regimes during the Cold War. With the delegitimation of the authoritarian state and the outbreak of democracy worldwide, human rights abuses may decline as predicted by the rhetoric in future decades.

In other fields, world polity processes have been shown to be consequential for outcomes on the ground. Improvements in outcomes occur as the net result of broad institutional shifts in which no one particular policy or action is essential (Schofer and Hironaka 2005). International treaties and discourses have indirect effects, such as 'naming and shaming', rather than more direct sanctions and enforcement (Drori et al. 2006). National policies that are criticized as ineffective may still result in improved outcomes within a decade or two (Liu and Boyle 2001). Over time, world polity pressures lead to the development of a 'virtuous regime' in which the goodness of a particular outcome becomes taken for granted. Once virtue has been declared, actors may find it increasingly difficult to justify departure (Schofer and Hironaka 2005).

Concluding Thoughts

With maturity, the world society literature is shifting focus – from original battles with functionalism and Marxism (which nevertheless continue to crop up under new labels) – to a more nuanced set of debates in a world where 'institutionalisms' of various sorts are increasingly common. A key fault line for future theory and research will likely be between more cultural/phenomenological institutionalisms and those that take a more purely actor-centric stance, such as the institutional traditions in International Relations. The world society tradition has generated novel predictions, in large part, by countering the endemic actor-centrism in much contemporary (especially American) social science. The continuing vibrancy of the world society tradition will likely hinge on continuing efforts in this vein, which differentiate the tradition from conventional institutional analysis.

Acknowledgement

We thank Colin Beck, Elizabeth Boyle and members of the Irvine Comparative Sociology Workshop for their insightful comments. We regret that we could not, in this brief review, do more than scratch the surface in terms of providing references to the outstanding theoretical and empirical work on this topic.

Further Reading

Drori, G.S. 2007: Institutionalism and globalization studies. In R. Greenwood, C. Oliver, R. Suddaby *et al.* (eds) *Handbook of Organizational Institutionalism*. London: Sage.

Frank, D.J., Hardinge, T. and Wosick-Correa, K. 2009: The global dimensions of rape-law reform: a cross-national study of policy outcomes. *American Sociological Review* 74: 272–290.

Jepperson, R.L. 2002: The development and application of sociological neoinstitutionalism. In J. Berger & M. Zelditch, Jr (eds) *New Directions in Contemporary Sociological Theory*. Lanham, MD: Rowman & Littlefield.

Jepperson, R.L. and Meyer, J.W. 2011: Multiple levels of analysis and the limits of methodological individualisms. *Sociological Theory* 29 (1): 54–73.

Krucken, G. and Drori, G.S. (eds) 2009: *World Society: The Writings of John W. Meyer*. Oxford: Oxford University Press.

Meyer, John W. 2010. World Society, Institutional Theories, and the Actor. *Annual Review of Sociology*, 36: 1–20.

Schofer, E. and Hironaka, A. 2005: World society and environmental protection outcomes. *Social Forces* 84: 25–47.

7

Studying Power

JOHN SCOTT

There are three dominant methodological traditions through which power is studied in empirical political sociology. The reputational approach looks at those who are believed to have power. Increasingly, however, it is thought that this is evidence only of images of power on the part of those asked. Structural approaches focus on strategic positions in the central organizations and institutions of a society. Decision-making approaches are based on the claim that the reputational and positional approaches ignore what actually happens when decisions are made. Scott favours the structural approach, arguing that it can, and should, incorporate the insights of the others: decision making can only be studied where there is understanding of the important structures within which decisions are taken; and perceptions of power can best be understood where there is independent knowledge of the positions people believe to be powerful.

The principal approaches to the study of power have generally been seen as bitter rivals and as offering mutually exclusive paradigms of research (Scott 2001). They have each come to be associated with quite distinctive methods of research and analysis. Indeed, it has even been claimed that the theoretical starting point determines not only the choice of research methods but also the substantive conclusions that can be drawn from the research (Walton 1966). To see things in this way is to put the point far too strongly. While there are certainly affinities between theoretical approaches and research methods, leading to distinctive research traditions, these are not tight and rigid connections. The merits and demerits of the various research methods can be considered independently of the particular theoretical approach adopted. In this chapter I concentrate principally on the virtues of one research tradition, but I take it as axiomatic that the theoretical approaches associated with these traditions must be seen as complementary perspectives rather than as all-or-nothing rivals (Moyser and Wagstaffe 1987).

The Wiley-Blackwell Companion to Political Sociology, First Edition. Edited by Edwin Amenta, Kate Nash, and Alan Scott.
© 2012 Blackwell Publishing Ltd. Published 2012 by Blackwell Publishing Ltd.

Table 7.1 Traditions and research methods

Research tradition	Paradigmatic study	Preferred research methods		
		Data collection	Data analysis	Object of analysis
Reputational	Hunter (1953)	Expert judgement, interviews	Voting, ranking, and rating scores	Images of power
Structural	Mills (1956)	Documents	Frequency distributions, social network analysis	Positions of power
Decision making	Dahl (1961)	Observation, interviews	Policy outcomes	Agencies of power

Three dominant research traditions have generally been identified in the study of power. These are the reputational approach, the structural approach and the agency or decision-making approach (Crewe 1974). Each of these traditions is associated with a study that exemplifies its research methods and techniques and that has provided a model for later researchers. Table 7.1 presents a simplified summary of the links between the research traditions and their preferred methods of research.

The reputational approach to power has as its main concern those agents who are *reputed* to be powerful. While it has often been assumed that this method can give direct evidence on actual power relations, it has increasingly come to be realized that, in fact, it evidences only *images* of power. Structural approaches to power focus directly on the attributes of strategic positions in the central organizations and institutions of a society. These positions are held to be central to the control of the resources that are the basis of power, and the occupants of these positions are the central actors in the exercise of power. Decision-making approaches have been based on the claim that reputational and positional approaches have been overly formalistic. They have looked at formal, official definitions of power and have ignored what really happens when decisions are made. Not all of those who occupy positions of formal authority will be equally involved in all the various stages of decision making, and the only proper way to investigate power, it is held, is to do so directly at its point of exercise.

My own position is that the structural approach has the most to offer to researchers on power and that it provides a basis for incorporating the insights of the rival approaches. It is possible to study decision making only if we have an understanding of the structure within which these decisions are made, and perceptions of power can best be studied if we have some independent knowledge of what it is that the participants are trying to perceive. The starting point for any study of power, then, must be a structural analysis.

Each tradition relies on particular techniques of data collection and data analysis, these techniques being very widely used in the social sciences. I will not attempt to give a comprehensive coverage of such techniques as survey methods, interview methods and the use of documents. Instead, I will concentrate on the features of these research methods that are most particular to the study of power and that raise particular issues in power research. As the focus of this discussion is on studying power, I have not discussed the research methods used in elite studies more generally, where the focus is not on power but on elite attitudes, values and behaviour (Putnam 1973; see also Moyser and Wagstaffe 1987, eds).

Power can be studied at a number of levels of analysis, and these will figure in this discussion. Some research has focused its attention on the national level, investigating power relations in and around the nation-state. An important tradition of research, however, has been concerned with power at the community level, in towns and cities within nation-states. There are, of course, important theoretical and substantive issues that surround the choice of an appropriate level of analysis, as well as about the extent to which global power relations should be considered alongside the national and the local. However, the research issues that arise in each of these areas are, in general, similar, and there is little need to make explicit reference to the level of analysis here.

Images and Decisions

The paradigmatic study for the reputational approach is that of Floyd Hunter (1953), for whom the central concern in a study of power was to identify those people who, according to general opinion in their community, exercise the greatest amount of power. It is perceptions or images of social positions and their occupants that are of interest to Hunter. In this respect, Hunter's work is similar to studies of images of class (Warner 1949; Lockwood 1966; Bulmer 1974) and of images of society more generally. In his work, however, he tends to gloss the distinction between images of power and the actual exercise of power. Hunter's 'positional' approach to power saw it as 'the acts of men [sic] going about the business of moving other men to act in relation to themselves or in relation to organic or inorganic things' (Hunter 1953: 2–3, emphasis removed). (Note that all the writers considered in detail here followed the sexist practice of referring to 'men' instead of 'people', and there is little or no discussion of the practices through which women have been excluded from power. In the direct quotations used in the rest of this chapter, I have left the argument in the words actually used by the researcher.) The resources that made such power possible were seen as being tied to social positions, and so the focus of any investigation must be on those who occupy prominent positions in various types of groups or associations. This starting point is the same as that of the structural approach, but Hunter wanted to move from structures to reputations.

In his study of community power in the financial, commercial and industrial centre of Atlanta, Georgia (called 'Regional City' in the original report), Hunter aimed to identify powerful individuals in four arenas of power – business, government, civic affairs and 'society leaders and leaders of wealth' (Hunter 1953: 169). He sought key informants in the leading organizations and associations in each of these arenas, asking them to name the chairmen and other leaders in the principal organizations in each of the four arenas of power. Many such office holders could, of course, have been identified from published documentary sources, as has been the case in more explicitly structural research, but Hunter was keen to tap into the knowledge and opinions of his key informants from the beginning.

The lists produced by the key informants were given to a panel of 'judges', whose job it was to use their knowledge to reduce them to a more manageable 'top ten of influence' in each arena. The panel of judges was supposed to be representative of the community in terms of religion, sex, age and ethnicity, and they were also supposed to be representative of business and the professions (though no attempt was made to ensure that they were representative of other occupational groups). The community influentials – seen as the holders of power – were defined as the 40 people who received the largest number of votes from the panel of judges. (Note, however, that while the panel of judges was supposed to be representative of middle-class opinion, there is evidence that they were far less representative even than this. Hunter found that no African Americans appeared on the list. This reflects, of course, the lack of power – real or reputed – held by African Americans in the southern states of America in the 1950s, but it also seemed, to Hunter, to reflect the unwillingness or inability of his key informants to recognize those African Americans who did achieve positions of power. To overcome this, Hunter made an ad hoc extension to his research by carrying out a parallel sub-study within the black community, arguing that there was a divided structure of black–white power. This argument is analogous to Warner's claims about black–white class relations in the Deep South (Warner 1936; see also Davis, Gardner and Gardner 1941).

This was, of course, an arbitrary limitation, and Hunter's claim that these people were typical of a larger group of powerful persons (Hunter 1953: 61) highlights a problem that occurs in all projects where only a sub-set of the powerful are studied. This is the problem of sampling. When a researcher does not cover the whole of the target population, whether by accident or design, it is important that the nature and representativeness of the resulting sample is examined. In general, it is preferable to use explicit sampling criteria in the first place, though this may not be possible when the size and composition of the target population are unknown or unspecified.

While it purports to investigate the actual holders of power, the reputational approach, at best, provides evidence on *images of power*. The images disclosed are those of the expert judges, or the larger social groups of which they are representative. As such, it is important for a reputational study to identify clearly its target group: Is the aim of the research to identify those that a whole society rates as the most powerful, or those that one class, sex or ethnic group within it rates as the most powerful? Such questions can be answered only on the basis of some knowledge about the actual structures of power and the wider social structure.

The paradigmatic study for the decision-making approach to power is that of Robert Dahl (1961), who was one of the earliest critics of Hunter and of structural approaches. Structural, or positional, approaches, he argued, presuppose that an elite exists, and a methodology that concentrates on top positions will inevitably conclude that an elite does, in fact, exist. The whole process, he argued, is circular. For Dahl, the existence of an elite had to be demonstrated through the direct investigation of decision making. He holds that 'A has power over B to the extent that he can get B to do something that B would not otherwise do' (Dahl 1957: 202–203), and this is studied by measuring the actual participation of position holders in specific key decisions (see Lukes 1974 and the 'Introduction' and the reprints of key contributions by Dahl, Lukes, and others in Scott 1994).

Paradoxically, Dahl also began his research with the identification of structural positions. His study of New Haven, Connecticut, in the 1950s identified a large number of positions that he thought had the potential for power and influence in the community. These included office holders in the city administration (elected and appointed), local businessmen and various 'social and economic notables'. The latter were large property holders and directors, and those active in 'Society' activities. While this starting point looks little different from that of Hunter, Dahl was not using it to delineate a group of actual power-holders. Rather, he wanted simply to identify a large population of *potential* holders of power, so that he could then go on and identify which of them were involved in the active exercise of power. This was the question that was to be investigated through an examination of their participation in the making of key decisions in the community.

Dahl's study of politics and his decision-making methodology have been emulated by many other political scientists and sociologists, though few have undertaken the kind of detailed and careful investigation of processes and policy outcomes that Dahl himself undertook. At the level of community power are studies by Vidich and Bensman (1968), Birch (1959) and Wildavsky (1964), while at the national level there have been Rose (1967) in the United States and Hewitt (1974) in Britain.

Dahl concentrated on a number of 'issue-areas' – urban redevelopment, local schooling, and nominations for political office – and within each of these he looked at specific decisions such as the formation of a Citizen's Action Commission, the redevelopment of particular streets and squares, the introduction of eye tests in schools, changes to educational budgets, policies for dealing with delinquency at school, nominations for election as mayor and proposals for a new city charter. Dahl and his researchers sought to use interviews, observations and documents to identify who proposed particular alternatives, who spoke in discussions, when and how proposals were modified or rejected, and who voted for each proposal when a final decision was arrived at. He concluded that a great many people were involved in initiating or vetoing proposals, and that they tended to be actively involved only in those areas where they had particular professional or occupational interests. Only the democratically elected politicians were centrally involved in more than one proposal (Dahl 1961: 181–183). The positional resources of the economic and social notables gave them only the *potential* for power, but very few of them either tried or succeeded in converting their potential into actual influence in decision-making processes. He further argued that political decisions were shaped by the lobbying and pressuring activities of a variety of groups. The outcome of decision-making processes did not uniformly express the interests or advantages of any one group. Power in New Haven was 'pluralistic' rather than elitist (see also Polsby 1980).

The problems with the decision-making approach are, of course, that there is no certainty that researchers will either get access to those who really make decisions or be able to uncover the key participants. To the extent that decisions are made behind closed doors, away from the glare of public scrutiny, then political scientists and sociologists are unlikely to be able to observe these decisions or to interview those involved (Bachrach and Baratz 1963, 1975). This critique points to the need to investigate the 'non-decision-making' processes that occur behind the scenes and that serve to keep some issues out of the overt decision-making process. From this standpoint, the 'potential' power inherent in structural positions has a far greater significance than Dahl allowed.

The necessity for a structural framework is also apparent in the need for an objective criterion for identifying which decisions are the most important or strategic in a community. Which decisions are important, and which are not, is a matter that can be decided only in relation to the overall structure of the society and the distribution of advantages and disadvantages within it. Without such information, the researcher may end up looking only at the marginal and unimportant decisions that the real rulers could safely leave to others. The implication of this kind of criticism, then, is that the very structural concerns that Dahl sought to eliminate must, indeed, find their place in a comprehensive investigation of power.

Structures of Power

If structures of power are to form the centrepiece of power research – and both Hunter and Dahl began with the identification of structural positions – how is this to be carried out? The paradigmatic study for this approach is that of Mills (1956), who used the positional method to study national-level power in the United States. Where Hunter and Dahl identified positions of power simply as their starting points, Mills saw this as central to the whole project. Power, he held, resides with all those 'who are able to realize their will, even if others resist it' (Mills 1956: 9). While the identity of the particular individuals is recognized to be important, it is the attributes of the positions that they occupy that are seen as more fundamental to power relations. Someone exercises power as an occupant of a particular position, subject to the constraint exercised by the occupants of other positions. Without their positions, individuals have no significant power.

Power is located in the top positions of the institutional hierarchies that define the social structure of a society, and the distribution of power varies with the shape taken by this structure. As the institutional hierarchies of a society become more centralized, so the distribution of power becomes more concentrated: 'As the means of information and of power are centralized, some men come to occupy positions in American society from which they can look down upon, so to speak, and by their decisions mightily affect, the everyday worlds of ordinary men and women' (Mills 1956: 3). Mills' central concept of the power elite follows from this view of power. The institutional hierarchies form a structure of power, and it is the overlapping and interlocking of their top positions that forms a power elite. A power elite, then, comprises the 'men whose positions enable them to transcend the ordinary environments of ordinary men and women; they are in positions that allow them to make decisions that have major consequences' (Mills 1956: 3–4).

Mills saw three institutional hierarchies at the heart of the power elite in the United States of the 1950s. These were the economic, the political and the military hierarchies. As the identification of positions of power was to be the heart of his study, Mills sought to be as comprehensive and as systematic as he could in his use of evidence. Instead of relying on the knowledge of key informants, he went directly to the documentary sources that provided a full coverage of these positions. Although his precise selection criteria varied from case to case, Mills did make great attempts to be systematic and rigorous in his data collection. In most cases, he collected data for the full set of positions over three generations.

Within the economic arena, Mills noted the twentieth-century growth of the corporate sector at the expense of personal, privately owned enterprises. He therefore focused his attention on those positions that formed what he called the 'corporate rich'. This category included holders of substantial wealth (termed the 'very rich') and holders of corporate office (the 'corporate executives'). The very rich were operationally defined as those men and women with assets of $30 million or more, and lists of names were compiled from a variety of official, corporate and secondary sources (on the use of documentary sources in power and other studies see Scott 1990). He defined 'corporate executives' rather loosely as the 'top two or three command posts in each of those hundred or so corporations which . . . are the largest' (Mills 1956: 126), and similar data on them were collected by his PhD student, Suzanne Keller.

This definition of corporate executives highlights a general problem in positional studies of power. This is the problem of defining and bounding the positions that are to be studied, sometimes referred to as the problem of system boundaries. While any such decisions are likely to be arbitrary, it is important that the criteria are both clear and consistently applied. For example, we must know whether the category of 'top' corporations includes the largest 50, 100, 200 or 500 corporations, and we also need to know by what criterion 'size' is measured. Similarly, we must know which actual positions are to count as the 'top' positions within them. Do we include just the president (chief executive), all the office holders or all the directors? There is no simple answer to such questions, as the boundary criteria that need to be used will vary from one situation to another.

In the political and military arenas, Mills focused his attention on what he called 'the political directorate' and 'the warlords'. The political directorate is a category that includes all the leading positions of state: President, Vice President, Speaker, Cabinet members, and Supreme Court Justices. His list also included a number of positions that had grown in importance in executive decision-making over the course of the century. These were the Under Secretaries, Directors of Departments, Members of the Executive Office of the President, and White House Staff. The warlords were all generals and admirals, including – most importantly – those holding office in the Pentagon. Like the political directorate, these office holders were identified from official documents that listed the positions and their occupants. As with the corporate rich, the boundaries of the 'top' positions in the political and military hierarchies were, inevitably, drawn arbitrarily, as a decision must always be made about which positions are important enough to include. An attempt to set out a framework for such matters in relation to identifying a political elite can be found in Giddens (1973a).

Mills' power elite comprised the overlapping groups of the corporate rich, the political directorate and the warlords. This emphasis on the analysis of overlapping memberships has been a central characteristic of structural studies of power. These studies have investigated the overlap among positions of power by the more or less systematic use of methods of social network analysis. Hunter had used these same techniques rather more systematically. He used rudimentary methods of social network analysis to construct sociograms of interaction among the reputedly powerful, concluding that there was evidence for the existence of various 'crowds' or 'cliques' within the leadership group (Hunter 1953: 77–78).

The systematic use of social network analysis has gradually become more central to structural research on power, as the advanced techniques developed since the 1960s have allowed more rigorous investigations into the formation of cliques and other sub-groupings. In social network analysis, individual positions are represented as points in a diagram or as rows in a matrix, while the social relations that connect these positions are represented as lines connecting the points or as the individual cells of the matrix. Mathematical techniques are now available to chart the size and structure of social networks through such measures as density, centralization and fragmentation (Scott 1991b; Wasserman and Faust 1994; de Nooy, Mrvar and Batagelj 2005). Density measures the coherence or integration of a network – how closely connected its members are. Centrality, on the other hand, concerns the relative prominence of members in the network. At an overall level, centralization measures examine the extent to which a network is organized around focal units. Particularly important measures in structural analysis are those that identify cliques, clusters and other sub-groupings that cross-cut the formal boundaries of institutions (Knoke 1994).

The most systematic and theoretically sophisticated examples of the use of the structural approach can be found in the work of Domhoff (1967, 1971, 1979, 1998, 2009) and those who have been influenced by him. In these studies, structures of powerful positions are investigated in relation to the social background and policy preferences of those who occupy them. Domhoff has explored the consolidation of capitalist class power through the formal and informal networks involved in the special-interest process, the policy-formation process, the candidate-selection process and the ideology process. In Britain, a similar approach has been used in works by Guttsman (1963), Miliband (1969) and Scott (1991c). Scott has shown that the 'old boy' networks of British politics can be explored through the structural analysis of power blocs and the structure of intercorporate relations in business. Such work has recently been enlarged in the growing number of studies into policy networks (see Marsh 1998).

The approach has been especially important in analyses of economic power in large corporations (see Mizruchi 1982; Scott and Griff 1984; Mintz and Schwartz 1985; Stokman, Ziegler and Scott 1985; see also Scott 1991a. Some of the key studies of political and economic elites using these methods can be found in Scott (1990, ed.). Such work has examined interlocking directorships and intercorporate shareholdings, showing the organization of economic power around structured relations between industrial and financial interests (Scott 1997). Central to many such studies has been a critical examination of the managerialist ideas of writers such as Burnham (1941) and Berle and Means (1932), who share many of the assumptions of the pluralist writers. Rejecting this point of view, the works of Mintz and Schwartz in the United States and Scott in Britain have documented the existence of structures of bank centrality through which finance capitalists are able to coordinate the affairs of the numerous corporate boards on which they sit. Through their interlocking directorships, these multiple directors become the most important force in the corporate power structure.

Conclusion

Each of the traditions that I have reviewed has produced important work, showing the potential and the value of the particular methods used to study power. However, each also has its limitations, and I have tried to sketch these out. The trite conclusion is undoubtedly that no one tradition has a monopoly of the truth, and they must, ideally, be combined in a single research design (Dowding 1996: 58ff and see also 1995 where he downplays the significance of structural concerns in an otherwise useful survey. This seems to be based on his appraisal of the limited results appearing in the relatively new area of policy network research). This is not to say that they carry equal weight. I have argued that the structural approach provides the best basis for integrating the results of research on participation in decision making and the images of power that motivate participants. It provides powerful techniques for mapping and measuring power relations, and it provides the essential framework for understanding processes of decision-making power.

Further Reading

Scott, J. (ed.) 1990: *The Sociology of Elites*, 3 vols. Cheltenham: Edward Elgar.
Scott, J. (ed.) 1994: *Power*, 3 vols. London: Routledge.
Scott, J. 2001: *Power*. Cambridge: Polity Press.
Wartenberg, T.E. (ed.) 1992: *Rethinking Power*. Albany: State University of New York Press.

8

Comparative Political Analysis

Six Case-Oriented Strategies

CHARLES C. RAGIN AND GARRETT ANDREW SCHNEIDER

It is commonplace to treat case-oriented comparative political analysis as a primitive form of quantitative research, analytically crippled by its focus on small Ns. It is not its focus on small Ns, however, that makes case-oriented analysis distinctive. Rather, it is its analytic logic, one that is especially well suited for theory building. The key difference between case-oriented work and conventional quantitative analysis is the fact that the former is largely concerned with the analysis of asymmetric set relations, while the latter focuses largely on the analysis of symmetric relationships among variables. In this chapter, we describe six case-oriented comparative strategies that illustrate its distinctiveness. Describing these strategies not only clarifies the logic of case-oriented comparative research, but also offers guidance to practising case-oriented researchers.

Context

Much of the discussion of comparative political analysis today remains mired in a dialogue with a 1994 text, *Designing Social Inquiry: Scientific Inference in Qualitative Research* (by Gary King, Robert Keohane and Sidney Verba). The recent publication of the second edition of *Rethinking Social Inquiry: Diverse Tools, Shared Standards* (Brady and Collier (eds) 2010), a collection of essays confronting *Designing Social Inquiry* from a variety of viewpoints, attests to the lasting impact of the latter. While *Designing Social Inquiry* is filled with useful suggestions and thoughtful reflection, it continues to promote the view that qualitative, case-oriented research is the simple-minded, unrefined, bastard cousin of quantitative, variable-oriented research. According to this view of comparative analysis, the key to the improvement of

The Wiley-Blackwell Companion to Political Sociology, First Edition. Edited by Edwin Amenta, Kate Nash, and Alan Scott.
© 2012 Blackwell Publishing Ltd. Published 2012 by Blackwell Publishing Ltd.

case-oriented research is for qualitative researchers to adhere as closely as possible to the well-known research template established by their quantitative cousins.

It is important to recognize that this view did not originate with King, Keohane and Verba. It has been around in various forms for decades. The closing chapters of Neil Smelser's (1976) landmark *Comparative Methods in the Social Sciences*, for example, makes the same basic argument, as does Przeworski and Teune's (1970) *The Logic of Comparative Social Inquiry*. Przeworski and Teune go so far as to argue that researchers should strive to remove proper names (e.g., 'China') from macro-comparative inquiry. Most comparativists to this day find this recommendation curious. Not only is case knowledge valuable, the best foundation for empirical generalization is in-depth knowledge of cases (Ragin and Schneider 2010). From this viewpoint, striving to remove proper names from comparative inquiry is about as sensible as trying to remove dates. In the abstract, this type of context-free social science might be appealing. However, most social scientists today remain committed to the accumulation of knowledge about phenomena that are firmly situated in time and place (Amenta 1991).

Our principal goal in this chapter is to provide further evidence that case-oriented inquiry is *not* the bastard cousin of quantitative research. We describe six case-oriented comparative strategies that illustrate its distinctiveness. Describing these strategies not only clarifies the logic of case-oriented comparative research, but also offers guidance to practising case-oriented researchers. Our approach contrasts with the usual practice, which is for qualitative researchers to judge quantitative research by the standards of qualitative research and vice versa. Both approaches come up short in this war of words. A more productive path is to recognize and celebrate their respective strengths. This chapter seeks to contribute to further progress on this path (see also Ragin and Becker 1992; Brady and Collier 2004; Mahoney 2010a; Bennett and Elman 2006).

Connecting Conditions and Outcomes: The Limitations of Correlation

Most quantitative techniques for assessing the relation between causal conditions and outcomes are based on the correlation coefficient or some other symmetric measure of association. Researchers are able to compute complex structural equation models, for example, armed with only a matrix of bivariate correlations and the means and standard deviations of the variables in the matrix (Bollen 1989). One feature that all symmetric measures share is that they give equal weight to an argument and its 'mirror'. For example, a researcher might argue that 'democracies with fractionalized elites are unstable'. The textbook method for testing this argument is to collect data on democracies, recording their degree of instability and their degree of elite fraction-alization. If the correlation between these two variables is positive, this evidence can be presented as support for the argument. However, notice that the correlation between stability and elite fractionalization tests not only the stated argument, but also its mirror, which is the argument that 'democracies with unified elites are stable'. While the mirror argument might seem inherent in the initial argument, the two can be separated.

For illustration consider Table 8.1: panel A, which shows a simple 2 × 2 table for the relation between elite fractionalization and political stability (hypothetical data). The table shows clearly that cases congregate in the unstable/fractionalized-elites cell and the stable/unified-elite cell, yielding a symmetric association of 0.320. In analyses of this type, cases in cells 2 and 3 count in the researcher's favour, equally so, while cases in cells 1 and 4 count against the researcher, again equally so. This table is consistent with both the researcher's stated argument (that democracies with fractionalized elites are unstable) and with its mirror (that democracies with unified elites are stable). A clear majority of the cases with unified elites are in the 'stable' row, and a clear majority of the cases with fractionalized elites are in the 'unstable' row.

Next consider Table 8.1: panel B. In this table, there is a statistically significant positive relationship between elite fractionalization and political instability, with a symmetric measure of association (0.313) about the same as in Table 8.1: panel A. In many quarters, the results in panel B would be considered completely equivalent to the results in panel A, for both show that the probability of instability increases with elite fractionalization. However, in panel B it is clear that most instances of elite fractionalization are politically stable. The strong association found in the data is in fact due to the very strong support for the mirror argument – that political stability is linked to having unified elites. Should this table count as support for the researcher's initial (as opposed to mirror) argument, that democracies with fractionalized elites are unstable?

To complete the picture, consider Table 8.1: panel C, which shows a third hypothetical distribution of cases. Again, there is a strong relationship between the two variables and the probability of instability increases with elite fractionalization, as in panels A and B. Again, the symmetric measure of association (0.342) is positive and about the same magnitude as in the other panels. It is clear in this table that there is

Table 8.1 Elite fractionalization and political stability

Panel A

	Elites unified	Elites fractionalized
Unstable democracy	8 (36%)	13 (68%)
Stable democracy	14 (64%)	6 (32%)

$N = 41$; symmetric association = 0.320

Panel B

	Elites unified	Elites fractionalized
Unstable democracy	2 (9%)	7 (37%)
Stable democracy	20 (91%)	12 (63%)

$N = 41$; symmetric association = .313

Panel C

	Elites unified	Elites fractionalized
Unstable democracy	13 (59%)	17 (89%)
Stable democracy	9 (41%)	2 (11%)

$N = 41$; symmetric association = .342

strong support for the researcher's initial argument; 17 out of 19 democracies with fractionalized elites are unstable. However, notice that the mirror argument, that democracies with unified elites are stable, is not supported. In fact, the majority of these democracies are unstable.

The point is a simple one, that the correlation coefficient and other symmetric measures of association pay scant attention to these subtle but important differences in argumentation and evidence. These measures are insensitive to the fact that many of the arguments that social scientists make are asymmetric and that it is possible to distinguish the initial argument from its mirror. Of course, researchers may formulate their hypotheses in a symmetrical manner, as in 'elite fractionalization increases the probability of democratic instability', but it is important to recognize that such arguments (1) are less empirically precise than asymmetric arguments, and (2) are more difficult to connect to empirical cases and empirical questions (e.g., 'Are democracies with fractionalized elites unstable?'). It is possible for the symmetric argument just described to be true, while most democracies with fractionalized elites are stable, as shown in Table 8.1: panel B. What matters most to the symmetric argument is *relative* levels of instability and the fact that these levels differ in the expected manner.

Connecting Conditions and Outcomes: The Case-oriented Template

When researchers study cases in an in-depth manner, they often focus on a change that occurred over a specific period of time, signalling some sort of shift or transformation (e.g., Skocpol 1992; Morgan and Prasad 2009; Stryker 1990; Bloemraad 2006; Chen and Weir 2009; Fourcade-Gourinchas and Babb 2002; Riley 2005; Steinmetz 2008; Mahoney 2010b; Swenson 2002). Accounts and explanations of these qualitative changes typically invoke specific *combinations* of causally relevant conditions that prompted the change. These combinations can be seen as *causal recipes* because all the relevant ingredients for change must be in place for it to occur. Specifying a causal recipe entails not only listing the relevant ingredients, but also identifying the processes and mechanisms involved in the production of the outcome (Steel 2004; Bennett 2008; George and Bennett 2004). Even as lists of combined conditions, causal recipes are pregnant with implications about processes and mechanisms (see, for example, Boswell and Brown 1999). The specification of a causal recipe for a given case may be considered a hypothesis relevant to other cases. In this way, the endpoint of a case study may be a testable hypothesis about other cases, especially when this endpoint is a more or less 'portable' causal recipe linked to a general outcome – a qualitative change experienced by other cases as well.

Consider 'Three Strikes and You're Out' in California, a mandatory minimum sentencing law enacted in 1993 (Brown and Jolivette 2005; Ehlers, Schiraldi and Zeidenberg 2004). Through analysis of a variety of case materials – newspaper articles, first-hand testimonials, public opinion surveys and economic, political, demographic and crime statistics – researchers have concluded that California enacted this change to its code because of (1) mobilization by interest groups and civic associations, (2) electioneering, (3) public fear of social disorder and (4) a sensational crime (Schneider 2008). This explanation cites a specific *combination* of conditions which have the character of a recipe: all four conditions were met simultaneously in the case of California, and together they explain the dramatic policy change and subsequent expansion of incarceration.

Using the analysis of California as a springboard, a researcher could move in either of two directions. The first possible direction would be to find other instances of punitive change to state-level penal codes and examine the extent to which they agree in displaying the same recipe: Do all (or virtually all) instances of punitive policy change display these four antecedent conditions? This strategy employs the common qualitative research strategy of 'selecting on the dependent variable', an approach that is almost universally, but mistakenly, condemned by quantitative researchers (see, for example, King, Keohane and Verba 1994; Geddes 1990; for a defence, see Dion 1998; Ragin 2000, 2008). The second direction would be to try to find other instances of California's recipe and examine whether these states also experienced punitive changes to their penal codes. In essence, the researcher would select cases on the basis of their scores on the independent variable. In this example, however, the 'independent variable' is a causal recipe with its four main conditions all satisfied. The goal of the second strategy would be to assess the sufficiency of the recipe: Does it invariably (or at least with substantial consistency) lead to punitive policy change?

Both of these strategies are set theoretic in nature and conform to the two general set theoretic approaches described in Ragin and Rihoux (2004) and Ragin (2008). The first is an examination of whether instances of the outcome (punitive change to the penal code) constitute a subset of instances of a combination of causal conditions. The researcher examines other states that introduced major changes to their penal codes, making them overwhelmingly more punitive, to see if the same combination of four ingredients existed in these other states. This demonstration would establish that the four causal conditions in question are consistent with necessity. The second is an examination of whether instances of a specific combination of causal conditions constitute a subset of instances of an outcome (punitive change to the penal code). The researcher would examine states that experienced the same coincidence of these four conditions, to see if they also instituted substantial punitive changes to their state penal codes. This demonstration would establish that the combination of causal conditions is consistent with sufficiency. It is also important to understand that from a case-oriented viewpoint, these two tasks – the assessment of sufficiency and the assessment of necessity – are distinct and should not be conflated.

Table 8.2 summarizes the case-oriented approach to assessing the connections between conditions and outcomes. It is important to understand that different ideas about the causal recipe in question motivate different research strategies. If the researcher suspects that the conditions identified in the recipe are necessary-but-not-sufficient, then the next analytic step is to examine other instances of the outcome (i.e., 'select on the dependent variable'). Specifically, the researcher seeks to certify that instances of the outcome reside in cell 2 of Table 8.2, with no cases in cell 1. Cases in cell 4 do not challenge the argument of necessity. By contrast, if the researcher suspects that the recipe is sufficient-but-not necessary, then the next analytic step is to examine other instances of the causal combination. Specifically, the researcher seeks to certify that instances of the causal combination reside in cell 2 of Table 8.2, with no cases in cell 4. Cases in cell 1 do not challenge the argument of sufficiency.

The key point is that in case-oriented research, the standard 2×2 table of outcome cross-tabulated against cause is disaggregated and partitioned because the different cells of this table have different interpretations and different analytic uses. This approach contrasts sharply with conventional variable-oriented research, where the usual endpoint of the analysis of a 2×2 table (or its correlational equivalent) is a global, symmetric measure of association describing the whole table, as illustrated in Table 8.1. It is also important to emphasize that these symmetric statistics reward researchers for having as many cases as possible in cell 3 (the null–null cell). By contrast, cell 3 plays no direct role in the case-oriented assessment of either the sufficiency or necessity of a causal condition or a combination of causal conditions.

Six Strategies of Case-oriented Comparative Analysis

Table 8.2 provides the framework for our presentation of six strategies of case-oriented comparative analysis. These six strategies focus explicitly on the problem of refining causal arguments. Each strategy offers a way to address what might be considered an empirical refutation of an initial argument. Three of these strategies are sufficiency centred and three are necessity centred. The key consideration is that it is very important to distinguish between situations where the focus is on sufficiency from those where the focus is on necessity.

Sufficiency-centred strategy #1: adding to the recipe

Consider the case-oriented researcher who initially believes that elite fractionalization is *sufficient* for democratic instability. Thus, instances of elite fractionalization should constitute a subset of instances of democratic instability, which is another way of stating that cases that exhibit elite fractionalization should also exhibit democratic instability. Assume the evidence is mixed and that some cases of elite fractionalization fail to exhibit instability. To resolve this contradiction, the researcher compares cases of elite fractionalization with and without the outcome, democratic instability, and tries to identify what was overlooked. The researcher concludes from this examination that elite fractionalization must be combined with having a multi-party system for instability to occur because the cases that combine these two conditions consistently

Table 8.2 Case-oriented research: assessing necessity versus sufficiency

	Causal recipe absent	*Causal recipe present*
Outcome present	Cell 1: cases in this cell challenge the argument of necessity but are not directly relevant to the assessment of sufficiency.	Cell 2: cases in this cell may confirm either necessity or sufficiency, depending on the researcher's goals.
Outcome absent	Cell 3: cases in this cell are not directly relevant to the assessment of either necessity or sufficiency.	Cell 4: cases in this cell challenge the argument of sufficiency but are not directly relevant to the assessment of necessity.

exhibit the outcome, while cases of elite fractionalization in two-party systems tend to be stable. Thus, this foray into the cases results in a recipe for democratic instability that is more elaborately combinatorial and less inclusive than the initial recipe.

This sufficiency-centred strategy is summarized in Table 8.3. The first panel shows the initial results; the second panel shows the researcher's resolution. Observe that in this investigation, the objective is to establish that the causal condition or recipe is a subset of the outcome, a pattern consistent with causal sufficiency. In effect, the goal is to empty cell 4 of cases. This resolution can be accomplished by making the causal argument more elaborately combinatorial, which shifts some cases from the second column (panel A) to the first column (panel B). If the researcher effectively empties cell 4 of cases by making the causal argument more elaborate and thus *less* inclusive, then an explicit, set-theoretic connection between cause and effect is established. The resulting causal argument is made more restrictive through the use of logical *and* (set intersection).

The shift from panel A to panel B in Table 8.3 moves cases not only from cell 4 to cell 3 but also from cell 2 to cell 1. Elaborating a causal argument in a combinatorial manner, therefore, may also reduce its coverage (Ragin 2008), which means that fewer instances of the outcome are explained. However, the cases that move from cell 2 to cell 1 do not challenge the sufficiency of the causal argument specified in panel B; they are simply not explained by the causal combination in question. From a purely statistical viewpoint (i.e., assessing the distribution of cases across all four cells with a symmetrical measure of association), the explanatory gain that accrues in the shift from panel A to panel B of Table 8.3 may be trivial. However, from a set-theoretic viewpoint, the difference is important and decisive, especially given the goal of using case knowledge to build theory. One of perhaps several recipes for the outcome has been clarified and refined.

Table 8.3 Sufficiency-centred strategy #1: adding to the recipe

Panel A. Initial results

	Elites unified	*Elites fractionalized*
Unstable democracy	Cell 1: 16 (40%)	Cell 2: 14 (70%)
Stable democracy	Cell 3: 24 (60%)	Cell 4: 6 (30%)

$N = 60$

Panel B. Resolution: a more elaborate combinatorial argument

	Elites unified or *two-party system*	*Elites fractionalized* and *multiparty system*
Unstable democracy	Cell 1: 22 (42%)	Cell 2: 8 (100%)
Stable democracy	Cell 3: 30 (58%)	Cell 4: 0 (0%)

$N = 60$

Sufficiency-centred strategy #2: narrowing the scope condition

The starting point of the second sufficiency strategy is the same as the first – a cross-tabulation showing that there are cases that combine elite fractionalization and democratic stability. The second sufficiency-centred strategy raises the issue of scope conditions (Walker and Cohen 1985; Goertz and Mahoney 2009): Are the cases included in the initial analysis all relevant to the argument in question? The researcher pays special attention to cell 4 cases (i.e., the ones that are inconsistent with the expectation that the cause is sufficient for the outcome) and assesses whether they are truly relevant to the investigation: Do they meet the researcher's scope condition? Should the scope condition be revised? If this assessment results in a narrowing of the scope condition, cell 4 may be emptied of cases, which in turn would establish that cases with the causal condition constitute a subset of cases with the outcome.

Table 8.4 illustrates the second sufficiency-centred strategy. Panel A shows the initial results, using data on all cases. After examining cell 4 cases, the researcher concludes that the argument applies only to 'new' democracies and not to 'established' democracies. Established democracies are therefore dropped from the analysis following this revision of the scope condition, and the analysis is recomputed, as shown in Table 8.4: panel B. Note that revising the scope condition may result in the removal of cases from other cells as well, for these newly designated 'irrelevant' cases could appear anywhere in the initial table. The N of cases drops from 60 in panel A to 45 in panel B, which from a probabilistic viewpoint is a substantial sacrifice of statistical power. From the viewpoint of formal hypothesis testing (especially as prescribed in textbooks on statistical analysis), redefining the set of relevant cases based on an examination of the evidence may seem opportunistic. It is important to keep in mind, however, the dynamic nature of case-oriented research, whereby investigators adjust their analytic strategies based on what they learn about their cases as the research progresses.

Table 8.4 Sufficiency-centred strategy #2: narrowing the scope condition

Panel A. Initial definition of relevant cases (all democracies)

	Elites unified	Elites fractionalized
Unstable democracy	Cell 1: 16 (40%)	Cell 2: 14 (70%)
Stable democracy	Cell 3: 24 (60%)	Cell 4: 6 (30%)

N = 60

Panel B. Final definition of relevant cases (young democracies)

	Elites unified	Elites fractionalized
Unstable democracy	Cell 1: 15 (43%)	Cell 2: 10 (100%)
Stable democracy	Cell 3: 20 (57%)	Cell 4: 0 (0%)

N = 45

Sufficiency-centred strategy #3: making the outcome more inclusive

The third sufficiency-centred strategy focuses on the outcome and how it is conceptualized. It is possible that the initial conceptualization is too narrow, and that it could be reconceptualized and operationalized in a somewhat broader and more inclusive manner. This reconceptualization, of course, would have important implications for the distribution of cases across the four cells of the table. In analyses of sufficiency, the focal cases are in cell 4. The third sufficiency-oriented strategy examines the outcome as initially conceptualized and asks whether the cell 4 cases experienced a lesser version. If so, then a broader, more inclusive definition of the outcome might redefine these troublesome cell 4 cases as instances, and the researcher could then transfer them from cell 4 to cell 2. The reconceptualization of the outcome might be as simple as lowering the threshold for what constitutes 'instability', or it might involve a qualitative expansion of the outcome.

Table 8.5 illustrates the third sufficiency-oriented strategy. Panel A shows the initial distribution of cases across the four cells, including the troublesome cell 4 cases. Panel B shows the impact of reconceptualizing the outcome, broadening it in a more inclusive manner. Specifically, the outcome 'instability' is recast as 'widespread distrust of government'. In this example, the cell 4 cases are successfully relocated to cell 2, thus emptying cell 4 of cases and establishing set-theoretic patterns consistent with sufficiency. Of course, this reformulation of the outcome also shifts cases from cell 3 to cell 1. However, from the viewpoint of sufficiency analysis, such transfers are largely neutral. This strategy is consistent with the 'retroductive' logic of qualitative research, where there is often a 'double fitting' of theoretical concepts and empirical categories (Ragin and Amoroso 2010), based on knowledge the researcher gains in the course of the research.

The distinctiveness of the case-oriented approach is further highlighted when attention is directed to the assessment of *necessary conditions*. The three necessity-centred strategies parallel the three sufficiency-centred strategies. However, the

Table 8.5 Sufficiency-centred strategy #3: making the outcome more inclusive

Panel A. Initial conceptualization of the outcome

	Elites unified	*Elites fractionalized*
Unstable democracy	Cell 1: 16 (40%)	Cell 2: 14 (70%)
Stable democracy	Cell 3: 24 (60%)	Cell 4: 6 (30%)

N = 60

Panel B. Re-conceptualized outcome (more inclusive)

	Elites unified	*Elites fractionalized*
Widespread distrust of government	Cell 1: 20 (50%)	Cell 2: 20 (100%)
Acceptance of status quo	Cell 3: 20 (50%)	Cell 4: 0 (0%)

N = 60

analytic focus is on a different set-theoretic relation, which in turn defines a different cell of the 2×2 table as problematic. Consider the case-oriented researcher who speculates that elite fractionalization is a *necessary condition* for democratic instability. Instances of democratic instability should constitute a subset of instances of elite fractionalization, which is another way of stating that instances of instability should share elite fractionalization as an antecedent condition and that, correspondingly, cell 1 of Table 8.2 should be empty. It follows that the researcher who is interested in establishing a necessary condition considers cases in cell 1 contradictory and must develop analytic strategies for emptying it.

Necessity-centred strategy #1: identifying a substitutable condition

Consider the case-oriented researcher who examines the connection between elite fractionalization and democratic instability, hoping to show that fractionalization is a necessary condition. Assume the evidence is mixed and that some cases of instability lack fractionalization as an antecedent condition. These cell 1 cases challenge the argument of necessity. To resolve the contradiction, the researcher compares instances of democratic instability with and without elite fractionalization. The key task at this point, assuming that theoretical and substantive knowledge support the idea that fractionalization is a necessary condition, is to see if there is some other condition that is somehow *causally equivalent* to fractionalization and is found in the cases of instability that do not exhibit fractionalization (cell 1 cases). In other words, is there a causal condition shared by the cases in cell 1 that is *substitutable* for elite fractionalization? When two conditions are substitutable as necessary conditions, if *either* is present, then the antecedent condition in question is satisfied.

Assume in this example that the researcher studies cases in cell 1, identifies 'economically dominant ethnic minority' as a substitutable necessary condition for elite fractionalization, and concludes that these two conditions are causally equivalent as necessary conditions for the outcome. The causal argument is then reformulated to state that the presence of either condition is necessary for democratic instability. This analytic strategy results in a recipe for the outcome that is *more inclusive* than the initial recipe. It is made more inclusive through the use of logical *or* (set union). This analytic strategy involves moving up the 'ladder of abstraction' (Sartori 1970) to a more general conceptualization of the relevant causal condition. For example, 'elite fractionalization' and 'economically dominant ethnic minority' might both be embraced by the umbrella concept 'potential for multiple sovereignty'.

This necessity-centred strategy is summarized in Table 8.6. Observe that in this investigation, the objective is to empty cell 1 of cases. This can be accomplished by reformulating the causal argument from a single condition to the satisfaction of either of two substitutable conditions, which in effect shifts some cases from the first column (panel A) to the second column (panel B). If the researcher effectively empties cell 1 of cases by making the causal argument more inclusive, then an explicit, set-theoretic connection between cause and effect is established.

The shift from panel A to panel B in Table 8.6 moves cases not only from cell 1 to cell 2, but also from cell 3 to cell 4. Elaborating a causal argument in a substitutable manner, as demonstrated in the table, therefore, can increase the number of cases with the causal condition that *lack* the outcome (in cell 4). However, the cases that move

Table 8.6 Necessity-centred strategy #1: identifying a substitutable condition

Panel A. Initial results

	Elites unified	Elites fractionalized
Unstable democracy	Cell 1: 5 (25%)	Cell 2: 25 (62.5%)
Stable democracy	Cell 3: 15 (75%)	Cell 4: 15 (37.5%)

N = 60

Panel B. Resolution: a more inclusive argument

	Elites unified and no dominant ethnic minority	Elites fractionalized or dominant ethnic minority
Unstable democracy	Cell 1: 0 (0%)	Cell 2: 30 (62.5%)
Stable democracy	Cell 3: 12 (100%)	Cell 4: 18 (37.5%)

N = 60

from cell 3 to cell 4 do not challenge the necessity of the causal argument specified in panel B. The cases in cell 4 meet this necessary condition but lack additional, unspecified causal conditions that would establish sufficiency. From a purely statistical viewpoint (i.e., focusing on the distribution of cases across all four cells), the gain that accrues in the shift from panel A to panel B of Table 8.5 may be trivial. However, from a set-theoretic viewpoint, it is decisive.

Necessity-centred strategy #2: narrowing the scope condition

This strategy exactly parallels the second sufficiency strategy. The key difference is that the focus is on cell 1 cases, not cell 4 cases. The researcher studies the troublesome cell 1 cases and asks whether they are truly relevant to the investigation: Do they meet the researcher's scope condition? Should the scope condition be revised? If they do not meet the initial scope condition or if it is apparent that the scope condition needs to be revised, then it may be possible to drop the troublesome cell 1 cases from the analysis, thereby establishing a pattern of results consistent with necessity. This second necessity strategy thus entails a respecification of the set of cases relevant to the investigation, making this set narrower and more tightly circumscribed.

Respecifying the set of relevant cases in this manner may result in the removal of cases from all four cells of the table, as illustrated in Table 8.7. In panel A, the scope condition is all democracies, and there are five cell 1 cases. Suppose the researcher determines that these five cases are all presidential systems. The researcher decides to restrict the necessary conditions argument to parliamentary systems, and all countries with presidential systems are therefore removed from the analysis. Panel B shows the result, a distribution of cases consistent with an argument of necessity. This reduction in the number of cases not only entails a loss of statistical power, it may also lead to only a trivial gain in explanatory power, considering the distribution of cases across all four cells of the table and using a symmetric measure of association. However, from a set-theoretic viewpoint, an empty cell 1 signals an explicit connection between the cause and the outcome, which could provide decisive evidence in favour of a necessary conditions argument.

Necessity-centred strategy #3: making the outcome less inclusive

Another necessity-centred strategy for addressing the problem of cell 1 cases is to examine them to see if they display outcomes that are different in some way from the outcomes displayed by cell 2 cases. This strategy parallels the third sufficiency-centred strategy presented previously, except that instead of making the definition of the outcome more inclusive, the researcher may adjust it so that it is less inclusive. For example, suppose the outcomes displayed by the cell 1 cases are weaker than, or not as pronounced as, those displayed by the cell 2 cases. If so, then the researcher might narrow the definition of the outcome, making it less inclusive, so that the cell 1 cases are excluded as instances of the outcome and thus transferred to cell 3.

The third necessity-centred strategy is illustrated in Table 8.8. The initial distribution of cases is shown in panel A, with five cases contradicting necessity (cell 1). The outcome in panel A is democratic instability; in panel B it is narrowed to cases of constitutional crisis. Countries with constitutional crises are a subset of unstable democracies; thus, there are fewer cases with the outcome in panel B than in panel A. Cell 1 is cleared of cases, establishing a pattern of results consistent with causal necessity. Of course, this reconceptualization of the outcome shifts cases not only from cell 1 to cell 3, but also from cell 2 to cell 4. From the viewpoint of conventional quantitative analysis, the shift from panel A to panel B may have at best a trivial impact on a symmetrical measure of association. However, from the viewpoint of necessity analysis, the gain is decisive.

Table 8.7 Necessity-centred strategy #2: narrowing the scope condition

Panel A. Initial definition of relevant cases (all democracies)

	Elites unified	Elites fractionalized
Unstable democracy	Cell 1: 5 (25%)	Cell 2: 25 (62.5%)
Stable democracy	Cell 3: 15 (75%)	Cell 4: 15 (37.5%)

N = 60

Panel B. Final definition of relevant cases (parliamentary democracies)

	Elites unified	Elites fractionalized
Unstable democracy	Cell 1: 0 (0%)	Cell 2: 22 (63%)
Stable democracy	Cell 3: 10 (100%)	Cell 4: 13 (37%)

N = 45

Table 8.8 Necessity-centred strategy #3: making the outcome less inclusive

Panel A. Initial conceptualization of outcome

	Elites unified	*Elites fractionalized*
Unstable democracy	Cell 1: 5 (25%)	Cell 2: 25 (62.5%)
Stable democracy	Cell 3: 15 (75%)	Cell 4: 15 (37.5%)

$N = 60$

Panel B. Reconceptualized outcome (less inclusive)

	Elites unified	*Elites fractionalized*
Constitutional crisis	Cell 1: 0 (0%)	Cell 2: 20 (50%)
No constitutional crisis	Cell 3: 20 (100%)	Cell 4: 20 (50%)

$N = 60$

Summary

Major contrasts between case-oriented and variable-oriented analytic strategies are clear in the examples provided. Conventional variable-oriented strategies use symmetric measures of associations which fail to distinguish between a causal argument and its mirror. Also, these measures focus on the distribution of cases across all four cells and are thus incapable of directly assessing either necessity or sufficiency. Case-oriented research, by contrast, (1) focuses on strategies that empty *either* cell 4 *or* cell 1 of cases, treating these as analytically distinct tasks, with the first focused on establishing sufficiency and the second on establishing necessity; and (2) may culminate in tabular patterns that from the viewpoint of variable-oriented research represent little or no explanatory gain. From a set-theoretic viewpoint, however, the difference may be decisive.

Conclusion

The case-oriented approach, in effect, deconstructs a key variable-oriented analytic device, the cross-case correlation, into two main components. Using the most elemental form of this device, the 2 × 2 table, this chapter demonstrates that conventional variable-oriented analysis conflates two very different research strategies. Sufficiency-centred strategies address causal conditions that constitute subsets of the outcome and thus focus on the second column of Table 8.2, while necessity-centred strategies address causal conditions that constitute supersets of the outcome and thus focus on the first row of Table 8.2. As illustrated in Tables 8.3 through 8.8, different ideas about the nature of the connection between cause and outcome motivate different analytic strategies.

The demonstrations offered in this chapter focus on the most elementary form of variable-oriented analysis, the 2 × 2 table. It is important to point out that these same issues arise in more sophisticated forms of analysis. For example, as shown in Ragin (2000, 2008), Pearson's correlation coefficient, which is used to assess the relationship between interval-scale variables, also conflates the two case-oriented analytic strategies described in this chapter. Using fuzzy sets it is possible to assess set-theoretic relations between case aspects that vary by level or degree, and thus to disentangle the two assessments central to the case-oriented approach (Ragin 2006). These fuzzy set-theoretic procedures exactly parallel those demonstrated in this chapter with crisp sets and 2×2 tables.

Further Reading

Dion, D. 1998: Evidence and inference in the comparative case study. *Comparative Politics 30*: 127–145.

Ragin, C.C. 1987: *The Comparative Method: Moving Beyond Qualitative and Quantitative Strategies*. Berkeley: University of California Press.

Ragin, C.C. 2000: *Fuzzy-Set Social Science*. Chicago: University of Chicago Press.

Ragin, C.C. 2008: *Redesigning Social Inquiry: Fuzzy Sets and Beyond*. Chicago: University of Chicago Press.

Rihoux, B. and Ragin, C.C. (eds) 2009: *Configurational Comparative Methods: Qualitative Comparative Analysis (QCA) and Related Techniques*. Thousand Oaks, CA: Sage Publications.

Part II

States and Governance

A. Formation and Form
B. Governance and Political Process
C. Violence and States

9

Theories of State Formation

GIANFRANCO POGGI

The state is not universal. It emerged in its modern form between the twelfth and eighteenth centuries in Western Europe. Poggi focuses on three principal accounts of its formation: (i) on the managerial perspective, which emphasizes the top-down aspect of the process: the establishment of increasingly effective political administration over larger and larger territories; (ii) on the military perspective which, following Weber, emphasizes the state's monopoly of legitimate violence, with particular reference to war; and (iii) on the economic perspective which, following Marx, sees the state as an outcome of class struggle between producers and exploiters in a capitalist mode of production. Poggi sees each of these perspectives as making important contributions to our understanding of state formation, and, indeed, to our understanding of all aspects of political sociology.

This essay gives a summary and highly selective account of the most significant sociological perspectives on the early and intermediate phases of (what one may call) 'statualization', a set of processes taking place in Western Europe between the twelfth and eighteenth centuries, in the course of which the practice of rule, as concerned a diminishing number of generally larger and more clearly delimited territories, became to a growing extent:

- depersonalized – that is, rule is (in principle) vested in offices rather than in physical individuals as such;
- formalized – the practice of rule increasingly refers to norms which expressly authorize it, mandate it, specify the modalities of its expression and control it;
- integrated – rule increasingly takes into account other aspects of the social process, recognizes their significance and makes some contribution to their persistence, while being at the same time

The Wiley-Blackwell Companion to Political Sociology, First Edition. Edited by Edwin Amenta, Kate Nash, and Alan Scott.
© 2012 Blackwell Publishing Ltd. Published 2012 by Blackwell Publishing Ltd.

- differentiated from them – rule, that is, addresses distinctive concerns and employs special resources (material and symbolic). Finally, it is
- organized – this expression suggests two related and at the same time contrasting phenomena: on the one hand, rule is exercised by and through a plurality of subjects (individual and collective); on the other, these subjects constitute together a single unit, which overrides their plurality.

Why Deal with These Matters?

As recently as 30 years ago, a work such as this one would probably not have contained an essay devoted to our present topic. At the time, political sociology largely left political institutions to political science. The latter, in turn, showed little concern with 'the state' as such, much less with the question of how it had developed. Subsequently, it fell largely to sociologists (though some of these were active both in sociology and in political science) to 'bring the state back in' (Evans, Rueschemeyer and Skocpol (eds) 1985). Some of them expressly thematized where, when, how and why the state had come into being and had become the prime political institution of modernity (see King and Le Galès, Chapter 10, in this volume).

The state was put on the scholarly agenda, from the 1960s on, by diverse developments. Some of these were of a pragmatic nature: for instance, the feeling that in the West the 'long boom' and the prevalence of social peace owed much to various forms of public intervention in, and regulation of, economic and social processes, which shifted and sometimes seemed to erase the state/society divide. On the radical side, some authors emphasized the role played by the welfare state in moderating social conflicts, while others wondered about how long it could continue to play that role.

There were also more specifically intellectual reasons for thematizing the state and its developments. In particular, for reasons not discussed here, the nature of modernity and the peculiar features of the West began to exercise the minds of some sociologists, and both these overlapping topics necessarily led to an increased awareness of how distinctive and significant Western political arrangements had been, from the Middle Ages on.

Much of the resultant work was inspired by a new appreciation of the theoretical legacy of Max Weber, emphasizing his explicit concern with juridical and political developments. Oddly enough, however, scholars who appealed chiefly, instead, to Marx's legacy also moved towards the same themes, in spite of the fact that previously the Marxist tradition had de-emphasized them. In the intellectual climate of the social sciences in the 1970s, marked by a hegemony of Marxism, in some form or other, much of what went under the name of 'state theory' was in fact a more or less sophisticated exercise in advanced Marxology, bent upon the peculiar task, say, of 'deriving the category of the state' from the concept of capital, or of commodity (Holloway and Picciotto (eds) 1978; Jessop 1982). But some Marx-inspired authors engaged in a less venturesome, more substantial inquiry into the phases and modalities of the development of the modern state. In fact, some of the more significant contributions to these topics come from authors who appeal to some extent, more or less expressly, to the Marxist tradition (Block 1987).

More recent impulses have come, on the one hand, from the growing significance of such concepts/phenomena as nationalism, citizenship or the public sphere; on the other, from the increasingly problematical nature of the relationship between 'state (or: politics) and markets'. The accounts of state development chosen for attention below emphasize in turn what one may call the managerial, the military and the economic aspects of 'the state's story'.

The Managerial Perspective

My chief witness concerning this view is a short work that has been largely ignored in the current discussion about that story: *On the medieval origins of the modern state*, by the American historian Joseph Strayer. One reason for putting it first is its explicit focus on the early phases of that story, coupled however with a suggestion that 'the modern state, wherever we find it today, is based on the pattern which emerged in Europe in the period 1100 to 1600' (Strayer 1970: 12). Over this time

> [w]e are looking for the appearance of political units persisting in time and fixed in space, the development of permanent, impersonal institutions, agreement on the need for an authority which can give final judgements, and acceptance of the idea that this authority should receive the basic loyalty of its subjects.
>
> (Strayer 1970: 10)

The book's relevance in our context rests on its focus on the top-down aspect of the process; that is, on the developing conceptions and practices concerning the political administration of larger territories. Strayer emphasizes both the traits common to most Western European experiences (for instance, the practices of consultation between rulers and other powerful individuals or bodies or the importance of law) and some of the contrasts relating to these matters between countries, especially England and France.

The key process, in Strayer's view, consists in the establishment of increasingly effective modes of management of larger and larger territories, put into place on behalf of rulers by growing bodies of professional administrators. He thus concerns himself to a large extent with the evolving practices relating to the recruitment, training and employment of those administrators, and with the distinctive practices which they develop (often quite self-consciously) and which later become to an extent traditional.

How distinctive and pointed this argument is, in spite of the low-key way in which Strayer advances, shows from what is missing from it – in particular, any bloody-minded, 'Schmittian' sense of the heroic distinctiveness of the political enterprise, of the centrality of the confrontation with 'the Other', of the momentousness and drama of political decision, of 'the demoniac face of power' (Ritter 1979).

As Strayer depicts it, the development of the modern state is chiefly an ongoing, low-profile process of inventing and adopting/adapting marginally (though sometimes markedly) more effective ways of collecting and husbanding resources, of controlling their employment, of providing services (especially judicial and 'police' services) to local communities. As he remarks pointedly, 'the first permanent institutions in Western Europe dealt with internal not external affairs. High courts of justice and

Treasury Departments existed long before Foreign Offices and Departments of Defence' (1970: 26).

The individuals active in these primordial offices play the key role in getting a population, in spite of its intense localism, to accept and value the existence of a centrally controlled framework of rule, to which it increasingly refers in defining its interests and obligations, and to develop a sense of trans-local commonality (this, Strayer argues, happened first in England). Thus, political units in the process of becoming states are not seen in the first place as conquering entities, but as the growing estates of dominant dynasties, assisted chiefly by managers intent, day in, day out, upon tending and increasing the dynasty's possessions.

Strayer refers occasionally to the role played in the above process by ecclesiastical personnel, who contributed to it on the one hand a distinctive concern with establishing and maintaining peace, on the other some critical resources, such as literacy and the use of Latin as a trans-local language; and a sense of what it means for a local collectivity (a parish, an abbey) to belong to a higher one (a diocese, the Church at large, a religious order as a whole).

Some years after the publication of Strayer's book, a distinguished legal scholar, Harold Berman, argued at length in an impressive book, *Law and Revolution*, a much stronger version of that argument. He does not simply point to the contribution made by ecclesiastics and their distinctive ways of thinking and acting to the construction of states, but holds that 'the first state in the West was that which was established in the church by the papacy in the late eleventh and the twelfth century' (Berman 1983: 276). This is chiefly because the Gregorian reformation made express and sustained use of sophisticated, text-based, secular, 'rational', institutionally differentiated legal discourse in order to institute, activate and coordinate ecclesiastical organs. Such discourse was later much used, in properly political bodies, to orient and control binding decisions, including those involving the threat of or the recourse to violence.

Although Strayer had already acknowledged the uses of law in the performance of managerial tasks, Berman follows and complements an earlier tradition of legal and constitutional history in emphasizing the wider significance of law in state-building. Why is law important, and particularly enacted, non-customary law? For one thing, it permits two contrasting requirements to be fulfilled: on the one hand it reduces the contingency in the conduct of public bodies and in the determination of the obligations of subjects/citizens towards them, by tying them to expressly promulgated commands valid in principle 'wherever and whenever'; on the other hand, each such law is itself contingent, for, by following certain procedural rules (themselves juridical in nature), it can be set aside by another one. Thus, administrative and judicial bodies can be programmed to act in predictable ways, but that programming is itself variable. Also, the validity of existent bodies of law can be extended to new territories, facilitating their incorporation in a given polity.

Furthermore, in the West, on various grounds, law long enjoyed high moral and cultural prestige. It is a sophisticated, highly literate, text-based intellectual product, which can be systematized, taught and examined. It can thus assist rulers and their top administrators in the process of selecting and training the specialized personnel who, through the first centuries of the modern state, are increasingly called upon to replace the feudal and the clerical elements in manning the political establishment. To this extent, Berman's sustained concern with the legal dimension in the development of papal institutions usefully complements Strayer's primary emphasis on other aspects of the management of royal territories.

The Military Perspective

The state is the central political institution; *qua* political, it has an intrinsic connection with violence, emphasized in a famous definition of the state by Weber, which Randall Collins has elaborated as follows:

> By 'state' we mean a way in which violence is organized. The state consists in individuals in possession of firearms and other weaponry and willing to put them to use: in the version of political organization found in the modern world, these individuals claim the monopoly of such use. [...] The state is, in the first instance, the army and the police.
>
> (Collins 1975: 181)

Although the distinction itself between army and police is a historical product, and can be institutionalized to a different extent, this statement suggests two different ways in which this theme can be elaborated: one which emphasizes primarily what we may call the 'internal' uses of organized violence – law enforcement, the repression and suppression of threats to the public order, by the police and the judicial system – and one which emphasizes its 'external' uses – war and the military establishment. But in the literature on state development the first mode of elaboration is much less significant, although significant moves in its direction could be derived, in particular, from Foucault's writings on punishment and surveillance. The second, on the other hand, has been much practised in the past, and recently has enjoyed something of a revival. It is, furthermore, more likely to inspire reflections about other significant themes of political theorizing, such as the moral significance of violence in general and war in particular, or such concepts as sovereignty, territory, the states system, political obligation.

In the context of the discussion about state development, the argument for the significance of war is straightforward. From the beginning, the modern state was shaped by the fact of being essentially intended for war-making, and primarily concerned with establishing and maintaining its military might. In turn, the fortunes of war played the decisive role in shaping the map of Europe and thus the original context of the states system, which found in war the irreplaceable instrument for periodically revising its equilibrium.

Early in the twentieth century Otto Hintze claimed most succinctly that according to all comparative scholarship, 'all state constitution is originally war constitution, military constitution' (Hintze 1970: 53). Later elaborations of this thesis emphasize not so much a direct link, say, between the distribution of military capacities within a population and the structure of the polity, but rather an indirect one: each state derives its institutional arrangements chiefly from the ways in which it goes about providing itself with 'the sinews of war' – the material resources necessary to equip itself militarily. Bertrand de Jouvenel's statement of the argument exemplifies this emphasis:

The intimate tie between war and power is a constant feature of European history. [...]
If a feudal monarchy succeeded in getting financial aids from the vassals at more and
more frequent intervals and could thus increase the number of mercenaries in its
employ, the others had to copy it. If in the end these aids were consolidated into a
permanent tax for maintaining a standing army, the movement had to be followed. For,
as Adam Smith remarked, 'Once the system of having a standing army had been
adopted by one civilized nation, all its neighbours had to introduce it; security reasons
made it inevitable, for the old militias were quite incapable of resisting an army of this
kind'.

(de Jouvenel 1962: 142)

A recent, very strong re-statement of this point, by Tilly (1992), suggests that state
structures at large be understood as secondary products of the rulers' efforts to provide
themselves with military resources. On the face of it, this might seem to apply only to
the core administrative and fiscal structures, those established in the early and middle
phases of state development; but one might argue that even arrangements typical of its
late phases, and apparently remote from military concerns, sometimes have a military
rationale. For instance, some of the early welfare state provisions introduced by the
British state were a response to the realization, in the course of the Boer War, that
many of the young males brought up in the industrial conurbations were in inadequate
physical condition, and thus poorly fit for fighting.

A significant component of this kind of argument has always been the connection
between the challenge of war on the one hand, and a tendency to tighten the hold of
the centre on the political organs of the periphery of the state. In other words, the
proximity, the awareness, the urgency of that challenge have generated and sustained the 'centralization trend' typical of maturing states. Note that this connection
is not a prerogative of European states; it can be found in the United States, a polity
originally designed in the express intent of transcending the European experience,
and operating in a very different geopolitical environment. For instance, Richard
Bensel (1991) emphasizes the role played by the American Civil War in fostering the
progress of central political institutions both in the United States and in the
Confederacy.

Two significant aspects of the military perspective on state development may be
noted. In the first place, its frequent emphasis on fiscal arrangements creates a kind of
thematic overlap with what I have called the managerial perspective. In the second
place, by the same token it also connects the study of political arrangements with the
arrangements dominant in two other spheres of social experience: on the one hand
the economy, on the other technology – particularly, of course, the technology of
warfare.

This last connection, in particular, is extensively explored in some of the more
sophisticated studies developing the military perspective. Warfare technology, itself, is
a complex matter: one aspect of it is strictly material, and has to do with the power,
precision, and other operational features of the military hardware; the other is largely
social, and is constituted chiefly by the ways in which military manpower is raised,
trained, deployed, organized, monitored, motivated, etc.

Recent studies have made much of the relationship between the early modern
'military revolution', characterized largely in material terms, and changes in the

political, fiscal, administrative arrangements of European states. The title and subtitle of Brian Downing's *Military Revolution and Political Change: Origins of Democracy and Autocracy in Early Modern Europe* neatly convey the message.

In fact, title and subtitle suggest two different emphases, in this book as well as in others adopting the same perspective: a (let us call it) 'narrative' emphasis, stressing continuities and discontinuities – of military practice in this case – and the relative adaptations; and a comparative emphasis, stressing instead the variations in those adaptations. In the latter perspective what matters are the different, indeed divergent ways in which rulers respond to developments in the technology (material and social) of warfare.

The broadest generalization suggested by writings advancing this perspective is that the military revolution makes it necessary for states, if they want to remain in business, to commandeer more resources than the arrangements inherited from the late medieval past can put at their disposal. Those arrangements (which can be subsumed under one variant or the other of the so-called *Ständestaat*, or 'polity of estates') must be either suppressed or complemented by others that increase the discretion of rulers and/or capitalize on the parallel process of economic modernization.

In most cases, the ancient pattern of decentralized military capacity and of ad hoc financial levies is replaced by one of three, all of which substantially increase the extraction of resources to be put to military uses. The main contrast lies perhaps between Prussia and England: the first develops a pattern of 'authoritarian' extraction, associated chiefly with a new, centrally imposed and run system of taxation; the latter, a pattern of 'negotiated' extraction, which involves first the court, later Parliament as the representative organ of society, and taps the new resource base constituted by an increasingly commercialized economy via both taxation and (increasingly) a flexible, responsible public debt system. But one must add at least the French pattern, whereby the monarch puts the state in hock by means of a ruinous process of indebtment with which taxation can never catch up.

One reason why much attention has been recently devoted to how such matters were settled in the seventeenth and early eighteenth century is the sense that each of the patterns (and their variants) makes a huge difference to the nature of the state at large, including whether, to what extent, at what point, it opens itself to constitutionalism, representative government, liberalism. (A book by Thomas Ertman (1997) is particularly significant in this context.) But of course the perspective also includes later developments in the relation between war and state making; in particular, it is often claimed that there is a significant connection between, at one end, the advent of mass armies in the late eighteenth and early nineteenth centuries, and continuing since then; at the other end, 'the entry of masses into politics' characteristic of the later part of the nineteenth and of the twentieth centuries. In other terms, the military perspective on state development lends itself to extensive and sophisticated elaboration (see in particular the arguments developed in Mann 1988).

The Economic Perspective

In the interpretation just discussed, the development of the modern state finds its basic rationale in a phenomenon – war – that is a (perhaps the) most significant aspect of the political sphere. The next interpretation, however, shifts the focus to a different sphere, the economic one, where take place the processes of production and distribution of material wealth, and which views as aspects and components of those processes, and of the resulting conflicts, political phenomena in general, and the formation and development of the state in particular. This line of thinking has as its main proponents Karl Marx and various thinkers chiefly inspired by him; thus my exposition of it must seek to convey, in however elementary a fashion, the main contentions of Marx's views on politics and the state (see Jessop, Chapter 1, in this volume).

Human life can only be sustained through labour. Beyond a minimal threshold of effectiveness, labour, in its interaction with nature, can yield a greater product than is strictly necessary to reconstitute the individual's capacity to labour, in the form both of product which is surplus to the consumption needs of producers and of embodied products of past labour to be used as instruments of further labour. But both surpluses, being objectified, can be taken away from those producing them, and put to the service, and placed under the control, of individuals not themselves responsible for producing them.

Typically, the privilege of consuming more than one contributes to the social production process is enjoyed by a minority who make the majority work to their own advantage; thus it is intrinsically invidious and contentious, and exposed to the risk of being challenged by the majority. On this account, the minority/majority relationship is always potentially unstable, and must be stabilized by processes external to those of material production: chiefly, the production of symbolic and ideological resources which moderate or divert the majority's resentment of and opposition to their condition, and an asymmetric allocation also of the capacity to exercise coercion.

This capacity (grounded on control over means of violence, including organization) may play either a direct role in the production/exploitation process (as in slavery or serfdom) or only (or chiefly) an indirect role. In particular, the 'feudal mode of production' required the overt submission of the producers to the political superiority of the exploiters, and to the threat of open coercion, because some means of production were under the producers' immediate control. This situation was compatible with (and indeed conducive to) the decentralization of authority, and of coercive resources, characteristic of feudalism in its political aspects.

However, in the capitalist mode of production, according to Marx, exploitation is achieved in a covert manner, not by expressly subjecting the producers to the exploiters, but by means of voluntarily entered, contractual relations between formally free individuals, once these have been dispossessed of any autonomous control over the means of production. This pattern required that rearrangement of political relations and of juridical arrangements which is the core of state development, at any rate in its domestic aspects. In particular:

- Capitalism entails production for the market, centred on exchange values, not on use. As such it requires orderly, purposefully organized cooperation within units and peaceable, market 'traffics' between units. An intrinsic aspect of state formation and of the unification of jurisdictions it involves is the widening territorial reach of power centres, which standardize and secure relations between many individuals across wide spaces, making production and exchange easier and more calculable, and more open to continuing rationalization.

- The development of the modern state is associated, particularly on the Continent, with two fundamental developments in the field of private law: the return to the absolute Roman conception of property (*dominium*), and the establishment of contract as the key device for the creation and transmission of rights. Both are indispensable to the mobilization of wealth and to the creation of contingent, open-ended, cash-oriented relations between exchange partners.
- In particular, the contractualization of employer/employee relations allows capitalists to dismiss any responsibility for the workers' livelihood, to treat labour (power) as commodity, buying it to the extent and for the duration required for production and in the light of present or expected market demand and on terms set in turn by the market. According to Marx, this construction of employer/employee relations is critical because it hides the intrinsically exploitative character of the employment relation, wherein the systematic inferiority of all employees (*qua* members of a class) towards all employers (*qua* members of a class) allows the latter to extract unpaid labour from the former, without seeming to.
- The secular movement from 'status' to 'contract' characteristic of modern law also leads to the emergence of a new kind of collective actor – *class*: a unit of a non-corporate nature, based purely on the convergence of the factual interests of its components, rather than on publicly recognized privileges. To this socio-economic development corresponds, in political terms, a long-run movement towards the formal equality of all citizens, which is characteristic of the state.

The absolutization of property allows the abolition of property forms of communal nature, and thus the expropriation of resources which previously allowed the members of subaltern groups to subsist autonomously, if only on a collective basis, forcing them into the new dependency characteristic of salaried labour. 'Absolute' property also entitles those who own it to a privileged claim on the deployment of that coercive power which the state has progressively monopolized and vested in the police and the judiciary. Furthermore, within the new places of production, and signally within the factory, it grounds a despotic control by the capitalist over the expenditure of labour power by workers and over their product, to the end of maximizing profit.

These aspects of state development in the political sphere constitute significant, indeed essential requisites of the formation and advance of the capitalist mode of production. Like other, pre-modern forms of political order, the state is thus critically implicated in upholding the central form of inequality, that constituted by the control, or the exclusion from control, over the means of production characteristic of a given situation: ruling practices secure the exploitation process and the advantages of the dominant minority. For the same reason, all significant changes in the socio-economic order presuppose a substantial development in the means and the relations of production, but must also have a political dimension, resulting in the changed nature of the ruling class. Thus, for all the differences it may reveal in its phases and in its locales, the modern state also entails the ascent of the bourgeoisie also to a dominant political role. In a famous sentence of the Manifesto, 'the government is but the executive committee of the bourgeoisie'.

For this very reason Marx, Engels and many Marxist authors display a certain interest in political developments, assuming that certain developments in the formation of public policies, and particularly those centring on the emergence of parties, would in turn play a role in the political dimension of the socialist revolution. However, Marx himself, at any rate from the mid-1840s on, paid little sustained attention to major changes in the institutional forms of the state. One might suspect that a more or less explicit economistic bias, while it allows Marx and others to develop (what strikes me as) an insightful view of the process of state development as a whole, seriously limits their capacity for appreciating some significant aspects of it.

At any rate, in the early twentieth century, following Hobson, Lenin interprets imperialism as the 'supreme phase' of capitalism, allowing the ruling classes of the West to delay its inevitable fate, and placing the class struggle on we would call today a global footing. By and large, Marx-inspired writers treat war as the extreme limit case of the conflict between 'national fractions' of capital over opportunities for accumulation and/or as ways of diverting the working masses from pursuing their class interest. They interpret fascism chiefly as a different, but not hugely different way of organizing and conducting the business-as-usual of the state in countries where financial capital has prevailed over other forms, and where the bourgeoisie feels particularly threatened by the class war.

Valuable as some of these interpretations may be, they mostly revolve on the question of what kind of political order is necessary for what kind of economic order. Since the latter is conceptualized in a rather simple way, as a succession of only four modes of production (ancient, feudal, Asiatic, capitalist), this mode of analysis becomes essentially unilinear, and pays little attention to the historical variants of the respective political orders – a lack of attention which in the twentieth century was to have unfortunate practical consequences, such as the early refusal of the communist parties outside the Soviet Union, but controlled by the Comintern, to take on board the gravity of the appearance of fascism, and to make a resolute stand for the defence of democratic institutions in the West.

But the interpretation outlined above is only a partial rendering of the Marxist perspective on state development, reflecting only its 'objectivist', systemic/functionalist side. Marx's own thinking has another side which emphasizes the class struggle, and acknowledges to some extent the plurality of its protagonists, the variety of the respective interests and the strategic component in their relations (which class allies itself with which, against which, with what success or lack of it). In this context, it can attribute some significance, among other things, to the various political arrangements associated with those strategies and with their outcomes.

Within the Marxist camp (broadly understood) the best work in this manner, as concerns our topic, is probably that done by Perry Anderson. However, an even more impressive, imaginative framework of analysis focused on classes and their strategies, and expressly concerned with varieties of political development and (among other things) of state construction, is embodied in a masterpiece by Barrington Moore, Jr: *Social Origins of Dictatorship and Democracy*. I wind up this essay by briefly considering this book because, while reflecting upon the early modern era, it is concerned chiefly with a later development, the commercialization of the countryside, and seeks to account for even later ones, such as Nazism and fascism, and the communist-led revolutions of the twentieth century. It also has an expressly comparative focus, as its title itself makes clear.

Moore's relationship to Marx and Marxism is complex. He shares that tradition's tough-minded emphasis on revolution and on revolutionary violence; the attribution to classes and class interest of the key role in historical development; the assumption that the key relationship between dominant and subaltern groups is one of exploitation, however masked by claims for the 'functional' contribution of the former to the welfare of the latter; the systematic discounting of the significance of 'values' and other cultural factors. However, as indicated above, he considers the countryside as the central stage of modernization processes, and landowners and peasants as its protagonists; he adds to these the ruler and its apparatus, and the town-based burgher and then bourgeois groups – but the working class is nearly nowhere, even in considering twentieth-century events.

Even Moore's construction of at any rate some moments in the development of the bourgeoisie is at variance with the standard Marxist construction. He somewhat half-heartedly concedes, in particular, that the French Revolution may be labelled 'bourgeois', but points out that the bourgeoisie in question had little to do with capitalism proper, and even less with industrial capitalism.

Furthermore, Moore problematizes the Marxist assumption that exploited and oppressed groups will revolt; he also has an acute sense of the contingent nature of major social developments and of the attendant ironies – see for example one of his chapter headings: 'England and the contribution of violence to gradualism'! It is again ironic that those revolutions in which peasants have played the most significant role (in the twentieth century, the Russian and the Chinese) are also those which in the end imposed on them the greatest costs and defeats. Even more significant, in our context, is Moore's sense that political institutions matter, and so do differences between them; particularly valuable are those that impose constraints on arbitrary rule, allow the development of just and rational rules, and give the populace some voice in their making.

Finally, as I have already suggested, Moore attaches great weight to the strategic components in the operation of major social groupings, and particularly to their positive or negative alignments and the resultant arrangements in the political sphere. The argument to this effect is (alas) too complex to be reviewed here. But when all is said and done, as I see the matter, *Social Origins*, in an original and sophisticated manner, interprets many critical aspects of political modernization, including some relating to the timing, nature and shape of state development, chiefly in the light of the interests of groups constituted around questions of control or exclusion from economic resources. On these grounds, it develops a significant, though of course controversial, interpretation of such events as the great revolutions of the twentieth century, and the rise of fascism and of collectivist states.

Conclusion

We have come a long way from a ruler's efforts to increase his dynastic patrimony and optimize its management at the very beginnings of the modern state, to mention an attempt to analyze some complexities in the nature itself of the state enterprise in its twentieth-century phase. In this manner, the proposed, simple tripartition between 'perspectives' adopted by major students of state development appears relevant not just to the topic of this essay but to others pursued in the volume.

One may ask oneself which of these perspectives appears more relevant and reliable. The answer would have to be, predictably, that each has something to contribute, and that one should attempt, if anything, to achieve a synthesis between them rather than compel a choice. Some recent works already mentioned expressly aim at such a synthesis: for instance, Tilly's utilizes insights proper to the military and the economic perspectives; and Ertman does the same thing within a framework which, by emphasizing the significance of administrative arrangements, may remind the reader also of the managerial perspective. And one may already see the elements of a masterful synthesis in some of Max Weber's many contributions to the topic, culminating perhaps in the wonderfully compressed version offered in 'The Profession and Vocation of Politics'.

Further Reading

Lachmann, R. 2010: *States and Power*. Cambridge: Polity Press.
Poggi, G. 1990: *The State: Its Nature, Development and Prospects*. Cambridge: Polity Press.

10

State

DESMOND KING AND PATRICK LE GALÈS

The question of the state remains central in the social sciences. The famous call for 'bringing the state back in' in the 1980s (Evans, Rueschemeyer and Skocpol, eds 1985) has been remarkably successful; it does not need repeating. Nor need we claim 'new' debates of the state as such. In this chapter we underline enduring aspects of state development, structure and significance for modern political systems and economies, and we rehearse some important developments in recent scholarly research on this key topic. Since research – both empirical and theoretical – on the state is abundant, our discussion here cannot claim to be exhaustive but it does convey a sense of the salient debates and identifies ways in which scholarly argument about the state is developing. That the state remains and will remain fundamental to political sociology, comparative politics, legal studies, political economy, public policy and international relations is not in doubt.

State Origins and Contemporary Relevance

Since the seventeenth century states have been the principal form of political organization within the international system. 'Peoples' who believed themselves to form a distinct nation fought enemies, overthrew imperial powers, petitioned Great Powers and later international organizations such as the League of Nations and its successor the United Nations, and staged secessionist struggles to achieve national self-determination. The purpose of such activities was to achieve status as a state recognized by other states and accredited in global organizations such as the United Nations (UN), World Bank and World Trade Organization (WTO) and acknowledged by regional institutions such as the Organization of American States (OAS) and European Union (EU). This aim inspires movements of peoples believing

The Wiley-Blackwell Companion to Political Sociology, First Edition. Edited by Edwin Amenta, Kate Nash, and Alan Scott.
© 2012 Blackwell Publishing Ltd. Published 2012 by Blackwell Publishing Ltd.

themselves to be distinct nations entitled to a separate state. East Timor (2002) and Kosovo (2008) are recent instances, bringing the total number of states to just over 190 (compared with 55 in 1914 and 69 in 1950). A new African state, South Sudan, appeared in 2011.

Defining a state and what states do

The Treaty of Westphalia ending Europe's bloody Thirty Years' War, agreed over three centuries ago, determined that international politics occurs primarily between states. States consist in:

- Units which recognize each other's independence in principle, though in practice many states violate other states' sovereignty on occasions.
- The legitimacy of a nation of people aspiring to the status of independent statehood – a trend that signalled the long-term demise of numerous multi-ethnic empires such as the Ottoman Empire.
- Presumption of internal sovereignty, or what scholars term a compulsory political organization, over which a state enjoys control, a feature made central to theoretical analysis by the German sociologist Max Weber (see Breiner, Chapter 2, in this volume). Over time, internal sovereignty extends to administrative control and competence across the state's territorial cartilage and bureaucratic capacity to raise taxes and to provide security for citizens against disorder, crime or illegal imprisonment.
- States operate as diplomatic actors in an international system of states, a system governed and regulated by international law and mediated through mass state membership in international organizations, principally the UN, but including regional alliances such as the African Union or OAS or military alliances such as the defunct pre-1989 Warsaw Pact and North Atlantic Treaty Organization (NATO).
- States demand allegiance from citizens, and while religion or ruling royal dynasties may be intricately interwoven with state identity, they are no longer the fundamental basis for a state's legitimacy. As the eruptions in Tunisia, Morocco, Egypt and Libya in early 2011 demonstrate, a state's legitimacy is a dynamic not a static quality and one open to challenge in all societies.

Established historically as international actors, states increasingly became institutions engaged with their citizens rather than just external relations. Hence the growth of tax-raising ability and expectation of public spending on military, social welfare and health care, and law and order.

State power and fiscal crisis

In the 1990s, debate about the state was shaped by scholarly exchange between those researchers emphasizing the eternal strength of the state and those making a living out of prophesying its demise in relation to globalization, or Europeanization, or region-alization trends. Books and articles speak volumes in this regard: 'the dismantling state'; 'the splintered state'; 'the virtual state'; 'the retreating state' (Strange 1996); 'the hollowing out of the state' (Castells 2000); 'the destatization process' (Jessop 2002). Some contributions attached a question mark to their polemic: 'the state, obsolete or obstinate?' (Hoffman 1995). Comparative political economy scholars in the vein of neo-institutionalism demoted the importance of the state as an actor in public policy and economic outcomes. This analytical demotion is made clear both in Crouch and Streeck (1997) and in Hall and Soskice's influential varieties of capitalism model (eds, 2001).

This question of whether the state has in fact disappeared either empirically or theoretically is no longer appropriate given the demands and responses to the Great Recession. The debate about the state is now framed as analysis of the 'restructuring of the state' to use Cassese and Wright's title of an agenda-setting book on the state (1997). Actors within the state are active agents in globalization processes (Jessop 2002; Brenner 2004). Some sections of the state are gaining ground and developing new forms of authority. The economic crisis since 2007/08 is a compellingly reminder of the role of the state at times of crisis, both of its key policy response role (as in the United States' Troubled Asset Relief Program 2008 in support of banks) and of its economic weaknesses and political vulnerabilities (in Greece or Belgium, for instance).

However, the analysis of the restructuring of the state is fraught with conceptual difficulties, including such questions as: Where to begin analysis? What is the appropriate length of time to consider a state development? What variables should be emphasized? What are the principal dynamics of change?

Beyond Europe: Diverse State Activity and Varieties of State Research

Some of the distinctive contributions to the state debate come from scholars benefiting from many years of intellectual engagement with this subject. A growing body of research examines the making and the evolution of the state in less linear ways in different parts of the world (Vu 2010). In particular, the conditions at the creation of states, their dynamics, and examples of state failures call on explanations and characterizations of states which are more and more divergent from the standard European nation-state seen through the experience of France, the United Kingdom or Germany. Some American historians and political scientists emphasize how the particular story and characteristics of the US state are germane to comparative studies.

Thus in a provocative paper, 'Ironies of state building', King and Lieberman use insights from the making of states in Eastern Europe to characterize the American state. They conclude (2009: 573) that 'without the development of a central bureaucratic state to enforce standards of democratic procedure (such as the Fourteenth and Fifteenth Amendments), the American democratization process would have remained incomplete'. This view of the American state as a key agent of democratization contrasts with the need to dilute and weaken the state elsewhere. This standardization activity is one of five distinct American state activities identified by King and Lieberman, the others being the American state's historical role in upholding racial segregation which ended in the 1960s, the fostering of public–private associational networks to develop public policy in a unique way, the administrative state with a distinct bureaucratic structure, and the multiple sites of power created by federal structures. These dimensions can easily be applied in comparative settings.

The accumulation of cases about state creation and transformations and the development of innovative comparative projects reveal a messier but also stimulating world of social science dealing with the state.

Failed states

For instance, the classic dichotomy strong states/weak states (Badie and Birnbaum 1982) has been more or less abandoned in favour of more nuanced typologies or a serious rethinking about key variables of stateness. Systematic comparative research about states in Asia, Latin America and Africa emphasize the role of colonial inheritance, the dynamics of religious influences and the effects of competition between parties and interest groups, that is, the role of internal actors in competition to shape forms of state simultaneously influenced by norms and forces from outside. An innovative literature is, for instance, engaged with state failures, the difficulties arising from some states' inability to collect taxes, to provide goods and services to the population or to protect the population. States or elites of the state may also be active in order to steal, to oppress, and to develop violence against their own population (Spruyt 2009).

Modern states act internationally and developed historically in part because of the way international society evolved. But it is in respect of their treatment of individual members and capacity to govern effectively and legitimately that ideas about state failure arise.

It is among many of the new states that the problem of state failure prevails. Mostly able to satisfy the criterion of territorial sovereignty, many of these new states fail to govern effectively across their geographic unit with respect to the following.

(i) *Violence*: The principal defining characteristic of a failing state is the presence of violence because of the state's inability effectively to exercise its monopoly on the use of legitimate violence. This failure translates into public disorder, severe and continuing danger to personal security and organized gangs paralleling the state's structures:

- Violence is continuing and systemic as for example in Angola and the Sudan. This can lead to collapsed states of which Somali is an example. The state's rulers are in constant war with violent challengers, failing to exercise authority throughout their geographic territory. Warlords dominate and there is no state presence to provide public goods or disarm the private armies. Control of peripheral areas by the centre is tenuous at best, as the internationally unrecognized territory of Somaliland in the old north of Somalia shows.
- Violence is widespread and consuming in large geographic parts of the failed state, as for instance in Burundi, Afghanistan and Sierra Leone; during the 1990s the Colombia government failed to control large parts of the state and between 1992 and 1997 the state in Tajikistan also lacked effective presence.

- Violence is anti-government and anti-state: it is mobilized and used to destabilize the existing government and regime; until the recent defeat of the Tamils in Sri Lanka their decades-long campaign threatened the state.
- Violence is often equivalent to civil war, as divisions rooted in ethnicity or religion or regions provide the basis for violent conflict as in parts of the former Yugoslavia or Kenya since its last election.
- Because of violence the state may effectively lose control of parts of the state, as seems to have occurred in Mexico in drugs-gang-controlled regions; such criminal gangs make lawlessness common and terrorize ordinary citizens. In the most extreme form 'shadow states' emerge providing some of the public goods – notably protection against violence – which the state traditionally provides, at a heavy fiscal price and under a regime of fear. Such privatized violence fundamentally challenges the idea and purpose of states. The European process of state formation, stretched over several centuries, consisted in part in the transfer of organized violence to the state's monopoly on legitimate force. In many failing states in Africa, the process is in reverse as groups in society deny the legitimacy of the state's monopoly and rival its organization with a shadow state based on its own exercise of violence.

(ii) *Dismantled states*: Beyond the problem of public order and violence, failed states manifest:

- Poor or absent infrastructure, with roads and other transport links destroyed from a combination of conflict and inadequate fiscal resources. Palestine is a glaring example as is Guinea-Bissau, the former Portuguese colony. Elections in June 2010 in Guinea-Bissau reminded the world of its parlous condition. One former finance minister characterized its state as 'in a phase of deliquescence;' in Guinea-Bissau the state has been dismantled. There is no electricity at night; violence is widespread and endemic with killings all the time and no state response, with the last three military chiefs of state murdered and the president shot dead. No president has completed his five-year term since the 'restoration' of multi-party rule in 1994, as the military effectively controls state institutions and power. It is a failed state, not just a weak one. According to the UN, its fragility is such that even drugs gangs have chosen other states as smuggling bases.
- The collapse of state revenues – such as Zimbabwe or Haiti – because rulers have siphoned off resources for personal profit and/or to pay off protectors. The prospective state South Sudan, independent from 2011 following a referendum on secession, is so fragile and potentially unstable as to be characterized as a 'prefailed state', since murderous inter-ethnic Lou–Jikany conflicts have increased despite the presence of UN peace-keepers and the Sudanese People's Liberation Army. The government of Southern Sudan does not inspire confidence: it received oil revenues and UN Food Programme aid yet has a humanitarian crisis level of malnutrition and state infrastructure outside the regional capital (Juba) is non-existent, any facilities a result of charities and foreign governments. This corruption and waste of oil resources bode ill for effective statehood.

- The collapse of educational and health systems, as physical infrastructure decays, salaries of key public-sector workers go unpaid and rampant inflation takes root.

Variations in stateness indicators

Research on the state has taken multiple foci. Consider a few instances.

The now classic 'fiscal-military model' of state (see Poggi, Chapter 9, in this volume) formation epitomized in particular in Tilly's work has been contested from all sorts of social science perspectives, including comparative historical sociology (Vu 2010; Jessop 2006). There is now a substantial gender literature about the state (Adams 2005 and Dean, Chapter 25, in this volume). STS (Sociology of Science and Technologies) scholars inspired by the work of Latour, Law or Callon but also Michel Foucault and Norbert Elias in particular emphasize the construction of states in relation to the emergence of different kinds of knowledge, technologies, representations, material-ities, networks, produced for instance by engineers or doctors (Baldwin 2005). Porter's (1995) or Desrosière's (1998) classic books on quantification and the production of figures have been crucial landmarks in the understanding of the state, echoing Weber's rationalization process or James Scott's argument about the modern state making society legible (1998). Carroll writes:

> The state can be understood simultaneously as an idea, a system, and a country, as a complex of meanings, practices, and materialities. The state idea has become a powerful discursive formation, a cognitive structure, and assemblage of institutions: the state system has become a vast organizational apparatus that is practiced with varying degree of coherence (and indeed incoherence) from the heads of executive agencies to the most mundane aspect of everyday life: and the state country is constituted through the materialities of land, built environment, and bodies/people, transformed by the co-productive agencies of science and government and rendered in the new forms of techno-territory, infrastructural jurisdiction and bio-population.
>
> (Carroll 2009: 592)

Research about the state has been significantly critically revised under the influence of cultural studies and post-positivist research scholarship (Marinetto 2007). In partic-ular, they have contributed to the deconstruction of the state as a stable institution. By contrast, they stress the fact that the state is a contingent form, always in question, always changing in response to discourse, a radical constructivist point of view. In their book *The State as Cultural Practice*, Bevir and Rhodes propose an alternative to positivism by defining the state through the meanings of its action, that is, 'the state appears as a differentiated cultural practice composed of all kinds of contingent and shifting beliefs and actions, where these beliefs and actions can be explained through an historical understanding' (2010: 8).

In parallel, constructivist sociologists have emphasized the historical specificity and contingency of processes leading to state formation in order to avoid either the reification of the state or to take the European-centric conception of the state for granted. Joel Migdal (2009) suggests differentiating at least between three waves of state formation in the twentieth century beyond classic European models: the post–First World War wave, the decolonization wave and the end of the Soviet empire. At each period, different forms of capitalism, national ideologies, norms of nation-states and power relations between states may explain the emergence of different processes of state making. Furthermore, timing of creation clearly affects the potential to become a failed state. Whether the 2011 democratic protests and government changes in the Middle East will constitute a continuation of Migdal's third phase of state formation or a fourth phase will engage scholars in the coming decade. Such comparative and historical works reveal the value of analysing a range of state emergence and trajectories, beyond the long-dominant European nation-state path. This irreducible contingency of state formation is central in comparative historical sociology research on the power of bottom-up processes, the fluidity of state-making trajectories and the diversity of historical experiences. In his work on African states J. F. Leguil-Bayart underlines hybrid processes related to diverse colonial experiences. His researchers emphasize intersection points between overlapping levels of institutional development and overlapping historical periods. Béatrice Hibou's collection on the privatization of the state (2004) is also anti-functionalist as she shows non-linear trajectories of state de-differentiation and transfers of functions to agencies or families (patrimony), focusing on different forms of interactions between states and societies in different parts of the world.

In other words, the state is complex and so is the analysis of the state (Migdal 2009).

Essentialism and the state

One radical solution with which to develop the same line of argument is to get rid of any definition in order to avoid essentialism. Quentin Skinner's method of 'ideas in context' leads to that conclusion. In a recent paper on the genealogy of the modern state, a follow-up to his classic books, Skinner makes the following point about the word 'state': 'I consequently focus as much as possible on how this particular word came to figure in successive debates about the nature of public power . . . to investigate the genealogy of the state is to discover that there has never been any agreed concept to which the word state has answered' (2009: 325–326). This is a fascinating intellectual journey but such radical constructivism does not help comparative research by generating clear hypotheses for research. The argument does have a logical rationale. However, moderate constructivism seems a more fruitful perspective to analyse contemporary changes.

Although neo-Marxist analysis of the state has lost salience (though it had not vanished), the current economic crisis shows the relevance of many Marxist insights about the state (see Le Galès and Scott 2010 for a fuller account of the issues raised in this section and Jessop, Chapter 1, in this volume). Marx was the first thinker to demonstrate that the self-regulated market – the putatively free and effective play of market forces – in practice requires the state. On Marxist and neo-Marxist accounts, the state played a key role, namely in the accumulation of capital and ideology, the latter a reflection of the dominant force in society. This argument has been applied in various empirical studies. For example, it features in Logan and Molotch's (1987) classic sociological study of urban growth coalitions and how urban real-estate markets operate in the United States. They empirically clarify the social role of the state in growth coalitions: the state first intervenes as guarantor of social order, namely through ideology and by regulating the various social interests (a classic neo-Marxist argument), as social order is an essential condition for real-estate investment; it later intervenes in the accumulation phase, by making below-market-price land or subsidies available to real-estate developers.

Those developments are also used in relation to the globalization of capitalism. Jessop (2002, 2007) and Brenner (2004) provide ambitious theoretical frameworks with which to analyse the transformation of the state under current conditions of capitalism. They argue that although the importance of the national-state-controlled scale of political power may be in decline, states are still very active and control many resources. To analyse the rescaling of the state these scholars develop a political economy of scale, or rather, *statehood*, based upon an analysis of the struggle to reorganize both statehood and capitalism following the destabilization of the nation-state's primacy in organizing both society and capitalism. They contrast the postwar Fordist Keynesian state with more competitiveness-driven approaches to the contemporary state. To stress that the state is a strategic site of structuration of globalization, such scholars highlight a strategic-relational approach to the state.

In contrast to anti-essentialist views, generations of legal scholars define the state in terms of an independent territory, an institutional apparatus of government and the source of the law. But beyond this, there is ambiguity about what should be analysed. The state theorist Bob Jessop poses the problem:

> Is the state best defined by its legal form, coercive capacities, institutional composition and boundaries, internal operations and modes of calculation, declared aims, functions for the broader society, or sovereign place in the international system? Is it a thing, a subject, a social relation or a construct that helps to orient political actions? Is stateness a variable and, if so, what are its central dimensions? What is the relationship between the state and law, the state and politics, the state and civil society, the public and the private, state power and micro power relations? Is the state best studied in isolation: only as part of the political system: or, indeed, in terms of a more general social theory? Do states have institutional, decisional, or operational autonomy and, if so, what are its sources and limits?
>
> (2006: 111–112)

As this quotation makes explicit, much of the confusion about the state, and the analysis of the contemporary restructuring process, derive from the variables but also from uncertainty about the most appropriate historical period to select to understand change.

Weber's Endurance

To address these sorts of empirical questions and analytical tasks, a return to the classic Weberian route retains its appeal. Although there is a debate about several definitions of the state, the well-known Weberian definition of the state in terms of political institutions and the attempt to monopolize violence is most widely employed by scholars (Weber 1978: 57); the definition has been refined in much work on state capacity (Hendrix 2010). The institutional dimensions of the state are key to Weber's account. In the macro-historical comparative sociology tradition, scholars emphasize the differentiation and autonomy of elites, separate from social or economic elites, professionals claiming a monopoly to be in charge of governing and developing specialized institutions (see Lachmann 2010). In that tradition of research, the key variable of the state is the construction of an autonomous political space and the differentiation of elites specific to the state. Of course, in this perspective, there are different types of state but this analysis gives little purchase on the contemporary restructuring of the state. What is central is the long-term construction of states, which are fundamental in structuring societies.

Adopting a similar Weberian line, du Gay and Scott (2010) argue that much confusion about the state derives from the choice of periods upon which scholars focus. They cast doubts on the literature dealing with the restructuring of the state because most of it tends to identify a high point of the state in the 1960s (a golden age according to the TranState programme in Bremen – see Leibfried and Zürn (eds) 2007) and to reify some post-golden-age period. They argue that this dichotomy is of limited value because both comparative macro sociologists of state formation and the scholars of the so-called Cambridge School have demonstrated in detail the gradual process of state formation, slowly reaching its modern form over several centuries. In other words, they argue, the relevance of short-term radical change to fundamental state form is likely to be weak. They also stress the fact that confusion is increased by the most recent developments of the state (such as the welfare state in the twentieth century). In other words, they criticize the choice made by many scholars to analyse the state first and foremost in terms of government rather than develop a richer sense of the actions and activities of the state. By contrast, they argue in favour of a parsimonious, quasi-essentialist definition of the state. The state is an independent coercive apparatus also defined by the centrality of the rule of law as argued by Gianfranco Poggi (1977). Defined in those terms, the state is about 'being' and the activities play no role. These authors thus rehabilitate Raymond Aron's concept of 'regime' to talk about the rest, including government. Beyond the fact that the relations between regime and state are not – as yet – clearly defined in this account, this definition implies that the development of government policies over the past two hundred years was of minor importance in comparison with the making of the state itself. It also means improbably that these developments are independent from the noble structure of the state and have no effects whatsoever on the state itself. Nevertheless, du Gay and Scott make a valuable case that it is useful to distinguish the state from the government in order not to assume that changes concerning governments automatically signal state changes.

Analysing state apparatus

Following this route leads to analysis of the apparatus of the state, the organization of the state. Many empirical projects, sometimes initiated by public administration scholars, have attempted to document the restructuring of the state bureaucracy, that is, the demise of amorphous hierarchical administration and ministries, of external services of the state and the rise of agencies – known as the agency-form of the state (Thatcher 2007) – and of auditing organizations (Hood 1998). In most European countries, how states reform themselves – reform of the public sector – has become a central political question. What Bezes (2009) has cleverly called 'Le souci de soi de l'Etat' is a good indicator of serious changes that even parsimonious Weberians find hard to put aside.

All in all, in the Weberian tradition, there is widespread consensus around a definition of the state understood in terms of relative monopoly and concentration of coercion. It is defined as a complex of interdependent institutions, differentiated from other institutions in society and legitimate, autonomous, based upon a defined territory and recognized as a state by other states. The state is also characterized by its administrative capacity to steer, to govern a society, to establish constraining rules, property rights, to guarantee exchanges, to tax and concentrate resources, to organize economic development and to protect citizens (Mann 1986; Tilly 2010; Levi 2002). Even the American state – often seen as an outlier – presents these broad Weberian features (Carpenter 2001; King and Lieberman 2009; Skowronek 2009) together with distinct public–private associational networks (Lieberman 2009) and social actors responding to signals in public policy about the need to reform (Dobbin 2009; Farhang 2010). The state takes different shape depending on historical periods, nationally distinct circumstances and political institutional structures, notably whether it is federal or unitary (Johnson 2007; Ziblatt 2006a).

Infrastructural power and the policy state

One group of scholars advocates studying the state with parsimony, concentrating on its basic institutions and functions, on its formation and the classic criteria of elite differentiation. However, it may also be fruitful to think about the state by looking at what it does, the activities, the interactions, the capacity to structure and steer society, as government – what is termed the 'policy state' (Skowronek 2009). In other words, the development of public policies over one century may not just be a strange appendix to the 'pure' state that could be easily terminated. What happens in the policy realm, in relation to politics, may have structural consequences for states, secession or sovereign bankruptcy for instance.

A useful point of departure is the sociologist Michael Mann's distinction between what he calls the *despotic power* of the state, that is 'the range of actions which the elite is empowered to undertake without routine, institutionalized negotiation with civil society groups', and the *infrastructural power*, that is, 'the capacity of the state actually to penetrate civil society, and to implement logistically political decisions throughout the realms' (1986 [1984]: 113). Combining those two analytically distinctive dimensions allows Mann to show, in his influential two-volume study of the state (1986 and 1993), the weakening of the first dimension and the strengthening of the second in relation to the rise and rise of public policies in Europe from the early twentieth century. This framework leads to typologies of state activities and policies such as Ted Lowi's widely used threefold categorization (1964). Many public policy scholars, neo-institutionalists in particular, have tried to show how the implementation of policies, their results, were crucial elements of the structuring of political conflicts, and to the legitimacy of the state (Duran 2009). Feedback from policies helps shape political conflict and subsequent policy.

Three very different research strategies are therefore at play in analysing the restructuring of the state. One is to concentrate on the classic question of elites and institutions, including the personnel of the state, in order to show the long-term resilience and robustness of the state. A second is, in contrast, to stress ever-changing configurations. A final strategy is to assume that the long-term entropy of the state has also had lasting consequences for the basic institutions and purposes of the state. Analysing the 'government' dimension of the state, the 'policy state' to take the phrase coined by Stephen Skowronek, may be central to understanding the institutional dimension of the state, even its survival. Policy successes and policy failures are not without consequence for the legitimacy of the state. In a number of cases, from the United States to Greece, Spain or Belgium, the sustainability of the state in its current form is at stake (Jacobs and King 2009).

In Western Europe and in the United States, empirical research points to different, sometimes contradictory directions, hence the research agenda defined in terms of restructuring of the state. A large body of research has tried to identify the failures of the state to govern. The contemporary debate about the state, greatly influenced both by comparative political economy research and by governance questions, tends to focus on the question of capacity. In the late 1990s, scholars identified the state's decreasing capacity to govern society as a crucial issue. The argument is well known: globalization trends, however contradictory they might be, may compel the state to force societal changes but they also make society more difficult to govern because of the rise of exit strategy, especially among firms and capital, and economic fluctuations affecting working- and middle-class incomes and employment prospects. The hidden – or not so hidden – secret of the state was therefore one of growing inability to govern society, to tax, to implement decisions, a question well identified by governance scholars (Mayntz 1993).

This issue prompted a new research agenda based upon classic questions associated with governance and government alike: not just who governs but how governments and various actors involved in governance processes operate. This is not as new an idea as some conjectured. Foucault in particular stressed the need to understand changes in governmentality and the theme was central for Miller and Rose (2008) when they started their research project on governmentality. However, to raise this issue is to underline that the governance research agenda is historically related to the 1970s research about public policy failures, well represented by the work of Pressman and Wildavsky (1973). One then wondered whether complex societies were becoming ungovernable or if, at the very least, governments and state elites were less and less able to govern society through the public administration, taxes and laws. Ever since, this debate has led to a dynamic governance research domain organized around the following questions: Can government govern, steer or row (Peters 1997)? Do governments always govern? What do they govern, and how? What is not governed? Can we identify dysfunctions of governments over time? Can groups or sectors escape from governments (Mayntz 1993)? What does it mean to govern complex societies?

Political economy scholars, emphasizing the significance of globalized capitalism for state activity and change, have stressed too the notion of a powerless state against global economic forces (as in the work of Susan Strange, for instance); or at the very least they see the state as heavily constrained by financial markets, the strategy of large firms or globalized exchanges. In a recent contribution to this debate, the sociologist Wolfgang Streeck (2010) has underlined the fiscal crisis of the state. If inheritance is a classic theme in public policy, Streeck shows, before the crisis, the structural development of public deficits in most developed countries followed by rising debt and dramatically reduced capacity to govern. Needless to say, this argument has not lost its force with the coming of the financial crisis.

Paralleling this trend is the expansion of the state into new activities (Jacobs and King 2009). States have become more intrusive or have developed new policies in matters of education, gender, discrimination and environment, but also security, defence or surveillance. New bureaucracies are employed in the field of auditing and control to change individual behaviour through mechanisms of sanctions and rewards (Le Galès and Scott 2010). In terms of relations between states and markets, neo-Marxist, Polanyian and neo-institutionalists have long stressed the fact that markets were sustained by state activities, policies, ideology and finances. As Levi rightly documents, the rise of market-making activities and policies has become a notable feature of state elites more influenced by neoliberal ideas. Both the Thatcher and the New Labour governments were characterized not only by privatization and the introduction of market mechanisms in the public sector but also by centralization and the development of a stronger and more authoritarian state (Gamble 1993, Faucher-King and Le Galès 2010). In the United States, a body of recent research finds similar apparently contradictory pattern (Jacobs and King 2009).

The financial and economic crisis since 2008 illustrates more than ever this apparent paradox of weakened states in relation to banks, hedge funds, or large firms escaping taxes. To survive, states had to bail out the financial sector and in numerous cases transfer the private debt to the public sector. Despite the structural weakening of financial state capacity, some attempts have been made to recover the infrastructural power of the state, to use Mann's turn of phrase. Again, innovations in public policies and activities of the state are probably very revealing of state restructuring.

Conclusion

What the Great Recession that commenced in 2008 demonstrates is both the power and the vulnerability of the modern state (see Crouch, Chapter 42, in this volume). States were buffeted severely by the economic crisis, most in advanced democracies forced into dramatic and extensive policy initiatives. Many of these latter involved hugely expensive public interventions into the private sector (though several such as the United States' Troubled Asset Relief Program (TARP) and the UK's semi-nationalization of two major banks have seen funds repaid to the state). It showed strikingly also the centrality of the state in these roles. The infirmity or incoherence of supranational bodies such as the EU or international organizations such as the WTO or World Bank as forums in which to develop effective policy exposed the shallowness of the alleged transnational and internal erosion of state institutions. State strength and capacity are challenged by the Great Recession but not the *role* of the state as the primary agent of policy initiator and legitimate authority for such responses.

The agenda of state research is exciting and varied. Scholars will spend many years excavating the precise mechanism and triggers through which the Great Recession occurred and integrating political economy and state theory in the process. The role of material interests, the competence of state institutions (such as central banks), the inadequacy or capacity of state regulatory institutions and the effect of long-term global shifts in power and resources from the West to the East will all feature in such accounts. Concurrently, the enduring Weberian-style questions about how states restructure their public-sector capacities and how states retain or augment legitimacy will remain central to these new empirical studies.

Further Reading

Jessop, B. 2007: *State Power*. Cambridge: Polity Press.

Jacobs, L. and King, D. (eds) 2009: *The Unsustainable American State*. New York: Oxford University Press.

Mann, M. 1984: The autonomous power of the state: its origins, mechanisms and results. *Archives Européennes de Sociologie 25*: 185–212. Reprinted in J.A. Hall (ed.) *States in History*. Oxford: Blackwell, 1986.

Migdal, J. 2001: *State in Society*. Cambridge: Cambridge University Press.

Scott, J.C. 1998: *Seeing Like a State*. New Haven, CT: Yale University Press.

Ziblatt, D. 2006: *Structuring the State*. Princeton, NJ: Princeton University Press.

11

Political Legitimacy

DAVID BEETHAM

Claims to political legitimacy try to ground the occupation of positions of political power, to show why they are rightful and why those subject to them should obey. Political sociology is concerned with their effectiveness; the conditions under which legitimacy is realized or eroded and what happens when it fails. The most important writer for the study of political legitimacy is Weber, who set the basic questions that must be addressed. Who is the audience for legitimacy claims: the general public or the administration? What is the relation between principles of legitimacy and the organization of systems of power? Weber's own typology of power systems is, however, inadequate to the variety of types that have existed in the twentieth century. Beetham refines it to account for differences between liberal democracy, Marxist–Leninism, theocracy, and fascism. He then discusses why it is that the liberal-democratic mode of legitimacy has become globally prevalent at the start of the twenty-first century.

Since the dawn of human history, those occupying positions of power, and especially political power, have sought to ground their authority in a principle of legitimacy, which shows why their access to, and exercise of, power is rightful, and why those subject to it have a corresponding duty to obey. Mostly such claims to legitimacy have been taken for granted by those involved in power relations. However, where the possession or exercise of power has been substantially contested, whether because it breaches some important interest or established principle of legitimacy, or the principles themselves have proved inadequate to new social circumstances and political forces, then serious reflection and argument about what makes power rightful has taken place. It has usually been the task of philosophers to elaborate such reflection into a considered theory or theories, and to test legitimacy claims against accepted standards of normative validity and discursive argument. From at least the time of the

The Wiley-Blackwell Companion to Political Sociology, First Edition. Edited by Edwin Amenta, Kate Nash, and Alan Scott.
© 2012 Blackwell Publishing Ltd. Published 2012 by Blackwell Publishing Ltd.

ancient Greeks onwards, the study of legitimacy has been central to the practice of political philosophy, through its analysis of normative principles of the right and the good.

The study of legitimacy as a subject for political sociology, by contrast, is comparatively recent, beginning only with the twentieth century. As befits a social science, political sociology's focus is much more empirical than the normative tradition of philosophy. Its concern is less with the abstract validity of legitimacy claims than with their acknowledgement by the relevant social agents, and with the consequences that follow from that acknowledgement for the stability of a system of rule and for the manner in which it is organized. Political sociology is concerned with questions such as: What difference does legitimacy make to the exercise of power? Who constitutes the audience for legitimacy claims? What happens when legitimacy is eroded, or is lacking altogether? What difference do the historically and socially varying bases or principles of legitimacy make to the manner in which political power is organized? Underlying all these questions is a more basic one: What exactly is 'legitimacy' as a subject for political sociology?

It was Max Weber in his *Economy and Society* (1978 [1922]) who made legitimacy a key subject in the systematic study of power relations and typologies of power, and hence a central concern for political sociology. Anyone who studies the subject has therefore to come to terms with what Weber wrote about it. In my view, two features of Weber's analysis are important and valuable, while others have proved misleading. The best way of introducing the subject, and debates about it, is to consider these features in turn.

First is what Weber had to say about the significance of legitimacy for power relations, and the instability of systems of authority where legitimacy is lacking. 'Custom, personal advantage, purely affectual or ideal motives of solidarity,' he wrote, 'do not form a sufficiently reliable basis for a given domination. In addition, there is normally a further element, the belief in *legitimacy*' (Weber 1978: 213). In other words, where there is general recognition of the legitimacy of authority, its commands will be followed without the widespread use of coercion, or the constant fear of disobedience or subversion. In this Weber was echoing an earlier observation by the political theorist Rousseau, who wrote that 'the strongest is never strong enough to be master, unless he transforms strength into right and obedience into duty' (Rousseau 1963 [1762]: 6).

However, a number of other social theorists have since challenged the assumption that a general recognition of the legitimacy of authority is necessary either to its reliability or to its durability. For most of human history, they would argue, systems of power have been maintained by the effective organization of the means of coercion. What has kept those subordinate in line has been their lack of any means of resistance, and, above all, their belief in their own impotence. This position has been put most forcefully by James C. Scott (1990: ch. 4). The point of the symbolic and ideological elaborations of authority, he argues, is not so much to convince the subordinate of the rightfulness of their subordination – claims which they are perfectly capable of seeing through – as to create an impression of impregnable power, which it is pointless to resist. It is this aura of impregnability, he argues, rather than of moral superiority, that is essential to the stability and durability of power. In so far as legitimacy claims matter, it is to the powerful themselves. It is they who need to be convinced of the rightfulness of their rule if they are to have the self-confidence to maintain it; they constitute the chief audience for their own legitimacy claims (see also Abercrombie and Turner 1978 and Barker 2001).

Now it should be said that Weber himself was aware of different levels of audience for legitimacy claims. In particular, he was insistent that it was primarily those who were involved in the administration and enforcement of a system of power who had to be convinced of its legitimacy, if the supreme power-holders were not to be vulnerable to a 'palace coup', or, as in the late Roman Empire, to any usurper who could offer the imperial guards more pay and booty. Moreover, he acknowledged that broader strata of subordinates might submit simply out of helplessness, because there was no alternative. 'A system of domination may be so completely protected,' he wrote, 'on the one hand by the obvious community of interests between the chief and his administrative staff as opposed to the subjects, on the other hand by the helplessness of the latter, that it can afford to drop even the pretence of legitimacy' (Weber 1978: 214).

Yet Weber regarded such a condition as the exception rather than the norm. The norm is for a system of power 'to establish and cultivate the belief in its legitimacy'. The reason is not far to seek. The more that a power structure is dependent on those subordinate to it for the achievement of its purposes, and especially where the quality of their performance matters, the more essential is it that the relationship is constructed according to an acknowledgement of reciprocal rights and duties such as only a principle of legitimacy can provide. This is particularly true of the modern state, which requires those subject to its authority not only to obey its laws, but to pay their taxes, cooperate with its policies and even to fight in its defence.

Take, for example, the payment of taxes. By definition, no-one likes paying taxes. But it makes an enormous difference to a system of tax collection if people acknowledge the right of the state to tax them and accept the system as broadly fair. Then the vast majority will pay up without demur. Naturally, the administrative arrangements will have to be efficient, and there will have to be compulsion at the margin to deal with backsliders, and to convince the rest that there are no 'free-riders'. But a state where people acknowledge no duty to pay taxes will have to engage in enormously expensive systems of enforcement, which will substantially reduce the overall take, and may even, as in contemporary Russia, compromise its capacity to raise taxes altogether. This means that the effectiveness and the legitimacy of a system of power are not distinct and separable elements, as many sociologists have assumed (see Lipset 1983: ch. 3). This is because the capacity of political authorities is also dependent upon their moral authority or standing among those whose cooperation is required for them to achieve their purposes. So the first main significance of legitimacy lies in the contribution it makes, alongside the organization of the means of administration and coercion, to the reliability, effectiveness and durability of a system of power.

The second important point Weber had to make about the significance of legitimacy concerned the relationship between the different ideas or principles of legitimacy and the way systems of power were organized in practice. 'According to the kind of legitimacy which is claimed,' he wrote, 'the type of obedience, the kind of administrative staff developed to guarantee it, and the mode of exercising authority, will all differ fundamentally ... Hence it is useful to classify the types of domination according to the kind of claim to legitimacy typically made by each' (Weber 1978: 213). Weber is highlighting two things here. All institutional arrangements for the organization of power embody legitimating ideas or principles, which determine how power is attained and by whom, how it is exercised and within what limits. Understanding institutions is therefore not just a question of giving an empirical description of how they operate, but of exploring the regulative ideas that help explain why they are organized as they are. And it follows, secondly, that we can most usefully construct a typology of different historical and contemporary power systems according to their different legitimating principles or ideas. It was on just such a basis that Weber organized his own political sociology in *Economy and Society*.

This is an important insight, which has significant implications for sociological practice, and relates to the broader Weberian method of 'interpretative sociology' (Weber 1978: 4–22). The limitation of it lies not in the method itself, but in the particular typology of power systems that Weber constructed from his threefold legitimating principles: traditional, rational-legal and charismatic, respectively (Weber 1978: 215–216). There is not space to explain fully here what is inadequate with this typology, but it can be summarized as follows: although the three legitimating ideas may help to define what is distinctive about modern, in contrast to pre-modern systems of law and administration, they provide a wholly inadequate basis for characterizing the different political regime types that have existed in the course of the twentieth century. Comparative political scientists who have tried to use the Weberian typology for this purpose have usually produced more obfuscation than light. It is not particularly helpful to be told that both liberal democracy and fascism are different variants of charismatic authority, one more rule governed than the other; or that communist systems comprised a unique combination of the traditional, rational-legal and charismatic types (Heller 1982).

To construct a more adequate typology we need to address a basic question: What exactly is it that makes political authorities legitimate, and acknowledged as such by those subordinate to them? The answer lies in an interpretative analysis of the grounds for that acknowledgement, which reveals that legitimacy is multidimensional, not mono-dimensional: it is constructed from rules, justifications grounded in societal beliefs and actions expressive of recognition or consent (Beetham 1991a: ch. 1). Political authority is legitimate, we can say, to the extent that:

1. it is acquired and exercised according to established rules (legality);
2. the rules are justifiable according to socially accepted beliefs about (i) the rightful source of authority and (ii) the proper ends and standards of government (normative justifiability);
3. positions of authority are confirmed by express consent or affirmation of appropriate subordinates, and by recognition from other legitimate authorities (legitimation).

The three levels are not alternatives, since all contribute to legitimacy; together they provide the subordinate with moral grounds for compliance or cooperation with authority. The fact that all are required is shown by the different negative words used to express the different ways in which power may lack legitimacy. If there is a breach of the rules, we use the term 'illegitimacy'; if the rules are only weakly supported by societal beliefs, or are deeply contested, we can talk of a 'legitimacy deficit'; if consent or recognition is publicly withdrawn or withheld, we speak of 'delegitimation'.

The most extreme example of *illegitimacy* is usurpation or *coup d'etat* – power attained in violation of the rules. Examples of *legitimacy deficit* are enormously varied: from situations where changing societal beliefs leave existing institutional arrangements unsupported, or those where people have widely diverging beliefs, say, about which state they should belong to; to situations where government is chronically unable to meet the basic purposes, such as welfare or security, which people believe it should. Legitimacy deficits usually only become critical when some performance failure of government exposes a fundamental doubt about its rightful source of authority (see Coicaud 2002 and Gilley 2009). Examples of *delegitimation* include acts of widespread public opposition to a regime, of which revolutionary mobilization is the most extreme example. Revolutions follow a typical course, from chronic legitimacy deficit of the regime (doubtful or disputed source of authority compounded by performance failure), through its delegitimation by mass oppositional mobilization which splits the governing apparatus, to an illegitimate seizure of power which heralds its reconstruction under a new set of legitimating principles.

The different dimensions of legitimacy outlined above constitute only the most general or abstract framework, the specific content of which has to be 'filled in' for each historical society or political system. They provide a heuristic tool to guide analysis. Is political authority valid according to the rules? The relevant rules have to be specified, their conventional or legal form established, the mode of adjudication appropriate to them determined for the given context and so on. Are the rules justifiable in terms of the beliefs and norms of the particular society, and are these norms relatively uncontested? We need to examine the specific beliefs current in the society about the rightful source of authority, on the one hand, and the proper ends and standards of government, on the other. Are there, finally, actions expressive of consent to authority on the part of those qualified to give it, as well as recognition by other authorities? Who counts as qualified, and what actions count as appropriate, will be determined by the conventions of the given society or system of power, as also what other kinds of authority there are whose recognition has legitimating force.

This overall framework can be used to construct a typology of twentieth-century political systems or regime types according to the different dimensions of legitimacy outlined: their characteristic form of law or legality; their distinctive source of authority; their publicly defined ends or purposes of government; and their typical mode of consent. The results of this typology are to be found in the Table 11.1, in which the different systems are portrayed in their most typical form ('ideal-typical' to use the Weberian term).

Military dictatorship has been included here as a limiting case of a non-legitimate political order, born of illegitimacy, and lacking both a rightful source of authority and any mode of expressed consent. Such legitimacy as military regimes have is based entirely on their purpose or mission – to save society from chaos – and is typically defined as transitional, to promote the restoration of a normal legitimate order. Like all regimes whose legitimacy is limited to the dimension of performance, they are vulnerable once performance falters and their failure exposes their lack of any valid source of authority. Legitimate political orders, in contrast, which are secure in their source of authority, are able to withstand shocks and performance failures, and to effect routine changes of administration which do not threaten the legitimacy of the system itself.

Table 11.1 Typology of twentieth-century regimes

Regime type	Form of law	Source of authority	Ends of government	Mode of consent
Traditional	Custom/ precedent	Hereditary/the past	Well-being within traditional order	Assembly of social elite
Fascist	Sovereign will	Leadership principle	National purity/ expansion	Mass mobilization
Communist	Sovereign will	Party monopoly of Marxist–Leninist truth	Building communist future	Mass mobilization
Theocratic	Sacred texts	Divine will interpreted by the hierarchy	Purifying moral order	Various
Liberal democratic	Constitutional rule of law	The people through competitive election	Individual rights and protection	Competitive election
Military dictatorship	Decree	None	Restore order and national unity	None

Use of the regime typology can help us to identify what is distinctive about the liberal-democratic mode of legitimacy, in comparison with others, and also help explain why it has come to prevail over the course of the twentieth century. It will be useful to start with its source of authority and mode of consent, since these are the most characteristic democratic features, and bring us to the heart of the difference with the other political systems. First, in liberal democracy the source of political authority lies with the people, and the right to rule derives from electoral choice, rather than from heredity and the past (traditional system), from the party's monopoly of the truth (Marxist–Leninism), from religious authorization (theocracy) or from the exceptional qualities of the leader (fascism). Ever since the principle of popular sovereignty was announced in the eighteenth century, who has counted as 'the people' has been a matter of contestation, as progressively those who have been excluded from the political nation – the propertyless, women, racial and other minorities – have demanded inclusion. At the same time, where the boundaries of the nation-state should be drawn has become problematized in a way it never was when the state was regarded simply as the property of the ruling family, and its borders could be altered at will, according to dynastic convenience or military conquest.

Many have argued that nationalism is the major legitimating idea of modern politics, and certainly it has been central in determining the spatial dimensions of the state, and which state people should belong to. It has also been widely used to bolster the legitimacy of rulers, especially non-democratic ones, and to delegitimize those who could be accused of selling out to foreign powers. Yet nationalism does not of itself provide any legitimating basis for appointment to political office, or for a particular kind of political system, and in this key respect it does not constitute an alternative, say, to communism. Moreover, since its legitimating force derives from the same principle as that of democracy – that political authority stems from the people – its articulation always invites the challenge that the people should express the 'nation's will' for themselves, through an electoral process, rather than have it merely proclaimed by higher authorities on their behalf.

This brings us to the second key feature of liberal-democratic legitimacy, which is the distinctive method through which consent is expressed to political authority. It is often argued that 'consent' as such is distinctive of liberal democracy, but this is mistaken. All political authorities throughout history have sought to bind in key subordinates through actions which express consent to, and confer public recognition on, their authority, and in so doing contribute to its legitimacy. Where systems differ is in who among their subordinates is qualified to give consent or confer recognition, and through what kinds of action. In a traditional system it is key notables who do so through swearing an oath of allegiance, kissing hands, or some other public symbolic act. In post-traditional systems those who are qualified include the population at large. In fascist and communist regimes, however, consent is expressed through acts of mass acclamation and mass mobilization in the regime's cause, which have their counterpart in the secret suppression of all dissent. What is distinctive about liberal democracy is that the process through which consent is conferred – popular election – is the same as that through which political authority is appointed in the first place, whereas in all other systems the expression of consent *follows* the process of appointment to office, which is determined by other means (heredity, priestly selection, inner-party choice, self-appointment etc.). So it would be more accurate to say that it is the popular *authorization* of government, rather than popular *consent* to it, that is the distinctive feature of liberal-democratic legitimation.

The two other dimensions of liberal-democratic legitimacy exemplify more the characteristically liberal than the democratic components of the portmanteau construct 'liberal democracy'. Its distinctive purpose of government lies in the protection of individual rights, initially the liberty rights of the eighteenth-century bourgeois revolutions, then increasingly also during the twentieth century the welfare rights of the social democratic tradition. This emphasis on individual rights contrasts with a variety of collective purposes characteristic of other regime types. And its distinctive mode of legality lies in the constitutional rule of law, in contrast to the customary law of traditional systems, the sacred law of theocratic ones, or law as the expression of sovereign will, whether of the leader or the revolutionary party, as in fascist or communist ones.

Why is it that the liberal-democratic mode of legitimacy, and form of political system, has become globally prevalent by the start of the twenty-first century? This is partly for negative reasons, that other forms of legitimate political order have proved ill-adapted to some key aspect of contemporary economic and social conditions, and have lost their internal legitimacy. The hereditary monopoly of political authority characteristic of traditional systems has proved vulnerable to the modern requirement of a career open to talent, and to popular demands for inclusion in the political process. The Marxist–Leninist goal of a communist society came up against the inherent limits of its system of economic planning, and the party's claim to exclusive knowledge of the workers' interests proved increasingly out of step with their own perceptions of them. The fascist pursuit of radical national goals has typically led to self-destructive wars; or, where these have been avoided, an authority vested in the person of an individual leader has proved unable to survive his death. Theocracies have proved vulnerable to fundamentalisms that have quickly forfeited popularity, or else they have provoked adherents of other faiths to open disaffection or civil war. Each system has had its own internal crisis tendencies, inherent in its legitimating principles or procedures, which have eventually proved terminal (Beetham1991a: ch. 6).

Liberal democracy has become prevalent, in contrast, because it has proved the only sustainable legitimate order compatible with the conditions of market capitalism, on the one side, especially in its most advanced form, and with the requirements of multicultural societies on the other. Market capitalism's anti-paternalist principles – individuals are the best judge of their own interests, are responsible for their own fate and are sovereign in the consumer market – have over time led to the demand for people to be sovereign in the political sphere also, and have undermined all paternalist forms of legitimacy, especially as education has become widespread. At the same time, the increasingly global dimensions of communication have made closed political systems, claiming a monopoly of information and ideology, unsustainable. Finally, the potential antagonisms between different communities cohabiting the same state, which are normal for most contemporary states, can only be peacefully resolved through the methods of dialogue and respect for equal rights, such as are intrinsic to liberal-democratic procedures.

The long-term superiority and survivability of liberal democracy's legitimating principles and procedures do not mean that they are themselves unproblematic. Indeed, they contain their own inherent crisis tendencies. One stems from the inescapable tension between the economic and social inequalities that are as intrinsic to capitalism as to pre-capitalist economic systems, and the equality of citizenship and political voice that democracy promises. This tension requires carefully crafted institutional compromises within the party and political system if it is not to prove unmanageable. The main alternatives are either a pseudo-democracy in which the mass of the people is effectively excluded from power and influence despite the formal exercise of the vote; or else a reversion to dictatorship, when the demands of the masses prove too threatening to the interests of economic and social elites. The second recurrent problem lies in the majoritarian procedure of democracy, which encourages political mobilization along ethnic lines in divided societies, and threatens the permanent exclusion of minorities from power and influence, with the prospect of consequent degeneration into civil war. Again, this requires carefully crafted institutional procedures, such as a form of consociational democracy, to resolve (Lijphart 1977).

It is important to stress, however, that liberal democracy's crisis tendencies, where they have not been institutionally resolved, have never proved terminal, in the sense that they have marked a transition to a different legitimate political order. At most they have led to the suspension of legitimacy, in military dictatorship or other forms of exceptional regime, whose rationale is precisely that they are temporary. These have usually ended in turn with attempts to restore the liberal-democratic form of legitimacy once more. In this sense the twentieth century, though not history itself, has ended with liberal democracy triumphant.

This dominant position has been reinforced at the international level also. For most of the past few centuries, recognition by the international state system has been an important contributor to the domestic legitimacy of states, particularly for newly established regimes. However, this recognition has simply required that regimes demonstrate a de facto capacity to exercise power within their territory, and especially within the capital city, and has been quite neutral as to the form of regime, which has been regarded as entirely a domestic matter. Increasingly, however, states are now being required to meet externally monitored legitimacy requirements if they are to achieve full international recognition. At first this has been a human rights requirement, according to the standards of the International Covenant on Civil and Political Rights, as it has increasingly become accepted that how a state treats its own citizens is no longer just an internal matter for the state concerned (Rosas 1995). Since 1989, however, the requirement that a state also meet liberal-democratic principles and procedures in its mode of political organization has started to become generalized as an internationally accepted norm. This norm provides strong external legitimation to domestic political forces engaged in democratization, and is also given practical effect through positive measures of democracy support and through negative pressure where aid, trade and debt interdependencies are involved (see Clark 2005).

The liberal-democratic principle of legitimacy has become most fully developed as an international norm within the European political space, as applications from the former communist countries to join the economic club of the European Union (EU) have been made dependent on prior membership of the Council of Europe, with its democracy and human rights conditions (Storey 1995). These norms have also been used to legitimate external military intervention in a sovereign European state, as in the NATO war against Yugoslavia over its treatment of the Albanian population in Kosovo. This war serves to mark the decisive shift in international norms away from the principle of unconstrained sovereignty on the part of states over their own internal affairs, regardless of how they treat their populations. It also underlines the deeply problematic character of external intervention, while states still retain a monopoly of physical force over their own territories. There is a serious disjunction, in other words, between the developing normative framework at the international level, and the means available to enforce it.

The development of a democracy and human rights 'mission' on the part of the EU has served to focus attention on the legitimacy of its own political arrangements, which is both contested politically and a source of disagreement among analysts. On the one hand are those who model the EU's authority on that of international institutions, whose legitimacy is derived from recognition by member states, and whose audience for legitimacy claims are the states' own bureaucracies. On the other hand are those who argue that the supranational dimension of the EU's institutions, and the impact its policy and legislation have on the lives of citizens, require a direct rather than merely indirect form of legitimation; and that this can only be constructed on liberal-democratic principles (see Beetham and Lord 1998: ch.1). At all events, it is clear that political legitimacy in the European political space now involves an interactive, two-level relationship, between the European levels and that of individual states. In this, the EU is simply the most developed example of what can be seen as a more general feature of political legitimacy in the contemporary world: it is no longer determined simply at the domestic level of the individual state, as it has been for the past few centuries, but is increasingly dependent also on the state's conformity to norms defined at the international level.

Further Reading

Barker, R.S. 2001: *Legitimating Identities: The Self-Presentation of Rulers and Subjects.* Cambridge: Cambridge University Press.
Beetham, D. 1991: *The Legitimation of Power.* Basingstoke: Macmillan.

Beetham, D. and Lord, C.J. 1998: *Legitimacy and the European Union*. Harlow: Addison Wesley Longman.

Clark, I. 2005: *Legitimacy in International Society*. Oxford: Oxford University Press.

Coicaud, J-M. 2002: *Legitimacy and Politics: A Contribution to the Study of Political Right and Political Responsibility*. Cambridge: Cambridge University Press.

Gilley, B. 2009: *The Right to Rule: How States Win and Lose Legitimacy*. New York: Columbia University Press.

12

Political Corruption

DONATELLA DELLA PORTA AND ALBERTO VANNUCCI

In parallel with growing social scientific interest in the topic of corruption, there has been a growing debate on the very definition of the phenomenon. True, there is a broad consensus on conceptualizing (political and bureaucratic) corruption as abuse by a public agent: 'corruption is commonly defined as the misuse of public power for private benefits' (Lambsdorff 2007: 16). However, this definition raises the problem of establishing the standards against which misuse of power can be assessed. Formal norms, public interest, public opinion – all might be included here. Moreover, abuses of power for private gain can assume different forms. Besides corruption in a strict sense, embezzlement, favouritism, nepotism, clientelism, vote-buying, fraud, extortion and maladministration are often used as synonymous or corresponding terms to describe corrupt relationships involving public administrators. Andvig *et al.* (2000: 14–17), for example, classify 'some basic varieties of corruption' as including very different phenomena, ranging from embezzlement (where no private agent is usually involved) to extortion (where no exchange takes place). This chapter examines the various forms of political corruption and the debates that surround the issue.

What Is Corruption?

In order to avoid (or at least, reduce) the risk of the concept of corruption becoming all-encompassing, we can differentiate the components of corruption adopting a principal–agent scheme (see, among others, Banfield 1975; Klitgaard 1988; Pizzorno 1992; della Porta and Vannucci 1999; Lambsdorff 2007). There are different kinds of illicit, dysfunctional or malfunctioning operations within the political and administrative realm, and corruption is one of them. As Bryce observes, '"Corruption" may be taken to include those modes of employing money to attain private ends by political means which are criminal or at least illegal, because they induce persons charged with

The Wiley-Blackwell Companion to Political Sociology, First Edition. Edited by Edwin Amenta, Kate Nash, and Alan Scott.
© 2012 Blackwell Publishing Ltd. Published 2012 by Blackwell Publishing Ltd.

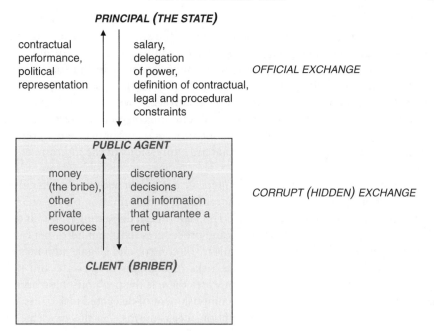

Figure 12.1 Public corruption within a principal–agent model

a public duty to transgress that duty and misuse the functions assigned to them' (Bryce 1921, 477–478).

In formal terms (see Figure 12.1), corruption can then be defined as:

(i) the *illegal* and therefore *hidden violation* of an explicit or implicit contract;

(ii) that states a delegation of responsibility from a *principal* to an *agent*, who has the legal authority, as well as official and informal obligation, to use his discretionary power, capacity and information in pursuing the principal's interests;

(iii) the violation occurs when the agent exchanges these resources in a (*corrupt*) *transaction*;

(iv) with a *client* (the *briber*), from whom the agent receives as a reward a quantity of money – the bribe – or other valuable resources.

In political and bureaucratic corruption, moreover:

(va) the principal is the *state* (in a democracy, the citizens), the corrupted is a *public agent,*

while in private corruption:

(vb) the principal is a *private actor* or *organization*, the corrupted is a *private agent.*

Within any private or public organization there are relations of a contractual nature between the agent, delegated to take specific decisions, and the principal, who delegates him/her. The latter can be a collective actor: in liberal democracies, politicians and bureaucrats are agents to whom the state – as a principal, that is, the sovereign people – delegates, through various mechanisms (electoral competition, public contest, lot etc.) the pursuit of public interest in the formation and implementation of public policies. The complexity of the tasks delegated to the agents makes a detailed list of clauses in the relations between the principal and the agent impossible. The distinction of roles and functions responds nevertheless to this fundamental distinction: the public agent does not act on his or her own account, but is delegated to accomplish those tasks that are expressions of the interests of his or her principal.

Any agent, however, also has private interests that do not necessarily coincide with those of the principal. An agent may, moreover, hide information on the characteristics and the content of their activities. To prevent this, in delegating power and tasks to the agent the principal stipulates rules and procedures that limit his or her range of discretion and develops various mechanisms of control and (legal, administrative, social, political) sanctions to reduce the risks of conflicts of (private and public) interests. Amongst these rules in modern states there is the prohibition on accepting illicit payments by other actors in the accomplishment of delegated tasks. Illegality is therefore an essential attribute of corruption. Legal norms – in this case, the norm prohibiting the agent's acceptance of 'bribes' in the exercise of his or her public duties – define constraints on the agent's activities in accordance with the principal's interests, as they are perceived and stated in a particular context. The very illegality of corrupt activities increases their transaction costs and expected risks, therefore generating a demand for protection within that murky environment. This implies a substantial difference in the social mechanisms regulating practices similar to corruption that are legal, such as clientelism, favouritism, etc. If they are exposed, such practices are sanctioned only by social stigma.

We, therefore, have corruption when a third actor enters and distorts the relations between agent and principal. The intervention of a client-briber pushes the agent to avoid the constraints and controls imposed by norms and procedures. The corrupter, by offering resources such as money or other utilities, succeeds in obtaining favourable decisions, reserved information or a broader protection of its own interests. In its elementary logic, the corrupt exchange is therefore a 'three-player game' in which an invisible and illegal exchange between an agent and a client-briber modifies the terms of the official contract to which the principal committed the agent in a way that is potentially damaging to the interests of the principal. Even though corruption can emerge also in private relations, the social sciences have focused on politico-bureaucratic corruption. While early research particularly addressed corruption in poor countries, often in authoritarian regimes, there is an increasing attention to corruption in democratic systems.

The exercise of public power in a democratic government can be conceived as a chain of principal–agent relationships between electorate, elected officials and bureaucrats, in their functional and hierarchical attribution of roles and functions. The collective nature of the *basic* principal – the sovereign people – makes it impossible to define unequivocally and contractually the interests and preferences whose realization is delegated to the agent. While bureaucrats are relatively limited in their activity by normative and procedural constraints, therefore, politicians can operate with a greater degree of discretion in the pursuit of some presumed 'true' general interest.

Where there is corruption in democratic government, the transaction between the corrupt agent and the client involves the exchange of *property rights* for *rents* created through the political process. Corruption, in fact, is 'actually just a black market for the property rights over which politicians and bureaucrats have allocative power. Rather than assigning rights according to political power, rights are sold to the highest bidder' (Benson 1990: 159; Benson and Baden 1985). State activity, like market exchanges, modifies the existing structure of property rights. Public agents use the coercive power of the state instead of voluntary transactions to allocate resources: the corrupters try to modify to their advantage the structure of property rights over resources that are either public or subject to public regulation. A rent is created through (a) the acquisition of goods and services paid to private actors above their market price; (b) the selling of licences for the use of public goods below their market price; (c) the arbitrary use of enforcement activities that attribute to public agents the competence to selectively impose costs or to reduce the value of some private goods (Rose-Ackerman 1978, 61–63). In such cases, corrupter and corrupted share between them property rights to the political rent thus created in ways that are hidden. The corrupted official obtains a part of the rent in return for his or her services (decisions, confidential information, protection), the aim of which is to guarantee or to increase the chances of property rights being granted. They are usually paid for their services by a monetary bribe, but sometimes also with access to other valuable resources (della Porta and Vannucci 1999: 35–37).

Using this model of corruption we can better distinguish it from other political misdeeds. Vote-buying, which is illegal in most states, is a subspecies of corruption: the agent is the citizen in his public role as a selector of the people's representatives, while the briber is the candidate or party who purchases his vote in exchange for money or other valuable resources. Other illegal activities are not structured in the same way as corruption. In cases of embezzlement, fraud and conflicts of interest, the agent misuses the principal's trust, but there is no third party involved. In extortion there is no exchange of rents, but rather the use of coercive power to extract resources from a private actor. In favouritism and nepotism – which are often not illegal, though they are generally considered morally blameworthy and therefore hidden – a 'client' (who can be a relative) induces the agent not to comply with his or her duties towards the principal, but no tangible resource is given in exchange: deference, gratitude and informal future obligations within familiar, political or personal networks are what is at stake here. Similarly, in clientelism the relationship is generally not illegal, while resources offered in exchange by the 'client' are political support or votes.

The informal obligations linked to clientelistic exchanges, favouritism and nepotism invariably present a potential for breaking promises: like corrupt dealings, the terms of their agreements cannot be enforced by public institutions (such as the judiciary and the police). Mistrust of counterparts, pessimistic expectations and opportunistic attitudes may then be fatal to these relationships, provoking their failure. Governance and enforcement mechanisms – administered by party organization and political machines and emerging within familiar linkages or through reputational assets – may nevertheless be available in these contexts. The illegality of corruption makes an important difference here, since in this case any mistake, quarrel, disagreement, misunderstanding, breach of trust or public denouncement might produce disastrous effects on the corrupt agent's career. They may not just lose an opportunity for profit, but violence and/or imprisonment too.

There is no doubt that corruption is an ongoing problem, to different degrees in different contexts. It is not confined to developing countries. Functionalist research was over-optimistic about its elimination. Functionalists suggested that corruption in developing countries had a number of positive functions in specific paths of modernization, 'oiling' blocked bureaucratic and political mechanisms which would otherwise have hindered development, modernizing the political system, lessening recourse to political violence, favouring social integration and economic capital formation (see, among others, Huntington 1968; Merton 1972; Leff 1964; Nye 1967; Lien 1986; and for a critical review, see Cartier-Bresson 1997, in particular pp. 52–55). It follows that: (a) since it contributes to the attenuation or solution of dysfunctional political and social processes which are its hidden generators, corruption tends to be a temporary and self-extinguishing phenomenon; (b) in more developed countries, corruption is a residual or marginal component of political processes, caused by a few 'black sheep', with few adverse consequences. In advanced liberal democracies in particular, the rule of law, the information activity of the media and the political control exercised by citizens should prevent systemic corruption from becoming established.

The benevolent prognosis of a 'transparent' modernization of third-world institutions, accompanied in their emancipation by corrupt-free first-world countries, has, however, been proved largely wrong. Not only is corruption still rampant in many developing states, but various international governmental and non-governmental institutions (such as the United Nations, the Organization for Economic and Co-operative Development and the European Union among the former, and Transparency International among the latter) have shown how elites in developed countries are *exporters* of corruption to poorer contexts – for example, where Western corporations obtain public contracts, pollute or get access to natural resources by paying bribes to local elites. Moreover, after the Clean Hands investigations in Italy and similar scandals in many other advanced liberal-democratic countries, the myth of a natural incompatibility between corruption and democracy has vanished. In fact, levels of corruption vary significantly among different democratic countries and, within them, within different sectors and public organizations. Nevertheless, democracy and corruption are related. Significantly, 'quality indexes' of democracy have utilized the variable 'degree of corruption' as one of the indicators of the quality of the rule of law and the democratic processes (Diamond and Morlino 2004).

Approaches to Corruption

To simplify somewhat, in the contemporary literature on corruption we can distinguish between three main general theoretical explanations: socio-cultural, political-economic and neo-institutional.

1. The socio-cultural perspective looks at differences in cultural traditions, social norms and internalized values that inform moral preferences and the roles of individuals belonging to different societies and organizations. According to this explanation, individuals are *pushed* towards corruption by internalized values and social pressures. Their sensitivity to opportunities for illegal enrichment depend on their moral standards and those of their peer group: 'for an individual, the moral cost is lower the more ephemeral circles of moral recognition offering positive reinforcement of respect for the law appear to him to be' (Pizzorno 1992: 46). Key terms associated with the socio-cultural approach are ethical norms, cultural values, traditions, civic culture. The crucial variables are operationalized in formal models as the *moral cost* of corruption, that is, the utility that is lost because of the illegality of an action. This moral cost increases with the sharing of a value-system that supports respect for the law. Individuals will suffer higher moral costs when, from the perspective of both their own ethical standards and those of their peers, corrupt behaviour involves a violation of values – such as commitment to public service, or to business ethics – which have been deeply internalized and constitute shared criteria of judgement. Moral costs in fact mirror social norms and ethical preferences and beliefs, as reflected in the *esprit de corps* and the 'public spiritedness' of officials, the political and civic culture, the political identity and 'moral quality' of the political class, the public's attitudes towards illegality and business ethics. Variations in levels of corruption observable across countries endowed with similar legal systems and formal institutions are then explained by differences in the size (and distribution) of moral costs, since 'people in a given society face the same institutions but may have different values' (Elster 1989: 39).

2. The economic approach emphasizes the crucial role of economic incentives and opportunities to engage in corrupt activities. People are *attracted* towards illegal practices by their *interests*, and the institutional opportunities to gain advantage from the exercise of public authority: 'A person commits an offense if the expected utility to him exceeds the utility he could get by using his time and other resources at other activities. Some persons become "criminals", therefore, not because their basic motivation differs from that of other persons, but because their benefits and costs differ' (Becker 1968: 172). In this perspective, corruption is considered to be outcome of rational choices, and its spread is determined by the structure of expected costs – the risks of being denounced and punished, the severity of the potential penal and administrative penalties – and the expected rewards as compared with available alternatives. Political economists have identified some opportunities and incentives that influence the individual calculus to participate in political corruption (Rose-Ackerman 1978), including: the costs of political mediation; the level and characteristics of state intervention in economic and social fields; the size of rents which can be collected by corrupt agents; the degree of discretionary power in the exercise of public authority; the relative efficiency and severity of various administrative and political controls; the types of the bureaucracy and procedures where corrupt exchanges develop (della Porta and Vannucci 1999). Klitgaard's formula – here

revisited – synthesizes the main variables influencing this economic calculus (Klitgaard 1988):

$$C = M + D + H - A$$

Levels of Corruption are proportional to Monopoly (the number of monopolistic positions in the public and in the private sector, implying the creation of rents), plus Discretion (the power to decide how to allocate rents), plus Hidden information (the capacity to use confidential information to influence the allocation of rents), minus Accountability (the effectiveness of state and social monitoring of agents' conduct). An element has been added to Klitgaard's formula: the list of potential corruption generators includes H, standing for hidden (that is, not publicly available) information. Bribes, in fact, can be paid not only to influence the exercise of a discretionary power, but also to have access to confidential information. The agent can sell this information, which has value for the briber since it offers him or her a competitive advantage, increasing his or her probability of gaining access to a rent following a certain official procedure.

3. The neo-institutional approach to corruption (see, among others, by Husted 1994; della Porta and Vannucci 1999; Lambsdorff 2007) does not consider only *external* variables – moral values or economic incentives – but also *endogenous* dynamics of corrupt networks and transactions. Once a certain organizational texture and 'cultural adaptation' to corruption has developed, governance structures and enforcement mechanisms provide internal stability to illegal dealings, reducing uncertainty among partners in relationships which appear more lucrative and less morally censurable. The co-evolution of economic incentives and cultural values, in other words, is path dependent. The heritage of corruption in the past produces *increasing returns* by neutralizing moral barriers, creating more profitable opportunities rooted in formal procedures and decision-making processes, providing organizational shields and mechanisms of protection against external intrusion by authorities, and reducing internal friction among corrupt actors. The influence of the legacy of bribery operates through several mechanisms. Widespread corruption generates 'skills of illegality', governance structures and informal norms whose force is based on adaptive expectations and coordination effects. Moreover, past corruption may influence its present spread through the activities of those implicated, who can use networks to obstruct judges' inquiries and strengthen expectations of impunity through law and procedural reforms.

What an individual may expect to obtain through involvement in a corrupt exchange – or, alternatively, through honesty – does not depend only on personal moral preferences and economic incentives but also on social interactions, the choices and actions taken by other agents, and the effects of these upon judgements concerning the individual's actions. For instance, where corruption is widespread, risks of being denounced by those engaged in illegal practices are lower; the lower the perceived moral barriers and social stigma of corruption, the higher the cost to be paid by those who try to remain honest. Conversely, when corruption is marginal, the search for a reliable partner in corrupt activities becomes more difficult, and reciprocal honesty becomes dominant thanks to self-fulfilling beliefs and a value-system sustaining transparent behaviour. Multiple equilibria – with ample variation in levels of corruption – are then possible in similar institutional settings, reflecting divergent beliefs and reciprocal adaptations of choices and preferences: 'people may have similar values, within and across societies, and similar institutional structures and yet, for accidental reasons, end up in different equilibria' (Elster 1989: 39–40).

As we shall argue below, the neo-institutional approach emerges as particularly useful in analysing the development of corruption.

Corruption in Complex Exchanges

Within a neo-institutional approach, political corruption is conceptualized as a complex system that develops its own 'rules of the game', that is, governance structures. Political corruption implies a complex web of exchanges of different resources, involving several actors, within which alternative norms and rules tend to emerge. In this complex web of relationships, a combination of *first-party* internalized mechanisms of self-sanctioning, reciprocal *second-party* bonds of trust, and other forms of *third-party* guarantees are needed, which allow the exchange of precarious property rights on political rents to be achieved. Various actors intervene at different points, supplying resources necessary not only to the successful conclusion of the hidden exchange, but also to guaranteeing its implementation: protecting actors from risks of external intrusion, ensuring the reinvestment of illicit capital and maintaining secrecy and silence (della Porta and Vannucci 1999). Additional players cannot easily be excluded from the expected benefits of the 'corruption game', since their involvement in the public decision making or their access to confidential information on illegal deals provides them with blackmailing power (della Porta 1992). In this case there are also illegal exchanges *internal* to each group of corrupt or corrupting agents, who have to share the expected benefits.

Often private citizens and entrepreneurs do not act as isolated counterparts in illicit deals. Entrepreneurs involved in corruption are sometimes organizers or members of explicit agreements through which information about public works is shared and bid-rigging is more or less scientifically managed. Repetition of the game is anticipated, and this reassures participants that individuals in the cartel will receive their share of profits. Cartels can obtain compliance by threatening potential free-riders with exclusion from the circle of 'protected' entrepreneurs. Moreover, cartels socialize individual entrepreneurs into norms of corruption, by justifying illegal payments as a necessity in order to 'stay in business'. Finally, cartels reduce the individual risks of singling out the politician or public administrator to bribe and bargaining over the amount of money to be paid, increasing the power of the 'private side' in the corrupt exchange through monopolistic practices.

Similarly, political actors involved in corrupt exchanges often simply cannot act autonomously, hiding their illicit activities from an inner circle of their own party's functionaries and leaders whose political support is necessary in order to enhance their role and career opportunities. Especially when corruption becomes widespread, parties may play an important role in organizing and monitoring the collection of bribes. First of all, they assure compliance through their control over public administration: 'rules' about bribes (with a 'price list' for different 'services') tend to be applied to large sectors of the public administration, weakening the 'exit' option for more honest or scrupulous firms. Parties may also socialize their members into corruption, framing it as 'normal business'. They may also reduce the risk related to the collection of information necessary to corrupt business, managing unofficial lists of loyal entrepreneurs (della Porta and Vannucci 1999).

Corrupt politicians need consensus in order to obtain the informal 'property right' to their official roles. In democratic systems this can be obtained via clientelistic exchanges with voters, using bribe-money to fuel political machines. Corrupt politician are normally very skilled in networking, building up circles of loyal supporters to whom they distribute favours (or even just promises of favours). Economic revenues from bribery are often reinvested in political activities, through which contacts are kept up and favours distributed in exchange for votes that reinforce the political power from which further money is illicitly gathered.

All these actors need 'cover-ups' and a certain degree of certainty in the corrupt exchange. They must minimize the likelihood of being reported and investigated, as well as of being cheated by partners. With threats and/or favours, the corrupt and corrupting agents must erect a wall of silence around their illicit dealings. This can be done by corrupting judges and/or the local press, but it may also require the involvement of bureaucrats, who know about hidden exchanges developing in their public structures. High-level bureaucrats, thanks to their specific skills and competences, could influence or jeopardize the corrupt deals. Alternatively, they may introduce valuable resources within the networks of corrupt exchanges: information on private partners and technical knowledge on norms and procedures. Moreover, bureaucrats, more permanently employed than elected politicians, can reduce the expected risks of breaking promises with entrepreneurial cartels; sometimes even directly collecting bribes which are then redistributed (della Porta and Vannucci 2005a).

The relationship between corrupted and corruptor may sometimes be made easier by the intervention of a wide range of brokers who specialize in illegal markets, where expected rewards, as well as risks, are generally higher. Middlemen may establish contacts between the two parties, looking for approachable and receptive partners, they may help conduct negotiations and physically transfer bribes. They also play an important role in socializing public and private actors into 'illegal' norms, and in reducing moral scruples as well as risks by collecting bribes, sometimes disguised in the form of formally legal payments for professional services.

When trust, repetition of the game, self-enforcing norms, and reputation are not sufficient to enforce illegal agreement, and avoid individual exit from secret exchanges, physical coercion may be required. Organized crime is therefore often an actor from whom corrupt politicians and cartels of entrepreneurs buy the resources of violence and intimidation needed to enforce their deals, to punish 'lemons' from free-riders and to discourage potential 'whistle-blowers'. Corruption networks are especially robust and durable where mafia bosses enter into the game, helping the career of political actors with the supervision of vote-buying activities and the direct influence

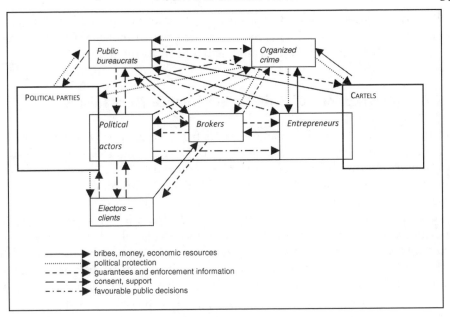

Figure 12.2 A complex network of corrupt exchanges

over packages of votes, and strengthening their reputation of being 'dangerous' to cross. Politicians and bureaucrats reciprocate by protecting mafia bosses from police investigations and allocating them bribe shares, as well as guaranteeing privileged access to public bids.

Figure 12.2 gives a synthetic overview of the multifaceted web of exchanges which can emerge from the interaction of different political and bureaucratic actors, political parties, cartels, brokers, citizens – in their alternate roles as electors, clients, vote-sellers, bribers – and organized crime. In order to understand the corrupt exchanges, we have to look not only at institutional and cultural constraints on the violation of the contract between the public administrator (the agent) and the state (the principal), but also at the involvement of actors skilled in delivering resources that are necessary for the development of corrupt exchanges. These resources lower the overall cost of illegal exchanges, by reducing their material risks as well as their moral costs. In fact, as actors multiply and the amount – as well as the variety – of resources at stakes increases, the increasing difficulty of anticipating possible opportunities and outcomes of illegal deals may actually discourage individuals from participating. Information, bargaining and policing costs of corruption are clearly related to the extension of the network of actors involved and the complexity of the decision-making context, which in a similar environment reflects the vague and sometimes obscure division of tasks, responsibilities and personal attributes among a wider number of individuals, increasing the risks of defection.

As in a well-functioning 'ordinary' market, however, so within the networks of corruption enlargement to new participants may induce some actors to specialize precisely in the production, 'advertising' and selling of resources to reduce uncertainty, favouring the convergence of expectations towards the desirable outcome of undetected corruption. Information and reputational assets, networking and illegal skills, trust and social capital, informal norms and constraints, protection, third-party enforcement: these are the most important resources that introduce a certain degree of 'order' and relative predictability within networks of corruption.

Institutions of Bribery: Governance Mechanisms

Institutions are the 'rules of the game in a society or, more formally, are the humanly devised constraints that shape human interactions', reducing uncertainty and trans-action costs (North 1990: 3). The function of shared beliefs about other players' expected choices is crucial for the understanding of institutional change: when observed actions do not meet anticipated results, a search for new models can lead (more or less rapidly) to the joint adoption of a new (relatively) consistent system of rules for action. From this perspective, an institution exists only when agents mutually believe in the summary representation (tacit or explicit) of rules which coordinate their beliefs: 'For example, even if the government prohibits the importation of some goods by a statutory law, but if people believe it effective to bribe customs officers to circumvent the law and make it a prevailing practice, then it seems appropriate to regards the practice rather than the ineffective statutory law as an institutions' (Aoki 2001: 13).

In illegal markets 'private-order' mechanisms and other governance structures assume a crucial role. The use of comparative institutional analysis seems to be particularly fruitful in this field. Investigating the institutional diversity and the complexity of organizational responses to the common problem of reducing the transaction costs of corrupt activities can shed light on the variables that influence the profound differences in the diffusion and in the characteristics of corrupt networks, recognizable also in similar political and administrative environments. In spite of high transaction costs, more or less complex networks of corrupt exchanges can develop with governance mechanisms that help to meet the 'demands' of protection of fragile and uncertain property rights. Such structures can sustain time-consuming bargaining activities in 'honest' trade relationships among different actors, generating stable expectations that constrain their actions within illegal contracts. Illicit markets are, therefore, structured by *informal* institutions and their enforcement mechanisms, which include self-sustaining illegal conventions, moral codes, self-enforcing contracts, norms of reciprocity, reputation, and third-party sanctioning, as well as several organizational architectures (limited in their scope or more elaborate and wide ranging), whose resources are used in order to protect illegal deals and corresponding property rights (Vannucci 1997).

Hidden markets for corrupt exchanges are characterized by three different – but interlinked – enforcement mechanisms that act upon:

  (a) *First-party control*, when the (illegal) norms and rules of behaviour are internalized by individuals;
  (b) *second-party enforcement*, when compliance is guaranteed by partners or indirect counterparts in corrupt exchanges;
  (c) *third-party enforcement*, which relies upon the intervention of external actors, capable of imposing compliance on those directly involved in the exchange.

First-party control occurs when the informal norms of corruption have been internalized to such an extent that their violation produces a psychic cost, such as feelings of guilt or discomfort. Enforcement becomes here self-enforcement: moral costs are not associated with a violation of the law, but with moral duties to respect the unwritten clauses of corruption contracts that we can call *immoral costs* (della Porta and Vannucci 2005b). When all partners (as potential cheats) in corrupt deals share similar internalized norms, exchanges can be successfully concluded. A potential basis for 'reliable' corrupt transactions is then the involvement of agents embedded in shared customs, ideological and cultural values (opposed to, or at least autonomous from, those embodied in the state's norms), which produce expectations of reciprocal implementation of corrupt agreements. One example here is the role of Italian party cashiers, who were chosen by leaders precisely for their high personal reputation for reliability in illegal transactions. They managed the flux of bribes and could easily conceal part of the illegal revenues to their party colleagues, being the only ones who possessed a detailed knowledge of the mechanisms governing their allocation (della Porta and Vannucci 1999: 97–99). Party cashiers acquired a favourable reputation in the market of corruption thanks to their observance of a peculiar norm of honesty, implying a complete respect for the obligations assumed in illegal transactions.

Internalized sharing of illegal codes and norms is, however, rarely sufficiently strong and generalized to discourage free-riders. *Second-party enforcement* occurs when sanctions are directly administered or credibly menaced by counterparts in corrupt exchanges (Ellickson 1991). The resources used to perform and enforce agreements are generally related to relation-specific expected advantages of a reiterated relationship. The establishment of personal trust can be interpreted in this perspective: when there are frequent bilateral opportunities for repeated interaction, being cooperative becomes an advantageous strategy, under the menace of termination of relationships (or other forms of retaliation) in the case of cheating. Moreover, the acquisition of a *reputation* of 'honesty' in illegal dealings, thanks to the circulation of information about previous behaviour within the restricted circles of actors involved in the corrupt game, facilitates the reduction of the expected risks of interactions in a wider network of exchange.

As the domain of the corruption network extends, raising the costs of the ex-ante gathering of information, identification of partners, monitoring and sanctioning of deceitful partners, the demand for guarantees and 'certainty' increases. A specialized third party, distinct from those directly involved in the corrupt deal, may then enter into the scene, selling his or her protective services. Either public (bureaucrats and politicians) or private (entrepreneurs, brokers and organized crime) actors may play this role, using different resources to impose costs on cheating or defecting partners. In this way they may secure a 'private-order' regulation of corrupt dealings. In illegal markets protectors are rarely neutral to the transacting parties: facilitators and enforcers of corruption contracts do not restrict themselves to prescribing rules for compliance, as in the idealized rule-of-law operations of a state. There are problems of reliability and incentive-compatibility in the activities of actors and organizations when they are involved in the market for corruption. In order to be credible guarantors, being accepted and trusted by corrupt actors, protectors have to control and exhibit specific resources: information and social contacts are required for brokers, control over political careers and public spending for party organizations, reputation for violence for criminal organizations, economic resources for entrepreneurs etc. Moreover, guaranteeing property rights and enforcing agreements has a cost, which is higher when dealings and resources are illegal or illegally acquired. At the same time, protection and regulation activity has 'public good' attributes that make them exploitable by free-riders to a degree. Third-party enforcers of corrupt dealings, with the exception of criminal organizations, do not use violent resources to gather compulsory payments for their protection services. They must therefore also police their 'extractive' activities, in order to motivate and monitor payments of protection-money. On the other hand, since the essence of protection consists in the capability to impose costs, partners of corrupt transactions must also be reassured that guarantors will not use their power in order to seize (instead of protect) their resources.

Conclusion: Systemic Corruption

We enter the realm of *systemic* corruption when the following conditions are met: (a) all, or almost all, activities within a public organization are oriented or related to the collection of bribes; (b) all, or almost all, the agents in the organization are implicated in an invisible network, which is regulated by unwritten norms and a commonly understood allocation of tasks and roles. Its activities include the collection of bribes and their distribution; the socialization of newcomers; isolation or banishment of 'honest' agents; measures of camouflage and protection from external inquiries; the definition of internal rules and their enforcement; (c) all, or almost all, private agents in contact with the organization know the 'rules of the game' and are willing to pay bribes in order to obtain the benefits allocated as a result of them; (d) third-party enforcers monitor and enforce respect for (illegal) norms, guaranteeing the fulfilment of corruption contracts and – eventually – imposing sanctions on 'opportunistic' cheating agents, free-riders and whistle-blowers.

Systemic corruption is not confined to developing countries, as is commonly supposed. It has found a fertile ground within public organizations in some advanced democratic countries. Because it is robust, self-reproducing and can easily become endemic, because it delegitimizes public bodies, and in light of the high economic and political costs it entails (including the costs of fighting it), corruption represents a significant threat to the stability of democratic institutions and to the success of democratization (della Porta and Vannucci 2011).

Further Reading

della Porta, D. and Vannucci, A. 1999: *Corrupt Exchanges. Actors, Resources, and Mechanisms of Political Corruption.* New York: Aldine de Gruyter.

della Porta, D. and Vannucci, A. 2011: *The Hidden Order of Corruption.* Burlington, VT: Ashgate.

della Porta, D. and Mény, Y. (eds) 1996: *Democracy and Corruption in Europe.* London: Pinter.

Heidenheimer, A.J., Johnston, M. and LeVine, V.T. (eds) 1989: *Political Corruption: A Handbook.* New Brunswick, NJ: Transaction Publishers.

Heywood, P. (ed.) 1997: *Political Corruption*. Oxford: Blackwell.

Johnston, M. 2005: *Syndromes of Corruption: Wealth, Power, and Democracy*. Cambridge: Cambridge University Press.

Kawata, J. (ed.) 2006: *Comparing Political Corruption and Clientelism*. Burlington, VT: Ashgate.

Klitgaard, R., MacLean-Abaroa, R. and Parris, H.L. 2000: *Corrupt Cities: A Practical Guide to Cure and Prevention*. Washington, DC: The World Bank.

Rose-Ackerman, S. 1999: *Corruption and Government: Causes, Consequences, and Reform*. Cambridge: Cambridge University Press.

13

Parties and Interest Intermediation

Herbert Kitschelt

There are two main ways of distinguishing parties from other techniques for pursuing political objectives: institutional definitions emphasize the arena in which collective political action takes place; functional definitions see parties as political alliances for solving problems of collective action and social choice. Kitschelt here combines the two approaches, asking: What are the institutional conditions under which the functional criteria for constituting a political party are met? Different institutional conditions result in different types of political parties: those with a programme that offer credible policy initiatives and clientalist parties that offer a direct exchange of goods for votes. In Europe, programmatic parties prevail and political sociologists have focused on their relation to social divides and cleavages. Another – oddly unrelated – field of investigation is that of party competition, primarily studied from a rational choice theory perspective. The study of party organization is rather underdeveloped – there has been a tendency to treat parties as unitary actors; the existing literature in political sociology is largely inspired by Michels' early work on party oligarchy. However, new controversies have been generated by debates over the precise form parties now take in postindustrial democracies. In the final section Kitschelt outlines two main alternative developments for political parties: the technocratic-monological model in which existing parties maintain their dominance aided by professional advice; and the postmodern pluralist interpretation which sees the potential for a proliferation of new parties appealing to an increasingly sophisticated and differentiated electorate.

Interest groups, social movements, and political parties are specific techniques individuals choose to pursue political objectives by pooling resources. People's goals are *political* when they seek authoritative decisions that are ultimately backed up by coercion in order to (re)distribute material or non-material life chances, rights and privileges. Whether political pursuits take the form of a *political party* hinges upon

The Wiley-Blackwell Companion to Political Sociology, First Edition. Edited by Edwin Amenta, Kate Nash, and Alan Scott.
© 2012 Blackwell Publishing Ltd. Published 2012 by Blackwell Publishing Ltd.

institutional or *functional* attributes that distinguish parties from other modes of collective mobilization.

Institutional definitions of political parties emphasize the arena in which individuals become collective political actors. Individuals form parties when they combine resources to compete for electoral office. The institutional definition of parties presupposes the existence of competitive, representative oligarchies or democracies. These polities confer civil and political rights on some or all competent adult members, including the rights to vote and run as candidates for legislative and executive political office, as well as the rights to articulate political demands, to assemble and to organize collectively.

Functional definitions conceptualize parties as political alliances that articulate and aggregate political demands, or, in a more current vocabulary, that solve problems of collective action and social choice in the pursuit of political goals (Aldrich 1995). Politicians solve a *collective action problem* by pooling resources under a partisan label: they make pursuing office more efficient for everyone without permitting free-riding. Parties may also solve a *social choice problem*: voters and politicians may have rather different personal preference rankings, but coordinate around one collective preference schedule we may call a party 'programme'. Anyone stepping too far away from that collective schedule or is unwilling to act on that schedule in legislative votes may lose membership of the party.

The functional definition of political parties is both wider and narrower than the institutional definition. On the one hand, it qualifies collective political mobilization as parties even *outside* the context of competitive oligarchies or democracies, provided such joint undertakings solve problems of collective action and social choice in the pursuit of political goals (e.g., the Bolsheviks in Tsarist Russia). On the other, it characterizes only a *subset* of politicians' electoral vehicles as political parties within competitive democracies, namely those that articulate *and* aggregate political interests. The empirical discrepancy between the entities that institutional or functional definitions identify as parties generates an interesting research question: What are the institutional conditions under which bands of office-seeking politicians will meet the functional criteria for constituting a political party? In a nominalist epistemology, conceptual definitions are a matter of taste, practicality and theoretical intuition. Once entities have been conceptually defined, however, understanding the way they relate to each other in the empirical world is a matter of developing theoretical propositions and testing them with empirical evidence.

I will first discuss conditions under which entities that qualify as parties by institutional criteria are also parties in the functional sense, that is, are primarily based on joint programmatic appeals. I then examine what sort of programmatic political demands structure party alternatives. This leads me to consider theories of party competition and party organization, followed by final thoughts on the current development of parties in developing and in postindustrial countries.

Before addressing these issues, let me note different respects in which parties may be analysed. They will appear implicitly and explicitly in my discussion, but do not organize the flow of the exposition. First, parties can be studied as individual entities and as elements of a party system in which several parties compete. Both levels of analysis may be intertwined. Second, at both levels, parties operate as (1) efforts to assemble coalitions of supporters, (2) strategic units in legislatures or executives and

(3) organizational structures with internal decision-making processes, or miniature polities. Both 'sociological' and economic bottom-up conditions, as well as political top-down strategies and institutional arrangements, may affect the behaviour of individual parties and entire party systems.

Programmatic or Non-Programmatic Parties

Politicians solve their collective action problem of running for office by investing in an administrative-technical infrastructure (clerical staff, communication technology, headquarters, public relations materials etc.) that enables them to harness economies of scale in advertising their candidates, to simplify the voters' choices by offering them recognizable labels on the ballot and even to monitor or physically ensure their supporters' voting turnout by delivering them to the polling stations. Parties solve their social choice problem by elaborating policy preferences across a wide range of issues, whether reached by broad internal deliberation or monocratic fiat issued by the leadership.

If politicians address neither the collective action nor the social choice problem, they have no party. We then encounter a situation of *individual representation* where personalities advance their political objectives based on personal public name recognition. Where politicians solve the social choice problem of rallying around a programme, but not the collective action problem of building an infrastructure to turn out the vote, they approximate the situation of *caucus or framework* parties common before the advent of universal suffrage; for example, in the British parliament of the mid-nineteenth century with rival legislative caucuses, but no external party organization.

In twentieth-century mass democracies with universal suffrage, electorally successful politicians almost always had to solve the collective action problems through organization building. But they do not necessarily solve the social choice problem as well. Political parties around the world often run without programmatic platforms that detail credible policy initiatives. Programmatic initiatives propose to compensate electoral supporters *indirectly* for their vote through policy changes that will affect citizens regardless of whether they did or did not support the party that won office. By contrast, parties without credible programmes may still attract voters by proposing to them a *direct exchange* in which citizens surrender votes, labour and financial support for parties, while the parties, through their public office holders, compensate these supporters through targeted personal monetary payments, gifts in kind, public-sector jobs, housing, favourable regulatory decisions or government procurement contracts. In direct exchange, only those voters who actually supported the ruling party or parties receive rewards. Under conditions of lacking credibility, direct clientelistic exchange may provide a new venue for parties to attract voters.

At least four theories, alone or in combination, vie to identify the conditions under which more clientelistic or more programmatic parties prevail (Kitschelt and Wilkinson 2007). First, *theories of development* argue that parties in poor countries generally, and parties catering to the poor more specifically, develop clientelistic linkages to their electorates. Poor citizens want benefits that yield immediate gratifications. They tend to discount the future and often rely on localized, face-to-face relations between patrons and clients. Conversely, wealthier and professionally skilled citizens, and especially in countries with greater affluence, find clientelistic inducements rarely a worthwhile pay-off (such as unskilled public-sector jobs or public housing).

Second, *statist theories* focus on the strategic choices of politicians with the introduction of universal suffrage (Shefter 1978). Where it preceded the rise of professional bureaucracies, insider politicians, originating from the pre-democratic oligarchy, availed themselves of state resources and patronage to build clientelistic parties. Where democratization precedes industrialization, like in the United States, clientelistic linkages may well pre-empt the formation of policy-oriented class parties by building constituencies attracted by targeted, contingent, patronage benefits. More generally, universal suffrage before professional state building undercuts program-matic partisan politics. This may apply to many contemporary Latin American, Southeast Asian and some Eastern European polities as well. Political economy comes into play here as well: the persistence of large state-owned, regulated or protected industries open to patronage may explain the tenacity of clientelistic practices in advanced industrial democracies (Austria, Italy, Japan). These arrangements come under duress through a growing urban professional middle class unaffiliated with the clientelistic party pillars of politics, exacerbated by the economic crisis of state-subsidized industries in the 1980s and 1990s.

Third, *institutionalist theories* argue that the programmatic cohesiveness of parties depends on electoral laws and executive–legislative relations. Where electoral laws personalize relations between voters and individual representatives, such as in first-past-the-post single-member district systems or in multi-member district systems with citizens casting votes for individual candidates, particularly if these votes accrue not to the party list as a whole (non-pooling), clientelistic direct exchange between con-stituencies and politicians is more likely. In a similar vein, presidential executive–legislative designs may encourage clientelism. The separation of purpose between elected presidents, serving a fixed term and responding to the national median voter, and legislators accountable to narrow legislative constituencies, may encourage the latter to emphasize clientelistic strategies (cf. Samuels and Shugart 2010). Presidents may be willing to provide funds for such strategies in order to build legislative coalitions supporting government programmes, but undermining the programmatic coherence of political parties along the way.

Finally, a fourth theory focuses on *ethnically divided countries*. Where mobilized ethnic groups build social and associational networks, contingent clientelistic ex-change can be monitored and sanctioned more easily. Ethnic organization helps to solve the problem of opportunism in contingent clientelistic exchange of votes for favours.

Beyond development, bureaucratization, democratic institutions and ethnic plu-ralism, however, the plain *political ideology* of a party may make a difference. Parties with universalist ideologies, such as market liberalism or Marxian socialism, tend to be more impervious to clientelistic practices than religious or ethnic parties. Never-theless, postindustrial changes in the political economy and exigencies of state professionalization, together with intense inter-party competition, may precipitate the decline of clientelism in a number of OECD countries.

The Nature of Programmatic Divisions

Inspired by the experience of European democracies in the twentieth century, most party theorists essentially take the prevalence of programmatic politics in which parties offer large-scale club and collective goods to broadly defined categories of voters along 'cleavage dimensions' for granted and primarily ask what sorts of dimensions are likely to dominate the democratic political struggle. Cleavages signal divides between groups in society. But this notion is very colourful and involves a great deal of conceptual ambiguity that requires clarification (cf. Lipset and Rokkan 1967). As a linguistic convention, let me distinguish between 'divides,' 'cleavages' and 'competitive dimensions' relevant for parties' programmatic appeals. Divide is the generic term for group differences based on citizens' personal traits (e.g., location in the social structure), organizational affiliations or attitudes and preferences (Bartolini and Mair 1990). Cleavages are those divides that are durable, usually because they 'entrap' individuals in certain social locations, such as class, or networks. *Social cleavages* are group divides in the social organization and public opinion outside party politics. *Political cleavages* are group divides mapped onto party alternatives. Not every social or political divide is a cleavage as well. For example, the question of left- or right-side driving in Sweden in the 1950s was a temporary divide that never crystallized to become a political cleavage. Furthermore, not every social cleavage translates into a political cleavage. For example, urban–rural divides have given rise to party alternatives only in a minority of West European democracies.

Competitive dimensions, finally, are only those political cleavages on which parties compete. They advertise positions in the expectation that they may sway voters one way or the other. Competitive dimensions thus involve voter elasticity, contingent upon politicians' programmatic appeals. Where voters are inelastic in their support profiles, political cleavages constitute *dimensions of identification* (cf. Sani and Sartori 1983). For example, religious devotion predicts party choice in many more democracies than the limited subset in which politicians consider religious-moral issues to be a competitive dimension in electoral politics.

The number of competitive dimensions in a democratic polity is typically smaller than the number of social and political cleavages. Some social cleavages never make it onto the map of political cleavages because the start-up costs of party formation are too high, the salience of the divide is too low, or existing parties have already partially incorporated the alternatives. Further, many political cleavages constitute dimensions of identification. Finally, politicians will do their best to combine salient political divides in mutually reinforcing programmatic packages in order to avoid intra-party conflict.

While restricting the range of partisan alternatives, voters may be amenable to this simplification of the political space because they have limited cognitive capacities to process partisan complexity. Conceptualizing political alternatives in packages on one or two dimensions is easy. Positions on a single dimension can be referred to in simple spatial left–right metaphors.

Sophisticated political sociologists always knew that neither a purely sociological bottom-up nor a purely political-elite-driven top-down theory of party competition could account for political cleavages and competitive dimensions (Lipset and Rokkan 1967). Lipset and Rokkan's famous four cleavage dimensions in European politics represent only *social cleavages*. The first two, the centre/periphery and the religious denominational or religious/secular divides, are associated with the national revolution of state formation in fifteenth- through twentieth-century Europe. The second set of urban/rural and social class cleavages relate to the social dislocations and conflicts brought about by the industrial revolution. Whether or not these social cleavages translate into political cleavages, let alone competitive dimensions, however, according to Lipset and Rokkan hinges on a host of institutional and strategic conditions.

Much of the literature since Lipset and Rokkan's seminal article has revolved around three positions: (1) *Persistent alignment*: Lipset and Rokkan laid out a configuration of voters around political party brand names that remain stable, one they had time to entrench themselves. (2) *Intermittent or continuous realignment*: Contingent upon changes in social structure and political economy, but also the strategic appeals of politicians from above, old and new voter groups, characterized by distinct bundles of interests, realign around partisan labels. (3) *Dealignment*: In an era of great mobility owing to the revolution in transportation and communication, stable relations between groups and parties will be replaced by single-issue-based, fleeting relations between citizens and parties. This detachment of parties from voters may be reinforced by a 'cartelization' of all relevant parties in a polity (Katz and Mair, 1995). As parties rely more on public funds than voter and activist contributions, their programmes converge and rupture the representative link presumed in the alignment literature.

From the vantage point of the new millennium, the original list of cleavages appears dated and historically as well as geographically contingent. Outside Western Europe, ethno-cultural cleavages that are not fully captured by Lipset and Rokkan's centre/periphery divide have certainly played an increasing role. The literature on social and political cleavage divides outside Western Europe is now growing, covering regions such as Latin America (Kitschelt *et al.* 2010) or Eastern Europe (Evans and Whitefield 1993; Kitschelt *et al.* 1999; Rohrschneider and Whitefield 2009). Within Western Europe, both processes of realignment and dealignment have proceeded that have shaken up established party systems.

One approach to the study of cleavages is inductive, based on survey research among citizens. While valuable, public opinion studies tend to inflate the number of cleavage dimensions, describe social divides rather than competitive dimensions and under-appreciate the *reductive effect* of political elites on the spatial complexity of party competition. Elite-centred approaches to determine the spatial structure of party systems, for example based on expert surveys or party manifestoes, typically find a lower dimensionality of party systems. My own favourite classification relies on three categories (cf. Kitschelt 1992). First, *distributive cleavages* concern citizens' desire for income ('greed') and derive from their market positions, based on their assets (skills, property), and their relations to the state. Class politics is a special case, but many other elements play a role (especially sector, firm, occupation and skill). 'Greed'-based cleavages concern the extent to which income allocation should be based on market contracting or authoritative redistribution of resources through the state.

Second, *socio-political cleavages* over the procedural governance of social organization ('grid') divide individualist and universalist libertarians who endorse a maximum of personal discretion over lifestyles and participatory decision making where collective coordination is necessary from collectivist and particularistic authoritarians who postulate the priority of binding collective norms and rules of conduct that cannot be violated and deference to political authorities. Third, *ethno-cultural cleavages* define group relations ('group') as whom to consider as member or citizen in a polity, as opposed those who are labelled as foes and outsiders. On this 'group' dimension, positions range from universalistic inclusiveness of all humankind to particularistic, ethnocentric, exclusionary positions, a tension that plays out in immigration policies and in deliberations about secession from, or integration of new peoples into, existing polities.

Group-, grid- and greed-based cleavages may be analytically distinct, but historical circumstances may often make them overlapping and mutually reinforcing, albeit in different configurations. Greed and group may be related. For example, where ethnic minorities arc both politically and economically disadvantaged, they may opt for a state-led distribution of scarce resources rather than market allocation. Conversely, ethnic minorities with economic advantages may favour spontaneous market allocation of economic assets. Much future research must account for contrasting alignments of political cleavages and their contribution to competitive dimensions in party systems, particularly in the more recently founded democracies.

Political scientists have considered both top-down, elite-led and bottom-up, mass-driven processes of political cleavage formation. Empirically, cleavage formation may involve both. Cleavages and people are not simply raw material in the hand of political elites to whom the capacity to shape and mould cleavages is then attributed (e.g., Przeworski 1985). But political cleavages are also more than a mere reflection of social structural trends in the structure of class, occupation or religion (cf. Elff 2007, 2009). Institutions, for example, such as electoral laws, mediate between social structure and party competition, albeit in complex ways that may defy a simplistic understanding of Duverger's Law (1954) about the relationship between institutions and party system format (cf. Cox 1997: ch. 11).

For example, to explain the rise of left-libertarian and right-authoritarian parties in postindustrial democracies, changes in the occupational structure, levels of education, and the role of women in business, politics and family organization itself may set the stage for the possibility of new partisan appeals. Whether and how such realignments occur, however, depends very much on the strategic configuration of established parties and the moves they undertake to secure their continued dominance, as especially the literature on the radical right has shown (Carter 2005; van der Brug *et al.* 2005; Arzheimer 2009).

The second perspective on party system change originates in Kirchheimer's (1966) catch-all thesis. It postulates that with increasing mass communication, physical mobility, and occupational fluidity, stable political alignments would melt away and make room for a pretty free-floating issue politics, enabling politicians to engage in 'catch all' strategies that assemble voters under the umbrella of a party however disparate their beliefs and orientations may be, as long as the party manages to invoke issues that resonate with different elements of the electorate.

While the demise of Marxian socialism, the change of the class structure of advanced capitalist democracies and the rise of mixed economies with comprehensive welfare states have certainly dismantled the programmatic alternatives on distributive politics that prevailed in West European democracies in the first half of the twentieth century, it is questionable, however, whether the party affiliations of electorates have become unstructured as a consequence. What observers in the 1960s and 1970s initially described as 'dealignment' has often turned out to be the beginning of a 'realignment' of political forces where distributive conflicts are cast in a new way and where they associate with new socio-political and cultural divides. Volatility in postindustrial democracies has indeed gone up, but to a far lesser extent than the dealignment thesis would call for.

Compared to postindustrial democracies, it is much harder to determine whether political cleavage alignments congeal in Latin American, Southeast Asian and East European party systems. Many of these polities exhibit strong incentives to build clientelistic exchange relations between voters and politicians that may inhibit the consolidation of programmatic cleavage dimensions. Furthermore, only the broad mobilization of socio-economic groups around recasting fundamental political-economic governance structures may make it possible to generate lasting partisan cleavage structures in the aftermath of major upheavals (cf. Kitschelt *et al.* 2010).

As a necessary, but probably insufficient condition of political cleavage building, democracies must have played the game of electoral competition over multiple rounds. Only then may sufficient proportions of the citizenry with relatively little political information and involvement have been able to acquire enough basic knowledge about their own preferences and the partisan alternatives that speak to them to stabilize political alignments. This process may reveal itself in a drop-off in electoral volatility, at least that share of volatility generated by support for new parties mobilizing outside existing alignments and appealing to voters primarily on charismatic personality or pure protest appeals.

Party Competition

The literature on political party alignments should have a natural affinity to the study of party competition, but these two fields have often remained divorced from each other. Whereas the former tends to attract political sociologists and comparative political scientists, the latter draws on economists and rational choice theorists broadly conceived. Whereas the former is more inductive, ad-hoc historical and empirical, the latter is more formal, general and deductive, but often void of empirical analysis (for an overview and self-critique, see Ordeshook 1997, especially 268–270, and Schofield 1997). More work needs to be done at the interstices of political sociology and formal theory of party competition and recent contributions by Adams, Merrill and Grofman (2005), Laver (2005) and Kedar (2010) show the way, albeit in highly distinct directions.

Pure formal theory, as first exemplified by Anthony Downs' (1957) approach, starts from a unidimensional policy world in which politicians can locate themselves wherever they wish and where voters support candidates who are closest to their own personal policy position in Euclidean terms. This proximity voting model, however, yields strange results, as Downs himself admits: two-party competition deprives voters of rational choice, because both parties will converge on the position of the median voter to obtain a majority, provided we buy into certain assumptions (such as non-abstention and non-entry of additional parties, short time horizons of maximization by both voters and politicians, and many more: see Grofman 2004). In multi-party systems, by contrast, Downsian voters can be rational by supporting a diversity of alternatives, each proximate to certain voter groups in policy preferences, but parties void these good intentions by the common need to form coalition governments again not straying far from the median voter. What is more, parties and voters appear to have been defying Downs' median voter theorem in two-party elections time and again, a fact that has contributed to the rise of the current literature in between behavioural and formal-rational models:

- Some share of voters may have passionate preferences that make them abstain and drop out of the electorate rather than vote for a party relatively closest, but absolutely far away from their preferred positions.
- Parties cannot move freely in the competitive policy space. They have to build up and defend programmatic reputations that make their strategic moves path-dependent, costly, and liable to discounting by voters.
- Neither parties nor voters (nor political scientists) can compute optimal equilibrium strategies for most real-life situations and therefore operate with behavioural decision rules of thumb as simplifying templates in an overly complex political world. These decision rules may themselves be subject to political debate and revision in light of observed past outcomes.
- Voters and politicians rarely calculate benefits simply over the choice for a single party or a single electoral period, but over coalitions of parties (or even coalitions of intra-party factions) and multiple rounds of elections in which parties may build up and change their reputations.
- Political actors are a heterogeneous bunch and party activists who contribute to parties, but for the most part do not aspire to run as prominent national candidates for electoral office themselves, may lead entire political parties to respond to the complexities of the competitive situation in distinctive ways that, at least with the benefit of hindsight, clearly subverted office- and vote-getting intentions.

Two behaviourally inspired theories have challenged other elements of the spatial models of party competition and called for amendments, if not fundamental revisions of the model. First, Budge and Farlie (1983) developed a salience theory of competition based on the assumption that most issues are valence issues such that voters agree on the desirable outcome (e.g., low unemployment), but ascribe different competence to political competitors in realizing such objectives. The competitive skill of politicians then consists in their ability to advance the salience of those issues for which their party 'owns' the credibility and competence attribution of the electorate and de-emphasize the issues owned by competitors. The problem of this theory is that issues can usually be mapped onto competitive dimensions (Hinich and Munger 1996) and thus can be understood in the spatial-positional model. Empirically, the investigations inspired by the valence/salience theory of competition employed measurement instruments that often led them back to spatial models, for example by coding a party's position on an issue in a manifesto, not simply the valence of the issue.

The other behaviourally inspired model of competition is a *directional theory* advanced by Rabinowitz and Macdonald (1989) and giving rise to a voluminous controversy (e.g., Westholm 1997; Merrill and Grofman 1999). Parties must express clearly non-median, though not extreme, positions on each side of an issue's positional mid-point to catch the voters' attention. Voters support the parties that have such stark positions on the side of the issue they are leaning towards, even if another party is spatially closer to the voters' position on the opposite side. While the directional theory may sometimes marginally improve our understanding of voting rationale, often enough its predictions are empirically trumped by simple spatial models of voting or provide only minor corrections (cf. Merrill and Grofman 1999; and Tomz and van Houweling 2008, 2009).

All of the sketched models of party competition take voter preferences on salient issues as given, but not as induced by party competition itself. Although there have always been claims that politicians shape social and political divides (e.g., Przeworski 1985), there is little systematic evidence of this being the case. For example, socialist class appeals could not rally the overwhelming share of the emerging working class in precisely those European democracies where the Catholic Church had begun early to organize the poor and eventually the industrial workers. The reverse does not apply: lower-class mobilization based on religious appeals was not prompted by the failure of socialist politicians to articulate a clear message. Nevertheless, as Lipset and Rokkan's (1967) work and that of later writers suggest, in the longer run, elite strategies at time t_1, such as the introduction of confessional schools or the construction of particular welfare state institutions, may have an impact on the nature and distribution of citizens' preference schedules many years later at time t_2. For all practical purposes, party politicians with relatively short time horizons of one or two electoral terms simply cannot hitch their electoral strategy to the expectation to induce a massive shift of public opinion towards what are outlier positions in the initial status quo. Thus, while ex post politicians' strategies leave their imprint on voter preferences, ex ante it is very difficult for politicians to choose competitive strategies with that purpose in mind. In the short and medium run, parties take the menu of policy issues as given, even though at the margin politicians and the mass media may manipulate programmatic impact on voting behaviour through strategies of information, priming, framing and persuasion.

Party Organization

Theories of political alignments and party competition tend to treat parties as unitary actors inside which the resolution of social choice problems leads to a single shared internal collective preference schedule. This idealization is useful for some purposes, but often unrealistic when studying parties' strategic choices in the electoral and the legislative arena. A theoretically guided literature on studying parties as internal polities with conflicts, competition, and coalition formation is still underdeveloped, but would nevertheless require a separate article. Both a more inductive, historical-comparative and a more formal, deductive literature take their clues from Michels' (1962 [1911]) seminal book on party oligarchy. According to Michels, democracies require mass-membership party machines. These, in turn, involve division of labour and delegation of decision making to leaders. For the sake of preserving their political office, the latter ultimately develop different interests than their rank-and-file followers and erect an oligarchy that supports the societal and political status quo, even if their constituencies and party activists demand radical social change.

The historical-comparative literature has developed numerous typologies of political party organizations (cf. Duverger 1954; Panebianco 1988). What underlies all these models, however, is the belief that in the late nineteenth and twentieth centuries, with the diffusion of universal suffrage as catalyst, the competitive struggle of parties necessitated the emergence of mass-membership parties capable of turning out the vote and 'encapsulating' electoral support, often in complex organizational webs which included economic interest groups and socio-cultural associations. With the advent of the modern mass media and the dissolution of tightly knit social subcultures, however, large party membership organizations have lost some, although not all of their political missions. Rather than physically turning out the vote, they provide the cadres of candidates for the large number of local and regional electoral offices that parties must fill and serve as recruitment pools for screening future political leaders who can transport the reputation of parties, among other tasks.

While docile card-carrying, but otherwise passive, party members are much more scarce in the early twenty-first than in the twentieth century, party leaders may in fact face more diverse, active and engaged party activists who exercise considerable capacity to move parties to and fro in the strategic manoeuvring of multi-party politics. More so than in the past, for parties to develop programmatic credibility in the eyes of strategically important voter constituencies whose members deliberately gear their partisan choices to party appeals, they may have to bind their hands by giving more leeway to activists in parties as lively micro-polities with intense debates and veto-players. An extreme version of this new dynamic of partisan politics may be postindustrial framework parties in which leaders, on one side, enjoy a measure of freedom in the choice of policy objectives vis-à-vis their members, but in which comparatively small and variable groups of rank-and-file activists, on the other, can selectively mobilize, team up with or supplant some elements of the leadership, and alter party strategy profoundly (cf. Kitschelt 1989a, 1994).

Much of the current analytical literature on party organization derived a simple model from Michel's theory, namely of a radical, ideology-inspired activist base of parties set against a moderate, pragmatic office-seeking leadership (May 1973; Panebianco 1988; Schlesinger 1984). This model may be more accurate in two-party systems in one-dimensional policy spaces, but makes little sense in multi-party systems in multiple dimensions, where activists could be preference outliers vis-à-vis the leadership in many different directions. Moreover, even in two-party systems the extent to which party rank-and-file activists are 'extreme' compared to the leadership varies across parties and time periods. What the coalitional structure of party activists is and how they relate to party leaders may depend more on political-economic and other exogenous societal developments than an invariable preference alignment induced by the hierarchical division of labour inside a political party (cf. Kitschelt 1989b).

As in the case of party competition, what is needed is a combination of insights flowing from the inductive, historical-comparative and the deductive formal literature to advance the analysis of party organization. The formal literature forces theorists to clarify their basic premises about the preferences and calculations of actors and the contingencies that affect their choices. The behavioural approach can explain how actors choose among alternatives under conditions of bounded rationality, based on beliefs, precedents and experiences, and thus do not take all the alternatives into account which a fully rational calculation of their best strategy of office-seeking would require. The behavioural models, however, have to identify how and why they restrain the feasibility set of the actors' consideration of alternatives against the backdrop of the underlying rational formal models.

Controversies about Parties in Postindustrial Democracy

Very few analytical subjects in the study of parties and party systems, and certainly none of those covered in this brief overview, are non-controversial. The prognosis of the perspective advanced here for postindustrial democracies is primarily one of 'party system realignment'. While old political-economic and cultural cleavages wane, new ones emerge, but in the particular environment of increasingly well-educated electorates smaller proportions of which are docile followers of large mass parties. This view has a variety of implications:

- Voters affiliate less with political parties based on socio-economic and cultural traits, but mediated through deliberate political preference profiles, albeit those may originate in distinctive socio-economic and cultural experiences.
- Particularly educated voters take the principal–agent relation in partisan politics seriously: they are not deferent, but mistrust parties and are ready to defect and switch to competitors, if their main concerns are not serviced by their past choices.
- In order to force parties to hear their voices, active citizens engage in many non-partisan political activities in interest groups and social protest movements.
- Because the political preferences of many voters have become more distinct, deliberate and intense, parties can aggregate successively smaller shares of voters. They move from being like encompassing department stores to becoming like 'boutiques'. Parties shrink because the distinctiveness of electoral constituencies imposes too many trade-offs on their appeals, when they try to reach broad audiences.
- Party system fragmentation and a certain measure of rising volatility are the implication of this tendency.
- The atrophy of mass parties coincides with an atrophy of mass membership, albeit the persistence of a core of party activists that may not be all that much smaller than in the mass parties of the past.
- Within these parameters, parties realign within a differentiated, at least two-dimensional space of competition in which questions of economic distribution form one dimension ('greed'), questions of socio-political governance (authoritarian-libertarian) a second dimension ('grid'), which is possibly fused or may be increasingly separated from a third dimension, namely the inclusiveness and exclusiveness of citizenship conceptions, concerning questions of immigration and multi-culturalism ('group').

The realignment perspective differs from two other perspectives in the recent literature on party systems (cf. Dalton and Wattenberg, 2000; Dalton 2003). The first is a dealignment perspective that claims many of the phenomena consistent with the realignment perspective to be consistent with its own interpretive scheme, but then also claims that voters choose parties based on single issues on a case-by-case basis devoid of underlying cleavage alignments, in a quasi-free-floating fashion. I see precious little evidence in favour of that perspective, as its distinctive implication, namely that voters' endowments and experiences in the economy (markets and occupations), on the one hand, and in the sphere of social reproduction (families and voluntary associations), on the other, are no longer systematically related to their political preferences and partisan choices. While old conceptions of social class and collective identities may no longer apply to postindustrial societies, new conceptions can reveal sharply articulated relations between social structure, political preferences and partisan choices, and even account for cross-national variance, as social structure may be mediated by the long-term, cumulative impact of national public policies, such as the development of welfare states.

The final perspective on political parties is that of the 'party cartel' thesis (Katz and Mair 1995, 2010). It, too, claims to find support in many of the phenomena that are also consistent with the realignment and dealignment theses, such as the waning of mass party organizations and the increasing diversification of citizens' political activities outside the sphere of electoral and party politics, including a certain cynicism and disaffection about party politics that comes with it. The cartel thesis, however, adds two distinctive elements, namely (1) that parties deploy public financing systematically as a way to make themselves independent of membership contributions and entry of new competition and (2) that parties converge in their policy positions, while voters do not, with the result of an intensifying failure of parties to represent popular preferences. What speaks against the first argument is that in fact in countries where public party finance has been most extensive citizens have supported the greatest diversification of party alternatives (cf. Kitschelt 2000). If cartel theorists embrace this as confirmatory evidence, showing that citizens are disgusted with established parties, their theory loses empirical bite: it would predict every possible outcome. What speaks against the second argument is that there is no evidence whatsoever that citizens' preferences are systematically further removed from their parties' preferences than in the past. On the most salient issues of greed, grid and group politics, the convergence of party leaders' and electoral supporters' preferences is still remarkable, and exceptions prove the rule: what was the gap between political elites across parties and their supporters on capital punishment in the past may be the discrepancy on the issue of European integration at the present time.

Few voices, however, expect the utter displacement of parties by other vehicles of interest, articulation and association, even though anti-party sentiments well up in many democracies. While democracy does not exhaust itself in elections and legislative manoeuvring where parties have their prime fields of activity, a democracy without formal rules of representation in legislatures, based on universal suffrage and the equal weight of each citizen's vote in the election of territorially based districts, is all but inconceivable. Corporatist governance of interest groups and direct democratic action by social movements may supplement the democratic process, but they cannot take over the task structure of parties in elections or legislatures.

Further Reading

Kitschelt, H., Mansfeldova, Z., Markowski, R. and Toka, G. 1999: *Post-Communist Party Systems. Competition, Representation, and Inter-Party Cooperation.* Cambridge: Cambridge University Press.

Mair, P. (ed.) 1990: *West European Party Systems.* Oxford: Oxford University Press.

14

Interest Groups and Pluralism

David Knoke and Xi Zhu

Interest groups in pluralist democracies aggregate and represent their members' political preferences. First, we define an interest group as a collective political actor seeking to influence governmental policy decisions. Next, we review recent research on US and European interest groups, highlighting their contexts and structures, strategies and actions, and influence on public policy outcomes. Then we assess policy network research as a distinct subfield that applies social network analytic methods to reveal how interest-group coalitions form and how their influence-activities affect policy decisions. Finally, we offer three suggestions for future directions in research on interest groups.

In pluralist democracies, organized interest groups aggregate and represent the political preferences of their constituencies. Their actions influence policy decisions that may benefit the public good or serve only narrow concerns. We concentrate on recent US and European interest-group research that extends understanding of these dynamics.

Interest Groups Defined

An interest group is a collective political actor that attempts to influence governmental policy decisions. Interest groups are typically formal organizations with a name and membership requirement. However, some groups lack bounded memberships, such as 'astro-turf' organizations fronting for wealthy individuals (in contrast to 'grassroots' groups with a broad membership). For example, during the 2010 elections, the conservative Tea Party movement was strongly supported by the advocacy wing of the Americans for Prosperity Foundation, an organization started by David Koch to

The Wiley-Blackwell Companion to Political Sociology, First Edition. Edited by Edwin Amenta, Kate Nash, and Alan Scott.
© 2012 Blackwell Publishing Ltd. Published 2012 by Blackwell Publishing Ltd.

further the environmental deregulatory interests of Koch Industries, an oil refinery and pipeline conglomerate owned by Koch and his brother Charles (Mayer 2010). We restrict our attention to voluntary associations whose members pool financial and other resources to engage in conventional political actions intended to influence policy decisions (Knoke 2001: 324). Excluded are voluntary associations without policy interests, such as fraternal, philanthropic or recreational goals. The primary vehicles for aggregating large corporate and small business interests are peak business associations and industry trade associations. For example, a month before the 2010 congressional elections, Rupert Murdoch's News Corp. gave $1 million to the US Chamber of Commerce, which advertised against Democratic candidates (Rutenberg 2010). Trade unions behave as interest groups when they lobby for favourable labour policies (Bradley *et al.* 2003).

Government agencies, legislative and regulatory bodies are usually conceptualized as targets of interest-group influence. However, governmental entities act as interest organizations by participating in coalitions or directly pressuring other governmental units. The National Association of Mayors lobbies on federal policies affecting cities, from transportation to police assistance and green energy. Similar associations promote the common interests of state legislatures, governors and local conservation districts. Social movement organizations (SMOs) are sometimes disregarded by interest-group analysts. An SMO is a formal group of activists trying to advance the interests of excluded or relatively powerless persons, such as ethnic and sexual minorities, animal rights, and migrant workers. Although SMOs frequently stage rallies and street protests, occasionally erupting into violent confrontations with authorities, many routinely engage in conventional tactics, such as petitions, media promotion, and litigation. Burstein (1998) made a compelling case that SMOs differ little from other types of interest organizations. Grossmann (2006) found few differences in political mobilization and representation between 92 environmental organizations and 1,600 other types of constituency interest organizations. Broad similarities occurred among 141 US advocacy organizations representing 19 ethnic group categories (Grossmann 2009). We concur that SMOs and interest groups are equivalent political actors.

Recent Research

The past two decades witnessed a surge of empirical research on interest groups in Europe and the United States, stimulated in part by integration of the European Union (EU) and rich data released under the US Lobbying Disclosure Act. We highlight three research areas: contexts and structures, strategies and actions, and influence on policy outcomes.

Contexts and structures

Recent work on the contexts and structures of interest-group pluralism includes the size of interest-group systems, institutional contexts of group formation, biases in interest representation, and group coalitions. Since the 1960s, the number of interest groups has grown substantially in both the United States and the EU (Walker 1991;

Baumgartner and Jones 1993; Baumgartner and Leech 1998; Greenwood 2003; Jordan and Maloney 2007). Parallel to this trend were declining sizes of other political organizations, such as political parties (Scarrow 2000). Knoke (1986) highlighted some historical events triggering the growth of US interest groups, including congressional reorganization, post-Watergate election reforms, waves of regulatory and deregulatory policies, an unravelling two-party system and ideological polarization. Mahoney and Baumgartner (2008) observed agreement among interest-group researchers that the development of interest-group systems was strongly influenced by the expanding size and breadth of government policy activities. Over time, comparisons of the United States and the EU consistently found that the number of interest groups and their scope of activities increased whenever the size of the government expanded. Baumgartner and Jones (1993) traced the development of US government activities and interest-group formation after the Second World War. They demonstrated that both expanded simultaneously, growing most quickly during the 1960s and 1970s, and slowing down after the late 1970s. Fligstein and Sweet (2002) and Wessels (2004) found a similar European pattern. Further, US federal policy activities both directly and indirectly affected interest-group mobilization at the state level (Baumgartner, Gray and Lowery 2009). Interest groups responded directly to federal policy by becoming more active in those issue-areas. The indirect effect was triggered by subsequent state legislative activities following the national-level policies.

Beyond general trends in system growth, researchers examined group formation by applying population ecology theory (Gray and Lowery 1996; Halpin and Jordan 2009). Population ecology departs from traditional treatments of interest-group formation, which emphasize incentive structures or political opportunities, by focusing on the institutional contexts. The rate at which a new type of interest group forms is affected by the density of this type within the entire interest-group population. Ecology theory predicts that the formation rate will be low when a new type of interest group is scarce, because the new type must justify its activities and gain legitimacy. The formation rate accelerates as legitimacy increases, but eventually the new type stops growing because competition resulting from a denser population constrains available resources. Several studies confirmed the predicted group formation pattern (Nownes 2004; Nownes and Lipinski 2005). Although current evidence is limited to interest groups working in specific issue-areas (e.g., gay rights), ecology theory remains a promising explanation for interest-group population growth.

One enduring effort is evaluating biases in interest representation. The bias question has important normative implications for pluralist theories because many scholars equate interest-group composition to political fairness. Berry (1994) identified two representation biases evident in the United States and EU. First, individual-level bias is the tendency for people with higher socio-economic status to participate more than lower-status people in interest-group activities. Second, organizational-level bias occurs when most groups are organized around business and professional interests instead of citizen interests (a.k.a. public interest groups, or 'PIGs'). Scholars have observed persistent organizational biases in both the United States and the EU (Baumgartner and Leech 1998). More than 70 percent of EU groups are business or professional organizations, while PIGs account for only 20 percent (Greenwood 2003). Business groups are not only larger, but have resource and expertise advantages, enabling them to exercise greater policy influence. Yackee and Yackee (2006), examining business interest advocacy on government regulations, found bias towards business interests in bureaucratic notice and comment rule making. Government agencies more often adjusted final rules to suit business interests, but not other expressed preferences. They concluded that these procedures did not succeed in 'democratizing' regulatory policy making. Persistently biased interest representation led pluralist scholars to abandon any presumption that proliferating interest groups equate to fair and representative politics (McFarland 2007).

Some researchers examined interest-group coalitions using social network analysis. Grossmann and Dominguez (2009) analysed US interest-group networks based on involvement in three types of political activities: endorsing the same candidates in primary elections, donating to the same candidates in general elections, and supporting the same legislative proposals. Interest groups were split into two coalitions polarized along party lines in primary and general elections, but not in legislative debates. In legislative debates, the structure of the interest-group network was organized by a core bipartisan coalition and a peripheral group of 'tag-alongs'. Winner-take-all elections force interest groups to make partisan choices, while law making is more multidimensional and encourages bipartisan cooperation.

Strategies and actions

The strategies that lobbyists employ to influence policy outcomes are a focus of much interest-group research. Whether examining external factors influencing interest-group strategies or internal group dynamics, recent research extends understanding of interest-group pluralism. Scholars challenged the conventional distinction between insider strategies (i.e., directly influencing decision making through contacts with the government) and outsider strategies (i.e., indirect influence through media or group-member mobilization). US and European researchers demonstrated that most interest groups deploy a wide range of lobbying tactics, including both direct and indirect activities (Baumgartner and Leech 1998; Binderkrantz 2005). In pluralist theories, most groups can gain some access to policy-makers. Yet, as political contexts around some issues grow more complex, 'insider' groups actively implement outsider strategies in their advocacy (Grant 2001). Binderkrantz (2005) used survey data on all Danish national interest groups to demonstrate that they use both direct and indirect strategies. Strategic choice depends on both political contexts and interest-group characteristics. Groups with privileged access to policy-makers pursue more activities targeting those officials, but absence of privileged access does not induce indirect strategies. Groups in competitive situations more actively pursue indirect strategies when facing challenges of attracting members.

Differing US and EU institutional contexts fostered diverging research on interest-group strategies and actions. Emerging multi-level EU governance structures and the Europeanization of interest groups inspired scholars to study cross-level 'venue-shopping' as an interest-group strategy. As EU institutions proliferate policy venues, what determines domestic interest-group decisions about where to attempt influence? Researchers offered somewhat contradictory perspectives on policy influence efforts at the supranational EU level. Eising (2004) found that groups unable to influence domestic policies often choose to mobilize at the EU level. In contrast, Grossman (2004) argued against overestimating interest-group ability to mobilize at the highest level due to EU-level barriers. Beyers and Kerremans (2007) suggested that choosing an advocacy level is shaped both by EU governance structural opportunities and by group embeddedness in immediate contexts, especially dependence on critical resources such as membership. Mahoney and Baumgartner (2008) proposed that future venue-shopping strategy research consider the political opportunity structures within which interest groups operate, such as number and openness of access points, political institutions and political climate.

In a long tradition of observing advocacy-related phenomena, US scholars sought to explain complex interactions among contexts, issues and interest-group actions. Several recent studies made important breakthroughs. Mahoney (2008) compared the advocacy strategies of US and European interest-group communities. She demonstrated that American and European advocates deploy similar tactics in argumentation, inside lobbying, and networking. They differ on lobbying approaches, targeting strategies, outside lobbying, and coalition building. Mahoney found US lobbyists more inclined to block policy proposals, target numerous policy-makers, bring issues to the public and construct coalitions. American groups are likely either to achieve all their goals or nothing, while Europeans tend to achieve partial goals. Mahoney's research highlighted the important effects of institutional characteristics and issue contexts on group advocacy behaviour.

In a relatively underexplored area, Beyers, Eising and Maloney (2008) called for more systematic research on intra-group dynamics and their relations to external activities. Strolovitch's (2007) work on intersectionality and interest representation of marginalized groups was an important advance. Strolovitch examined how advocacy groups represent interests and differentially benefit their constituencies. She found that advocacy organizations devote great efforts to issues affecting the majority of their members. But, much more energy is expended on issues affecting advantaged subgroups than those affecting disadvantaged, marginalized subgroups. Interest groups engage in different activities across various issues. For example, groups tend to engage in costly actions, such as litigation and coalitions, to fight for issues benefiting advantaged subgroups but not for issues addressing marginalized subgroup interests. Group leaders generally believe that benefits will trickle down to the disadvantaged if their efforts on behalf of majority or advantaged subgroups succeed.

Influence

In pluralist theories, interest groups play a critical role in democracies because they purportedly represent popular interests and serve as intermediates between citizens and policy-makers. Consequently, the legitimacy of pluralism depends on how much influence interest groups wield and how power is distributed among them (Baumgartner and Leech 1998; Dür and De Bièvre 2007a). Classic pluralists proposed an equilibrium model of political forces to explain interest-group emergence in democratic polities. People form groups and mobilize politically whenever their interests are threatened. In the absence of barriers to mobilization, opposing interests tend to counterbalance and constrain one another's influence. This dynamic leads to solutions that optimize the needs and desires of the citizenry (Truman 1951). Such benign views were challenged on their assumption that all affected interests would be naturally mobilized and fairly represented (Schattschneider 1960).

Moving beyond normative questions, recent research concentrated on identifying the conditions shaping group capacity to exercise influence. Dür and De Bièvre (2007a) classified explanatory factors as institutions, group characteristics and issue-specific factors. First, government institutions affect relationships between interest groups and decision-makers, which in turn affects group potential influence. The US electoral system amplifies politicians' dependence on interest-group resources to finance campaigns, thus enhancing group influence over electoral politics. In contrast, coalition governments, often found in European parliaments, may reduce political parties' reliance on interest-group resources and thus weaken group clout (Mahoney 2008). Second, such interest-group characteristics as resourcefulness, strategies and political positions (relative to other groups and government agencies) affect group influence. Influence may also depend on whether a group represents diffused or concentrated interests because diffused interests are more difficult to mobilize (Dür and De Bièvre 2007b). Third, scholars argued that interest-group influence varies significantly across issue-areas. Depending on an issue's place on the political agenda and how much controversy it ignites, an issue may provoke weak or strong counter-mobilization, which in turn affects how much influence a particular group achieves (Baumgartner and Jones 1993). Analysing a random sample of 137 issues in US interest-group activity reports filed in 1996 under the Lobbying Disclosure Act, Baumgartner and Leech (2001) documented a highly skewed distribution of group involvement across issue-areas. The top 5 percent of issues attracted more than 45 percent of lobbying activity, whereas the bottom 50 percent attracted less than 3 percent of lobbying. This distribution implies that issue context affects how groups allocate attention and influence resources. Dür and De Bièvre (2007a) suggested that public attention also amplifies the difficulties that specific groups encounter when trying to exert pressure.

Although researchers have long attempted to assess interest-group influence on specific policy decisions, little evidence has accumulated (Baumgartner and Leech 1998; Dür 2008a). Dür (2008a) noticed that researchers often reported contradictory findings from different settings while addressing the same research questions. For example, researchers found that concentrated interests considerably influenced some EU policy areas, but had limited influence in other areas (Bandelow, Schumann and Widmaier 2000; Michalowitz 2007). Dür (2008a) discussed obstacles that possibly hinder research consensus, including disagreements in defining influence, the complexity of influence pathways and difficulties in measuring interest-group influence. He suggested overcoming the measurement problem by combining multiple methods and collecting larger-scale data sets (Dür 2008b).

Policy Networks

Policy network analysts apply social network methods to identify important actors participating in policymaking institutions, to describe structural relations in policy fights and to explain policy outcomes. Achieving these objectives requires understanding the formation and transformation of policy networks, showing how political communication shapes policy proposals, and revealing how interest-group coalitions and influence processes lead to specific policy decisions. Over the past four decades, policy network research has generated new concepts and principles for studying policy events and demonstrating their usefulness (Knoke 2011).

Lobbying coalitions

A policy network is a bounded set of actors connected by one or more relations. Kenis and Schneider (1991: 26) defined it as 'a relatively stable set of mainly public and private corporate actors' whose linkages 'serve as channels for communication and for the exchange of information, expertise, trust and other policy resources'. Actors are typically organizations, such as interest groups, legislative institutions, executive agencies and regulatory bodies. Laumann and Knoke (1987) argued that substantive issues define the boundary of a policy network, which they termed a policy domain, a policy system whose participants are interconnected by political relations. Policy actors socially construct a domain's boundary by 'mutual recognition that their preferences and actions on policy events must be taken into account by the other domain participants'. Examples of policy domains include education, agriculture, welfare, defence (Laumann and Knoke 1987), health, energy, transportation (Burstein 1991: 328), labour (Knoke *et al.* 1996), telecommunications and homeland security (Knoke 2004).

Policy network analysis treats a relation (a specific type of tie, such as information exchange) between a pair of interest organizations as the basic unit of analysis. The overall pattern of present and absent ties among all participants comprises policy network's social structure. 'The perceptions, attitudes, and actions of organizational actors are shaped by the larger structural networks within which they are embedded, and in turn their behaviors can change these network structures' (Knoke 2001: 63–64). The probability of persuading legislatures or agencies to make policy decisions favourable to group interests increases when organizations pool their political and material resources. Hence, the primary political subgroup within a policy network is the lobbying coalition. Coalition partners all prefer the same event outcome, such as a proposed legislative bill, are connected by communication ties and coordinate their lobbying and other influence activities, such as media outreach and membership mobilization (Knoke *et al.* 1996: 22). By combining finances, expertise and political experience, coalitions can construct an efficient division of labour. Some interest groups mobilize their members to phone and e-mail legislators, other organizations use knowledgeable research staff to produce credible data, yet others raise campaign contributions.

Although lobbying activity should not be viewed as blatant vote-purchasing (Browne 1998), a winning coalition often makes a more persuasive case for its preferred policy outcome than does its opponents on substantive, technical-scientific, economic, social and, most importantly, political criteria. Illustrating these dynamics, on the eve of a crucial House of Representatives floor vote on regulatory reforms of the finance industry, Rep. John Boehner, the Republican minority leader, huddled with more than a hundred industry lobbyists and conservative political activists in a Capitol Hill strategy meeting. 'We need you to get out there and speak up against this', he said, according to three witnesses (Lipton 2010). Although the House Democratic majority carried that particular decision, Boehner's close-knit alliance of lobbyists and former aides representing large corporations, nicknamed 'Boehner Land', helped accelerate campaign fundraising for a Republican takeover in the 2010 House elections. With Boehner as the new House Speaker, his inner circle of lobbyists and former aides would wield great influence during legislative efforts to roll back the Obama Administration's policies.

Policy network research

Network studies of pluralist policymaking by sociologists and political scientists emerged in the 1970s and 1980s in the United States, Germany and the United Kingdom (Börzel 1998; Knoke 1998). The initial project, a community power structure study of a small German city, revealed how multiplex ties (communication, resource exchanges, influence reputations) among its elites shaped collective actions on community policies (Laumann and Pappi 1976). This approach was subsequently replicated in two small Illinois cities (Laumann, Galaskiewicz and Marsden 1978; Galaskiewicz 1979). Next, an 'organizational state model' of national policy domains examined networks in the US national energy and health policy domains (Laumann and Knoke 1987). Replications included a comparative investigation of labour policy domains in the United States, Germany and Japan (Knoke *et al*. 1996), and interest-group representatives in the US energy, health, agriculture and labour policy domains (Heinz *et al*. 1993). Key actors are labour unions, business associations, corporations, PIGs, state and local government associations, executive agencies and legislative committees. Because organizational interests diverge, no core groups can control or dominate policymaking. Instead, short-term opposing coalitions form to take collective actions in attempts to influence outcomes of specific policy events. After a policy decision occurs, coalitions disperse and new policy events attract other combinations of interest organizations. Despite such unstable microstructures, durable cleavages may emerge and persist, such as business-versus-union conflicts in labour policy and pharmaceuticals-versus-consumers in health-care policy domains.

German conceptualizations of policy networks originated with Laumann and Pappi (1976) and Lehmbruch's (1989) depiction of the West German federal system as generalized exchanges among interest organizations, resulting in interlocking autonomous policy networks. German scholars tended to view networks as a distinct governance form, an alternative to strongly centralized hierarchies and deregulated markets for settling policy disputes between the state and civil society (Börzel 1998). Absent a central authority capable of imposing national policy solutions, cooperative policy coalitions provided informally institutionalized structures for the complex negotiations required to reach acceptable policy decisions (Kenis and Schneider 1991; Marin and Mayntz 1991). The EU increasingly proliferated new policy domains and dispersed resources among public and private interest organizations. Overloaded national governments were compelled to cooperate with interest organizations during policy formulation and implementation. Volker Schneider's comparative studies of German and EU telecommunications and dangerous-chemicals policy domains exemplified the Germanic approach to policy networks as a distinctive governance form (Schneider 1986, 1992; Schneider, Dang-Nguyen and Werle 1994). He uncovered diverse governance mechanisms – from formally institutionalized advisory bodies, to working committees, to informal and secretive groups – that co-opted interest groups in policymaking.

UK political scientists tended towards more theoretical and narrative accounts of policy networks rather than formal social network analyses of inter-organizational relations (Rhodes 1990; Thatcher 1998). They conceptualized the 'policy community', a self-organizing network encompassing agents of government bureaucracies and pressure organizations. Networks grew increasingly prevalent in the British human services sector as governmental ministries, interest organizations and informal actors collaborated to manage a 'hollowed out state' (Marsh and Rhodes 1992). Marsh and Smith (2000) proposed a dialectical change model positing interactions among a policy network and its actors, its social contexts and its policy outcomes. They applied the dialectical model to explain transformative changes in UK agricultural policymaking since the 1930s, and UK policy on genetically modified crops and food (Toke and Marsh 2003). Kisby (2007) advocated adding 'programmatic beliefs' as antecedent ideational contexts in the dialectical change model.

Research on policy networks continued apace in advanced nations; for example, US water policy (Scholz and Wang 2006), Canadian biotechnology policy (Montpetit 2005), British hospital construction (Greenaway, Salter and Hart 2007), Greek rural development (Papadopoulos and Liarikos 2007) and Czech social welfare (Anderson 2003). The EU became fertile ground for policy network studies, with research on higher education (Lavdas, Papadakis and Gidarakou 2006), genetically modified foods (Skogstad 2003), industrial regulation (Coen and Thatcher 2008), European integration, agriculture and immigration (Kriesi, Adam and Jochum 2006). Most encouragingly, policy networks of non-Western nations slowly emerged: Chilean free trade negotiations (Bull 2008); Egyptian and Ethiopian water policies (Luzi *et al.* 2008); and Mexican forestry policy (Paredes 2008). Finally, some projects investigated global or transnational policy networks (Witte, Reinicke and Benner 2000) and international policy networks (Kohlmorgen, Hein and Bartsch 2007).

Future Directions

Our suggestions for future directions: First, study how changing institutional conditions affect interest-group actions. Second, compare interest groups and policy networks cross-nationally. Third, improve interest-group theories.

On 21 January 2010, the US Supreme Court transformed how interest groups participate in American elections. Its 5–4 ruling on *Citizens United v. Federal Election Commission* struck down McCain–Feingold Act prohibitions on organizations spending money on candidates for office. The policy change appeared slight: 'The day before the *Citizens United* decision, corporations had the constitutional right to spend unlimited funds telling voters that "Candidate Smith hates puppies." *Citizens United* added only protection for these corporations to convey an incremental "Vote Smith out" exhortation' (Levitt 2010). However, the ruling immediately impacted the 2010 national elections through unrestricted and undisclosed spending by corporations, unions and other groups. Interest-group spending on advertisements quintupled to $80 million compared to the 2006 midterms, with Republicans raking in 87 percent of funds (Farnam and Eggen 2010). Interest groups structured as non-profits were not required to disclose their donors in filings. President Obama complained of foreign sources illegally channelling money through the US Chamber of Commerce, allegations it denied (Shear 2010). The *Citizens United* ruling offers a unique natural experiment for investigating how altering institutional rules affects interest-group actions and outcomes, both electorally and legislatively. Ironically, donor secrecy renders data accuracy more problematic!

The 'comparativist turn' in EU interest-group research was clearly the past decade's major development (Beyers *et al.* 2008: 1293), but sovereign nation-states remain crucial loci for interest representation. Researchers must conduct more cross-national investigations of interest-group systems – particularly contrasting non-pluralist and non-Western polities – to improve understanding of how pluralist and elite-dominated institutions differ in policymaking processes and outcomes. Multidisciplinary teams of country specialists, possessing skills in survey research and policy network data collection, are indispensable for such projects. Unfortunately, too many studies continue to examine only single cases, with little effort devoted to integrating empirical findings or building a shared research agenda. Baumgartner and Leech's (1998) observation, that interest-group research tends to produce too many investigations answering overly narrow questions, leading to findings 'elegantly irrelevant' to one another, still aptly characterizes the field. Another assessment concluded, 'much we study, little we know' (Beyers *et al.* 2008). Making dramatic progress requires better interest-group theories to guide the selection of cases, measures and propositions. A unified grand-theory of everything is implausible, but middle-range interest-group theories might be feasible if analysts would collaborate in developing rigorous concepts, principles and frameworks with hypotheses amenable to empirical testing. Without theory-driven research, the accumulation of knowledge about interest groups will remain agonizingly slow.

Further Reading

Baumgartner, F.R. and Leech, B.L. 1998: *Basic Interests: The Importance of Groups in Politics and in Political Science*, Princeton, NJ: Princeton University Press.

Beyers, J., Eising, R. and Maloney, W. 2008: Researching interest group politics in Europe and elsewhere: much we study, little we know? *West European Politics* 31: 1103–1128.

Grossmann, M. and Dominguez, C.B.K. 2009: Party coalitions and interest group networks. *American Politics Research* 37: 767–800.

Mahoney, C. and Baumgartner, F.R. 2008. Converging perspectives on interest group research in Europe and America. *West European Politics* 31: 1253–1273.

15

Elections

Jeff Manza

Political sociological research on elections has been primarily concerned with investigating the underlying social bases of party support. Three issues are of central concern. First, there are important questions about voters, both individual voters and members of key electoral groups (in particular, classes, genders, religious traditions, and a wide range of other social groups over whom parties compete for votes). Second, political sociologists have been interested in questions about the consequence of elections: how much and to what extent do elections, as opposed to other political factors, influence police and political outcomes? Finally, the institutional context in which elections are contested varies.

In democratic polities, elections matter. They decide who governs, providing a critical mechanism for translating citizens' preferences into public policies. Elections also provide clues about underlying political trends. Critical sources of information can be unearthed in the details of election surveys: How are social groups aligned? Where do the votes come from, that is, which major social groups supported which parties or candidates? How do differences in turnout and/or the changing size of important voting blocs influence outcomes and impact the possibilities for the future? Understanding the social profiles of political parties – and how they change over time – is important because once in power, parties and political leaders enact policies that will tend to reward their supporters. The study of these 'social' bases of elections has thus been one important part of the tradition of voting studies, and the one to which political sociologists have traditionally devoted the bulk of their attention.

The range of questions that political sociologists typically ask about elections are broad in scope. Three issues are of central concern. First, there are important questions about voters, both individual voters and members of key electoral groups (in particular, classes, genders, religious traditions, and a wide range of other social

The Wiley-Blackwell Companion to Political Sociology, First Edition. Edited by Edwin Amenta, Kate Nash, and Alan Scott.
© 2012 Blackwell Publishing Ltd. Published 2012 by Blackwell Publishing Ltd.

groups over whom parties compete for votes). Second, political sociologists have been interested in questions about the consequence of elections: how much and to what extent do elections, as opposed to other political factors, influence police and political outcomes? Finally, the institutional context in which elections are contested varies. For example, legislatures can be elected through proportion representation, single-member districts or 'mixed' systems. Electoral systems vary in terms of their party systems, both in terms of how many parties seriously contest for votes and seats.

In this essay, I discuss some of the most important aspects of each of these questions, in order to provide an introduction to the study of elections from a political sociological perspective. To keep the discussion manageable, my focus is on research and findings for the established 'rich' democracies of Western Europe and North America, although many of the same points could be made about some of the newer democracies in Eastern Europe, Asia and Latin America.

The chapter is organized as follows. I begin with a brief discussion of why elections matter. I do this because much of the scholarly foci of political sociologists in recent years has largely centred on other topics; far fewer sociologists systematically study elections than a scholarly generation ago. That said, the field has been revived in recent years by the introduction of new methods, theories and insights, and the remainder of the essay provides a discussion of several of the most significant of these directions. In part two, I review what we have learned about the changing social bases of contemporary political life as read through democratic elections. Significant developments in the party systems of rich democratic countries have appeared. Among the most notable have been declining electoral support for socialist and traditional 'left' political alignments, the rise of what are sometimes called 'neoliberal' political formations, and changing issue contexts in which elections have been fought. Finally, the chapter concludes with a brief discussion of some of the questions at the cutting edge of contemporary research, and how political sociologists are pursuing them.

Why Elections?

Elections are of interest to political sociologists for three main reasons: first, because it is clear after a generation of research on policy outcomes that who wins elections does in fact deeply influence policy outcomes; second, because political sociology's focus on the causal importance of political institutions finds important expression in the electoral context; and third, because election results provide one of the clearest (and well-measured) sets of signals about how important social groups are parented to political life.

Elections influence policy outcomes

Let's start with why elections matter for policy outcomes. The answer would seem, on the surface, to be fairly obvious: elections matter because they determine who governs. If the ultimate purpose of having democratic elections in the first place is to allow ordinary citizens a say in the policies made by their government, then there should be some clear connection between election outcomes and policy. But the straightforward impact of elections has not always been so clear. Across the world, the election of either conservative or social democratic governments often disappoints their followers. Even dramatic changes in partisan control of government, such as the election of free-market conservative Margaret Thatcher in the United Kingdom or socialist François Mitterrand in France in the late 1970s and early 1980s respectively, may not produce nearly as much shift in policy as one might guess (see Pierson 1994).

But a generation of scholarship has explored the impact of partisan control over government, and the fruit of this work suggests quite clearly that it does (e.g., Hicks 1999; Huber and Stephens 2001). Perhaps the best overall indicator of the impact of election outcomes can be seen in the case of the welfare state. Where social democratic parties have long governed, welfare state benefits tend to be more universal, more generous and less subject to means-testing, and tend to be more egalitarian in their treatment of men and women (e.g., Esping-Andersen 1990). In polities where religious parties, such as Christian democratic parties, have been dominant but in close competition with left parties, social spending has been relatively generous but historically skewed towards re-enforcing traditional family forms. By contrast, in countries with weaker social democratic traditions, mostly notably in countries like the United States, Japan, Canada and Australia, social spending is lower, more subject to means-testing and less likely to produce egalitarian outcomes.

Perhaps the critical test of the hypothesis that elections matter arises in the United States. There, a two-party system in which both parties compete closely in efforts to attract centrist voters would seem to provide the least room for election outcomes to matter. The old joke about the American two-party system is that it consists of 'Tweedledum' and 'Tweedledee', that is, that the parties are largely indistinguishable from one another. Yet even in the American context, research strongly suggests that it makes a substantial difference whether Democrats or Republicans govern. One line of recent work has examined the impact of partisan differences in control over government in an era of rising inequality. Income inequality has grown rapidly since the early 1970s, but that rising inequality has occurred primarily during periods in which a Republican president was in office (Bartels 2008; Kelly 2009). This is particularly the case with respect to tax policy, where key changes under Republican leadership led to rising inequality. On other important issues, such as incarceration rates (and drug policy in general), anti-discrimination law and enforcement, business regulation and some social issues (notably abortion policy at the state level), evidence has now accumulated suggesting that partisan control matters as well (see, e.g., Jacobs and Helms 1996; Brooks 2006; Hacker and Pierson 2010).

Research on the connection between elections and policy outcomes is now moving into a second generation of scholarship, where more fine-grained hypotheses are being proposed and tested. In particular, analysts are reconceptualizing the complex interplay between institutional and political factors (Kelly 2009), as well as re-thinking key outcomes such as how we think about welfare state outputs (Garfinkel, Rainwater and Smeeding 2010), the complexity of labour market policies (Rueda 2008), the role of 'corporatist' political arrangements (Kenworthy 2004), and paying more attention to how public opinion and elections are related to one another and ultimately policy outcomes (cf. Erikson, MacKeun and Stimson 2002; Brooks and Manza 2007).

Electoral institutions matter

If election *outcomes* seem to matter for important kinds of public policies, it is natural to ask, *how* do they matter? One answer concerns the institutions of democracy, or more specifically, how election results translate into the creation of a new government. There are several ways in which democratic elections can be formally contested (Powell 2000), and then there is also a variety of underlying informal and cultural contexts in which elections are typically held (Tilly 2007). These institutional factors shape the party systems (for example, by creating high or low barriers to entry) as well as the impact of elections on policy.

How did these different institutions arise? The spread of democracy, conventionally measured by the existence of regular and honest elections with turnover of parties in office, universal suffrage, the right of anyone to run or form a party and a free press to cover it, has been uneven over the course of the past 150 years (Markoff 1996; Dahl 1998). The institutions of democracy were robustly established at the turn of the twentieth century in more or less the form they are found today, in only a small handful of countries. Even in these countries, most of which were in the Anglo-American world, the franchise had not been fully extended nor had some of the most important institutions of contemporary elections (such as the mass media) developed in their modern form. In the 1930s, a wave of authoritarian reversals dramatically reduced the number of democratic countries in the world, and much of the period after the Second World War was marked by democratic stability in Western Europe and North America and authoritarian governments elsewhere. But the recent period beginning in the 1980s, and especially since 1989, represents a clear high-water mark of democratic governance. The vast majority of countries around the world are now plausibly able to make at least some claim to being 'democratic'.

Beyond the question of whether democratic elections are held at all is the critical institutional context within which members of national legislatures are chosen. The institutions of democracy were robustly established at the turn of the last century in some countries, but not all. As electoral systems were debated, a key question was whether the elections would take place in single-member districts (most common in the Anglo-American world) or through systems of proportional representation (where the percentage of votes won by each party would determine the number of seats it would win). Eventually, a variety of systems mixing features of majoritarian and proportional representation emerged as well, although some type of proportional representation remains the dominant system throughout the world.

The research literature in comparative political economy strongly suggests that proportional representation (PR) systems are more likely to produce strong welfare states and public policies encouraging more egalitarian income distributions than are majoritarian systems (Swank 2002; Persson and Tabolini 2004). PR systems seem to promote universalism in part because legislators do not represent individual districts. They also typically ensure a broader presence of parties across the ideological spectrum (Lipjhart 1999). One estimate holds that the strict majoritarian institutions employed in American elections may account for as much as half of the differences in welfare spending in the United States versus Western Europe (Alesina and Glaeser 2004: ch. 4). To be sure, this conclusion has to be qualified in a couple of ways: in particular, the choice of electoral system is itself subject to other political factors (and occasional revision). Still, the conclusion that electoral institutions matter and that PR systems foster more egalitarian policy outcomes is now clear.

Another, less often studied (at least in relation to stable democracies) but clearly important question is whether democratic institutions are 'clean' or contain significant forms of 'patronage', subtle exclusions of some groups of citizens, or otherwise fail to foster trust and cooperation among citizens (cf. Amenta 1998; Tilly 2007). Patronage-based electoral systems – where rewards in the form of jobs or benefits are exchanged for votes through one mechanism or another – are common around the world. Whether because of patronage or other forms of corruption, electoral institutions that do not foster trust have proven inherently unstable, and encourage political actors to mobilize other ways to bring about social change. By contrast, social revolutions, or even significant revolutionary movements committed to the violent overthrow of the government, have not been found in any fully democratized country since the Second World War (Goodwin 2001).

Elections as indicators of group-based political trends

The final reason elections are important to political sociology is that election outcomes – or more specifically, election surveys – provide important clues about the political alignments and beliefs of key social groups (for recent assessments of the literature, see Evans 2010; Franklin 2010). Political divisions along class, religious, racial and ethnic, linguistic, national or gender lines have often led to enduring voting patterns. Elections are one place where such social divisions can be peacefully deployed, as well as measured and studied over time. The classical theory of group alignments held that once a group became embedded in the party system, it tended to endure and reproduce itself in the absence of some source of political change. The logic was that party leaders and candidates make similar group-based appeals and policy commitments at each election that are sufficient to 'remind' voters of their usual preferences, and a pattern set in that seemed to hold alignments in place pretty robustly in most democratic countries for several decades in the middle part of the twentieth century. Evidence of changing group alignments in many countries over the past three decades provides strong evidence that the historical patterns are indeed changing in response to broader social and political shifts. I explore some of those changes in the next section.

Social Forces and Elections

Are workers significantly more likely to support left parties, and affluent people to support conservative parties? Do highly religious voters align with conservative or religious parties, or do their 'class' interests trump their religious beliefs? What other types of group-based divisions are significant sources of political alignment? The most important of such group-based divisions came to be known as 'social cleavages', enduring forms of group differences in electoral preference grounded in a society's social structure (Lipset 1981 [1960]). Any enduring and significant social cleavage, whether based on class, race/ethnicity, linguistic preference, region, gender or religion, will exhibit varying degrees of expression in political conflicts at four distinct levels:

(1) social structure; (2) group identity; (3) political organizations and party systems; and (4) public policy outcomes (cf. Bartolini and Mair 1990; Manza and Brooks 1999: ch. 2). Social structural divisions give rise to groups of people with shared interests or statuses. Societies – even those as similar as the rich democratic countries of Western Europe and North America – will vary in the types of divisions embedded in social structure. While class and gender may be universal, there is considerable variation in other social structural divisions. For example, in the case of religion in some countries a single denomination (the Catholic Church in Italy, Ireland or Belgium, the Anglican Church in Britain, the Lutheran Church in Sweden) has the allegiance of most citizens who claim a religious identity, while in others a competitive religious marketplace can be said to exist where two or more religious blocs compete for members (e.g., Germany, the Netherlands or the United States).

Although the primary focus of most research has been on how members of significant groups vote, the impact of social cleavages on elections broadens quite considerably when we think about how *likely* members of a particular group are to actually vote, as well as how large the group is. A good way to think about how social forces matter for elections is to think about them dynamically, and ask two questions: where do the votes come from, and how has that changed over time? (see Manza and Brooks 1999: ch. 7 for fuller elaboration). This can be broken down into three smaller questions: (1) Who votes? (2) How are important social groups aligned with parties? (3) How has the size of key groups (and their change over time) impacted parties and elections?

Who votes

In some rich democracies, turnout in national elections is very high (80 percent or more). When turnout is at those levels, turnout rates among groups tend not to vary much. But it has long been understood that in elections where turnout is far from universal (either in countries with low turnout for national elections, or in local or other low-stakes elections in high-turnout countries), resource-rich groups vote at higher rates than more disadvantaged groups. For example, in the United States, a country with low rates of voting (adjusted turnout rates in presidential elections have been between 55 and 60 percent in recent elections), there is typically a large turnout gap (25 percent or more) between the highest turnout group within a cleavage category (such as professionals versus unskilled workers in the case of the class cleavage, or Jews versus those with no religion in the case of the religion cleavage). In all of these cases, group differences in educational attainment are especially important, and mediate but do not explain all of the differences between the groups.

One of the most striking trends in recent years has been evidence of declining turnout in many of the established democracies (Franklin 2004). Although the source of this decline is debated, the fact that it is as widespread as it appears to be suggests that downward pressures on participation are both general and substantial. Analysts have focused on a number of different issues in accounting for turnout decline (cf. Lijphart 1997). Turnout is highest in countries with mandatory turnout, although most have abolished those rules (most recently, in Italy and the Netherlands). Turnout is lower when national elections are held on a working day (as in the United States) versus on either a weekend or national holiday (Freeman 2004). One compelling thesis that has been advanced more recently is the role of declining 'social capital' among groups, specifically those related to social networks that promote political participation, such as in close-knit neighbourhoods or communities (see, e.g., Abrams 2010). The decline of organized labour has also been an important factor in almost all countries (Western 1997); unions are especially effective in organizing their members to vote, even when representing workers with lower education levels that might otherwise reduce their participation. The upshot is that to the extent that turnout decline in the rich democracies continues, patterns of unequal turnout (as in the United States) are likely to grow.

Voting behaviour

The second leg of the triad concerns the actual voting behaviour of key social groups, historically the heart of the political sociology of elections. Three issues are important: (1) How and when do key social groups become politically aligned? (2) How large are these differences? (3) How have they changed over time?

It is somewhat difficult to provide a comprehensive summary of the origins of enduring social cleavages in electoral contexts, as there is considerable cross-national variation. What is clear is that the timing and sequencing of the development of political parties are a key part of the explanation for how and why electoral cleavages take the form that they do. When the right to vote and a multi-party system arose together, early socialist and labour parties were considerably strengthened by the struggle to extend the franchise to the working class, advantages that they would preserve for many decades and which would drive high levels of class-based voting cleavages (Przeworski and Sprague 1986; Rueschemeyer, Stephens and Stephens 1992). In other countries, national or religious cleavages were as strong or even stronger, leading to a different pattern of cleavage politics (cf. Lipjhart 1979; Nieuwbeerta, Brooks and Manza 2006).

The general question of the size of cleavage impacts is also difficult to generalize across the democratic world. It would hardly be surprising to note that cleavages are larger in places where they are embedded most successfully in the party system, and/or when they continue to be 'activated' in particular electoral campaigns. The class cleavage tends to remain strongest, for example, in countries where unions are strong and party systems are organized along class lines. These organizational features – rather than the level of inequality per se – have been consistently strong predictors of the level of class voting (e.g., Evans 1999). In fact, one of the great paradoxes of class voting is that it is often highest in countries with the lowest levels of inequality, such as in Northern Europe!

Finally, turning to the question of change over time in group alignments, a wide range of scholars have argued that traditional group-based political alignments have begun eroding in recent decades. Some have argued that in recent decades a kind of 'new politics' has emerged, one rooted in conflicts over lifestyles, identities, symbolic conflicts and national identity rather than traditional social identities and social structural factors (Inglehart 1997). The rise of green parties and the increased attention paid by the major parties to new political concerns provides one expression of its potency (Dalton 1996). Another would be the resurgence of right-wing parties in many countries, who may draw support across the spectrum, including among working-class voters for anti-immigrant appeals (Bornschier 2010).

The empirical evidence in support of the theory that traditional voting blocs are dealigning is somewhat mixed. But as we approach the beginning of the second decade of the twenty-first century, it is now clear that important changes have occurred. The most careful research finds some evidence of declining levels of class voting, although not in all countries and not to the same extent (Evans 1999; Houtman, Achterberg and Derks 2008). Social democratic parties across Europe and elsewhere must win votes from middle-class voters to stay competitive. Conversely, conservative parties are winning more votes from non-traditional sources such as working-class voters, sometimes in response to nationalist or anti-immigrant appeals, but also by building a more diverse base for anti-tax, anti-government policy ideas.

The lively and ongoing debate concerning the fate of the class cleavage in British politics provides a good example of the increasingly complex overall picture. The historic pattern of strong working-class support for the Labour Party and equally strong middle-class support for the Conservatives long appeared among the most robust in the democratic world. The influential and innovative research of Anthony Heath and his colleagues presented persuasive evidence that while there had been fluctuation in the degree of class voting, no overall net decline could be discerned, for the period from the early 1960s onwards through the early 1990s (e.g., Heath, Jowell and Curtice 1991). The most recent assessments of Heath and colleagues, however, extending their analysis through the elections of Tony Blair and New Labour, find greater evidence of the erosion of the overall level of class voting (Heath, Jowell and Curtice 2001). A number of other studies employing slightly different models or assumptions, including our own research as well as those studies including even more recent elections, have also found even more evidence of decline in class-based voting in Britain (Nieuwbeerta, Brooks and Manza 2006; Evans and Tilley 2011).

While it would be wise not to overstate the inevitability of these trends, it is nonetheless worth exploring some of the dynamics of declining class voting. Some theories point to changes in the social structure of the rich democracies. For example, rising levels of citizen affluence and increasingly upward inter-generational social mobility appear to be pushing the children of working-class families into more conservative political alignments. The break-up of stable working-class communities, rising economic instability and the decline of unions has surely contributed to changing working-class alignments (and pushed at least some working-class voters into supporting right-wing parties). Increasing average levels of education are thought to provide voters with the ability to reason about political decisions above and beyond simple class-based heuristics. And many middle-class voters have shifted their support to centre-left parties at least in part out of concern for non-materialist 'social' issue positions (the rise of the so-called 'second left'). While no one of these factors by itself is decisive, in varying combinations they have worked to reduce traditional class politics (for a recent review, see Houtman *et al.* 2008: ch. 1).

Parallel research and arguments about the religious cleavage have also been advanced. Virtually every country in Western Europe has a significant religious party, or parties with significant religious roots (Britain is an exception). These parties are generally located on the centre-right of the political spectrum, and usually known as Christian Democratic parties. In terms of the overall impact of religious identities on voting behaviour, as with class so too with religion: there is evidence of declining religious voting, at least as measured at the denominational level (see Manza and

Wright 2003; Norris and Inglehart 2004). The magnitude of changes in the alignment of religious groups and parties has varied, depending on the structure of the religious field. For example, analysts generally find that Catholic countries, religiously divided countries or countries without a state church have higher levels of religious division in voting behaviour than countries with a state-sanctioned church that claims the allegiance of most citizens. Declining church attendance and rising rates of secularism have reduced the impact of religion on voting behaviour, although this also opens up the possibility of new political divisions between those who are churched (in whatever denomination) versus those who are not.

Perhaps the most wide-ranging debates about religion and voting have taken place in the United States. Here, the rise of a 'new Christian Right' (NCR) has been widely publicized, and viewed by many analysts as exerting a significant force on the party system (particularly inside the Republican Party). However, some of this impact has been exaggerated. Religious party activists associated with NCR groups have become more prominent over the past 30 years, and some have exerted enough influence in local or state Republican Party organizations to pull the party to the right on social issues like abortion. But their impact on voting behaviour has not been huge. Many evangelical Christians support Democratic candidates, and much of the apparent shift of Southern evangelicals towards the Republican Party has been part of a larger *regional* realignment of American politics that proceeded independent of increased religious political activism (cf. Hout and Greeley 2006).

The most striking change in the social foundations of voting behaviour in recent years has involved the rise of a new gender cleavage. During the 1950s, prevailing wisdom held that women supported centre-right parties *slightly* more than men, and data in many countries seemed to bear this out. However, this 'traditional' gender gap has been called into question by empirical evidence of a leftward shift in women's voting patterns across advanced industrial nations, starting in the 1980s. Comparative researchers have now converged on a near consensus that there has in fact been a rise in the so-called 'modern' gender gap, in which women have grown more left-leaning than men in their attitudes and their vote choices (see Inglehart and Norris 2003).

A broad array of factors may have contributed to this significant shift in women's voting behaviour (see Manza and Brooks 1999: ch. 5; Inglehart and Norris 2003). Many analysts have looked to the transformation of women's roles in both family and society – including women's lower socio-economic status, rising rates of divorce and non-marriage and rising rates of labour-force participation by women – which have worked in combination to push women towards greater support (relative to men) for left-of-centre parties. Although most agree that the structural factors outlined above are significant, still other researchers ask *how* these changes in women's life situations are translated into new forms of political behaviour. Some studies have credited the women's movement with raising the feminist consciousness of women by making the structural changes in their lives more salient and by infusing these changes with an explicit political relevance. Still others have examined the development of feminist consciousness itself as the source of the modern gender gap, although studies have produced mixed findings. Finally, a number of recent studies have found evidence of a distinct *generational* gender gap, in which younger cohorts of women in particular are significantly more left-leaning than men.

Group size and 'total' cleavage impact

The final source of change in the social profile of party support arises from changes in the demography of electorates. Many of these changes are well known. Probably the most critical have been changes in the class structures of the rich democratic countries over the past hundred years. The share of the population employed in agriculture has plummeted, and parties drawing significant vote shares from farmers have suffered. In the late nineteenth and early twentieth centuries, the rapid rise in the proportion of manufacturing workers fuelled the growth of the social democratic electorate. Today, we see the declining share of unionized blue-collar workers in the electorates of the rich democracies and the rising share of secular voters across Europe (and to a lesser, but still significant, extent in the United States).

Looking at the big picture, it is clear that however we think about it, social divisions in the electorate remain important sources of voting behaviour and electoral change, even as the specific patterning of groups and votes has changed in significant ways since the 1970s. Some of the changes we are observing in the social bases of voting are linked; it is almost certain, for example, that the increase in the gender gap is associated with the decline of class voting; as economies shift the mix of jobs towards a higher proportion of service-sector jobs and labour-force participation of women increases, one 'traditional' pattern declines but a new one opens up. This does not necessarily mean that there will be a definitive swing towards the left or the right; the vote shares of centre-right and centre-left parties have fluctuated over the past three decades without showing marked change. But the changing composition of the parties – where the votes come from – is likely related to changes in party platforms and campaign strategies. It is hard to imagine, for example, the shift of social democratic parties towards the political centre without understanding the steady change in the underlying foundation of their electorates. The only thing we can be certain about is that these changes will continue for the foreseeable future, and are well worth paying attention to alongside our usual interest in who wins the election.

The Future of Election Studies in Political Sociology: The Return of Contextual Analysis

In this concluding section, I want to turn briefly to some comments about the place of political sociology, and sociological ideas, in the study of elections as a whole. While the classical political sociological traditions and questions outlined in this chapter continue to be vital topics of investigation, the most influential work in the field of election studies long ago migrated from political sociology to political science. Indeed, one highly stylized view of the history of the field of voting studies holds that while the paths charted by the early political sociology of voting behaviour – with their characteristic focus on social groups and networks – dominated the agenda, these approaches already began to give way in the late 1950s to purely individual-level approaches to understanding political behaviour. In particular, the appearance of Anthony Downs' *An Economic Approach to Politics* (1957) and Angus Campbell and colleagues' *The American Voter* (1960) would sweep the field of voting studies. Campbell and his 'Michigan School' colleagues' social psychological framework moved the social context of political behaviour to the 'back-end' of the 'funnel of causality', suggesting that group influence on elections manifests itself largely in individual identification with group categories ('I am a worker'). By the late 1970s, rational choice theory largely inaugurated by Downs was increasingly displacing Michigan-style voting studies, sharpening the turn towards individual-level assumptions and moving even further away from the contexts of individual voting behaviour.

In spite of their many other differences, both the social psychological approach of the Michigan School and RCT (Rational Choice Theory) share the view that it is the preferences and partisan histories of individuals – not the social groups they are embedded in – that provide the key to unlocking the mysteries underlying vote choice. The rapid move to intellectual dominance of the field of political behaviour first by the Michigan School and later RCT had a transformative effect. In the 40 years following the publication of the two landmark texts, virtually all of the major or influential works on voting built upon the foundations of one or the other. At the same time, political sociologists abandoned the field of voting studies altogether (see Manza, Brooks and Sauder 2004).

Yet over the past decade, a renewal of interest in how the *social* context of politics matters has begun to reemerge. A couple of major motivations for its re-emergence can be identified. First, the insights of individual-level models long dominant in political science have not been able to satisfactorily answer some important empirical puzzles. For example, why is turnout higher in some countries or regions than others? Or why are the class cleavages in voting often higher in countries with less inequality than those with more inequality? Both of these puzzles have remained impervious to individual-level analysis and theory. For example, Americans do not vote at dramatically lower rates than Europeans because they are less well educated, less informed or less interested in politics. Controlling for these individual-level factors will simply not explain the enormous cross-national differences. At the same time, within-country analyses have cast doubt on whether institutional differences alone are sufficient: for example, while in many parts of the United States voter registration requirements may reduce turnout, a number of states have moved towards same-day registration that has had at best a mixed impact on turnout (see Freeman 2004 for a review). In the case of class voting, without an analysis of the context provided by strong or weak unions and social democratic parties it is impossible to understand – purely from the standpoint of individual voters – why class voting does not increase as inequality increases.

Given such shortcomings, renewed interested in how the *social contexts* of politics matters has begun to reappear. Recent scholarship is returning to examine the neglected role of social groups, social networks and organizational contexts in shaping the patterning of political participation and voting behaviour (e.g., Leighley 2001; Zuckerman 2006; Mutz 2006). In particular, evidence is beginning to mount suggesting that interpersonal discussion networks are important influences on political behaviour (Huckfeldt and Sprague 1995; Mutz 2006). Baldassari and her colleagues (Baldassari and Berman 2007; Baldassari and Gelman 2008) develop models of opinion polarization that arise out of network processes. Weeden and Grusky (2005) propose to move the analysis of class politics to the level of occupation, where individuals interact most closely with one another and are most likely to develop group consciousness.

While this work is still in its infancy, it suggests enough promise to lead us to suspect that a rethinking of the relationship between political sociology and the orthodoxies of political science in the field of voting studies is in the offing. Combined with changes in party systems in many democratic countries, this suggests the possibility of fruitful new investigations. Given this, research on elections and the social bases of voting and political participation is likely to remain an important topic in the field of political sociology.

Further Reading

Bartels, L. 2008. *Unequal Democracy*. New York: Russell Sage Foundation Press.

Franklin, M. (ed.) 2004. *Voter Turnout and the Dynamics of Electoral Competition in Established Democracies Since 1945*. New York: Cambridge University Press.

Manza, J. and Brooks, C. 1999. *Social Cleavages and Political Change*. New York: Oxford University Press.

Norris, P. 2004. *Electoral Engineering: Voting Rules and Political Behavior*. New York: Cambridge University Press.

Zuckerman, A. (ed.) 2006. *The Social Logic of Politics*, Philadelphia, PA: Temple University Press.

16

War

ANTOINE BOUSQUET

The study of war as an object of social theory has in recent decades finally begun to receive the attention that such an enduring and multifaceted phenomenon merits. Indeed, the history of armed conflict is closely connected to the emergence of the modern world, the rise of the nation-state and the development of industrial capitalism, as the work of prominent historical sociologists has now shown. The ways in which societies fight and organize military force can thus shed invaluable light on their wider social and cultural dynamics, revealing the workings of some of their most intimate mechanisms of social power and the roles played by discipline, rationalization and technoscience. Further analytical challenges await those scholars seeking to grapple with the ongoing transformations of war in a globalizing world, from the changing relations of military institutions to civil society in the developed world to the occurrence of 'new wars' and the resurgence of non-state actors contesting the state's monopoly on violence.

While war seemingly has been a perennial feature of human societies as far back as we can trace them (Keeley 1996), it has been the recipient of surprisingly limited socio-logical analysis until recently. Despite abundant evidence to the contrary throughout the twentieth century, sociology in the main inherited one of the most prevalent assumptions of social theorists in the nineteenth century, namely that of the archaic character, and thus increasing irrelevance, of war. It was then widely held, including by critics of capitalism such as Marx, that the emerging global order of bourgeois societies, bound by trade and commerce and guided by rational economic self-interest rather than by dynastic pride or religious zealotry, was inherently pacifistic (Mann 1984). Subsequent neglect of the question of war in sociological scholarship may therefore be at least partly accounted for by the lasting legacy of the habits of thought of its founding figures in this respect. Furthermore, in making relations between state and society its central focus,

The Wiley-Blackwell Companion to Political Sociology, First Edition. Edited by Edwin Amenta, Kate Nash, and Alan Scott.
© 2012 Blackwell Publishing Ltd. Published 2012 by Blackwell Publishing Ltd.

political sociology has generally located its analysis at the level of the internal dynamics of bounded political communities, a restriction that allows at best for only a partial understanding of a phenomenon pitting such groups against one another.

The younger discipline of international relations was explicitly founded to undertake the task of studying the external relations of states with each other and took as one of its central ambitions to understand and limit, if not entirely prevent, the recurrence of interstate war. While disagreements abound among scholars over the causes of war and the means and likelihood of averting it, the latent possibility of armed conflict is generally seen as a fundamental structural condition of international politics. However, in making the international its *raison d'être*, the discipline has in turn all too often eschewed consideration of the domestic sphere, without which any rounded understanding of war is all but impossible. Perhaps for this very reason, war per se is rarely the focus of study in the field and generally considered to be only of interest to students of military strategy. And while any sociological study of war will necessarily entail some engagement with strategic thinking given its predominance within military institutions, the primary concern of strategic studies is with the narrow question of the most efficient and successful deployments and uses of military force, with wider social processes considered only insofar as they directly impact on the above.

Historians are by nature less instrumentally minded and more naturally inclined to consider both the wider contexts in which specific wars have taken place as well as their finer details. However, we find here again within the field an unfortunate division of academic labour, which has seen military history and broader social history develop into distinct traditions that have by and large avoided meaningful dialogue and potentially fruitful cross-pollination. Many strands of historical writing have thus tended to treat wars as essentially episodic bouts of organized violence interrupting the regular course of political and social life. Accordingly, while wars have been considered worthy of in-depth research as to their causes and their aftermath by historians of this disposition, the assumption that the conduct of wars is itself so different from ordinary social life has fuelled the notion that they have little to tell us about contemporary society as a whole. Conversely, military history has largely evolved as a separate sphere of historical research from that of the rest of the field, with a tendency among practitioners to focus on narrow areas of expertise, most frequently accounts of battles, tactical manoeuvres and the decisions of military leaders that have been dubbed, essentially pejoratively, 'drums and trumpets' history. All too often, this literature has been reticent to engage or take on any of the findings in wider historiography and the social sciences (Black 2004).

Twenty years ago, Martin Shaw could thus incisively sum up the essence of this enduring blind spot in the scholarship:

> Most thinkers about society have not been able to grasp the huge problem which war poses for our understanding of society in general: they have marginalized it, treated it as exceptional, abnormal, etc. Most thinkers about war, on the other hand, have tended to treat it as if it were a self-contained process, certainly depending on society for its resources, but ultimately operating according to its own laws ... The problem of war and society can therefore be seen as a dilemma, the horns of which have been tackled separately by social and military theory, but the heart of which has rarely been exposed.
> (1988: 10)

A growing if unsystematic realization of the deficiencies of existing accounts of war in the aforementioned fields can be dated to back to the late 1970s, leading to a first wave of influential publications in the following decade. Some earlier moves had been made in the area of military history, notably through the figure of Michael Howard, who had expressed discontent with the state of his discipline as far back as the 1950s and had with *The Franco-Prussian War* (1961) undertaken to provide an account of the political and social context of the conflict. Howard subsequently observed in his synthetic *War in European History* (1976) that:

> to abstract war from the environment in which it is fought and study its techniques as one would those of a game is to ignore a dimension essential to the understanding, not simply of the wars themselves, but of the societies which fought them ... War has been part of a totality of human experience, the parts of which can be understood only in relation to one another.
>
> (ix)

If this last sentence would be worthy of being enshrined as the guiding motto for any serious sociological engagement with war and notwithstanding the significance of his contributions to advancing military history, Howard's work essentially remained within the conventional historiographical tradition centred on narrative and shunning any explicitly theoretical approach to the subject matter. The study of war would thus await the engagement of sociologists and more theoretically inclined historians to receive its proper treatment as an object of social theory. The first prolific site of such an encounter was to be the nexus point of war with two other classical concerns of sociology, namely capitalism and the nation-state.

War, Capitalism and the Rise of the Nation-State

The growth in interest for war within political sociology was sparked by a wider critique of historical materialism and its reduction of the state to a superstructural effect of economic forces and mere instrument of class rule. Drawing on Weber, scholars such as Anthony Giddens and Michael Mann argued for the autonomy of the modern state as a process of monopolization of violence and internal pacification characterized by the development of centralized bureaucratic power and distinct from, if necessarily entangled with, the emergence of capitalism. Crucially, they also perceived that concomitant to the domestic monopolization of violence by territorially bounded authorities was an increase in the intensity of armed conflict between such entities. The role of the bureaucratic state as a formidable war machine would therefore have to be a significant feature of any complete social theory.

In *The Nation-State and Violence*, Giddens thereby sought to approach 'surveillance and control of the means of violence' as 'independent influences upon the development of modernity' from those of capitalism and class conflict (1985: 2). As for Mann, he laid out his case for a reconsideration of the role of the state in sociological analysis in a few important pieces such as 'Capitalism and Militarism' (1984) and 'The Autonomous Power of the State' (1986 [1984]), subsequently deploying those insights in his ambitious and yet to be completed trilogy *The Sources of Social Power* (1986, 1993). In the first of those contributions, Mann found that militarism is neither caused nor remediated by capitalism but rather that its origin is to be found in the contingent persistence of a multi-state system that predates capitalism and in which 'warfare has been a normal, and often rational, element throughout recorded history' (1984: 45). The industrial and technological power unleashed by capitalism did nevertheless enable the tremendous escalation in the destructiveness and reach of war, all the way to the nuclear sword of Damocles that now permanently hangs over the world. However, in seeking to wrench militarism from economistic interpretations, Mann ends up adopting a position very close to that of international relations realists and their view of ceaseless competition between states in an anarchical international system, a view that is habitually attacked for both its alleged reductionism and neglect of the domestic and ultimately tells us little about war itself.

Rather than assume a perennial multi-state system that would give states their militarist character, it may be preferable to develop a more sophisticated account of the co-evolution of domestic and international spheres and the regulation of violence this division both required and sustained. Indeed, the monopolization of violence by states cannot be properly understood with exclusive reference to processes internal to them but must also be situated in the context of the emergence of a modern system of states that established the rules and norms of behaviour that still structure contemporary international relations. The domestic elimination and co-option of potential rivals and recalcitrant remnants of the feudal era was thus mirrored by the joint efforts of states to disarm and delegitimize transnational non-state actors such as pirates and mercenaries so that violence in the modern era was progressively 'dedemocratized, demarketized, and territorialized' (Thomson 1996: 4). The ascent of the state form as the sole legitimate wielder of force was hence the outcome of a global systemic process that participated in the very constitution and reproduction of the partition between domestic and international. It is this multifaceted process at the origin of the modern world that the scholarship that followed these early efforts has contributed to unearth.

As early as 1975, Charles Tilly had famously quipped that 'war made the state and the state made war' (1975: 42), but a full fleshing out of this statement would await his widely hailed monograph *Coercion, Capital, and European States* (1992) in which he charted the intertwined historical development of systems of coercion and capital, thereby complementing and advancing the work of Giddens and Mann. An intricate set of feedback loops and push–pull dynamics linking the state, war and capitalism thus seem to have driven the emergence and development of the modern world, establishing a set of mutual dependencies that precludes any reduction to a single monocausal determinant (see Poggi, Chapter 9, in this volume). While Tilly rightly insists on the various concatenations of political, military and economic factors that historically produced more or less 'coercion-intensive' and 'capital-intensive' paths of development in different geographical locales, a general account of these interdependencies can be garnered from the now considerable literature on the subject.

Owing to the entanglement of causal factors, there is no 'proper' place at which to begin such an account but, given our present concern, one could start with the growth in armies and the adoption of gunpowder weapons that characterized the European 'military revolution' of the early modern period (Parker 1996; Gat 2006). The rising cost of war and resulting demands on taxation associated with it could only be borne by expanded state bureaucracies capable of improving the efficiency and reach of their revenue-raising powers and of establishing standing armies (Dandeker 1990). This mounting military expenditure and the related economies of scale were naturally to the disadvantage of smaller political entities such as the wealthy city-states of Italy and the Low Countries which had previously successfully relied on costly mercenary forces to preserve their autonomy. Successive conquests and annexations consequently saw the number of separate political entities in Europe fall from around 500 in 1500 to a mere 25 by 1900 (Porter 1994: 12). Control over large pacified territories by powerful central-ized authorities promoted the flourishing of agriculture, industry and commerce along with greater monetization of their economies, in turn increasing the wealth available for taxation that could be used to further strengthen the state and sustain its military competitiveness (Tilly 1992). Military force, and notably its naval arm, was also instrumental in securing trading posts outside Europe, safeguarding the transit of goods by sea and opening up new parts of the world to capitalism and thus taxable revenue, whether through naked imperialism or any variety of means short of it (McNeill 1982). Each of these processes therefore sustained and stimulated the others, combining together to give birth to our modern world characterized by capitalist economies, strong centralized states and a dramatic development of the means available for war.

Bruce Porter (1994) further proposes a noteworthy typology of successively dominant state forms in which each new extension of popular political participation and state welfare provision is accompanied by concomitant increases in the commitments de-manded in the pursuit of war. From the Peace of Westphalia of 1648 to 1789, the dominant state form in Europe was the dynastic state, whether in its constitutional or absolutist variants. Generally led by monarchies that could often count on little more than acquiescence from their subjects, the ability of such states to wage sustained military campaigns was severely limited. With the French Revolution and Napoleonic Wars, the nation-state gained ascendance, grounding its legitimacy on the notion of popular sovereignty and the supposed identity of cultural communities and territory, thereby unleashing nationalist passions that could be channelled into armed conflict. Finally the World Wars and their unprecedented mobilizations of society are linked to the rise of the collectivist state with its wide-ranging interventions in the economy and the welfare of its citizens, of which totalitarian regimes are for Porter simply perverse mutations.

The argument over the autonomy of the state that largely initiated this rich vein of scholarship seems today to have largely swung in favour of its proponents, integrated as it has been into a number of sophisticated Marxist accounts. David Harvey has notably articulated in his recent work a dialectic between distinct territorial and capitalist 'logics of power', the former referring to 'the political, diplomatic and military strategies invoked and used by a state' as it seeks to exert control over a territory and its resources and the latter to the flow of economic power 'across and through continuous space, towards and away from territorial entities . . . through the daily practices of production, trade, commerce, capital flows, money transfers, labor migration, technology transfer, currency speculation, flows of information, cultural impulses and the like' (2005: 26).

If this reassessment of the role of state power against a certain brand of crude economic determinism represents a major and salutary advance in political sociology, it however only offers a partial understanding of the phenomenon of war and its place in the modern world. As Shaw puts it, a state-centred social theory 'is not the same thing as a social theory of war, since it will not necessarily explain how warfare has become a central determinant of social and political relations' (1988: 28). The contours of such a theory begin to emerge when we consider the modalities taken on by the mobilization and organization of armed force and how deeply intertwined they have become with the wider rationalization of social life, the production and diffusion of scientific knowledge, and the very mechanisms of power operative within modern societies.

Rationalizing Military Force: Discipline, Medicine and Technoscience

Max Weber famously noted that alongside modern bureaucratic forms of organization came a highly rationalistic disposition to the world and the practice of war has been no exception. Clausewitz's famous statement that war is an 'an extension of policy by other means' is above all a plea for armed force to be wielded rationally and only insofar as it serves the interests of the state, this most bureaucratic of institutions. In this call for the submission of war to *raison d'état*, Clausewitz was thereby exhibiting a typically modern disposition towards instrumentalist rationality. In contrast, traditional aristo-cratic views of warfare as an existentially meaningful activity that defines a warrior class and is to be pursued for its own sake have been increasingly marginalized within modern societies (Coker 2002). But rationalization has not been restricted to the determination of the utility of force; it has also extended to the very way it is produced, managed and deployed. Thus Jeremy Black has noted that the organization of armed forces has to be understood as 'an aspect of, and intersection and interaction with, wider social patterns and practices, leading to the social systematization of organized violence', and which is to be at least in part accounted for by 'the systematization of knowledge, such that it is possible better to understand, and thus seek to control, the military, its activities and its interaction with the wider world' (2000: 29).

The role of discipline as a means for the control and rationalized management of individuals is here crucial. Weber had already observed that in the military 'the masses are uniformly conditioned and trained for discipline in order that their optimum of physical and psychic power in attack be rationally calculated' (1948: 254), further noting that 'the discipline of the army gives birth to all discipline', including that which made possible the modern capitalist factory (p. 260). If first and foremost a history of the penal institution, Michel Foucault's *Discipline and Punish* (1977) developed this original insight in its account of the role of disciplinary techniques in the militaries of the early modern era. These included schemes for the spatial distribution and enforced enclosure of bodies (whether on the battlefield or in the barracks), a microphysics of power governing the posture, gait and corporeal movements of soldiers through systematized drilling, and a generalized surveillance that ensured compliance with the above through regular examination and systems of reward and punishment for either conforming to, or deviating from, the desired behaviour. While their sophistication may have since grown and other methods of social control have supplemented them, these basic principles have remained remarkably unchanged to date, a testament no doubt to their effectiveness in assembling obedient and proficient fighting units. McNeill (1995) has notably shown how rhythmic coordination and 'muscular bonding' have long served to produce and sustain *esprit de corps*.

One of effects of the total mobilization of societies brought about by modern war has been to forge increasingly close alliances between military endeavour and apparently antithetical domains, such as that of medicine. The human body is here again simultaneously grasped as an object of scientific knowledge and focal point of power relations. The scale and intensity of industrial warfare effectively provided vast laboratories for the trialling of medical techniques and institutional practices for the treatment and rehabilitation of battlefield casualties as well as the general sanitary management of the population (Cooter, Harrison and Sturdy 1998). One can for example trace major advances in emergency surgery, anaesthetics, transportation of blood, prosthetics and plastic surgery to the horrific human cost of armed conflict. Instrumental rationalization prevails here again, as with the system of triage that was increasingly formalized from the nineteenth century onwards and according to which the allocation of limited medical resources is determined through the sorting of patient intake by order of priority of treatment. While in civilian life triage habitually means providing preferential treatment to those patients to whom it will make the greatest immediate improvement in their prognosis ahead of the lightly injured and walking wounded, in battle 'reverse triage' can, when deemed necessary, be employed to identify those soldiers who can most quickly be patched up and returned to action. A similar rationale has permeated the treatment and recovery of medical (and increasingly psychiatric) patients behind the frontlines, with doctors being tasked with returning soldiers to combat status as promptly as possible and rooting out any malingering by recalcitrant recruits. The discovery made through mass conscription that large segments of the population were unfit to fight owing to poor health was a major motivation for the development of national health policies calling upon medical expertise to design and implement large-scale campaigns dedicated to vaccination, personal hygiene, diet and exercise. Despite the obvious tensions between the Hippocratic Oath's paramount concern with the well-being of patients and the instrumental imperatives of war, medical knowledge and practice thus came to acquire de facto a supervisory and regulatory power that made them essential components of national preparation and mobilization for war.

Another facet of the rationalization of warfare is to be found in the oft-observed increase in technological intensity and sophistication characteristic of modern industrialized war. Although discussion of the role of technology in war has a lengthy tradition in military history, it has tended to suffer from the almost exclusive focus on the impact of technology, and particularly weapon systems, on tactics to the detriment of developments in logistics and mobilization. Studies of this nature have a marked propensity to view technological change as an exogenous factor to military practice, frequently lapsing into technologically deterministic accounts in which the appearance of new technologies, in particular those of an offensive nature, induce fundamental transformations in the conditions of war. Changes in tactics and organizational arrangements are here viewed merely as subsequent adjustments to a new technological reality. The origins of technological innovation are rarely questioned and the wider social and cultural contexts are generally only treated in terms of the extent to which they facilitate or impede the adoption of inevitable changes in the practice of warfare. This attitude weighs heavily on current debates about the future of the military, with advocates of a 'revolution in military affairs' arguing that information technology and precision-guided munitions will automatically ensure complete dominance to those armed forces that adopt them (Owens 2001).

To these reductionist accounts must be opposed a richer understanding of tech-nology 'as a certain kind of know-how, as a way of looking at the world and coping with its problems' (van Creveld 1989: 1). Indeed, military developments with political and social ramifications as significant as strategic bombing or nuclear deterrence are only made possible through the establishment of vast socio-technical systems in which the aeroplane and the nuclear bomb are respectively only particular elements inte-grated and co-evolving alongside many others. An understanding of the deployment and evolution of such assemblages relies less on sorting technological from social entities, since neither can function without the other, but on tracing the guiding principles and rationalities overseeing their design, implementation and operation. One of the keys is the ordering role played by scientific rationalism in shaping military organization, the predictive triumphs and technological prowess of modern science enduringly exerting a powerful hold on the imaginations of military practitioners seeking to bring control and predictability to the battlefield. Thus they have drawn on successive techno-scientific paradigms to frame their understanding of armed conflict and marshal men and materiel into fearsome war machines, from the clockwork armies of Frederick the Great and thermodynamic engines of mechanized war to the cybernetic architecture of nuclear deterrence and 'chaoplexic' networks of the Internet age (Bousquet 2009).

That all the rationalizing schemes discussed in this section have been frequently undone in the heat of battle or resisted in various ways by their designated agents, just as the course of individual wars has regularly escaped from their would-be political masters, is not to be doubted. Clausewitz himself was well aware of the limitations imposed by passion and chance on any purely rational designs for war. Nonetheless, we should not lose sight of their wider sociological relevance since 'at one level, the study of Western warfare becomes an aspect of the history of systems as well as of power' (Black 2004: 11).

The Transformation(s) of War: Armed Conflict in the Twenty-First Century

In the wake of the Cold War, Martin Shaw (1991) proclaimed the advent of 'post-military society' in the West, by which he meant the end of the mass mobilization associated with total war and a decline in the influence of martial values on the rest of the population. If subsequent events, including the declaration of a 'War on Terror' whose remit and global stretch appears as unlimited as those of the Cold War, have dispelled any wider illusions that war itself was being consigned to the historical scrapheap, Shaw's analysis still largely stands, capturing as it does certain aspects of the profound transformations that war has being undergoing in recent decades.

For one, Europe finds itself today in the remarkable, and certainly historically unprecedented, situation in which interstate war between any of its nations is not only deemed unlikely but quite simply unimaginable, at least for the foreseeable future. Conscription and universal military service have been abandoned in favour of smaller professional armies in almost all Western nations. The sociological makeup and organizational culture of contemporary 'postmodern militaries' (Moskos *et al* (eds) 2000) is also changing, with these institutions placing increasing value on its personnel possessing such skills as technical proficiency, diplomatic nous and media savviness as well as opening themselves, admittedly not without some reluctance, to female and gay recruits. As Shaw points out, fears of a 'militarization of society' – perhaps most clearly embodied in the fascist regimes of the first half of the twentieth century – have given way to the reality of a 'civilianization of the military' (73) by virtue of which armed forces are increasingly expected to conform to values prevalent in civilian life.

The origins of this evolution are partly to be found in the developments of warfare that followed the Second World War, most notably in the area of nuclear weaponry. Although there were a number of near-misses during the Cold War, the development of vast nuclear arsenals effectively rendered total war as it had been waged in the two World Wars impracticable owing to the intolerable catastrophic losses it would have certainly entailed for all parties. Just as it signified a decline in the utility of mass conscription armies, the nuclear balance of terror could simultaneously only be sustained by complex socio-technical assemblages of mass destruction whose deterrent power depended on their ability to reliably and without delay initiate their terrible work if called upon to do so. This created an unprecedented degree of dependence upon a techno-scientific elite tasked with designing and maintaining these systems and whose backgrounds and proclivities bore little in common with those of traditional military men. More generally, the increasing reliance of militaries on technologically intensive systems and the heavy logistical and bureaucratic chains necessary for their operation has carried with it a requirement for much more specialized and highly educated personnel, the vast majority of whom never serve in a direct combat role.

If it brought the immediate nuclear deadlock to an end, the unwinding of the Cold War merely accelerated these trends as Western militaries threatened by huge budget cuts sought to redefine their role in their new geopolitical environment. An array of novel threats were identified, leading to operations ranging from suppressing illegal immigration and the drugs trade to peacekeeping, humanitarian intervention and state building, all of which took militaries far away from their conventional war-fighting missions and required a wide range of new skills and competences from their forces. If the 'Global War on Terror' has since restored a questionable sense of overarching unity to their operations, there is no indication that it has been accompanied by a diminishing complexity of their operational environments or reduction in the myriad tasks asked of them.

Indeed, it has been argued that the face of war has been undergoing even more profound transformations at the turn of the millennium, the full extent of which are being most clearly realized outside the West. For van Creveld (1991), the Clausewitzian interlude during which war was essentially the preserve of states wielding armed force for political ends is drawing to a close. In its place we find an array of non-state actors ranging from guerrillas and terrorists to bandits and pirates engaged in protracted civil wars in the developing world and opportunistic raids and attacks on the developed world. Mary Kaldor (1999) takes a similar tack in opposing 'old wars' pitting states against each other in increasingly destructive trials of strength over territory and 'new wars' driven by murderous politics of identity and predatory economic gain that blur the line between war and crime.

This alleged decline of interstate war echoes the wider claims about the demise of the nation-state made within the debates surrounding globalization and indeed global processes are central to most accounts of the new wars. Kaldor speaks of a phenomenon of 'global dislocation' in which global forces are 'breaking up the cultural and socio-economic divisions that defined the patterns of politics which characterized the modern period' (73). Ethnic conflict is thus understood in terms of particularist reactions to the social and cultural anomie generated by globalization, exploited by endangered political elites seeking new forms of legitimation and leading to the erection of mythified communities and identities that demand the forcible purging of foreign elements, as in the former Yugoslavia or Rwanda. A globalized political economy is also thought to sustain the new wars, be it through competition for control over natural resources and export commodities, the global arms trade and private military industry, or remittances and assistance from foreign diasporas and governments. Rather than being excluded from it, contemporary war zones are thus found to be very much inserted within globalization, thereby creating all manner of incentives for the persistence of conflict – war as 'a continuation of political economy by other means' as Cramer (2006) would have it. This has led scholars such as Mark Duffield to warn against viewing war in the developing world as irrational 'expressions of breakdown or chaos' but rather as marking 'the emergence of new forms of protection, legitimacy, and rights to wealth' (2001: 3), however different these may seem from those characteristic of the modern nation-state.

One may well be tempted to infer from all this that the constellation that brought state, war and capitalism into a mutually supportive alignment in the early modern period is now setting on the historical horizon. Rather than lead to the emergence of strong central authorities governing over defined territories, war in large parts of the developing world seems to be resulting in greater political fragmentation in which warlords are able to prosper under the cover of persistent low-intensity conflicts by tapping into global markets. The state's monopoly of violence further appears to be fraying in the face of the resurgence of piracy and the catastrophic forms of terrorism espoused by non-state actors bent on acquiring weapons of mass destruction. Even the most functional states of the developed world seem to have acquiesced to the return on the scene of mercenary forces in the form of private military companies (Singer 2003).

It is, however, no doubt premature to write off the state just yet and certainly opportune to remind ourselves that the return of major interstate armed conflict would unleash destruction on a scale that would dwarf anything non-state actors could conceivably muster. Globalization is not strictly speaking a new phenomenon and has in fact long shared a common history with that of war (Barkawi 2005). Nevertheless, the multifaceted manifestations of war today more than ever demand of us a sophisticated theoretical engagement, not only because a mitigation of their terrible human cost may well hinge upon it, but also because no intellectual discipline with an ambition to grasp our world in its totality can hope to dispense with it.

Further Reading

Black, J. 2004: *Rethinking Military History*. London: Routledge.

Bousquet, A. 2009: *The Scientific Way of Warfare: Order and Chaos on the Battlefields of Modernity*. New York: Columbia University Press.

Kaldor, M. 1999: *New and Old Wars: Organized Violence in a Global Era*. Cambridge: Polity Press.

Mann, M. 1988: *States, War and Capitalism: Studies in Political Sociology*. Oxford: Blackwell.

Tilly, C. 1992: *Coercion, Capital, and European States, AD 990–1992*. Oxford: Blackwell.

17

Terrorism

Jeff Goodwin

When states or armed rebels indiscriminately attack civilians, they generally attack civilians who support and/or have a substantial capacity to influence opposing states or rebel movements. Overthrowing, defeating or strongly pressuring such states or movements is the primary goal of terrorism, which is thus a kind of *indirect* warfare. 'Categorical' terrorism – violence against a whole category of non-combatants – will generally be employed against non-combatants who support states or rebel movements that themselves perpetrate extensive, indiscriminate violence against non-combatants who support their armed enemies. By contrast, categories of civilians which include significant numbers of allies or potential allies (or which can be strongly influenced by non-violent appeals or protests) will not be attacked by states or rebels.

Like 'democracy', 'power', 'class', and other 'essentially contested' concepts, there is no universally accepted definition of 'terrorism'. And yet an explanation of terrorism requires a clear definition, even if, empirically, terrorism is not always easily distinguished from cognate phenomena.

I define terrorism as *a strategy characterized by the deliberate use of violence against, or the infliction of extreme physical suffering upon, civilians or non-combatants in order to pressure or influence other civilians and, thereby, governments or armed rebels*. Terrorism is thus a strategy that may be employed by states or rebels and by ideological moderates as well as 'extremists'. This definition directs attention to the killing of civilians in conflicts between two or more armed actors, state or non-state. This strategy does not encompass all types of political violence against non-combatants, including, for example, state violence against an oppressed ethnic group which is not aimed at pressuring a state or movement supported by that ethnic group (e.g., Nazi violence against Jews). This definition of terrorism encompasses (1)

The Wiley-Blackwell Companion to Political Sociology, First Edition. Edited by Edwin Amenta, Kate Nash, and Alan Scott.
© 2012 Blackwell Publishing Ltd. Published 2012 by Blackwell Publishing Ltd.

violence or other lethal actions against non-combatants by rebel groups (i.e., 'terrorism' as many if not most people think of it) but also (2) violence or other lethal actions by states or allied paramilitary forces against non-combatants in conflicts with rebels and (3) violence or other lethal actions by states against non-combatants in international conflicts. 'State terrorism' is important to consider for a number of reasons, not least because state violence against non-combatants has claimed many more victims than has rebel violence against non-combatants (see, for example, Herman and O'Sullivan 1989: chs 2–3; Gareau 2004).

This definition of terrorism stipulates that terrorism involves violence against or the infliction of suffering upon non-combatants, thus differentiating terrorism from conventional and guerrilla warfare directed against armed actors (however literally terrifying these may be), whether waged by state or non-state actors. What we must explain in order to explain terrorism, accordingly, is not why states or political groups sometimes resort to violence, but why they employ violence against civilians or non-combatants in particular. Indeed, one virtue of this definition is that it squarely focuses our attention on violations of the idea (and the ideal) of *non-combatant immunity* – the principle that non-combatants should never be targeted in wars or civil conflicts. Non-combatant immunity is a fundamental principle of 'just war' theory and international law, including the Geneva Conventions.

Two Types of Terrorism

Two types of terrorism need to be analytically differentiated, both of which differ from conventional and guerrilla warfare, insofar as the latter are directed against the combatants or armed forces of a state or rebel movement (see Table 17.1). Of course, as Black points out, 'those popularly known as guerrillas may sometimes engage in terrorism [when they attack civilians], and those popularly known as terrorists may

Table 17.1 Three types of armed struggle

Targets of state or rebels		
Combatants	*Non-combatants*	
Armed rebels	Politicians, rebel political leaders	Anonymous members of an ethnic group, nationality, social class, or other group
Government soldiers and security forces	State officials, bureaucrats	
Paramilitaries	Leaders/activists of competing oppositional groups	
Armed civilians	Collaborators Common criminals	
[1. Conventional/ guerrilla warfare]	[2. Selective/individualized terrorism; i.e. targeted assassination]	[3. Categorical/indiscriminate terrorism]

sometimes engage in guerrilla warfare [when they attack military facilities or personnel]' (2004: 17).

One type of terrorism, which we may call 'selective' or 'individualized', is directed against non-combatants who are targeted because of their individual identities or roles. These individuals typically include politicians and rebel political leaders, competing oppositional leaders and political activists, collaborators and spies, unsympathetic intellectuals and journalists, and common criminals who prey upon the state's or rebels' supporters. This type of terrorism – essentially a strategy of 'targeted assassination' or 'extrajudicial execution' – was employed by some nineteenth-century Russian revolutionaries, a number of anarchist groups and several radical European groups of the 1960s, and, more recently, by US and Israeli 'counterterrorism' forces.

Targeted assassination or selective terrorism is very different from 'indiscriminate' or what I term 'categorical' terrorism, which is directed against anonymous individuals by virtue of their belonging to a specific ethnic group, nationality, social class or some other collectivity. This type of terrorism – with which this chapter is especially concerned – is typically called indiscriminate or 'random' terrorism because it makes no distinctions among the *individual* identities of its targets. In another sense, however, such terrorism is *very* discriminate, being directed against specific categories of people and not others. For this reason, I believe 'categorical terrorism' is a more accurate label than 'indiscriminate terrorism' for this strategy.

Following the general definition of terrorism given above, categorical terrorism may be defined as *a strategy characterized by the deliberate use of violence against, or the infliction of extreme physical suffering upon, civilians or non-combatants who belong to a specific ethnic group, nationality, social class or some other collectivity, without regard to their individual identities or roles, in order to pressure or influence other civilians and, thereby, governments or armed rebels*. In much, if not most, popular discourse, as well as for many scholars (e.g., Turk 1982; Senechal de la Roche 1996; Black 2004), 'terrorism' is basically understood as what I am calling categorical terrorism. 'Indiscriminate' violence, that is, is seen by many as an essential property of terrorism.

There is substantial variation in the extent to which states and rebel movements employ categorical terrorism as a strategy in conflict situations. Of course, both states and rebels generally employ a range of both violent and non-violent strategies in pursuit of their goals, and their mix of strategies typically changes over time. Some states and rebel groups have perpetrated extensive categorical or indiscriminate terrorism. Others have been much more selective or individualized in their use of terrorism, and some (e.g., the Sandinista National Liberation Front in Nicaragua) have employed virtually no terrorism to speak of. The Provisional Irish Republican Army (IRA) and Basque Homeland and Freedom (ETA) are borderline cases. Between its founding in 1969 and a cease-fire in 1997, the IRA typically engaged in attacks on security forces as well as some selective terrorism, but it also occasionally carried out bombings and other sectarian killings of ordinary Protestants in both Northern Ireland and Britain, especially during the height of 'the Troubles' in Northern Ireland during the mid-1970s (English 2003). Historically, ETA has directed most of its violence against the Spanish military and police presence in the Basque region and against politicians of parties that oppose Basque independence. However, it has also engaged in occasional bombings and attempted bombings against ordinary civilians (Clark 1984).

Two Theories of Terrorism

How have social scientists and other analysts attempted to explain why states or rebels employ terrorism? Many theories have been proposed, but here I will focus on just two important theoretical claims: (1) terrorism is a product of the *weakness and/or desperation* of rebels or states, and (2) much terrorism is *a retaliatory response to terrorism* by one's armed enemies (be they states or rebels). While these claims offer important insights into terrorism, they are ultimately unsatisfactory.

Perhaps the most common idea about what causes terrorism is the notion that oppositional movements turn to terrorism when they are very weak, lack popular support, and yet are desperate to redress their grievances. A similar argument has been proposed as an explanation for state terrorism, emphasizing that states turn to terrorism – or 'civilian victimization' – when they become desperate to win wars (Downes 2008). This claim – or rationalization – also seems very popular among many groups and states that employ terrorism. The core idea here is that states and rebels who lack the capacity to pressure their opponents non-violently or through conventional or guerrilla warfare, or who fail to attain their goals when they *do* employ these strategies, will turn to terrorism as a 'last resort'.

Disaffected elites turn to terrorism, according to Crenshaw (1981), because it is easier and cheaper than strategies that require mass mobilization, especially when government repression makes mass mobilization difficult if not impossible. 'In situations where paths to the legal expression of opposition are blocked, but where the regime's repression is inefficient, revolutionary terrorism is doubly likely, as permissive and direct causes coincide' (Crenshaw 1981: 384). Rebel groups will presumably employ categorical terrorism, moreover, because it is generally even cheaper and more efficient than selective terrorism. For example, there may be only fleeting opportunities available for assassinating a particular politician or competing opposition leader, but setting off a bomb in a pub or bus may be relatively simple and will also produce more casualties.

There are a number of logical and empirical problems with this 'desperation' theory of terrorism. Most importantly, the theory seems simply to assume that desperate state officials or rebels would view attacks upon ordinary civilians as beneficial instead of detrimental to their cause. But even if terrorism is cheaper than many other strategies, why employ it at all? We need to know what beneficial consequences state officials or rebels believe their attacks on specific categories of civilians will bring about. How exactly will these attacks advance their cause? Why would officials or rebels not assume that attacks on civilians would undermine their popularity? Or create more – and more determined – enemies from the civilian population they are attacking?

Second, there does not in fact seem to be a particularly strong empirical relationship between the organizational strength of states and rebel groups, on the one hand, and their use (or not) of terrorism, on the other. For example, the US government was hardly desperate when it imposed economic sanctions on Iraq during the 1990s, which resulted in the deaths of more than half a million people (Gordon 2010). (Although these sanctions did not entail direct violence against Iraqi civilians, they fit our definition of terrorism because they deliberately inflicted extreme physical suffering upon non-combatants.) The Liberation Tigers of Tamil Eelam (LTTE) in Sri Lanka, furthermore, were a very powerful rebel movement during the 1990s according to most accounts. The LTTE sometimes even waged conventional warfare against Sri Lankan government forces. Yet the (predominantly Tamil) LTTE also occasionally engaged in indiscriminate attacks on ordinary ethnic Sinhalese civilians, and it did so long after it decimated rival Tamil nationalist groups (Bloom 2005: ch. 3). The desperation theory does not tell us why.

One can also point, conversely, to relatively *weak* states and rebel movements that have *eschewed* terrorism. Perhaps the best example of the latter is the armed wing of the African National Congress (ANC) in South Africa. In 1961, as many of its leaders were being arrested and many others driven into exile, the ANC established an armed wing called *Umkhonto we Sizwe* ('Spear of the Nation' or MK). The ANC explicitly adopted armed struggle as one of its main political strategies. By most accounts, however, MK failed to become an effective guerrilla force, as the South African Defence Forces were simply too strong and effective. And yet MK did *not* adopt a strategy of terrorism, despite the fact, as Gay Seidman points out, that, 'In a deeply segregated society, it would have been easy to kill random whites. Segregated white schools, segregated movie theaters, segregated shopping centers meant that if white deaths were the only goal, potential targets could be found everywhere' (2001: 118). However, as Davis notes, 'since the exile leadership sought to portray the ANC as a principled and responsible contender for power, it imposed restrictions against terrorist tactics that specifically targeted noncombatant whites' (Davis 1987: 121).

In short, weak states and rebels do not necessarily adopt a strategy of terrorism, and strong states and rebels do not necessarily eschew this strategy. As Turk concludes, 'Because any group may adopt terror tactics, it is misleading to assume either that "terrorism is the weapon of the weak" or that terrorists are always small groups of outsiders – or at most a "lunatic fringe"' (1982: 122).

The main insight of the desperation theory of terrorism is that states and rebel groups *do* often seem to take up arms after they have concluded that diplomacy and non-violent politics cannot work or that they work too slowly or ineffectively to redress urgent grievances. But notice that this does not tell us why armed actors would employ violence against non-combatants as opposed to conventional or guerrilla warfare. Moreover, the argument that attacking 'soft' targets such as unprotected civilians is cheaper and easier than waging conventional or guerrilla warfare does not explain why states or rebels would *ever* bother to wage conventional or guerrilla warfare. The argument implies that rational people would *always* prefer terrorism to these strategies, which is clearly not the case. In sum, the most we can say is that weakness and desperation may be a necessary but not sufficient cause of terrorism in some instances.

A second common view of terrorism is that it is *a retaliatory response to terrorism*. Leftist and radical analysts of terrorism often make this claim about oppositional terrorism, and it is emphasized by Herman and O'Sullivan (1989). They suggest that the 'retail' terrorism of oppositional groups is caused or provoked by the 'wholesale' or 'primary' terrorism of states, especially powerful Western states, above all the United States. The terms 'wholesale' and 'retail' are meant to remind readers that state terrorism has been much more deadly than oppositional terrorism.

This claim certainly has an intuitive plausibility. Why else would oppositional groups turn to a risky strategy of violence – why would they risk their necks – except when they confront a government or state that is unmoved by non-violent protest and indeed itself employs violence against peaceful protesters? Deterring such state violence, or perhaps simply avenging it in a bid to win popular support, would seem to be reason enough for opposition groups to employ violent strategies. And yet, as a general explanation of terrorism, this hypothesis is also beset by both logical and empirical problems.

It is certainly true that indiscriminate state violence, especially when perpetrated by relatively weak states, has historically encouraged the development of rebel movements (Goodwin 2001). But why would these movements attack and threaten ordinary *civilians* as opposed to the state's armed forces? In other words, if they are responding to *state* terrorism, would not rebels employ violence against *the state* – and just the state? State terrorism, that is, would seem more likely to provoke rebels to employ guerrilla or conventional warfare than terrorism.

Empirically, one can also point to rebel organizations that have arisen in contexts of extreme state violence which have nonetheless eschewed a strategy of terrorism. For example, Central American guerrilla movements of the 1970s and 1980s, including the Sandinistas in Nicaragua and the Farabundo Martí Front for National Liberation in El Salvador, confronted states that engaged in extensive violence against non-combatants, yet neither movement engaged in much terrorism. In fact, the Sandinistas engaged in virtually no terrorism at all. Another such example is, once again, the ANC in South Africa. Interestingly, Herman and O'Sullivan's book devotes considerable attention to both South African and Israeli state terrorism (1989: ch. 2). And yet, while they note the 'retail' terrorism of the Palestine Liberation Organization during the 1970s and 1980s – emphasizing that Israeli state terrorism was responsible for a great many more civilian deaths during this period – they do not discuss the oppositional terrorism in South Africa which their theory would seem to predict. In fact, as we have noted, the ANC simply did not carry out much terrorism. State terrorism, clearly, does not *always* cause or provoke oppositional terrorism.

Having said this, it is indeed difficult to point to a rebel group that has carried out extensive terrorism which has *not* arisen in a context of considerable state violence. For example, the rebels in French Algeria, the West Bank and Gaza, Sri Lanka and Chechnya who engaged in extensive categorical terrorism are drawn from, and claim to act on behalf of, populations that have themselves suffered extensive and often indiscriminate state repression. The question is what to make of this correlation. Why, in these particular contexts, have rebels attacked certain categories of civilians as well as government forces? To answer this question, we need a different account of terrorism.

A Relational Theory of Terrorism

To explain terrorism, our main task must be to determine why and under what conditions armed actors (state or non-state) regard the killing of ordinary civilians as a reasonable (although not necessarily exclusive) means to advance their political agenda. It also behooves us to consider why and under what conditions armed actors consider terrorism an unreasonable and perhaps even counter-productive strategy.

I outline below a 'relational' theory of terrorism (see Tilly 2004) in which social relations among key actors – states, armed rebels and civilians – carry the primary explanatory burden, as opposed to ideas and ideologies. The presence (or absence) and the nature of social ties (whether conflictual or cooperative) between armed actors (states or rebels), on the one hand, and different kinds of civilians, on the other, provide the main incentives or disincentives for terrorism.

We can begin to move towards a better understanding of terrorism – particularly categorical terrorism – by considering the precise *categories* of civilians or non-combatants which states and rebels (sometimes) target for violence. Why and how states and rebels come to see particular non-combatants as enemies is something the aforementioned theories generally do not examine. Yet, clearly, states and rebels do not indiscriminately attack just *any* civilians or non-combatants. Indeed, both states and rebels are also usually interested in winning the active support or allegiance of certain civilians. So which are the 'bad' or enemy civilians whom they attack?

When they employ a strategy of categorical terrorism, states and rebels generally attack or seek to harm civilians whose support or acquiescence is valuable to their armed enemies. These are civilians who support enemy armed actors in different ways and/or have some capacity to influence the actions of an enemy state or rebel movement. Attacking such civilians is a way to attack indirectly one's armed opponents. Indeed, the main strategic objective – the primary incentive – of categorical terrorism is *to induce civilians to stop supporting, or to proactively demand changes in, certain government or rebel policies or to change the government or rebel movement itself.* Categorical terrorism, in other words, mainly aims to apply such intense pressure to civilians that they will either demand that 'their' government or movement change or abandon certain policies or, alternatively, cease supporting the government or rebels altogether.

States' and rebels' calculations about whether they should employ categorical terrorism as a strategy are strongly shaped by social and political contexts. An adequate theory of terrorism needs, first and foremost, to specify the key contextual factors that create incentives or disincentives for states or rebels to choose terrorism as a strategy. Before I turn to a discussion of the contexts that encourage and discourage terrorism, let me pause briefly to clarify precisely what my theory of terrorism is attempting – and *not* attempting – to explain.

Figure 17.1 presents a simplified model of political tactics. Concrete tactical actions or operations – involving specific techniques and technologies, divisions of labor, site

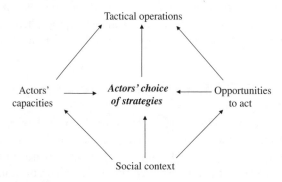

Figure 17.1 A model of political tactics

selection, timing etc. – are *not* my concern here. An adequate explanation of tactical operations would not only have to consider the political strategies that actors have chosen, but also their capacities to act in specific ways (determined by their skills, access to resources etc.) and the situational opportunities (or absence thereof) for specific tactics. What my theory of terrorism seeks to explain, by contrast, is *why and in what contexts state or non-state actors choose a strategy of terrorism* (perhaps among a mix of strategies), recognizing that this choice is also likely to be influenced by their capacities and situational opportunities. In sum, I am not interested in explaining this or that terrorist act per se. Rather, I want to explain why some states and rebels choose to kill non-combatants as a political strategy. Absent this strategic choice, terrorist actions or operations simply do not occur, given that my definition of terrorism stipulates that violence against civilians must be *deliberate or intentional* to count as terrorism. 'If we want to understand the choice of terror', Walzer has written, 'we have to imagine what in fact always occurs … A group of men and women, officials or militants, sits around a table and argues about whether or not to adopt a terrorist strategy' (2004: 57). Perhaps there is an argument; perhaps there is not. But a choice is made.

I propose that there are three general contextual factors that most strongly influence the probability that states or rebels will view non-combatants as enemies and, thus, employ a strategy of categorical terrorism against them. First, and most importantly, there is an incentive for states and rebels to employ terrorism against civilians who support violence by 'their' states or rebels. By contrast, terrorism is discouraged when violence by armed enemies is opposed by significant numbers of civilians (or is limited or non-existent).

Rebel movements, for example, that have employed a strategy of categorical terrorism have typically emerged from populations that have suffered extensive and often indiscriminate state repression (for example, in French Algeria, the West Bank and Gaza, Sri Lanka and Chechnya). In these contexts, moreover, there was also *substantial civilian support* for or acquiescence to that repression 'on the other side' (by European settlers, Jewish Israelis, Sinhalese and Russians, respectively). Indeed, the governments that carried out the repression in these cases had (or have) a substantial measure of democratic legitimacy among civilians. Democratic rights and institutions, in fact, are often effective at creating the impression (especially at some social distance) of substantial solidarity between the general citizenry and 'their' states. When extensive and indiscriminate state violence is supported by civilians and/ or orchestrated by democratically elected governments, it is hardly surprising that rebel movements would tend to view both repressive states *and* the civilians who stand behind them as legitimate targets of counter-violence, which typically begins, and is justified, as 'self-defence'. Nor is it surprising that *retribution* for such violence would be directed at civilians as well as at the enemy state's armed forces. For it would also be reasonable under these circumstances for rebels to conclude that attacking civilians might cause the latter to put substantial pressure on 'their' states to change their ways. Extensive state ('wholesale') terrorism seems to beget extensive oppositional ('retail') terrorism, in other words, in contexts where there is *a citizenry with significant democratic rights*. The latter would appear to be a common if not necessary precondition for extensive categorical terrorism by rebel movements (see Pape 2005; Goodwin 2006).

This also helps us to understand why rebels who are facing an authoritarian or autocratic regime often carry out very little terrorism. Categorical terrorism is much more likely when an entire ethnic group or nationality is supportive of a government as compared, for example, to a small economic elite or the cronies of a dictator. (In fact, all major cases of categorical terrorism seem to have entailed the use of violence against, or infliction of harm upon, a large ethnic or national group.) For example, the Sandinista Front in Nicaragua carried out virtually no terrorism during their armed conflict with the personalistic Somoza dictatorship, an otherwise bloody insurgency during which some 30,000 people were killed (Booth 1985). Civilians who supported the dictatorship consisted of a tiny number of Somoza cronies and a loyal elite opposition, both of which were drawn mainly from Nicaragua's small bourgeoisie. Virtually all other civilians in Nicaragua, from the poorest peasant to Somoza's bourgeois opponents, were viewed by the Sandinistas as potential allies, and indeed many would become such. Had the Somoza dictatorship been supported by more people – a larger social stratum, say, or a substantial ethnic group – then the Sandinistas (other things being equal) might very well have employed terrorism more frequently than they did.

Civilians may support the violence of 'their' states and rebels, and thereby incentivize terrorism, in three main ways – politically, economically and militarily. First, terrorism is likely to be employed against non-combatants who *politically* support – or at least do not actively oppose – one's armed enemies. In this context, terrorism is a reasonable strategy (other things being equal) to weaken civilian political (or 'moral') support or tolerance for violence. By contrast, terrorism is much less likely to be employed against civilians who do not politically support – or are substantially divided in their support for – one's armed enemies.

Secondly, terrorism is likely to be employed against non-combatants who *economically* support armed enemies by, for example, supplying them with weapons, transportation (or the means thereof), food and other supplies needed to employ violence. In this context, terrorism is a reasonable strategy (other things being equal) to weaken civilian economic support for violence. By contrast, terrorism is much less likely when soldiers are supplied by foreign states or non-state allies or through covert, black markets.

Thirdly, terrorism is likely to be employed, pre-emptively, against non-combatants who may *militarily* support armed enemies by, for example, being required to serve an obligatory tour of duty in a state or rebel movement's armed forces or by serving voluntarily in a state or rebel reserve force, militia or paramilitary force. In this context, terrorism is a reasonable strategy (other things being equal) to pre-empt or weaken civilian participation in the armed forces of a state or rebel movement. By contrast, terrorism is much less likely when civilians are not required to serve as warriors for states or rebels or show little interest in doing so – and may be actively resisting such service.

Terrorism is also likely to occur in contexts in which armed actors have begun to attack the civilian supporters of their armed enemies, presumably for one of the three reasons just given. In this context, terrorism is a reasonable strategy (other things being equal) to deter terrorism by armed enemies, thereby protecting one's civilian supporters, or, alternatively, to avenge such terrorism, thereby winning or reinforcing the political support of civilians who feel they have been avenged. By contrast, terrorism is much less likely when armed actors are not attacking the civilian supporters of an enemy state or movement – even if they are otherwise at war with an enemy state or movement.

Finally, terrorism is *less* likely to occur in contexts in which civilians have a history of politically supporting or cooperating with opposing states or rebels – which is another way of saying that some significant fraction of civilians has defected from 'their' state or rebel movement to the 'other side'. Such civilians are not simply opposing the violence of 'their' state or rebels – which, as noted above, would itself make terrorism against them less likely – but are also actively supporting the warriors who are fighting 'their' state or rebels. In this context, categorical terrorism would clearly *not* be a reasonable strategy (other things being equal) for the warriors who are supported by the dissident fraction of such civilians. Such categorical terrorism would not only put at risk the support that these warriors are receiving from the dissidents, but would also make it much less likely that additional civilians would defect from 'their' state or rebels. By contrast, terrorism is much more likely (other things being equal) when civilians have not and do not support or cooperate with opposing states or rebels.

The existence of a significant fraction of dissident civilians explains why the African National Congress (ANC) – the leading anti-apartheid organization in South Africa – rejected a strategy of categorical terrorism against white South Africans. The ANC eschewed this strategy even though the apartheid regime that it sought to topple employed very extensive state violence against its opponents. This violence, moreover, was clearly supported (or tolerated) by large segments of the white, especially Afrikaner, population. The Nationalist Party governments that unleashed the security forces against the regime's enemies were elected by the white population. So why did the ANC adhere to an ideology of 'multi-racialism' and refuse to view whites as such as enemies? The answer lies in the ANC's long history of collaborating with white South Africans, especially of British background – as well as with South Asian and 'coloured' (mixed race) South Africans – in the anti-apartheid struggle. Especially important in this respect was the ANC's long collaboration with whites in the South African Communist Party. Tellingly, an important, long-time leader of MK, the ANC's armed wing, was Joe Slovo, a white Communist. (Try to imagine an Israeli Jew leading Hamas's armed wing or an American Christian directing al-Qaeda!) For the ANC to have indiscriminately attacked South African whites would have soured this strategic relationship, which, among other things, was essential for securing substantial Soviet aid for the ANC. In sum, given the long-standing multi-racial – including international – support for the anti-apartheid movement, a strategy of categorical terrorism against white civilians made little strategic sense to ANC leaders.

Figures 17.2 and 17.3 provide graphic illustrations of the preceding claims about the contextual incentives and disincentives for terrorism. Figure 17.2 portrays the structure of a *symmetrically* terror-prone conflict, that is, a two-party conflict in which the armed actors on each side are likely to employ violence against non-combatants on the other side. Two features of this structure are important: First, the boundaries between the states or armed movements and the civilian populations on each side are blurred, that is, the armed actors are well embedded in the civilian populations. This is meant to represent the fact that civilians support and/or can influence the state or armed movement on each side. Second, the boundaries between the two sets of actors

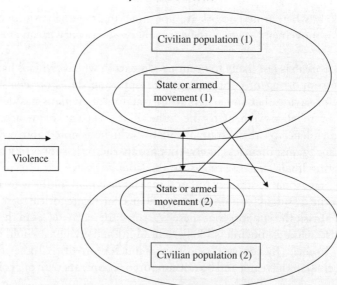

Figure 17.2 The structure of a symmetrically terror-prone conflict

are clearly distinct; the two sides are politically (and otherwise) distant from each other. In this context, when the armed actors have cause to fight, they are also likely to try to kill civilians or non-combatants on the other side, given that the latter are supporting their armed enemies. This structure of conflict is commonly found in international wars and in ethnic and/or nationalist conflicts.

Figure 17.3 portrays the structure of an *asymmetrically* terror-prone conflict, that is, a two-party conflict in which only *one* of the armed actors is likely to employ violence against non-combatants on the other side. The structure of this conflict differs from the previously discussed one in two ways: First, the boundaries between what I have labelled *state or armed movement (1)* and *civilian population (1)* are not blurred

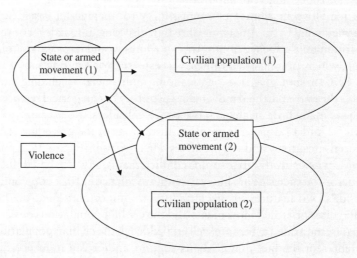

Figure 17.3 The structure of an asymmetrically terror-prone conflict

but quite distinct; the state or armed movement, in this case, is not well embedded in a civilian population. This is meant to represent the fact that *civilian population (1)* does *not* support or have the capacity to influence *state or armed movement (1)*. In fact, this state or armed movement uses violence to oppress or control *civilian population (1)*. Second, *state or armed movement (2)* is not only embedded in (i.e., supported by) *civilian population (2)* but is also connected to *civilian population (1)*. This is meant to represent the fact that some significant fraction of *civilian population (1)* is politically allied to or cooperates with *state or armed movement (2)*. In this context, when the armed actors have cause to fight, *state or armed movement (1)* is also likely to try to attack *civilian population (2)*, given that population's support for its armed enemies, but *state or armed movement (2)* has no incentive to attack *civilian population (1)*, given its political ties to that population.

Conclusion

By way of conclusion, let me try to demonstrate how the theory outlined here helps to explain why al-Qaeda and affiliated or similar Islamist groups have carried out extensive categorical terrorism in recent years, including the attacks of 11 September 2001 (9/11).

Al-Qaeda's political project is best described as pan-Islamic, viewing itself as a defender of the transnational *umma* or Muslim community. In al-Qaeda's view, this multi-ethnic, transnational community is currently balkanized and violently oppressed by 'apostate' secular and 'hypocritical' pseudo-Islamic regimes, from Morocco to Mindanao, as well as by the 'Zionist entity' in Palestine. And standing behind these regimes – and occupying Iraq and Afghanistan – is the powerful US government (and, to a lesser extent, other Western governments, especially Britain). This understanding that the United States is the ultimate power which is propping up repressive, un-Islamic regimes in the Muslim world is the fundamental source of al-Qaeda's conflict with the United States. Al-Qaeda believes that until the US government – the 'far enemy' – can be compelled to end its support for these regimes – the 'near enemy' – and withdraw its troops and other agents from Muslim countries, local struggles against these regimes cannot succeed (Gerges 2009).

But why does al-Qaeda kill ordinary, 'innocent' Americans in addition to US armed forces? Why would al-Qaeda target the World Trade Center, for example, in addition to US political and military installations? Shortly after 9/11, Osama bin Laden described the rationale for the 9/11 attacks in an interview that first appeared in the Pakistani newspaper *Ausaf* on 7 November 2001:

> The United States and their allies are killing us in Palestine, Chechnya, Kashmir, Palestine and Iraq. That's why Muslims have the right to carry out revenge attacks on the U.S. . . . The American people should remember that they pay taxes to their government and that they voted for their president. Their government makes weapons and provides them to Israel, which they use to kill Palestinian Muslims. Given that the American Congress is a committee that represents the people, the fact that it agrees with the actions of the American government proves that America in its entirety is responsible for the atrocities that it is committing against Muslims. I demand the American people to take note of their government's policy against Muslims. They described their government's policy against

Vietnam as wrong. They should now take the same stand that they did previously. The onus is on Americans to prevent Muslims from being killed at the hands of their government.

(Quoted in Lawrence 2005: 140–141)

Bin Laden believes that it is reasonable to kill ordinary American citizens, then, because they pay taxes to and otherwise support an elected government, which makes Americans responsible for the violent actions of this government in Muslim countries (and, indirectly, of governments supported by the United States) (Wiktorowicz and Kaltner 2003: 88–89). Al-Qaeda views ordinary American citizens, in other words, not as 'innocents', but as morally responsible for US-sponsored 'massacres' and oppression of Muslims in a number of countries.

This idea has also been articulated by Mohammad Sidique Khan, one of the four suicide bombers who killed more than 50 people in London on 7 July 2005. In a videotape broadcast on al-Jazeera television in September 2005, Khan said, 'Your democratically-elected governments continuously perpetuate atrocities against my people all over the world. And your support of them makes you directly responsible, just as I am directly responsible for protecting and avenging my Muslim brothers and sisters' (quoted in Rai 2006).

To be sure, al-Qaeda's precise strategic goal in attacking US citizens remains unclear: Was 9/11 a reprisal for massacres carried out or supported by the United States? Was 9/11 meant to 'wake up' Americans to what their government was doing in the Islamic world, in the hope that they would force it to change its policies? Or was the goal perhaps to provoke a violent overreaction by the US government, luring it into Afghanistan, where it would become bogged down (like the Soviet Union before it) in an unwinnable war? What is certain is al-Qaeda's belief that it is logical and reasonable for it to attack ordinary Americans in order to bring about a change in 'their' government's policies.

As in similar cases in which states or rebels have turned to a strategy of terrorism, al-Qaeda has concluded that the violence directed against its constituents has widespread civilian support – or, at least, is widely tolerated – in the United States. At the same time, al-Qaeda and its Islamist sympathizers obviously do not have the type of history of political collaboration with American citizens which might lead them to reject a strategy of categorical terrorism; language, religion and, above all, US government policies have created a formidable chasm between the two. The confluence of these factors, as elsewhere, has strongly encouraged, and continues to encourage, al-Qaeda's terrorist strategy against non-combatants in the United States and allied countries.

Further Reading

Bloom, M. 2005: *Dying to Kill: The Allure of Suicide Terror*. New York: Columbia University Press.

Downes, A. 2008: *Targeting Civilians in War*. Ithaca and London: Cornell University Press.

Gerges, F. 2009: *The Far Enemy: Why Jihad Went Global*, 2nd edn. Cambridge: Cambridge University Press.

Goodwin, J. 2006: A theory of categorical terrorism. *Social Forces* 84(4): 2027–2046.

Herman, E. and O'Sullivan, G. 1989: *The 'Terrorism' Industry: The Experts and Institutions That Shape Our View of Terror*. New York: Pantheon.

Pape, R. 2005: *Dying to Win: The Strategic Logic of Suicide Terrorism*. New York: Random House.

Tilly, C. 2004: Terror, terrorism, terrorists. *Sociological Theory* 22(1): 5–13.

18

Globalization and Security

DIDIER BIGO

How has security become associated with globalization, with risk management of international terrorism, migration, drug trafficking and human trafficking? How has it escaped the bounds of the nation-state? Bigo argues that it is as a consequence of, on the one hand, a meta-narrative, or (in Bourdieuian terms) a *doxa* that naturalizes a new assemblage of (in)security practices reconfigured after September 2001. On the other hand, the acceptance that insecurity and risk management have 'gone global' is a consequence of the competition and strategic alliances between diverse public/private agencies that operate across borders, exchanging information, databases and 'know-how' in ways that are extremely difficult to contest, especially as they are generally kept hidden from public view. The linking of globalization and security is a consequence of networks of transnational guilds, experts in security, for whom discourses of global (in) security are a resource that enables them to expand their operations and to compete in a transnational field to assess priorities and propose preventive solutions to perceived dangers, even to the detriment of the rule of law, human rights and national sovereignty.

'Globalization' and 'security' are both weighty terms with diverse and contradictory meanings (Bigo and Tsoukala 2008). It would seem to be impossible to find an agreement about them, but when they are put together, as if by magic, 'globalization and security' captures the imagination of a variety of actors and seems to push them to agree that global security is one of the most important challenges of our world. How is this possible? How does 'global (in)security' become one of the most important questions of our time?

In the first place, it is important to understand the current conjuncture in terms of how narratives have come together – from the Iranian revolution, the end of the Cold War, the fear of illegal migrants and the fear of terrorism; how they have merged, and

The Wiley-Blackwell Companion to Political Sociology, First Edition. Edited by Edwin Amenta, Kate Nash, and Alan Scott.
© 2012 Blackwell Publishing Ltd. Published 2012 by Blackwell Publishing Ltd.

created the possibility of shifting from one threat to another. It seems as if they are all aspects of the same generalized insecurity. Along with the emergence of global networks, these narratives form what I call, following Latour, an '(in)security assemblage' (in preference to my previous formulation, 'insecurity continuum') (Latour 2005; Bigo 1996). This assemblage creates the conditions for diverse agencies to extend their operations, and to transfer the legitimacy of their original missions to other domains and scales: the police go abroad; the military operates inside territorial borders; intelligence services exchange personal data across borders all over the world. Public and private agents work together, creating para-private organizations. The temporary alliances that emerge are the result of competition between agencies in which each of them considers that what is at stake concerning (in)security is vital. Different agents understand their actions as a response to violence and insecurity whose scale is now 'global'.

The 11th of September 2001 (9/11) is seen as the proof of the truth of this narrative about the emergence of global (in)security, which we can analyse as a form of *doxa* in Bourdieuian terms (Bourdieu 1980a). Deconstructing discourses that trace the origin and spread of the globalization of (in)security from the events of 9/11 is not enough to dissolve them. Even correlating them, as in the Foucaultian approach, with forms of organization and material infrastructures in terms of techniques of government is not sufficient. What is necessary is to understand that these practices are linked to the rise of transnational guilds of experts of security, who have the last word over the truth concerning the evaluation of the future dangers and the construction of categories of danger and desirability.

To be sure, many scholars have criticized the idea that 9/11 marks a radically new period (Borradori, Habermas and Derrida 2003; Žižek 2002). Some have argued, quite rightly, that the fusion of war and crime does not arise from the objective reality of the emergence of al-Qaeda, nor even from new wars and hyperterrorism, but from the transformation and extension of discourses of threats, even a form of governmentality of late modern society based on risk management (Amoore and de Goede 2008; Aradau and van Munster 2007). However, such critical approaches do not always themselves escape from the doxa of the assemblage of (in)security practices. There is a tendency in this work to accept that both insecurity and risk management have 'gone global', when what is needed is close analysis of the particular narratives and discourses that produce this effect. In addition, it is far from evident that critique is sufficient to destabilize the belief of the general public in the growing connections between globalization and dangers. The Foucauldian approach of tracing the origins of the discourses of insecurity practices and showing their connection with emerging networks and organizations of risk management is important, but it becomes politically significant only if it leads to an assessment of who is involved in developing these narratives, and what are the interests at stake in their construction. The governmentality of global risk has a politics. That is why, in what has been called the Paris school of security studies, we have insisted on the importance of the emergence of a transnational guild of diverse professional managers of unease, and the structural de-differentiation of the social universes dealing with danger (military, intelligence, police, border guards, but also bank analysts, insurance companies and so on) to explain the emergence of this overall discourse formation or doxa of global (in)security (CASE Collective 2006; Bigo and Tsoukala 2008; Williams 2008; Bigo *et al.* 2010).

The Doxa of a Global (In)security

For many in the academic community, who simply believe political professionals and civil servants of the most 'advanced liberal societies', 9/11 is the origin of awareness of the globalization of (in)security. In some ways, this vision is not wrong, even if the simplicity of the logic can be contested. The impact of 9/11 has been to create a 'theory effect' which may not be accurate but which is believed as such. A *doxa* was born, creating a common-sense understanding that we live today in a radically new period, 'post 9/11', which marks the death of national security and its rebirth as global security, requiring collaboration between states and the reframing of 'internal' and 'external', public and private. It is understood, for example, that the rule of law represented by international treaties has to be adapted to enable effective intelligence gathering. Under the 'charm' of this account of history, each local event after 2001, even petty crime on occasion, is read as a 'sign' of the local materialization of a global causality of danger rather than as a product of other local events.

From 11 September – or rather from 14 September when the US Congress granted George Bush special powers as President overseeing 'the global war on terror' (Dal Lago and Palidda 2010) – a standard narrative condensing many diverse and competing stories which had existed from the end of the Cold War became the *epitome* (the condensed version of a sacred text) of the dogma of global (in)security. In this narrative (which actually comes from a quasi-religious belief about the coming of Armageddon), the period immediately after the 'attacks' is described as a period of doom in which no state (not even the most powerful) enjoys a monopoly of violence or is in control of its own territory. Therefore collaboration between and beyond states to prevent the eruption of catastrophic violence is absolutely necessary for the salvation of the world. The narrative is so powerful that no argument is necessary beyond description; images are sufficient to 'act' (Williams 2003). As Derrida immediately perceived, a series of images of the Twin Towers falling now stand in for the full story (Borradori, Habermas and Derrida 2003). The evocation works so well because it connects the personal memories of each individual – what they were doing that day, when they heard or saw the images of the fall of the Twin Towers on TV – with the collective narrative of the end of a traditional understanding of (national) security.

This epitome works through its repetition and local variations in many different social universes. 'The traditional understanding of what it means to speak of war, of crime, of state security, of sovereignty has collapsed in the same second as the towers', said one of the senior intelligent analysts in charge of US counterterrorism that we interviewed in 2002 in Washington (Bigo, Bonelli and Delthombe 2008: 165). 'We have dust all around. Political science is at ground zero. Then we have to rebuild everything and to adapt to a new world, global and profoundly insecure', said a key national adviser of the US Security Council to a meeting of top-level academics in Brussels the same year (Bigo *et al.* 2008: 29). Tony Blair and Georges Bush have repeated the same story. The belief that an era was at an end was also shared by sociologists, like Ulrich Beck, who said that on 11 September: 'the difference between war and peace, the military and police, war and crime, and national and international security are, from within and without, completely annulled' (Beck 2003: 257).

For this very long list of experts, 11 September 2001 signals, then, the birth of a new form of terror in the global age, creating waves of intimidation that governments have to prevent through cooperation. In this new world, small groups of terrorists must be taken seriously. The old mechanisms no longer work: deterrence is not possible because these actors are irrational; and in the future they will have access to weapons of mass destruction. The globalization of insecurity is first and foremost the product of 'stealth' enemies, enemies that, because of their size and mobility, cannot be detected. Emergency is a permanent task for governments. Prevention is the key word for the new regime of management of insecurity.

In quite all the official meetings about international security, we find experts and academics singing in chorus. The world is globalized, the boundaries between states are permeable, the mobility of people is the new absolute danger. Some conclude that each individual must then be treated as a potential suspect, to be placed under strict surveillance and control. The Bush Administration followed this line, supported by academics, with well-known illiberal practices resulting, not only at home, but abroad (Bigo *et al.* 2008). Other academics have tried to cope with the 'new situation' in more nuanced, but equally illiberal ways, speculating, for example, on the necessity and limits of torture (Dershowitz 2007; Ignatieff 2004). In both cases international treaties, covenants, agreements and even constitutions are considered to be out of date and in need of new interpretations. This is especially the case where they concern foreigners, asylum-seekers, migrants or foreign-born citizens.

In this new global era, the fundamental basis of the rule of law, including habeas corpus rights, have been challenged. For Amitai Etzioni, for example, even if he was critical of the invasion of Iraq, the survival of the human species facing nuclear terrorism supposes that security must be paramount: 'Security drives democracy, while democracy does not beget security' he says (Etzioni 2007: ix). Security does not depend, 'as followers of narrow realism might have it, only on the security of the United States and its allies. The "primacy of life" principle is global; it places a responsibility on the major powers not only to ensure basic security to their own people, but also to contribute to the basic security of other peoples' (Etzioni 2007: 193). Global security overrules national sovereignty. Following this principle, the sovereignty of states is no longer sacrosanct: military intervention may be justified on moral grounds. State sovereignty is redefined as state responsibility, and states that do not fulfil their obligations may legitimately be disciplined by other states (Deng *et al* 1996; Badie 1999). With a different tone to Etzioni, Mary Kaldor has also contributed to systematizing the discourse on global (in)security, linking security and global protection. Her concern is with new wars and the fusion of war and crime (Kaldor 2000). The responsibility to protect then becomes the responsibility to intervene where, for example, violations of human rights, especially in case of genocide or massive war crimes, are going on, or where there is a threat of nuclear terrorism. In fact, to be consistent, it may be necessary to act *before* the crimes happen; a kind of *preventive punishment* for an act not yet accomplished. The duty of responsibility must also be a *duty to prevent*. Those who are responsible must calculate the risks that a people within a state territory may be killed, and intervene under conditions of uncertainty, as often there is not time to gather knowledge in the face of dangers of this scale (Feinstein and Slaughter 2004). Human security and state security become the twin faces of global preventive security and its politics of emergency.

For all these actors the world is on the verge of a catastrophe: from repeated genocides, nuclear terrorism, the rise of organized crime, massive flows of migrants and refugees, and now, beyond human actors, from climate change or epidemics of new viruses. Whatever they are discussing, these experts propose a 'global' approach because insecurity is at a global scale, whether the threat is al-Qaeda, nuclear, bacteriologic or chemical terrorism, global organized crime, destabilization of financial markets, cyber wars attacking critical infrastructures, trafficking of diverse sorts (fissile materials, drugs, arms, money), including trafficking of persons (migrants, asylum-seekers, women and children) and their local exploitation, or natural catastrophe in virus mutation from animals to human, tsunami and water heights, or degradation of the environment (water, air and atmosphere). They contribute, therefore, to a *new doxa, a new common sense* that takes for granted, beyond the discourse on terrorism, the *rise of insecurity at the world level*, transforming the humanity of the planet into a single 'survivor' struggling with the imminence of Armageddon. The future is a 'future perfect', a future already known. It ends with the destruction of humanity if the necessity to prevent and protect against evildoers of all sorts and against global catastrophes is not recognized by the population of the world and if the experts and elites do not stop framing issues in national terms.

What emerges, then, from this cloud of discourses, whose topics are hugely heterogeneous in terms of discipline, focus and scale, is a shared sense that collaboration is an 'absolute necessity', a matter of urgency. What becomes central is the feeling that we are living in exceptional times, a time of non-calculable risks that, failing politics and negotiations, technology will permit the experts to predict and prevent, as long as all the information is gathered, exchanged and transmitted. There is a convergence between the mentality of the engineer, who insists on early warning indexes, and the manager, who insists on the necessity to develop planetary consciousness. A certain form of governmentality, different from that which supported sovereignty, discipline and biopolitics, is taking shape under the sign of the future perfect that Philip K. Dick explored in *The Minority Report* (Dick 2002).

Is it then possible to disagree in the face of this cloud of discourses and the connections made between them through the insecurity assemblage? Or is disagreeing only a sign of being outdated, sovereignist, techno-pessimist? Is it really possible to set up a space of discussion, scientific and social, around 'purely' techno-scientific questions where all experts share knowledge and find solutions by prioritizing the dangers, profile suspicious persons and create technologies to deal with 'multi-risks'? Or is there a de-polarization of choice, as the meaning of the future is kidnapped, and the spokespersons of a secure humanity try to persuade us that they speak for our own good? The best way to address these questions is to return to the origins of these discourses concerning the globalization of security. We need to ask who is saying what. Who authorizes himself to be the spokesperson of the global security, and how?

The Roots of Global (In)Security: A Transnational Guild of Experts Willing to Monitor the Future

A small group of academics has reacted against the 'fact' that a new form of violence has emerged globally. They considered that this story has been used to develop a politics of fear, emancipating governments from the rule of law, justified by an exceptional moment of emergency that enables the reframing of norms of freedom, security and democracy (Guittet, Perier and Bigo 2005; Agamben 2005). They were among the first to challenge the legitimacy of the narrative of 11 September 2001, and to question this *epitome*. They insisted on the permanent exception enacted in this discourse and its consequences. Some agreed with Agamben that under this regime of exception, human beings were all becoming *homo sacer*. Liberal wars appear to be war of the human 'species' purifying itself from evil in this view (Dillon and Reid 2001; Dillon 2007). In what has been correctly portrayed as a development of biopolitics of liberal wars, protection and prevention become a duty for those responsible for the management of populations; they must act according to their predictions of the future to ensure security (Huysmans, Dobson and Prokhovnik 2006).

This debate concerning the state of exception is now well known. But the critique of the exception as danger is insufficient if it does not displace the exception as routine. Too often a managerial discourse concerning risk is seen as a solution to risk, as long as this management is more 'democratic' and less 'exceptional', in other words sufficiently routinized to be acceptable, and sufficiently effective. The problem with this debate is that the discourse of exceptionalism shares in the *doxa* that the globalization of security is a *turning point* in the history of humanity (and, indeed, a postmodern return to religious wars, which were foremost for Hobbes when discussing the Leviathan) (Neal 2009). It shares with the *doxa* the idea that we are leaving the Westphalian period for an unknown global era which looks like a coming anarchy where the 'community' of states no longer controls the use of major technologies of violence.

It is this *doxa* we must resist. Ideas about the globalization of (in)security are insufficient to analyse the practices through which it is produced. Risk management may be more prominent after 11 September 2001, but it is not new. The idea that we are in a new era of globalized (in)security serves the interests of diverse experts of security who are finding ways to collaborate with new partners, locally, nationally, internationally. The internal struggles amongst these groups, and the search for allies beyond the national arena, are the key elements that have enabled the emergence of the narrative of globalized (in)security. Whereas leading agencies within nation-states were designated to *limit* competition between services, across borders they have *expanded* rivalries (Bonditti 2001).

Transnational links between specialized agencies have transformed the notion of government, diminishing the capacities of elected politicians to steer the ship in one direction, by splitting bureaucracies. In this way the role of specialized professionals is further enhanced. In the European Union (EU), for example, the councils of Justice and Home Affairs or of Agriculture work to the detriment of the national position determined by Berlin, Roma, Bucharest or even Paris and London. Solidarities in the world of experts of (in)security have shifted from *nations to professions*, or more precisely to groups sharing similar activities (crafts), as in the pre-revolutionary meaning of 'corporation'. Hence, 'guilds' of specialists: guilds of border managers, guilds of intelligence services, guilds of risk managers, guilds of police with military status. The principles governing the worldview on (in)security are to be found in the oppositions between transatlantic networks of intelligence and policing which privilege coercive prevention on both sides of the Atlantic, and transatlantic networks of judges and activists emphasizing rule of law and respect for international treaties. This is why the opposition between the United States and the EU in terms of security policies is always a caricature. The United States and the EU have no homogeneous policy opposing Mars to Venus, warriors to peace lovers, neo-cons to democrats, wrong-doers to ethical people. In questions of security the policies of each country are not so much determined by governments and their professionals of politics, as by the struggles and alliances between local segments of transnational networks: of police-men, intelligence services, border guards, military officials, those representing the security industry, diplomats, risk analysts and so on. These networks of transnational guilds are often formalized by the existence of clubs or organizational structures (especially in the case of the EU), but they may also be more informal, as in the case of exchange of information between intelligence services following their own agenda, with or without the knowledge of their own governments, and often beyond legality (as Dick Marty, Claudio Fava and Martin Scheinin have shown) (Bigo *et al.* 2008: 31).

These guilds share the same beliefs and solutions, even if their internal experts belong to different nationalities, and they disagree with other specialized transna-tional guilds, themselves composed of diverse national experts. This is why I use the notion of a *transnational field of (in)security professionals* to analyse the impact of policies against terrorism, refusing popular ideas of a rift across the Atlantic, or the emergence of an hegemonic United States imposing a coalition of the willing, or even the more subtle ideas of global imperial power realized through a politics of permanent exception governing humanity biopolitically. To speak of a transnational field implies that the practices of power circulate along specific groups and determine who has authority and who is excluded from determining (in)security. But this does not imply a new form of homogenization at another scale. The practices are scattered, dispersed as in a Foucauldian *dispositif*, and they produce a normalization of the majority and a ban for minorities associated with insecurity and undesirability. These practices of (in)security are no longer homogenized by national governments, and they are certainly not globalized. We are after the globe and before the world (Walker 2010). We are in a world where boundaries do not form circles or bubbles with a clear inside and outside. Boundaries are now more like in a Mobius strip, maintaining a difference between an inside and an outside, but creating ambiguities about their location, depending on the position of the observer (Bigo 2006).

So there is not a clear-cut opposition between the United States and the EU in terms of value and civilizations, friends and enemies. Boundaries evolve along the positions and interests of the institutions constructing them, and only a detailed genealogy of each 'new' terminology permits us to understand how they assemble themselves into the *doxa* of global (in)security.

Perhaps one of the oldest cases of the creation of oppositions between different transnational experts, which then enabled the structuring of alliances, was created around the analysis of the Iranian Revolution of 1979. That analysis brought together the military and civil strategists of the Cold War on one side, and on the other the Special Operation Forces and the counter-insurrection specialists inherited from colonial and US interventions in Latin America. Delegitimated with decolonization and the Viet Nam war, counter-insurrection and anti-subversive specialists saw in the idea of a terrorism network with a stronghold in one country that would spread across the world a way to challenge the alternative vision of terrorism as an indirect and secret war between the major powers of the Cold War. They pushed the notion of terrorism as a form of 'real war' in contrast to that of nuclear deterrence as a 'false war', and they argued that they were more important for the new world than traditional soldiers in uniform. Throughout the 1970s and 1980s groups of experts in counterterrorism gathered to share their common perspectives and fears, and created a stock exchange of confidential information about suspects that the judiciary refused to investigate for lack of evidences. Strong bureaucratic coalitions emerged across the different departments of Justice, Defense and State in the United States and they developed their own networks of correspondents abroad. We know now how they succeeded in gaining the upper hand on strategies of conflicts in Iraq and Afghanistan. During the same period, police and intelligence networks from the Cold War were also reinventing themselves through anti-terrorist collaboration. The Drug Enforcement Agency, the National Security Agency and the Echelon network also extended their links abroad and these transatlantic ties were very strong until the late 1970s (Nadelman 1993). Professionals from the United Kingdom, the Netherlands, Belgium, Switzerland and Israel were included in the English-speaking intelligence community of the white commonwealth under a US leadership, which accorded to the United Kingdom a special relationship.

The initiative to build what became known as 'the third pillar' of the EU, dealing with 'internal security' as well as external, severed these transatlantic ties during the 1980s with the formation of a 'European' or 'Schengen' entity of policing. In Europe, assemblages of insecurity took a particular path, with growing fear of open borders in the mid-1980s, and the discourse of the 'security deficit' linked to the removal of internal border controls (with fears of Italian mafia arriving in France, Turkish migrants moving to United Kingdom, British football hooligans everywhere). In Europe, this development was the product of institutionalized professions like customs or border guards who were threatened by the idea of the removal of border controls. They did not share fears of global networks of terrorism coming from Middle East, and were more interested in local forms of extreme nationalism – which were also labelled 'terrorist' (Bigo 1996).

Police, customs officers and intelligence services met at the European level to consider how the opening of internal borders was creating a 'security deficit'. In Europe links developed through police liaison officers, clubs and groups, and by exchange of information through interoperable databases. The Trevi group was one of the initiators of new developments in insecurity, developing a series of 'warnings' and 'safeguard measures'. Under the heading of 'European internal security', the control of transnational flows of persons was added to traditional tasks of combating crime, and the missions, and sometimes even the professions, of customs officials, border guards and police were altered. They became obliged to exchange information about people (e.g., in the SIRENE system linked to Schengen). The analysis of different forms of crime and migration using the very same computer techniques and the very same databases (in which files were separated but where interoperability was immediately conceived as a mere operator) has been crucial in this respect (Bigo 1996).

In the United States the expansion of police and intelligence data bases existed too, reinforcing the transnationalization of guilds of specialists, but their transnational networks were more connected with the prevention of drug trafficking, especially on the border with Mexico, focusing for a while quite exclusively on cocaine (Andreas 2009). In Australia it was the indigenous peoples and, after that, migrants who were considered as a central threat, not terrorism or drug trafficking (Rajaram 2004). But the structuration, through international meetings like the G7–G8, of so-called links between terrorism, drug trafficking and illegal migration developed all through the 1990s (Scherrer 2009)

Post-9/11 the links between the United States and Europe have been partially reconstituted, but with different modalities of functioning (Carrera and Guild 2004; Dal Lago and Palidda 2010; Bigo *et al.* 2010). The transnationalization of exchanges of personal data by intelligence services on terrorist suspects works only if the different intelligence services accept as true the information they are given by their counterparts. Even if personnel have doubts, they are more or less constrained to inscribe in their lists of suspects the names given by the other services. A narrative of 'trust' between professionals enters into competition with the older one concerning 'national interest' and 'state sovereignty'. These exchanges are certainly asymmetrical, and their credibility depends on reliability of their sources, but they cannot function without reciprocity. There has been a transformation in terms of the number and quality of the exchange of data between European member states, and even more so in the case with the US agencies (some European services will share their information only on a base of mutual recognition or acceptance that their own priorities have to be considered as well as the 'global' agenda). The legitimacy of these exchanges becomes even more complicated when the exchange of personal data concerning suspects of terrorism takes place with agencies that are even less democratically accountable. Libya, Russia, China, Pakistan – all have put their own 'suspects' on these lists, and they have often been accepted as such (where more names are seen as improved efficacy of the lists). In some cases political opponents have become potential terrorists on Western lists, in the case, for example, of Chechens and Uighurs. In such cases, these states have 'sold' their own fears in response to the fears of Western states concerning radical Islam.

Such exchanges have been not only about information-knowledge but also about know-how and techniques of interrogation. Contrary to the discourse of the 'coalition of the willing', they have not resulted from a cooperation between the good cops (and intelligence services) versus the evildoers. They have been the result of strategies of competition, distinction and symbolic hierarchies between services, creating a kind of 'stock market' of exchange of fears, generating interdependency between intelligence services, and resulting in chains of illiberal practices, beginning with widespread lists of suspects themselves, multiplication of 'errors' and complicity in extraordinary renditions and torture (Bigo *et al.* 2008). Transnational expert groups and/or regular meetings between these agencies have been set up that go beyond exchanges of information through databases, proliferating not only in counterterrorism, but also concerning the so-called globalization of drug trafficking, money laundering, illegal migration, human trafficking, false documents. In each case there has been a new proliferation of automated lists of suspects and undesirable people. An industry of surveillance and computerization developing data mining and software for modelling and predicting behaviour has provided technologies for constituting these lists, which at the same time reinforce belief in their efficiency that is not supported by evidence. Techno-futurologists have been central in the framing of discourses concerning global insecurity and the need for global protection through prevention and prediction. A mapping of the main experts and professionals of security shows the relations between the different police clubs, formal groups of the EU, intelligence services on both sides of the Atlantic, and private companies working on banking and security industry (Bigo and Olsson forthcoming).

So many works have demonstrated these elements that it is a shame that the discourse of global (in)security is still so alive, including in the academic community. A counter-narrative based on precise ethnographical analysis of each local case of violence has been unable to undo the 'magic' of the association between globalization and security. Maybe, in a provocative way, Arjun Appadurai's analysis of India can be generalized. If these beliefs are so popular that nobody can discuss their truth, it is because they concern the 'fear of majorities of becoming minor (culturally or numerically)' (Appadurai, 2006: 83); fear that explains their willingness to use violence and discrimination against foreigners and actual minorities they suspect of becoming majorities. Is the future of India that of Europe and North America in this respect?

In conclusion, then, the narrative of global (in)insecurity is the effective creation of experts and spokespersons of bureaucratic (public and private) agencies who compete to define what is a threat, what is risk, and what is fate. The practices it engenders do not reflect a real fusion of war and crime, but the entanglement of the police and military through the role of intelligence services that are transformed into the foreseers of one future, the one that will happen, the future perfect, the one in which technology could reverse time and read the future as the past. According to the *doxa* after 11 September 2001, the globalization of dangers is a response to a threat to global security. In contrast, I argue that the convergence of military, intelligence and police activities, subordinating other means of everyday surveillance to their own purposes, is the result of a de-differentiation between internal and external security. This, in turn, is not the result of a transformation of political violence. It is the product of institutional practices of (in)securitization that define security and insecurity. To understand the transnationalization of the field of managers of unease, it is necessary to analyse in detail, to map, to trace the web of security institutions (both public and private) that has developed beyond national borders, through liaison officers of different kinds and through computer links as well as through 'internal service diplomats', forms of policing at a distance and transnational intelligence services. It is through this transnationalization that security is being disentangled from state sovereignty, not because fears global dangers are justified.

Further Reading

Bigo, D. and Tsoukala, A. 2008: *Terror, Insecurity and Liberty. Illiberal Practices of Liberal Regimes after 9/11*. New York: Routledge.

Dillon, M. 2007: Governing terror: the state of emergency of biopolitical emergence. *International Political Sociology* 1(1): 7–28.

Dal Lago, A. and Palidda, S. 2010: *Conflict, Security and the Reshaping of Society; The Civilization of War*. New York: Routledge.

19

Incarceration as a Political Institution

SARAH SHANNON AND CHRISTOPHER UGGEN

The prison is a significant social and political institution that is not only shaped by cultural and political forces, but in turn shapes the political and social lives of those who have been imprisoned. In this chapter, we discuss the theoretical backdrop for imprisonment as a political and cultural force worldwide. In doing so, we consider variation in imprisonment rates over space and time, selection into prison and the effects of incarceration on human and social capital. We conclude with an examination of the particular case of the United States to illustrate the social and political consequences of imprisonment.

Incarceration as a Political Institution

Scholars of punishment have called imprisonment 'intensely political,' owing to the politicization of crime policy and sweeping changes in sentencing patterns that have increased both the use of imprisonment and the length of incarceration for those convicted of crime (Jacobs and Helms 2001; Garland 1990; Savelsberg 1994; Chambliss 1999). Theories and empirical studies of punishment show how dynamics of politics and power shape incarceration patterns (Garland 1990; Foucault 1977; Barker 2009; Beckett and Sasson 2000; Tonry 1996, 2004; Gottschalk 2006; Sutton 2000), which in turn play a key role in state efforts to maintain control and establish legitimacy (Foucault 1977; Savelsberg 1994; Garland 1996, 2001; Jacobs and Helms 1996; Simon 1993; Sutton 2000; Beckett and Western 2001; Greenberg and West 2001; Jacobs and Carmichael 2001; Page 2004). Imprisonment is fundamentally an exercise of power and is therefore influenced by the political forces, policy choices, public sentiment, and media interpretations that drive political actors in modern society.

The experience of incarceration also shapes the political behaviour and attitudes of those who have been confined (Manza and Uggen 2006; Clear 2007; Travis 2005).

The Wiley-Blackwell Companion to Political Sociology, First Edition. Edited by Edwin Amenta, Kate Nash, and Alan Scott.
© 2012 Blackwell Publishing Ltd. Published 2012 by Blackwell Publishing Ltd.

Internationally, nations vary along a continuum of those who allow prison inmates to vote to those who bar all prisoners from voting (Uggen, Van Brakle and McLaughlin 2009). For example, over 5 million Americans are ineligible to vote owing to a felony conviction (Manza and Uggen 2006). In addition, research suggests that ex-prisoners are less trusting of government, less likely to think that they can influence politics, less engaged in political conversation and far less likely to participate politically than those with no prior involvement in the criminal justice system (Manza and Uggen 2006).

The prison is also bound up with other major social institutions as a powerful force of punishment that extends beyond its physical boundaries. Theoretical explanations for the use of prison as punishment posit several causal mechanisms, including class struggle (Rusche and Kirchheimer 1968; Melossi 1985; Western and Beckett 1999; Beckett and Sasson 2000), power regimes (Foucault 1977) and the interaction of culture and politics (Garland 1996, 2001; Jacobs and Helms 1996; Savelsberg 1994; Sutton 2000; Barker 2009). In this chapter, we elaborate the theoretical case for imprisonment as a political and cultural phenomenon, viewing the prison as a significant social and political institution. We also consider variation in imprisonment rates over space and time, selection into prison and effects of incarceration on human and social capital. Using the particular case of the United States, we conclude with a discussion of the political consequences of imprisonment.

Why Prison?

Social theorists have attempted to explain the rise in modern incarceration, especially in light of pronounced race, gender and class disparities in imprisonment. Rates of incarceration are increasing worldwide, but in some geographic areas more than others (Walmsley 2009). Figure 19.1, a cartogram depicting international incarceration rates in 2008, demonstrates the wide-ranging variation in international incarceration rates. Cartograms are maps that distort land area based on an alternative statistic, in this case incarceration rates. As a result, the sizes of the nations in the map are altered to reflect their rate of incarceration relative to other countries with similar rates. As compared to a more typical map of the world based solely on land area, this cartogram depicting incarceration rates brings high-incarceration nations, such as the United States, into bold relief, while nations with low incarceration rates, such as Canada and many nations in Europe and Africa, nearly disappear on the map. Other nations that are large in land area but lower in incarceration rates, such as China and India, are also noticeably diminished in size. The United States appears bloated on the cartogram, having the highest total rate of incarceration (756 per 100,000) in the world. Despite the fact that prison populations are growing worldwide, the United States outpaces every other nation, exceeding incarceration levels of other democratic nations by five to seven times (Walmsley 2009). Only two other nations have incarceration rates greater than 600 per 100,000: Russia (629) and Rwanda (604).

To explain this variation in incarceration rates around the world, scholars have compared national crime rates. Farrington, Langan and Tonry (2004) examined cross-national crime patterns in seven countries to see whether higher rates of crime explain higher national incarceration rates. Because robbery is most consistently measured across countries, robbery rates provide a useful measuring rod for

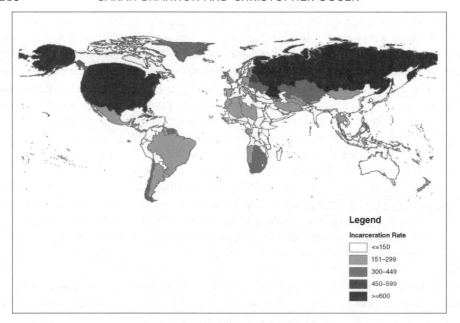

Figure 19.1 Cartogram of world incarceration rates, 2008
Source: Based on data from World Population List (8th edn). International Centre for Prison Studies

comparing national crime rates. As Figure 19.2 shows, the United States has one of the lower robbery rates among the seven nations compared. Low-incarceration countries such as the Netherlands and Canada have the highest robbery rates.

However, an examination of conviction rates (Figure 19.3) and total time served in prison shows that the United States ranks among the highest countries on these

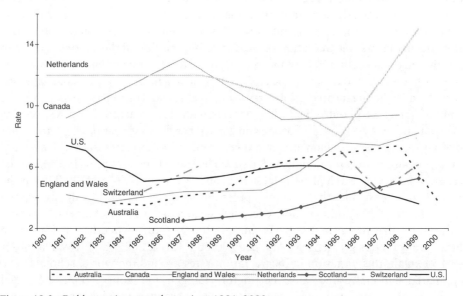

Figure 19.2 Robbery crime rates by nation, 1981–2000
Source: Adapted from David P. Farrington, Patrick A. Langan and Michael Tonry (eds) *Cross-national Studies in Crime and Justice* (Washington, DC: US Department of Justice, 2004)

measures. Studies within the United States have also shown that imprisonment is influenced by broader social processes, such as exposure to police surveillance (Beckett, Nyrop and Pfingst 2006; Tonry 1996), rates of conviction (Bridges and Steen 1998) and varying sentencing patterns (Steffensmeier, Ulmer and Kramer 1998).

From this study, it appears that involvement in crime alone does not explain who goes to prison. If cross-national differences in incarceration rates cannot be explained by differential crime rates, other political and cultural factors must be at play.

Incarceration in comparative perspective

At the macro level, scholars of punishment have sought to explain broader social trends influencing modern incarceration. Others have explored how such trends are filtered through particular political and cultural contexts, resulting in varied policies and practices of incarceration. Empirical studies have explored how macro trends in politics and culture have influenced penal policy using comparative studies of political traditions, legal structures and cultural influences (Sutton 2000; Savelsberg 1994). To explain the growth of incarceration, scholars have sought to link penal practices to larger social projects of political and cultural identity. As Garland (1990: 276) notes,

> In designing penal policy we are not simply deciding how to deal with a group of people on the margins of society – whether to deter, reform, or incapacitate them and if so how. Nor are we simply deploying power and economic resources for penological ends. We are also and at the same time defining ourselves and our society in ways which might be quite central to our cultural and political identity.

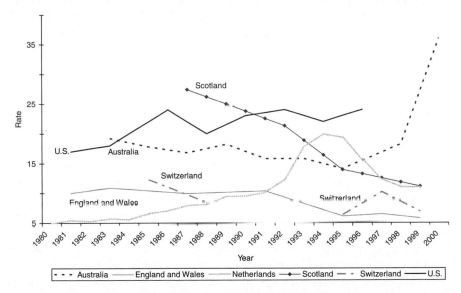

Figure 19.3 Robbery conviction rates by nation, 1981–2000
Source: Adapted from David P. Farrington, Patrick A. Langan and Michael Tonry (eds) *Cross-national Studies in Crime and Justice* (Washington, DC: US Department of Justice, 2004)

Scholars have forwarded global explanations that include adaptations to the risks of late modernity, the devolution of the welfare state and the rise of 'hyper-ghettos,' neoliberal economics and political strategies (Garland 2001; Wacquant 2001; Western and Beckett 1999; Simon 2007).

For example, Garland (2001) argues that the punitive turn towards imprisonment in the United Kingdom and the United States was precipitated by changes in structural and cultural forces from the 1960s onwards, including increasing crime rates, urban decay, changes in family structure and declines in economic prosperity, as well as shifts in cultural sensibilities, such as growing pessimism and distrust of the state. Combined with critiques of the rehabilitative model of incarceration from academics, prison rights activists and the political right, these forces helped drive various adaptations in the practice of punishment which include more punitive sentencing policies, the war on drugs and increased focus on containing and managing rather than rehabilitating criminals. The prison is an 'indispensable pillar of late modern social life' because it has become a way of addressing the anxieties and risks of contemporary life in the modern West (2001: 199).

In a study comparing five Western democracies (Australia, Canada, New Zealand, the United Kingdom and the United States), Sutton (2000) notes that imprisonment rates have risen in most Western democracies, although at a more moderate rate than in the United States overall. Further, these countries share similar demographic and political influences, but appear to have differential levels of incarceration. Sutton examined economic trends, social welfare spending and political factors in these five nations and found that prison growth slows when legal employment opportunity expands, but increases with declines in welfare spending and right party rule across all nations. The effect of decreased welfare spending was especially strong in the United States. Sutton argues that the diffuse administrative structure of the United States can lead to more highly politicized, localized and particularistic social policies that may amplify the effects of these factors as compared to other Western nations. Similarly, Savelsberg (1994) compared the relative impact of government structures, public opinion and cultural ideologies on imprisonment in Germany and the United States, finding that differences in institutional arrangements help account for variation in penal policy between the two nations.

Indeed, others have highlighted particular historical and political factors that have contributed to higher incarceration rates in the United States. Wacquant (2001) points to the rise of the urban ghetto and the dismantling of the welfare state as drivers of incarceration rates. According to Wacquant, the extreme racial disparities in prison populations demonstrate that mass imprisonment is the fourth in a series of social institutions, starting with slavery, designed to control African Americans as a subordinate caste. Prior to the 1970s, policy-makers attempted to ameliorate poverty and racial inequality through social welfare policies. Wacquant argues that neoliberal economic changes and the dwindling social safety net of welfare programmes since that time has led to the 'hyper-incarceration' of blacks as a means of managing and obscuring these disparities. Others have forwarded explicitly political arguments for the rise of retributive penal policies. Scholars have demonstrated how 'moral panics' – public scares over particularly egregious crimes – are used by politicians to gain electoral advantage (Cohen 1972; Beckett and Sasson 2000). Beckett (1997) argues that politicians capitalized on racialized political rhetoric and media attention in order to enact 'tough on crime' policies through the 1990s, which helped shore up their own political capital. Similarly, Simon (2007) posits that politicians increasingly frame non-criminal policies using the same rhetoric of retribution. In schools and the workplace, the language of crime and punishment is used as a tool to interpret and address non-crime problems, a practice Simon calls 'governing through crime'. Common in these analyses is that change in penal policy is driven by political strategy, not by an actual increase in crime.

Imprisonment and local political contexts in the United States

In light of the exceptional growth in US punishment rates, a special focus on that nation is merited. Over the past three decades, a large-scale transformation of the rationale of punishment has taken place in the United States. Historically, legal and philosophical justifications for punishment have included retribution, incapacitation and deterrence (Pincoffs 1966). While retribution focuses on matching the punishment to the crime, incapacitation and deterrence emphasize the prevention of crime through physical restraint or fear of punishment. For most of the twentieth century, rehabilitation of individual prisoners was the central goal of incarceration, implemented through indeterminate sentences, treatment and education programmes within prisons, and state parole boards (Rothman 2002). Since the mid-1970s, however, changes in sentencing laws have led to the dismantling of the 'rehabilitative ideal' and a turn towards retribution as the rationale for punishment through the establishment of determinate sentences and 'get tough' polices such as three strikes laws and mandatory minimums. Apart from an uptick during the Great Depression, the incarceration rate between 1925 and 1972 held steady at about 100 inmates per 100,000 population. From 1973 to the present, however, incarceration has climbed sharply at an average rate of approximately 6 percent per year, as illustrated in Figure 19.4. By the end of 2008, the US incarceration rate including prison and jail inmates was 754 per 100,000, with a total of 2.3 million people serving time (Sabol, West and Cooper 2009). The increased use of prison as punishment and longer prison sentences have fueled the rising incarceration rate. Feeley and Simon (1992) have argued that these developments characterize a 'new penology,' which focuses on the containment and management of dangerous populations rather than the reform of individuals.

A growing line of inquiry questions the utility of overarching theories of the transformation of criminal punishment and, rather, seeks to understand how such political and cultural processes take place within specific regional and local contexts (Lynch 2010; Tonry 2009). As Lynch notes, the dominant narrative of the decline of the rehabilitative ideal in the United States over the past three decades assumes that such practices were widely held and practised in similar ways across regions and localities, which was clearly not the case in her study of Arizona. Similarly, Tonry argues that explanations dependent on macro-level social and economic trends, as outlined above, do not hold true in all contexts, even in cases where theoretically they should. As a result, these authors assert that attention to regional and local variation in politics and culture is instrumental to understanding criminal punishment.

At the national level, Tonry (2009) argues that a distinctly 'paranoid' American style of politics combined with conservative religious moralism, racial inequality and

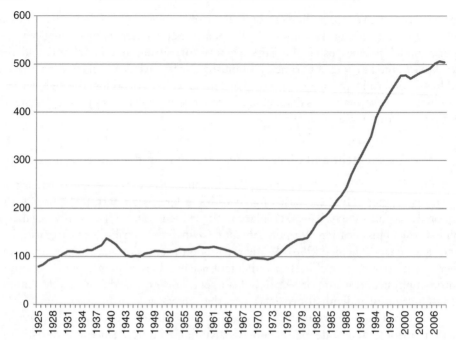

Figure 19.4 US prison incarceration rate, 1925–2008
Source: Based on data from Bureau of Justice Statistics

outmoded constitutional arrangements facilitate the enactment of laws that appeal to public emotions and short-term political agendas. In their study of US election cycles and imprisonment rates, Jacobs and Helms (2001) noted that incarceration increases during Republican presidencies. In addition, during presidential campaign cycles, incumbents from both political parties vie for votes by enacting more punitive policies. Jacobs and Helms call this a 'political-imprisonment cycle' in which partisan and electoral factors both impact incarceration (2001: 190).

Studies have also sought to explain variation among US states in rates of incarceration, noting that differences in economics, crime rates, demographics and sentencing laws can lead to diverse practices among localities (Zimring and Hawkins 1991). As Figure 19.5 shows, individual states within the United States vary substantially in the use of imprisonment. This cartogram, like Figure 19.1, distorts the land area of US states based on their incarceration rates. In doing so, the map dramatizes the immense variation among the states in levels of incarceration. While the world map in Figure 19.1 tells the story of US exceptionalism on the world stage, Figure 19.5 demonstrates that incarceration in the United States in not merely a national-level phenomenon. Rather, factors influencing incarceration function at the state level in markedly different ways.

As compared to the world cartogram, in which many nations' incarceration rates fall into the lowest category of 150 per 100,000 or less, no US state has a rate in that range. As Figure 19.5 shows, incarceration rates are much lower in the Northeast (306) and Midwest (393) than in the South (556). States such as Minnesota (179), North Dakota (225), Utah (232) and much of New England shrink significantly, while

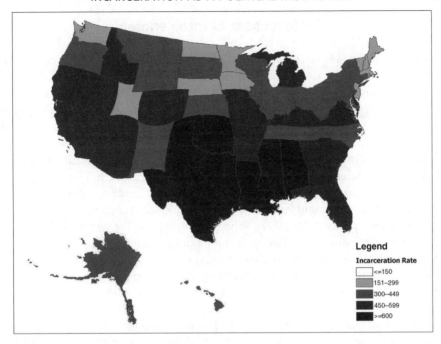

Figure 19.5   Cartogram of US incarceration rates by state, 2008
Source: Based on data from Bureau of Justice Statistics

high-incarceration states such as Louisiana (853), Mississippi (735), Oklahoma (661) and Texas (639) swell in size. The states with the strongest recent growth trends (e.g., Minnesota, Iowa, New Hampshire) tend to have lower base rates, while states with the slowest growth rates tend to be those with higher corrections spending as a percentage of their total state budget (Pew 2008).

Greenberg and West (2001) argue that varying religious and political cultures between states shape differences in penal decision making. For example, they found that incarceration rates were higher in states with higher levels of violent crime, suggesting that more punitive public sentiments in these states contribute to a rise in imprisonment as a response to greater violence. Barker (2006) examined case studies of three states (California, New York and Washington) and found that political context affects incarceration rates depending on levels of citizen participation. Barker's analysis of Washington State shows that, contrary to expectations, greater public participation in government can decrease incarceration rates. Gilmore's (2007) analysis of the 'prison fix' in California suggests that governments may turn to imprisonment as a way to address fiscal crises. In California's case, the prison expansion helped alleviate unemployment and, in some communities, buffer the impact of the economic downturn. Similarly, Lynch (2010) found that cultural values particular to Arizona, such as distrust of government and traditional punitiveness, helped facilitate prison expansion as a means of promoting economic development in rural locales. Taken together, such studies suggest that political context shapes incarceration rates in ways that cannot be accounted for from a macro-level framework. Incarceration is an institution that is shaped by multiple social forces, including economics, politics and culture that vary across national, regional and local jurisdictions.

Consequences of Incarceration

Increased incarceration rates over the past three decades in the United States have created a population of about 4 million ex-prisoners (Uggen, Manza and Thompson 2006). In addition, more than 11 million US residents are former felons, whether previously incarcerated or not. Adding together current and former felons, the number tops 16 million, which totals about 8 percent of the adult population, one-fifth of the African American population and more than one-third of the African American adult male population. Incarceration is by no means the only form of punishment imposed by the state. Concomitant with the growth of imprisonment has been the rise of community corrections – probation and parole. About 5.1 million Americans (1 in 45 adults) were under community supervision in 2008 alone, 84 percent of whom were on probation (Glaze and Bonczar 2009). When combined with the number of individuals incarcerated in prisons and jails, over 7 million adults (about 1 in 31) in the United States are under the supervision of the criminal justice system. However, these overall numbers obscure the differential impact of incarceration on low-income and minority populations (Clear 2007; Western 2006). For example, in 2004 about 7.5 percent of the total adult population in the United States had a felony conviction on their records as compared to 33.4 percent of African American adult males (Wakefield and Uggen 2010). In addition, while the vast majority of the prison population remains male (Sabol, West and Cooper 2009), women's incarceration has been growing faster than men's in recent years (Heimer and Kruttschnitt 2005; Kruttschnitt and Gartner 2005). Recent research has also documented the proliferation of hybrid forms of punishment that combine administrative and civil laws to 'banish' persons with criminal backgrounds from some public spaces (Beckett and Herbert 2009).

Short of the death penalty, however, imprisonment is the most severe penalty at the state's disposal. Incarceration removes people from the general population for extended periods of time, severing their ties to family and other forms of social support as well as from significant social institutions such as the labour market (Braman 2004; Clear 2007; Pager 2007; Travis 2005; Western 2006). This growth in the number of individuals who have been incarcerated or otherwise supervised by the criminal justice system has had far-ranging social and political consequences for individuals, families and communities.

Social consequences of incarceration

Although our focus is on political and civic effects, a substantial body of research has documented the 'collateral consequences' of imprisonment in terms of labour market opportunities, family, and health of former prisoners. These effects are present at both the macro and micro levels. For example, high levels of incarceration artificially lower the unemployment rate by removing large segments of working-age men from labour-force counts (Western and Beckett 1999). However, incarceration also impedes the employment prospects of individual ex-prisoners by reducing wages and lifetime earnings (Pettit and Western 2004; Waldfogel 1994; Western 2002; Western 2006) and providing a 'disqualifying credential' in the form of a criminal record (Pager 2003, 2007). These effects vary significantly by race, such that African Americans suffer the most severe attenuations of earnings and employment as compared to whites and Latinos (Western 2006; Pager 2007).

Incarceration also impacts families by lowering marriage rates, increasing single-parent families and concentrating poverty among women and children (Western and Wildeman 2009). This is especially true for African Americans and those living in disadvantaged neighbourhoods (Western and Wildeman 2009; Clear 2007). Approximately 2.2 million US children have a parent in prison (Western 2006; Wildeman 2010). Children with incarcerated parents have been shown to suffer detrimental consequences, including increased aggression and delinquency, decreased educational attainment and increased social isolation and stigma (Murray and Farrington 2008; Foster and Hagan 2007; Hagan and Palloni 1990; Wakefield 2007; Wakefield and Uggen 2010; Wildeman 2010). Parental incarceration is associated with poor mental and behavioural health in children (Foster and Hagan 2007; Parke and Clarke-Stewart 2003; Wakefield 2007; Wildeman 2009; Wakefield and Uggen 2010). Families suffer other informal costs, such as stigma and loss of social support (Comfort 2008; Braman 2004). Moreover, families and communities are at greater risk for negative health outcomes given the detrimental effects of imprisonment on the physical and mental health of inmates (Massoglia 2008a, 2008b; Schnittker and John 2007; Massoglia and Schnittker 2009). As with labour market and family effects, African Americans are at greater risk for poorer health, given their disproportionate exposure to incarceration (Massoglia 2008a).

Most importantly for our purposes, communities with high levels of incarceration are at greater risk for social instability and diminished political and civic engagement (Clear 2007; Manza and Uggen 2006). Problems associated with re-entry of ex-prisoners fall disproportionately on low-income urban neighbourhoods. For example, some neighbourhoods in Cleveland and Baltimore have more than 18 percent of male residents incarcerated, and one in five adult males in Washington, DC are behind bars on any given day (Clear 2007). Similarly, over half of all prisoners released in Illinois and Maryland return to the cities of Chicago and Baltimore, respectively. Within these urban areas, one-third of returning prisoners are concentrated in a handful of neighbourhoods (Travis 2005). All of these factors point to the far-ranging effects of punishment in the United States, especially among minority populations and low-income communities. Imprisonment thus interacts with other major social institutions, such as the labour market and the family, to exacerbate inequality.

Political consequences of incarceration

There is substantial evidence that incarceration is not only influenced by politics, but also has political implications for the individual as well as at the state, national and international levels. Felon disenfranchisement affects 1 in 40 (about 5.4 million) adult Americans who are unable to vote because of a felony conviction (Manza and Uggen 2006). States vary in policy regarding felon voting, however. Maine and Vermont have no restrictions on felon voting, allowing even current prison inmates to vote. Other states bar only inmates from participation, others prohibit all inmates and probationers, and a few exclude even ex-felons from voting regardless of sentence completion (Manza and Uggen 2006). These felon voting restrictions clearly influence state and national politics. Disenfranchisement of current and former felons has impacted the results of multiple elections nationwide, including the 2000 Presidential outcome (Manza and Uggen 2006). Had former felons been allowed to vote, at least seven Senate elections between 1978 and 2000 would probably have turned in the Democrats' favour. As a result, Democrats might have held control of the Senate throughout the 1990s (Uggen and Manza 2002). Internationally, felon disenfranchisement policies have been linked with low political and economic development, high ethnic heterogeneity and punitive criminal justice policies (Uggen, Van Brakle and McLaughlin 2009).

In addition to civic participation, incarceration rates impact government spending and the allocation of political influence and resources. In 2006, federal, state and local governments combined spent a total of about $68 billion on corrections (Bureau of Justice Statistics 2009). States spent just over $40 billion on corrections, $33 billion of which was spent directly on imprisonment. This is a 548 percent increase in corrections spending since 1982. Clearly, incarceration is a major source of government expenditure at all levels.

But more than economic resources are at stake in the growth of incarceration in the United States. The decennial census, which determines allocations of federal and state funding streams, is also distorted by incarceration. By law, prisoners are counted in the census based on their current residence in prison, not where they lived prior to incarceration (Lotke and Wagner 2003; Lawrence and Travis 2004; Clear 2007). The federal government disburses more than $140 billion via formula-based grants determined in part by census data (Lawrence and Travis 2004). These grant funds are used for programmes such as Medicaid, foster care, adoption assistance and social services block grants. At the state level, census counts determine allocations of funding for community health services, transportation, public housing and other essential services. Given that a high proportion of prisoners come from low-income, under-resourced and high-poverty communities, counting them for census purposes in locations outside of their home communities can shift the distribution of economic and social service resources away from already distressed urban areas (Clear 2007).

Census counts also determine political boundaries and representation (Lotke and Wagner 2003). The federal as well as state governments use census data to determine legislative redistricting. At the national level, incarceration has very little impact on representation given that most prisoners are confined within their home states. At the state level, however, political representation can be significantly affected by counting prisoners in prison facilities rather than their home communities (Lotke and Wagner 2003). As with economic appropriations, the distribution of power at the state level can be transferred from predominantly urban areas where most prisoners originate to outstate areas where they are imprisoned.

In the light of such far-reaching impacts of incarceration on civic participation as well as allocation of political power and economic resources, it is clear that the prison's reach is indeed long in the United States, shaping the political and social lives of individuals, communities, states and the nation in profound ways.

Conclusion

In this chapter, we have argued that the prison is a major social and political institution. Imprisonment is not only shaped by but also determines political, cultural and economic conditions. Incarceration is itself an institution that interacts with other social institutions in complicated ways. This reality necessitates a broader vision of the prison as a form of punishment, as well as a comprehensive assessment of the political, economic and social impacts of incarceration at multiple levels of analysis.

Social theorists and researchers have sought to explain why the United States has achieved such a comparatively and historically high rate of incarceration over the past three decades. Explanations have ranged from macro-level theories that attempt to take account of global processes, such as neoliberal economics and social conditions of late modernity, to empirical studies examining or comparing specific nations, regions or states. Some scholars argue persuasively that, while macro-level social, economic and political factors may play a role, they are almost always filtered through the unique cultural and political landscapes of specific localities. Incarceration is an institution that is shaped by the political and cultural forces at play within nations, regions, states and even smaller jurisdictions.

Nevertheless, incarceration is not simply an institution shaped by politics; it in turn shapes the political, social and economic lives of individuals, families and communities. From employability to civic participation, incarceration leaves an indelible mark not only on the men and women who experience prison, but also those to whom they are connected in their families and neighbourhoods. Imprisonment impacts the political power and government resources allocated to particular jurisdictions. As a result, imprisonment is a complex, multifaceted and powerful political institution in the United States and worldwide.

Further Reading

Garland, D. 2001: *The Culture of Control. Crime and Social Control in Contemporary. Society.* Chicago: University of Chicago Press.

Manza, J. and Uggen, C. 2006: *Locked Out: Felon Disenfranchisement and American Democracy.* New York: Oxford University Press.

Sutton, J.R. 2000: Imprisonment and social classification in five common-law democracies, 1955–1985. *American Journal of Sociology* 106: 350–386.

Wacquant, L. 2001: Deadly symbiosis: when ghetto and prison meet and mesh. *Punishment & Society* 3: 95–133.

Western, B. 2006: *Punishment and Inequality in America.* New York: Russell Sage Foundation.

Part III

The Political and the Social

A. States and Civil Society
B. The Politics of Identity and Action
C. Citizenship

20

Culture, State and Policy

Brian Steensland and Christi M. Smith

Since the 'cultural turn' of the 1970s, scholarly conceptions of culture have changed significantly. This chapter outlines these changes and illustrates how they have been refracted in the cultural analysis of politics. Conceptual innovations have reformulated long-standing perspectives on national culture, status politics and political symbolism. Newer lines of analysis emphasize the influence of discourse and cognition. Promising research in this vein centres on state formation and state policy making, topics that serve as focal points for an agenda that pushes cultural analysis in productive directions.

Introduction: The Cultural Analysis of Politics and the State

Over the past generation, scholarly conceptions of culture have changed significantly. The 'cultural turn' of the 1970s established an intellectual framework that displaced views of culture prominent during the post-Second World War era. Cultural analyses of politics have refracted these changes. Older notions of political culture have been recast and more recent conceptual innovations have opened up new lines of inquiry and argument. These changes have penetrated the study of politics to varying degrees. Relative to research on social movements, studies of the state have been slow to incorporate these trends. The state continues to be seen as dominated by objective interests and instrumental rationality and therefore seems inimical to cultural analysis. Yet as this chapter will illustrate, processes of state formation and policy making serve as promising focal points for a research agenda that pushes cultural analysis in productive directions.

The older, now largely discredited conception of culture was heavily influenced by Talcott Parsons' structural-functionalist perspective (Parsons and Shils 1951). In Parsons' framework, culture was a well-integrated system of values, norms and

The Wiley-Blackwell Companion to Political Sociology, First Edition. Edited by Edwin Amenta, Kate Nash, and Alan Scott.
© 2012 Blackwell Publishing Ltd. Published 2012 by Blackwell Publishing Ltd.

symbols that served as society's master coordinating system. Individuals internalized widely held societal values, and their actions, guided by these values, then reproduced social organization at the macro level. Prominent studies of politics incorporated Parsons' cultural model. Against arguments that focused on economic structure, party systems or patterns of industrialization, these studies emphasized the role that national values played in political development (Lipset 1963), democratic governance (Almond and Verba 1963) and welfare state formation (Rimlinger 1971).

The 'cultural turn' that began in the 1970s reacted against and subsequently superseded this prevailing view of culture. The newer approach to culture contains a number of interrelated facets (see Smith, 2001, for a concise overview of these trends). First, the dominant imagery of culture as widely shared and socially integrating has been supplanted by views of culture as fragmented, multiple and contested at both the collective and individual levels. Social groups have subcultures that are distinct from, and often opposed to, other subcultures (Hall and Jefferson 1976). This multiplicity provides individuals with access to a variety of cultural repertoires that they utilize as befits their situational context (Swidler 2001). To the extent that culture *is* widely shared, scholars recognize this as an outcome to be explained rather than a state of affairs to be assumed. Second, following Geertz's (1973) seminal scholarship, the locus of culture in empirical analysis has shifted from individuals' internalized states to publicly available cultural practices. Third, the type of culture that orients analyses has shifted from normative values to collective schemas and discursive formulations. Fourth, because culture is seen as essentially contested terrain, studies give greater attention to the connections between culture, power and inequality (Bourdieu 1990; Foucault 1980). Fifth, and perhaps most fundamentally, the dominant imagery of the culture–structure relationship has changed. Most sociologists of culture see culture as neither the master coordinating system in social life (as in Parsons) or as an epiphenomenal reflection of society's material base (as in classic Marxism). Rather they see social structure as mutually constituted by material resources and the cognitive schemas through which they are understood (Sewell's 1992).

These broad conceptual shifts within the sociology of culture manifest themselves in the study of politics in two key ways. Scholars have reformulated well-established perspectives, such as those on national culture, status politics and political symbolism. Beyond this, newer lines of analysis centred on discourse and shared cognition have emerged. Exemplary here are studies of the state that have argued for the causal influence of political discourse, political ideas and constitutive schemas on state processes.

Contemporary Perspectives on National Culture, Status Politics, and Symbolism

A number of important ways of thinking about the cultural dimension of politics pre-date the cultural turn. While these remain important touchstones for analysis, they have been reformulated in light of recent trends within the sociology of culture. For instance, the studies of political development inspired by Parsons based their accounts on the idea that societal values shape national political development. More contemporary work continues to recognize the importance of cultural differences at the level of nation-states, but recasts those differences in various ways as national culture. Dobbin (1994) argues that national political culture explains the differing patterns of industrial policy during the railroad era in the United States, Britain and France. Yet rather than invoking national values, he defines 'political culture' as the ways in which industrialists and government experts perceived economic and industrial problems, and how the prevailing means–ends designations in each country delimited particular solutions to those problems. Lamont and Thévenot (2000) centre their analysis of French–US civic differences in terms of 'national repertoires' that include institutionalized cultural categories and dominant modes of justification and evaluation. In her account of the rise of right-wing movements in Europe, Berezin (2009) emphasizes national 'consolidation regimes' in contrast to studies that highlight the role played by partisan politics. Countries that have fused national culture and political institutions, such as a strong national identity and the provision of social security, are more likely to produce nationalist movements as a response to globalization and immigration. Consolidation regimes produce cultural relations that mitigate or exacerbate reactionary sentiments.

Another influential approach to political culture is the 'status politics' perspective that Gusfield (1963) developed in his analysis of the temperance movement in the United States. He argued that political conflict was as often rooted in conflict between status groups – who sought political objectives that reaffirmed their position in the status hierarchy – as in class-based competition over economic resources. More recent analyses along these lines have drawn conceptually from the work of Bourdieu (1990), whose analysis of social conflict and reproduction in terms of habitus, fields, and forms of capital represents a synthesis of Marxian and Weberian perspectives. Beisel (1997) extends Bourdieu's approach to social conflict in her analysis of anti-vice campaigns in late nineteenth-century America. Elite groups in northeastern cities protected their class privilege with claims about aesthetics, fine breeding and natural hierarchy. Yet their interests were also fundamentally status based – rooted as they were in concerns about family reproduction and perceived threats to social rank. Elites' support for moral crusades against pornography, gambling and contraception bolstered their claims on both material and symbolic resources. Steinmetz (2007) employs Bourdieu's approach to status competition in his comparative analysis of nineteenth-century 'native policy' in three German colonies. Colonial states were political fields in which acute knowledge of indigenous culture was the symbolic currency. Through acts of policy making, German colonial elites sought social recognition by demonstrating their ethnographic capital.

A third long-standing perspective on political culture focuses on the role that symbols and ritual play in politics. Representative of this long-standing interest is Edelman's (1964) book, *The Symbolic Uses of Politics*. While not denying the instrumental side of politics, Edelman argued that political activity also contains an important expressive dimension. Elections have ritualistic components, political conventions affirm group sentiments and public policy acts as a 'condensation symbol' that evokes a variety of emotions and associations among the electorate. Contemporary scholarship downplays the singular meaning of any particular symbol and instead points to the multi-vocality of political symbols and the strategic virtues of ambiguity. Kertzer (1988) observes that political symbols do not always derive their influence by imposing a consensual meaning upon things; rather their power derives from their ability to generate sentiments of group solidarity in the absence of shared understandings. Wagner-Pacifici and Schwartz (1991) illustrate such processes in their analysis of contestation over the Vietnam Veterans Memorial.

Recent studies turn the analysis of ritual on its head as well. They demonstrate how ritual can be used not only as a vehicle for social integration but as an instrument of subjugation in the hands of the elites and an instrument of protest and resistance in the hands of the marginalized. Wedeen (1999) documents the former process in her analysis of the Assad regime in Syria. The regime devoted extensive resources to enforcing tired and transparently phony ritualized acts. But in doing so, President Assad dramatized the power of his regime through its ability to compel people to avow the absurd. Ritual served as a social control mechanism to elicit compliance. Taylor *et al.* (2009) examined the dramaturgical motives underlying same-sex wedding ceremonies in San Francisco. They found that gay couples who saw dubious value in the institution of heterosexual marriage nevertheless participated in same-sex wedding ceremonies as an instrumental and expressive protest tactic that further catalyzed gay rights activism. This work is situated in a long-standing line of inquiry into expressive and ritualized dimensions of resistance (Hall and Jefferson 1976; Willis 1977).

New Lines of Inquiry on Political Processes: Discourse, Ideas, Schemas

Beyond revising long-standing approaches to culture and politics, contemporary studies have brought attention to discourse and shared cognition to the forefront in new ways. Useful here is Campbell's (1998) discussion of culture operating in the foreground or background of political life. Elements of culture in the foreground are explicit. They are mentally available to actors to utilize. Elements of culture in the background are tacit. They operate as cognitive assumptions or categories of knowledge rather than as explicit arguments, and are thus less amenable to easy articulation. While both types of culture exert influence on politics, a common distinction is to treat discourse as a resource that actors strategically deploy (foreground), while cognitive processes operate in either the foreground or background, depending on whether the analytic focus in on 'ideas' (foreground) or 'schemas' (background).

Political discourse

There are two prominent streams of research that examine the role of discourse on politics: studies of framing and studies of narrative. Frames are typically seen as being put to strategic use. Treatments of narrative are more diverse, depicting it as either a strategic resource or as more constitutive, depending on the concept's specification.

In studies of politics, framing refers to the discursive process of highlighting particular problems, solutions, moral evaluations or collective identities for the purposes of motivation and persuasion. Research on collective action frames and policy frames has drawn out the explanatory value of this concept. The study of collective action frames is now well established within the literature on social movements, where the framing concept was introduced to help explain membership recruitment and collective mobilization. In a seminal article, Snow *et al.* (1986) describe four different strategies of 'frame alignment' that social movement entrepreneurs employ to draw people into participation. Each involves creating congruence between the interests of potential members and the objectives of the movement. Their analysis opened the way for greater attention to the influence of culture on social movement processes (see Benford and Snow 2000 for a review). In examinations of public policy, Gamson and Modigliani (1989) developed the concept of policy frames to help explain trends in public attitudes towards complex legislative issues. In their study of attitudes towards nuclear energy, they argued that the 'interpretive packages' advanced by political actors construe the stakes of social issues in strikingly different ways. Changes in public attitudes can be seen as a function of the symbolic contests between groups over whose framing of an issue prevails. Gamson (1992) extended this approach by using focus groups to examine how attitudes towards social issues were influenced by a combination of personal experience, conventional wisdom and policy frames in the media.

Recently studies have moved analyses of framing in two directions. First, scholars have sought to integrate the influence of framing on movement outcomes with the impact of more 'structural' factors, such as the resources available to social movements and the opportunities available to them in the political environment. For instance, McCammon *et al.* (2007) analysed factors that contributed to the success of the women's jury movement. They found that discursive framing of the issue mattered, alongside other factors such as political opportunities and legal constraints. Second, scholars have treated patterns of policy framing as an outcome of interest in their own right. This is based on accumulating evidence that political discourse impacts citizens' policy preferences (Chong and Druckman 2007). This evidence then begs the question of what factors explain patterns of policy framing. Steensland (2008a) evaluated the joint influence of two such factors: the composition of actors who receive coverage in the media and the diffusion of ideas in the broader political environment. His analysis revealed that diffusion mattered overwhelmingly for how welfare reform was framed in the United States. A cross-national comparison of the United States and France found that four factors influence patterns of media discourse on social issues: national cultural repertoires, the legal environment, the degree of media autonomy and the country's position in the global system (Benson and Saguy 2005).

Beyond studies of framing, the concept of narrative has advanced studies of political discourse in productive ways. While definitions vary somewhat, the main thing narrative does is emplot social action in a temporal, story-like cultural framework. Narratives typically contain sequential ordering, claims about causality, a cast of characters, a point of view and normative evaluations. In her analysis of storytelling in politics, Polletta (2006) observes that narratives can be seen as a 'master' type of discourse: they comprise other forms of discourse, serve as vehicles for cultural power and provide the components for collective action frames. Her empirical analyses underscore the strategic uses of narrative, such as when black leaders invoke the legacy of Martin Luther King, Jr in Congress to help bolster their claims as heirs to the civil rights movements, or when citizens employ narrative in public deliberative forums in attempts to garner agreement.

Narrative contributes to understanding a variety of political processes, including collective identity formation, interest definition and the workings of ideology.

For instance, Steinmetz (1992) argues that narrative contributes to working-class formation under the following conditions: when social class is the key organizing principle for individual and collective stories; when events that are central to class identity are highlighted and discussed in positive terms; when the causal accounts used to explain social phenomena emphasize class relations; and when the class basis of group histories is fully elaborated, so that the group will be able to resist alternative accounts of history or group identity. While this framework pertains to social class, the model is generalizable to other social categories, such as gender, race or religion. Narrative also plays an important role in shaping group interests. Gerteis (2007) documents this process in his analysis of interracial organizing among the Knights of Labor and the Populists in the late nineteenth century. Their adherence to a group narrative based upon civic virtue led them, against prevailing norms, to seek common political cause with black workers. Immigrant workers, on the other hand, though no less 'wage slaves' than blacks, were deemed unfit as political allies because they were not viewed as capable of upholding the duties of republican citizenship. The dominant narrative of civic virtue shaped these groups' coalition-building preferences.

Ideology is a notoriously slippery concept (Eagleton 1991). Yet it can be productively recast as what Somers (1999) refers to as 'meta-narrative', which is akin to Bourdieu's (1990) notion of 'doxa'. The benefit of doing so stems from the ability to disaggregate some of ideology's component parts to show how narratives generate taken-for-granted meanings that privilege some group interests over others. Somers takes 'Anglo-American citizenship theory' as her case. In her reading, the embrace of this Lockean theory of state–society relations has been the main culprit in the subordination of 'civil society' and citizenship to the market side of the market–state dichotomy. Analytically, Somers deconstructs the historical roots of this ideological framework by showing how it comprises two distinct cultural elements: binary oppositions that situate natural rights in the private realm rather than the public realm, and a narrative that naturalizes the market by temporally associating it with an authentic and true 'state of nature' while simultaneously casting the state as an unnatural and arbitrary modern intervention. Thus meta-narratives (or ideologies) can be seen as dually constituted by binary oppositions and the narratives that emplot them. Somers and Block (2005) employ this framework in their analysis of welfare reform discourse in the United States and Britain over a 200-year period. They contend that to understand the continuing efficacy of the 'perversity thesis' – the idea that welfare benefits exacerbate the problems they aim to solve – across two centuries, two continents and a variety of social conditions, it is essential to understand the epistemological structure of anti-welfare discourse – in particular, how the perversity thesis reframes potentially disconfirming evidence in its favour through a 'conversion narrative' based on social naturalism.

Ideas and constitutive schemas

The sociological approach to cognition views thinking as a property of social groups, or 'thought communities', such as those based on nationality, religion or social class (Zerubavel 1997). This contrasts with approaches that focus on universalistic features of the human mind or that treat cognition as personal and idiosyncratic. Shared cognition and collective representations are clearly consequential for politics. Within political sociology, a growing body of work employing these concepts has examined transformations in the structure of the state – both the early stages of state formation and the policy-making processes of mature states. Work in this area can be differentiated by whether it is oriented by 'ideas' or 'constitutive schemas'. While it is important not to overdraw this distinction, these two veins of research have different intellectual origins, orient themselves differently vis-à-vis other types of explanations and challenge mainstream (i.e., non-cultural) perspectives on policy making to different degrees.

Research on the role of ideas in policy making is rooted within the historical institutionalist perspective, and the meaning of 'ideas' is typically akin to formal knowledge among experts. As historical institutionalism took an ideational turn, ideas were initially integrated in analytic frameworks as an outcome influenced by other factors. Institutional factors, such as state capacity, constrained the types of ideas that emerged in policy domains (Steinmo, Thelen and Longstreth 1992). In her analysis of employment policy in the United States, Weir (1992) referred to the process as 'bounded innovation'. As state actors came to play a larger role in explanations of policy development, however, scholars began to recognize that the actions of state actors themselves were under-theorized. In his discussion of this shortcoming, Hall (1993) developed the idea of 'policy paradigms' to provide leverage for understanding decision-making processes among policy-makers. Put simply, policy-makers have ideas about the world that guide policy development within institutional constraints. Importantly, these ideas vary across groups. So when confronted with the same economic problem, committed Keynesian economists are likely to develop policy solutions different from those of committed monetarists. In the area of foreign policy, Goldstein and Keohane (1993) developed a similar idea, which they termed 'roadmaps'. They underscored the significant role that epistemic communities play in bringing different cognitive roadmaps to bear on policy formation. Since the mid-1990s, scholarship on ideas and policy making within the historical institutionalist school, much of it by political scientists, has been steadily growing (see Béland 2005 for a review).

Beyond treating ideas primarily as formal knowledge, there are a few things to note about this approach. In many formulations, most explicitly early on, the impact of ideas is juxtaposed with the impact of actors' interests. This implies that interest definition happens outside of cultural influences. When it comes to incorporating ideas into models of policy making, the causal imagery is one of interactions between independent factors. Experts' interests are channelled by the roadmaps or paradigms that prevail in particular epistemic communities. Thus 'ideas' are added to the historical institutionalist framework without substantially altering it.

This stands in contrast with scholarship oriented by a deeper and more diffuse notion of culture that is perhaps best described as 'constitutive schemas'. The roots of this approach are multifaceted, found in the cognitive turn within psychology and anthropology (DiMaggio 1997), poststructuralism (Foucault 1980), practice theory (Bourdieu 1990) and feminist theory (Fraser 1989b). A few things set it apart from the research on 'ideas'. First, the focus on collective schemas directs attention to the structure of knowledge as much as to the content of knowledge. A hallmark of this research tradition is attention to how information gets mentally sorted into interconnected categories (D'Andrade 1995). The insight here is that mental categories systematically bias perception, reasoning and motivation. This emphasis is particularly attractive to scholars interested in the interrelations between social categorization schemes – such as those concerning race, class, gender or citizenship – and the state. Second, in this view, culture is more diffuse than expert ideas. It is widely shared by the public and it is interwoven into the fabric of language, legal rules, institutional practices and group identities. Therefore schemas are reflected in formal knowledge, such as experts' policy paradigms, but their influence is not restricted to them. Third, attention to schemas provides a different type of leverage for understanding the mechanisms of power. While studies oriented by 'ideas' typically conceptualize ideological influence as a function of the groups who advance particular ideas, an approach based on collective schemas is more likely to decentre actors in its analysis, seeing power in the social distinctions that structure perceived reality. Finally, this approach sees deeply held schemas as constituting social life. So rather than introducing culture as a factor that interacts with other, so-called non-cultural factors, such as interests and institutional patterns, collective schemas constitute those factors at a fundamental level. There is no non-cultural way in which groups define their interests. Indeed, it is only through cultural processes that groups can even define themselves (Melucci 1996).

In his volume *State/Culture*, Steinmetz (1999) contends that this constitutive view provides the sharpest point of contrast with alternative conceptions of culture and competing approaches to the state. In opposition to 'objectivist' views of the state, cultural scholars argue that the state and its power are dialectically related to, and permeated by, culture. Bourdieu's (1999) approach to the state is illustrative. He outlines a recursive view of culture and the state in which the state is a fundamentally cultural construct, albeit one that constructs itself over time. The state's power relies on cultural representations of 'the state' that it creates itself through a concentration of coercive, economic, informational and symbolic power. Thus empowered, the state creates the conditions for 'pre-reflexive agreement' within the citizenry. Commonsense understandings of the world are politically produced by processes that themselves rely on antecedent categories of perception that make state actions appear legitimate. Foucault's view of power provides a kindred but distinctive view. While he generally viewed exertions of power as diffuse and largely without agents, his later lectures on governmentality recognized an important place for the state (Foucault 2009). Yet rather than seeing the state as a central agent of top-down social control, he saw it as a conduit for the manifold disciplinary practices and mentalities in day-to-day life that render citizens governable.

Though the constitutive view of culture sees culture and the state as interpenetrating, it does not preclude casual cultural arguments about state processes. Indeed, constitutive views may provide some of the best leverage for making causal claims, as long an analysts, following Kane (1991), distinguish between culture's analytic autonomy (a heuristic construct) and its concrete autonomy (an empirically observable condition). Recent empirical work on state formation has moved this explanatory agenda forward. Loveman (2005) takes a constitutive view of symbolic power in her examination state administrative efforts in nineteenth-century Brazil. She examines a negative case in which Brazilian overtures to extend the state's administrative scope were stymied by popular revolts. Paying close attention to causal sequencing and comparative cases, she argues that Brazil's early failures to accumulate symbolic power hindered its accumulation of administrative and coercive power. Gorski (2003) extends Foucault's ideas about discipline and governmentality in his analysis of state formation in early modern Europe. He argues against mainstream accounts that emphasize the impact of class relations, the world system or fiscal-military capacity. Instead he examines the disciplining power of Calvinism, which reformed individuals from within through religious self-discipline and reformed society at large through technologies of observation and surveillance within ecclesiological communities. This infrastructure of religious governance, Gorski argues, became a template for the rise of modern nation-states throughout Europe.

Studies of contemporary social policy have demonstrated the explanatory value of constitutive schemas based upon race, gender and the work ethic. Skrentny (2002) shows how the implicit racial schemas held by policy experts shaped the evolution of minority rights policies in the United States during the 1960s and 1970s. He places 'policy meanings' at the centre of his account. These meanings are constitutive – they define the identity and boundaries of groups, shape strategic interests and constrain legitimate political action. The success of various minority groups – including Hispanics, white ethnics, and gays and lesbians – in achieving government protections depended on how political elites perceived these groups' similarities to blacks based upon their 'deservingness'. Subconscious cognitive categories and comparisons play a central role in his analysis. Likewise, research on gender and social policy has generated a number of insights about cultural influences on policy outcomes. This scholarship draws from work in poststructuralist and feminist thought that empha-sized categories, discourse and power. Binary gender-based distinctions influence the definition of needs (Fraser 1989b), normative views of labour market participation and 'care work' (Orloff 1999), and perceptions of dependency (Gordon 1994) – all of which shape patterns of social provision (see Padamsee 2009 for a review).

Steensland (2008b) applies a constitutive view of culture to welfare reform in the United States during the 1960s and 1970s. The specific case is the rise and fall of guaranteed income proposals, which aimed to ensure economic security for all American families regardless of labour market participation. Cultural categories of deservingness, based on perceived adherence to the work ethic, served as the ultimate obstacle to the passage of these policies. Put simply, guaranteed income proposals would have eradicated the categorical distinction between the deserving and unde-serving poor in government welfare policy. The fact that the proposals placed the deserving and undeserving poor in the same government programme led to what Mary Douglas calls 'symbolic pollution' – the 'impure' status of one category contaminated the 'pure' status of the other. Because categories of deservingness defined perceptions of poverty and social policy among experts and the public alike, this symbolic contamination shaped the interests and identities of key collective actors. Symbolic pollution led the nation's most influential business federation, the US Chamber of Commerce, to oppose the proposals, not on the basis of their economic interests, but on the basis of the cultural threat to labour market functioning that the Chamber perceived in the legislation. Symbolic pollution also shaped the collective interests of the 'deserving' working poor, who never rallied to support the proposals, even though it was in their direct economic interest to do so. They feared the stigma of receiving 'welfare' benefits. Categories of deservingness biased the thinking of government policy-makers, even sympathetic ones who wanted to erase the distinction between the deserving and undeserving poor, and they help explain the jarring disjunction between the substance of presidential plans and the public symbolism projected in presidential discourse.

Future Directions

Recent trends in the cultural analysis of politics suggest two productive directions for future work. First, one of the emerging trends of the past two decades has been a reassertion of claims about the causal influence of culture on mainstream political outcomes, such as social policy development, state formation and political gover-nance. After the demise of the 'national values' approach to cultural analysis in the late 1960s, much of the energy within the sociology of culture concentrated on the 'production of culture' perspective, which treated culture as an outcome to be explained as a consequence of other factors (see Peterson and Anand 2004). In studies of politics, this meant that analysts sought to explain patterns of political culture as outcomes, such as in Luker's (1984) penetrating analysis of the abortion debate in the United States. Yet more recently, as some of the scholarship discussed here suggests, studies have used the conceptual tools of the cognitive and linguistic turn to return to a more causally oriented agenda (also see Adams, Clemens and Orloff 2005). The number of studies that focus on culture's explanatory role in politics is growing, but it still remain an 'outside' perspective within political sociology, so more empirical research devoted to this explanatory agenda is needed.

Second, while the trend towards discursive and cognitive views of culture has been salutary for empirical research, it has pushed other dimensions of culture to the margins, particularly culture's normative and affective dimensions. Here research on the state could draw important lessons from the social movements literature, which has begun to redress this shortcoming by paying greater attention to the role that emotions play in motivating political action (Goodwin, Jasper and Polletta 2001). Gould's (2009) analysis of ACT-UP, the direct-action AIDS movement, is exemplary. She develops the idea of the 'emotional habitus' and illustrates its influences on collective action. Groups cultivate emotional dispositions among their members, only partly consciously, until members' affective responses come to feel like second nature. These sentiments play a key role in shaping activism, particularly by shaping activists' views of the political horizons – the possible, the desirable and the necessary. In research on the state, questions of motivation have received scant attention relative to more phenomenological questions concerning reality construction. Greater attention to normative commitments and affective responses can provide a valuable point of entrée for considering motivations, not just among grassroots activists, but among all political actors.

Further Reading

Adams, J., Clemens, E.S. and Orloff A. (eds) 2005: *Remaking Modernity: Politics, History, and Sociology*. Durham, NC: Duke University Press.

Johnston, H. and Klandermans, B. (eds) 1995: *Social Movements and Culture*. Minneapolis, MN: University of Minnesota Press.

Skrentny, J.D. 2002: *The Minority Rights Revolution*. Cambridge, MA: Harvard University Press.

Somers, M.R. and Block, F. 2005: From poverty to perversity: ideas, markets, and institutions over 200 years of welfare debate. *American Sociological Review* 70: 260–287.

Steensland, B. 2008: *The Failed Welfare Revolution: America's Struggle over Guaranteed Income Policy*. Princeton, NJ: Princeton University Press.

Steinmetz, G. (ed.) 1999: *State/Culture: State-Formation after the Cultural Turn*. Ithaca, NY: Cornell University Press.

21

Civil Society and the Public Sphere

LARRY RAY

Although these concepts have different origins and connotations, they are closely related in contemporary theory, especially in the work of those drawing on Habermas's writings. 'Civil society' refers to processes of social differentiation in modern European societies in which political power was separated from other activities, so that the state became a distinct area of society among others. In seventeenth-century political philosophy, 'civil society' came to be understood as essential to good government. In the critical tradition inaugurated by Hegel it is seen more problematically as an area of conflict as well as of ethics. For Marx it was equivalent to bourgeois society, an arena of class oppression and illusory emancipation. In Eurocommunism and the anti-communist movements of Eastern Europe in which it was recently revived, it is again seen in a positive light: as the social space between the state and the economy within which voluntary associations can discuss and act to link public and private concerns. This assumes that civil society necessarily creates an active public sphere. Ray distinguishes two models, 'Civil Society I' and 'Civil Society II'. According to the first, a democratic polity is secured by a dense network of civil associations that generate 'social capital'. This claim may not be justified, especially given the complexity and fragmentation of contemporary societies. According to the second, more explicitly normative model, what is needed is the generation of an alternative public sphere of autonomous self-organizing groups that will limit state power. This model may be quite particular to the situation in Eastern Europe from which it emerged. Ray outlines a number of important difficulties for the concept of civil society: the feminist critique of its gendered nature; the way in which the public sphere has failed to develop in post-communist societies; the over-simplification of the binary opposition of civil society and state and the homogeneity of community it assumes. It is further problematized by processes of globalization that undermine the liberal democratic state on which the existence of civil society has historically depended.

The Wiley-Blackwell Companion to Political Sociology, First Edition. Edited by Edwin Amenta, Kate Nash, and Alan Scott.
© 2012 Blackwell Publishing Ltd. Published 2012 by Blackwell Publishing Ltd.

Both the concepts of civil society and the public sphere are fluid, problematic and open to various, sometimes conflicting interpretations. Although the concepts are closely related in contemporary debates, especially among writers drawing on Habermas, they have different origins and connotations (Seligman 1995). For Habermas the public sphere, which emerges prior to civil society, is 'a domain of civic communication and cultural contestation' whereas civil society refers to 'specific forms of mobilization and citizen participation which have some relation to the state' (Delanty 2001). The notion of an active public sphere in which citizens engage in reasoned argument over affairs of state and morality derives from (idealized) notions of the ancient Greek polis in a political tradition running through Machiavelli and Rousseau to twentieth-century theorists such as Arendt and Habermas. Central concepts are *virtue*, the moral requirement to be a good citizen, and rational debate. Ideas of public disputation, activity and ideally (if not neces- sarily) face-to-face contact imply a small-scale, relatively homogeneous society. This was the kind of city-state republic, participatory rather than procedural, envisaged by Rousseau (Patomáki and Pursianen 1999). Civil society, by contrast, refers to more complex, organic and differentiated orders. Certainly, 'civil society', like 'public sphere', originates in Greek and Roman political philosophy (Aristotle's *politike koimonia* and Cicero's *ius civile*) but is more closely identified with eighteenth-century political philosophy. The emphasis here was on the importance of a realm of privacy, economic exchange and association, and consequently the limitation of the state. For many (though not all) theories of civil society the freedom to enter into private contracts is important, which associates the concept with the growth of the political power of the bourgeoisie in Europe. Despite these different emphases, though, many theorists understand civil society as a public realm of voluntary association essential for the stability of democracy.

Civil Society and Social Differentiation

The concept of 'civil society' refers to the processes of social differentiation associated with the emergence of modern European societies. With the depersonalization of political power, separated from the familial rights of monarchs, barons and landlords, the idea of the state as the personal property of the sovereign and benefice of officials slowly gave way to the idea of impersonal rule bound by rules. In the process, sovereignty was transferred from the figure of the monarch to the state, which also underwent a process of differentiation, into administrative, judicial, representative, functions. Further, the development of trade, commerce and markets increased the complexity of economic organization while establishing the dual notion of social activity, divided into political and civil roles. 'Civil society' described the new commercial social order, the rise of public opinion, representative government, civic freedoms, plurality and 'civility'. Thus civil society depicted a realm of contractual and voluntary relationships independent of the state, which thereby became merely one area of social activity among others. At the same time, political economy and philosophy began to address the question of the social context for the existence of the state (political society), the nature of which was no longer taken for granted. In particular, Enlightenment social theory (e.g., Montesquieu 1949; Rousseau 1963;

Condorcet 1976) regarded the despotic state as an enemy of human progress and well-being and began to examine the social conditions for democratic or constitutional forms of government.

The origins of contemporary usage can be found in seventeenth-century political philosophy. Thomas Hobbes' theory of the sovereign state (Leviathan) was premised on the existence of two branches of society – political and civil – tied by a 'social contract' between subjects and the state. Hobbes constructed a hypothetical 'state of nature' in which essential human tendencies posed an ever-present threat to social peace, where 'the life of man was solitary, poore, nasty, brutish and short' (Hobbes 1994 [1660]: 71). However, rationality and mutual self-interest persuaded people to combine in agreement, to surrender sovereignty to a Common Power, the state, established by covenant to constrain those who would otherwise violate the social peace. With the social contract came a separation between political and civil society – two systems in which 'men [are] joyned in one Interest' as parts of the body (1994 [1660]: 131). The political system was constituted by the sovereign power and civil society by subjects 'among themselves'. Although the political system was the dominant part, this expressed the idea of differentiated civil and political life as mutually sustaining systems, in which the realm of private activity, while governed by sovereign laws, was otherwise bound only by conscience (in foro interno) and the rules of civic association.

Disputing Hobbes' negative views of human nature, John Locke's concept of the social contract further enhanced the status of civil society, as a space of association, contract and property regulated by the law. 'Those who are united into one body, and have a common established law and judicature to appeal to, with authority to decide controversies between them and punish offenders, are in civil society one with another; but those who have no such common appeal... are still in the state of Nature' (Locke 1980: para. 87). Leaving the state of nature for Locke involved entering a commonwealth of men of property who contract authority to the state for their self-protection, but they do not do so unconditionally. Law is derived from God-ordained natural rights, which inhere in civil society, to which the state is ultimately answerable. Unlike Hobbes' Leviathan, which was the *product* of a covenant but not a *party* to it (and hence not bound by it), Locke's constitutional state was constrained by the law, violation of which rendered it non-legitimate.

In Hobbes and Locke though, despite differences between them, civil society was an aspect of government (Locke used political and civil society interchangeably), while in subsequent theorists, such as Adam Ferguson, it became an autonomous sphere separate from the state. The development of civil society for Ferguson reflected the progress of humanity from a simple, clan-based militaristic to complex commercial society. However, this process of social differentiation and loss of community threatened increased conflict and weakened the social fabric. Civil society, with a strong connotation of 'civility', has the potential to establish a new order requiring dispersal of power and office, the rule of law and liberal (i.e., tolerant) sentiments, which secure people and property without requiring obligations to friends and cabals (Ferguson 1966: 223). Again, civil society is inseparable from good government, but more than this, the reference to 'friends and cabals' indicates an important point that is sometimes missed in subsequent debates. Civil society does not refer to just *any* kind of informal or private social relations, which exist in all societies, but to morally guided, rule-following relations that make possible anonymous social exchanges. It thereby facilitates social integration in impersonal and potentially conflictual situations.

The implicit tension here between the new conflicts of commercial society and the moral demands of social peace appeared explicitly in Hegel, for whom civil society was divided between ethical life (*Sittlichkeit*) and egotistical self-interest. Civil society is understood here more as a process than in Hobbes' rigid system. Objective Spirit achieves self-knowledge through differentiation into discrete spheres, which none-theless form a totality. In the family, socialization towards moral autonomy trans-formed biological and psychological needs into individual desires. But in complex societies, private life is transcended through association in civil society, the sphere of production, distribution and consumption, which meets a system of needs that are modified and multiplied in the process. It has its own regulatory institutions (Justice, Public Authority, Corporations) guided by morality, although they remain instru-ments for achieving personal, egotistical ends. To some extent, Hegel's view of civil society anticipated Marx's critique of class polarization and dehumanization, as 'the conflict between vast wealth and vast poverty steps forth, a poverty unable to improve its condition. . . [which] turns into the utmost dismemberment of will, inner rebellion and hatred' (Hegel 1967: 149–151). However, this will be overcome if the consti-tutional-legal state (*Rechtsstaat*) synthesizes ethical life with the public domain of civil society while transcending them. Differences of class, rank and religion dissolve in universal law and formal rights.

By regarding civil society simply as the equivalent of bourgeois society, an arena of conflict, class oppression and illusory emancipation, Marx only partially echoed Hegel's view and disregarded the latter's concept of civil society as *Sittlichkeit*. His critique of civil society was in part a critique of the limitations of Hegel's *Rechsstaat*, in which formal legal equality is merely an illusory dissolution of differences of class, rank and religion, which masks their perpetuation within civil society. In part too, though, it involved a fundamental rejection of the very process of social differentiation into institutional orders (such as private life, the economy, and civil and political association) that Hegel and most eighteenth-century theory had taken for granted. For Marx, the proletarian victory would substitute for the old civil society a classless association in which there would be neither political power nor the antagonisms of civil society (Marx 1978: 169). Marx's vision of communism was radically de-differentiated, in which boundaries between the civil and political, like those of class, nation and religious difference, wither away. It drew on Rousseauian and radical Jacobin concepts of a public sphere of equals, along with anti-modernist nostalgia for a lost unity of humanity (Gellner 1994), rather than an organic concept of socially differentiated networks.

For much of the twentieth century the concept of civil society passed into disuse. There is some irony in that despite Marx's pejorative treatment of the term, its revival in the later twentieth century was a result first of the attempts by Eurocommunist parties to devise new strategies in the 1970s and second of its popularity among the anti-communist movements in Eastern Europe. Eurocommunists (especially the Italian Communist Party), theoretically informed by writers like Gramsci, Bobbio, Althusser and Poulantzas, offered an alternative to Soviet Marxism's economistic reductionism and simplistic polarization of social and political conflicts. Gramsci had conceived of civil society as the sphere of non-corporeal forms of class rule, a cultural space between state and economy. Here the proletarian party could wage a cultural and ideological war to undermine the hegemony of the ruling class, creating a counter-hegemony of workers' clubs, social and educational organizations, assisted by the activity of 'organic intellectuals'. This restated the centrality of processes of social differentiation and situated civil society within a cultural and institutional realm rather than the economy. Despite the effectiveness of this strategy in bringing various social movements and parties into loose coalition and debate, it already pointed towards a post-Marxist politics in its abandonment both of materialism and centrality of proletarian class struggle.

The second revival of civil society theory was encouraged by the collapse of communism and its use by writers such as Vajda (1988), Konrad (1984), Fehér and Heller (1986) and Havel (1988) to capture the essence of dissident politics. Theorists such as Rödel, Frankenberg and Dubiel (1989), Arato (1981) and Cohen and Arato (1992) excavated the concept of civil society during the disintegration of state socialism, combining ideas of radical civic republicanism with Habermas's procedural discourse ethics. The central idea of these theories was to identify a social space for public discussion, of voluntary citizens' associations that was neither narrowly merged with the market, nor an adjunct to the state. Again with Eastern Europe in mind, Sztompka (1993: 73) argued that civil society was the key to closing the chasm between public and private realms, involving pluralism of voluntary associations, interest groups, political organizations, local communities, markets and representative democracy as institutional arrangements linking the public and personal choices of active and informed citizens. But this kind of analysis assumes that civil society necessarily creates an active public sphere when the assumptions underlying the two ideas may differ significantly. So, when does 'civil' become 'political'?

Civil Society and Public Sphere

Clearly, for many writers, the concept of 'civil society' lies at the centre of concerns with self-government, activism and privacy, separation from the state, human rights, free economic initiatives and the definitions of the social itself (Keane 1988: 20). But there are various ways of connecting all these, which imply different understandings of social organization, sometimes called 'Civil Society I' and 'Civil Society II' (e.g., Foley and Edwards 1996). There is further the question of whether models advanced are theorizations of existing social processes or normative visions of a possible future.

One argument ('Civil Society I') runs from the Scottish moralists (such as Ferguson) through de Tocqueville (1946) and Durkheim (1969 [1898]) to contemporary writers such as Robert Putnam (see Begnasco, Chapter 22, in this volume). According to 'Civil Society I', a democratic polity is secured by being embedded in dense networks of civil associations, such as clubs, trade associations, voluntary societies, churches, parent–teacher associations, sports clubs and the like, that generate 'social capital'. The denser the networks the more secure are the bridges between civic life and political associations along with institutions of the state. Active, voluntary and informal groups and networks make for more stable democracy and protect against incursion by the state. The bridges envisaged here are based on institutional links along with shared moral and civic values of reciprocity (e.g., Bryant 1995). Civil society in this sense has a recursive property; it protects against state incursion yet strengthens the (liberal democratic) state. Conversely, the absence of civil society is both an explanation and reinforcement of authoritarian yet ineffective government.

This view is consistent with the notion of organic, complex societies with high levels of social differentiation. Gellner (1994: 99–100) writes of modern 'man' as 'modular', that is, having the capacity to combine associations and institutions without these being total and underwritten by ritual. Civil society creates a social 'structure. . . not atomized, helpless and supine, and yet the structure is readily adjustable and responds to rational criteria of improvement' (Gellner 1995: 42). Civil society as a network of institutional and moral links is not monolithic but accommodates a plurality of 'groups within groups, their sense of identity. . . always multi-layered' with many possible 'we-images' along with corresponding images of the other (Mennell 1995). 'Civil Society I' is less a definable social space so much as a complex web of processes and connections. In this vein, Habermas separates the social into two parts – social integration through normative communication within the lifeworld, and system integration through money and power. The lifeworld (within which Cohen and Arato situate civil society) is further differentiated into implicitly known traditions (culture), the medium of communication (society) and social identities (personality), each of which undergoes yet further internal differentiation. The potential for the expansion of public spheres exists as social movements form at contested boundaries between system and the lifeworld. An example would be environmental protests over, say, nuclear reprocessing, that force open debates about the rationality and morality of projects previously driven by technological and financial criteria.

However, the question remains as to the extent to which a public sphere of active citizens in the Arendtian or Habermasian sense is consistent with development of complex and multi layered societies. Habermas's (1989) well-known critique of the erosion of the public sphere in late capitalism claims that the commercialization of mass media replaced rational and unconstrained debate by public opinion research, through which political parties 'extract' loyalty from publics in an instrumental fashion. At the same time, increasing state intervention and the growing interdependence of research and technology resulted in a process of 'technicization' whereby questions of moral value and political controversy were converted into managerial technical or planning processes (see Ray 1993: 51–53). This critique can be extended to the erosion of public space by post-Fordist urban restructuring and flexible accumulation (see for example Brenner and Theodore 2002). As physical space is privatized and occupied by city-centre and out-of-town consumption complexes the 'publicness' of urban space is eroded. Voyce (2006) argues that 'One of the spatial consequences of globalization is the tendency of "public" space to come increasingly under the control of private corporations'. The classic example, he continues, is the shopping mall where public amenities are subsumed within private space, often no political activity is allowed, charities must pay daily rates to collect, and surveillance and regulation replace public discourse and activity. At the same time cultural space is increasingly eroded by media networks interested only in advertising revenue. So in the place of democratic public participation we have 'reality TV' that creates a public spectacle of voyeurism and humiliation. These shows mobilize voting, which offers the promise of participation, but is actually a medium of surveillance since the act of voting provides demographic data about voters (Andrejevic 2003: 161).

Commercialization thus further undermines the public sphere. However, although Habermas opens the way to this kind of critique, he also regards social steering by both the market and state as unavoidable (1987: 339), so it is not entirely clear whether he is describing a pathological and reversible process or essentially depicting the condition of modernity. If it is the latter, then ideas of a reconstructed public sphere of active citizens may be utopian and nostalgic.

Further, with the decline of a constitutional public sphere there is a danger, as a number of commentators have noted, that local social loyalties can lead to the fragmentation of civic groups into warring factions that actually increase the risk of public violence (see for example Mennell 1995; Foley and Edwards 1996). Ethnic and religious solidarities that undermine multinational and secular states are often cited in this context (e.g., Kaldor 1993 and Sivan 1989, respectively). However, civil society theorists would generally counter this by stressing what Cohen and Arato (1992: 421) regard as essential to civil society, namely reflection on the core of collective identities and their articulation within democratic politics. In particular, following Habermas, the crucial factor here is that we inhabit a world of morally mature post-traditional ethics, in which public debate is constrained by procedural rules. Social integration requires not that we agree over substantive matters of identity and opinion but on the rules through which public debate and conflict will be conducted. Indeed, according to Misztal (1996: 197), it is the *disengagement* of political and juridical institutions from the lived bonds of solidarity that is a failure of 'Civil Society I', that promotes new exclusive communities of trust, such as ethnic nationalism.

A second approach to the relationship between state and civil society ('Civil Society II') is associated particularly with the anti-communist movements in the 1970s and 1980s, where the role of civil society is explicitly normative. Rather than embedding political processes in supportive but constraining civic networks, this conception regarded civil society as a harbinger of a new type of society – anti-political, authentic, and based on informal social solidarity. The spaces of civil society and public sphere here were often fused in that the private realm of autonomous self-organizing groups was to become an authentic public sphere alternative to the state. For Arato (1981) the seeds of new civil society germinated in *samizdat*, self-defence movements (such as the Polish KOR), the idea of self-managing democracy and permanent rights theory (Fehér and Heller 1986). Thus social movements such as Solidarity aimed to limit the state, or bypass it altogether through alternative networks, but not to seize it as an instrument of coercion, and in this sense they were quite different from earlier and more traditional revolutionary movements (Pelczynski 1988). The early Solidarity programme of *podmiotowość* (self-management) was a radical alternative to Western democracy as well as to Soviet-type socialism. The democratization of the economy was understood as part of a decentralized social order of autonomous subsystems, managed along the lines of professional self-government (Glasman 1994). These notions of self-government transcend the liberal dichotomy of public/private by bringing rational democratic procedures into everyday life, through extrapolating the networks and practices of intellectuals in the parallel polity. Cohen and Arato (1992) argue that the new public spheres in Eastern Europe could provide a model for a more general idea of civil society that is appropriate in the West too. However, they also warn against an overly polarized view of 'civil society vs. the state' that was derived from a particular historical context. In contrast to the highly differentiated view outlined above, the 'eastern European' model over-unifies civil society in a false solidarity and risks blocking the emergence of societal and political pluralism (1992: 67).

Critiques of Civil Society

It should be clear from the foregoing that civil society is an ambiguous if seductive concept and this has attracted considerable critique. Two types of critique are particularly important. First, there is the accusation that its utopian promise is flawed, in some ways echoing Marx. Second, there is the charge of ambiguity – that the complexity of the social is better appropriated through other frameworks.

The 'Marxist' critique is echoed in various ways. Feminist critics have argued that the gender-neutral language of civil society and public sphere conceals how the role of citizen has been linked to the capacity to bear arms, which has been predominantly a masculine role (Fraser 1989b). This fusion of citizenship, militarism and masculinity reinforces the male occupation of the public sphere that is inscribed into the public/private dichotomy, resulting in a civil contract amongst brothers combined with the feminization of the private sphere (Pateman 1988; Okin 1991). Habermasian distinctions between public and private roles treat the family as a black box in which patriarchal power remains invisible. The male citizen-speaker role links the state and the public sphere to the family and the official economy while the worker-breadwinner role integrates the family with the economy and the state, confirming women's dependent status in each. Thus the exclusion of the family from the realm of civil society is interpreted by some feminists as the exclusion of women from this sphere, although the subordination of women in the family means that this is not a voluntary society but is (or at least in the past was) rather based on obligations that were enforced through patriarchal power (Himmelfarb 2000). The exclusion of the family from civil society then renders women invisible in civil life while occluding the enforced subordination of women within what are apparently voluntary associations. It is not clear, though, whether these criticisms negate the very ideas of civil society and the public sphere or whether inclusive non-gendered institutional forms might be possible.

Another line of critique addresses the rediscovery of civil society in anti-communist social movements. After the fall of communism some of the enthusiasm for civil society dissipated in the wake of the political demobilization and the emergence of new elites. For Tamás (1994) the revolutions of 1989 were made by the private sphere against the public with its 'rational utopia' communism. However, the language of civil society was a myth, invoking a 'tale of a non-coercive political order of mutual non-hierarchical contract'. Indeed, for Lomax (1997) the early popular enthusiasm was betrayed by the post-communist intellectual elite, who appropriated the term 'civil society' but demobilized society and failed to develop civil initiatives and popular participation. A similar point is addressed in Ray (1996: 200–28). Hann sees no evidence to support the notion that an effective civil society 'in the sense of public sphere' has been able to develop in Hungary in recent years. Rather, like Lomax he suggests that the term was appropriated by urban intellectuals to bemoan the fact that (especially rural) people were less willing than previously to display deference to cultural elites. However, Bernard (1996) more optimistically suggests that the initial phase of post-communist depoliticization is temporary and public life will be reinvigorated around new interest cleavages. However, the more pessimistic conclusion as to the fate of post-communist civil society is echoed by the former activist in Polish Solidarity, Adam Michnik, who says:

> We thought that our revolution. . . in the name of freedom and normalcy, will be not only velvet and bloodless but also free from. . . superstition. But the collapse of communism brought ethnic chauvinism, bloody wars and religious intolerance. . .their legacy has been (in different measure) radicalism of revenge (seeking out 'former communists'), nostalgia for the past in the face of corruption and uncertainty, and crass commercialism.
>
> (2001: 3)

Even if there is some exaggeration in this, as Ray (2009) argues, the sense of disappointment with the utopian promises of 1989 has prompted the emergence of social movements that seek to pursue other utopias of community and solidarity.

Secondly, it is claimed that civil society (II especially) assumes a homogeneous community and takes too little account of functional differentiation and the interpenetration of state and society in complex societies (Seligman 1993). Hann (1995) argues that the model of civil society vs. the state is derived from the pre-industrial history of the West and is too simplistic to examine the complex interpenetration of state and society. Citizens confront different authorities via a series of roles – taxpayers, proponents of resolutions, voters, writers of letters to editors, supporters of interest groups etc. – that are divided according to the requirements of the political system (Luhmann 1982: 153). The binary opposition of civil society and the state could be described in terms of what Luhmann calls a political code, which simplifies and steers otherwise highly complex communications. As such, it operates as a rhetorical counter to the sovereignty of the state, which invokes the myth of the collective sovereign 'people'. But any attempt to make this a reality, such as the unconstrained communication (supposedly) envisaged by Habermas, or the permanently open democracy of civil societarians, would be chaos (Luhmann 1982: 287–288). Again, the breadth of the meaning of 'civil society' is a source of ambiguity, giving it a nebulous and undifferentiated character (Ely 1992). This may be particularly so with Habermasian accounts (e.g., Cohen and Arato 1992) that insert the concept of the public sphere into the domain of potential communicative ethics, thus merging civil society with the routine linguistic practices. Others regard the concept as meaningless since the very existence of civil society presupposes the state, that is, a state bound by legality that will not trample over civil rights (e.g., Kumar 1993).

Global Civil Society?

The concept of civil society discussed so far exists within the boundaries of the nation-state, which many argue has been undermined by the process of globalization. The extent to which this is occurring is a matter of controversy and should not be exaggerated. However, there may be a general trend towards 'de-statization of the political system', reflected in the shift from govern*ment* to govern*ance* (Jessop 1999) where the state's role is increasingly one of coordinating multiple agencies, institutions and systems coupled through reciprocal interdependence. According to this account, the state becomes one agent among others operating in sub-national, national and international domains. If this is the case then the notion of a 'state–civil society' polarity is clearly not complex enough to grasp current intersections between the governmental and non-governmental. In this context some writers nonetheless suggest that a transnational or global civil society may be emerging. There are several possibilities here:

- Statist concepts projected and reproduced on the world stage along with shared norms, international social networks, multi-level democratic systems and an equalization of human rights (e.g., Walker 1994; Held 1995a). A post-state global civil society develops based on recognition of inalienable human rights no longer tied to specific states or national membership (e.g., Frost 1998).
- Novel forms of civic sociality are facilitated by communication technologies along with decentralized, lateral organizational forms (Ahrne 1996).
- Global social movements establish new networks, resources and social capital, providing the infrastructure for global democratization (Walker 1994; Smith 1998).
- A 'cosmopolitan civil society' that is largely an aspiration rather than already realized; as Beck and Grande (2007: 2) put it, 'Europe is Europe's last politically effective Utopia', meaning that the project of a post-national European community is politically possible although does not yet exist.

However, an alternative scenario is an implosion of civil society, as the relation between the state and civil society envisaged by the theory is inverted. The realm of the state, which was formerly 'exterior' to civil society, is becoming localized and hence 'interior' to the realm of private interests (civil society), which becomes global, through transnational capital. Thus the local state may lose its cohesion and become a set of 'disaggregated agencies' rather than the centre of distributional politics (Miller 1993: 222). At the same time, identity and lifestyle politics, community orientations and movements supersede instrumental class and welfare politics. Since civil society was symbiotically located between institutions of the state, corporations and everyday life, globalization weakens the civic sphere as it dislocates the pattern of these relations. One consequence of this is that the nation-state cannot sustain social welfare, and people's vulnerability to effects of the market is increased. The role of civil society as intermediary between state and individual weakens while processes taking shape in the global arena impact on everyday life. Capital gains maximum mobility across national boundaries, taking command of *space* in a way that voluntary organizations rooted more in locality and *place* cannot do (Harvey 1994: 238). Delanty (2001) concludes that there is potential for a global public sphere of communication and public contestation while remaining more sceptical of the possibility of global civil society.

Evaluation

Where do these observations leave the idea of civil society? I tried to indicate earlier that some accounts of civil society allow for, indeed are premised on, an organic differentiated society. To some extent, critics of the concept are reacting to utopian versions ('Civil Society II') that detach the concept from the state. On the other hand, the complex intersections of global and local processes and the increasing functional differentiation of societies make problematic polarities (civil society/state) drawn from an earlier stage of social development. Civil society and public spheres are best viewed as multiple processes rather than as 'sites', and as anonymously interlocked subjects and flows of communication, rather than homogeneous communities (Habermas 1992). A central theme in civil society theory, and indeed in sociology as a whole, has been the importance of embedding processes of money and power in supportive but constraining cultural and normative systems. Where civil society is positioned between the economy and polity, rather than being absorbed into either, it is possible to explore the mediating processes that connect institutional spheres to limit the extension of one into the other. Where (as is common in post-communist societies) the boundary of the state and private activity is unclear, with few mediating institutions, the result is low trust, weak legitimacy, high crime and corruption. As a counter to these, social organizations and non-governmental organizations (NGOs) often strive to generate a culture of civic regulation and public accountability, such as the umbrella of anti-corruption organizations in Bulgaria, Coalition 2000. This is not to propose civil society as a panacea, but an important factor in structuring social outcomes.

If civil society is viewed as mediating other institutional orders, then one should be sceptical of ideas of a post-state or global civil society. The pursuit of interests arising from the system of needs takes place within a framework of procedural rights that allow the articulation of substantive differences of interests, roles, values, and membership of voluntary associations. Without juridical processes against which alleged violations can be protested, the 'civil rights' enjoyed are very weak. So the existence of civil society does not just require the existence of non-state organizations (which would apply to Lebanon in the 1980s or to internet chat rooms) but an acceptance of rules of behaviour by both government authorities and citizens that self-limit their mutual claims (White, Gill and Slider 1993: 226–229). Further, the self-limitation of power does not arise spontaneously from the process of functional differentiation (as Luhmann suggests, 1982: 214) but implies a procedural threshold sustained by the diffusion of power through the social system. This can only occur, as Offe and Preuss (1991: 161) argue, when power is embedded (*Vegesellschaftet*) in social norms and networks, local and diverse public spheres. Despite the diffuse meanings to which the concept of civil society is open, it captures crucial features of contemporary societies in which social integration is dependent on the fixing of public institutions in cultural and moral systems of regulation. These in turn presuppose the presence of social networks and active public citizens.

In this volume Colin Crouch (Chapter 42) points out that in the wake of the post-2008 financial crisis there has been a process of displacement of oppositional political activity from parties to civil society organizations and social movements, such as environmentalists, defenders of workers' rights, general opponents of large concentrations of power – critical of corporate behaviour. However, he also points out that important though these are, the struggle between them and the corporations is highly unequal. At the same time, in late 2011 the elected government of Greece has, under intense pressure from EU and financial institutions, given way to a coalition committed to drastic austerity. Meanwhile the democratic process in Italy has essentially been suspended in favour of a 'government of technocrats' that will again steer through drastic public spending cuts. This is in some ways a nascent revisiting of the bifurcation between state and civil society that was discussed above in relation to collapsing communism. What the outcome of these processes will be for European and North American capitalism will become clearer over the coming years. However, this chapter suggests that an active civil society interlocking with an open public sphere is the surest basis for a democratic polity, which may be under considerable strain during the current crisis.

Further Reading

Chambers, S. and Kymlikca, W. (eds) 2002: *Alternative Conceptions of Civil Society*. Princeton University Press.

Edwards, M. 2004: *Civil Society*. Cambridge: Polity Press.

22

Trust and Social Capital

Arnaldo Bagnasco

'Social capital' describes a resource that facilitates action that is neither individual, nor physical, but inherent in social relations. In Coleman's influential account, he used it to criticize the individualist bias of classical and neoclassical economics while preserving the rational actor paradigm. For him 'social capital' is generated by authority relations, relations of trust, and unilateral transfers of control over resources; and, since it depends on networks, stable relations, ideology and other factors, it may be created, maintained and/or destroyed. From his research on the comparative institutional performance of regional governments in Italy, Putnam concludes that social culture was a crucial variable in explaining differences between them. He sees higher levels of 'civicness' – solidarity, mutual trust, and tolerance promoted by values, norms, institutions and associations – as enhancing governments' capacities to implement political choices. Fukuyama has explored how economic efficiency depends on social capital – the capability of people to work together to achieve shared goals. The form and extent this takes varies according to national culture, religion and family values. Bagnasco argues that the concept of social capital is a useful tool for political sociology in that it enables the exploration of the relation between state and civil society. However, Putnam's and Fukuyama's accounts underestimate the role of politics in creating and sustaining it. Coleman's idea of social capital, based on action theory, is much more useful in this respect

The term 'social capital' is a relatively recent addition to the language of sociology and political science. It was probably used for the first time by Jane Jacobs (1961: 138). In her studies on the crisis of American cities, Jacobs stressed society's loss of self-organizational capability in neighbourhoods built without a care for the perverse effects of economic action. The subsequent literature continued to place the onus on informal aspects – seen as latent components and crucial resources for the functioning of society, hence as social capital – of relational structures in highly organized

The Wiley-Blackwell Companion to Political Sociology, First Edition. Edited by Edwin Amenta, Kate Nash, and Alan Scott.
© 2012 Blackwell Publishing Ltd. Published 2012 by Blackwell Publishing Ltd.

societies. The subject of trust as a resource for action has also been widely developed in recent social research. Here I speak of trust only in so far as it is used to formulate the notion of social capital.

In the first section, I define the concept and examine the theoretical perspective that derives from it, with special reference to the studies of J. Coleman, the scholar most committed to the theoretical foundation of that perspective. I then present two of the most important applications of the concept to political sociology, showing how the new idea casts new light on the relationship between civic culture and the performance of political institutions, and how it can be applied to comparative analysis of capitalism in a period of difficulty for traditional political economy. In conclusion, I add a few critical observations on the future of the perspective.

A New Term in Social Theory

The economic concept of capital refers to a stock of resources that can be used to produce goods and services for the market. It is usual to distinguish between financial capital and physical capital. Speaking of the quality of labour, Becker (1964) and other authors introduced the concept of human capital to explain wage differentials depending on investment in worker training. The idea of social capital is a further extension of the original concept of capital; it is not necessarily applied to economics, but seen more generally as a resource that facilitates action.

James Coleman introduces the concept by speaking precisely of a specific resource that facilitates action, one that is 'lodged neither in individuals nor in physical implements of production', but 'inheres in the structure of relations between persons and among persons' (Coleman 1994: 302).

To reason in terms of social capital is to see society from the point of view of the action potential which individuals draw from relational structures. Observed in this way, social capital seems not so much a specific object as a vantage point on society as a whole or, at any rate, on a vast, hard-to-define set of social phenomena.

Coleman claims he borrowed the concept from Loury (1977, 1987), who uses it to describe the relational resources, useful for the development of children, which families find in specific communities. He also explains that, among the first authors to use the concept explicitly, were Bourdieu (1980b), Flap and De Graaf (1986), Schiff (1992) and Putnam (1993), but also that a great deal of research by anthropologists and sociologists moves in the same direction without using the term. For example, the notion of the embeddedness of economic transactions in stable social relations, which Granovetter (1985) borrows from Polanyi, can be traced to the more general notion of social capital.

Coleman first used the concept to address the problem of the formation of human capital (Coleman 1988), but he only defines it comprehensively in *Foundations of Social Theory* (1990; see also 1994). Here his general aim is clearly to construct a complex social theory criticizing the individualist bias of classical and neoclassical economics, while preserving the rational actor paradigm. The rational choice perspective of sociologists differs today from that of economists in so far as it sees organizations and social institutions as contexts that affect choices and produce systemic effects (1994: 166). As we shall see, the concept of social capital is a keystone in this perspective.

Coleman begins to build his theory by imagining actors with resources over which they have control and in which they have interests. Since actors have interests in events that are under the control of others, they engage in exchanges and unilateral transfers of control that lead to the formation of permanent social relations. According to this logical sequence, authority relations, relations of trust and the consensual allocation of rights that establish norms thus arise as the components of the social structure. These elements, however, may be seen both as components of the social structure or system and as resources for individuals pursuing their own ends. The term 'social capital' describes these resources, which vary from person to person.

For individuals, social capital is an appropriable social structure. Authority rela-tions, relations of trust and norms are forms or generators of social capital. For actors, social capital materializes in the network of relations of which they are a part, and through which they activate resources for their own strategies. Structures thus contain forms of social capital that can be activated by actors.

- *Credit-slips*, that is to say credit based on obligations to pay back. One example is the rotating loan association described by anthropologists, in which groups of friends and neighbours contribute a sum of money every month and take turns in using the central fund. Such a credit association requires a high level of trustworthiness and the extent of credit-slips on which individuals can draw at any time varies greatly. A patriarch, for example, held a large concentration of social capital. As Weber has shown, the destruction of this social capital was decisive in allowing individualist strategies to contribute to the development of capitalism.
- *Information channels*, which can be established to cut the cost of information, using networks of relations that exist for other purposes.
- *Norms and effective sanctions*, as in special norms and relative forms of social control whereby self-interest should be adapted to the interests of the collec-tivity. It must be remembered, however, that just as norms constrain deviant actions, so they may also constrain innovativeness.
- *Authority relations*, which transfer rights of control. Even vesting authority in a charismatic leader is a way of creating social capital.
- *Appropriable social organization*, an expression used to define the possibility of appropriating an entire fabric of relations for other purposes than the ones for which it was initiated. In many cases, this possibility is connected to what anthropologists refer to as the multiplexity of relations among people bound together in more than one context (i.e., family, work, religion and so on).

If the social capital presented so far may appear to be a sort of by-product of social structures, other forms exist which derive from specific investment in the setting up of structures to generate them. This is the case of specifically created *intentional organizations* – associations and organizations in the narrow sense. I shall return to this point later, since Coleman's critical perspective reflects the tension that exists between intentional organizations and other forms of social capital.

Social capital has the properties of a public good: namely, it is inalienable and it is not the private property of the persons who benefit from it; it is useful for certain purposes but not for others and, as circumstances change, it may lose its effectiveness. More generally, it can be created, maintained and destroyed. We can list some of the factors that trigger these processes:

- *The closure of social networks*, due to which all or most actors are bound together. Closed structures increase possibilities for reciprocal monitoring, generating expectations and mutual norms and improving the trustworthiness of the environment. Networks are an important variable and deserve further exploration.
- The *stability of relations* in the course of time. The mobility of individuals tends to destroy social capital. The only exception is formal organizations in which positions remain, even though their incumbents change.
- *Ideology*: the Protestant doctrine of the individual's separate relation to God, for example, is a cultural factor that inhibits the creation of social capital.
- Additional factors that reduce mutual dependence among people include affluence and government aid. The ruling principle is that 'the more extensively persons call on one another for aid, the greater will be the quantity of social capital generated' (1990: 321).

I have dwelt on Coleman's theory not only because of its quality, but also because it is continually referred to in the subsequent literature. Deviations have, however, appeared whose scope has not always been appreciated. The references which follow must, therefore, be taken as examples of important and paradigmatic applications of the theory of social capital to political sociology, but also as variations on it.

Civic Culture as Social Capital

Robert Putnam conducted a major research programme on the comparative institutional performance of regional government in Italy (Putnam 1993). By 'institutional performance', he means the capacity of regional governments to implement political choices. Putnam sets out from the idea that, despite the fact that regions have the same institutional set-up, differences in context mean that institutions work in different ways. Following Almond and Verba (1963), he explores the hypothesis that political culture may be the decisive variable in explaining differences in performance. In their study of five countries, Almond and Verba introduced a typology of political cultures that breaks down into 'participants' (rational and informed) and 'subjects' (who display trust in authority and deference). A combination of the two defines the civic culture typical of well-established democracies, such as the United States and Britain. The lack of both dimensions defines a 'parochial' type that, according to the authors, is characteristic of Italy.

Putnam reveals sharp differences in performance from one region to another, and seeks to explain them according to higher or lower levels of 'civicness', by which he means the fabric of values, norms, institutions and associations which permit and support civic commitment, the distinctive features of which are widespread solidarity, mutual trust, and tolerance. Civicness is also the opposite of Banfield's 'amoral familism', based on the principle of 'maximizing the short-term material advantages of the family nucleus, seeing as everyone else does' (Banfield 1958: 85). In the survey he conducted in a poor southern Italian village in the postwar years, Banfield attributed the community's failure to mobilize to address problems to this cultural complex. Civicness, on the other hand, is Tocqueville's 'personal interest seen in the proper sense' or interest evaluated in the context of a wider public interest.

Putnam establishes the relationship between civicness and institutional performance through a set of statistical correlations between indicators, while seeking to control other variables. He thus identifies four macro-areas in which the quality of institutional performance corresponds to the level of civicness present. He then goes back eight centuries in search of the roots of these differences. In the twelfth century, Italy was divided into two consolidated political systems: the Norman monarchy in the south and the free communes in the centre-north. The first was hierarchical and autocratic, the second republican and egalitarian, the product of free bargaining. Two different systems subsequently evolved, each according to its own logic, the first accumulating experience of 'vertical' cultures and institutions, the second of 'horizontal' ones. As early as the fourteenth century, it was possible to observe the four macro-areas that stand out today for their different levels of civicness, and which, with the odd adjustment, substantially reiterated primordial differences.

Putnam brings his study to an end by returning to the theory of social capital, referring in particular to Coleman. Different levels of institutional performance (but also, according to the author, of economic development) depend, in the final analysis, on different endowments of social capital. One conclusion is that both states and markets operate more effectively if the context has a rich civic tradition, that is to say an important legacy of social capital. This means that social capital contributes as much as, and perhaps more than, economic and human capital to modernization and development. In conclusion, the building of the necessary social capital is the key that opens the door of democracy.

Putnam's research has since become a benchmark for the development of the theory of social capital. It has also had a major impact on the political debate. It is almost as if the author suggests we observe America from Italy, an approach which has fuelled a lively discussion on the progressive loss of social capital in his own country (Putnam 1995, 1996).

Making Democracy Work has been praised (cf. Laitin 1995), but also criticized (e.g., Goldberg 1996; Tarrow 1996). No-one questions the importance of civic culture (or social capital) in political processes, but what is in doubt is the role to attribute to civic culture in the processes analysed and the relationship between this dimension and other aspects of social structure. One is perplexed by Putnam's final explanation of a cultural *longue durée* that is reproduced in processes of socialization and social control. True, the history of cultural characteristics moves slowly, but the persistence and variation of such characteristics need to be explained, hence the need to observe the combination of social interplay and the concrete choices of actors in successive moments. Political action tends to be underestimated, but ought to be revalued, as should the true extent of economic processes. Putnam 'explains too much' with social capital, reconstructing history to fit the concept itself.

Social Capital and the Political Economy of Capitalism

In recent decades, the comparative analysis of the institutional set-ups of different national capitalisms has established itself in social research. Shonfield's essay on modern capitalism (1965) may be regarded as the point of departure for a vast literature, developed with a variety of theoretical tools (for a summing-up, see Trigilia 1998). *Trust* by Frances Fukuyama (1995) is the first attempt to apply the social capital perspective.

Fukuyama begins by observing that national political and economic institutions are converging, with economies increasingly oriented toward the market and integration in the global capitalistic division of labour. Social engineering has failed and the state is withdrawing from the economy. The idea that healthy political and economic institutions depend on a healthy, dynamic civil society is enjoying a revival. Civil society – firms, associations, schools, clubs, trade unions and so on – is founded, in turn, on the family, the centre of any society's cultural socialization, values and moral precepts.

The economic and political convergence of the different countries brings to light the awareness and importance of cultural differences, which are firmly rooted in religion. Economic efficiency can be obtained inside groups in which persons work well together on the basis of common values; it depends, that is, on their endowment of social capital or, in other words, the capability of people to work together in groups and organizations in pursuit of common goals. This capability corresponds to mutual trust, the expectation of correct and cooperative behaviour by others, which ultimately depends on the sharing of norms and values and on the ability to subordinate self to group interest. The accumulation of social capital is a lengthy, complex and essentially spontaneous process. Politics is capable of destroying it unheedingly or, at best, struggles to preserve it. Culture, seen as an inherited ethical habit, thus plays a decisive role.

Different societies enjoy different endowments of social capital, and an abundance or paucity of trust is a function of different ethical codes that may be traced to different family cultures. The family may provide the basis for successful forms of small-scale enterprise, as in the industrial districts of central and northeastern Italy, where a kind of familism is at work that extends to the local community, albeit hindering more complex economic organizations. Large corporations find fertile cultural ground in countries such as Japan, Germany and the United States, where the family has never been a cultural impediment to extended forms of association, which are fostered by other cultural factors (by Protestant sects in the United States, for instance). Southern Italy and Russia, areas without strong families or more extended networks of trust, are examples of narrow familialism, hence their backwardness and the presence of a criminal economy within them. It is worth noting that China, France, southern Italy and other societies in which trust is low had experiences of strong political centralization which exhausted the social capital available there. This is not the case of Japan, the United States and Germany.

Each national capitalism thus has a place of its own in the international division of labour. The specific culture of each selects a specific industrial structure option from those defined by markets and technologies, and the industrial structure, in turn, determines the sector of the global economy in which the country in question can achieve success.

Comparative political economy has developed different models of regulation and allocation to address problems of system integration (for example, a specific combination of aggregate economic variables which allows growth and stable employment) and social integration (for example, cultural and political acceptance of the redistributive combination obtained). This analytical school has accompanied the political experience of European forms of Keynesian capitalism. European models of economic regulation have accumulated inefficiencies and rigidities, and are ultimately jeopardized by the process of globalization which, other problems apart, has reduced the regulatory scope of national states. The most liberalist economies are the ones that are performing best at the moment.

Fukuyama's response to the new challenge is to use the idea of social capital for comparative analysis, thus liquidating the European model and allowing the 'virtuous' American model to return to centre-stage. In this ambitious programme, he produces a large-scale synthetic framework joining past and future and backed by references to a vast literature. His book has also enjoyed great success outside academic circles, and thus deserves careful critical attention.

A Tool to be Handled with Care

The conceptual pairing of state and civil society has taken on a variety of meanings. One way of using it today is to identify the limits of politics. If politics organizes a society as a whole, civil society expresses capability and spaces for social self-organization. The concept of social capital has allowed us to explore these spaces. The collapse of communist systems and the problems encountered by Keynesian capitalism provide food for thought about the role of the state and politics in social organization. But exactly what role politics has to play remains an open question. Oddly enough, the first two comprehensive applications of the concept of social capital to political issues underestimate this problem.

Putnam assesses the performance of institutions, but fails to consider how the process of the building of the modern state has influenced the formation or the preservation of certain cultural traits (Tarrow 1996). Fukuyama defines the space of politics in a negative sense. He is not clear about what he wants politics to do; all he says is that it has to intervene as little as possible and avoid causing damage, because political action constantly risks destroying social capital. The welfare state, he argues, has often consumed social capital; by distributing subsidies it has destroyed fabrics of community self-help. It is, admittedly, important to call attention to the possible perverse effects of political action and society's loss of self-organizational capability (cf. also Ostrom 1994), but to do so is not to define the tasks of politics. Indeed, such an attitude is de facto negative and prejudicial.

Both authors shift their focus from politics to culture so that, for them, the question of social capital boils down to culture's functions for social integration. Albeit addressing different themes, both ultimately trace social capital to a shared culture. For Putnam, civic culture explains not only institutional performance, but also economic development. In the final analysis, Fukuyama's model explains the state and functioning of the economy in terms of market mechanisms; the reasons for adjustment to the market, he concludes, reside in culture, seen as an inherited ethical habit. This habit is the source of trust, and hence constitutes basic social capital. Both authors are attracted by the long-term duration of original cultures, and argue that historical events may have influenced the evolution of the original model, but we get the impression that everything – or almost everything – was destined to develop the way it has anyway.

To stress the limits of these applications and grasp the potential of social capital for political analysis, let us return to Coleman. Earlier I spoke of the tension that Coleman establishes between intentional organizations and other forms of social capital. In reality, he centres his attention on social capital as a by-product of social structures and the informal aspects thereof. Why?

The answer lies in the 'replacement of primordial social capital' (1990: 652): namely, the social capital that used to be typical of small-scale traditional societies and now thrown into crisis by modernization. Here Coleman proves to be an heir to the classical sociologists who built the categories of modernity by difference from those of traditional society, for which they show a certain nostalgia (Nisbet 1966). The *Gemeinschaft–Gesellschaft* pairing (Tönnies 1974 [1887]) is paradigmatic in this sense, although Coleman chooses to recall Weber and his idea of modernity as rationalization-bureaucratization (Weber 1978 [1922]). The lingering problem, however, is that something needs to be replaced. Modernity fails to produce the resources it needs for integration, yet wastes others. This idea recurs today in several authors. For Habermas, capitalism lives off cultural resources that it finds in previous forms of society and consumes but fails to reproduce (Habermas 1976). On closer scrutiny, Coleman is not unduly concerned with the survival of traditional elements, although he regards them as important. He turns his attention instead to the small-scale spontaneous society of *today* in the rationalized, large-scale society of *today*. He is one of those sociologists who have rediscovered the world of direct, face-to-face interaction and how it helps us understand a society made up largely of remote, indirect interaction managed in large-scale, formalized systems of interaction (e.g., Giddens 1984; Luhmann 1984). How to fit interaction and society, micro and macro, into the analysis is an open question which every generation of sociologists posits in different ways. The perspective of Coleman's general theoretical construction moves from micro to macro. But he is also interested in the consequences of macro for micro – the destruction of small-scale social capital in formalization processes – and micro for macro – the utility for social integration of the social capital produced in direct interaction.

The difference between Coleman's idea of social capital and those of the applications described thus becomes clear. It is a basic difference of methodology and has far-reaching analytical consequences. Coleman adopts a paradigm of action, Putnam and Fukuyama a deterministic, causal paradigm (Boudon 1982). Putnam and Fukuyama develop their explanations exclusively in relation to previous situations and conditions: a certain family structure and culture, for example, foretells company size. Their analysis defines differences and explains them with correlations of this type, but the actors tend to leave the stage. Both authors know full well that the historical process intervenes to redirect lines of development at particular moments, but their references exclude individual or collective subjects oriented towards strategies that they attempt, with varying degrees of coherence and awareness, to implement in a concrete situation that at once limits them and opens alternative possibilities. This way of reconstructing historical connections and, above all, this type of attention to the present, which enhances analysis and introduces the actor to situations that are not necessarily closed, do not seem to interest them. The general limit of their deterministic approach is that, at best, it describes a correlation between phenomena but without explaining it and, sometimes, struggles to define which variable in the correlation is independent and which dependent. So is it civic culture that explains the efficiency of democratic institutions or vice versa (Barry 1970)? The fact is that the presumption that explanations are possible without real actors, their definition of the situation and intentional strategies typically lapses into hyperfunctionalism and hyperculturalism. The actors that emerge are hyper-socialized, passive agents of economic and cultural structures.

It is possible to discuss the utility of the two paradigms at length, but it is more important now to show the differences and comparative advantages of the case in point. In an age of uncertainty and differentiation, Coleman comes out on top. In his perspective, social capital is essentially a stock of relations that an actor has for his or her own purposes, and which are effective since they are based on a specific culture, but also on the form of the network or other factors still. It is no coincidence that Coleman only cites examples of possible different forms of social capital. His focus on networks of relations as opposed to culture is an attempt to leave room for strategic actors, closed as little as possible in stereotyped role behaviour, and protagonists of a fabric of relations in autonomous, combinatory forms. Coleman's perspective seeks to grasp progressive adjustments, combinations of different re-sources and 'code games' rather than repetitions of crystallized cultural patterns. Developed coherently, this perspective is concerned more with the production of culture than its reproduction.

The first attempts to apply the theory of social capital to political sociology have brought to light often neglected aspects of social processes and helped to revive the political debate. Alas, their anti-political prejudice undermines the utility of the discussion. No-one today questions the need to reappraise civil society's self-organizational resources, to redesign the methods and bounds of politics and to reassess the utility of the market. The theory of social capital offers the analytical resources to support these convictions. It is odd, however, that its applications have been so keen to show that politics consumes social capital, yet say so little about how it might help create it. Are we positive that welfare systems have not helped to preserve or create social capital in Europe? Are we so sure that politics in America has destroyed more social capital than the market? Towards the end of his book, Fukuyama briefly acknowledges that, albeit compatible with many institutional set-ups, capitalism consumes social capital. But is it possible to find compatible set-ups of economic growth and social integration without reappraising the regulatory role of politics?

The idea of social capital has made headway in research and has been applied in fields as diverse as the labour market, the school careers of children, the misconduct of professionals, the economic behaviour of immigrants, social mobility and so on.

Simultaneously, a theoretical formulation of a 'paradigm' for social capital is being developed (see Portes 1998; Sandefur and Laumann 1998) which is sure to direct research on the old and new issues of political sociology. In substance, the concept of social capital appears useful for analysis of political phenomena, but it needs to be perfected. Far from being overburdened with duties, it has to be handled with care.

Deregulation, and after

A long phase of economic deregulation ushered in increasing globalization and the increasing centrality of financial operations in the overall economy, processes that in turn, in the long run, led to the worst economic crisis since the Second World War. This transformation of capitalism began early in the 1980s and the damage it has caused includes, from our perspective, the destruction of a large amount of social capital. Mistrust has grown towards economic institutions, political systems and their capacity to cope with difficult times. Flexible capitalism destroyed robust networks of relationships, and hindered the creation of durable and strong new networks. Richard Sennett (1999) has pointed out the risks of 'corrosion of character', an inability to make long-term plans for one's life and to maintain self-confidence across continuous changes in employment, residence and social relations, possibly with long stretches of unemployment; Sennett's work dates before the severe financial crisis that exploded in 2007, which very probably aggravated the risks he feared. The corrosion of character is the subjective counterpart to what loss of social capital is for the web of relationships in a social environment.

I will not be pessimistic, but optimism requires imagining a path back to a more regulative role of politics. The search for a new balance between the state and the market is currently on the agenda of most advanced capitalistic countries: capitalism may indeed be coming to a new turning point. In the opinion of many, we cannot afford an economy that works well only with a large number of temporary jobs, eating away the social fabric and spreading the corrosion of character syndrome: we risk a consolidation of the trend described in France by R. Castel (2009), a polarization between *citoyens par excès*, with access to resources and able to cope with deregulated environments, and many *citoyens par défaut*, without stable resources and constantly seeing both their market opportunities and their rights to social citizenship diminished. Even a healthy economy, capable of planning long-term investment and not just short-term speculation, that is, a new economy that can sustain itself without consuming resources it cannot reproduce, needs new political regulation. Of course, we cannot turn back to old recipes, but new recipes will need to tackle, among other things, the issue of how to create social capital, suitable for the new environment.

This is the problem and the task that Coleman called 'rational reconstruction of society', an organizational and political style of institutional design aimed at the development of cooperative interaction contexts, partly planned and partly open to spontaneous adaptation; an appropriate mix of formal and informal social capital.

Acknowledgement

Translated by John Irving.

Further Reading

Portes, A. 1998: Social capital: its origins and applications in modern sociology. *Annual Review of Sociology* 24: 1–24.

Putnam, R. 1993: *Making Democracy Work: Civic Traditions in Modern Italy*. Princeton, NJ: Princeton University Press.

Woodcock, M. 1998: Social capital and economic development: towards a theoretical synthesis and policy framework. *Theory and Society* 27(2): 151–208.

23

The Media and Politics

JOHN B. THOMPSON

All forms of mediated communication involve the transmission of information or symbolic content through time and space. They create forms of interaction in which participants are unlikely to confront each other directly 'face-to-face'. This is not new, but these forms of interaction have been transformed in various ways by the rise of the so-called 'mass media' and by the proliferation of new media in recent decades. Empirical studies of the effects of the mass media on the political process have tended to focus on their impact on attitudes and behaviour, especially voting behaviour in elections. Also important is their effect on the electoral practices of candidates and political parties. The proliferation of new media associated with digitization and the Internet has created new modes of communication and information dissemination that supplement or bypass traditional media channels, thereby opening up new possibilities for politicians to reach out to citizens but also new arenas for individuals to exchange information among themselves. A wider question is that of how the development of the media, old and new, has altered the very relationship between rulers and ruled. Developing Habermas's idea of the public sphere, Thompson argues that the development of communication media has created new forms of publicness which are no longer linked to sharing a common locale. While this means that politicians have become increasingly sophisticated at manipulating their public images, it also makes politics more open and accessible than ever before.

The Nature and Development of the Media

The term 'media' is commonly associated with particular forms of communication which have become pervasive features of contemporary societies, such as newspapers, magazines, radio, cinema and television. But these particular forms of communication represent only some of the many ways in which information and symbolic content can

The Wiley-Blackwell Companion to Political Sociology, First Edition. Edited by Edwin Amenta, Kate Nash, and Alan Scott.
© 2012 Blackwell Publishing Ltd. Published 2012 by Blackwell Publishing Ltd.

be fixed in technical media of various kinds and transmitted to others, or stored for subsequent use. In the most fundamental sense, the term 'media' refers to these various kinds of material substrata and the institutional forms by means of which information and symbolic content can be fixed and transmitted to others. Hence the use of paper for writing, the use of the telephone for communicating with others and the use of computer technologies for storing and exchanging information all involve the use of media in this sense.

One characteristic which is common to all forms of mediated communication is that they involve the transmission of information or symbolic content through time and space. The use of communication media enables individuals to transmit information and symbolic content to others who are situated in distant contexts. Hence, the use of communication media involves the creation of forms of interaction which are rather different from the forms of interaction which take place in the shared locales of everyday life. Much everyday interaction is 'face-to-face interaction', in the sense that it takes place in a localized setting in which individuals share a common spatial-temporal framework and confront one another directly. But mediated interaction is 'stretched' across space and perhaps also time; the participants may be situated in distant and diverse contexts, and they are unlikely to share a common spatial-temporal framework.

Understood in this broad way, communication media have been part of social and political life for several millennia. The development of systems of writing in Mesopotamia and Ancient Egypt, and the use of clay, stone, papyrus and paper for recording and transmitting information and symbolic content, involved the use of communication media in this sense (Innis 1950). But the invention of the printing press in the fifteenth century, and the subsequent rise of the printing and publishing industries, marked the beginning of something new. Thanks to the techniques of printing, it was now possible to reproduce multiple copies of texts relatively cheaply, and hence to make them available to a plurality of recipients in a commercially profitable way. The techniques of printing spread rapidly throughout Europe in the late fifteenth century, and by the sixteenth century there was a flourishing trade in books, pamphlets and other printed materials. In the early seventeenth century, regular journals of news began to appear in various European cities: these 'corantos', as they were called at the time, were the precursors of the modern newspaper. By the early eighteenth century, a variety of daily and weekly newspapers were well established in most major European cities.

The rise of media institutions concerned with the production and diffusion of books, newspapers and other symbolic material represented an important development. The gathering and circulation of information and symbolic content was increasingly linked to a range of institutionalized activities which were oriented towards the production of symbolic goods and their exchange in the marketplace. When we speak of 'the media' today, we are often referring to these institutions and their products. (They are also commonly described today as 'the mass media' or 'mass communication', although the term 'mass' can be misleading.) These institutions and their products have several important features. In the first place, these institutions are, for the most part, commercial organizations which are oriented towards financial gain. They use technical media of various kinds to produce symbolic goods which can be sold or otherwise distributed to individuals in a way that generates some kind of financial return. A second feature of media institutions is that their products are generally oriented towards a plurality of potential recipients. These goods are produced in multiple copies or transmitted to a multiplicity of receivers in such a way that they are available in principle to anyone who has the means, skills and resources to acquire them. Moreover, the flow of media products is a structured flow, in the sense that they are often produced by organizations which are largely responsible for shaping the product and its content, and then sold or transmitted to individuals who are primarily recipients. Of course, recipients can influence the production process in various ways, but this capacity is generally quite limited.

While the origins of media institutions can be traced back to the rise of the printing and publishing industries in late medieval and early modern Europe, the media have changed in many ways since the early nineteenth century. Three changes have been particularly significant. First, media institutions have become increasingly commercialized, and some have been transformed into large-scale commercial concerns. This transformation was due partly to a series of technical innovations in the printing industry, and partly to a gradual shift in the financial basis of the media industries and their methods of generating revenue. Through processes of growth and consolidation, large-scale communication conglomerates have emerged. These conglomerates – such as Time Warner, Disney and Rupert Murdoch's News Corporation – have today become key transnational players in the production and circulation of information and communication (Herman and McChesney 1997; Bagdikian 2000).

A second and closely related development was the globalization of communication and the emergence of global communication networks. In earlier centuries, printed materials were commonly transported over large distances and across the boundaries of kingdoms and states. But in the course of the nineteenth century the international flow of information and communication assumed a much more extensive and organized form. The development of international news agencies based in the major commercial cities of Europe, together with the expansion of communication networks linking the peripheral regions of empires with their European centres, established the beginnings of a global system of communication and information processing which, in the course of the twentieth century, became increasingly ramified and complex.

The third development was the emergence of electronically mediated forms of communication. Telegraph and telephone systems were introduced in the nineteenth century, and by the 1920s viable systems of radio broadcasting had been developed. Television broadcasting began after the Second World War and expanded rapidly in the 1950s. More recently, many media systems have been transformed by the development of new forms of information processing based on digital systems of codification – the so-called 'information revolution'. Digitization has led to the growing convergence of information and communication technologies on a common digital system of transmission, processing and storage. Information and symbolic content can now be converted rapidly and relatively easily into different media forms, and this in turn has blurred the traditional boundaries between different sectors of the media industries. Moreover, the dramatic expansion of the Internet from the early 1990s onwards has generated a plethora of new channels of communication and information dissemination, transforming the information environment for the rapidly growing numbers of individuals across the world with access to the Internet and enabling them to communicate in new ways.

The Media and the Political Process

It has long been recognized that the development of the media has important implications for the nature of politics and the political process. Early liberal thinkers, such as James Mill and John Stuart Mill, regarded an independent press as a crucial component of a liberal democratic society. They saw the free expression of opinion through the organs of an independent press as a vital means by which a diversity of viewpoints could be expressed and the abuses of state power by corrupt or tyrannical governments could be checked. A free and independent press would play the role of a critical watchdog, scrutinizing and criticizing the activities of those who rule (J. Mill 1967; J.S. Mill 1972).

Other social and political thinkers have taken a less sanguine view. Among the early critics of the media were Max Horkheimer and Theodor Adorno, two authors associated with the Frankfurt School of critical social theory. Writing in the 1930s and 1940s, Horkheimer and Adorno feared that the development of the media – or what they called 'the culture industry' – would lead to an increasingly oppressive social and political order. They used the term 'culture industry' to refer to the commodification of cultural forms brought about by the rise of the entertainment industries in Europe and the United States in the late nineteenth and early twentieth centuries. The cultural goods produced by these industries are standardized and rationalized commodities which are shaped primarily by the logic of capital accumulation. These goods would not stimulate critical thinking in audiences or readers but would, Horkheimer and Adorno feared, render individuals less capable of autonomous judgement and more dependent on social processes over which they have little control. Individuals would be increasingly assimilated to the social order by their very desire for the objects produced by it (Horkheimer and Adorno 1972; Adorno 1991).

The gloomy prognosis of critics like Horkheimer and Adorno presumed that the media were capable of having a quite powerful impact on the attitudes and behaviour of ordinary individuals. Whether this was true, however, and the precise nature of the impact that the media might have, were primarily empirical questions which required careful investigation. A good deal of empirical research has been done in an attempt to answer questions of this kind. Among other things, researchers have tried to determine whether the media have a discernible impact on the outcome of elections, and whether election campaigns conducted in the media have a significant impact on the decisions of voters. Studies of this kind have yielded relatively few clear-cut and generalizable conclusions. Given the complexity of electoral processes and the wide range of factors which are likely to affect outcomes, it is perhaps not surprising that researchers have found it difficult to isolate the effects of media coverage and campaigns. But the early studies did tend to suggest that the impact of the media on electoral outcomes was less significant and less direct than many commentators had supposed.

One of the first major studies of the media and elections was carried out in the United States by Paul Lazarsfeld and his associates in the 1940s and 1950s (Lazarsfeld, Berelson and Gaudet 1948; Katz and Lazarsfeld 1955). Lazarsfeld and his associates were particularly interested in why people changed their voting intentions during election campaigns. Initially they studied the 1940 presidential election and found that exposure to media campaigns produced little alteration in people's voting intentions. Instead, the key factor influencing changes seemed to be other people. They also found that some people were particularly influential in this regard, and that these 'opinion leaders' were more likely to be influenced by the media. So Lazarsfeld and his associates put forward a model of what they called 'the two-step flow of communication': ideas flow from the media to opinion leaders, and from these opinion leaders they flow to other sections of the population. This model suggested that the impact of the media on most ordinary individuals was largely indirect: it was mediated by the social groups to which they belonged and by significant individuals with whom they interacted in their day-to-day lives.

The work of Lazarsfeld and others in the 1940s and 1950s seemed to show that the power of the media to change people's views was relatively limited. Media messages, it seemed, were much more likely to confirm and reinforce pre-existing attitudes and beliefs than to change them; minor alterations might occur, but conversion to fundamentally different points of view was rare. 'Persuasive mass communications functions far more frequently as an agent of reinforcement than as an agent of change', concluded Joseph Klapper in a text which became a standard reference work in the field (Klapper 1960: 15). But the thesis of minimal consequences, together with the research on which it was based, has been criticized on various grounds (see, for example, Gitlin 1978). The emphasis on short-term changes of attitude might well obscure a range of more subtle influences, and the circumstances in which elections take place today might differ in significant ways from the social and political contexts in which Lazarsfeld and others carried out their research. More recent studies have highlighted a number of important ways in which the media can shape political processes.

One important line of research, initiated in the 1970s by Maxwell McCombs, Donald Shaw and others, has focused on the phenomenon of 'agenda setting' (McCombs and Shaw 1972; Dearing and Rogers 1996; McCombs 2004). Like Lazarsfeld and his associates, McCombs and Shaw were interested in the impact of the media on people's attitudes during election campaigns. They knew there was little evidence to suggest that the media directly changed people's attitudes on a significant scale, but McCombs and Shaw hypothesized that the media would set the agenda for political campaigns, influencing the salience of particular issues. In other words, while the media may not be very successful at telling people *what* to think, they may be quite successful at telling them what to think *about*. In their study of a sample of voters during the 1968 US presidential campaign, McCombs and Shaw found a high correlation between the issues emphasized by the media and the issues which voters regarded as important, a finding which they viewed as consistent with the agenda-setting hypothesis. Subsequent studies have explored the relations between news stories in the media and public attitudes on drugs, crime, race, environmental issues and so on. These studies show that, in some cases, particular events can act as 'triggers' which play a key role in putting the issue on the media agenda, and thereby turning them into public issues.

Another factor which has been explored by recent research, and which is relevant to the impact of the media, is the changing social composition of the electorate. In the period immediately after the Second World War, there was a relatively strong sense of party identification among voters in Britain, the United States and elsewhere. This strong sense of party identification, cultivated in family contexts and local communities from an early age, might well have limited the capacity of electoral campaigns in the media to produce significant effects. But from the 1960s on, this strong sense of party identification has been eroded to some degree. The traditional working class has declined, and traditional links between social classes and political parties have weakened. At the same time, there has been an increase in the proportion of 'floating voters' who are not firmly committed to any particular party. There is some evidence to suggest that the electoral choices of floating voters are more likely to be influenced by the media coverage of an election than the choices of committed voters (Harrop 1986; Miller 1991). In the run-up to the 1987 British General Election, for example, the swing to the Conservatives was much stronger among uncommitted voters than among the committed, and uncommitted voters who read the *Sun* or *Star* – two tabloid newspapers which supported the Conservatives – were more likely to swing in this direction than other uncommitted voters (Miller 1991: 194–195). Of course, evidence of this kind must be treated with caution, since it is extremely difficult to isolate the effects of any single factor. But the evidence lends some support to the view that, in a political environment characterized by a weakening of traditional party loyalties and the declining significance of social class, the potential for using the media to influence electoral outcomes at the margins – especially among floating voters – may be growing.

Whatever the precise impact of the media on the electoral choices of voters, it is clear that the existence of the media has altered the electoral practices of candidates and political parties. Elections are increasingly fought on the terrain of the media, as candidates and parties rely increasingly on media coverage and campaigns in order to present themselves and their policies to the electorate. Elections have become media events. The rise of television has accentuated this trend and has, in turn, altered its character. With the growing significance of television, politicians and parties have come to rely increasingly on techniques borrowed from advertising in order to 'sell' themselves to voters. This practice became increasingly common among US presidential candidates from the 1950s on. Candidates began to employ media advisers who were trained in advertising, and spot advertisements on television became an increasingly central feature of election campaigns (McGuinnis 1970; Jamieson 1984). Television advertising now consumes a very large share of campaign budgets in both presidential and congressional elections. In Britain and many other countries, there are much stricter controls on the ability of candidates and parties to advertise on television. But some provision is usually made for candidates and parties to present themselves and their policies to the electorate via televised broadcasts.

The use of advertising techniques has also contributed to the rise of what has been called 'political marketing' (O'Shaugnessy 1990; Maarek 1993). Political marketing involves more than just the use of television advertisements (or party political broadcasts) to promote the images and policies of candidates (or to attack their opponents). It also involves the use of techniques drawn from the world of commercial marketing to tailor the product to the needs and tastes of consumers. The use of political marketing techniques has become a common feature of American election campaigns, but marketing techniques have also become increasingly prevalent in

Britain and elsewhere. The British Conservative Party under Margaret Thatcher relied heavily on the marketing expertise of Saatchi and Saatchi, the London-based advertising agency, to develop its campaign strategy for the General Election of 1979 and subsequent elections (Scammell 1995). And the reorientation of the Labour Party under Tony Blair, aimed at restoring Labour's electoral credibility after four successive General Election defeats, was based on the extensive use of methods of market research.

Since the early 2000s, the Internet has played an increasingly important role in electoral campaigns. Political parties and campaign organizations have made increasing use of the Internet to reach out to potential supporters, organize campaigns, mobilize voters and solicit donations. This was a key feature of the electoral campaign of Barak Obama in the run-up to the US presidential election in 2008. In both the primary and the presidential campaign, Obama's organization made extensive use of the Internet and of computerized systems of information to raise funds and mobilize support. During the primary Obama raised nearly $340 million (by 30 June 2008), substantially more than Hillary Clinton's $233 million, and 88 per cent of Obama's funds came from individual donations; nearly half of these were less than $200 and three-quarters were less than $2,000. There is some evidence to suggest that effective use of the Internet by the Obama campaign was responsible for a substantial proportion of these small donations (Castells 2009). The Obama campaign also used the Internet extensively to disseminate information, feed material both to the mainstream media and to countless web sites, organize activists, coordinate activities and establish personalized connections with millions of actual and potential supporters.

The Media and the Transformation of Public Life

While the role of the media in elections and election campaigns has been a major focus of attention for scholars interested in political communication, it is also clear that the significance of the media for politics extends well beyond the relatively limited sphere of elections. The rise of communication media has altered the very nature of politics and the ways in which political leaders relate to those over whom they rule. These changes are part of a broader transformation in the nature of public life. The distinction between 'public' and 'private' has a long history in Western social and political thought, and these terms have acquired various senses (see Bobbio 1989; Habermas 1989; Thompson 1995). In one sense of the term, 'public' means 'open' or 'available'. What is public, in this sense, is what is visible or observable, what is performed in front of spectators, what is open for all or many to see or hear about. What is private, by contrast, is what is hidden from view, what is said or done in secrecy or behind closed doors. In this sense, the public–private distinction has to do with publicness versus privacy, with openness versus secrecy, with visibility versus invisibility.

The development of communication media has altered the publicness or visibility of actions or events in a fundamental way. (For a more detailed discussion of this point and of the consequences which follow from it, see Thompson 1995, 2005.) Prior to the development of the media, the publicness of actions or events was linked to the sharing of a common locale: an event became a public event by being staged before a plurality of individuals who were physically present at the time and place of its occurrence. This 'traditional publicness of co-presence' was tied to the characteristics of face-to-face interaction. But the development of communication media – beginning with print, but including the more recent electronic media – created new forms of publicness which were no longer linked to the sharing of a common locale. An action or event could be made visible and observable by being recorded and transmitted to others who were not physically present. These new forms of 'mediated publicness' did not entirely displace the role of the traditional publicness of co-presence. But as new media of communication became more pervasive, the new forms of mediated publicness began to supplement, and gradually to extend and transform, the traditional form of publicness.

The changing nature of publicness has altered the conditions under which political power is exercised. Political rulers and leaders have always sought to construct self-images and manage the ways in which they appear before others, but the development of communication media has changed the nature and scope of this activity. Prior to the development of print and other media, political rulers could generally restrict the activity of managing visibility to the relatively closed circles of the assembly or court. There were occasions, such as coronations, victory marches or royal progresses, when rulers appeared before wider audiences. But for most individuals in ancient or medieval societies, the most powerful rulers were rarely if ever seen. With the development of new means of communication, however, political rulers had to concern themselves increasingly with their self-presentation before audiences which were not physically present. Monarchs in early modern Europe, such as Louis XIV of France or Philip IV of Spain, were well versed in the arts of image making; their images were fabricated and celebrated not only in traditional media, such as paint, bronze and stone, but also in the newer media of print (Elliott 1985; Burke 1992). The subsequent development of electronic media (radio and especially television) created powerful new means for political rulers and leaders to construct their images, to communicate with distant others and to appear before them in ways that were simply not possible in the past.

These new media of communication required new modes and styles of self-presentation. The traditional forms of political speech making – the fiery rhetoric of the speech delivered to an assembled crowd, for example – were not necessarily suitable for the new kinds of communicative situations created by electronic media. The radio allowed for a more conversational style in which political leaders could address others in a more direct and personal way; the fiery rhetoric of the impassioned speech was exchanged for the conversational intimacy of the fireside chat (Jamieson 1988). Television accentuated this trend and added the symbolic richness and immediacy of the visual image. Hence, political leaders could now address distant others with the kind of directness and intimacy characteristic of face-to-face inter-action, but in a way that was freed from the constraints and reciprocity of conversation in a shared locale. The impersonal aloofness of most political leaders in the past was increasingly replaced by a new kind of mediated intimacy through which political figures could present themselves not only as leaders but also as human beings, as ordinary individuals who could address their subjects as fellow citizens, selectively disclosing aspects of their lives and their character in a conversational or even confessional mode. And given the capacity of television to convey close-up images, viewers could now scrutinize their leaders' actions, utterances and appearances with the kind of close attention once reserved for those with whom one interacted intimately in the course of one's daily life.

Under these radically altered conditions of public life, the management of visibility and self-presentation through the media has become an integral and increasingly professionalized feature of government. The conduct of government requires a continuous process of decision making concerning what is to be made public, to whom and how, and the task of making and executing these decisions is increasingly handed over to a team of specialized personnel who are responsible for managing the relation between the government and the media. Since the early 1970s, US presidents have relied heavily on the White House Office of Communications to perform this task. Established by Nixon in 1969, the Office of Communications employs a permanent staff which is concerned with coordinating the flow of information from the White House to the media, planning interviews and television appearances by Administration officials and developing a long-term media strategy (Maltese 1994). Part of the task of the Office (and similar organizations elsewhere) is not only to control what Administration officials say and how they appear in public, but also to try, as far as possible, to influence what the media say about them (to 'spin' the story), so that the Administration will appear in a favourable light.

However, despite the efforts of governments and political leaders to manage their visibility in the mediated arena of modern politics, this is an arena which is strewn with dangers and risks. Political leaders must constantly be on their guard and employ a high degree of reflexivity to monitor their actions and utterances, since an indiscreet act or an ill-judged remark can have disastrous consequences. The mediated arena of modern politics is open and accessible in a way that traditional assemblies and courts were not. Moreover, given the development of new technologies and the sheer proliferation of media organizations, channels and sources, it is simply not possible to control completely the flows of information and the ways in which political leaders become visible to others.

Leaks, gaffes, scandals: these and other occurrences exemplify how difficult it is to control information and manage self-presentation in the age of mediated visibility. The example of scandal is particularly interesting, both because the phenomenon has become so widespread today and because its consequences can be so disastrous for the individuals concerned. Scandal is not a new phenomenon; the concept can be traced back to ancient Greece, and the word became increasingly common in European languages from the sixteenth century on. But the rise of the modern phenomenon of mediated scandal dates from the late eighteenth and early nineteenth centuries (Thompson 1997, 2000). A mediated scandal is a distinctive type of event which involves the disclosure through the media of an activity that transgresses certain norms, an activity which had previously been hidden (or known only to a small circle of people) and which, on being made public in this way, may give rise to public criticism and condemnation that can have damaging consequences for the individuals concerned. Disclosure through the media endows these hitherto private activities with the status of public events: they are now visible, observable and knowable by thousands or even millions of others who become spectators of activities which they did not and could not have witnessed directly. There is a continuous line of development from the scandals of the late nineteenth century – such as the scandal that destroyed the political career of Charles Parnell, the charismatic leader of the Irish parliamentary party at Westminster – to the scandals which have become such prominent features of political life in recent decades, from Profumo and Watergate to the Clinton–Lewinsky scandal and the MPs' expenses scandal, to name but a few.

The prevalence of political scandals is symptomatic of the transformation of visibility brought about by the rise of the media and it demonstrates how difficult it is to control the flow of information and maintain a veil of secrecy around the private activities and conversations of political leaders and others today. We now live in an age of high media visibility, and those who hold or aspire to positions of prominence in public life find themselves acting in an information environment which is very different from that which existed several centuries (and even several decades) ago. The public domain itself has become a complex space of information flows, and given the proliferation of media and networks of communication, it is much more difficult today for political actors to throw a veil of secrecy around their activities, much harder to control the images and information that appear in the public domain and much harder to predict the consequences of such appearances and disclosures when they occur.

Further Reading

Castells, M. 2009: *Communication Power*. Oxford: Oxford University Press.

Iyengar, S. and McGrady, J.A. 2007: *Media Politics: A Citizen's Guide*. New York: W. W. Norton.

Jamieson, K.H. 1988: *Eloquence in an Electronic Age: The Transformation of Political Speechmaking*. New York: Oxford University Press.

Negrine, R. 2008: *The Transformation of Political Communication: Continuities and Changes in Media and Politics*. Basingstoke: Palgrave Macmillan.

Scammell, M. 1995: *Designer Politics: How Elections are Won*. Basingstoke: Macmillan.

Thompson, J.B. 1995: *The Media and Modernity: A Social Theory of the Media*. Cambridge: Polity Press.

24

Imagined Communities

ALAN FINLAYSON

An imagined community is a kind of everyday social and political theory about what and whom to value and why. Durkheim's opposition between mechanical and organic solidarity recognizes the continuing 'moral' function of collective belonging and, in modernity, the primary way in which this has been imagined is through the nation. National imagining, as Gellner argued, is made necessary by industrial modernization and possible by, as Anderson argued, the spread of print-culture. But imagining such community is not a mere reflex. It is a conscious attempt to answer problematic questions about the legitimacy of modern states and their policies. Indeed, some theorists suggest that modern ideology is nothing other than the process of imagining community. As new means of communication make possible the 'deterritorialization' of cultural practices and experiences, some analysts posit the emergence of a global imagined community. But these new technologies also make possible the invention or reinvention of all sorts of local or particular imagined community. The relationship of these two processes is a vital topic of political sociological research.

A difficulty for theories and analyses of 'community' is that community is itself a kind of social theory. In declaring the presence of a community we propose a way of comprehending and evaluating social relationships. Believing that we share interests with others, or that we interpret the social world in similar ways, we then attribute such commonality to something deeper (history, culture, tradition, values, spirit) which gives the community shape and purpose. An imagined community, then, is a group of people who not only draw on the same set of symbolic resources when articulating their sense of identity but, additionally, recognize and value that commonality which they regard not as an outcome of certain social facts but as their cause. For that reason community is not simply one form of identity that rivals others

The Wiley-Blackwell Companion to Political Sociology, First Edition. Edited by Edwin Amenta, Kate Nash, and Alan Scott.
© 2012 Blackwell Publishing Ltd. Published 2012 by Blackwell Publishing Ltd.

but, rather, a way in which identities of various kinds are apprehended and their significance inferred.

The challenge for the political sociology of imagined communities is: firstly, to make sense of the social and historical conditions of possibility for such imagining; secondly, to comprehend the intellectual needs it might satisfy; thirdly, to identify its political implications. In this chapter we will begin exploring these challenges by examining how some influential classical sociological theories conceptualized community. We will then examine debates about the primary form of modern imagined community – the nation – and in the process identify some of its social and historical determinants. We will then look at how imagined community has seemed to provide an answer to some intellectual problems of political theory and practice, before looking directly at its ideological aspects and, finally, reflecting upon contemporary and possible future developments.

Community and Social Thought

At the end of the nineteenth century Tönnies (1974 [1887]) famously defined 'community' by contrasting it with 'association'. The former was organic and moral, the latter contractual and amoral. The forms of association encouraged by modern life and embodied in the state, he argued, were 'estranged' from community life. The force of convention prevailed over consensual ethical harmony. Such a diagnosis of the decline of community is reflected throughout modern social thought and criticism, from Weber's theories of rationalization and disenchantment to the injunction to revive 'community spirit' characteristic of contemporary communitarian social and political thought (see Etzioni, 1995; Kenny, 2003).

The contrast of 'natural' or 'traditional' community with soulless and anomic modern life is a commonplace that shapes the contemporary social and political imagination. We cannot accept it at face value. Significantly, in contrast to Tönnies, Durkheim proposed that solidarity in small-scale 'traditional' societies was 'mechanical' (a conformity born of necessity), and contrasted this to the 'organic' connections of modern societies. An effect of the contemporary division of labour, he wrote, was 'to create in two or more persons a feeling of solidarity...to cause coherence among friends and to stamp them with its seal' (1933: 56). In place of uniformity and convention, he argued, modern societies are composed of differentiated and specialized individuals who can come to recognize their mutual dependence on each other. That recognition has 'a moral character, for the need of order, harmony, and social solidarity is generally considered moral' (1933: 63). The conclusion is that the 'collective consciousness' of 'traditional' community is not destroyed by modern life. Rather, it becomes transcendental and universal, embodied in 'the cult of individualism' and normatively expressed in liberal civil law.

What Durkheim understood was that in contemporary societies the formation of communities is more than an anthropological reflex. It has a self-conscious and moral aspect and is connected with rational administrative and legal systems. Consequently, the way in which community is imagined is a fundamental political issue. While social solidarity in industrial societies is, for Durkheim, rational rather than mythic, it is also the case that 'there can be no society which does not experience the need at regular intervals to maintain and strengthen the collective feelings and ideas that provide its coherence and distinct individuality' (1995: 425). Such practices are today important forms of political invention and intervention, and also of its contestation. The political sociology of imagined communities must therefore investigate the production of collective sentiments and ideas, their basis in social organization and the affective or ideational work they do; the ways in which persons come to consciously believe in a common bond and how this is connected to larger moral and political claims. In the modern period the primary example of this process has been the nation-state.

Nationalism

Ernest Gellner (1983) argues that industrial societies' need for a new kind of shared culture is the primary cause of modern nationalism (see also Schwarzmantel, Chapter 29, in this volume). Agrarian society, he argues, was localized and hierarchical. The ruling class was rigidly separated from the peasantry and a clerical elite monopolized literate culture. But where agrarian society was static, industrial society is fluid, characterized by a division of labour, 'which is complex and persistently, cumulatively changing' (Gellner 1983: 24). This variability requires facilitation from a set of generic codes – a basic training in a high culture of literacy and numeracy that is applicable across occupational fields and which generates a level of commonality that transcends the particularity of artisan labour. Thus: 'in industrial society, notwithstanding its larger number of specialisms, the distance between specialists is far less great. Their mysteries are far closer to mutual intelligibility, their manuals have idioms that overlap to a much greater extent, and re-training, though sometimes difficult, is not generally an awesome task' (Gellner 1983: 26–27).

According to Gellner, the state, holding 'the monopoly of legitimate education', is the only institution capable of creating this universal high culture. Culture and politics thus become combined, since for any culture to persist it must have its own 'political roof'. Nationalism creates the nation and it does so in response to the disruptions and transformations of industrialization that throw rigid social positioning into question.

It is not always clear if, in Gellner's argument, nationalism is a by-product of modernization or part of how modernization is propagated. Historical examples suggest that claims could be made either way in different cases. Nationalism has often emerged as a force opposed to modernization and, as John Breuilly remarks, it 'cannot originate as a deliberate project of modernization unless one attributed phenomenal clairvoyance as well as power to nationalists' (Breuilly 1996: 156). This is one reason why, in opposition to Gellner, Anthony Smith (e.g., 1998, 1991, 1995) emphasizes the significance of pre-modern social forms for understanding nationalism. He argues that scholars confuse modern state formation with the building of national communities. Where some focus on the instrumental aspect of nations, their usefulness in advancing certain elite claims, Smith shows how this is too insensitive to the nature of mass support for nationalism which has a strongly affective aspect and is not concerned with satisfying only 'rational' aims. As Walker Connor has stressed, the nation is a 'psychological bond' defining a people, differentiating it from others and cohering in 'the subconscious conviction of its members' (Connor 1978; see also 1994). Smith argues that a pre-modern core of ethnic identification (an *ethnie*) forms the basis for the deeply held sentiments out of which nationalism develops, and that such communities have been present throughout human history. Indeed, for Smith, ethnicity is a key mode of social organization. Careful to reject the argument that nationalism is simply primordial or perennial, he suggests that '*ethnies* are constituted not by lines of physical descent but by the sense of continuity, shared memory, and collective destiny'. These derive from shared experiences, such as warfare or colonization, that generate a strong sense of belonging, and the myths and rituals that reproduce it. Where these become embedded in centralized administrative systems (such as those based on religion) they foster homogeneity and give to social organization an ethnic core.

In a third approach to nationalism, Benedict Anderson (1991) has persuasively argued that the imagined community of the nation is rooted in a new conception of temporality which finds unconnected people across differentiated space occupying the same time. They all live, he suggests, in a simultaneous 'meanwhile'. This development derives from the spread of print-capitalism which, in order to create viable markets, assembled varied dialects into more homogeneous languages, creating a bridge between elite clerical Latin and diverse popular vernaculars. In then providing those markets with newspapers, periodicals, novels and so forth, print-capitalism not only brought individuals information about others in the same linguistic community but also the experience of living in the same moment as them, thinking about the same things and sharing preoccupations. The convergence of capitalism and printing made it possible to imagine a community of more people than one could possibly meet and come to know.

Gellner, Smith and Anderson propose markedly different theories of the emergence of nations and nationalism. However, they all indicate some of the social-historical conditions that made this new form of community possible – historical experience allied to social transformation and new means of communication – and also the important connections between these and forms of political and economic organization. Nationalism both emerges from and institutionalizes systems of communication that made it possible for diverse peoples to share in an imagining of community. In many nineteenth-century European nationalisms, promotion or protection of the national language was central. For instance, Irish nationalists revived Gaelic language and culture as part of their political project; Fichte demanded the expunging from the German language of all 'alien' French words; the codification of French nationality after the Revolution involved the standardization of the language through the replacement of regional dialects with Parisian French. More broadly, shared ethnic culture and tradition are to some extent 'invented' or at least reworked by political and cultural elites (Hobsbawm and Ranger 1983), and one of the crucial roles of nationalist ideologues is to gather and codify the traditions and rituals of an assumed national people, be it the revival of traditional sports or the codification of a vernacular literature (see Hutchinson 1987).

Contemporary states still often act in ways intended to reproduce and sustain such a national culture. For instance, 'heritage' in the form of architecture or 'natural' woodland can be seen as the embodiment of the national spirit and its preservation proof of the national loyalties of the representatives of the state (Wright 1985). School curricula (especially literature and history) are often a battleground for shaping and defining the nation (Clark 1990; Crowley 1991). Various forms of culture may be understood to reproduce or challenge visions of national community – novels, dramas, films, television, popular music (e.g., Cairns and Richards 1988; Bhaba 1990; Helgerson 1992; Carter, Donald and Squires 1993; Higson 1995). National governments often implement policies to prevent the dilution of national culture by foreign cultural forms. In France quotas are imposed on radio stations to guarantee air-time for French language pop and rock music, and free trade in films has been a major stumbling block in international trade agreements. To understand imagined communities we need to examine the everyday cultural phenomena that reinforce a sense of national belonging – what Billig (1995) calls 'banal nationalism'. But above all we need to understand the relationships of governments, cultural institutions and the symbolic contents of nation-ness. That requires us to consider not only the underlying cultural-historical determinants of imagined national communities but also the ways in which these provide answers to questions characteristic of modern political thinking.

Political Legitimacy and Imagined Community

In an argument reminiscent of Anderson's (but developed earlier), Nicos Poulantzas found that the national standardization of language was 'necessary not only for the creation of a national economy and market, but still more for the exercise of the state's political role. It is ... the mission of the national State to organize the processes of thought by forging the materiality of the people-nation' (1978: 58). He concludes that monopolization and standardization of forms of communication are some of the means through which the state produces a communal identity from which it then attains legitimacy. From a different starting point John Breuilly reaches a similar conclusion (1982: 393), arguing that nationalism helps to explain the relationship of the modern state to society by making government appear as a natural historical development rooted in the authenticity of the community. Similarly, Smith advances a moderate defence of nationalism and nationality, arguing that it is politically and socially necessary, helping to ground principles of national sovereignty and so protect groups while promoting interdependence (Smith 1995).

What these varied but overlapping claims point to is the fact that the imagined community of the nation, as well as a manifestation of deep-rooted and wide-scale social and cultural transformation, was also a way in which individuals addressed political and philosophical questions those same transformations threw up. If state power could no longer be legitimated by appeals to divine or monarchical descent, how could it be justified? Modern liberalism sought to ground authority in rational recognition of a natural law or morality and of the self-interest satisfied by signing up to the social contract. But the political advance of such claims was also sustained by inventions of, and appeals to the ancient liberties and rights, as well as the innate disposition of, those who were part of the imagined national community (and distinct from those who lay without).

It is in this context that we should appreciate Weber's insight that the concept of nation belongs 'in the sphere of values' (Weber 1948). An imagined community carries within it something more than a content-less commitment to belonging. To belong is also to be attached to some set of values or practices that receive their validation from the very fact that they are expressions of the community, reaffirmed daily in the hearts, minds and activities of its members. To recall Durkheim, the necessity of mutuality in small-scale societies is replaced in the modern nation-state by a conscious sense of organic interdependence. That nation-state in turn attains legitimacy for itself, and also for its policies, by showing how these are rooted in the spirit of national culture and community.

Once we recognize the interaction of claims about community, legitimacy and particular social values, we can investigate their varied instances. For instance, Hall (1978; CCCS 1982) showed how political arguments about crime and deviance in 1970s Britain were shaped by concepts of nationhood and race. Such discourses, Gilroy argues, involve 'a distinct theory of culture and identity which . . . views nations as culturally homogeneous "communities of sentiment" in which a sense of patriotic belonging can and should grow to become an important source of moral and political ideas' (1987: 59–60).

Communities function by defining boundaries and policing them; boundaries shaped by the dual axes of similarity and difference (Cohen 1985). Consequently we must attend to the intersection of imagined community with other ideological configurations and in particular to who is and is not included. For example, we may ask if a particular idea of community specifies gender or sexual roles (see Parker *et al.* 1992; Yuval-Davis 1997). Early nationalism in Ireland built itself on the projection of the nation as a suffering woman and mother to be defended by her noble Gaelic sons. Such a notion was codified in the 1937 constitution where the roles and rights of women were clearly specified (Finlayson 1998a). Salecl (1993) shows how gender was important to the nationalism of the new states of the former Yugoslavia. Here it intersected with claims about religion and sexual morality. The intersection of sexuality and national community can also be observed in British politics (see A-M. Smith 1995).

Nationalism, as Anderson argued, is 'a cultural artifact' that is 'capable of being transplanted with varying degrees of self-consciousness to a great variety of social terrains, to merge and be merged with a correspondingly wide variety of political and ideological constellations' (1991: 4). That is why we often find nationalism to be a hyphenated phenomenon: socialist-nationalism, liberal-nationalism, pan-Arab-nationalism and so forth. The political sociology of imagined communities has to look further than this, investigating the ways in which community is linked to all sorts of political project. For the community is not simply imagined as a generalized form of existence. It is always a particular community (say, the Irish or Indian people) in possession of, and defined by, specific values or characteristics. Furthermore, nations are not the only instances of political imagined communities. Some feminisms have founded themselves on an imagined community of all women, while movements based around sexual orientation have also found it necessary to propose the existence of, as one slogan has it, a 'queer nation'.

All sorts of political ideology legitimate their claims through an identification with the intrinsic spirit of a community. By secreting themselves within such a projected essence ideologies may render themselves apparently natural (Finlayson 1998b). The identity of that community and its values thus becomes central to political contestation of all kinds. Politicians, activists and spokespeople claim to articulate the feelings of 'the community' and to mobilize action around a concept of communality, be it rooted in a particular ethnicity, social class or gender (see Finlayson, 2003). The ubiquity of this process perhaps suggests that it is yet more fundamental to the ways in which individuals relate to their political society. And that is certainly the implication of some contemporary approaches to the theory and analysis of ideology.

Ideology and Imagined Community

Where social integration is forged through mechanical necessity the primary focus of the communal imaginary is the disruptive gap between people and unpredictable nature. This takes the symbolic form of the totem and social relations understood via nature. The community is built around beliefs that mediate the group's relationship to the natural environment. But in contemporary complex societies the terrain of the communal imaginary is the relation between people. We must ground our relationship to the world but also our relationship to potentially unpredictable others by creating an imaginary community mediated through the dimensions of time and space. It is in this sense that community may be understood as intrinsically ideological.

For instance, Balibar (1995) argues, adapting Marx, that ideology involves the representation of particulars as universals. The modern state, he writes, is 'a man-ufacturer of abstractions precisely by virtue of the unitary fiction (or consensus) which it has to impose on society'. This entails an abstracted and fictive community that 'compensates for the real lack of community between individuals' (1995: 48). In Lefort's terms there is a 'projection of an imaginary community under the cover of which "real" distinctions are determined as "natural", their particularity is disguised under the features of the universal . . . the imaginary community rules over individuals or separate groups and imposes behavioral norms upon them' (Lefort 1986: 191). Ideology then may be nothing other than the imagining of community. Modern societies are forced continually to re-imagine the grounds of their legitimacy in the form of visions of community that also specify the roles the subjects of that community must aspire to.

Psychoanalytic philosophers such as Slavoj Žižek see such phenomena as instances of 'ideological fantasy'. This is not something that merely mystifies or masks the truth. It is 'an illusion which structures our effective, real social relations' (1989: 47). From this perspective the ideology of imagined community might be what makes such social relations possible. But for Žižek this would be an imagined unity that compensates for the lack that is the absent core of all social identity. In a related formulation Ernesto Laclau (1996) proposes that 'the nation' is an ideological 'empty signifier' standing in for the lost unity of the community and linking together hegemonic discourses. He argues that contemporary populist politics are a radical attempt to ground legitimacy in the fact of the community and its innate will, imagining a level at which all 'the people' are equivalent to each other and opposing them to an antagonistic illegitimate power such as that of 'the elite' (Laclau 2007).

The argument of these theorists of ideology is that ways of imagining community are not just one aspect of modern ideological thinking but central to it. Imagined community is part of the 'logic' of contemporary politics (see Glynos and Howarth 2007). On the basis of some shared experience or outlook a more fundamental equivalence is posited and from it are derived claims about the legitimacy of political demands. Political sociology has to study the interaction of technologies, histories and emotions with such political activities, tracing out their sources, trajectories and effects.

Imagined Community after the Nation

As we have seen, many theories of nations and nationalism emphasize the extent to which systems of communication (in the first instance printing) made it possible to imagine community on the national scale (also Deutsch 1966). The predominantly national basis to media institutions certainly has made them of tremendous importance in the maintenance of national community. Television, for instance, has been understood as a means of integrating millions of domestic, family units into the rhythms and experiences of a national imaginary (Ang 1996: 5) and of creating national experiences – the coronation of a monarch, the swearing in of a president – that 'integrate societies in a collective heartbeat and evoke a renewal of loyalty to the society and its legitimate authority' (Dayan and Katz 1992: 9). This is what Baudrillard called 'the *mass communication effect*' (1998: 107).

However, as media products and markets become more globalized (in both their production and dissemination) they bring about, it is argued, a deterritorialization of cultural space. Products are severed from specific locations, and, in the attempt to be marketable internationally, become ever more generalized in content (Herman and McChesney, 1997). On the one hand, that might promise only a homogenized vapidity to which nobody feels allegiance. Doug Kellner (2002) claims that 'a new global culture is emerging as a result of computer and communications technology, a consumer society with its panorama of goods and services, transnational forms of architecture and design, and a wide range of products and cultural forms that are traversing national boundaries and becoming part of a new world culture...'. But it might also portend a new kind of global imagined community. Through becoming conscious of a 'simultaneous meanwhile' at a global level we can come to experience some measure of emotional affinity with those who are otherwise distant, a kind of 'popular cosmopolitanism' (Nash 2003). Increasingly, as governmental institutions become detached from national communities, political and social theorists are proposing ways of formalizing such a global cosmopolitanism, giving it institutional but also cultural and ideological legitimacy (e.g., Brown and Held 2010; Held 2010), although others suggest that this may be nothing other than a way of legitimating 'interventions' motivated by economic or political self-interest (see Archibugi 2003; also discussion in Fine 2007).

But the same processes that make possible this homogenization or cosmopolitanism also energize particular imagined communities, freed from the constraints of time and space. For instance, global diasporas may remain in regular, even permanent, contact with their home countries, living under one state while consuming and producing the imaginary of another. As Marie Gillespie has noted: 'improved access to, speed and effectiveness of transport, communication and information systems has enabled a strengthening of transnational kinship, religious, economic and political networks, leading to powerful globalizing alliances as well as troubling polarizations...'. Indeed, parts of a diaspora may, despite living apart from a national state, still exercise influence upon its domestic politics, acting as what Jean Seaton has termed 'external republics... groups of immigrants who remain fiercely committed to the communities from which they have come, and the ways of life they leave behind' (1999: 256). This is a kind of 'nationalism at a distance' and can be a powerful influence, especially in conflict situations. In short, media globalization and its effects on imagined communities are multidirectional and multidimensional (see also Appadurai in Nash 2000: 110–114).

Contemporary communication systems are the locus of very varied forms and scales of communion. Subcultures can form around media products and fan groups, giving members a sense of identity and connection based on the intensity of shared feelings – what Grossberg calls 'affective community'. Although through the internet the physical space and presence of community is dissolved, a language of renewed intentional community greatly shapes discourses on information technologies (e.g., Rheingold 2000). Political movements seek to regenerate themselves as virtual town halls, and it is undoubtedly the case that communities of some kind can form online where the boundaries of public and private, self and social identity are blurred (Lange 2008a), forming communities out of subjective taste (Lange 2008b). It may even be the case that, for instance through the mechanism of online 'commenting', behaviours are policed, generating communities not only of affect but also of value (Lange 2007).

However, as we have argued, the involvement of people in a communal activity and even the development within it of a value-system or shared set of symbolic resources are not sufficient to make an imagined community. They lack the commitment to a 'something' that underlies the community and which can be imagined to be its true source; they also lack the entanglement of that idea with broader practices of ideology and legitimation. Often communal sentiments online are intensifications of forms of imagined community that exist independent of digital life.

Conclusion

Cohen claims that 'the reality of community in people's experience inheres in their attachment or commitment to a common body of symbols' (1985: 16). Stuart Hall goes further when he writes that '... people participate in the idea of the nation as represented in its national culture. A nation is a symbolic community' (Hall 1992b: 292). Both recognize that community is not purely a 'function' of sociological or anthropological necessity. It involves an element of active imagination, commitment and participation. This is the truth behind Renan's (1990) famous (but otherwise obscure) definition of a nation as 'a daily plebiscite'.

In this sense community is a kind of everyday social theory about the derivation of social values and the significance of relationships. In imagining a communal connection we consciously affirm the significance of some relationships – often above others – and we posit a natural basis to political organizations and ethical prescriptions. For this very reason the community we imagine – its values and its import – is always at the heart of political and ideological contestation, institution building and policy formation. The political sociology of imagined community must attend to the technologies, mechanisms and institutions that make this possible but also to the affects it sets in motion and the complex relations it may have to competing political ideologies.

Today global processes may cut across but also intensify feelings and practices of imagined community. However, while part of the logic of community is to swallow up and obliterate differences, communities are also always particular. The development of a global imagined community will proceed at the same time as the invention or reinvention of a range of local imagined communities advancing their own specific cultural and political claims. This complex dialectic remains a pressing topic for investigation by political sociologists.

Further Reading

Anderson, B. 1991: *Imagined Communities*, 2nd edn. London: Verso.

Billig, M. 1995: *Banal Nationalism*. London: Sage.

Brown, G.W. and Held, D. 2010: *The Cosmopolitanism Reader*. Cambridge: Polity Press.

Gellner, E. 1983: *Nations and Nationalism*. Oxford: Blackwell.

Smith, A.D. 1995: *Nations and Nationalism in a Global Era*. Cambridge: Polity Press.

25

Gender, Power, Politics

JONATHAN DEAN

Contemporary gender relations are shaped by a plethora of contradictory social and political forces encompassing (among others) feminism as a transnational political movement, diverse modes of globalization and resurgent gender traditionalisms. Against this backdrop, current scholarship on gender, power and politics argues that gender is central to understanding social and political life, and seeks to conceptualize the contradictions and 'messiness' that mark contemporary gendered power relations. In this chapter, I place particular emphasis on one aspect of this 'messiness', by examining some ways in which forces of progressive and conservative constructions of gender relations are not necessarily external to one another, but are intertwined and co-constitutive. The chapter explores different framings of the intertwined character of ongoing dynamics of gender retrenchment and liberalization in relation to four key issues in the current literature, namely the state, the 'transnational', new feminine subjectivities and agency/resistance.

This is an exciting yet confusing time for the study of gender within the social sciences. This is partly because contemporary gender-aware social and political analysis explores the ways in which the gendered present is marked by complex forms of liberalization (with new openings for a progressive gender politics) and by diverse processes of gender retrenchment and re-traditionalization (via the consolidation of global gendered inequalities and the gendered impacts of neoliberalization). Thus, there is a strong emphasis on complex intertwinings of conservative and progressive elements in current gendered power formations. Current research from a gender perspective is thus often geared towards the difficult task of mapping the paradoxes, contradictions and points of unevenness in contemporary gender formations.

The Wiley-Blackwell Companion to Political Sociology, First Edition. Edited by Edwin Amenta, Kate Nash, and Alan Scott.
© 2012 Blackwell Publishing Ltd. Published 2012 by Blackwell Publishing Ltd.

In very general terms, the emergence of these double-edged dynamics of retrench-ment/liberalization as central to current gender analysis has been made possible by a number of theoretical and empirical shifts in recent decades, which are now com-monplace narratives in feminist work. To put it simply, one might say that early feminist interventions into the theorizing of power and politics drew attention to the presence of gendered power-laden practices across a variety of domains within civil society (Millett 1970; Dworkin 1981). Although some of these analyses were charged with framing patriarchy as a historically invariant power structure (Aker 1989), they coincided with a broader problematizing of sovereign conceptions of power (Foucault 1978; Lukes 1974) as well as a burgeoning concern with forms of power and governance that exceeded the spatial and juridical reach of the nation-state. Conse-quently, interventions from gender-sensitive perspectives both enabled, and were themselves influenced by, an increasing interest in forms of power manifest in ambiguous sites of contestation often spatially located in places hitherto regarded as beyond the disciplinary purview of political sociology (and political science more broadly).

It is partly against this broadly 'post-Foucaultian' backdrop of shifting concep-tualizations of gendered power relations that the analysis of instances of the double-edged logic of retrenchment/liberalization becomes possible. Crucially, if – as Judith Butler (1993) argues – power is not exercised from a single privileged location, but, rather, is practised and reworked in a diverse range of sites, then forms of power come to be seen as incomplete and potentially riven with gaps, slippages and inconsistencies. While Butler rightly sees a transformative political valence to this, one must be alert to the possibility that seemingly progressive modalities of gender politics will also be marked by points of unevenness, rendering them potentially open to unforeseen inegalitarian consequences and re-articulation within conservative forms of gender discourse. Taken together, these theoretical interventions foreground the unevenness and variability of constructions of gender hierarchy in different contexts.

In particular, there is now widespread acceptance of the view that gender-based research cannot be carried out in isolation from the analysis of other axes of inequality, particularly those centred on race, class and sexuality. The popularity of the notion of 'intersectionality' in contemporary gender studies is testament to this. Intersection-ality is typically traced back to Kimberlé Crenshaw's (1991) work on the dynamics of racism and sexism in violence against women of colour, but is now such common currency that it is arguably *the* hip buzzword in modern-day gender studies (Davis 2008). The term is appealing as it provides a helpful way of framing the interlinked nature of different axes of oppression, and it seems limitless in its applicability to empirical contexts. However, there remain significant ambiguities about its method-ological aspects, although, paradoxically, Davis argues that this very ambiguity partially accounts for its popularity. Furthermore, Jennifer Nash (2008) – in a critical engagement with the term – has pointed out that intersectionality, when used in academic feminist discourse, implicitly uses the figure of the 'black woman' as its main referent, often leading to a romanticization of the epistemic privilege of black women's experience.

So while intersectionality might be a problematic term, its popularity can none-theless be read as indicative of a broader attempt in gender studies to come to terms with the 'messiness' of current constructions of gendered power relations. The rest of

the chapter explores this 'messiness' by mapping out double-edged logics of retrenchment and liberalization in relation to four key themes in current literature on gender,
power and politics. These are: first, feminist theories of the state; second, gender and
the transnational; third, new femininities; and finally, the question of agency and
resistance. While acknowledging the worrying proliferation of often inventive forms
of gender retrenchment transnationally, I argue that the prevalence of these double-
edged logics should prevent us from succumbing to the temptation of political
defeatism, and that the intensification of complex forms of gender retrenchment and
liberalization renders transnational social and political gender analysis more pressing
and urgent than ever.

Gender and the State

Even though one of the key insights of feminist theory has been to 'decentre' the state
in analyses of power and politics, an equally key insight from feminist theory has
been to highlight how the state itself is a profoundly *gendered* set of institutions: its
practices, structures and modes of discourse are imbricated in prevailing gender
inequities, and – particularly in the context of increasing militarization – the state's
self-understanding is frequently linked to aggressive forms of masculinity (Cockburn
2007). Furthermore, feminist theory has brought to light the diverse ways in which
the state itself is a key actor in the construction of gender relations more broadly.
While remaining ever critical of the state and its functions, much recent feminist
work eschews a sweeping anti-statism, and instead draws attention to the multiple
ways in which state institutions contemporaneously provide spaces for new forms of
progressive gender politics while also constructing and enforcing multiple forms of
gender retrenchment.

If early feminist thinking tended to foreground 'the state' as a somewhat monolithic
agent of patriarchal domination (Ferguson 1984; MacKinnon 1989), more recent
work has tended, to use Johanna Kantola's (2006) terminology, to frame states both as
internally differentiated (differences *within* states) and as different from one another
(differences *between* states). Partly taking inspiration from accounts of the 'woman-
friendly' Nordic welfare (as different from the more gender-conservative liberal states)
(Hermes 1987), much recent work on gender and the state is concerned with broad
comparative analyses of different manifestations of 'state feminism' in different
contexts (though usually in the global North).

The 'state feminism' literature emphasizes how recent forms of state reconfiguration in the global North (in part linked to the so-called 'hollowing out' of the nation-
state) have created new opportunities for feminist intervention at local, national and
supranational state level (Banaszak, Beckwith and Rucht 2003; Outshoorn and
Kantola 2007). These works argue that new forms of multi-level governance have
coincided with a renewed 'gender awareness' within a range of state institutions,
partly motivated by a sense that crises of state legitimacy to some extent derived from
their upholding of the gender hierarchies that feminism sought to contest. For
instance, Kantola (2006) outlines how a prevailing discourse of openness and
accessibility in the post-devolution context in Scotland has provided possibilities for
feminist progress (particularly around the issue of domestic violence). Elsewhere,

Squires (2007a) maps the spread of new forms of policy instruments (including gender mainstreaming and gender quotas) aimed at rectifying state legitimacy in the face of feminist critiques, while Sylvia Walby (2002) – affirming a cautious optimism running through much state feminism literature – makes a case for framing the spread of discourse around 'women's human rights' within the European Union and United Nations as a crucial discursive resource capable of injecting renewed vigour into feminist movements transnationally. And at UK national level, Joni Lovenduski (2005, 2007) draws attention to, amongst other things, the streamlining of equalities legislation via the 2007 establishment of a single equalities body (the Commission for Equality and Human Rights), as well as the successful establishment of a network of Members of Parliament, women's policy agencies and feminist non-governmental organizations (NGOs) which has been able to push successfully for pro-feminist change at national state level across a range of issues.

However, as indicated, there is much emphasis on the ways in which these very processes of liberalization and increasing 'gender awareness' within particular types of state institution may paradoxically lead to stagnation of feminist progress and to diverse forms of gender retrenchment. If this gender awareness and liberalization occurred partly in response to crises of state legitimation, then states opening up to feminist demands can contribute to a perceived 're-legitimization' which may militate against further progressive gender transformations. For example, while Lovenduski (2005) writes extensively about gender mainstreaming in UK state institutions, she also mentions how the gendered cultures of British political institutions remain largely intact: paradoxically, her work suggests that partial feminist success has created a sense that the gender question in British politics is now 'over', offsetting any perceived need for further interrogation of the gendered aspects of the British state.

Other examples of increasing gender awareness on the part of state institutions paradoxically stifling progressive gender transformations include Jyoti Puri's (2006) analysis of self-defence training classes run by the police station for Crime Against Women in Delhi. Puri highlights how, while the classes fostered forms of empowerment and self-determination among women, they precluded acknowledgement of the structural factors contributing to widespread violence against women. Elsewhere, Gayatri Spivak (2002) notes that while global state-sanctioned efforts to improve girls' education may be read as an instance of feminist success, such a view overlooks the ways in which such education programmes are geared towards enabling women's participation in global processes of neoliberalization. Finally, both Judith Butler (2000) and Wendy Brown (2005) have noted how the passing of legislation enabling marriage or civil partnerships for non-heterosexual couples (a seemingly progressive reform) nonetheless has inegalitarian implications. They argue that the passing of such legislation expands the regulatory purview of the state, and pushes forms of kinship and sexuality that do not conform to the model of the monogamous couple further to the margins of cultural and legal intelligibility. Thus, although I have highlighted a number of new possibilities for feminist intervention into various kinds of state institutions, and an increased mainstreaming of gender-related issues at different levels of governance, I have stressed how these very dynamics of liberalization are themselves liable, paradoxically, to consolidate forms of gender retrenchment and sexual conservatism.

Gender and 'the Transnational'

The double-edged character of contemporary thinking about gender, power and politics is particularly prescient when we turn our attention to the question of the 'transnational'. Very broadly speaking, current feminist debates surrounding the transnational can be said to have arisen from two separate but overlapping sets of concerns. These are, first, an increasing interest in the gendered aspects of globalization and its implications for gender scholarship, and, second, a series of theoretical shifts arising from critiques of forms of Western bias, imperialism and ethnocentrism in Anglo-American feminist theory.

While the notion of the 'transnational' is profoundly contested, we can nonetheless trace two dominant uses of the term in contemporary feminist discourse, which roughly correspond to the two sets of concerns mentioned above. Firstly, 'transnational feminism' often refers to an increasing move towards forms of feminist mobilization across and beyond the borders of the nation-state. Here, it denotes the ways in which a variety of social and political aspects of globalization have been enabling for feminist activisms. In this respect, transnational feminism can refer to the use of new media technologies by feminists to generate instances of cross-border mobilization, or, more usually, it refers to feminists using new political opportunity structures linked to new forms of supranational governance (including the UN and regional bodies). In most instances, the UN Fourth World Conference on Women in 1995 in Beijing is treated as a turning point, as the founding moment of current forms of feminist transnationalism. In this context, then, the 'transnational' is invested with a positive valence: it signifies the ways in which feminists have creatively appropriated aspects of globalization.

Valentine Moghadam (2005), for example, emphasizes how feminist appropriation of increasing cross-border communication has destabilized North–South hierarchies in feminist politics and facilitated the consolidation of links between feminism and other progressive struggles. On the enabling role of supranational institutions, Margaret Snyder (2006; see also Walby 2002) paints an extremely upbeat picture of a strong growth of women's movements working in partnership with the UN across the world in the 1990s and early 2000s, while an increasing 'gender awareness' at national level within electoral democracies prompts Mona Lena Krook (2008) to argue that current campaigns around gender quotas constitute part of a new global women's movement.

While it is indisputable that certain dimensions of globalization have created new political opportunity structures for feminist mobilization, it should come as no surprise that a number of cautionary notes have been sounded. There is, of course, something paradoxical about the fact that these new forms of feminism have emerged partly as a consequence of the very same forms of globalization that have contributed to a retrenchment of gender inequalities (through, for instance, the intensification of global care chains and reductions in welfare spending). To give one example, Breny Mendoza (2002), in an analysis of feminist transnationalism in Latin America, points out that feminist NGOs have in some cases directly benefited from neoliberal modes of deregulation, as funds are delegated from the state to non-state service providers. In addition, both Mendoza and Desai (2005) express reservations about the domination of new forms of feminist transnationalism by a relatively small elite group of globetrotting feminist professionals.

Finally, the status of the 'transnational' as something of a buzzword in feminist academia risks foreclosing a genuinely critical engagement with the term (as, in some senses, one cannot *not* affirm the 'transnational'). Despite this, the notion of the transnational (conceived in terms of new cross-border feminist mobilization in politics and knowledge production) can be seen as problematic: the 'transnational' is often framed as the site of new forms of feminist politics, such that, from a Western feminist perspective, the appeal of the 'transnational' lies in part in its capacity to offset narratives of declining feminist mobilization and radicalism in the global North (Tripp 2006; Dean 2010). Such a view re-instates the hegemony of Western feminist temporalities and spatialities, especially when – as is often the case – 'transnationalism' simply seems to refer to feminist mobilization in the global South, and not to forms of feminist politics that are genuinely *trans*national (Mendoza 2002: 309).

However, it is helpful to distinguish the above sense of transnationalism from a notion of the 'transnational' as referring to critiques of unitary, Western-centric formulations of the feminist political subject. This line of thought is typically traced back to Chandra Mohanty's groundbreaking 1986 article 'Under Western Eyes' (reproduced in Mohanty 2003) which took issue with the Anglo-American notion of a 'global sisterhood': the latter, Mohanty argued, presupposed a unified global feminist subject, but which was in fact firmly rooted in a specifically Anglo-American framework and thus tended to colonize and marginalize the voices of Third World women. Common to this formulation of transnational feminism, then, is a concern with forms of feminist political articulation that establish connections between feminist struggles in diverse spatial locations, but without bracketing out the specificities of local knowledges and experiences.

This form of feminist transnationalism emphasizes solidarity rather than unity or feminist separatism (Mohanty 2003; Yuval-Davis 2006) and conceptualizes transnational feminist politics as a difficult and fraught process of articulation between disparate feminisms and other oppositional political struggles. I would argue that this is a more useful formulation of 'transnationalism' than that referred to above: it helps foster a critical stance towards contemporary feminist practices and seems more firmly grounded in the double-edged nature of contemporary gender politics. And, as one might expect, it can lead to (productively) diverse conclusions about the present state of feminist political mobilization across borders. Mohanty's recent (2003) work outlines how trends such as increasingly technocratic forms of management in the US higher education sector and the global intensification of capitalist relations of production have impacted deleteriously on women's movements. By contrast, Kathy Davis (2007), employing a notion of transnationalism as grounded in careful processes of negotiation and translation between disparate grassroots feminist groups, presents a helpful account of the multiple ways in which the Boston Women's Health Collective's classic 'second-wave' feminist text *Our Bodies, Ourselves* has travelled across national borders, and been creatively reworked within diverse vernacular gender cultures. Davis explicitly frames her analysis as a hopeful one, and argues powerfully that the movement of *Our Bodies, Ourselves* across national borders should not be read as a form of American imperialism, but as a transnational feminist success story, characterized by the production of an imagined feminist community (to use Benedict Anderson's famous phrase) via creative forms of cross-border translation and negotiation.

The framing of *Our Bodies, Ourselves* as a feminist success story is further testament to the double-edged nature of contemporary gender regimes. On the positive side, globalization has increased the political opportunities for cross-border mobilization between feminists and, as we saw in the section on state feminism above, has coincided with a partial opening up of supranational institutions to a progressive gender politics. However, the very same dynamics that enabled the emergence of these forms of feminist politics are also central to logics of neoliberalization and ongoing gender retrenchment. Consequently, it is imperative that we avoid the triumphalism of some affirmations of feminist transnationalism, while also acknowledging and affirming the possibility of the emergence of productive new opportunities for transnational feminist theory and practice.

New Femininities

The literatures on both state feminism and transnational feminism are partly concerned with making sense of a range of contemporary power relations in which elements of feminism (traditionally an oppositional discourse) are routinely invoked in a range of sites within mainstream public life. A similar set of concerns pervades a wave of recent work on reconfigured feminine subjectivities. The 'new femininities' literature seeks to conceptualize the ways in which the profound gender upheavals arising from globalization, neoliberalization and 'second-wave' feminism have impacted upon contemporary feminine subjectivities (primarily in the global North). As one might expect, this is a complex and contested terrain, but it is one in which, again, the double-edged character of contemporary gender formations very much comes to the fore. More specifically, the 'new femininities' literature grapples with the paradox that feminism often appears to have been at once very successful, and yet at the same time seems to have been relegated to the margins of cultural intelligibility, a situation characterized by some authors as specifically 'post-feminist' (McRobbie 2009; Levine 2008; Tasker and Negra 2007). Within this broad terrain, a number of recurrent themes emerge. These are, first, that contemporary young womanhood in the global North enjoys a range of freedoms that were unavailable to previous generations of women (particularly with regard to education, employment and sexuality); second, that the public sphere is replete with intensifying forms of regulation of feminine subjectivities (tied up with other identity categories such as class, race and sexuality), and, third, that the public sphere and contemporary femininities are predicated on a widespread disavowal of feminism.

Despite the striking recurrence of these key themes, there is much disagreement about their implications. One can read the increased acceptability of women's participation in (for example) the labour market and higher education as indicative of feminist success. Even the perceived disavowal of feminism as a political movement in much of the global North need not necessarily indicate feminist failure. Instead, it could be read as a 'maturing' of feminism as a social movement such that it has now been mainstreamed into the everyday practices of femininity (Nash 2002; Genz 2006). However, the proliferation of overt heteropatriarchal representations of female sexuality and forms of re-traditionalization have prompted some authors to claim that the current cultural terrain is resolutely anti-feminist (Whelehan 2000).

However, most current academic work on feminism and femininity rejects framing the gendered present as overtly anti-feminist. Rather, it tends to see contemporary femininities as constituted by an ambivalent set of discourses that blur the feminist/anti-feminist divide, and conceptualizes feminism as operating 'in and against' normative femininity (Gill 2007; Budgeon 2001; Aapola, Gonick, and Harris 2005). Consequently, as with the arguments about the state and the transnational described above, contemporary Western femininities are marked by a complex series of double movements in which the invocation of feminist discourses is itself used in the service of forms of gender retrenchment and re-traditionalization (Adkins 1999). This is the key argument of Angela McRobbie's recent (2009) book *The Aftermath of Feminism*, which – referring primarily to the UK and drawing largely on Butler and Foucault – describes how discourses of female individualization are marshalled and promoted at the same time that feminism proper is disavowed. McRobbie argues that although feminism has a shadowy, spectral existence, it is constructed as being at odds with the forms of individualization and sexuality necessary to 'count' as an intelligible feminine subject. Furthermore, much 'new femininities' literature draws attention to how the foregrounding of empowered, individualized white femininities (young women as 'subjects of capacity') naturalizes and legitimates new forms of hostility towards working-class women given their perceived lack of the requisite material and cultural capital necessary to successfully embody the normatively feminine (Skeggs 2005; Tyler 2008).

Thus, contemporary Western femininities are marked by a complex interplay between feminism and gender conservatism, perhaps arising from the fact that the dust produced by the gender upheavals of the late twentieth century has not yet settled. In this context, the pervasive attempts to disarticulate feminism and femininity – combined with forms of gender re-traditionalization and increasingly pernicious forms of regulation of female sexuality – might occasion a pessimistic view. However, one might also claim that recent attempts by young women in the UK and elsewhere to affirm feminism in the face of its widespread disavowal, alongside new forms of mobilization against hegemonic representations of female sexuality, again point to the double-edged nature of the gender regime (Dean 2010). While in some cases feminism is invoked in the service of its undoing, paradoxically, that very undoing may provide motivation for a renewed commitment to feminist mobilization.

Agency and Resistance

So far, I have drawn attention to a number of ways in which the gendered present is marked by ambiguous forms of gender retrenchment and liberalization. In light of this, we may want to ask: What are the implications of this 'messiness' for our theorizations of feminist resistance and political intervention? It is in responding to these questions – concerning the nature of agency, politics and resistance – that some of the most interesting recent developments in feminist theory have taken place.

Feminist theory has always been critical of dominant understandings of agency in political theory, particularly those framed by notions of the (implicitly masculine) unencumbered self (see, for example, Wilson 2007). However, when it comes to substantive theorizations of agency, the picture becomes less clear. This is in part because while notions of agency and autonomy have come under attack from feminist critics, thinking about conditions for improving women's agency has also been a central concern for feminist theory and politics (Mackenzie and Stoljar 2000). In addition, transnational feminist interventions have highlighted how, from the perspective of some feminists in the global North, women in the 'third world' have often been problematically framed as lacking agency and in need of the salvation of the enlightened first-world feminist (Mohanty 2003). Furthermore, intersectional perspectives have brought into view the raced (and sometimes classed) dynamics of women's agency.

These concerns have brought about a number of consequences. First, partly in response to the critiques advanced by authors such as Mohanty, feminist analysis (particularly of gender relations in the global South) has often dug deep in search of moments of resistance and non-compliance with patriarchal norms in difficult circumstances. Such understandings of agency tended to be predicated on a conflation of feminist agency with feminist resistance: that is, the presumption that agency only occurs when patriarchal norms are contested, resisted or subverted, a view predicated on a somewhat romanticized notion of women's agency (Abu-Lughod 1990). In this vein, a provocative recent work by Saba Mahmood (2005) prompts us to ask: What would it mean to decouple agency from resistance? What if forms of agency can be located in practices that do not necessarily contest patriarchal norms? Mahmood provides a theoretical critique of the tendency to conceptualize agency in terms of a complicity/subversion binary, alongside an empirical analysis of an urban women's mosque movement in Cairo (part of a broader Islamic Revival movement) seeking to foster forms of conduct and ethical dispositions in line with Islamic piety. Mahmood argues that while the practices of piety depart significantly from feminist conceptions of agentic resistance, the women she studied nonetheless exercised complex forms of agency in the development and negotiation of pious subjectivities.

Mahmood's analysis suggests that it is nonsensical to think in terms of an absolute presence or absence of agency. Rather, agency consists in the ongoing negotiation of one's position in gendered power relations, which at any given time may consist of elements of both subversion and complicity. Consequently, agency and feminist political action/resistance cannot be seen as coextensive. However, this leads to the question of what would it mean to exercise a specifically *political* or resistant mode of agency.

One of the most persuasive recent answers to this difficult question is that offered by Linda Zerilli (2005). Drawing on Hannah Arendt (a divisive figure within feminist political theory), Zerilli argues for a total abandonment of a sovereign conception of the feminist subject. She claims that attachments to sovereign notions of agency were evident in the anxiety induced by the 'postmodern' attack on the sovereign feminist subject, and the presumption that this would prove debilitating for feminist political action. In opposition to such a view, Zerilli claims that feminist political freedom involves not the articulation of demands on behalf of a sovereign subject, but rather the collective imagining and creating of new 'ways of being' in the world. Crucially, this means that feminist political action is always a 'worldly', grounded practice, but has a dynamic, ungraspable element to it, involving complex processes of negotiation and interaction with others. To illustrate: we tend to think of Anglo-American feminism as having followed a certain almost teleological trajectory: women's autonomous consciousness-raising led to a burgeoning feminist awareness which in turn led to gendered analyses of dominant power structures. However, an implication of Zerilli's intervention is that there was nothing inevitable about the trajectory of 'second-wave' feminism: the women involved did not 'know' in advance their position in history, and nor did they require a strong conception of feminist subjectivity in order to act. To claim that a sovereign subject is a necessary precondition for political action is, Zerilli argues, a denial of the irreducible contingency and unpredictability of feminist politics.

While Zerilli's decoupling of political action from sovereign agency might sound somewhat counter-intuitive, her account ties in well with the double-edged character of much contemporary gender analysis, resonating with the work of authors such as Mohanty and Yuval-Davis who argue that feminist politics is – and always has been – an unpredictable business, involving complex dynamics of articulation across geographical and discursive space. Fundamentally – and perhaps in opposition to those for whom the 'postmodern' attack on the feminist subject is a tragic loss – feminist politics can never proceed from a position from outside power, but is always constituted in and through dominant power relations, and is thus a never-ending process of articulation, subversion and contestation.

Conclusion

The story I have told is one of an increasing emphasis on complex dynamics of gender retrenchment/liberalization, and the intertwining of progressive and conservative constructions of gender. It is in some respects a story of a shift away from grand explanatory conceptions of theory, and a move towards more empirically based, located forms of analysis. This of course is a simplification, and as with any story of the current trajectory of gender in the social sciences it is marked by exclusions (Hemmings 2005). Indeed, while one could frame this story as one of loss, here I have framed it largely as a story of progress. However, this is not a naive or celebratory account of feminist progress. One could claim that the double-edged nature of power perhaps means that we have 'lost' a notion of pure feminist politics, but a positive spin would be to say that the failure constitutive to power means that the possibilities for productive feminist intervention are potentially infinite. While – as Kathy Davis (2007) remarks – the poststructuralist urge to locate forms of complicity even in practices that seem to be at first glance innocuous may engender a degree of resignation, one might just as easily claim that an equally strong poststructuralist injunction is to locate points of failure and unevenness in power structures that may at first seem overarching. The increasing awareness and visibility of this constitutive unevenness may therefore seem daunting, but it renders the analysis of contemporary structures of gendered power relations as important as ever.

Further Reading

Staeheli, L.A., Kofman, E. and Peake, L.J. (eds) 2004: *Mapping Women, Mapping Politics: Feminist Perspectives on Political Geography*. New York: Routledge.

Ferree, M.M. and Tripp, A.M. (eds) 2006: *Global Feminism: Transnational Women's Activism, Organizing and Human Rights*. New York: New York University Press.

Blakeley, G. and Bryson, V. (eds) 2007: *The Impact of Feminism on Political Concepts and Debates*. Manchester: Manchester University Press.

Phillips, A. (ed.) 1998: *Feminism and Politics*. Oxford: Oxford University Press.

26

Class, Culture and Politics

Mike Savage

Class analysis has historically been central to debates in political sociology. Social class divisions, notably those between middle and working classes, have long been recognized to be one of the central cleavages in voting behaviour throughout the world (see Lipset 1960; Evans 2005). Class has exerted considerable influence on the organization of pressure groups and political parties, especially when they were institutionalized into corporatist political regimes such as those characteristic of European nations in the third quarter of the twentieth century (e.g., Middlemas 1980; Crouch 1977). Class relationships have been seen as playing a decisive role in the historical formation of political regimes (famously, Moore 1966 on *The Social Origins of Dictatorship and Democracy* and Thompson 1966, on *The Making of the English Working Class*). Yet, with ample evidence pointing towards class dealignment in voting patterns, and with the weakening of labour movements and socialist parties in most parts of the world, influential commentators have pointed to 'the end of class' (e.g., Beck 1992). New kinds of 'post-materialist', 'identity' or 'lifestyle politics' (Inglehart 1990; Giddens 1991), the rise of social movements and the growing interest in the cosmopolitan political agenda provoked by the 'war on terror' (Beck 2005) all appear to indicate a fundamental reworking of the political landscape. Yet, very recently a new paradigm has emerged, which has 'had a profound influence on class theory and research over the past ten years or so' (Atkinson 2010: 10). This is 'cultural class analysis', the key elements of which I elaborate in this chapter. Originating in the reception of Bourdieu's sociology in the anglophone social sciences, this work has spawned influential studies of the relationship between class, culture and politics that have energized debates in social stratification and proved inspirational to a significant group of younger scholars. And, although originating as a scholarly academic movement, the destabilization brought about by the financial crisis from 2008, and in particular public concerns about the 'super rich' and evidence from many nations of escalating social polarization (see notably Wilkinson and Pickett's (2009) *The Spirit Level* which has been a bestseller in the UK), has made its concerns more publically visible.

The Wiley-Blackwell Companion to Political Sociology, First Edition. Edited by Edwin Amenta, Kate Nash, and Alan Scott.
© 2012 Blackwell Publishing Ltd. Published 2012 by Blackwell Publishing Ltd.

The first part of my chapter analyses the main differences between traditional 'class formation' perspective on class and politics associated with the canonical sociological figures of Marx and Weber, and the newer formation of 'cultural class analysis'. I will show an important shift in the kinds of relationships between politics and class that are conceived in these two approaches. The second part of my chapter explains how cultural class analysis emerged out of an Anglophone appropriation of Pierre Bourdieu's concepts, and will reflect on the place of politics in this intellectual movement. Given that Bourdieu's work is provocative and controversial, and attracts keen enthusiasts as well as fervent critics, I try to pull out the core elements of his thinking for an understanding of politics and class. The third part of the chapter explores how these concerns have been taken up within sociology and elaborates some of the key research exemplars that have demonstrated the value of this perspective. The fourth and final part of my chapter examines methodological and analytical debates within this paradigm, and offers a summary assessment of its future prospects.

From Class Formation to Cultural Class Analysis?

Table 26.1 schematically lays out key theoretical, substantive and methodological differences between two paradigms in class analysis. These are firstly the 'class formation' approach, which dominated in the third quarter of the twentieth century and which proved a springboard for the emerging European social sciences which were expanding rapidly in these years (see Savage 2010), and secondly 'cultural class analysis' which has come to the fore in the past decade.

Table 26.1 Schematic differences between class formation perspectives and cultural class analysis

Issues	Class formation	Cultural class analysis
Theoretical underpinning	Marx, Weber	Bourdieu, feminism
Perspective	Structural	Relational
Empirical focus	Occupations and communities	Lifestyle, consumption, education
Main interest in	Working (and subaltern) class	Middle (and dominant) class
Interests in political mobilization	Labour movements, political parties, rebellion and revolution	Neoliberal markets, media representations, social movements
Class consciousness	Overt, widespread, politicized	Indirect, 'misrecognized'
Driving force	Interests	Recognition
Relationship to other inequalities	Class centrism	Intersectionality (class articulates with gender, ethnicity, age, etc.)
Methods for analysis	Historical case studies, community studies, variable-based survey analyses	Ethnography, case studies, multiple correspondence analysis
Disciplinary bases	History, politics, sociology	Sociology, cultural studies, geography
Heyday	1950–1975	2000–?

The class formation paradigm can be seen, in David Lockwood's (1995) terms, as fundamentally defined by the 'problematic of the proletariat'. Here, the burning question, shared by Marxists and social democrat 'revisionists' alike, was to understand the political potential of the working class to change society 'progressively'. This concern had long been central to socialist and labour politics (see Savage 2008), but probably the first major intellectual statement of this 'class formation' approach was T.H. Marshall's influential lecture on 'Citizenship and Social Class', given in 1949. He asked the fundamental question as to how the working classes were to become full citizens of their nations. His answer, famously, was that only by expanding citizenship to include social welfare would it be possible for the working class to belong. Through this move, class was seen as fundamental to questions of political integration and solidarity, and sociologists were encouraged to reflect on how a progressive politics could be forged through working-class mobilization and engagement.

Theoretically, the main tension within this class formation school was between those learning towards a Marxist, and those attracted to a Weberian position. This difference mapped onto to the difference between communist or left-wing socialist politics on the one hand, and Fabian or social democratic politics on the other. Marx emphasized that class formation was an inherent feature of capitalist society, and that structural antagonisms between capital and labour were bound to give rise to social, cultural and political tensions. The most celebrated studies of this kind were by the labour historians Edward Thompson and Eric Hobsbawm, who diluted the Marxist view that revolutionary politics was inevitable in favour of more historically nuanced accounts that recognized that contingent historical processes might affect working-class insurgency and protest. Thompson's (1966) emphasis, however, that the working class was fundamentally important in the shaping of modern democracy, was emblematic of this approach.

In fact, from the 1960s it was Weberian scholars who became more prominent in pursuing this class formation perspective, especially in the expanding and fashionable discipline of sociology. Here, scholars such as David Lockwood (1957), John Goldthorpe (1980) and Anthony Giddens (1973b) drew on Weber's differentiation between economic and social class to insist that there was no necessary reason to expect structural antagonisms to give rise to class consciousness and political mobilization. Instead, attention needed to be focused on the kind of 'proximate' social relations which might facilitate this, with research here centring on social mobility, the structure of industrial relations, and community life.

This research tradition was especially strong in the UK, but also had a marked impact internationally. It spawned entire academic sub-disciplines, such as in social history, in industrial relations and in cultural studies. It generated methodological advances, notably in the use of large-scale survey analysis to address political partisanship (e.g., Butler and Stokes 1971) and social mobility (Goldthorpe 1980; Halsey, Heath and Ridge 1980). In its more Weberian aspects it generated a subtle, empirically sensitive approach to social and political mobilization. An interesting diversionary route was also taken from the later 1970s by writers from the Marxist tradition, notably Erik Olin Wright, who broke free from a reliance on the reductionist labour theory of value to champion 'game theoretical' approaches to exploitation (Wright 1985). These recognized a greater diversity of class positions, and the fact that class consciousness and political mobilization could not be read off from employment relations. This more pluralistic Marxist work inspired significant studies that were attuned to the variability of forms of political mobilization.

The fundamental stumbling block for this class formation paradigm, however, was that it depended on the viability of some kind of visible and coherent working-class political movement, on which it could comment. The emergence of neoliberal political regimes from the later 1970s, the dismantling of corporatist politics in much of continental Europe and especially the collapse of communist regimes in Eastern Europe from the later 1980s dealt a deathblow to the 'problematic of the proletariat'. From this moment, it proved difficult to sustain the view that the 'traditional' working classes were plausible political harbingers of change. Rather, they appeared as defenders of an old industrial order, as in the heroic but ultimately futile attempt of the National Union of Mineworkers to defeat the Thatcher government's pit closure programme in the early 1980s.

For these reasons, many commentators preferred to emphasize the 'end of class' as a central social and political division. In the absence of evidence that the working class was a key political agent, it seemed at best arcane, and at worst an irrelevance, to spend time worrying about the conditions in which they might, in principle, be politically engaged. During the 1980s and 1990s, the dominant motif, both in sociology and politics, stressed the declining importance of class on politics.

The emergence of a new 'cultural class analysis' programme can be attributed to a growing interest in the middle classes. Studies of the middle class were far from new (e.g., Lockwood 1957; Crompton and Jones 1984) but they had previously been couched in terms of interests in proletarianization, where the main question was whether they would be downgraded into the working class. From the mid-1980s, however, as a direct counterpart to studies of the working class, a new kind of research interest emerged which took it as given that the professional and managerial middle classes were the beneficiaries of economic change and were destined to remain as advantaged groups in the coming political climate. The question instead was how far they were likely to be harbingers of cultural change, political innovation and social unrest, and how far they were supporters of the status quo. Lash and Urry (1987) identified this 'service class' as carriers of a new kind of 'postmodern' culture that embraced pluralistic values and tastes. My own *Property, Bureaucracy and Culture: Middle Class Formation in Contemporary Britain* (Savage *et al.* 1992) offered a systematic overview of the changing fortunes of the middle classes in Britain, including a discussion of their political proclivities, such as their interest in social movements, and saw their changing composition and character as central to an analysis of social change in contemporary societies.

This interest in the middle classes was strongly based in the UK, but has been evident in numerous other parts of the world, not only in Europe but also in the United States (Lamont 1992), South America (Mendez 2008) and Australia (Martin 2003). Collectively this generated a critical interest in 'the problematic of the middle classes' and how best to see their role in shaping society. It also explicitly drew on the sociological theory of Pierre Bourdieu, and thereby established a link between debates on class politics and cultural sociology that had hitherto been absent. Previously, Bourdieu's sociology, though influential, had been focused either on his studies of education or on specific cultural fields, and had not been integrated into the study of class and stratification. Subsequently, this cross-fertilization proved to be very fertile, and staked out the parameters for the emerging 'cultural class analysis' paradigm in a number of different national contexts. For Crompton (2008: 102), 'Bourdieu's approach has been enormously influential across a range of different fields (. . .) in sociology and cultural studies (. . .) as well as in class and stratification'. For Butler and Watt (2007: 5), Bourdieu's work has 'developed a sociological approach which transgresses many, if not all (. . .) boundaries (leading to) a more synthetic approach which has also seen a blurring of boundaries with cognate disciplines and fields'.

Let me therefore review Bourdieu's legacy in greater detail.

Bourdieu and Social Class

Bourdieu's influence has been usefully identified by Bottero (2005) as linked to his support for a relational perspective on social inequality, rather than one which depends on a theory of social structure, such as that developed by Marx or Weber. As she summarizes,

> In structural approaches groups are defined as socially distant if they are very *different* to each other (in terms of class, gender or race categories), in relational approaches groups are defined as socially distant if they are held to rarely associate with each other.
>
> (Bottero 2005: 7).

This relational approach is developed by Bourdieu through his 'field analysis' (Thomson 2008), whereby he sees social relations as akin to a sporting contest, where players compete for position and advantage. Social life is organized around different arenas in which we recognize rules that allow us to gain position, advantage and resource. These might be concerned with the labour market, for instance (where we learn that to get a good job we need better qualifications, experience or skill, and if we do not play by these rules, we will probably not succeed very effectively in getting the best jobs). It follows that Bourdieu does not see classes as defined by an underlying social structure, but rather in more fluid terms, through a competitive process of striving and social closure. It is a model which to some extent he draws from a literary tradition such as that sketched out in Marcel Proust's *In Remembrance of Things Past*, with the careful 'social dances' which are lavishly portrayed there. But this conceptual frame also explains another important feature of Bourdieu's approach: that whereas the class formation tradition thought it was likely that members of the disadvantaged classes would feel deprived by their position, Bourdieu thought it equally, if not more likely, that they would blame themselves for their lack of success, and this 'internalization of disadvantage' would often prevent overt conflict from surfacing.

It is a central feature of Bourdieu's argument that players do not compete equally, but that those endowed with greater 'capital' possess advantages that allow them greater opportunity to sustain their privileges over time. These advantages may be evident within the field itself, in bestowing resources to allow certain combatants the means to succeed within the parameters of the sporting contest itself, but also might be convertible into other fields. Bourdieu identifies three main kinds of capital: economic, cultural and social. Let us consider the latter first, since there is an important contrast here with the influential perspectives developed by Coleman and Putnam (see Bagnasco, Chapter 22, in this volume for discussion). Bourdieu identifies social capital when there are social networks amongst privileged groups which allow them to 'pull strings' for each other. He thus sees it as a means by which the powerful look after each other. Two important points follow from his account. Firstly, we see a characteristic aspect of Bourdieu's thinking which sets him apart from the class formation perspective, namely that he does not see the social conditions of the working or popular classes as conveying effective means of solidarity or social cohesion, but in fact thinks they are more likely to be atomized and fragmented (see especially his powerful testimony here drawn from interviews with disadvantaged and disempowered French citizens in *The Weight of the World*, Bourdieu 1999). It is both cause and effect of their advantages that the wealthy and powerful have social ties to each other that allow them to cohere and effectively interrelate with one another. Secondly, however, Bourdieu is sceptical of the systemic importance of social capital, which explains why it features relatively little in his most famous text, *Distinction*. His argument is that social privilege is far too endemic for it to be explained simply by social capital, which can better be understood as a residual variable, evident in a few cases. He would hence be highly sceptical of the recent championing of social capital as an effective device to allow social mobility as espoused by Coleman, for instance.

Bourdieu explains systematic inequalities in terms of the operation of economic and cultural capital. The first of these is the relatively straightforward suggestion that money, wealth and income impart advantages to their possessors. Here, he is largely stating a widely accepted economic truth. It is his concept of cultural capital that is more challenging, and this has attracted greater attention. Rather than seeing cultural values and practices arising on the basis of a class position, as with the class formation school, he instead sees them as (semi-) autonomous from economic determinants, and having their own 'rules of the game', in which culture itself can be defined as a field. Here, it is those who are endowed with the scholastic capacity to distance themselves from everyday constraints, so that they can look at cultural artefacts abstractly, who are better placed to define legitimate taste, and these are the dominant players within the cultural world.

Having completed this thumbnail sketch of Bourdieu's arguments (and see the discussion in Weininger 2005; Silva and Warde 2010; Grenfell 2008; Swartz 2007), let me pull out their significance for the 'cultural class analysis' paradigm. Bourdieu's focus is on how the privileged develop and retain their advantages. Here his most explicit engagement with political sociology is in his account of what he terms 'the field of power', most notably in his book on *The State Nobility*. Here he sees those vested with differing amounts of economic and cultural capital contesting for relative advantage between themselves, but also in terms of being able to secure access to the state and 'political capital', the competency to mobilize masses in social space. Here the political field in general, and the state in particular, are seen not as institutional monoliths, but as spheres in which mobilization and contestation between privileged groups – who nonetheless ultimately share a dominant position over the popular classes – take place. In this neat approach, Bourdieu recognizes the genuine existence of tensions and conflicts amongst the 'political classes', while also recognizing that they share certain values.

Bourdieu himself discusses this in the brilliant last chapter of *Distinction*, on the 'political field'. Here he draws attention away from the familiar political sociology question of whether people from different classes support left- or right-wing parties. Rather, he starts from a different place. Ruminating on the apparently minor point (which has subsequently become a major concern) that those who are in lower-class positions are more likely to offer 'don't know' responses in opinion polls, and are more likely to be politically disengaged, Bourdieu sees the extent to which people feel politically entitled as fundamental to the political field. 'The right to speak' is even more significant than whether one speaks from a feminist, conservative, socialist, liberal, or any other perspective. And, in many democratic nations, Bourdieu notes, large numbers of people do not think they do have the right to speak. Their lack of capital and their marginalized position in social space have made them internalize their own lack of right to a view. It is this that speaks to the true power of class.

Bourdieu's account, written in 1979, was remarkably prescient at hinting towards issues of political disengagement, cynicism and disaffection that have gathered considerable pace over the past three decades. Yet, whereas proponents of social capital theory such as Putnam (2000) blame disengagement on secular social changes such as greater use of television, commuting, and changing family dynamics, Bourdieu is clear that it is the product of class domination. It is this analysis of how the unequal distribution of cultures of entitlement, shame and respect are implicated in the political agenda that lie at the centre of the cultural class analysis paradigm.

Exemplars of 'Cultural Class Analysis'

Having sketched out the key ideas that Bourdieu has elaborated, let me now review some of the ways that his work has been influential within the 'cultural class analysis' paradigm. These can best be grouped in three areas. Firstly, we can see a new interest in the 'politics of identity'. The key work here was Beverley Skeggs' *Formations of Class and Gender*, which had a profound influence on encouraging feminists to recognize the strong articulation of class with gender. Skeggs' ethnographic study of young working-class women in the English Midlands during the later 1980s and early 1990s showed that 'Class was completely central to the lives of the women ... Lack of alternatives was one of the central features of being working class; they rarely had the potential to re-valorize their classed subjectivities' (Skeggs 1997: 161). This exclusion led the young women to embrace feminine and respectable identities as an attempt to 'trade up', to find some lever they could pull which could give them a modicum of legitimacy in the eyes of the powerful. But this was ultimately a fraught and self-defeating politics.

Skeggs' work was important in drawing attention to the bodily and mundane feelings of shame, guilt, desire and fantasy which class invokes. 'The way class was experienced was through affectivity, as a "structure of feeling". This was the emotional politics of class fuelled by insecurity, doubt, imagination and resentment' (Skeggs 1997: 162). This kind of intimate 'bodily class politics' has been subject to important research over the past decade, especially by feminist writers, for instance in the studies of Walkerdine (2002) and Lawler (2000). It contrasts a privileged class, comfortable with (even if anxious about) themselves, and large numbers of disadvantaged people who pay the price for their exclusion in the shame and sense of inadequacy that they experience on a daily basis.

A second area of development has been explorations of the mundane ways that the privileged perpetuate their advantages. The point here is that they do not need to do this by mobilizing as specifically 'middle class' people, but rather that their dominance is so entrenched in the routine workings of institutions that simply 'playing the system' effectively is enough to allow them to succeed. The most discussed instance here is in educational institutions such as schools and universities, where educated middle-class parents are effective in acting as rational consumers, able to strategize about which schools to send their children to, and how best to interface with the school and its teachers to ensure their children do 'well' (see variously Ball 2003; Reay 1998). The contrast here distinguishes 'effective' and 'ineffective' parents, so naturalizing and internalizing social inequalities into the personal qualities of the parents themselves. Given that educational attainment remains highly uneven, with little sign of a decline of the relative advantages of the advantaged middle classes over the past decade, this is a telling example

A further instance of this process comes from research on neighbourhood change and housing. One of the major empirical difficulties for those arguing that we are becoming 'classless' is that patterns of residential segregation are not only marked, but are in some respects intensifying, for instance with gentrifiers displacing poor urban residents in city centres. This is another kind of cultural class politics, in which the educated middle classes feel entitled to possess houses appropriate for 'someone like me'. Savage, Bagnall and Longhurst (2005), in their study of middle-class residents in Greater Manchester, call this a form of 'elective belonging', in which the 'choice' of a place to live brings together similar kinds of people. This has also been explored by Burrows and Gane (2007) as allowing the socio-spatial sorting of people into ever more refined residential locations as they use postcode classifications to 'self select' where to live. This is a further example of the way that the educated middle classes use their reflexivity to routinely, though also unobtrusively, position themselves in superior ways. As Atkinson (2010: 71) puts it:

> not only would a certain amount of both economic and cultural capital be required to realize a fully 'reflexive' pursuit of different lifestyles but also, because of this fact, the reflexive construction of one's lifestyle would for the most part be perceived through the lens of the habitus of those with less cultural capital as 'not for the likes of us'.

Thirdly, we can identity an important body of work examining the strategies of elites. The class formation paradigm had largely ignored elites, in part because they were too small to readily show up in national random sample surveys (see Savage and Williams 2008). The ruling class was also often identified as a kind of status throwback to the older aristocratic order (see e.g., Sampson 1962; Scott, 1982) that would lose its prestige and position in a marketwise society. Researchers influenced by Bourdieu's own work on elites have emphasized that elites are not a status throwback but actively make themselves, by deploying their various capitals as effectively as they can and by converting their capitals where this is possible (e.g., Hjellbrekke et al. 2007). In keeping with the general disavowal of the importance of social capital, this literature draws attention to the relative sparseness of the social networks of elites, but (drawing on Burt's theory of structural holes) suggests that intermediaries who can bridge different elite groups may be able to wield undue power and influence (see the discussion in Savage and Williams 2008).

A fourth area is particularly important in relating cultural class analysis to the older 'class formation' tradition. This is the increasingly extensive international research programme which seeks to map cultural tastes and practices, and which assesses how far they overlap with those that Bourdieu discussed in *Distinction* (see notably Bennett *et al.* 1999, 2009; Prieur, Rosenlund and Skjott-Larsen 2008). This research is important in two ways. Firstly, it allows us to see how far we can still see cultural activities as bestowing cultural capital, and secondly, it allows us to assess the extent to which such differences may overlap with social class inequalities.

In much recent cultural sociology, it is assumed that Bourdieu's concept of cultural capital is necessarily associated with 'high', snobbish or elite culture, as exemplified through an appreciation of classical music and the literary canon. Thus, proponents of the 'cultural omnivore' argument argue that Bourdieu's concern is with snobbish, 'highbrow' culture, as manifested by a liking for classical music (especially) and other forms of traditional culture (e.g., Peterson; Peterson and Kern 1996; Chan and Goldthorpe 2007). Such cultural sociologists thus see the existence of more hybrid cultural tastes, in which people might like elements of both high and popular culture, as necessarily marking the erosion of cultural capital.

Cultural class analysis researchers recognize that the nature of cultural capital dissected by Bourdieu in 1960s France may not be that which operates today. The cultural infrastructure of France in the 1960s was very different from today. Only a small proportion of the population had television sets. The very concept of the personal computer (as opposed to the mainframe) was unimaginable. The flowering of youth culture which had opened up in this decade and which animated student politics and social movements during this decade was a recent phenomenon that had not been critically digested. In the intervening decades, social changes associated with neoliberalism and financialization have been much discussed by social sciences. Given the scale of technological and social change, it would be remarkable if Bourdieu's account of cultural capital could be simply upheld.

A series of recent studies, notably Bennett *et al.*'s (2009) *Culture, Class, Distinction*, have shown that in fact, despite increasing cultural hybridity, there remain marked patterns of class inequality in cultural taste, and there remain crucial divides which are rarely crossed by the educated middle classes. Cultural capital now seems more associated with the ability to appropriate cultural artefacts 'reflexively' and 'discerningly', showing awareness that one is aware of the cultural coding of these artefacts. An interesting example is the way that young professionals are often happy to knowingly watch what they regard as 'crap TV', so showing an awareness of the codes used to classify programmes. Although there is more research to be done, there seems clear evidence that even in a cultural world increasingly shaped by media, forms of cultural capital can still be detected.

Discussion and Conclusion

I have shown that the cultural class analysis paradigm has emerged in the past decade as a serious and important intervention, with considerable relevance for political sociology. We can best understand this paradigm as a classic sociological riposte to the kinds of institutional and individualistic currents that predominate in political science. Researchers within the cultural class analysis paradigm emphasize that political institutions work in a social context in which individuals are differentially endowed with capital, and that the scope of an expansive political sociology needs to be extended to include these wider social processes which escape the awareness of institutional analysis (as well as politicians and 'educated' opinion). One might read this current of work as a reprise of Steven Lukes' (1974) celebrated insistence that there are three dimensions of power, and that we need to be alive not just to open contestation (the first 'face'), or even the controlling of agendas (the second 'face'), but also the way that large numbers of people with interests in changing the political order do not feel they have distinctive interests of their own (the mobilization of bias, the third 'face').

This analogy is pertinent because one of the problematic issues facing the cultural class analysis paradigm is the same one that Lukes faced, and which subsequent literature exposed as his Achilles' heel. This is the thorny problem of attributing 'objective' interests to groups who are unaware of (or 'disidentify' from) them. I have shown that a key feature of the class analysis paradigm is the way it has shown that the lack of overt class consciousness should not be read at face value, but can be taken as evidence for the power of class itself as a doxa. In the hands of sociologists such as Skeggs (1997) and Lawler (2000) this exposure is subtle and well worked through because it demonstrates ethnographically how such disidentifications are imbricated in the difficulties of people's lives. But there still remains the danger of a cavalier treatment of popular identities, which too easily reads into them disavowals and disidentifications that are projections by the researchers themselves. One of the attractive features of Bourdieu's thinking is the way that he sidesteps the need to overtly impute 'interests' to social agents through his deployment of field analysis, with its sporting analogy, and the emphasis on struggles over recognition and position, but not all commentators are convinced that he avoids a reductionist tendency (e.g., Joas and Knobl 2009; Jenkins 1992).

A second key issue is the need to take institutional analysis more seriously. As I have emphasized, the focus of Bourdieu's thinking, and that of his followers, is to emphasize the different endowments of capital that various agents can mobilize. His focus is on those who are effective 'players' and those who are not, and who do not feel they have a full right to compete. However, amongst those who do feel they are 'players' there can be intense competition and indeed such disputes are central to institutional politics. As we have seen, Bourdieu addresses this tension through his celebrated differentiation between 'cultural' and 'economic' elites in his account of 'the field of power'. But this is too restrictive a focus. Subsequent research suggests that there might actually be considerably more overlap between these groups (e.g., Bennett et al. 2009, on the UK). There is also evidence that 'technical' and 'scientific' expertise – which has become very significant over the past century – cannot be straightforwardly defined as the same kind of cultural capital as that which is associated with the arts and humanities (see Savage 2010). Contests amongst the privileged may (arguably) take a number of forms and these might be highly significant in shaping institutional forms, policies and key actions. In principle, field analysis could be a highly useful tool for unravelling such internal tensions and contests, but there needs to be more work on this, and in particular on looking at how the institutional processes themselves structure the 'field of power'.

A third issue for cultural class analysis consists of developing adequate strategies for comparative analysis, which do not assume that nations are bounded societies (see Urry 2003). There is an emerging sociology which explores the formation of trans-national fields, notably Fligstein's (2008) study of how increasing numbers of professionals and managers operate on a Europe-wide basis and regularly travel and communicate across national boundaries. This leads to the suggestion that the fields for different social groups may be organized at different kinds of scales, and that this scalar organization might be highly significant for the operation of fields themselves. This issue requires recovering a greater interest in the relationship between spatial and social processes (see Savage 2011 for an attempt to recover the importance of Bourdieu as a 'lost urban sociologist').

These three challenges all raise substantial theoretical and methodological issues. But none of these, on the face of it, is insuperable. They hark back to the need for a fuller and more developed understanding of the interplay between the sociological minutiae of everyday life and the study of political life than has been the case in recent years. But this is not simply a matter for academics to resolve. The increasing lack of 'connection' between the lives, beliefs and actions of increasingly sequestered political elites and those of 'ordinary' citizens is a marked feature of politics today. Challenging this boundary depends on forging a more effective kind of political intervention. But it also demands intellectual energy and resources, and it is my contention that cultural class analysis paradigm is a vital platform to build this from.

Further Reading

Bennett, T., Savage, M., Silva, E.B., Warde, A. *et al.* 2009: *Culture, Class, Distinction*. London: Routledge.
Bourdieu, P. 1986: *Distinction*. London: Routledge.
Savage, M. 2000: *Class Analysis and Social Transformation*. Milton Keynes: Open University Press.
Skeggs, B. 2004: *Class, Self, Culture*. London: Routledge.

27

The Politics of Ethnicity and Identity

ALETTA J. NORVAL

The theorization of ethnicity is bound up with political concerns and normative judge-ments, visible in the different approaches developed over time. Traditional views range from primordialism to instrumentalism, with the former treating contemporary forms of ethnic expression as a reactivation of older, sometimes biological relations, while the latter reduces ethnicity to a resource available for use by different interest groups. Primordialism is essentialist: it ignores the complexity of the historical conditions under which ethnicity becomes significant and overstates the internal homogeneity of ethnic identities. Instrumentalism is nominalist: it suggests that ethnic identification is impor-tant only insofar as it is based on more material phenomena. The third main position on ethnicity – constructivism – emphasizes the historical and political processes whereby ethnic identities are formed and situates them in relation to other identities: racial, sexual, national or gendered. Constructivism itself takes a variety of forms, ranging from a materialist post-structuralist theory to linguistic monism. The former suggests that 'the body' is important, but that markers of race and ethnicity are historical, social and political rather than natural. It is concerned with hybridity, diaspora, displacement and the politics of cultural difference, in which pluralism is radicalized in order to democ-ratize potentially exclusionary identities.

Ethnicities Old and New

We are suggesting that a new word reflects a new reality.... The new word is 'ethnicity', and the new usage is the steady expansion of the term 'ethnic group' from minority and marginal subgroups... to major elements of a society.

Glazer and Moynihan (1975: 1)

The Wiley-Blackwell Companion to Political Sociology, First Edition. Edited by Edwin Amenta, Kate Nash, and Alan Scott.
© 2012 Blackwell Publishing Ltd. Published 2012 by Blackwell Publishing Ltd.

The new politics of representation [...] also sets in motion an ideological contestation around the term 'ethnicity'. But in order to pursue that movement further, we will have to re-theorize the concept of difference.

(Hall 2003 [1989]: 93)

For intellectual reasons, it is interesting to return to the literatures that first alerted us to the presence of ethnicity as a novel form of identification. Such a return does not seek to rediscover its purported origins, but to remind ourselves that the theorization of ethnicity, multiculturalism and the emphasis on a politics of identity/difference, so acutely present in our contemporary world, all have long and difficult trajectories. A few remarks on these trajectories are necessary so as to situate current attempts at theorization in a proper context. In particular, it is important to note that the history of the theorization of ethnicity is not a progressive and cumulative one. Rather, it is intimately bound up with political concerns and normative judgements. Consequently, any attempt to reconstruct its trajectory should take a genealogical form. That is, it has of necessity to start from where we are, from our current concerns and our present commitments, so as to make visible the conditions under which particular theoretical accounts of ethnicity emerged and became disseminated. It is not possible to achieve anything approaching a full account of the complex genealogy of the uses and abuses of this term. To do so requires an investigation of the structural, historical and academic contexts of emergence and surfaces on which it has been inscribed, as well as a full critical assessment of the achievements and failures of the politics and theories of ethnicity. In its stead it may be useful simply to remind ourselves of some of the main outlines and features of this trajectory. In this chapter I will trace out the movement from primordialist and instrumentalist approaches to ethnicity, to a more general engagement with questions of difference. I will give particular attention to the contribution of accounts of difference, drawing on post-structuralist and post-colonialist theorizations that treat ethnicity as one amongst many possible forms of identification. In so doing, I aim to supplement these approaches with a consideration of the politics of difference, and its implications for the treatment of ethnicity.

Traditional debates on ethnic identity can be situated on a continuum of views ranging from primordialism to instrumentalism. That is, from views that ethnic identity stems from the givens of social existence – blood, speech, custom – which have an ineffable coerciveness in and of themselves (Geertz 1973: 259), to a view that ethnic identity is nothing but a mask deployed strategically to advance group interests that are often economic in character. The primordialist thesis, first discussed by Shils (1957) and elaborated upon by Geertz in the early 1960s, was and remains influential in discussions of ethnicity. One of the most prolific commentators on nationalism and ethnicity during the 1980s and 1990s, Anthony D. Smith (Hutchinson and Smith 1996: 6), treats contemporary forms of ethnic identification as nothing but a resurgence of more primordial identifications associated with 'ethnies'. Despite the emphasis in his work on the symbolic dimensions of identity, such as myths of common origin and shared historical memories, Smith retains an emphasis on the enduring, and even pre-modern, character of ethnicity. That is, modern forms of ethnic expression are ultimately a reactivation of older, more primordial forms. Diverging from this more culturalist turn, the 1980s also witnessed a recasting of primordialism in a sociobiological form. Van den Berghe (1986), for instance, argues that ethnicity has to be understood on the basis of kinship relations. Ethnicity for him is a manifestation of nepotism between kin that has a genetic basis. Consequently, ethnogenesis and transmission depends on 'successful reproduction': ethnicity 'always involves the cultural *and* genetic boundaries of a *breeding population*' (1986: 256). Primordialist approaches have been criticized, in particular, for failing to account for change, for working with overly static conceptions of ethnicity, and for naturalizing ethnic groups (Jenkins 1997: 44). More specifically, while sociobiological approaches are questioned for their biological reductionism, ethnosymbolic primordialists have been taken to task for an overemphasis on symbolic phenomena at the expense of material factors in the constitution of ethnicity. By contrast, an emphasis on the role of material interests stands at the heart of instrumentalist approaches.

Instrumentalist approaches treat ethnicity as a resource for different interest groups. Analytical emphasis, in this case, falls on analysing and uncovering the process through which elites mobilize groups so as to further their own self-interest. Instrumentalism, drawing its initial inspiration from the work of Barth (1969), treats ethnicity as essentially malleable and thus open to elite manipulations. Like primordialism, instrumentalism is not a homogeneous category. It encompasses both neo-Marxist and rational choice approaches. In the case of the former, ethnicity is viewed as an instrument to allow mobilization around interests that are, ultimately, grounded in social class (Wolpe 1988). Hence, ethnicity is reduced to and explicated in class terms. Something similar occurs in rational choice approaches where ethnicity is analysed from the perspective of rational actors who choose to join groups to secure specific individual ends (cf. Hechter 1986). Both of these types of analysis signally fail to treat ethnic identification as worthy of analysis in and of itself. As a consequence, identity and identification are reduced to a level of analysis which is deemed to be somehow more fundamental and politically more significant than ethnic identity itself.

This somewhat stale debate between primordialists and instrumentalists may be recast in order to throw more light on what is at stake in the discussion, and to bring us closer to contemporary theoretical debates on identity in general, and ethnic identities in particular. In order to do so, it is useful to concentrate on the question of the 'reality' of ethnicity. From this vantage point, it is possible to discern at least three diverging positions on ethnicity. In the first case, ethnicity is treated as natural, as a given and as a nodal point around which identity is organized. This nodal point has an historical value: it is the core of identity, regardless of historical context; it acts as an indicator of a homogeneous group identity; it is politically, socially and culturally salient regardless of the specific context under analysis. The essentialism is particularly evident in primordialist approaches to ethnicity. The main problems with treating ethnicity in an essentialist fashion consist in denying the complexity of both the specific historical circumstances under which ethnicity comes to be a significant phenomenon, and the lack of internal homogeneity of ethnic identities. In the second, ethnicity is not accorded any reality of its own. Ethnicity is merely a marker for deeper, more significant social divisions. Since it is something purely epiphenomenal, this marker is manipulable. Elites are argued to be in a position to mould popular feelings through the use of ethnic symbols to achieve ends unrelated to those symbols. This *nominalism* about ethnicity is characteristic of instrumentalist approaches. It suffers from a reductionism that naively suggests that the force of ethnic forms of identification arise entirely from external inducement. The obverse side of this assumption suggests that were we to understand this process properly there would be nothing of significance left to engage with: ethnicity will simply dissolve.

Since the mid-1980s there has been, primarily as a result of an increasing engagement with post-structuralist theories, a significant shift away from both axes of this debate. Both the primordialist/essentialist and the instrumentalist nominalist positions have come under fire from a third position, namely, *constructivism*. While there are many different forms of constructivism or contextualism, commonly held tenets include, *inter alia*, arguments for a context-sensitive theory which is attentive to the complexities of processes of identity formation, and to the hybridity of identities, while not ignoring the political significance of ethnic forms of identification. In other words, there is, first, a shift away from the assumption of the ahistorical and given nature of ethnic identity, towards an emphasis on the analysis of the historical and political processes and practices through which it comes into being. Second, there is a break with the assumption that ethnicity is in and of itself, always, the core organizing feature of identity. This pluralization has shifted attention towards other forms of identification, be they racial, sexual, national or gendered, in short, to a preoccupation with question of *difference*. Simultaneously, it has facilitated a more politically sensitive and nuanced approach to the question of ethnicity. While not assuming that it would always be politically significant, there has been a break with the instrumentalism of the nominalist position. That is, the emphasis on the constructed character of ethnic identities has also led to an acknowledgement that whether or not such identities will be politically salient is an entirely contextual matter.

From Identities to Identification

Every social community reproduced by the functioning of institutions is imaginary... it is based on the projection of individual existence into the weft of a collective narrative, on the recognition of a common name.... But this comes down to accepting that... only imaginary communities are real.
                                                                    Balibar (1991: 93)

Despite these advances, much of the current theorization of the phenomenon of ethnicity has remained trapped in the strictures of a distinction, widely deployed in the social and human sciences, between the objective and the subjective. Separating the subjective and the objective on the grounds of the assumption that the former is 'purely personal' and the latter is a 'given' simply reintroduces the problematic features of the primordialism/instrumentalism divide through the back door. What is needed is a rethinking of the relation between the subjective and the objective, so as to facilitate an engagement with the social and political processes shaping ethnic forms of identification.

Recasting this distinction has been made possible by the theorization of the imaginary constitution of society (cf. Anderson 1991; Castoriadis 1987; see Finlayson, Chapter 24, in this volume), a view that contains the possibility of a break with the topographical conception of the social underlying the traditional subjective/objective distinction. On this reading, far from simply 'given', objectivity is nothing but that which is socially constituted, and which has become *sedimented* over time. The feature of 'objectivity', thus, may be attributed to any sedimented social practice or identity.

Positing objectivity in this manner has the further consequence of opening the space for the thought of *desedimentation*: any sedimented practice may be put into question by political contestation. And once its historically constituted character is revealed, it loses its naturalized status as 'objectively given'.

The consequences of this shift for the analysis of the phenomenon of ethnicity are far-reaching. Once the givenness and objectivity of identity are put into question, and a purely subjectivist account of ethnic identity is problematized, the way is open to develop a theoretical account of ethnic *identification*. As Ahmed (1997: 157) argues, when we can no longer assume that the subject simply 'has' an identity in the form of a properly demarcated place of belonging, what is required is an analysis of the process and structures of identification whereby identities come to be seen as such places of belonging. However, this recognition of the importance of identification should not overshadow differences of approach amongst constructivist theorists.

Different Forms of Constructivism: From Linguistic Monism to Post-structuralism

Constructivist positions take many forms, ranging from linguistic monism, where linguistic construction is taken to be generative and deterministic, through instrumentalist accounts such as those discussed earlier, to fully fledged post-structuralist approaches. The difficulties arising from linguistic monism are many. First, if the act of construction is understood as a purely verbal act, it is unclear how such an act would be linked to materiality since ethnic markers place certain limitations on what could be 'constructed' verbally. Second, as with instrumentalist accounts, construction is still understood as a unilateral process initiated from above, thus reinforcing a top-down view of the production of ethnic identity which leaves little, if any, space for human agency and resistance. Third, both of these positions fail to account for the force of ethnic identification by treating it either as a matter of individual choice or as a matter of elite manipulation.

In order to outline an alternative, post-structuralist account of constructivism, it is necessary to specify clearly what main features such a position would have to contain. As argued earlier, it has to break with the view of ethnic identity as either imposed or merely subjective. It must, therefore, provide us with an account of the subject and of identification which takes cognizance of wider power relations while not treating such identification as if it were imposed on passive subjects. It must, in addition, be able to address the complexity and hybridity of identities, while avoiding linguistic determinism. It must, therefore, contain a plausible account of materiality and its role in the production of images for identification. The latter is especially important if one is to accommodate the force of racialized identities without giving way to the spuriousness of a sociobiological approach.

Racialized Identities: The Question of Materiality

Theorists such as Wallman (1978) and Eriksen (1993) have argued that physical appearance should be considered as only one possible marker of ethnic boundaries amongst many, and that ideas of race may or may not be an important factor in ethnic politics. These insights resonate with those developed from within post-structuralist theorization of identity/difference more generally. Once one moves towards a constructivist analytic proper, neither race nor ethnicity can be treated as natural givens. Indeed, both result from complicated processes of production and identification. Whether such identification takes a racialized or an ethnicized form, or both, is a matter largely if not solely of historic-political circumstances (Mason 1999: 21). Omi and Winant (1986), for instance, concentrate on the racialization of identities in the United States; Hall (1996) treats the movement towards hybrid ethnic forms of identification in the United Kingdom; and Norval (1996), Howarth (1997) and others investigated the complex interpretation of racialized and ethnicized forms of identification in apartheid South Africa.

Two areas in particular have to be addressed if the constructivists analytic is to be deepened in a post-structuralist direction that emphasizes the need to avoid a pure contextualism. The first concerns the theorization of the presumed materiality of the body, and of any other 'physical' markers. The second is related to the first. It concerns the theorization of the politics of ethnicity. In terms of the former, Alcoff's work on racial embodiment and Butler's on the body is particularly significant. The need to deal with 'the body' arises, *inter alia*, from objections against early constructivists that seemingly ignore the material visibility of colour and of cultural practices and tend to absorb them into accounts of the linguistic meaning conferred upon such phenomena. In *Bodies that Matter*, Butler (1993: 30) argues that, in order to counter such linguistic determinism, one needs to recognize that the theoretical options 'are not exhausted by presuming materiality, on the one hand, and negating materiality, on the other'. Rather, matter must be understood as always *positioned or signified as prior*. The body signified as prior to signification is then always already an effect of signification. In this manner, she puts into question the brute givenness of matter, and by implication of the body, and of colour. In arguing that signifying acts delimit and contour matter she does not also suggest that the body, colour and matter do not matter. From this quite abstract starting point, it is necessary to move towards a more phenomenological approach to the body, an approach that would allow us to come to grips with the effects and the production of effects arising from embodiment.

It is here that Alcoff's work is significant, for it begins to develop an account that is both less abstract and politically more sensitive to the issues at stake (Alcoff 1999a, 1999b). She suggests that a phenomenological approach may render our tacit knowledge about racial embodiment explicit (1999b). It may, for instance, uncover the ways in which we, without being explicitly conscious of it, read and interpret bodily markers as significant. These markers are not in any sense natural or given. She concentrates on the visual registry of embodiment, a registry which, she argues, is historically evolving, culturally variegated, but which, nevertheless, has a powerful structuring influence on individual experience. The account offered by Alcoff has the further advantage of being genealogical and thus critical in character. The phenomenological descriptions, far from naturalizing and consolidating racism, reactivate the contingency of the visual registry and have, at least, the potential to disrupt the naturalization of radicalization.

A phenomenological approach to the racialized body can further be developed by drawing on recent work on embodiment and corporeality that sees the body not merely as passive transmitter of messages but as playing 'an active role in the generation of perceptual meaning' (Coole 2005: 128). On this understanding, it is important to give attention to what is called 'bodily knowing', a practical reasoning gathering together disparate elements into 'existentially meaningful forms' (Coole 2005: 128) The body here is treated as active, capable of choices and innovations, even though those are inevitably circumscribed and limited by sedimented practices. Conversely, it also takes account of the fact that the body situates subjects in time and space, and has an 'outside whose inter-subjective significance eludes conscious control'. Finally, Coole also highlights the importance of embodiment as a reminder of one's own frailty, vulnerability to suffering and pain, and the political stakes of corporeal politics.

Thus, to point to the formation of racial or ethnic identities in this sense, and to the fact that attention needs to be given to the materialization of categories such as the body, colour and other ethnic markers as a result of political practices, is not also to assert that they are unimportant or irrelevant. Similarly, to emphasize the contingency of socially inscribed identities does not mean that they are fungible, that they may be picked and chosen as if from a supermarket shelf. To the contrary, it directs attention to the historical, social, ad political processes through which images for identification are constructed and sustained, contested and negotiated. One consequence of this shift towards identification is that the focus of analysis of ethnic identities is laterally displaced. It is no longer adequate simply to ask 'in whose interest are ethnic identities constituted?' Rather we need to inquire into the processes through which ethnicity becomes a significant site of identification that may or may not entail a construction of the 'interests' of a particular group, and that may or may not become a site of political contestation. This is perhaps the most significant element of the politics of ethnic identification today. Claims and demands made in the name of ethnic groups cannot be understood without giving attention to the dimension of identification. As Gooding-Williams (1998) puts it, to the first-person perspective, one which notes and engages with the way in which individuals contribute to the formation of their own (racial) identities. As he shows through his analysis of, *inter alia*, the writings of Du Bois, once this is acknowledged, a whole world of new possibilities and impossibilities is opened up (Gooding-Williams 1998: 24). Hence, identification, while it may be closely associated with felt discrimination and the unequal distribution of resources in society, cannot be reduced to the latter. Moreover, it requires careful, systematic and nuanced analysis.

Hybrid Ethnicities: Rethinking Pluralism

The problem of reductionism occurs, not only where ethnicity is reduced to other modes of identification based, for instance, upon class, but also where there is an over-concentration on the presumed homogeneity of ethnic identities. Such an emphasis on homogeneity, purity and authenticity always occurs at the expense of the recognition of difference and diversity, and has its roots in the manner in which 'plurality' was thought of in early accounts of ethnicity. Jenkins (1997: 25) points out that the conceptual replacement of the 'tribe' by 'ethnicity' was accompanied by the development of the idea of a 'plural society'. Both of these changes were related to the changing postwar world and the loss of empire. In particular, it addressed the need to conceptualize, within the colonial administrative and institutional frameworks, the convergence of separate institutions for 'Europeans' and urbanized local groups on the one hand, and 'tribespeople' on the other. Thus, while the term 'ethnicity' was an analytical category within urban anthropology with which to make sense of these new social and cultural formations (Eade 1996:58), the term 'plural society' (taken over from Furnivall's analysis of colonial policy in Southeast Asia in the 1940s) had to capture the institutional incorporation of different ethnic groups into a single state (Jenkins 1997: 26). The idea of a plural society was created in opposition to the European ideal of homogeneous nation-states. However, this recognition of plurality at the level of state institution was based upon a homogenizing account of identity, both of the ethnicities of the colonized and of the nationhood of the colonizers. More recent developments in post-colonial theory have sought to overcome the problems associated with the assumptions underlying this model. In particular, new theorizations have problematized the idea that only 'minorities' of 'third world' peoples have ethnicity, as well as the assumption that European nations were indeed internationally homogeneous.

Contemporary post-colonial theories of identity are explicitly situated within the context of contemporary concerns with diaspora, displacement, and the politics of cultural difference. So, for instance, one finds an emphasis on displacement as the starting point for rethinking questions of identity in the work of Hall, Spivak and Bhabha. Hall utilizes this perspective to extricate the concept of ethnicity from its anti-racist paradigm, 'where it connotes the immutable difference of minority experience'. It then becomes a term which takes into account the historical positions, cultural conditions and political conjunctures through which all identity is constructed. It becomes a concept connoting the 'recognition that we all speak from a particular place, out of a particular history, out of a particular experience [...]. We are all, in a sense, *ethnically* located and our ethnic identities are crucial to our subjective sense of who we are' (Hall 2003 [1989]: 94). For Hall, as for Juteau (1996: 55), what is important is to show the extent to which ethnicity is not the exclusive characteristic of the other. It marks every identity as such.

Bhabha, by contrast, continues to focus on the consequences of displacement for the *minority* subject. His development of the concept of 'hybridity' serves to act as a signifier of the irreducibility of cultural difference (1994b: 37). Before exploring this any further, it is worthwhile noting that, as with other terms in this debate, that of hybridity has a longer history. As Papastergiadis shows, hybridity has shadowed every organic theory of identity, and was deeply inscribed in nineteenth-century discourses of scientific racism where it served as a metaphor for the negative consequences of racial encounters (1997: 257–279). However, for Bhabha hybridity is precisely *not* to be understood as a mixture of pre-given identities or essences. Rather, it signifies the attempt to capture the non-purity of identity, the non-coincidence of the self with itself, and the unhomeliness of existence which arises as an effect of colonial power. The production of hybridization, moreover, 'turns the discursive conditions of dominance into the grounds of intervention' (Bhabha 1994b: 171). It is from here that the concepts of homogeneous cultures and national communities, the very logic of identity conceived as pure, intact and self-sufficient, is being challenged and subverted. Bhabha thus moves almost seamlessly from a conception of hybrid identities exemplified in the experience of displacement, to a politics of resistance, based on transgressive discourses aiming to unsettle liberal multiculturalists and assimilative political strategies. Bhabha has frequently been criticized for his easy celebration of the condition of displacement, unhomeliness and hybridity, and for the naivety of the politics that follows from it (Ahmed 1997: 153–167; Papastergiadis 1997: 267; Norval 1999). Suffice it to mention here that the disruption of old certainties and traditional identities by no means leads inexorably to an acceptance of greater diversity.

The idea of hybrid identities does, nevertheless, have important consequences for our understanding of ethnicity. As Bhabha (1994a: 269) notes, it forms a response to the initial pluralism that marked the questioning of homogeneous identities. The shift away from 'class' and 'gender' as primary conceptual categories has resulted in an awareness of the multiple subject positions – generational, gendered, racial, locational – that inhibit any claim to identity. Thinking about identity in terms of hybridity moves beyond this pluralism of identities to focus attention on the 'interstitial moments or processes that are produced in the articulation of "differences"' (1994a: 269). As a result, the analytical questions that we seek to answer now are related to the formation of subjects that become possible in the overlapping and displacement of domains of *difference*. Difference here is not a reflection of pre-given ethnic traits set in sedimented traditions. Rather, it is to be conceived of as a complex process of negotiation, the outcome of struggles and antagonisms with dominant traditions that open up spaces through which dominant designations of difference may be resisted and recast. However, while Bhabha offers a theoretically sophisticated account of the inherently fissured nature of identity, he lacks the tools to address the complexities and ambiguities of the political struggles that emerge from these spaces. To be able to address these questions, the study of ethnicity and identity must relinquish its isolation from political theory and engage with the wider theoretical concerns and conditions under which it may become politically salient.

Conclusion: Relocating the Politics of Ethnicity

The politics of ethnicity, all too often, is associated with a study of 'conflict' and its regulation in deeply divided societies (cf. Lijphart 1977; Horowitz 2000 (1985); McGarry and O'Leary 1993). It presupposes ethnicity and sets out to develop mechanisms to 'accommodate' it. The assumptions on which this paradigm rest have been problematized along with the conception of homogenous, given identities, treated as if they were of necessity incommensurable; this approach perpetuates rather than accounts for the myths which have fed conflictual relations. As Taylor (1999: 123) remarks, we need to break free of the belief that 'race' and 'ethnicity' are simply forces that we 'encounter' in politics. Instead, we need to engage with the difficult issue of learning to distinguish between a politics that arises from the legitimacy of difference and a politics resting on coercive unity. This, in turn, necessitates an engagement with the question of democracy, since a politics of legitimate difference can only avoid the problem of coercive unity in so far as it is inserted into a *democratic* context, a context in which identity is open to challenge, negotiation and renewal. While accepting that an understanding of the hybridity and ambiguity of identity in no way leads inexorably to a democratic politics, a democratic context – more than any other – facilitates accentuating 'exposure to contingency and increases the likelihood that the affirmation of difference in identity will find expression in public life' (Connolly 1991: 193).

This is where accounts of the need to move away from more traditional accounts of pluralism become pertinent (Norval 1993; Bhabha 1994a). The radicalization of traditional pluralism is akin to what Connolly (1995: xiv–xv) has called a process of active *pluralization* that seeks to turn an appreciation of established diversity into an active cultivation of difference. Pluralization, in this sense, would refer to subjecting static conceptions of 'cultural diversity', based on categories such as gender, race, class and ethnicity as givens, to the disruptive effects of a conception of difference as irreducible, and to actively cultivating the visibility of the deeply split nature of identity politically. Such an active cultivation of difference is necessary, first and foremost, because there is always the danger that ethnic forms of identification may become exclusionary and self-enclosed. This possibility arises from the very context in which ethnic forms of nationalistic projects emerge. There is, moreover, the danger that ethnic identifications *already* contain exclusions within them. That is why it is not enough to focus analytic attention on the articulation of ethnic demands against assimilative of homogenizing state projects. The democratic logic must go all the way down. All forms of identification must not only be open to critical interrogation, but if they are to be democratic, should foster and encourage it.

Further Reading

Alcoff, L.M. 1999: Philosophy and racial identity. In M. Bulmer and J. Solomos (eds) *Ethnic and Racial Studies Today*. London: Routledge

Coole, D. 2005: Rethinking agency: a phenomenological approach to embodiment and agentic capacities. *Political Studies* 53: 124–142.

Connolly, W.E. 1995: *The Ethos of Pluralization*. Minneapolis: University of Minnesota Press.

Gooding-Williams, R. 1998: Race, multiculturalism and democracy. *Constellations* 5(1): 18–41.

Hall, S. 1996: Politics of identity. In T. Ranger, Y. Samad, and O. Stuart (eds) *Culture, Identity and Politics. Ethnic Minorities in Britain*. Aldershot: Avebury.

Howarth, D. 1997: Complexities of identity/difference: black consciousness ideology in South Africa. *Journal of Political Ideologies* 2(1): 51–78.

Jenkins, R. 1997: *Rethinking Ethnicity. Arguments and Explorations*. London: Sage.

28

Race and Politics

JOHN D. SKRENTNY AND RENÉ PATNODE

Race or race-like categorizations are factors in politics throughout history and all over the world. Political elites use race categorizations, as well as ethnicity and nation, as cleavages for exclusion, domination and hierarchy. Race has been a part of the politics of immigration, where states choose who can and cannot become a member of a polity. Though still an axis of domination, the past several decades have seen regulatory efforts at ameliorating racial inequality. Though varying globally, social movements and political officials in the United States pioneered a distinctive approach heavily dependent on regulations and often using racial categorizations to move beyond race.

Social scientists and historians have shown that race, or race-like categorizations, are factors in politics throughout history and all over the world. Related to ethnicity and nation, race is typically a cleavage of exclusion, domination and inequality, though patterns are highly variable. The very conceptions of race, and racial mixing, also vary considerably over time and space, and even between groups in the same society. Racial and ethnic exclusions are typically highly salient in the politics of immigration, when the constitution and identity of the nation itself are at issue. Though always a cleavage of inequality, the trend in race politics, especially since the middle of the twentieth century, has been the development of policies designed to ameliorate this inequality. Here, the United States was an early leader, though social movements and political officials institutionalized a distinctive approach heavily dependent on regulations and often using racial categorizations to move beyond race.

The Wiley-Blackwell Companion to Political Sociology, First Edition. Edited by Edwin Amenta, Kate Nash, and Alan Scott.
© 2012 Blackwell Publishing Ltd. Published 2012 by Blackwell Publishing Ltd.

Race and Ethnicity in Global and Historical Perspective

There is considerable debate as to how exactly scholars should define the terms race and ethnicity. Brubaker (2009), for example, disputes the utility of maintaining distinct terms for what might ultimately be two sides of the same analytical coin. However, given their widespread usage in the literature, we shall adopt the definitions supplied by Cornell and Hartmann (1998), which in turn owe a debt to Weber (1948) and Schermerhorn (1978). In this view, ethnicity refers to the cultural and familial ties that bind a people group from a presumed shared past. As such, ethnic relationships are strongly felt by the group's members and thus are powerfully motivational. In contrast, race refers to phenotypical differences – most notably skin colour, but also hair, eye shape, etc. – that serve as characteristics for classifying individuals. Nationalism, Cornell and Hartmann argue, is commonly based on ethnicity, but is distinctive. It 'typically involves the effort by a people to determine their own destiny and free themselves from external constraint, to overcome internal divisions and unite, and to express their sense of themselves and their cultural heritage' (Cornell and Hartmann 2007: 36). Distinct from ethnicity, nations have this political aspiration, and the peoplehood may be based on something other than shared ancestry or blood.

Cornell and Hartmann note that, in the real world, race and ethnicity may be difficult to distinguish. For example, racial processes have led to the creation of the group known as Black Americans, but this group nonetheless demonstrates a culture particular to them. Conversely, members of an East Asian ethnic group might differentiate themselves from other East Asian groups on the basis of physical build.

Still, we may use race, ethnicity and nation fruitfully as ideal types of categorizing behaviour to highlight their real-world complexity. Race is *typically* based on perceived phenotypes and is ascribed, and ethnicity is *typically* based on perceived cultural and ancestry similarity and is asserted. Nationalism is *typically* based on ethnicity, though it can be based on race or on neither category. These identities and categories are thus negotiated through the process of 'social construction'.

For our purposes, recognizing the distinction between ethnicity and race is helpful because it gets at a very political issue: the very notion that race is an assignable identity implies coercion of some form or another. Coercion in turn is a typical property of governmental control, that is, the formalized control of one group by another. In politics, racism, the term denoting this control, is more than just the simple calculus of prejudice added to power; it expresses more completely the ideology underlying systems of power, which in turn simultaneously draws from and feeds popular prejudice (Bonilla-Silva 2003). Conversely, ethnicity is an identity around which members can rally to oppose such control. Thus both forms of identity are intimately connected with political institutions. It does not mean that governments do not coerce or ascribe identities to ethnic groups, but only that this is more typical of racial politics, and could imply a racialization process.

States make race as a categorizing principle in a wide range of contexts across time and space. Though the sociological literature frequently depicts race as the product of developments in Western ideology from the seventeenth and eighteenth centuries (see, for example, Omi and Winant 1994), race-like categorization can be found in diverse political systems and throughout history. For example, Brubaker, Loveman and Stamatov (2004) linked the construction of categories of people to an innate human psychological need to organize reality. Hahn (2001) finds the presence of racism in the European Middle Ages, and A. Smith (2002) argues that concepts of ethnic groups and ethno-centricism even among non-elites existed well before that. A focus on modern, Western racism may obscure larger processes of boundary construction, particularly political ones, that have historically undergirded race-like domination around the world.

Dikötter's (1994) research on China provides an enlightening illustration. In addition to a long history of alternating between acceptance and expulsion of foreign cultural influence, and a general view of foreigners as 'barbarians', the urban Chinese, and East Asians more generally, have long equated the white and black duality with that of good and evil. They have also disparaged individuals with dark skin because of its association with lower-class agricultural work. Also, one can only partially attribute the later evidence of racist discrimination against African immigrants within China (such as the anti-African-student demonstrations in the 1970s and 1980s) to the importation of Western beliefs; to the extent that racist beliefs have been imported, they appear to have linked or meshed with indigenous racism (Sautman 1994). Similar patterns of racial and/or ethnic politics can be found in Horowitz's exhaustive (2000 [1985]) study of ethnic conflict in the developing world, where some ethno-racial hatreds have been long-standing. Though Western racism may affect non-Western polities in profound ways – consider Kim's (2008) study of how globalization has enabled US racism to influence South Korean attitudes – societies outside the West may develop their own racist or race-like ideologies and form hybrids with Western racial conceptions.

Racial Orders, Racial Domination, Racist Discrimination

Though racial politics can be found around the globe and throughout history, the form that racial ideology takes and how it might become part of the foundation of a political system is highly context-dependent. The way that race patterns politics is a 'racial order' and it may be stable or not. Omi and Winant's (1994) analysis of the US case shows how both majority and minority members of the political community seek to change the way the American 'racial formation' articulates the meaning of race. In the American context, King and Smith (2005) argue that political development can be understood in terms of two evolving though still competing racial orders: a 'white supremacist' order and an 'egalitarian transformative' order. Though one may be dominant in a particular historical period or geographical region, this does not mean that the other is entirely absent. In a detailed study of race politics in Britain and France since the end of the Second World War, Bleich (2003) shows how the availability of ideological frames concerning race can shape the development of racial policy. He found that Britain, particularly in the 1960s and 1970s, utilized frames from the American example and thus tried to wipe out employment discrimination through civil legal action sponsored by state bureaucracies, whereas France sought to distance itself from Nazi Germany by criminalizing expressed racism. Thus, context determines how actors conceptualize racism and how they can respond to it in complex ways.

Racial orders and racial discrimination may vary also in the ways people and policies identify races. Race may be understood as discrete categories in a particular context, or there may be 'colourism' – the view of race as a spectrum between two extremes. Which conception is dominant may matter for opportunity, conflict and other dynamics. It may be that countries that feature colourism (e.g., Brazil and other Latin American societies) tend to have less explicitly racial policies (Schermerhorn 1978), but this would not necessarily mean that racial discrimination does not exist. Indeed, when a society is characterized by colourism, the lack of clear boundaries can hinder the development of identities and therefore social movement responses that seek to change the racial status quo. Conversely, societies ordered by clear lines (e.g., the United States and South Africa) tend to have strong identities on both sides, which can polarize racial conflicts, leading to ongoing cycles of oppression and resistance (Marx 1998). At the same time, even though the United States may have a 'one-drop rule' regarding black identity (Davis 1991), there is evidence that colourism and discrete racial categories are not exclusive even among blacks (Hochschild and Weaver 2007), and that the discrete lines dividing blacks and whites in the United States may be blurring (Lee and Bean 2010).

Strong racial identities in turn can lead to interaction effects with other highly salient political identities. Glenn's (2002) study of citizenship and labour in the American South (African Americans), Southwest (Latinos) and Hawaii (Native Hawaiians) uses a cultural lens to understand racial and gender domination. She structures her comparison through the analysis of race and gender politics in representation (symbols, language and images that express race and gender meanings), micro-interaction (focusing on social norms) and social structure (rules regulating power). This multifaceted approach allows a rich exploration of how dominant groups used citizenship laws to exclude – both in the law itself, or in the implementation of law that was equal on its face.

As the notion of hierarchy implies, race is also strongly correlated with class, and figures prominently in class identities in political action. Greenberg (1980) notes how all three British classes (industrialists, workers and peasants) in the nineteenth century all found the suppression of blacks to be in their interests and made use of the government to enact those interests. Gilroy (1987), also writing about class-conscious Britain in the mid- to late twentieth century, argues that observers may confuse race with class in so far as they have similar properties; he claims both are *sui generis* social phenomena that feature distinct and contextualized historical trajectories and serve as bases for political organization (p. 27). Thus he recommends adopting a broader definition of class to encompass any such phenomenon.

Race, Nation and Immigration

As they all are ways of conceptualizing 'peoplehood' (Lie 2004a), race, ethnicity and nation are all related and linked. The racial aspects of nationhood, as well as the hierarchical aspects (Seol and Skrentny 2009a), are most discernible or salient when polities confront immigrants. Government control of immigration and citizenship through policy allows states to determine who may be a member of the national community, who is excluded as a racialized 'Other', and how the national culture will be shaped in the future (Huntington 2004).

Studies of immigration policy, particularly in the United States but elsewhere as well, explore this narrative from different angles. The historical record reveals many efforts to make the American nation through immigration. King (2000) and Zolberg (1999) show how US immigration policy moved to exclusions and quotas in the 1880s and 1920s based on lawmakers' perceptions of the assimilability of different nationalities and races. Ngai (2004) explores the history of restriction and the creation of 'alien citizenship' – a racialized category where Asians and Latinos have formal citizenship but whom Americans nevertheless viewed as alien. Similarly, the British in the mid-twentieth century often conflated dark skin with the foreign, and thus unassimilable, nature of immigrants owing to Britain's imperial past (Gilroy 1987). Some scholars see European Union (EU) racial politics shaping immigration policy. For example, Geddes (2003) argues that the existence of the Schengen Agreement, allowing free movement throughout continental EU member states and a few non-members effectively, creates new borders around a racially white 'supranation'.

But the bigger story here, especially in the West, is that despite evidence for continuing racial discrimination and hierarchy, racial diversity is growing rapidly. Some of this growth occurred after the Second World War and consisted primarily of former colonial subjects. In the contemporary period, as in the past, around the world immigration restriction policy has failed to keep out undesired flows of immigrants (Cornelius and Tsuda 2004), especially in the US case (Andreas 2009), forcing states to confront populations that employers may desire for their cheap labour but who are not invited to be full members. Joppke (1999) argues that liberal institutions, and in particular independent courts, have allowed the settlement of large numbers of former guest workers, other economic migrants and asylees. Resistance to growing numbers of Muslim immigrants has created racial and ethnic tension along with religious conflict, with much attention directed at symbols of difference, and in particular the veil worn by many Muslim women (Joppke 2009).

In Asia, the ageing, industrial states of Japan and South Korea manifest the racial politics of immigration through their myths of ethnic homogeneity (Lie 2004b) and resistance to immigrant settlement (Seol and Skrentny 2009b). Both states also seek to fill low-skilled labour needs by relying on co-ethnic foreigners – ethnic Japanese South Americans for Japan (Tsuda 2003) and ethnic Korean Chinese for South Korea (Seol and Skrentny 2009a).

Responses to immigration such as these remind us to consider processes of ascription. The presence of racial and cultural Others serves to reinforce national identity and continually remake racial politics. As Triandafyllidou argues (2001), nationalism always develops in response to perceived competition – economic, cultural, social or otherwise – from a national or ethnic group that may be external to a nation or within it. The 'Significant Other' may dominate domestic politics and play a major role in defining national identity, as blacks did for much of American history. However, as the historical context develops, the Significant Other might change. One could argue, for example, that radical Islamists or the Chinese have now replaced the USSR and have ascended to the role of an external Significant Other in the American case.

Triandafyllidou's point helps one understand nationalism as a racializing act. Given that nationalism involves political action by definition, by assessing nationalism, one may be assessing the relationship between race and politics on a fairly large scale.

We may see nationalism in the responses to immigration in a variety of contexts, also in the more general instances of cultural protectionism that can drive foreign policy as it has done in China since antiquity, in the sense of moral and ethnic superiority that underlaid European colonialism and foreign political domination, and in the ethnic violence that continuously occurs throughout the world. While there is academic debate regarding whether nationalism, like race, is a modern phenomenon (see, for example, Anderson 1991, Connor 1994, Hechter 2000, among many others), the roots of the Othering process that underlies both race and nation have existed for much longer (A. Smith 1986).

One last aspect of nationalism that suggests its connection to race concerns the fact that any act of either racism or nationalism involves people, both the elite and the ordinary. Discourse and commands may originate from elites but those on the ground ultimately utter and execute them; successful racial and nationalistic projects need mass support. Racial, ethnic and national identities are *felt* by many and not just a handful of intelligentsia and politicians (Connor 1994).

The Amelioration of Racial Inequality in the United States: The Centrality of the Regulatory Approach

There is an enormous body of research on race and politics in the United States. This work, some of which is cited above, finds much in the US case that is typical, such as the foundational role of racial domination in politics, the institutionalization of both discrete racial categories and colourism in defining groups, and the use of immigration policy to define a racialized and ethnicized nation. But the United States has shown a relatively distinctive approach to addressing racial inequality and conflict.

There are many ways for states to promote racial equality. China has favoured an approach where minorities, including the immigrant Koreans, have some autonomy to manage their own affairs in particular areas (Kaup 2002; Mullaney 2010). Post-Second World War France, in contrast, assiduously avoids any racial or ethnic categorizations in law and favours a strong, universalist, integrative approach with a robust welfare state (Hargreaves 1995; Bleich 2003; Fassin and Fassin 2006). What may be distinctive about the US case, however, is the reliance on 'civil rights' regulation to ameliorate racial inequality and racial conflict, and in particular, a willingness to categorize by race in inequality-ameliorating regulations. In the US case, equality and integration are to come about from both 'colour-blind' and 'race-conscious' regulations rather than social policy spending. The goal of policies designed to achieve 'equal opportunity' is to give all groups an equal chance to succeed – and to fail. Civil rights regulations succeed when the wealthy, the middle class and the poor are all racially integrated.

The American state's move to promote racial equality occurred in interaction with the global context. Civil rights groups had fought for change throughout American history, but it was the Second World War's battle against a racist dictator, and ensuing creation of a global human rights culture, that created conditions for civil rights progress (Dudziak 2000; Skrentny 2002). A rich area of research with significant engagement with race and politics explores the social movements that emerged in this context and their efforts to create legal structures guaranteeing equal rights and full citizenship.

To be sure, this work may downplay the role of race even while examining groups organized around race in various ways; the thrust has been to use race and civil rights movements as cases to develop theories and concepts of wide generalizability. For example, McAdam's important (1982) study of the black civil rights movement made a significant contribution that bridged social movement studies and political sociology by demonstrating how attention to 'political opportunities' helps explain the emergence of social movements. In this view, we can understand the rise of black challenges to Jim Crow racial discrimination and push for civil rights regulations by showing how increasing access to political elites, growing allies, and intra-political elite conflict allowed the movement, which had long been fuelled by desire for change, to finally emerge. Yet Lee (2002) and Sugrue (2008) also show how grassroots organizations helped to change public attitudes towards racial inequality, and also the views of political elites as well. The story of black civil rights in the United States, then, is one of interaction over time between movements, elites and the public.

Another approach to civil rights politics examines how the American state implemented civil rights regulations once on the books, as well as their successes and failures. The issues explored vary from the impacts of the policies on equality and race relations (e.g., Reskin 1998) and the impacts of policies on organizations (Edelman 1992; Dobbin 2009) to the role of the new inequality-ameliorating policies (as opposed to racist policies designed for domination) in creating and defining racial categories. In these studies, there may be complex policy feedback effects where policies define the groups in question and these group-defining effects shape the later politics of policy development.

This is most apparent in the politics of affirmative action in the United States. Despite strong resistance to policies that targeted African Americans, and a hard-fought battle to force passage of even the 'colour-blind', classically liberal Civil Rights Act of 1964, by the early 1970s, the US state had created a panoply of affirmative action regulations to ensure equal opportunities (Graham 1990; Skrentny 1996; Pedriana and Stryker 1997, 2004; Sugrue 2008). Affirmative action created the political and legal category of 'minority' and targeted African Americans, Latinos, Asian Americans and American Indians for opportunities in employment and, through the power of targeted procurement and loans and technical aid, business development (Skrentny 2002, 2006). These policies were expansive, and included groups, such as Asian Americans, that had not been prominent movement actors or insider lobbyists though they themselves have experienced often brutal discrimination in the past. Yet there were limits as well. Mostly Catholic white ethnic groups as well as Jewish Americans lobbied for inclusion in the regulations but were denied. Similarly, the Small Business Administration denied Iranian and Afghan Americans access to special programmes and benefits (La Noue and Sullivan 2001). US administrators, supported by courts, moved to race-conscious civil rights regulations in other areas as well, including desegregation of schools and drawing voting lines to increase the chances of minorities being elected (Graham 1990). The move to race-conscious regulations failed for housing regulations, however, in part due to the placement of civil rights authority in a housing bureaucracy that had conflicting goals – race-consciousness did not extend to laws prohibiting discrimination in housing (Bonastia 2006).

Race categorization in civil rights law can, once established, impact race and ethnic politics. As already noted, groups that civil rights administrators excluded mobilized into action, but the categorizations also affected the politics of groups who *were* included. In a classic example of a policy feedback, Padilla (1985) shows how affirmative action categories affected Latino politics. The various Latino subgroups, especially Mexican Americans, Puerto Ricans and Cuban Americans, traditionally organized (like Asian and American Indian subgroups) around nation or tribe. By examining city politics in Chicago, Padilla shows how Mexican Americans and Puerto Ricans were able to unite and fight in their common struggle against discrimination when affirmative action policies helped focus their interests on a common policy goal.

The other major area of racial inequality amelioration, outside of civil rights regulations, where states draw racial lines through policy and law is in the census. Scholars and activists have sometimes exaggerated the importance of the census as an independent variable in racial politics in the United States, especially since the advent of racial categories for civil rights law. Census counts do play a role in some aspects of discrimination law, however, and being counted and having federal statistics that dramatize inequality can be a important resource for disadvantaged racial and ethnic groups in American politics since the civil rights era (Skerry 2000).

Nevertheless, most studies explore the census politics that create the racial categories and the fight to be counted accurately in order to ameliorate racial inequality. Nobles (2000) offers a comparative study of census race categories in the United States and Brazil, revealing how census bureaux make race a political reality, and showing how race categories are the outcomes of political struggles or domination rather than objective realities or defined by science. Williams (2008) shows the limits of state racial categorizations to define the thinking about race as discrete categories as she examines the pressure groups and politics behind the decision to give the 'mark one or more' race option for mixed-race Americans on the 2000 census.

Also, a substantial literature on race politics does not examine the development of inequality-ameliorating civil rights regulations but instead examines how social welfare policies, ostensibly to promote equality for all, in fact had significant racial effects, often to enhance the privilege of whites. Whether or not these policies were shaped with racial considerations in mind is disputed. There is a debate, for example, on whether or not we can best understand the shape of welfare policy in the United States by interpreting the founding policy decisions through a racial lens – did Social Security disfavour occupations (such as agricultural labour) that were dominated by African Americans for racist reasons (Lieberman 1998), or were these occupations disfavoured for other reasons, as revealed through comparative analysis (Davies and Derthick 1997)? The clearest statement for the view that universalist policy had profound racial effects may be Katznelson's provocatively titled *When Affirmative Action Was White* (2005), which shows how policies such as the GI Bill, ostensibly benefiting all veterans, in fact concentrated its considerable positive impacts on white men.

Another approach to understanding how race matters in the amelioration of racial inequality explores how race factors into democratic politics. Unlike states with parliamentary systems, non-white candidates have to win office, or non-white voters have to win influence with white candidates, in winner-take-all elections. There is large literature in the United States on how race, among other factors, affects or is correlated with liberal or conservative attitudes on non-racial issues (Tate 2010), willingness to vote for white and black candidates (Reeves 1997), the behaviour of elected officials (often called 'descriptive representation'; Tate 2004) and how the race of elected officials affects the views and behaviours of voters (Bobo and Gilliam 1990; Hajnal 2006). Frymer (1999) challenged conventional thinking about party politics in the United States, which had given little attention to the ways that race affected party strategy and coalition building. He showed how Republicans cede the black vote to Democrats and Democrats fear that attending to black interests will drive away white voters, rendering blacks a 'captured minority', for whom the party system does not allow a voice on a par with that of other interests.

A particularly vibrant area in the study of racial inequality and democratic politics is the study of public opinion towards racial groups and racial issues. The goal here is to discern patterns in attitudes towards race and/or the interaction of racial attitudes with policy preferences to understand the dynamics of attitudes, racial orders and policy development. In some of these studies, there is an assumption that at least to some extent public attitudes drive voter behaviour and then policy. According to 'symbolic racism' theory, white Americans view black Americans to be lacking in traditional values such as work ethic, individual responsibility and the ability to defer gratification. These attitudes – or more precisely, these meanings that many whites perceive in blacks – are correlated with opposition to policies to benefit blacks (Kinder and Sanders 1996). In Bobo's (2001) and Bobo and Tuan's (2006) view, the driving force behind white opposition to policies to benefit blacks is not a liberal ideology but perceived threat to white status, which he bases on Blumer's (1958) 'group position' theory of prejudice. In Bobo's approach, racial orders and racial hierarchy helps us to understand attitudes towards public policies that maintain that order.

There is also evidence that policies drive attitudes rather than the other way around. Sniderman and Piazza (1993) and Sniderman and Carmines (1997) argue that white opposition to policies such as affirmative action is due to conservative principles, rather than racial animus. But one of Sniderman and Piazza's more striking findings is the result of a 'mere mention' experimental research design. That is, Sniderman and Piazza gave one group of respondents a survey that asked for attitudes regarding whether or not African Americans were lazy and irresponsible. They gave to another group surveys that asked for views towards policies giving racial preferences to blacks in government jobs before asking about African American work ethic. Results showed that asking about racial preference policies led to a greater percentage (43% from 26%) of whites indicating that they believed African Americans to be lazy and irresponsible. Taken together, these studies indicate a complex feedback loop between racial orders, racial prejudice and public policies.

Conclusion

Though spread around the world by Western colonization and imperialism, there is ample evidence that many non-Western states already had (and continue to have) racial and ethnic politics, and that both have existed for a very long time. It is the form that changes, and scholars of race, ethnicity and nationalism are showing in new ways how these related concepts of peoplehood order politics. The trend in the past several decades is for states to develop policies to work against the patterns of racial domination and inequality that are so prevalent. Research from the United States indicates a preference for a regulatory approach and little aversion to using racial categories to promote equality rather than to maintain domination. Yet this approach's reliance on explicit racial categorization is frequently under attack, and it not clear if the United States will maintain it. There is also a large and growing body of research on a crucial question for twenty-first-century racial politics: how developed states may address their increasing racial diversity as immigration brings new workers and their families and mitigates demographic decline. The current US approach may appeal to other societies as a middle course that encourages integration and recognizes difference without promoting separatism. The universalist, colour-blind policies of France provide an important counter-model. Comparisons assessing the causes and impacts of the world's various policies to ameliorate racial inequality will be an especially vibrant area of research in the coming decades.

Further Reading

Bleich, E. 2003: *Race Politics in Britain and France: Ideas and Policymaking since the 1960's.* New York: Cambridge University Press.

Dikötter, F. 1994: *Discourse of Race in Modern China.* Stanford, CA: Stanford University Press.

Glenn, E.N. 2002: *Unequal Freedom: How Race and Gender Shaped American Citizenship and Labor.* Cambridge, MA: Harvard University Press.

Nobles, M. 2000: *Shades of Citizenship: Race and the Census in Modern Politics.* Stanford, CA: Stanford University Press.

Skrentny, J.D. 2002: *The Minority Rights Revolution.* Cambridge, MA: Belknap Press of Harvard University Press.

29

Nationalism

Its Role and Significance in a Globalized World

JOHN SCHWARZMANTEL

The study of nationalism and the debate about its significance in an increasingly globalized world remain key areas of controversy in political sociology and social science in general. One important starting point for understanding the role of nationalism remains Ernest Gellner's modernist analysis, though this has been criticized by those who emphasize the pre-modern origins of nations. Those who see the processes of globalization as eroding the centrality of the nation-state and who criticize what is called 'methodological nationalism' are challenged by theorists who deny that such processes establish the irrelevance of the nation-state or the superiority of cosmopolitanism as a political goal. Nationalism remains highly significant in the contemporary world, taking in many cases violent forms but also deployed as an effective discourse of protest and self-determination in opposition to homogenizing globalization. In contrast to its earlier historical role in forging larger units of political and social solidarity, nationalism in the contemporary world is a more fragmentary and fissiparous force. Civic forms of nationalism face serious challenges in contemporary societies of multicultural diversity but still provide important sources of democratic solidarity.

Nationalism in a Globalized World

The analysis of nationalism continues to be a growth area in the social sciences. This may seem paradoxical in an ever more globalized and cosmopolitan world, in which advanced technologies of communication and constant world news typify the compression of space and time that are hallmarks of globalization. Some theorists, like Eric Hobsbawm, see the ongoing scholarly concern with nationalism as a case of the 'owl of

The Wiley-Blackwell Companion to Political Sociology, First Edition. Edited by Edwin Amenta, Kate Nash, and Alan Scott.
© 2012 Blackwell Publishing Ltd. Published 2012 by Blackwell Publishing Ltd.

Minerva' phenomenon, in which scientific understanding of some aspect of social and political life is only possible when the object of study loses its significance; only then does it become possible to study it in an objective and disinterested fashion (Hobsbawm 1990: 183). Yet this seems a contestable judgement in the light of the undoubted and continuing capacity of nationalism to move people to political action, for good or ill. Many theorists speak of a crisis of the nation-state and focus on the divorce between effective power, exercised by global economic forces, and the limited capacity of the nation-state to control that power. Nevertheless, nationalism continues to have significant effects, and in a globalized world the appeal of national identity, often defined in ethnic or cultural terms, is still powerful. It resonates as a possible refuge against the way in which globalization threatens to sweep away markers of identity that give people a sense of their distinctiveness in an increasingly homogeneous world. Such national identity is often purchased through a visceral hostility to some 'Other' or outsider group seen as threatening the purity of national identity and also competing for the welfare that citizens of wealthier nations have so far enjoyed. Thus in many cases nationalism seems inherently connected with violence and inter-communal conflict. Recent discussion has focused on what Michael Mann calls the 'dark side of democracy' where 'ethnos' does not coincide with 'demos' (Mann 2005). In such situations, ethnic groups wish to make the state a vehicle for the power of their particular ethnic or cultural membership. This means the marginalization or in many cases victimization of members of other ethnic groups who inhabit the same territory or who are members of the same state. This then raises the question of whether nationalism can take more 'civic' or inclusive forms which bring citizens together in a democratic unit irrespective of their ethnic identity, or whether nationalism is always fated to regress to a more ethnic form with increasingly exclusive and xenophobic aspects.

The ongoing scholarly debate testifies to the problematic and multifaceted nature of nationalism and to its continuing capacity to move people to action. It further raises larger questions of the role of national identity in a more cosmopolitan world. The first task must be to define the nature of nationalism and its role in contemporary politics, before analysing the problem-areas of the discussion. Is nationalism a force of diminishing significance in the contemporary world, and how does it relate to ideas of cosmopolitanism and broader concepts of global civil society? Does nationalism inevitably lead to violence, or is this only true of its more extreme ethnically based forms? Does the nation-state still have a significant role to play in a globalized world, or are we inexorably moving to what Jürgen Habermas has called a 'post-national society' (Habermas 2001) in which global identities and new political institutions are emerging to play the role which the nation-state formerly carried out in the era of modernity?

Defining and Analyzing Nationalism

The debate continues between those so-called 'primordialists' who see the nation as a unit existing in some form long before the onset of modernity, and those 'modernists' for whom the nation is a modern creation, dependent on technologically advanced means of mass communication (Ozkirimli 2010: chs 3 and 4; see also Chapter 24 this volume). These means of communication give rise to a literate population where 'the nation' is not limited to an elite group but includes the broad masses of the people. Many scholars accept the classic analysis of Ernest Gellner that defines nationalism as a movement that seeks to link the cultural unit of the nation with the political unit of the state (Gellner 2006). Gellner's approach sought to differentiate the varying conditions under which this 'marriage' of state and nation took place. He argued that the significance of such a link of nation and state varied in time and place. In the classic nation-state of Western Europe a population with a relatively high degree of cultural homogeneity was ruled over by an effective and unified state apparatus, and therefore the union of state and nation was rather an unproblematic affair. This was contrasted by Gellner with two other types of situation. The first was represented by the nationalisms of Italy and Germany where a high degree of mass literacy and cultural homogeneity existed but what was needed was a unified state to provide a political 'roof' for the cultural or linguistic nation. By contrast, in what Gellner called 'Hapsburg and points East' forms of nationalism, neither a culturally unified population nor an independent and effective state apparatus existed. In such circumstances nationalism as a political and cultural movement had a more difficult task, a higher mountain to climb, involving both the creation of a mass modern culture as well as a state to protect and develop it. This explained the propensity of such forms of nationalism to depart from liberal values and to assume more extreme forms.

Gellner saw nationalism as the means through which societies made the transition from pre-modern agrarian society to its modern industrial form. Nationalist movements aimed at the creation of a common high culture, which Gellner labelled as a 'cultivated or garden culture' contrasted with the 'wild varieties' of localized and differentiated vernacular cultures (Gellner 2006: 48–51). Nationalist 'awakeners' sought to achieve mass literacy and education in order to diffuse awareness of a shared culture. Yet, according to Gellner, such a common education in which people of a given territory could, literally and metaphorically, speak the same language was a necessary condition for industrial society in which individuals would need to be mobile, changing locality and shifting jobs. This contrasted with pre-industrial or agrarian society where the dominant groups did not share the same culture as those over whom they ruled. In such an agrarian society there was no need for a common high culture, and nationalism was neither possible nor necessary. In such a 'modernist' analysis, nationalism accompanies and fosters the transition to industrial society, almost in a functionalist mode: nationalism brings into being the common culture needed for industrial society, and aims to give that culture the political protection of a unified state apparatus which in turn can develop further the educational system of the nation-state and instil ideas of common citizenship and national solidarity.

The impression should not be given that Gellner's view of nationalism set the terms for an unquestioned modernist paradigm for the interpretation of nationalism and its significance. His perspective has been criticized from a number of points of view. Theorists like Anthony Smith propose that nations are much older than the modernist paradigm suggests (Smith 2004; Roshwald 2006). They argue that in order to comprehend the hold of nationalism in the modern world we have to understand the ethnic origins of nations and reject the view of the nation as an essentially modern construction. To these criticisms are added others that take issue with the view (held by Gellner and other modernists like Hobsbawm) that nationalism was originally and classically exemplified by nation-states like those of England and France. Tom Nairn's influential analysis of 'the modern Janus' sees nationalism as typified by German nationalism in the late nineteenth century (Nairn 1981: ch. 9). This was a movement of 'periphery' against 'core', a movement that wanted to modernize Germany and catch up with the already unified nation-states of Western Europe. For Nairn, nationalism is like the two-faced Roman god Janus, looking forward to modernity but at the same time harking backward to national traditions, possibly invented ones, which were used to 'invite the masses in to history' by appealing to a sense of community and folk tradition in a popular, indeed populist, way. Nairn's analysis remains suggestive because it points to the emotional use of myths and symbols in nationalist movements, thus departing from Gellner's possibly over-rational dissection of nationalism and underestimation of its ideology. This line of critique is shared by those who place themselves in the 'ethno-symbolist' school (Smith 1998: ch. 8). Such critics emphasize the symbolic and emotive elements in nationalism, which, they claim, have far deeper ethnic and historical roots than can be explained by modernist theorists.

A further strength of Nairn's analysis is that it points to the ways in which nationalism can slide into extreme forms, as in the cases of Nazi and fascist varieties of nationalism. The desire to catch up with more 'advanced' areas is often combined with feelings of hostility and '*ressentiment*' against those more advanced areas, as analysed by Liah Greenfeld in her study of nationalism opening up 'roads to modernity' (Greenfeld 1992). Nairn shows how nationalism can combine such feelings of resentment with the power of a modern state apparatus in a highly explosive combination, as witnessed by German Nazism and fascism in general: 'Seen in sufficient historical depth, fascism tells us more about nationalism than any other historic episode' (Nairn 1981: 347). His theory thus illuminates the 'dark side' of nationalism, its capacity to mobilize popular feeling against rival nations and against those perceived as the 'Other' in ways which supplement the more benign perspectives on nationalism held out by Gellner and Hobsbawm. The interpretations of nationalism by the latter theorists imply that once the movement to industrial society has been achieved on a global scale, nationalism will be a force of declining significance and no longer constitute, as Hobsbawm puts it, 'a global political programme as it may be said to have been in the nineteenth and earlier twentieth centuries' (Hobsbawm 1990: 181). However, not only the significance of fascist and populist styles of nationalism but also the ongoing explosions of ethnic and national tensions throughout the contemporary world suggest that the fire of nationalist passion is far from dying out. The aim therefore must be to suggest how the debate on nationalism in academic analysis, mirroring real-life politics, has moved on from the confrontation between primordialists and modernists, important though that still is, and to show what are the current contested issues in the field of nationalist studies.

Nationalism and Cosmopolitanism

The debate has developed from one between 'primordialists' and 'modernists' to one over the significance of nationalism in a seemingly more globalized and cosmopolitan world, though there are several sets of issues that cannot fit in easily to a simple line-up of 'nationalists' versus 'globalists'. Those who highlight the crisis of the nation-state suggest that the marriage between nation and state central to Gellner's analysis, and to that of modernist perspectives in general, is now in terminal dissolution. This is so for several reasons. In the first place, there has been a divorce between politics and power: the former remains in the framework of the nation-state and its institutions while effective power has moved to the supranational sphere, exercised by corporations and a global elite, notably in the field of economic decisions. The nation-state on this analysis is in a weakened position and less able than it used to be to provide its members with control over the economy and with the package of benefits derived from membership of the national 'community of citizens' (Schnapper 1994). This is part of the argument put forward by Habermas in his discussion of what he calls 'the post-national constellation' (Habermas 2001). While in the era of modernity the nation-state was able to achieve a '*Schliessung*' or closure in the sense of democratic control of economic forces, this is no longer possible in a globalized world. The search must therefore be for another type of 'closure' which could only take the form of institutions of a supranational or perhaps 'post-national' kind, even if such institutions exist at the moment in embryonic form or not at all.

Those who hold such a post-national perspective accept that the nation-state was a success story in the period opened up by the American and French Revolutions. It provided the framework for the capture of democratic rights by the mass of the people. Beyond that, it was able to foster a common culture, political rather than ethnic, through a state-sponsored and state-controlled educational system. Equally importantly, the nation-state was able to create a unified internal market and to compete internationally with other states to offer its citizens a degree of economic welfare. As the demands of the masses increased, the nation-state turned into a welfare state offering not only political rights but also integration into a community of citizens in which guarantees were provided for economic security and a modest degree of redistribution of wealth. In this respect then, the nation-state and the civic nationalism that went with it were very successful in creating a national community, politically unified and culturally relatively homogeneous, in which political citizenship had developed into social citizenship, following the celebrated formulation of T.H. Marshall (Marshall 1950).

Those who follow what can be broadly called a 'post-national' line of thought accept that this was the historical record of civic nationalism and the inclusive nation-state. However, they point to two aspects in which this is now in crisis. The first is the one just discussed, in which economic power has evaded the grasp of the nation-state, leading to the separation of power from politics. The second relates to issues of cultural homogeneity and the cultural basis of the nation-state, also analysed in Habermas's concept of post-national society. Without creating a mythical picture of a golden age of the nation-state, it is true that the nation-state rested on a relatively homogeneous common culture. This involved shared symbols of national identity and a widely accepted common 'narrative' of national history, even if such a history contained elements of myth, invention and fabrication that sometimes bore a slender relation to historical reality. Ernest Renan argued in his famous lecture of 1882, '*Qu'est-ce qu'une nation?*' (Hutchinson and Smith 1994), that national histories often depended on forgetting infamous incidents as well as glorifying heroic moments in a nation's history. However, the debate in present-day social science focuses on issues of multiculturalism and the changing character of national culture. Adherents of the post-national persuasion suggest that the nation can no longer be realistically seen as the community of those sharing a common culture and accepting the same narrative of national history, since this is no longer appropriate to a much more diversified citizen body of varied ethnic origin and character. Whereas the classic nation-state relied on common traditions, enforced and inculcated by the state and its education system, this is no longer possible in societies marked by immigration and diverse cultural and ethnic loyalties. In Habermas's terminology, the idea of a *Volksnation*, a community of descent marked by a common ethnically based culture inherited by all its members through the mere fact of being born into that community, is no longer a viable basis for the contemporary nation-state. Not only is it implausible because the citizens of the nation do not share common descent or culture in an age of mass migration and globalization, but in the light of Nazi and fascist forms of the *Volksnation* such a conceptualization of the nation should be avoided, even if it were more feasible in contemporary conditions (Habermas 1996). Attempts to develop a wider European loyalty could be seen as suggestive of wider post-national affiliations replacing or at least supplementing those of the nation-state.

In the light of these post-nationalist arguments, the contemporary debate evokes two contrasting responses. One takes the path of cosmopolitan democracy, the other of a qualified defence of a form of civic nationalism. The former is exemplified by those like Daniele Archibugi who articulate the idea of a 'global commonwealth of citizens' (Archibugi 2008). This perspective suggests that the nation-state cannot be the framework for democratic politics and that new institutions need to be developed which create forms of solidarity that the nation-state used to provide, but which it can no longer effectively do. One of the most influential recent statements of cosmopolitanism comes from David Held, who takes his inspiration from Kant in his insistence on the need for 'cosmopolitan democratic law' to guarantee citizenship rights within frameworks of international law (Held 1995b: ch. 10). In rather different, though not incompatible vein, some forms of cosmopolitanism link up with a positive view of the alternative globalization movement as the agents and articulators of this new vision of politics, with some commentators seeing in this movement a form of 'cosmopolitanism from below' (Kurasawa 2004), distinct not only in its aims but in its means as well. The aim would be one of a global commonwealth of citizens realizing in a new form older socialist ideas of internationalism and solidarity. The means or agencies are new forms of 'transnational activism' in which activists based in their local or national communities interact with each other in a global movement that can develop a new global solidarity (Tarrow 2005). In various ways, therefore, these perspectives deploy an ethical idea of cosmopolitanism to criticize what are seen as the outmoded and narrow limits of nationalism and seek to develop categories seen as more appropriate to a critical view of a globalized world.

It is necessary here to make a distinction between *globalization* and *cosmopolitanism* as rivals to nationalism and to the nation-state. The former refers to flows of economic power and market forces that operate across and beyond the nation-state. Cosmopolitanism, on the other hand, refers to an ethical and moral stance that refuses the idea of giving preference to fellow nationals. It is based on a universalist perspective, highlighting the idea of fundamental human rights held by individuals everywhere and giving priority to the safeguarding and guarantee of such rights wherever and whenever they are infringed. The cosmopolitan vision, as Beck calls it

(Beck 2006), rejects what he and other theorists label as 'methodological nationalism', by which he means the assumption that the nation-state represents the 'normal' framework both of political activity in the real world and of academic analysis of politics. The critique of 'methodological nationalism' is intended to provide a different conceptual framework for the analysis of politics and social movements. This would cease to accept the primacy of nationalism and the nation-state, even if the latter has, since the seventeenth century, been a crucial unit of world politics in the Westphalian model of international relations. Krishan Kumar draws attention to the fact that while 'as ideological formations, nations and nationalism may well have occupied centre-stage in the modern world order', they shared this place with empires whose legacy of multiculturalism and diasporas has profoundly marked present-day nations and the problems they face today (Kumar 2010: 139). This suggests that a simple antithesis between, on the one hand, the period of modernity seen as one of nation-state predominance and, on the other, a post-modern period of cosmopolitanism is too crude an antithesis, and one into which some critics of 'methodological nationalism' are themselves prone to fall (Chernilo 2006).

In opposition to these cosmopolitan perspectives are those articulated in equally diverse ways by those theorists who defend the value of forms of civic nationalism. Those who fall into this category do not deny the transformations that come under the general heading of globalization. Nor do they deny the significance or value of cosmopolitan affiliations which link people and movements across national borders. This debate therefore is not one that opposes in a simplistic fashion 'nationalists' against 'cosmopolitans'. In the words of Craig Calhoun, 'cosmopolitanism and nationalism are mutually constitutive and to oppose them too sharply is misleading' (Calhoun 2007: 13). Theorists like David Miller and Craig Calhoun insist that the nation-state remains important in ways that are ignored by the above-mentioned critics of nationalism and of so-called 'methodological nationalism'. David Miller argues that the nation and national identity bring with them a sense of reciprocity and mutual support which are necessary bases for a democratic society, especially one in which a welfare state serves to iron out some of the inequalities inseparable from market society (Miller 2000). In similar vein Craig Calhoun maintains that nations remain significant because 'nationalism is a reminder that democracy depends on solidarity' and 'nationalism offers both a mode of access to global affairs and a mode of resistance to aspects of globalization' (Calhoun 2007: 166).

On this view, nationalism remains relevant in an age of globalization because it can provide resources for democratic solidarity that resist the homogenizing effects of globalization in its neoliberal form. Calhoun maintains that the nation can be an integrating institution even if, as he concedes, such integration has sometimes taken repressive forms in which minority cultures have been subordinated. However, a national public culture can develop by achieving solidarity through a dialogue between different groups, integrating them into a national public culture: 'national arenas for public culture are important and may achieve solidarity amid contest and diversity' (Calhoun 2007: 162). This is clearly a more positive view of nationalism, seen as taking civic and political forms that demarcate it from the exclusivist ethnic types of nationalism that are hardly compatible with the aspiration towards democratic equality. Such perspectives on nationalism indicate the need for a form of solidarity which nationalism can provide, recognizing distinct national cultures and particular shared histories that are far from being eroded in an age of globalization. Civic nationalism thus gives expression to universal values and to basic human rights, but validates and enforces those rights within a particular territory and with reference to distinct national histories, thus bridging the gap between an abstract universalism and national specificity.

The significance of these critics of cosmopolitanism is that they modify or decon-struct the opposition between nationalism and cosmopolitanism. While a commitment to defence of human rights everywhere is a strong ethical stance, it does not rule out more localized commitments at the level of the nation-state which can be based on national symbols and a shared history, both of which may be better able to motivate citizens than more abstract and universal ideas of cosmopolitanism. While Habermas has been cited above in connection with his ideas of 'the post-national constellation', he can also appear here in a rather different context. Habermas's idea of 'constitutional patriotism' (*Verfassungspatriotismus*) is a version of the civic nationalism concept in which members of the nation are united not by descent or shared ethnicity, but by adherence to democratic values and constitutional norms (Habermas 1996). Current discussion of the value of such 'constitutional patriotism' focuses on whether these values are in themselves too abstract to unite citizens in the community of the nation, and whether they need a supplement of ideas of a particular history to give more emotional force to the perhaps too rationalistic perspective of a purely civic nation-alism (Canovan 2000). Proponents of civic nationalism have to meet the charge that the civic values that they invoke could equally well form the basis for a cosmopolitan perspective of universal human rights. In this way civic nationalism shades off into the post-national perspectives described earlier, and this indeed seems to be the trajectory taken by Habermas's own thought in this area.

Nationalism, Violence and Fragmentation

The arguments analysed above pitted globalists and cosmopolitans on one side against proponents of civic and democratic forms of nationalism on the other. Recent work in the politics and sociology of nationalism has also focused on the tendency of nationalism to take extreme forms when one ethnic group uses the state as the weapon to enforce its supremacy against other ethnic or cultural groups living on the same territory. This has been exemplified by the cases of 'ethnic cleansing' in former Yugoslavia or the inter-communal violence in Rwanda. Nationalism can erupt in violence when particular national or cultural groups perceive a mismatch between their desire for recognition and their demand for at least some degree of self-rule or autonomy, on the one hand, and on the other their membership of a state which does not concede such recognition and autonomy in sufficient degree. When political groups can claim with a degree of plausibility that their national identity is not recognized by the state of which they are part, and when they argue that such a state is dominated by those of another (majority) ethnic group, this is a recipe for violence.

It seems clear that the post-nationalist or cosmopolitan perspective fails to come to terms with the continuing desire of national groups to achieve the twin goals of cultural recognition and some degree of political self-rule or autonomy. When the road to achieve those ends is blocked, often by the dominance of a majority or rival ethnic group, nationalism explodes in violence and is associated with many of the most intractable conflicts in the contemporary world. Academic analysis of these problems mirrors political realities, and focuses on ways in which nationalist demands can be met, or at least 'steered' into paths of peaceful non-violent political debate. In the context of the European Union (EU), it is possible to argue that the emergence of a new supranational European loyalty could create a 'Europe of the regions', in which regional loyalties and inter-regional cooperation (say between industrially developed regions like Catalonia and the North of Italy) replace the centralizing grip of the nation-state. This would be a perspective in which the nation-state is transcended by supranational loyalty from above (a European identity) and by regional loyalties from below. However, it has not escaped notice that so far the attempt to develop a European identity beyond the level of elites has had only limited success, perhaps not surprisingly because of the greater reserves of common history and institutional penetration still held by the nation-state.

The spread of globalization does not therefore seem to have sounded the death-knell of nationalism. Nationalism can take regressive and populist or even xenophobic forms appealing to those who are rendered insecure by the development of global-ization. This accounts for the nationalism of radical-right groups, typified by the French *Front National* or the British BNP, who propose a mythical view of an ethnically pure nation and seek to channel social discontent into hostility to the immigrant or foreign worker. Contrasted with this is the nationalism of national groups and parties like those in Scotland (Scottish National Party) and in Catalonia, representing 'nations against the state' (Keating 2001). Such forms of nationalism seek to renegotiate the terms of membership of the minority nationalism in the wider multinational state, with secession as either the ultimate threat or bargaining tool, or in more moderate form such nationalist movements demand a greater degree of autonomy and devolution of power. This issue has a wider significance since it applies to a whole range of nations (Britain, France, Spain) which developed the idea of an imperial mission and thus exemplified what Kumar calls 'imperial nationalism' (Kumar 2006). Such nations have to find new bases of solidarity in a post-imperial and multicultural society. The 'nations within the nation' such the Scots and the Catalans question the value of their membership of the wider nation of which historically they were part, whether willingly or reluctantly. Nationalism in the contemporary world thus has a definitely fragmenting impetus, contrasted with nationalism in its nineteenth-century heyday when its dynamic was oriented towards the creation of larger units. In the present situation nationalism seems to have taken on increasingly fissiparous forms, where particular cultural or national groups demand a degree of self-rule. This may impose strains on the idea of a multicultural or civic form of nationalism, though movements like the Scottish National Party deny that they represent any form of closed or ethnic nationalism.

On a more global scale, nationalism remains powerful as a discourse of politics that taps in to wider themes of self-determination, defence of particular cultures, and resistance to the all-pervasive spread of globalization that threatens to annihilate the distinctiveness of national cultures and identities. Such themes are given more resonance in a context of attempts, as in Afghanistan and Iraq, to spread democracy worldwide and to impose a particular model of democracy. Nationalism can function here in terms of a rhetoric of resistance to such attempts and a protest against a homogenizing process of globalization. It has preserved its power to mobilize people in the name of self-determination against newer and more informal kinds of imperialism or superpower domination.

Conclusion: Nationalism, Dying or Resurgent?

The key issue of contemporary analysis is not the question of whether nationalism is dead, since it clearly survives. Indeed the paradox of nationalism is that as a phenomenon it is itself global since there seem to be few, if any, parts of the world from which a sense of national identity is absent. The focus of contemporary discussion is the question of whether the nation-state and its hitherto dominant role in political life are being challenged by new identities both beyond and within the nation-state. Culture is increasingly global and hybrid in an age of CNN, MTV and other global and deregulated media, so that the idea of a cohesive and distinctive national culture is much less appealing. The economy has long ceased to function within the bounds of the nation, and as for citizenship, within the EU political and legal rights are increasingly dependent on the supranational framework of the EU. Within and below the nation-state, the rise of ethnic and sub-state cultural identities suggests that the old civic nationalist aspiration to tie people in to a common national and civic identity is in many cases more difficult in a more multicultural and diverse world. Civic nationalism still remains significant, as shown by the survival of ideas of solidarity based on shared political rights within a particular national territory, whether that is with reference to France, the United States or nations like Canada or Australia. These all preserve a sense of national identity that spans the ethnic divisions of a culturally diverse society. Yet such civic nationalism has to be sustained under conditions of greater diversity and arguably in situations where there is greater reluctance to assimilate a common culture and accept its integrating symbols in an unproblematic way.

By way of conclusion it may be said that it is premature to write the obituary of either nationalism or the nation-state. The nation-state still offers a framework of institutions and cultural identity that has powerful reserves of shared history and solidarity behind it. Ideas of cosmopolitanism remain rather abstract and lacking in institutional realization. While nationalism remains a threat to democratic community if the nation is defined in ethnic terms, some form of civic nationalism still has much to offer as a force for integrating citizens into shared democratic procedures and sentiments of reciprocity and mutual support. The democratic nation-state may need to be conceptualized in new ways as a state in which different cultural and ethnic groups find recognition and respect. However, even in such a multicultural democracy a form of civic nationalism would still be needed as a powerful force for some kind of broader democratic solidarity. Attempts to ignore or suppress national cultural identity can only lead to violence, and this is one of the challenges to the contemporary liberal-democratic state. The problem of liberal democracy is to allow for the recognition of different cultural and national identities while at the same time seeking to achieve some overarching political community which prevents citizens from remaining 'sealed off' in particular limited cultural groups. Civic nationalism still has a role to play in this context. Moreover, the connection of nationalism and themes of self-determination is still a powerful one, so that the discourse of nationalism preserves an appeal, even – or perhaps especially – in a globalizing world. Political sociology and social science in general still have much to do to assess the role of nationalism throughout past history and, equally importantly, explain its survival in a more cosmopolitan world.

Further Reading

Calhoun, C. 2007: *Nations Matter. Culture, History, and the Cosmopolitan Dream*. London: Routledge.

Gellner, E. 2006: *Nations and Nationalism*, 2nd edn, introduction by John Breuilly. Oxford: Blackwell.

Harris, E. 2009: *Nationalism. Theories and Cases*. Edinburgh: Edinburgh University Press.

Ozkirimli, U. 2010: *Theories of Nationalism. A Critical Introduction*, 2nd edn. Basingstoke: Palgrave Macmillan.

30

Religion and Political Sociology

Valérie Amiraux

Public conversations on religion-related subjects are taking place everywhere and mostly in a sensational register, feeding a global political anxiety. Religion has also made a comeback in social sciences as an incontrovertible part of social life. This chapter provides the coordinates for a better mapping of religion, alongside the classical tradition in political sociology, considered as a legitimate and unavoidable object of study for the discipline. These coordinates must include social forms and experiences, issues of power and control within and over religious organizations, the link between religion and politics and the development of individual religious behaviours in social contexts, and it should also favour a comparative perspective. This chapter explores first the issue of the definition of religion as an epistemological challenge for political sociology before moving on to review and contrast North American and European scholarship on religious developments in modern societies.

I've spent a lot of time over the past months thinking about what happened to McCann and me last winter in Sophis: asking myself what it was the Truth Seekers did to us there, and how. Could any group of rural religious cranks really have driven a well-known sociologist out of his mind, and his assistant almost out of the profession?

(Alison Lurie, *Imaginary Friends* (1967: 3))

Liberation theology, headscarf, burqas, Danish cartoons, the war on terror... and 9/11, but also the Moonies, the Iranian Revolution, and a variety of issues from comic strip controversies to family law questions ('sharia courts'), blasphemy, the Rushdie affair, polygamy, new religious movements, sectarian mortifère movements, public discussions on abortion, euthanasia or cloning, the role of religious groups and

The Wiley-Blackwell Companion to Political Sociology, First Edition. Edited by Edwin Amenta, Kate Nash, and Alan Scott.
© 2012 Blackwell Publishing Ltd. Published 2012 by Blackwell Publishing Ltd.

churches in the Eastern and Central European democratization process; worldwide, religion has become contentious in relation to the expression of specific forms of religiosity. The hypothesis of an irremediable decline of religion in secular public spaces has in particular been counterbalanced during the 1980s, against the expectations driven by the secularization thesis. Since the early 1990s, European secular public spaces have for instance taken a radical turn in dealing with the growing visibility of Muslims, and have become intolerant towards Muslim forms of religiosity, increasingly regarding them as cultural, social and political pathologies (Amiraux 2011).

The position religion occupies in the analytical vocabulary of political sociology is a complicated one, to say the least. Sociology initially emerged as a science of modernity pointing throughout the nineteenth and twentieth centuries to a 'crisis scenario' (Pollack 2008) predicated on the decrease of religion's social significance. It looked at the birth of rationality in the modern secular state and tried to understand the nature of the social bond in these emerging modern societies (urbanized, industrialized, rational and plural). But religion still animates many contemporary societies and political scenes. Since the works of the founding fathers – Weber, Comte, Durkheim, Marx in particular but not only – relations between religion and social togetherness have been a continuous subject for analysis. However, social anxieties relating to this terrain have multiplied, and the attendant political concerns renewed themselves and intensified. Religion's significance, role and value for the social sciences remain therefore a core object for interrogation, ontological, epistemological and methodological: Which definition should prevail? How can political sociology do justice to the intricate and multiple dimensions of religion? What should social scientists look at when seeking an overview of religion in today's world? This series of questions is rendered more difficult to answer within a political sociology perspective by the sheer publicity and politicization that has elevated them, over the past three decades, to the epicentre of public life, front stage on the social scene. Indeed, public conversations on religion-related subjects are taking place everywhere and mostly in a sensational register. It has become part of common knowledge: everyone has something to share on the subject of religion, his/her own and the other's. In the meantime, the interest in religion in the social sciences 'has now returned to a position close to the center of intellectual curiosity about the forces shaping socio-cultural life in the early twenty-first century' (Beckford and Demerath (eds) 2007: 3).

This chapter does not set out to answer these questions, nor to exhaustively survey the extremely rich and varied web of references that crisscross the field of study of religion in political sociology. Our aim is rather to provide the coordinates for a better mapping of religion, alongside the classical tradition that is tackled earlier in this volume, considered as a legitimate and unavoidable object of study for political sociology. These coordinates must include social forms and experiences, issues of power and control within and over religious organizations, the link between religion and politics, the development of individual religious behaviours in social contexts, and the connection between individual identity and one's life course as scrutinized in multiple specific case studies (Beckford and Demerath 2007). This chapter begins by exploring the issue of the definition of religion, before moving on in its second part to review North American and European scholarship on religious developments.

Questions of Definition, Problems of Perspective

When approaching the teaching of religion, it is essential to vary one's material and illustrative examples in order to open up the student's imagination to what constitutes 'the religious'. Every scholar has his/her own trick. Beaman (2008), for instance, usually works with a fictive religious group, the 'Church of the Holy Shoelace' (nothing wrong with an approach that induces immediate sympathy from students), to beckon her students. She then invites them to wonder: Should we stick to what we see? Do religious rites and practices suffice in analysing religion's role either in society or in individual lives? What makes a religion true for its believers? What difference does it make when believers do not practise? How do the devout become members of a community? What meaning does this have for them, and/or the rest of society? Where does religion fit in? Are religious people sincere in believing what they advocate? How does religious practice impact on other social behaviours? The awkward issue of definition may seem too basic, even altogether redundant. But the question does not confine itself to the classroom context, and has posed a challenge to all the disciplines of the social sciences. This epistemological challenge has also become part of the daily routine of judges, lawyers, public officials, doctors and social workers confronted with having to decide whether or not people may have the right to wear a headscarf, file a complaint for religious instead of ethnic discrimination, be granted refugee status, close their shops on certain days, obtain their divorce, etc. Defining religion is no longer exclusively a scholarly duty and a pedagogical exercise, but has become an everyday requirement for many social agents, in particular in the courtroom.

Part of the difficulty of definition relates to religion's diverse modes of expression. Indeed, one of the major shifts between the sociology of the founding fathers and today's discipline is the demise of insular religious dogma. This has come about through an intense religious vitality which has given rise to numerous new movements and forms of spirituality, expressed either individually or collectively and in some cases outside the traditional forms of religious organization (churches, sects). Gone are the days when an entrenched religion could claim an ultimate truth in a politically bound and territorially limited society. Instead we see the emergence of what has been described as a religious market further elaborated upon in terms of globalization (Beyer 2001; Lehmann 2002). Religion has thereby become 'an infinitely varied subject that interacts in a myriad different ways with the cultural, ideological, political and economic systems that surround it' (Davie 2007: 209).

Religion is also about belief and faith, practices and rituals that create a link with the sacred. It is primarily the field of experiencing the sacred but, as Talal Asad puts it, there cannot be a universal definition (2003). Religious manifestations are rich, diversified and multiple. Should one approach them in the first instance as exclusively linked to traditional established places of worship or include the constellation of passions and beliefs that have sprung up everywhere, including a spectrum of beliefs expressed independently from any relation to a deity? This is about individuals as well as communities. Religions are not simply constituted by ideas and opinions, but manifest themselves as a way of life, through the performances required of believers by their convictions. Though invisible for the most part, or to be more precise, having no empirical existence, these beliefs are not fictions. The sacred reality of the believer's praxis can still be described, even when religious motivations, religious experiences and emotions include miracles and apparitions. Last but not least, religion refers to divergent ideas about the right way in which to live (Berger talks about 'structures of plausibility'). However, the terminology deployed (denomination, faith, religious community/society, worship, sect) and the consequent categorization of ways of talking publicly about religion remains stubbornly nationally defined and distinctive to specific nation-states and cultural universes (Robbers 2005).

A final problem in defining religion is establishing its very nature. Can its essence be captured in its external characteristics and manifestations? This definitional problem is complicated by the flourishing multiplicity of ways to live and practise, which is a major outcome of globalization in the field of religious pluralism. The concrete experience of pluralism and diversity forces us to contend with the content of competing messages, but also teaches us how to cope *in concreto* with differences of practice inside one's own preferred rituals. If we cannot sum up the constellation of definitions that as a result flood the domain of the study of religion in the social sciences, we can extract some of the main elements that make it possible to work on it from a political sociology perspective. It is for example useful to distinguish between the practice of religion, that is, the 'religious vitality' that embraces religious observance but also spirituality (belief and practices), and the social significance of the influence that a religion exerts on the other parts of society (Herbert 2003: 5–6).

Two main types of definition have so far been deployed, a functional one and a more substantive one (Droogers 2009: 269). The former has given birth to a literature that largely reduces religion to its institutional definition (a believer is a practitioner), religion being referred to as productive of a social order. In the latter, ethnographic perspectives on lived religion have been more frequently used to make sense of the various ways of carrying out the practice of one's beliefs in one's daily activities (Bender 2003). Another variation on this functional versus substantive definition of religion highlights the tension between belonging (involving a reading of the relationship of an individual member to his or her religious institution: How do religious institutions work? How do they keep their members?) and believing (emphasizing the more internal or intimate part of one's belief). European Values Surveys have for instance helped to document a decline of Christianity in the European Union (EU) since the 1950s that has been labelled as the 'unchurching of Europe' (Ashford and Timms 1992). The decline in Christian membership has tended to confirm the description of Europeans' attitude towards religion as driven by a 'belonging without believing' dynamic (Davie 1994). Here the notion of belonging brings together many important aspects, including the transmission of religious culture to one's children through the extension of a chain of memory (Hervieu-Léger 2000). Clarke considers that this particular moment invites scholars to distance themselves from an institutional approach to religion and move towards a more 'organic concept' (2009). This means jettisoning a perspective exclusive to Christian-Western societies that insists on drawing a limited horizon around the complexity of religious phenomenon, in favour of a global framework that includes other perspectives among the epistemological premises of its analysis (Casanova 1994; Roy 2010). Such a move would also hasten the development of a more cognitive approach to religious belief.

To fully savour the significance of these comments regarding the burden of Christianity as a dominant framework for dealing with religion at large and religious otherness in particular, we turn to Benhabib's useful distinction between *observers* as authors of the narratives and the *social agents*, participants in the culture, who experience traditions, stories, rituals, symbols, tools, etc. not in terms of a narrative account as a compacted whole, but rather as the horizons of life. She elaborates for instance on the Hindu practice of *sati* according to which a widowed wife immolates herself by ascending the burning funeral pyre of her husband. This rather marginal practice to many Hindus came to be regarded as a central Indian tradition when its meaning and status entered into negotiations between British colonials and local Indian elites. Benhabib explains how the colonial administrators were driven by their own moral and civilizational revulsion when confronted with this not religious but merely cultural practice 'considered odious or offensive to human dignity' (2002: 12). They were equally concerned that their outlawing of it could lead to political unrest. If a practice was considered central to believers, some tolerance was to be shown. They investigated the status of *sati* as 'religious practice', looking to find a justification for it in religious scripture. In this they directly followed the Christian model (by analogy between systems of faith). Unable to identify any scriptural evidence, they proceeded nevertheless to codify the practice, '(. . .) and, above all, discrepancies in local Hindu traditions that varied not only from region to region but between the various castes as well were homogenized' (Benhabib 2002: 5–6).

This brings us to a rather convenient definition for all manner of situations. It takes religion as 'a system of beliefs and practices oriented toward the sacred or supernatural, through which the life experience of groups of people are given meaning and direction' (Smith 1996: 5). Belief is of particular importance insofar as it encompasses a wide spectrum of differing worldviews and ways of performing them (Roy 2010). Its cognitive and pragmatic dimensions are priority targets for political sociology looking at religion today.

Scholarship and Religion

Theories, paradigms and types of analysis focusing on religion in the social sciences have never strayed far from the conceptual terrain of secularization and individualization. These two notions are also key to grasping the difference between European and North American ways of working on religion in political sociology.

Secularization: the way out?

Secularization as a European paradigm has been severely taken to task over the past two decades for failing to account for the divergent roles religions may play in societies, but also because, during the 1980s, quite unexpectedly, religion made its comeback at the forefront of various forms of political activity all over the world, either as an object of contestation or as a subject in contestation following a 'deprivatization' movement (Casanova 1994). Within the secularization paradigm, where it is taken for granted that the influence of religion over a society has become less significant, belonging to a religion is assumed to have become a mainly voluntary affair, the possibility of choice even being protected through a set of constitutional fundamental rights (freedom of conscience).

The social impact of secularization, however, is scarcely a uniform matter: think only of the hugely differentiated impact of modernization in Latin American, Japan, South Africa, Western Europe or the Middle East. Thus the critique of secularization as the sole paradigm with which to analyse religion in public life began by pointing to the centrality of its functional definition of religion (focus on dogmas, obedience of the practitioners, institutions, ritual practices) and the insufficient attention paid to the variety of roles that could be associated with religion in these various contexts. Some of the critics of the secularization paradigm denounced the wilful blindness that secularization as a paradigm had exerted over social scientists at large (Wald and Wilcox 2006); while others set about deconstructing the 'death of God' and shifting the focus from the public spaces and state regulation of religion to the conditions of belief in the Modern Age (Taylor 2007) or chose to elaborate a 'spiritual' secularism (Bhargava 2010). Eisenstadt, comparing various historical settings, proposed the notion of 'multiple modernities' to resist prevalent intellectual traditions and in particular the idea of an equivalence between 'western civilization' and modernity, as well as the hegemonizing and hegemonic assumptions of the Western programme of modernity (Eisenstadt 1973, 2000). Important voices on this include Asad and others who pointed to the dislodging of the meaning of secularization by insisting on the pluralizing formations of the secular (Asad 2003; Brown 2009), a perspective that held considerable empirical sway over non-Western fields of study (Mahmood 2005). In the early twenty-first century, this secularization perspective has been, so to speak, effectively disengaged from its exclusive focus on the role of the state (as regulator, legislator, a producer of norms and values) and redirected to a more precise investigation of the lived experience of believers and unbelievers. In fact, as critics of the secularization narrative have often argued, the declining impact of religious beliefs is found particularly in the public sphere while it is assumed to be less evident in matters relating to the private: modern citizens, in particular in Western contexts, are supposed to relate to society as autonomous, responsible, reflective entities (Halman and Pettersson 2003). Individual morality has become a personal concern, as is personal religiosity, no longer requiring regular attendance at places of worship. But again, it is not as simple as it seems. The role that believers accord their religion varies according to multiple social cleavages, from class to ethnicity and denomination.

Secularization has often gone together with the privatization of beliefs as one solution to cultural conflicts (Barry 2001). Politics, culture and social morality come to be conceived of as independent of any religious influence. Morality in this process becomes a personal as opposed to a collective concern. These secular strains in scholarship that have dominated the field until recently must be recognized for what they are, since they have imposed quite specific cognitive frames on the other religions, even when studies were carried out in non-Western contexts. Core themes recur throughout, such as the decline of the authority and power of religious institutions in public life (both in the institutional and socio-structural dimension); the effect of social differentiation (tracing the decline of the influence of religion on different sectors of social life, in particular on education); the decline of individual involvement in religious practices owing to social integration (societalization); together with a general rationalization of public life. Today, however, secularization points us to a process whereby religious thinking, practice and institutions lose their political significance but not their social relevance.

European and North American views of religion and society

As an outcome of secularization, the religiously plural social context operates as a frame in which multiple ways of being a believer and member of a faith community are made possible and can be expressed. This is consistent with the idea of the positive freedom and expression of an individual's fundamental rights through choice (to believe and not to believe). Pluralization informs the diversification of the ways in which one can express one's religious belonging, either in resisting modernity or in part embracing its discourses and even in becoming radicalized. Beliefs are diversified, faiths have split, but the need for meanings remains central to an individual's social positioning (Taylor 2007).

A spectrum of rites, practices and modes of belonging is the hallmark of twenty-first-century religions. Their higher visibility does not coincide with the idea of the intensification or the return of the religious that for a while attracted scholarship. Rather this more explicit public presence challenges the confines of the secularization narrative. Many national political spaces have their experience of pluralism, not only Western societies. In modernized European societies based on the principle of autonomous individuals associating through citizenship and individual respect for specific common rules, the idea of keeping one's distance from religious institutions goes hand in hand with an increase in do-it-yourself approaches in religious matters. The resulting increase in individualization was particularly strongly manifested in the United States, becoming one of the central theoretical paradigms organizing political sociology in its study of religion (Warner 1993). To sum up, the rational choice perspective has been the central motto for this literature in which the believer deploys strategy and otherwise mobilizes resources as a perfectly rational agent in order to maximize profit and avoid losses (Bruce 1999; Goldstein 2006). In this project, the religious satisfaction of the individual is perfectly reconcilable with the metaphor of a religious market (the supply-side model).

The difference between EU and US scholarship on religion follows from these divergent interpretations of secularism. To put it concisely, the vitality of the religious sector in the United States contrasts strongly with its lethargy in Western European societies (Hammond and Machacek 2009: 400). The role of the state has been identified as part of the explanation: highly regulating the religious field in Europe while being altogether less invasive in the North American context. The religious vitality of the US people has been particularly thoroughly investigated, more specifically the role that religious and civic commitment plays in equipping individuals with the knowledge they need to launch themselves into society at large. This constitutes a major difference in the scholarship: while, in the US-based context, part of the literature emphasizes the idea that religious-based groups of committed people may contribute strong social ties to their societies, this has been comparatively undervalued and under-researched until relatively recently in the European context, when it arose in the context of the Fall of the Wall (Müller 2008) and also through closer study of ethnic community settlements with dynamic religious vitality, whether applied to Muslims, Sikhs or African Evangelists.

In North American scholarship, the distinction between public (state) and civic (secular) can be found in two rather different discourses: on the one hand the privatization thesis mentioned earlier (Luckmann 1967; Chaves 1994) and, on the other, study which takes as its object the way in which religious groups (private, civic) reach out into the public realm (Smith 1996; Wiktorowicz 2004). For instance, the civic interaction of religious groups is surveyed in order to assess its impact in terms of 'social capital' (as developed by Putnam) and to track the way that religion helps people to 'spiral outward' (Lichterman 2005) in their social relations. In European contexts, the religious individual is looked at through the lens of his or her personal autonomy and the limit a state might pose to this, the limit being perceived as in most cases illegitimate. States, for example, might regulate private clothing associated with religious practice as in the series of burqa rulings that are popping up all over the EU. In July 2010, the Pew Research Center's Global Attitudes Project released the result of a survey that illustrates this divergence in the two political cultures with respect to religion. Asked about their approval or disapproval of the French Bill that would make it illegal for Muslim women to wear full veils in public places, majorities in France (82%), Germany (71%), Britain (62%) and Spain (59%) declared that they would support such a ban in their own country; while only 28% of the US sample said that they could approve it.

Generally speaking, the US approach to religion has long drawn on political science to better understand the interaction between religion and political behaviour. Religion is regarded as the source of certain political attitudes and socially related behaviours, adding further sub-categories to the classical taxonomy (ethnic, age, gender, class, etc.) (Manza and Wright 2003). A large literature has analysed the connection between the resilient religious affiliation after the Second World War (Lipset 1996) and the historical prevalence of a strong overlap between religious and political affiliations, in order to assess the significance of splintering affiliations (based on a functional definition and relying on church attendance, doctrinal beliefs, denomination groups, contextual aspects of congregational memberships) as powerful predictors of US voting behaviour (Manza and Wright 2003). For European scholars, the dominant reading of religion in the social sciences has followed a more socio-historical trajectory. In both contexts, however, the major challenge presents itself as a disconnection between meaning and norms as experienced at an individual level. Authors have talked of a micro-secularization perspective, of a 'deregulation' of the religious market, or classically of 'individualization'. Still, the invitation to place the individual's ordinary experience of religion at the core of its episteme remains a crucial challenge to political sociology on both sides of the Atlantic. Such a development would also construct a bridge to a much-needed broader process of capillarization of religion as a social phenomenon.

Increasingly, current classical concepts seem insufficient to support a satisfying study of religion in its contemporary complexity. The sociology of religion is indeed in the middle of something of a paradigmatic crisis (Riesebrodt 2008). Discussions about religion in the modern world are very different from the ones that experts of religion have been studying ('Why this mismatch?' asks Davie 2007). It is a mismatch that somehow illustrates the intensification of the 'latent schism between religious and secular worldviews' (Mahmood 2009: 66). Alongside the call for a more organic approach to religion (in opposition to functional and substantive ones), US scholars have recently expressed the need for a 'strong program' in the sociology of religion which would recognize religion as an independent rather than a dependent variable (Smilde and May 2010).

The principal advance occurring throughout this discipline is better scrutiny at the level of individual belief, consciousness and practice at a grassroots level, but within a political sociology perspective. Works rich in ethnography have for instance been emerging in a steady stream. So following a tradition in the sociology of culture in particular inspired by Bellah, Lichterman examines the processes through which religious groups bring religion into the civic arena, while signalling to themselves and others that they are religious groups by deploying 'quiet signals of religious identity' in carrying out their civic obligations (Lichterman 2005). The notion of agentivity has also become paradigmatic in this renewal based on ethnography, as well as the theoretical framework of collective action and social movements, mostly in non-Western contexts (Wiktorowicz 2004).

Religion as a capillary social object

The idea that religion works in contemporary societies by following a 'capillarity dynamic' arises from a variety of sources. First, it follows from the suggestion that 'religion' is making its entry into disciplines where it used to be rather discrete (law, philosophy, economy). Religion and politics, still a troubling relationship viewed from the secularization perspective, is probably the most investigated topic in all the various contexts. It brings in the analysis of different actors, including states, and religion-based groups, while looking at the relationship of religious individuals to politics, mostly through the analysis of religion as an indicator of political attitudes and behaviours. It even ventures, in some contexts, into what is happening in people's private rooms and intimate practices as an example of a 'repoliticization' of the private and religious spheres (Casanova 1994). Queer studies and intersectionality have also made their entry into the field. Recent reflections on homonationalism, inspired by the seminal work of Puar (2007), examine the intersection of the broad structures of racism, neoliberalism and class exclusion that underwrite 'homonationalist config-urations' in which the rehabilitated figure of the 'queer' is transformed into a border differentiating in hierarchical terms Western liberal democracies from the rest of the world. Puar points out the racist or racial dimension of homonationalism insofar as it tends to exclude specific groups, in her eyes most notably Sikhs, Jews, Muslims (Puar 2007). 'Intimate citizenship practices' have thus been elevated into discriminating variables that measure the capacity of certain individuals to become European citizens or Europeanized. Concrete examples abound that clearly confirm the diverse ways in which homonationalism is enmeshed in securitization, counterterrorism, nationalism and citizenship (Haritaworn 2010). This complements the more classical work on religion looking at fundamentalism and radicalization as an effect of the globalization and politicization of religion.

The role played by law in framing public problems related to religion, either under the human rights rubric or in relation to culture, is also a relatively new preoccupation, given that religious freedom (as commonly defined in most secular constitutions) has not previously featured among the more controversial fundamental rights (Grimm 2009). Looking at the interaction of law and religion today means on the one hand regarding the impact religion may have on legal systems, and on the other, analysing the way certain religious groups and religious individuals rely on law to advance their claims and procure respect for their rights as believers. Questions arise around the ability of certain groups to develop the legal competences to build up a case: 'One concerns who has standing to take legal action against minority faiths; another concerns admissibility of evidence in matters dealing with small unpopular faiths. A third important issue concerns the general approach taken toward religion and religious groups within a society' (Richardson 2009: 423). This study covers the legal reality of the existence of established hierarchies of religion, which brings us back to the earlier concern about definition. Groups claiming status as a religion (think of Alevis or Baha'is) have to fit within a hierarchical scheme that matters when it comes to fundraising, building places of worship, training religious clerks and educating children. Looking at the nexus of law and religion also prompts reflection on the admissibility of evidence in matters dealing with the smaller, less popular faiths. Liberal states condemn certain practices that enter the spotlight of public life mostly through the glare of controversy, and welcome others in the name of neutrality. What is the logic and internal coherence of liberal neutrality? Can secular legal traditions be fair to religion?

Conclusion

Religion is no longer marginal to political sociology as it is not marginal to social life. It is slowly moving from being conceived of as the cause of something else and as an intermediary object of study, to a proper object of study in its own right capillarized within multiple sectors of social and political life. The epistemological and method-ological preconditions for a better knowledge of its political and social meanings still need improving, in particular a more systematic comparative perspective. On this point, the founding-father traditions may need to be revitalized. The central paradigms (secularization and privatization/individualization) have been challenged in many respects by the pluralization dynamic of new religions in the global-institutional faith landscape. The legal regulation of religious diversity, whether in national or international jurisdictions, tends to confirm the legitimacy of certain religious signs (Christian signs in Europe, for example) by qualifying them as 'cultural', while it marginalizes others by qualifying them as 'political'. Through secularism, constitutional traditions work somehow as guarantors of cultural homo-geneity (Mancini 2009). So not only is religion central to the social sciences research agenda, but it has gained a politically loaded status that makes its messages hyper-sensitive for publics at large.

Returning to the pedagogical challenge mentioned in the introduction, we need to dig into research with the same appetite that we look for appealing material that can register the complexity of religion as social fact in all its current complexity. *Big Love*, the HBO TV polygamist melodrama featuring the family life of the Henricksons – fundamentalist Mormons in Utah, has it all. The ritual addictiveness of the series stems from its portrayal of the complicated social and family life of Bill, father and potential prophet, and his three wives and numerous children. They are unchurched Mormons living in Salt Lake City out of the compound. The tie binding them to their initial community of belonging is essential to the narrative, an active theme in the drama throughout its four seasons. We contemplate a dynamic and intense family life mixed with up with a religious commitment that is taken completely seriously. The TV drama represents in fact a relatively exhaustive, beautifully illustrated handbook of the sociology of religion, including chapters which embrace not only such classic content as prophecy, dogmas, rituals, education, transmission, the link with tradition, un-churching, the creation of a new church, the experience of religious pluralism and competition, but also more functional and contemporary themes, such as legal constraints, politicization, public controversies around polygamy, gender relations, political participation, etc. Religion presented in *Big Love* exceeds the strict frame-work of polygamy. But the Henricksons have their say too ('Mormons don't eat salmon', says Barb, Henrickson's first historical wife), which somehow might drive political sociologists out of their minds, as Lurie justifiably imagined.

Acknowledgement

The author wishes to express her warm thanks to Rosemary Bechler for her meticulous editing of this text.

Further Reading

Ammerman, N. (ed.) 2007: *Everyday Religion: Observing Modern Religious Lives*. Oxford: Oxford University Press.

Beckford, J. and Wallis, J. (eds) 2007: *Theorising Religion: Classical and Contemporary Debates*. Aldershot: Asghate.

Côté, P. and Richardson, J. 2001: Disciplined litigation, vigilante litigation, and deformation. Dramatic organization change in Jehovah's Witnesses. *Journal for the Scientific Study of Religion 40*: 11–26.

Fernando, M. 2010: Reconfiguring freedom: Muslim piety and the limits of secular law and public discourse in France. *American ethnologist 37*(1): 19–35.

Jonker, G. and Amiraux, V. (eds) 2006: *Politics of Visibility. Young Muslims in European Public Spaces*. Bielefeld: Transcript Verlag.

31

Body Politics

Roberta Sassatelli

Sociology has questioned the epistemological status of the scientific study of the body, so opening up the space for exploring the political implications of bodily representations and practices. Although the body–power relation was marginal until the work of Foucault and feminist theorists, classical social theory also contributed to its emergence as a problem. In Marx's writings on labour as a corporeal process and those of Weber on discipline, the body is seen as transformed into an instrument. In other social theory, however, such as Elias's work on body rationalization, Goffman's understanding of the symbolic functions of bodily comportment and Bourdieu's theory of embodiment and mimesis, the body is also the paramount symbol of the subject's self-possession and degree of civilization. Much of Foucault's work is concerned with modern operations of power in which body and knowledge are central, including discipline, surveillance, medicalization and confession. Under the influence of the poststructuralist turn influenced by Foucault, feminism has confronted the body more directly than it did previously. For poststructuralist feminists, gender is not the cultural representation of biological sex, but rather the process that produces the possibility of two distinct sexes. The postmodern 'plasticity' of sex, crucially articulated in the work of Judith Butler, is also taken up in studies of technology, notably that of Donna Haraway in her discussion of 'cyborgs'. In general there has been a trend away from considering the body as a by-product of domination, towards seeing it as the focal point of conflicts over power.

A host of contemporary phenomena, ranging from AIDS to women's rights and assisted reproduction, from gay and lesbian movements to the Human Genome Project, have fore-grounded the body–power relation. Rather than formulating encompassing body typologies (Turner 1996), sociological theory has questioned the epistemological assumptions involved in the production of natural facts, decentring the physical body of the bio-medical sciences and exploring the political

The Wiley-Blackwell Companion to Political Sociology, First Edition. Edited by Edwin Amenta, Kate Nash, and Alan Scott.
© 2012 Blackwell Publishing Ltd. Published 2012 by Blackwell Publishing Ltd.

implications of body representations and practices. Social constructivism has spread its wings across the wide variety of bodily experience. Bodies have acquired a history (Feher *et al.* 1989; Porter 1991). They have become political not only because they are shaped by productive requirements or constrained by moral rules, but also because their 'naturality' is traced back to claims to truth reflecting power differences. Together with bodily matters occupying pivotal positions in political struggles, criticism of binaries such as culture/nature, body/mind, gender/sex, male/female, other/self has flourished (Rorty 1980; Butler 1990; Laqueur 1990). While calls for an embodied approach to social life are multiplying, corporeality itself, the way we perceive and define what it is to have and to be a body, has been problematized (Crossley 2001). Its links with different dimensions of power – be it discursive, social or strictly political – are being explored in an effort to specify how the present social order is reproduced and to what extent it can be challenged. Body politics indeed refers both to the processes through which societies regulate the human body or use (part of) it to regulate themselves, and to the struggles over the degree of individual and social control of the body, its parts and processes. In other terms, it covers the two sides of the power–body relations: the powers to control bodies on the one side, and resistance and protest against such powers on the other.

Mapping body politics is an exercise in complexity reduction. The territory is, above all, unstable, not least for its recent consolidation as something to be mapped. The body politics coordinates have been explicitly charted as a result of two major theoretical earthquakes – the work of Michel Foucault and the development of feminist approaches. Still, although the body–power relation has long been ancillary to other social scientific frames, much of classical sociological thought has contributed to its emergence as a problem in its own right (Turner 1996).

Discipline, Civilization and Taste

The concern with the relationship between the changing needs of an emerging industrial society and its disciplinary techniques stems from the rise of sociological reflections. The standing that Karl Marx assigned to labour as a corporeal process goes well beyond the creation of economic value. Through labour human beings can either realize themselves in harmony with nature or be alienated from themselves and their bodies, as in the capitalist mode of production. With the development of manufacture, the labourer 'performs the same simple operation' all his life, becomes 'detail labourer' and converts 'his whole body into the automatic, one-sided implement of that operation' (Marx 1976 [1867]: 458). The modern machinery-based factory is even more oppressive, reducing to a minimum the resistance the 'naturally elastic' barrier of the human body. Factory discipline 'exhausts the nervous system to the uttermost; at the same time, it does away with the many-sided play of the muscles, and confiscates every atom of freedom, both in bodily and in intellectual activity' (1976 [1867]: 548). Capitalism thus steals corporeality its meaning: the worker 'only feels himself freely active in his animal function – eating, drinking, procreating, or at most in his dwelling and dressing-up, etc.; in his human functions he no longer feels himself to be anything but an animal' (Marx 1981 [1844]: 66). Marx proposes the idea that the boundaries between animality and humanity are socially constructed. This construction is, however, the result of domination and exploitation, something to be criticized on the basis of a truly human and natural way of being in one's own body and deploying one's own labour.

Rather like Marx, Weber considers the modern factory as an example of the rational conditioning of work performances. However, as a 'uniform', 'exact', 'consistently rationalized' and 'methodically trained' conduct, discipline is both present in every society whenever masses are to be governed steadily and acquires a special character in modern times (Weber 1978 [1922]). Modern bureaucratic discipline is both rationalized and relies on people's aspirations, working through the subjects rather than simply upon them. Weber's analysis is rich in power effects: ascetic discipline worked for certain groups as a means of social mobility, crystallized into refined means of bureaucratic domination and promoted reformist attitudes legitimizing social change in the name of ever-greater rationalization. Owing to 'sober and rational Puritan discipline' Cromwell's 'men of conscience' were, for example, technically superior to their opponents the 'Cavaliers', undisciplined 'men of honor'. Furthermore, like Bell's (1985) medieval 'holy anoretics' who managed to transcend their female disadvantage, demonstrating spiritual superiority via methodical self-starvation, the bourgeoisie ascetic regime legitimized their social advancement. If the 'de-naturalization' of the body realized through extraordinary conducts works to set the 'chosen' apart, protestant 'worldly asceticism' tempers the repressive elements of religious asceticism, contrasting with the deployment of one's own professional vocation and demands that everyone be a *virtuoso* (Weber 2002 [1920]). Weber thus begins to show the extent to which certain forms of body government may work as techniques of both power and empowerment even in the age of secularization.

Body government is explicitly linked to the political by Norbert Elias. Elias traces body rationalization back to the advent of the modern nation-state while retaining a dynamic framework implicating embodiment in the struggles amongst individuals and groups. Historicizing the idea that our civilization is built upon the repression of instincts (Freud 1976 [1930]; Elias 1994 [1939]) shows that changes in the shape of political control brought about by the monopolization of physical violence gave way to pacified social spaces enforcing cooperation less charged with emotions and resulting in a change of personality structure: constraints through others are converted into self-constraints. The transformation of the ruling nobility from a class of knights into a class of self-restrained, calculating courtiers is conceptualized as both an example and a catalyst for such civilizing process. The courtization of the nobility takes place together with an increased upward thrust by bourgeois strata with the necessity on the part of the former to distinguish themselves from the latter. An unconsciously operating 'repulsion of the vulgar' and an 'increasing sensibility to anything corresponding to a lesser sensibility of lower-ranking classes' permeate the conduct of life of the courtly upper class, and this 'good taste' also represents a prestige value for such circles (1994 [1939]: 499). Through an imitation–emancipation dynamic, the 'code of conduct', which the leading bourgeois groups develop when they finally take over the function of the upper class, is the product of an 'amalgamation' of 'refinement' and 'virtue'.

Elias's theory of civilization suggests that in the historical development of the West a particular 'civilized' bodily conduct has become widespread. In contemporary society the 'pattern of self-control' has become 'all-embracing', having to be deployed towards every person. Above all, it has become 'more complex' and 'highly differentiated' to accommodate increased functional differentiation and the emergence of a public/private divide. Spaces for the 'controlled de-control of emotions' like sport and a variety of 'pleasurable' and 'exciting leisure pursuits', substituting for what is 'lacking' in everyday life, become more important (Elias and Dunning 1986). Such a picture contrasts with Freudian visions of repression, as well as Marcusian utopias of liberation (Marcuse 1969). Indeed we may consider that while individualization, affect control, formality and a higher shame threshold have become mankind's 'second nature', the de-naturalization of the body may take the shape of practices inspired by an idealized tribal communion, informality or even excess and the grotesque (Bataille 1985; Wouters 1986). Similar practices appear, on different occasions, as forms of resistance and subversion attempting to redefine society's power structure, or as functional to its reproduction. Many commentators have associated the former with community circuits and the latter with commercialization (Lasch 1979). Still, research on subcultural forms, amateur practices, sporting activities and so on shows that embodied pleasures mediated by consumer goods are by no means merely oppressive. For example, fitness practices as conducted in commercial premises may be organized in ways that foreclose or facilitate a reappraisal of received body ideals (Sassatelli 2010). On their part, ostensibly counter-cultural bodily conducts or drastic body modification have been indicated as politically ambivalent. Working as a desire-producing machine allowing for the experience of Dionysian communality and a de-subjectified state of ecstasy, the rave scene appears to be based on a politics of difference that is indifferent to all political values other than the new (Jordan 1995). Scarification or extreme piercing on the verge of 'neo-primitivism' makes clear that the body is a potential site of resistance to standardization and yet may be depoliticized as private symptom of disquiet or incorporated into the mainstream as exotic (Favazza 1996).

The trajectory indicated by the classics is twofold. On the one hand, the body is transformed into an instrument for work and labour, a utility, a function. On the other, however, the body continues to operate as the paramount symbol for the subject to demonstrate his or her being self-possessed, civilized or otherwise valuable. The symbolic function of bodily demeanour has become prey for micro-sociological approaches to identity, notably in the work of Erving Goffman. As individuals' vulnerability in face-to-face interaction becomes ceremonial and locally specific, a finer body language develops. Ever more sophisticated bodily markers indicate both 'diffuse social statuses' and individual 'character', that is, the actor's 'conception of himself', his or her 'normality' or 'abnormality' (Goffman 1963a). Modern selfhood is itself only understandable in relation to the ceremonial distance that individuals keep during interaction. The 'air bubble' around the body helps projecting a 'sacred', 'elusive', 'deep' self (Goffman 1967; 1963b), something which may well constitute the taken-for-granted basis for human rights to hold still in Western affectivity (Schneider 1996). Body language, however, can only to a degree be spoken strategically. As a language it talks of the subject beyond his or her intentions, and as a body it is never silent: '(a)lthough an individual can stop talking he cannot stop communicating through body idiom, he must say either the right thing or the wrong thing. He cannot say nothing' (Goffman 1963b: 35).

Like Elias, Goffman implies that with modernity there has been a shift in the attitudes towards natural functions that is by no means power-free. We could say with Georg Simmel (1997 [1908]: 118) that the modern general 'aspiration to hygiene' is accompanied by embodied social distinctions to the point that 'the social question is not only an ethical one, but also a question of smell'. The perceptions of dirt and cleanliness have been exposed as varying between cultures and across time, being implicated in power structures (Douglas 1966). Mary Douglas, in particular, has shown that as 'a system of natural symbols' the individual body is a metaphor for the vulnerabilities and the anxieties of the political body making. If what is inside and outside the body provides a language for discussing what is inside and outside the social, it would be a mistake to think that the contemporary confinement of purity to the scientific domain of the 'hygienic' marks a break with previous moralism. Indeed, the morality of bodily codes is powerfully illustrated by the potency of AIDS epidemics as a metaphor of decadence and deviance (Sontag 1988). And the very notion of epidemics can be extended to include many aspects of embodiment, including fat, with obesity increasingly represented as an infectious disease, unevenly distributed across the globe and the social classes so as to reflect differentials in value and standing (Gilman 2009).

For all its force the metaphorical approach may risk figuring practical activity and the body merely as representation. Bourdieu has tried to illuminate the circular process whereby social practices, as organized in specific fields such as sport, education etc., are incorporated into the body, only then to be renewed through body competences and inclinations (Crossley 2001). Re-elaborating on the notion of 'techniques of the body' as mimetic *habitus* assembled for the individual 'by all his education, by the whole society to which he belongs, in the place he occupies it' (Mauss 1973 [1936]: 76), Pierre Bourdieu (1977a) has composed his theory of practice with a concern that human experience is not to be understood in terms of cognitive and linguistic models, but in terms of embodiment and mimesis. These are, in turn, implicated in a set of classificatory systems which 'are not so much means of knowledge as means of power, harnessed to social functions and overtly or covertly aimed at satisfying the interests of a group' (Bourdieu 1986: 477). Although accused of ignoring dissent and social transformation, Bourdieu has helped conceptualize taste as embodied disposition that works as symbolic power naturalizing the existing system of power differences. For Bourdieu, the state of the body is itself the realization of a 'political mythology': lifestyle regimes reflect the cultural genesis of tastes from the specific point within the social space from which individuals originate – they are incorporated through the most elementary everyday movements inculcating the equivalence between physical and social space. Even 'in its most natural appearance... volume, size, weight, etc.' the body is a social product: 'the unequal distribution among social classes of corporeal properties' is both realized concretely through 'working conditions' and 'consumption habits', and perceived through 'categories and classification systems which are not independent of such distribution' (Bourdieu 1977b: 51).

Emphasis on embodiment is fundamental in this context to understand the depth of habitus as much as subjects' capacity or necessity to alter or negotiate it to enhance subjectivity or indeed to protect it. For example, marrying Bourdieu's with Giddens' (1991) theory of 'reflexive individualization' we may consider that certain advantaged social groups – such as the so-called cultural intermediaries – busily engage in body projects to alter their bodies and reappraise their taste so as to produce more marketable selves, something that adumbrates their collaboration in a broader process of self-commodification whereby self-actualization is realized through the embracement of market variety, novelty and abundance (Sassatelli 2007). On a different account, we may return to Elias's and Goffman's concern for the way bodies and selves are fundamentally, if institutionally, co-constituted. Survivors' accounts from Nazi camps, for example, point to the centrality of changing and negotiating body habits (Shilling 2008). Survivors had by necessity to develop a habitual attention to any opportunities that arose to attend to immediately body needs, such as feeding as adequately as possible. This was associated not only with becoming a physical body, but also with a heightened sense of specific body parts (notably the stomach). Feeling the body in this way, however, was not necessarily a process of being reduced to the body; on the contrary, survivors attempted to negotiate the possibility of maintaining a sense of future and self-respect through whatever care of the body was allowed. Thus participating in the ritual of washing (although in cold, dirty water) was viewed as a symbol and an instrument of moral survival.

Biopower, Surveillance and Medicalization

A focus on the institutional conditions for the production of subjectivity through bodies brings us to Michel Foucault's work. Much of Foucault's work strives to illustrate modern operations of power in which body and knowledge are central to produce subjectivity. Despite a number of criticisms – for attributing primacy to the discursive over the non-discursive realm; for over-stretching the notion of power; for reducing the subject to the body and the body to a passive text; or for bestowing a somewhat essentialist quality of resistance to subjugated forms of embodiment – Foucault's work has been pivotal in recognizing that the body is directly implicated in a political field. Power relations do not simply 'repress' it, they rather produce it, having 'an immediate hold on it; they invest it, train it, torture it, force it to carry out tasks, to perform ceremonies and to emit signs' (Foucault 1977: 25). Power, in turn, operates as a 'microphysics', as strategies and tactics working at an intermediate level between body and institutions, through everyday practices. Foucault has thus helped place emphasis on local and intimate operations of power, widening the scope of the political, something which has influenced, if not satisfied, a number of critical approaches.

In *Discipline and Punish* Foucault (1977) continues the classical preoccupation with the modern transformation of the body into a useful and docile instrument. Organizations such as schools, hospitals, armies, factories and prisons are described as disciplinary institutions consolidating routinary systems of power working through the embodiment of self-surveillance. The mechanized organization and routinized training intimated by Marx and Weber is thoroughly analysed by Foucault's description of discipline as coordinating people's movements and functions through time and space. Foucault, however, considers the body, rather than the subject, as the direct object of control. All disciplinary institutions may indeed be understood as laboratories where a new form of political rationality developed. The modern notion of sovereignty is coterminous with a shift from the right of death to the power over life, a 'biopolitics' consisting of an investment in the human body (conceived as an object to be manipulated) and of an interest for the human kind (with scientific categories such as population and species replacing juridical ones as objects of political attention).

The idea that the modern nation-state consolidates itself by stimulating life to grow into prescribed forms has been widely influential. Foucault himself addressed welfare provision and the whole idea of tutelary public authority as related to an open-ended expansion of the conduct of government (Foucault 1988a). Rather than an 'étaticization' of society, however, Foucault suggests the inclusion of the state in a particular style of political reasoning defined as 'governmentality' or the presumption that life conducts can, should and must be administered by authority (Foucault 1991; see also Hindess, Chapter 4, in this volume). Indeed, through a multifarious network of governance, regulatory interventions are increasingly important in the management of human bodies and the boundaries of their normalization. This includes practices as diverse as insurance technologies (Defert 1991); diffuse, localized and internalized techniques governing consumption of allegedly dangerous products such as alcohol (Valverde 1998); medical regulation concerning the boundaries of life (euthanasia and abortion on the one hand, see Shakespeare 1998; assisted reproduction on the other, see Hendin 1997); within life (gender arrangements, including the regulation of sex-change procedures, see Holmes 2002) and across life (organ donation and transplant for example, see Lock 2002).

Such normalization practices of course elicit struggle and resistance – witness the emergence of intersex activism (Chase 1998) or disability activism (Shapiro 1993) campaigning for the consolidation of a national and international jurisprudence concerning the redefinition of civil and human rights – in a continuous social and cultural dialectic. Still, emphasis on such dialectic may erase the role that physical violence still has in contemporary forms of government. While Foucault's work allowed him to consider how specialized disciplinary discourses and institutions realized the power to govern life, Giorgio Agamben (1998) has maintained that sovereign power, or the power to take life away, has never vanished and, like disciplinary power, it has become regionalized. Considering recent developments in body politics in the global arena and international law, he suggests that rather than a shift from sovereign power to disciplinary power, we witness a 'thanatopolitics': the creation of special 'state of exceptions' where the sacredness of life is suspended and 'emergency powers' are legitimated. The permutation of power into discipline is thus ultimately sustained by a new form of sovereignty with the regionalized creation of lawless zones, both within and without the frontiers of the nation-states. These are justified by the need to protect the value of life, and yet any human life that gets trapped within them is liable to be killed, or left to die or be kept barely alive without incurring any crime.

Whatever the definition of the political, nothing can illustrate better the insidious duplicity of biopolitics than the analogies between the eugenic measures developed in many Western countries and those developed by the Nazi dictatorship (Burleigh and Wipperman 1991). Initially fuelled by hopes to eradicate defective genes, a huge number of persons were sterilized without their consent from the beginning of the century up to the early 1960s in the United States, mostly belonging to social groups considered racially inferior, such as African Americans and Native Americans (Reilly 1991). Attention to the link between population control and racial issues has recently been renewed by the development in Western countries of an intense debate about migrations, migrants and refugees. In this context, Foucaultian approaches may provide an historically based perspective on racialized social relations, starting from the establishment of a colonial order where the European individual and political bodies are set against a savage 'other' (Stoler 1995). As African people were turned into commodities in the Atlantic slave trade, Western countries identified some specific bodily differences to justify their subjugation: dark skin was at the negative pole in the dichotomy of white and good versus black and evil, broad facial features stood for excessive sexual appetites, unruliness or stupidity, muscularity cried for hard labour. The body is the central site for the process of racialization whereby bodily differences are inscribed with social meaning and value. Even today, blackness is often constructed as being trapped within the web of nature while the white body has freedom of movement, and moves so as to disembody itself, locating whiteness (and masculinity) firmly within modernity and rationality (Hill 2004). Black embodiment still arguably battles against what Frantz Fanon (1967) suggested characterizes black consciousness: the perception that black embodied subjectivity is objectified in representation, rather than posited as the subject of experience. Bodies and their attributed qualities may thus still function, in the case of coloured people as of women, as hints to cast doubts on a subject's capacity to stand as fully as possible as valuable, responsible and reliable citizens.

Together with the objectifying qualities of modern political rationality, Foucault envisaged subjectifying ones: a shift in the notion of sovereignty is echoed by a shift in the notion of subjectivity, from subjects with ascribed identities to free citizens who are asked to produce themselves. Foucault's later work does not do without the body, though. It rather shifts to the modern preoccupation with uncovering one's 'true' self predicated on body–mind dualism. In *The History of Sexuality* he addresses the practices by which individuals were led to acknowledge themselves as 'subjects of desire', where desire located in the body contains 'the truth of their being, be it natural or fallen' (Foucault 1985: 5). The development of psychoanalysis epitomizes the fact that the 'truth' of individuals is no longer linked to their position in the universal order of things, but is constructed around a normalizing notion of inner responsibility requiring an endless hermeneutics of the self. While psychoanalysis is part of the 'confessional' machinery that it ostensibly redresses, repression is not accounted for as an historical fact. On the contrary, power takes on a productive character as testified by the 'multiplication of discourses concerning sex' in the fields of exercise of power which 'exploit it as the secret' (Foucault 1978: 17, 35). While in the Greco-Roman tradition sexual intercourse was part of a regime of life governed through a measure/excess dialectic, with modernity it was inscribed in a therapeutic model working on the basis of the normal/pathological distinction (Foucault 1978, 1985). The web of scientific practices operating on the body produced a '*scientia sexualis*' constructing sexuality as an empirical and natural object of enquiry and as the secret essence of the individual. Once again truth is revealed as an historically specific category: the body has no inherent truth; rather, truths on the body are constructed through various categorizing strategies.

Even Foucault's earlier works on the medicalization of insanity and the birth of medical discourse may be included in this picture if we consider that modern political rationality not only makes organic life enter the art of the possible, but also does so by employing and negotiating with a number of expert discourses. In particular, a concern with medical truths implicated in a network of power relations is developed in the *Birth of the Clinic* (Foucault 1973). Examining medical treatises, Foucault analyses the metamorphosis which leads to the establishment of pathological anatomy: disease becomes a 'collection of symptoms' necessarily expressed in the human body and integral to the disease itself rather than an abstract pathological 'essence'. This is accompanied by a medical 'gaze that dominates' the body by rendering its depth a visible object, with the anatomy lesson becoming itself a powerful representation of political power as in Rembrandt's famous painting. When the notion of a pathological essence infiltrating the body is replaced by the idea of the body itself becoming ill, death is transformed into disease and degeneration, a dispersed and uneven failure of the body. This opens the space for the medicalization of death, for its treatment as dirt, and for the institutionalization of the dying (Aries 1978; Elias 1994 [1939]). This in turn is coupled with ageing being increasingly seen as disease, whereby 'ageism' – or a cultural bias against ageing – is realized through both institutional practices such as health care and subjectivity, with old people internalizing negative messages about their bodies and selves (Gilleard and Higgs 2000). As we shall see in the next paragraph, ageism is particularly evident in the case of women's bodies: older women hardly find cultural endorsement in public images, with the older female body being the other of the 'beauty myth' through which women are invited to look at themselves.

Feminism(s), Gender and Technologies

Since its emergence feminist thought has conceived the body as a site of female oppression. The term body politics was a slogan for the feminist movement in the 1970s to campaign for abortion rights, to denounce violence against women and the objectification of their bodies. However, while early socialist-feminists were striving to counterbalance the gender-blindness of much classical sociology by conceptualizing the interdependence of capitalism and patriarchy and male domination over female bodies and selves, more recent works confront gendered bodies as primary sites of ordinary, minute subjection in practices of body care, maintenance and beautification, as sites of emotions facing increasing commercialization in the global arena, and sites of extensible capacities facing technological developments (in reproduction, production, communication and representation).

Firstly, contemporary feminist research has considered the minute and mundane practices that associate women with the body, confining them to a life centred on its maintenance (Bordo 1993; Weitz 1998). Plastic surgery in particular has been studied as its social acceptance has grown, being perceived as a site of both female subjugation and female negotiation of empowerment utopias (Davis 1995). These feminist concerns can now be usefully matched by research addressing masculine embodiment in its own right. If the ways men inhabit their bodies have emerged as correlated to patriarchy, studies addressing traditional symbols of masculinity such as muscles, and less obvious areas of male involvement such as fashion, show that old visions of masculinity are negotiated in the face of the changing power balances between the sexes (Segal 2007). In the 1990s new gender cultures within advertising agencies themselves have contributed to the development of new visions of masculinity

(Nixon 2003). For example, the 'new lad' and the 'new man' portrayed by much recent British commercial advertising are respectively characterized by an openness to pleasures previously marked as taboo for men, and by a partial loosening of the binary codes that regulate the relationships between the sexes as well as heterosexual and homosexual masculinities. All in all, alongside hegemonic masculinity and femininity, ads have thus conveyed non-traditional images of gender to the wider public, even if only to attract the attention of a distracted spectator or to bestow the thrill of the forbidden on a brand. These may be subversive, often marginal images, showing deviant masculinity and femininity, playing with sexual ambiguity, homosexuality, drag imagery and camp culture (Lewis and Rolley 1997). In this context, Susan Bordo (1999) has moved to acknowledge that the male body as represented in popular culture and advertising is also increasingly objectified, with selfhood being reduced to a surface to present. Still, feminist researchers insist that the burden of the body is heavier on women: new forms of sexism are seen as bourgeoning when young women claim their commoditized, eroticized bodies as capital to gain the favours of otherwise powerful men (Walters 2010).

Secondly, contemporary feminist and gender studies have considered how the commercialization process differently invests women's embodied capacities and emotional codes on a global scale. As Arlie Russell Hochschild (2003) has shown, especially among the upper middle and upper strata of the US and European populations, there is a trend for the commercialization of care which produces differentiated femininities: as care (for children, the old, the sick) is not rewarded as much as market success, care jobs in the home are typically carried out by female migrants, who are often portrayed as essentially more 'caring' than Western women. In a characteristic essentialist move they are portrayed as having bodies which are naturally 'made to love', while Western professional women may be portrayed as pressured for time, oriented towards their kids' achievement and incapable of being relaxed, patient and joyful – with the result that both femininities are devalued as either marginal or questionable. Indeed, in recent years, much of the work con- ducted on gender not only considers its interesectionality with race or ethnicity, age and class, but also engages with the increasingly intrusive global arena whereby gendered embodiment, of masculinity as well as femininity, is negotiated also in relation to the movements of corporate capital and its restless pursuit of cheap labour (Connell 2005).

Thirdly, as I will come back in the close of this paragraph, technologies have been studied as way to extend, alter and develop bodily capacities, notably impacting on what have long been perceived as the 'natural' limits of gendered embodiment. This area of studies has notably been furthered by theoretical developments within gender theory that extended social constructivism from bodily symbols, demeanour and rituals to 'the body' itself. Indeed, it is important to notice that contemporary feminism has developed a criticism of the earlier gender/sex division that inscribed sex in a dehistoricized biological difference. This has altered the way we approach body politics, making of plasticity and its limits an eminently political issue. In fact, despite scepticism about Foucault's inattention to the condition of women, the poststruc- turalist turn within feminism has changed the framing of gender while retaining it as its key organizing category. Together with a politics stressing the diversity amongst women (hooks 1982), gender has become understood not as a cultural representation of a biological given, but as the process that produces in the body the possibility of two distinct sexes. The biological foundation is exposed as only apparently clear: gendered bodies are unstable cultural constructions, whose purpose is to delimit and contain the 'threatening absence of boundaries between human bodies' (Epstein and Straub 1991). This has given way to rethinking gender/sex as a semiotics of corporeality constituting identities and self-representations.

The author most associated with such a poststructuralist turn is Judith Butler. In *Gender Trouble* Butler (1990) proposes to deconstruct the system of signs through which feminine identity has been linked to the heterosexual matrix. Considering gender as a performative, something which 'is always a doing, although not a doing by a subject that comes before the deed', Butler insists that as a 'continuous discursive practice', gender 'remains open to intervention and re-signification' (1990: 25, 33). Having dismissed expressive notions of femininity, she believes that the realization of a feminist politics of the body is to be built upon the same technologies and everyday practices inscribing gender/sexuality onto the body. Subversive performances such as cross-dressing are thus contemplated as revealing the 'imitative nature' of gender. Despite the lack of sociological analysis, Butler's agenda implies an emphasis on how different social contexts offer local rules consolidating gender through ritualistic repetitions. Drawing on Bourdieu's *habitus*, in her later work Butler stresses that this consolidation takes the shape of a social 'materialization of corporeality whereby "the force" of the performative is never fully separable from bodily force' (Butler 1993: 9; 1997: 141). As Bourdieu (1998) himself writes, using amongst others Nancy Henley's work on body politics and non-verbal communication (Henley 1977), gender cannot be reduced to a voluntaristic act, being consolidated both in matter – posture, demeanour, size etc. – and in symbols – classifications and categories – which speak of the subject. As noted by Iris Marion Young (1990a), studies in the use of space suggest that men and women use space in different ways which fix different embodied selves: on average, women walk with a shorter stride than men, hold their arms close to their bodies, avoid meeting the gaze of others in public spaces, use their arms to shield themselves and draw back from objects thrown to them rather than reach out to get them. These female ways of body-space articulation amount surely to a bodily idiom that can be ritualized in performances and hyperitualized in visual imagery, particularly advertising (Goffman 1979), but they are also deeply experienced as unconscious, un-reflected corporeality. Butler's subversion is thereby revealed as fragile, always in danger of surreptitiously reproducing dualism. Still, her theoretical move clearly signals the aspiration to recuperate corporeality in a post-dualistic fashion. To this end the body/power relation is openly constructed in such a way that the body is the weaker, plastic term of the equation, with the result that some feminists have accused her of endorsing a postmodern paradigm of plasticity that obliterates 'real' differences.

Butler has been crucial in consolidating the study of the politics of sex and sexuality. The normative convergence of the male/female dichotomy and heterosexuality was already implicit in Foucault's (1980b) presentation of the memories of Herculine Barbin and, above all, it was clearly related to performativity in Harold Garfinkel's (1967) well-known essay on Agnes. Here Garfinkel analyses how Agnes, an 'intersexed' person, tries to 'secure her rights to live in the elected sex status', learning to be a woman while presenting herself as a 'natural' one. Agnes's struggle for a sex-change operation that would satisfy her male boyfriend too shows the potency of the male/female duality and discloses the performative, imitative nature of femininity without assimilating all attributes or performances. Above all, the different chances available to Agnes and to the nineteenth-century hermaphrodite Herculine show that the plasticity of the truth of the body has penetrated materiality, consolidating paths for unprecedented physical transformation.

An approach to plasticity is developed in Donna Haraway's work on 'cyborgs'. Haraway (1991) argues for a feminist agenda addressing the cultural politics of an info-technic society that has modified the 'nature' of the organic. The 'cyborg', as a 'hybrid of machine and organism', is at the same time a 'creature of reality' – witness the diffusion of prosthetic medicine – and a 'creature of fiction', an 'imaginative resource'. As such, it works as a political platform to rethink the boundaries between animality and humanity, the artificial and the organic, the physical and non-physical. In particular, the 'cyborg' is set as a creature of a post-gender world providing an 'argument for pleasure in the confusion of boundaries and for responsibility in their construction' and a new 'ontology' for an 'oppositional' and 'utopian' politics (Haraway 1991: 150–151). Despite its proclaimed utopian tone, Haraway's work has offered a new perspective on how technology, traditionally identified as oppressive for women and alien to them, may become a major source of female resistance. Feminists have reappraised the potential of assisted reproduction. Approaches stressing that pre-natal medicine and assisted reproduction are forms of patriarchal domination undermining women's rights, displaying dangerous continuities with eugenics, producing anxieties and dependency, and depoliticizing social differences (Scutt 1990) have been questioned by those who salute new reproductive technologies as postmodern forms of deconstruction allowing for new ways of being (Farquhar 1996).

It is important to notice that rather than simply being blurred, the key analytical categories organizing our world and deriving from the division between technology and nature are being reconfigured and fought over. New technologies provide for new ways of conceiving the subject, ways that, like in the case of those geared towards gathering information about genetic risk (Novas and Rose 2000), draw the subject back to the body only to fragment or objectify the body into a myriad of parts or processes at the molecular level. More broadly, new technological domains are ambivalent spaces. The idea that new information technologies offer a world of masquerade in which we can represent our bodies with complete flexibility does not mean that the body is transcended altogether or that the heterosexual ideology disappears (Slater 1998). The representation of technology is itself ambivalent. In contemporary science fiction, dualistic thinking is articulated differently but it is not eluded (Holland 1995), while the popularization of genetics does not do without a rhetoric of nature and the (re)generation of value differences (Nelkin and Lindee 1995).

Concluding Remarks

Human bodies have been seen as clay, moulded by political and economic constraints. With an emphasis on the power effects of classificatory systems, bodies have also been conceived as symbols speaking of the place their bearers occupy within the social order as well as of what counts as order and disorder. More recently, bodies have been described as texts, emphasizing not so much their metaphoric quality, but rather readership and persuasion, the power to create reality through interpretation and representation. The immateriality discerned in textuality has been amended by a notion of the body as mimesis, whereby the body is practised in everyday life, shaped by dealing with the situations, rules and classifications encountered. Despite their differences, Foucault, Bourdieu and Butler seem to incline towards such notion. Furthermore, although each emphasizes different aspects of power – respectively biopolitics as part of governmentality, taste as related to political economy and symbolic power, the incorporation of binaries and classificatory power – they all try to widen the notion of power from its confinement to the political strictly conceived.

The map that I have been drawing is therefore both a topographic device and a trajectory for navigation. Within the social sciences, sociology in particular, there has been a general move away from considering the shaping of the body merely as a ghastly by-product of domination – like in Marx's analysis of the physical effects of factory work – and towards the designation of embodiment as a crucial aspect of social struggles and structure. What body politics teaches us is that the body is a battlefield, moulded by conflicts between groups with different values and different political and economic interests. Furthermore, the body – its images, definitions, boundaries etc. – is itself the focal point for conflicts over the shape of power, for the modern power to govern life can only crystallize a variety of identities which in turn become the basis for resistance against it. This seems to require a new conception of politics, one which considers, to restate Foucault, that we have become very peculiar animals, animals in whose politics our own life as living beings is put into question. This should help us consider the ambivalence of plasticity. Body politics is coterminous with the progressive consolidation of a notion of the body as plastic, both in its meanings and its materiality. To be sure, plasticity often takes the explicitly programmatic tone of a political project. Precisely because of this we cannot be satisfied with its location as the blind spot of our reflection on the body–power relation and should address the ways in which it is implicated in formations of both domination and freedom.

Further Reading

Brook, B. 1999: *Feminist Perspectives on the Body*. Harlow: Addison Wesley Longman.
Burkitt, I. 1999: *Bodies of Thought. Embodiment, Identity and Modernity*. London: Sage.
Harvey, J. and Sparks, R. 1991: The politics of the body in the context of modernity. *Quest 43*: 164–189.

32

Citizenship and Welfare:
Politics and Social Policies

SVEN HORT AND GÖRAN THERBORN

The welfare of the people is an ancient political norm, much older than citizenship and civic rights. Modern social rights did not, as a rule, develop as citizens' rights, but as rights of classes and of other social categories. Despite the widespread politics of anti-welfare, social welfare has grown in various political contexts and forms. In the last quarter of the twentieth century, social policy became the focus of a vast body of international, comparative research in sociology and political science. The overall trajectory of this still-expanding scholarly enterprise may be outlined in the shape of three generations of investigation, each with a characteristic empirical focus and geopolitical orientation, and set in a specific socio-historical context.

The welfare of the people is an ancient Eurasian political norm of government, probably more controversial in political argument today than a millennium ago, though still a respectable ideological position. The interpretation and the pursuit of the norm have, of course, varied enormously over time as well as across space. The coming of industrial capitalism in the nineteenth century was an historical watershed. Welfare and citizenship did not develop in tandem in spite of their association in Greco-Roman antiquity; an association carried over into the Roman Empire's provision of 'bread and circuses' to its citizens. Nor is their relationship very close today. Welfare is for the most part not a right of citizenship.

Virtually all economically developed states have become welfare states in the sense that a majority of government expenditure goes on the welfare of the population; on its education, health, social security and social care. Naturally, then, social policy and

---

The Wiley-Blackwell Companion to Political Sociology, First Edition. Edited by Edwin Amenta, Kate Nash, and Alan Scott.
© 2012 Blackwell Publishing Ltd. Published 2012 by Blackwell Publishing Ltd.

welfare states have become major research topics of sociology and political science. Like all fields of science and scholarship, social policy studies have their controversies and their field dynamics. However, the area is less ridden with ideological division than are many other fields of politics and policy. Most social policy researchers have basically viewed it positively.

Politics

Targets of welfare: duties and rights

In the beginning there were duties, not rights. These duties pertained to the rulers and to the pious. They derived from political ethics and from religion as obligations without human accountability and redress. But they were no less significant for that.

The classical Greek *polis* was there for the common good of its citizens, as was the Roman Republic: 'our aim in founding the city is not to make one group outstandingly happy, but to make the whole city as happy as possible', Plato has Socrates declaring in *The Republic* (Plato 2001: Book 4, 420b). This idea of common wellbeing was carried into the Hellenistic kingdoms, into the Roman and the Byzantine empires, and from there into medieval European political thought (Hahm 2000). The welfare or well-being of the subjects of emperors, kings and other rulers was a moral duty of the prince, or of the 'guardians' of Plato's Republic. 'The aim of the ruler should be to secure the wellbeing of the realm whose government he undertakes' was Thomas Aquinas's summation of medieval thought (Aquinas 1959: 6). Common welfare constituted *the* distinction between a legitimate monarch and a tyrant: 'That which makes government unjust is the fact that the personal aims of the ruler are sought to the detriment of the common welfare' (Aquinas 1959: 8–9).

Basically the same norm of rulership is found in all the major ethical and religious traditions of Asia, from the Rigveda and Confucius to Islam (Mabbet 1985). Relief from hunger and indigence, dispensation of justice and protection of comfort and prosperity were normatively expected. Crop failures and other national disasters were often interpreted as indicators of misrule. Institutions of charity, food buffer stocks, quarantines, flood control and so on developed long before modern times. Elizabethan England, for example, instituted a stern public Poor Law provision.

Caring for the poor was a duty of the pious; an obligation stressed in all the major religions. Giving alms or charity to the poor brought the benefactor closer to heaven or nirvana. This was a tenet most doctrinally central in Buddhism and Islam though not accepted within Protestant Christianity, which did not, however, completely reject compassion with the poor (Kersbergen and Manow 2009).

In pre-modern times, targets of welfare practice were mainly the subjects as a whole, and, more specifically, the poor. There were also the infirm former soldiers of the ceaseless wars of the time for whom, for example, Louis XIV built the magnificent Hotel des Invalides in Paris. This latter concern has been carried on up to the present day, by the United States in particular with its very comprehensive Veterans Pensions Program introduced after the Civil War. A century ago this was the most extensive pensions programme in the world (Skocpol 1995) and it can still be traced in the form of the generous, fully publically funded Veterans' Administration.

The early modern revolutions reaffirmed the ancient commitment to 'general' or 'common' welfare in the Preamble to *The Constitution of the United States of America* (1787) and in the version of the French *Declarations of the Rights of Man and of the Citizen* ratified by the National Convention (1793), and now as commitments of the people or the nation itself. However, with and after the French Revolution the reasons and the targets for social concern shifted. Most importantly, there was a turn from the duties and responsibilities of just and benevolent rulers and of prosperous true believers to the rights of the poor and the suffering. This social turn was of course related to the politics of bourgeois revolutions, to the commitment to constitution-alism and to the rule of law, the *Rechtsstaat*. However, this should not be interpreted as a rise of social citizenship in any concrete or explicit sense. The notion of social citizenship made an early appearance in revolutionary France where Article XXI of the *Rights of Man and the Citizen* (1793) declared that society is 'obliged to provide subsistence to all less fortunate citizens [*citoyens malheureux*]' by procuring work or assuring means of existence to those who cannot work. A system of social security and of public health care was legislated for in 1794. Adequate administrative as well as financial resources were lacking though, and the social dynamic went out of the Revolution. These projects came to nothing (Hatzfeld 1971). Citizenship had to wait another 150 years before coming to the forefront of social policy in the aftermath of the Second World War. Citizenship never became the dominant notion of social rights, although recent issues of immigration has made it more salient in a way T.H. Marshall could not possibly have foreseen in his famous 1949 lecture.

If social rights did not develop as citizenship rights, how did they develop? Three phenomena have trumped citizenship in most of the modern period in almost all countries: class, population and categorical groups (mostly based on occupation).

The new industrial working class was an important protagonist as well as a target of modern social policy, and the international model of the continental European welfare state grew out of conscious institutional and political efforts to minimize the ascendancy of the working-class movement, in particular in Germany. In 1871 a key adviser to the victorious German nation-builder chancellor Otto von Bismarck witnessed close-up in occupied France the insurrectionary potential of the working class in the Paris Commune, as well as the relatively developed institutions of social insurance, namely, the artisanal *mutualités* or friendly societies. National class integration by state-organized social insurance became a German export industry of the Wilhelmine Reich (Alber 1982), reaching as far as Japan. Within the European working-class movement, industrial safety – notably, labour inspectorates and oc-cupational injury insurance – was a priority. Here Britain, whose factory inspectors provided important source materials for Karl Marx while writing *Capital*, was the trailblazer.

The German class model was substantially modified, both in Scandinavia and in the British Empire (cf. Baldwin 1990). In neither of the latter areas was the industrial working class so demarcated from other popular traditions, of agrarian or urban petit-bourgeois radicalism, nor growing so rapidly as a class-conscious, Marxist-led class-for-itself. In Scandinavia and in Britain alleviation of poverty was more important to reformers than taming the dangerous industrial workers. But they were referring not to citizens, but to 'workmen' (Lloyd-George 2000 [1908]). The Swedish Pensions Bill of 1913 became the world's first universal scheme, not as a civic right but as a pragmatic conclusion of class analysis. Already in 1888, the Workers' Insurance Committee had concluded that workers and 'persons of similar standing' comprised 95% of the population, a recognition of the strength of agrarian populism. In the final parliamentary deliberation on the Pensions Bill in 1913, it was concluded that it would simply be unnecessarily bureaucratic and costly to exclude a tiny minority of rich people from the pensions system.

Conscript armies and industrial warfare brought the quantity and the quality of nation-state populations into high politics. This was voiced eloquently as an imperial concern in the British Poor Law Report of 1909 (Bruce 1968: 156) in the wake of the inglorious Boer War. The eugenic movement for genetic upgrading of the population developed in Britain soon after, and became a major political force in the 1930s. With powerful liberal reverberations, from Switzerland to the United States, and an integral part of fascism both in Italy and Germany, population-driven social policy was developed most extensively in Sweden. The only global rival to the Beveridge Report as a social policy bestseller was Gunnar and Alva Myrdal's *Crisis of the Population Question* (1934), which set the agenda of an extensive Swedish social policy for a decade. In its emphasis on promoting voluntary parenthood, this social policy thrust was unique in supporting women's employment and cautiously opening up to abortion rights.

Categorical groups were defined by generation, sex and occupation; primarily by the last which derived from pre- and early industrial occupational associations and mutual aid societies, above all of artisanal character. A considerable proportion of social policy has been aimed at providing categorical groups of the latter type with public rights and public financial support. Their predominance has been a characteristic of Latin/Mediterranean European and Latin American social entitlements, with their enclaved and fragmented working classes.

Social rights have also been bound up with residence, with *denizenship* rather than citizenship. Secular poor law rights were usually linked to parish/municipal residence, encouraging attempts to shift costs by moving the poor on to other parishes. The Chinese *hukou* system, which initially sharply distinguished the rights of rural and urban citizens, is a very important determinant of welfare in China. Residents of provinces, cantons or states often have specific rights of care and, in affirmative action nations like India or Nigeria, particular rights to higher education and to jobs. The narrow citizenship-based policy of 'guest worker' immigration, pioneered by Switzerland and developed by Germany and Austria from the early 1960s, was not adopted in the rest of Europe.

The historical record shows that civic social rights are surprisingly limited and rarely explicit or implemented. They are not even mentioned among the 'three guiding principles' of the *Beveridge Report* (2000 [1942]: 144). Universal access as a citizenship right was, however, enshrined in the postwar British National Health Service; once an admired international model adopted in the communist countries of Eastern Europe and occasionally west of them (e.g., rather late in Latin Europe) but now abandoned or under siege East and West. The system still survives in the UK but under bizarre financial rules, under which the hospital with one of the highest death rates in the 2000s was promoted to 'foundation' status for its financial rectitude (Healthcare Commission 2009). Most welfare state benefits base their claim rights on social insurance contributions, not upon citizenship. Others, means-tested, are meant for the poor only.

The politics of welfare

Comparative political sociology of welfare has, on the whole, been mainly interested in possibly explanatory background variables, and much less in the political process. A good example here is a Swedish project and volume directed and edited by Stefan Svallfors: 'The three concepts of our analytical framework are orientations, social cleavages, and political institutions' (Svallfors 2007: 9, italics omitted). Other works may be summed up in terms of foci on values, including religion, parties and legal heritage. The reason is, of course, that most scholars in the field have been interested mainly in social policy outcomes rather than politics.

The rich institutional literature has demonstrated that welfare state developments have been patterned by constellations of class cleavages and broad value orientations, and significantly affected by party and legal systems. But we may also ask: What kind of politics has driven welfare forward? What kind of politics has decreased 'common' or 'general' welfare? The answers to the first question, which may be distilled from the vast body of political historiography as well as of social institutional research, are:

- *Philanthropic concern* with poverty, misery and disease has been one driving force, going back to ancient religious and political norms, pushed by social reformers – more often secular or lay than clerical – of various kinds operating in the public sphere from the nineteenth century onwards. It has tended to be most effective when (also) concerned with externalities of misery, as in urban reform and public health. While its political forms were very often linked to, were often driven by, preoccupations with social conservation and stability, philanthropy is a significant orientation in several different prosperous milieus.

- Explicit *popular demands* were crucial in concerns with industrial safety, in particular outside Britain and its strong philanthropic current, and for unemployment insurance. Their significance has continued – for example, a Trade Union Congress demand in getting the Beveridge Committee set up and demands by the manual workers' confederation, LO (Swedish Trade Union Confederation), which brought general superannuation onto the Swedish political agenda in the 1950s. Popular demand politics has been hampered in driving welfare expansion by difficulties of political articulation among the poor, the sick, the unemployed and the discriminated. Progressive political parties, the British Labour Party in particular, have been crucial in bringing together philanthropy, popular concerns and policy expertise.

- Initiatives by *national leadership* have sometimes been important but relatively few first-rank politicians have directed social policy. Bismarck in Germany, Lloyd-George and later Aneurin Bevan in Britain, Jorge Battle in Uruguay and Gustav Möller of the Swedish Social Democratic Party are exceptions in more than a century of worldwide social policy.

- While the size and composition of the political franchise have certainly been important, as stressed in the institutional literature, specific *elections* have generally been surprisingly ineffectual for institutional change. An electoral social cycle has, however, developed in which existing benefits tend to rise in election years. An exceptional example of decisive elections took place in Sweden between 1957 and 1960. There was a referendum on superannuation in 1957 followed by an extraordinary parliamentary election in 1958, and a consolidating election in 1960, which together established a comprehensive public system of occupational pensions and redrew the lines of cleavage in Swedish politics, bringing the bulk of white-collar employees into the social democracy camp for a generation.

- *Group lobbying* was historically important in providing state subsidies and sponsorship of voluntary insurance societies. Social group lobbying accounts for the repertoire of segmented social group rights above all in Latin America and in Latin/Mediterranean Europe, from French Metro drivers to Greek trombone players. Advocacy groups later became important components of the social field almost everywhere, also confronted by powerful anti-welfare lobbies.

- Social rights have become a quite complex configuration of qualification criteria, benefit kinds and benefit levels. All this calls for *technical expertise*, which is another crucial variable of welfare politics. It has a powerful inbuilt bias of institutional conservatism and historical path dependency. In the disciplinary field, Theda Skocpol (1995) was a pioneer in drawing attention to this, but few have followed her lead.

- *Mass protests* have occasionally punctuated social policy making. As might be expected from its political tradition, France has provided the most telling examples. Most significant were the trade-union-orchestrated protests in 1995 against cuts to existing pension rights. In the end, they brought down the government as well as the proposal, resulting in an election that the socialist opposition won.

The political economy and political ethnicity of anti-welfare

Successful politics of anti-welfare, of reducing the living standard of poor, often of ordinary people, does not accurately mirror the politics of welfare. Criticism of public social generosity and of social rights has been a constant of modern times, but is often confined to the privileged minority and its intellectual admirers and hangers-on (cf. Rothstein 1998). In its effort to stem the rise of public expenditure on welfare, over the long run of modern politics anti-welfare has been a political loser. In 1930 public social transfers amounted to 0.6% of the American gross domestic product (GDP), for instance, in 1960 they amounted to 7% and in 1980 and 1990 to 11% (Lindert 2004, Vol. 2: 195). On average, in 1950 the four large Western European states (France, West Germany, Italy and the UK) spent 10% of their still war-ravished GDP on public social transfers; in 1980, 17% (Kohl 1985: 266). As we shall see, expansion did not stop there. However, a Whig interpretation of social progress would not do justice to the actual social record either. Significant also are a political economy and a (usually ethnically coloured) politics of stigma in anti-welfarism.

On the whole, it can be said that a successful politics of anti-welfare has almost always had to resort to the 'dismal science' of economics to force its advance. In the Depression of the 1930s, the response of cutting unemployment benefits and other social entitlements was the predominant 'Treasury view' (Keynes). The economic crisis of the 1970s/early 1980s was used and invoked in many countries across the globe as a rod for anti-welfare policies. However, it failed to stop public disbursement from growing. In the poor world, from Africa to post-communist Balticum, after the 2008 crisis, the economists of the International Monetary Fund have been major players in anti-welfare politics. At the time of writing, crisis-mongering, feeding on the Greek public deficit, is being utilized to motivate curtailments of social rights and has been endorsed by several elections: in the UK, the Netherlands and the Czech Republic. As in the 1980s, a British Tory-led government is in the vanguard of anti-welfare, invoking an alleged economic argument for there being 'no alternative'. The economics of anti-welfare is usually argued in terms of priority and/or incentives. The living conditions of people below the prosperous middle class are less urgent than reducing the public deficit and/or curbing inflation. If the labour conditions and social benefits of the non-prosperous are too good, they have little incentive to work hard and long for profitable wages, but if the prosperous are taxed too highly they are assumed to work less.

Anti-welfare politics is also, secondly, thriving by turning the classical pro-welfare coalition of the people against the privileged on its head: into a cleavage of decent working people against the fraudsters and the lazy. This *politics of stigma* is most easily achieved when an ethnic divide can be deployed against the latter; against, for example, immigrants, blacks, gypsies. The 1960s tilt of the US AFDC programme, from primarily benefiting white widows to mainly supporting unmarried black mothers, turned 'welfare' into a dirty word in American English. In 2009 the Obama Administration's plans to make health insurance all but a civic right could be successfully demonized as an outreach to the undeserving poor and immigrants at an outrageous cost to deserving Americans. Recent mass immigration into Western Europe, and the ethnic politics of the post-communist East, has propelled ethnic divisions into social policy there too. Where the socio-political field is very diverse and fragmented, as in the United States, sectional anti-welfare lobbies have often proved powerful veto groups.

Welfare States and Their Study: Three Postwar Generations of Comparative Research

Before a roster of welfare states with extensive social policies was established and consolidated, social policy studies were mainly the domain of insurance experts, labour economists and social reformers. The topic was largely outside both political science and sociology. T.H. Marshall's 1949 lecture (Marshall 1950) was a singular exception. This situation changed in the 1970s following the extraordinary social policy expansion of the 1960s, whereupon comparative social policy has become a major area of political sociology. One way of cutting a short, accessible path through this rich field of research is to divide it up into three generations of investigation, each with a characteristic predominant shaped by an agenda-setting piece of work; a focus which is geopolitical as well as analytical.

1. An American world of spending

The patterning of the worldwide growth of public social security efforts became the successful object of Harold Wilensky's pioneering study *The Welfare State and Equality – Structural and Ideological Roots of Public Expenditure* (1975), the foremost example of the first generation of welfare state studies. Analytically, it focused on public spending and its roots in industrialization and demography; geopolitically, it looked at the world from an American vantage point. This book spanned all five continents (though China was represented by Taiwan) and included data on social spending and social welfare programmes in 64 countries. In analytical terms, he made a distinction (p. 138) between four types of welfare state: democratic (31 countries), totalitarian (8 countries), authoritarian oligarchic countries (17) and authoritarian populist states (8). The last two types were not really part of his analysis, and very little was said about the differences between the first two apart from their most obvious Cold War aspects. Wilensky then narrowed down his sample by focusing on the 22 most advanced states: 19 Western countries including Israel, and 3 East European countries (Czechoslovakia, Poland and Hungary). There he stressed the similarity, or convergence, of the core welfare states.

The context was an American-centred world with a Cold War divide combined with a degree of détente, and a takeoff of public social commitments in the rich countries starting in the 1960s. By 1980, social expenditure (including education) accounted for about 60% of all public expenditure in developed capitalist countries, including the United States (OECD 1985).

2. Social rights: the beacon of Northern European social democracy

European reaction to this analysis was critical. It was challenged by a considerable number of scholars, in particular from West German and Scandinavian universities and research institutes. The argument was that social expenditure figures did not say much about welfare state developments but institutional arrangements and their effects on social relations did. Social rights independent of market status, 'decommodification' – a term first promoted by Claus Offe – were proposed, indexed and popularized as an alternative analytical focus.

Gösta Esping-Andersen's seminal *The Three Worlds of Welfare Capitalism* (1990) became the centre point of this second wave of research. The conventional sample had shrunk to 18 or fewer Western countries. Japan was included, Israel gone, and the rest of the world had disappeared altogether. Twelve West European countries were the objects of documentation and analysis in Peter Flora's monumental but unfinished *Growth to Limits* (1986–1987).

The background now was a social and cultural independence of Western Europe from its powerful and affluent American uncle, and an historical peak of labour movement influence, including of social rights inspired by it or trying to cope with it. Trajectories of suffrage, varieties of party cleavages (and of electoral strength in particular) and patterns of unionization became key explanatory variables (Korpi 1983). Not convergence but differences among the Western welfare states were emphasized. The 'three worlds' of North Atlantic welfare states provided a widely influential typology of differences. In addition to the Anglo-Saxon liberal male welfare breadwinner model, the spotlight was turned on two other welfare regimes and their expansions: on the one hand, the hierarchical and stratified continental or conservative traditional family-oriented welfare state of German provenience, and, on the other, what was now seen as the archetypical modern welfare state, namely the egalitarian Scandinavian or social democratic model of generous and general social entitlements and with a state feminist gender-equality approach (Lewis 1992). This was followed by the discovery of a special Southern European type: a second-class version of the conservative-continental, and, a few years into the 1990s, by a post-socialist model in Central and Eastern Europe. The 'encompassing' Scandinavian welfare state is the most elaborate one emerging from the dataset focusing on welfare coverage, redistribution and citizenship rights skilfully created and collected in Stockholm, Sweden by Walter Korpi and his many collaborators (e.g., Korpi and Palme 2003).

At the start of the neoliberal onslaught and of capitalist 'globalization', the focus of welfare state research had turned inwards, towards the small North Atlantic slice of the world.

3. Sustainability and globality

Since the early 1990s, the tenor as well as the geography of comparative welfare state research has changed dramatically, following the rest of the world into 'globalization' (Rieger and Leibfried 2003). The guiding analytical question is no longer welfare state expansion, whether by spending or by decommodifying social relationships. The issue now is one of sustainability. Can the welfare state maintain itself in the face of neoliberal political attacks, of globalization of capital power and of social dumping, in competition with economically ambitious regimes of insecurity and mass poverty, under conditions of demographic ageing and in view of ecological questioning of the sustainability of a globalization of the Northern level of consumption? Esping-Andersen (1996) edited one of the first major reconsiderations, in connection with the World Social Summit in 1995. The global sustainability of the European welfare state soon became a preoccupation of European comparative scholars. On the whole, the conclusion so far of this third generation of social policy scholarship has been that developed welfare states have maintained themselves, and that institutional changes should be seen as reconstructions rather than dismantling (cf. Leibfried and Mau 2008, Vol. II).

Social issues, policies and institutional arrangements in almost all parts of the world are now brought into the mainstream of research (Haggard and Kaufmann 2008). In a new global perspective, Ian Gough has broadened the comparative conceptual framework into one of 'welfare regimes', where the well-known welfare state regimes coexist with 'informal security' and 'insecurity' regimes (Gough 2004: 32ff). Global social policies, by international organizations such as the World Bank, the International Labour Organization and regional transnational actors, are also being highlighted by research. Global research is still heavily dependent on Euro-American institutions and funding, but the background and experience of researchers are widening geographically (Midgley and Tang 2010). In the 2000s, social entitlement and social services are growing in most parts of the world, crisis-ridden post-communist Eastern Europe being the main exception (Aidukaite (ed.) 2009).

Looking ahead: New Constellations of Rights and Duties

The industrial welfare states have proved remarkably resilient in the face of the vast structural changes brought about by de-industrialization and capitalist 'globalization', and in facing the ideological and political assaults of aggressive neoliberalism. Social expenditure and civilian public expenditure as a whole of the rich OECD economies have stayed, nay climbed further, on their historically high plateau reached by industrial forces of welfare and equality at the peak of their influence and power around 1980. It is unlikely that public social expenditure will be pushed down to its 1980 level in the foreseeable future. In 2005 average welfare expenditure among the G7 countries was 21.9% of GDP, as compared to 16.5 in 1980 (http://stats.oecd.org). Electoral democracy and a large senior citizenry pose limits to anti-welfare onslaughts.

The forms of change of social welfare institutions over the past century have been notably path-dependent despite strong international attention to fashionable national models; Germany in the late nineteenth and early twentieth centuries, mid-twentieth-century Britain, later on the 'Nordic model' and the more specific policy planks of the neoliberal era such as Pinochetista private pensions from Chile touted by the World Bank (1994) and US Clintonite 'workfare'. There has been emulation, but rarely without national accents. Any number of examples illustrate this path dependency. The segmented German social insurance systems survived the Nazi era in spite of strenuous efforts by one component of the regime, Robert Ley and the German Labour Front (DAF) (Gründger 1994: 139ff). For all the admiration bestowed upon it, the Beveridge project was adopted nowhere in postwar continental Europe. Even in Britain itself, the 'plan' of the Beveridge Report was never implemented according to prescription. The World Bank private pensions offensive scored in Latin America and in post-communist Europe, but it stalled not only in Western Europe but also, so far, in American Social Security. In Chile itself it has been inserted into a larger public system, and in Argentina privatization has been revoked.

Currently, welfare state policies are spreading to new countries of developed industrial capitalism such as South Korea (Kwon 2005). India has an array of social policy schemes, and China is returning to social policy. In short, the safest bet on the future of social policy is that it will continue to comprise the bulk of state expenditure and efforts of developed states, and that it will expand with economic development in Asia, Latin America and Africa (cf. Olivier and Kuhnle 2008).

The social rights of citizenship, which once were thought to reach maturity in the most developed welfare states, are, however, facing a problematic future. They are attacked from one side and questioned from another. They are attacked by neoliberals and by the latter's 'human face', 'Third Way' followers, for not pushing people into the labour market for a living and into the financial market for their pension.

The core features of advanced twenty-first-century welfare policies are no longer the risk presented by industrial workers. The current concerns are, firstly, old age, and, secondly, work–family balances of women and men (cf. Esping-Andersen 2009). Retirement age, pensions systems, health care, and social care of the elderly are the frontlines of social politics and policy. Ageing, as a mass demographic phenomenon, raises a set of social issues which are also going to knock hard on the doors of Chinese policy-makers very soon as an effect of the tough and successful one-child policy. The end of the classical bourgeois family, which became an ideal for the working class, the massive entrance of women into the labour market, the belated male discovery of the vast pool of female economic talent and plummeting birth rates in Europe and Japan have made work–family balance a second major social concern, bringing issues of parental leave and child care onto the mainstream agenda. The American push of poor single mothers onto the labour market has made day-care for children a public policy issue in the United States, although hardly a major provision (Ziliak 2009: 20). These two policy complexes are unlikely to decline in importance over the new century, at least not under conditions of political democracy. With the extension of human life expectancy, and with the stretch of human social capacity and resources at both ends, into computer-savvy childhood as well as into sexually active old age, inter-generational relations and conflicts are likely to come to the fore.

Thomas Marshall's 1949 Cambridge lecture on *Citizenship and Social Class* (Marshall 1950) set itself against the background of an 1873 lecture by the economist Alfred Marshall on *The Future of the Working Classes*. The gist of the latter was the forward march of equality towards a state where 'by occupation at least, every man is a gentleman'. The latter Marshall had the brilliant idea of transposing 'the modern drive towards social equality' into 'an evolution of citizenship' (Marshall 1950: 8). Citi-zenship may indeed be seen as a legally codified form of existential equality (cf. Therborn 2006: 7–8). But as an interpretation of the new Beveridgian welfare state it was a bit bogus, as we noted above.

But the main point here is a different one. There is no longer 'a drive towards social equality' in general, although there is one in terms of existential equality of gender and sexuality, and, with many more qualifications, of race and ethnicity. In terms of income, the boot is on the other foot. Since about 1980, in most, if not all, cases income inequality among citizens is increasing, and the gap between the richest and the poorest on the planet is widening.

Social citizenship rights are further questioned from two other angles. One raises the issue of obligations to qualify for entitlement. Two such obligations have come into the foreground in the 1990s and 2000s. One is a duty of active job search and of accepting whatever low-paid job is offered. This has hitherto been applied on the largest scale and with greatest stringency in the United States. In milder forms it is becoming popular among European politicians of the right. How successful it has been in its own terms, and how coercive it is, remain controversial. A quite different twist to it is given in Latin America, in Brazil with its *bolsa familia* programme in particular. There your duty is to your children. Poor parents get a crucial federal benefit provided they see to it that children get vaccinated and attend school. This policy is almost universally regarded as a great success, helping millions of families rise above the poverty line and substantially increasing school enrolment and attendance.

The implications of citizenship have also come up for discussion because of the return of mass international migration after the lull of the second third of the twentieth century. Non-citizens, especially denizens or long-term residents, have been accorded social rights, of various kinds, in Europe and North America (see Soysal, Chapter 34, in this volume), and the European Union (EU) means social rights for citizens residing in other member states. However, with immigration becoming increasingly contro-versial, there is a rising tendency to draw a sharper and thicker line of demarcation between national citizens with rights and non-citizens with fewer or no social rights. In the member states of the EU this is mediated by Union membership, with the bridge drawn up in front of extra-EU immigrants (from poor countries).

At a global level, on the other hand, we are witnessing an updating of the moral precepts of the ancient *polis* and of the ancient kingdoms. While there are no effective global human social rights, the rulers of this world are held to have a duty to provide some relief to the poorest and the most suffering of the world. The duty to secure the sustainability of decent social life on the planet is also increasingly discussed (cf. Gough and Therborn 2010).

Modern politics and policies of social rights constitute a delimited field, encroached upon but still largely intact, of time and territory between vague and elusive duties of ancient rulers and of a post-modern 'international community' or 'global civil society'. In the past, the practical value of the duties of the powerful and privileged was modest, and the rights people got had to be fought for. The twenty-first century does not look different in that respect.

Further Reading

Esping-Andersen, G. 1990: *The Three Worlds of Welfare Capitalism*. Cambridge: Polity Press.

Gough, I. and Wood, G. with Barrientos, A. *et al.* 2004: *Insecurity and Welfare Regimes in Asia, Africa and Latin America: Social Policy in Development Contexts*. Cambridge: Cambridge University Press.

Korpi, W. and Palme, J. 2003: New politics and class politics in the context of austerity and globalization: welfare state regress in18 countries, 1975–95. *American Political Science Review* 97(3): 425–446.

Marshall, T.H. 1950: *Citizenship and Social Class*. Cambridge: Cambridge University Press.

Rieger, E. and Leibfried, S. 2003: *Limits to Globalization. Welfare States and the World Economy*. Cambridge, Polity Press.

Wilensky, H. 1975: *The Welfare State and Equality*. Berkeley: University of California Press.

33

Citizenship and Gender

Ruth Lister

Feminist scholarship has revealed how citizenship has been male, in theory and practice. Central to this is the gendered public–private dichotomy, which has contributed to women's admission to citizenship on male terms and also to the way their exclusion has generally been ignored by citizenship theorists. Citizenship is a contested concept, with roots in the very different traditions of liberalism and republicanism. Both rights and responsibilities have been reinterpreted by feminist scholars. The three main feminist approaches to citizenship are 'gender-neutrality', working with a model of women as equal with men; 'gender-differentiation', working with a model of the sexes as different; and 'gender-pluralism', in which both women and men are seen as members of multiple groups. Lister argues that the re-gendering of citizenship requires a synthesis of these approaches together with change in public and private spheres to enable both women and men to combine paid work and caring responsibilities.

'Is citizenship gendered?' The answer to this question, posed by Sylvia Walby (1994), has to be a resounding 'yes'. Citizenship has always been gendered in the sense that women and men have stood in a different relationship to it, to the disadvantage of women. Yet, for much of its history, a veil of gender-neutrality has obscured the nature of this differential relationship. Today, as feminist theorists have stripped away this veil, the challenge is to reconceptualize citizenship in gendered terms in the image of women as well as men. We are thus talking about citizenship and gender from two angles: as an historical relationship and as a normative or political and theoretical project.

This chapter will discuss each in turn. It will focus in particular on the key debates around what we might call the 're-gendering' of citizenship. These relate to the meaning of citizenship itself and, more centrally, to the nature of this 're-gendering': is

The Wiley-Blackwell Companion to Political Sociology, First Edition. Edited by Edwin Amenta, Kate Nash, and Alan Scott.
© 2012 Blackwell Publishing Ltd. Published 2012 by Blackwell Publishing Ltd.

the aim a genuinely 'gender-neutral' or a 'gender-differentiated' model? Or can we, as I shall argue, avoid getting stuck in this particular formulation of the traditional 'equality' vs. 'difference' dilemma through a synthesis of the two and through a pluralist 'conception of citizenship which would accommodate all social cleavages simultaneously'? (Leca 1992: 30).

Citizenship and Gender: An Historical Relationship

Citizenship as both a theory and a practice operates simultaneously as a force for inclusion and exclusion, both within and at the borders of nation-states (see Soysal, Chapter 34, in this volume). Women have been denied the full and effective title of citizen for much of history, ancient and modern. The twentieth-century mainstream theorization of citizenship has tended to ignore the ways in which women's gradual achievement of civil, political and social rights often followed a different pattern from men's. Likewise, it has tended to dismiss women's earlier exclusion as an historical aberration, now more or less effectively remedied. Thus, for example, Adrian Oldfield asserts that it does not 'require too much imagination... to extend the concept of "citizen" to include women'; leaving aside Machiavelli and even allowing for the 'citizen-soldier', there is, he claims, 'nothing aggressively male' about the concept (1990: 59).

The excavations of feminist scholarship have, on the contrary, revealed how, in both theory and practice, despite its claims to universalism, citizenship has been quintessentially male. While the purpose of these excavations has generally been to spotlight women's exclusion from citizenship, critical studies in masculinities are beginning to problematize the other side of the gender equation: men's relationship to citizenship. Jeff Hearn (2001: 248), for instance, argues that 'to gender citizenship more fully... [means] making the theorizing of men more critical and more explicit', but in a way which also decentres men and which acknowledges their social heterogeneity. An example is Paul Kershaw's work, which explores 'male citizenship dysfunction' with regard to 'care irresponsibility' and violence (Kershaw, Pulkingham and Fuller 2008: 186, 184).

The exposure of the quintessential maleness of citizenship helps us to understand that women's exclusion (and the chequered nature of their inclusion), far from being an aberration, has been integral to the theory and practice of citizenship. Nowhere was this more obvious than in classical Greece where the active participation of male citizens in the public sphere was predicated on women's labour in the 'private' domestic sphere, which rendered them as unfit for citizenship. The public–private dichotomy, and the male–female qualities associated with it, stands at the heart of the gendered citizenship relationship. On the 'public' side stands the disembodied citizen *qua* man who displays the necessary qualities of impartiality, rationality, independence and political agency. This is upheld by the 'private' side to which embodied women are relegated and from whence they are deemed incapable of developing the 'male' qualities of citizenship (Pateman 1989). The continued power of this deeply gendered dichotomy has meant that women's admission to citizenship has been on male terms. It has also meant that much mainstream theorizing about citizenship continues to discount the relevance of what happens in the private sphere to the practice of citizenship in the public sphere (Lister 2007). Thus, for example, it ignores the ways in which the gendered division of labour in the private sphere shapes the access of both women and men to the public sphere and to the political, economic and social rights of citizenship which derive from such access (Lister 2003). Related to this is a lack of interest in time as a resource for citizenship (Bryson 2007). Feminist citizenship theory has also drawn attention to the implications for citizenship of conflicts over the terrain of women's bodies in both private and public spheres. In other words, it emphasizes the embodied nature of citizenship (Lister 2009).

Why Re-gender Citizenship?

For some, the historically gendered nature of citizenship, together with its inherently exclusive tendencies at the boundaries of nation-states, renders it a concept of little value for contemporary feminism. This rejection of the very concept of citizenship is rarely articulated in print, although Gillian Pascall (1993) expresses deep ambivalence about a concept that is so problematic for women. Likewise, Anne Phillips has warned that 'in a period in which feminism is exploring the problems in abstract universals, citizenship may seem a particularly unpromising avenue to pursue' (1993: 87). Nevertheless, it is an avenue that has become positively crowded by feminist scholars, in a wide range of countries, intent on re-gendering citizenship from the standpoints of women (for an overview, see Voet 1998; Lister, 2007).

This feminist preoccupation with citizenship in part reflects a wider desire to (re) claim concepts that have been hijacked in the interests of men. Citizenship is a pivotal contested concept in contemporary political and social theory. As such, feminists cannot afford to be absent from the contest. More positively, citizenship is seen by many as an analytical and political tool of considerable potential value (Walby 1994; Lister 2003; Yuval-Davis 1997; Voet 1998). It has also been deployed by a range of social movements, in which women are active, reminding us that women do not necessarily claim citizenship simply as women but as, for example, black women, disabled women or lesbian women.

Given citizenship's status as a 'contested concept', it is hardly surprising that the issue of how to re-gender it is not straightforward. The debates can be grouped around two questions concerning the nature of citizenship and the nature of its re-gendering.

The Nature of Citizenship

First, however, the literature increasingly recognizes that citizenship is a contextualized as well as a contested concept. As Birte Siim warns, 'there is no universal story about gender and citizenship. The story about the constraints and possibilities for the inclusion of women in full citizenship... needs to be told from different national contexts' (2000: 3). A cross-national study of gendered citizenship in Western Europe illustrates how 'as lived experience, citizenship cannot be divorced from its context – temporal and national. Diverse aspects of gendered citizenship are salient at particular periods of time in different countries' (Lister *et al.* 2007: 1).

As a theoretical concept, one reason why citizenship is contested is that it has its roots in two very different, and at times antagonistic, political traditions: liberalism and civic republicanism. The former casts citizenship as a *status* involving, primarily, rights accorded to individuals; the latter casts it as a *practice* involving responsibilities to the wider society (Heater 1990; Oldfield 1990). Whereas, under classical liberalism, rights were confined to the civil and political spheres, the twentieth century saw their extension to the social sphere and more recently their embrace of new categories, such as reproductive rights, demanded by social movements. Within civic republicanism, the citizen is primarily a political actor, exercising 'his' civic duty within the public sphere. In the late twentieth century, though, the more prominent duties discourse centres on work obligations as one element in what has been described as a communitarian strand to citizenship (Lister *et al.* 2007).

Rights

Until relatively recently, it is a rights discourse which has been more dominant. Women have struggled to achieve equal rights with men in the civil, political and social spheres as crucial to their achievement of full citizenship. Although some contemporary feminists reject a legal rights discourse as individualistic and male-inspired, many others acknowledge 'the dual nature of the law – as an agent of emancipation as well as oppression' and that, for all its shortcomings, it 'has played a vital role in securing for women the prerequisites of citizenship' (Vogel 1988: 155). There has thus been a rich debate within feminism about the status and nature of citizenship rights, as well as about the value of deploying a rights discourse (Hobson and Lister 2002).

Out of this debate has emerged the idea of embodied rights, in particular the right to bodily integrity (Lister 2009). Naila Kabeer writes that 'women have been able to gain recognition and ratification for new kinds of rights, rights which reflect an "embodied" rather than a disembodied understanding of what it is to be human, and hence an embodied rather than an abstract, view of citizenship' (2005: 11). Examples are reproductive rights, rights connected with domestic violence and what have come to be known generically as 'sexual rights' (Richardson 2000).

Political participation

From the perspective of re-gendering citizenship, there have been two main sources of challenge to a rights-based approach, centring on political participation and on promoting care as a citizenship obligation. In a text on feminism and citizenship, Rian Voet argues that 'instead of seeing citizenship as the means to realize rights, we should see rights as one of the means to realize equal citizenship. This implies that feminism ought to be more than a movement for women's rights; it ought to be a movement for women's participation' (1998: 73). She goes on to argue that having acquired citizenship rights, it is the exercise of those rights, especially in the political sphere, which is crucial to the full development of women's citizenship as part of what she calls 'an active and sex-equal citizenship' (1998: ch. 11).

The most forceful case for a feminist civic republican model of citizenship is that made by Mary Dietz. She advocates 'a vision of citizenship' which is 'expressly political' and, more exactly, 'participatory and democratic'. In this vision, politics involves 'the collective and participatory engagement of citizens in the determination of the affairs of their community' and we conceive of ourselves as '"speakers of words and doers of deeds" mutually participating in the public realm'. It is only, she contends, when active political participation is valued as an expression of citizenship, in contrast to the 'politically barren' construction of the 'citizen as bearer of rights' alone, that feminists will 'be able to claim a truly liberatory politics of their own' (1987: 13–15). Other feminists, sympathetic to Dietz's vision, such as Anne Phillips (1991, 1993) and Iris Young (1990b), nevertheless caution against an uncritical reading of civic republicanism that, *inter alia*, defines the political in narrow terms and ignores the domestic constraints on many women's political participation.

Responsibilities

Central to these domestic constraints is the unpaid care work that many women still undertake in the home. Under present models of citizenship, such work does not tend to appear in the pantheon of citizenship responsibilities as does paid work, nor does it carry the same access to social rights. This has led some feminists, such as Pascall (1993), to be wary of claims to citizenship based on duties. In contrast, feminist theorists such as Nancy J. Hirschmann (1996), while critiquing notions of citizenship obligation grounded in social contract theory, have instead posited more relational conceptualizations, which value care. Diemut Bubeck has suggested that by focusing on citizenship obligations, feminists can turn conventional understandings of citizenship on their head through the introduction 'of a revised conception of citizenship in which the performance of her or his share of care has become a general citizen's obligation' (1995: 29; see also Kershaw, 2006).

A Critical Synthesis

Most would accept that citizenship involves a balance of rights and responsibilities; what is at issue is where that balance should lie and what should be the link, if any, between them. With regard to whether the re-gendering of citizenship is better pursued in terms of citizenship as a status or as a practice, my own position (echoing that of, for example, Chantal Mouffe 1992) is that we need a critical synthesis of the two. While the rights and participatory approaches to citizenship have developed along separate parallel tracks, they are not necessarily in conflict. On the contrary, they can be seen as mutually supportive, even if a tension remains between their primary concerns with the individual or the wider community. The development of women's position as citizens in the twentieth century can be understood as the outcome of the interplay between women's exercise of their political capacities and their emergent social rights.

The re-gendering of citizenship needs, first, to embrace both individual rights (and in particular social and reproductive rights) and political participation, broadly defined to include informal modes of politics, and, second, to analyse the relationship between the two. The notion of human agency helps us to knit the two together. Citizenship as participation can be understood as an expression of human agency in the political arena, broadly defined; citizenship as rights enables people to exercise their agency as citizens. As citizenship rights remain the object of political struggles to defend, reinterpret and extend them, a dynamic is set in motion in which the rights and participatory elements of citizenship stand in a dialectical relationship with one another. Re-gendering citizenship in this way is particularly important in challenging the construction of women (and especially 'minority group' women) as passive victims, while not losing sight of the structural and institutional constraints on their ability to act as citizens.

The Re-Gendering of Citizenship

The different approaches to the re-gendering of citizenship can be summed up under the three headings of 'gender-neutrality', 'gender-differentiation' and 'gender-pluralism'. The first works with a model of women as equal with men; the second with a model of women as different from men, thereby reflecting the long-standing 'equality vs. difference' debate within feminism. In the third model both women and men are members of multiple groups and/or holders of multiple identities. Individual theorists do not always fit neatly into any of the three categories, so that any views cited here should not necessarily be taken as definitive of the particular author's thinking. In my own work, I have attempted to develop a 'woman-friendly' conceptualization of citizenship that draws on aspects of each of these models (Lister 2003).

The gender-neutral citizen

The model of the gender-neutral citizen (or more accurately 'ostensibly' gender-neutral citizen) is most commonly associated with liberal feminism, although it is not necessarily confined to it. The emphasis is on equal rights and equal obligations. The gender of the citizen should be irrelevant to the allocation and exercise of these rights and obligations. From the time of the French Revolution to the present day, some feminists have used the egalitarian and universalistic promise of citizenship in the cause of women's emancipation and autonomy (Voet 1998).

In the political sphere, this has meant an emphasis on women's full and equal participation in formal politics, first through the winning of the vote and then through formal political representation. Women's representation in parliament and government has been pressed as a matter of equality and justice rather than as a means of promoting a particular set of interests or a 'different' way of doing politics (see Squires, Chapter 41, in this volume).

In the social sphere, the priority has been to enable women to compete on equal terms with men in the labour market. This in turn opens up access to the social rights of citizenship linked to labour market status through social insurance schemes. In both cases, women are better able to achieve the economic independence seen as critical to full and effective citizenship. This approach prioritizes effective sex discrimination and equal pay legislation combined with 'family-friendly' employment laws and practices, which enable women to combine paid work with their caring responsibilities in the home. Its logic underlies the social security rules operative in many countries, which require lone mothers and fathers claiming Social Security to be available for paid work (once their children reach a certain age, which in a number of US states is as young as 12 weeks) on the same basis as unemployed people.

While traditionally proponents of a gender-neutral citizenship have tended to focus on the changes in the public sphere necessary to achieve this ideal, today there tends to be a greater recognition of the changes which also need to be made in the private sphere, most notably in the gendered division of labour. A more equitable division of labour is, for example, central to Susan Moller Okin's vision of the 'genderless' family and society, which she sees as crucial to the transformation of women's position as citizens (1989: ch. 8). Likewise, Anne Phillips, one of the more prominent exponents of a gender-neutral citizenship, places great emphasis on a more equitable domestic division of labour as providing the context in which 'the notion of the citizen could begin to assume its full meaning, and people could participate as equals in deciding their common goals'. Phillips' 'vision is of a world in which gender should become less relevant and the abstractions of humanity more meaningful'. However, she acknowledges that in the transition to such a world, an emphasis on sexual differentiation is necessary in order 'to redress the imbalance that centuries of oppression have wrought' (1991: 7).

Phillips is thus well aware of the dangers of a gender-neutral model of citizenship in a gender-differentiated world and of lapsing into a false gender-neutrality that in practice privileges the male. Others see such dangers as inherent in an ostensibly gender-neutral conception of citizenship. Ursula Vogel, for instance, dismisses as 'futile' any attempt to insert women into 'the ready-made, gender-neutral spaces of traditional conceptions of citizenship' which are a chimera (1994: 86). Kathleen B. Jones is critical of gender-neutral approaches which require women to mould themselves to fit a citizenship template which has developed in the interests of men and which ignore 'the ways in which gender, as a socially constructed, historical reality, reflects different ways of being and knowing that fundamentally affect the practice and meaning of civic duties and responsibilities, and the enjoyment of civil and political rights' (1988: 20)

The gender-differentiated citizen

In an exploration of the possible meaning of citizenship in a 'woman-friendly polity', Jones contends that:

> a polity that is friendly to women and the multiplicity of their interests must root its democracy in the experiences of women and transform the practice and concept of citizenship to fit these varied experiences, rather than simply transform women to accommodate the practice of citizenship as it traditionally has been defined.
>
> (1990: 811)

Jones is primarily concerned with women's *political* citizenship. The dilemma she poses is 'how to recognize the political relevance of sexual differences and how to include these differences within definitions of political action and civic virtue without constructing sexually segregated norms of citizenship?' (1988: 18). Historically, attempts to incorporate sexual 'differences within definitions of political action' tended to be rooted in 'maternalist' arguments for treating motherhood as the equivalent of a male civic republicanism grounded in active political participation and the ability to bear arms. Motherhood represented the embodiment of difference, for only women, *qua* mothers, could bear the next generation of citizens (Pateman

1992). Another strand in maternalist thought made the case for women's full political participation with reference to the qualities and gifts that women could bring to politics as mothers.

Within contemporary feminism, this argument is echoed in Sarah Ruddick's exposition of 'maternal thinking' which she defines as 'the intellectual capacities [a mother] develops, the judgments she makes, the metaphysical attitudes she assumes, the values she affirms' (1989: 24). Although Ruddick does not herself write explicitly about citizenship, other 'social feminists', such as Jean Bethke Elshtain, have made the connection for her. It is in Elshtain's work that the torch of political maternalism burns brightest among late-twentieth-century feminists. She celebrates mothering and the private familial sphere in contrast to a negative picture of 'an ideal of citizenship and civic virtue that features a citizenry grimly going about their collective duty, or an elite band of citizens in their "public space" cut off from a world that includes most of the rest of us' (1981: 351).

The maternalist approach has been attacked by those who see it as constructing the 'sexually segregated norms of citizenship' which Jones warns against. As Carol Pateman (1992) has reminded us, it is just such sexually segregated norms that have served to subordinate and marginalize women as political citizens. Dietz rejects 'maternal thinking' as the basis for citizenship on the grounds that it reinforces 'a one-dimensional view of women as creatures of the family' and that it does not 'necessarily promote the kind of democratic politics social feminism purports to foster'. On the contrary, she argues that the exclusiveness and inequalities of power associated with the mother–child relationship make it a poor model for democratic citizenship (1985: 20; 1987).

In the face of the critique of a maternalist construction of citizenship, a number of feminists, sympathetic to some of the values promoted by maternalism, are arguing for a non-maternalistic conceptualization of difference in politics around the broader notion of care and an ethic of care, which is not confined to women. This is underpinned by a commitment to human interdependence rather than a concern with (in)dependence, as in the gender-neutral model (Sevenhuijsen 1998). The case for care as a resource for political citizenship has been put by Bubeck (1995) on the grounds that the private concerns, values, skills and understandings associated with the practice of caring can all enhance public practices of citizenship. One arena in which they can do so, in particular, is that of informal, often community-based, politics, which is often grounded in concerns which derive from women's responsibilities for care (Lister 2003). Part of Jones' case for a gender-differentiated citizenship is the need for 'a new grammar and ethos of political action' which incorporates women's political activities rather than simply mirroring male definitions of what counts as politics (1988, 1990: 789).

The momentum for the incorporation of care into our thinking about citizenship is, though, stronger in relation to social citizenship. Again, historically maternalism has played a pivotal role in attempts to forge a gender-differentiated conceptualization of social citizenship. In the early twentieth century, in a number of countries, certain feminists drew on maternalist arguments to make the case for women's access to social rights. For instance, in both the United States and Britain, the campaign for the endowment of motherhood drew on the imagery of motherhood as national service, the equivalent of men's military service, in the construction of their citizenship (Pederson 1990; Sarvasy 1992).

Today, a number of feminists are drawing on feminist theorizing around care to make the case for the incorporation of 'care in the definition of citizenship, so the rights to time to care and to receive care are protected' as part of a more inclusive approach to citizenship (Knijn and Kremer 1997: 357). One policy implication often drawn is that those who stay at home to provide care should receive payment. Others, while agreeing with the need to place more value on care for citizenship, are worried lest such payments should undermine women's claims to citizenship through equal participation in the labour market.

Thus even if the care approach, by focusing on women's responsibilities rather than their supposed qualities, and by acknowledging that care is not gender-specific, is less vulnerable than maternalism to a biological essentialism that freezes the differences between women and men, it still shares certain risks with it. These are the risk of marginalization, mentioned earlier, and also the risk of ignoring the differences between women. Some disabled feminists, for instance, reject the very language of care as casting disabled people in the role of dependants and argue that the discourse of caring is incompatible with a commitment to disabled people's rights to be equal, participating, citizens (Morris 2005).

More broadly, Mouffe criticizes those who attempt to replace the false universalism of traditional conceptualizations of citizenship with 'a sexually differentiated, "bi-gendered" conception of the individual and to bring women's so-called specific tasks into the very definition of citizenship'. Instead of 'making sexual difference politically relevant to its definition' she argues for 'a new conception of citizenship where sexual difference should become effectively nonpertinent' (1992b: 376).

The gender-pluralist citizen

This is not an argument for gender-neutrality but for what Mouffe terms 'a radical democratic conception of citizenship' (1992b: 377). She interprets the feminist struggle for women's equality not 'as a struggle for realizing the equality of a definable empirical group with a common essence and identity, women, but rather as a struggle against the multiple forms in which the category "woman" is constructed in sub-ordination'. Thus she favours 'an approach that permits us to understand how the subject is constructed through different discourses and subject positions' against one 'that reduces our identity to one single position – be it class, race, or gender' (1992b: 382). Mouffe's concern is with citizenship as a political practice and as a 'common political identity of persons who might be engaged in many different purposive enterprises and with differing conceptions of the good, but who are bound by their common identification' with pluralist democratic values (1992b: 378).

Mouffe explicitly distinguishes her own pluralist position from that of Iris Young who proposes a 'group differentiated citizenship'. In the name of a 'heterogeneous public that acknowledges and affirms group differences', Young makes the case for a 'politics of group assertion' which 'takes as a basic principle that members of oppressed groups need separate organizations that exclude others, especially those from more privileged groups'. To this end, 'a democratic public should', she contends, 'provide mechanisms for the effective recognition and representation of the distinct voices and perspectives of those of its constituent groups that are oppressed or disadvantaged' (1990b: 10, 167, 184).

A key criticism which has been made of Young's proposal is that it runs the danger of freezing group identities, suppressing differences within groups and impeding wider solidarities (Mouffe 1992: 376; Phillips 1993). More fluid pluralist approaches, which are less prone to these dangers, have been articulated around the notions of a 'politics of difference' (Yeatman 1993), a 'transversal politics' (Yuval-Davis 1997), a 'politics of solidarity in difference' (Lister 2003) and a 'reflective solidarity' (Dean 1996).

Gender-pluralist approaches are best equipped to accommodate the range of social divisions, such as sexuality, class, 'race', ethnicity, religion, (dis)ability and age, which intersect with gender to shape the citizenship of women and men. They are reflected in a growing literature, which explores the intersections between migration, citizenship and gender (see, for instance, Tastsoglou and Dobrowolsky, 2006; Lister *et al.* 2007). One example, a study by Umut Erel of migrant Turkish women in Germany and Britain, argues explicitly for 'intersectionality as an epistemology for citizenship practice' (2009: 193). Erel's study explores how 'migrant women's experiences of intermeshing social divisions of ethnicity, gender, class, sexuality, ability and age structure their citizenship status and practices'. (*ibid*) She contends that 'if we recognize the central role of boundary making processes for the constitution of groups of citizens and within these groups, debates on citizenship should not treat the experience of multiple group identities and multiple exclusions as exceptional but rather as central for theorizing' (2009: 193).

Gender-pluralist approaches have been instrumental in the widespread acceptance among critical citizenship theorists of 'the importance of accommodating some form of differentiated citizenship' (Isin and Turner 2002: 2). For feminists, they help to diffuse the gender binary at the centre of the equality vs. difference dichotomy. However, they do not offer guidance on one of the key questions for the re-gendering of citizenship which it raises: the respective value to be accorded to unpaid care work and paid work in the construction of citizenship responsibilities and rights. And a purely pluralist approach means that citizenship no longer offers a universal yardstick against which marginalized groups can stake their claim (Pascall 1993). A gender-pluralist approach, therefore, represents only half of the re-gendering equation.

Towards a woman-friendly citizenship

Key to the other half of the equation is the reconstruction of citizenship's yardstick so that it no longer privileges the male through its false universalism. This means, in particular, the incorporation of care as an expression of citizenship, in line with the gender-differentiated model. However, this must not be at the expense of undermining progress towards gender equality and therefore the gender-neutral model cannot be totally discarded. What is needed is a synthesis of the two, within the framework of gender-pluralism, which, in the words of Pateman, enables 'the substance of equality [to] differ according to the diverse circumstances and capacities of citizens, men and women' (1992: 29). Pivotal to the construction of the synthesis is the disruption of the public–private divide in recognition of the ways in which the interaction between public and private spheres sculpts the gendered contours of citizenship. From a policy perspective, this means, above all, measures to shift the gendered division of labour and to create the conditions in which both women and men can combine paid work and caring responsibilities (Lister 2003; Kershaw 2006). Thus the re-gendering of citizenship will require change in both public and private spheres and in men's as well as women's relationship to citizenship.

Further Reading

Erel, U. 2009: *Migrant Women Transforming Citizenship*. Farnham: Ashgate.

Lister, R. 2003: *Citizenship: Feminist Perspectives*, 2nd edn. Basingstoke: Palgrave.

Lister, R. 2007: Citizenship. In G. Blakeley and V. Bryson (eds) *The Impact of Feminism on Political Concepts and Debates*. Manchester: Manchester University Press.

Lister, R. Williams, F., Anttonen, A., Bussemaker, J. *et al.* 2007: *Gendering Citizenship in Western Europe*. Cambridge: Policy Press.

Siim, B. 2000: *Gender and Citizenship*. Cambridge: Cambridge University Press.

Voet, R. 1998: *Feminism and Citizenship*. London: Sage.

34

Post-national Citizenship:
Rights and Obligations of Individuality

YASEMIN NUHOĞLU SOYSAL

Predominant conceptions of citizenship treat it as national, denoting a territorially bounded population with a specific set of rights and duties. Immigration challenges the premises of this nation-state model. In the postwar era, individual rights have been increasingly legitimated as 'human rights' at the transnational level. Furthermore, as in the case of the European Union (EU) for example, political authority is increasingly dispersed among local, national and transnational political institutions. In terms of rights and identity, the development of post-national citizenship involves the extension of rights to non-citizen immigrants, which blurs the dichotomy between nationals and aliens. Mobilization around claims to collective rights generally involves particularistic identities, but they are connected to transnationally institutionalized discourses and agendas of human rights, sometimes invoking the rights of the individual to cultural difference. Furthermore, this mobilization is often organized and directed beyond the nation-state, towards transnational jurisdictions. However, Soysal argues that post-national citizenship does not imply the end of the nation-state, which remains important to the organization of rights and the safeguarding of national cultures; nor does it herald a global society. It is rather a paradoxical and contradictory process, but it does require that sociologists take transnational institutions and discourses more seriously than has previously been the case.

Citizenship is back with a vengeance. Since the 1990s, it has made its way in noticeable strides into the discipline of Sociology. One point of entry is the comparative and historical studies, either reconceptualizing the Marshallian concept of citizenship as a more dynamic and relational one (Turner 1989; Somers 1993) or re-narrating the

The Wiley-Blackwell Companion to Political Sociology, First Edition. Edited by Edwin Amenta, Kate Nash, and Alan Scott.
© 2012 Blackwell Publishing Ltd. Published 2012 by Blackwell Publishing Ltd.

development of welfare and women's rights in the right historical order (Barbalet 1988; Fraser and Gordon 1992; Orloff 1993; Skocpol 1996). The other is a growing literature on immigration and citizenship (for reviews see Kymlicka and Norman 1994; Shafir 1998; Bloemraad, Korteweg and Yurdakul 2008). Immigration provides a productive viewpoint to study citizenship since it challenges the very premises of the nation-state model that we political sociologists take for granted in our work.

Our theories are stubborn in assigning the nation-state a privileged position as a unit of analysis, even when conversing about global processes such as immigration. By doing so, they axiomatically embrace the dichotomy of citizen and alien, native and immigrant. This not only generates analytical quandaries as transnational institutions and discourses become increasingly salient, but also renders invisible changes in national citizenship and new formations of inclusion and exclusion.

The predominant conceptions of modern citizenship, as expressed in both scholarly and popular discourses, posit that populations are organized within nation-state boundaries by citizenship rules that acclaim 'national belonging' as the legitimate basis of membership. As such, two foundational principles define national citizenship: a congruence between territorial state and the national community; and national belonging as the source of rights and duties of individuals as well as their collective identity. Hence, what national citizenship denotes is a territorially bounded population with a specific set of rights and duties, excluding others on the ground of nationality.

In the postwar era, a series of interlocking legal, institutional and ideological changes affected the concept and organization of citizenship in the European state system. A crucial development regards the intensification of the discourse and instruments on the individual and her rights. As sanctified across a range of sites, the individual has come to constitute the target of much of the legal and policy regulations (Meyer *et al.* 1997; Beck 2007). In particular, the codification of 'human rights' as a world-level organizing principle in legal, scientific and popular conventions signals a significant shift in the conceptualization of rights. Individual rights that were once associated with belonging to a national community have become increasingly abstract and legitimated within a larger framework of human rights.

As legitimized by international codes, standards and laws, the principles of human rights ascribe universal rights to the person. Even though they are frequently violated as a political practice, human rights increasingly constitute a world-level index of legitimate action and provide a hegemonic language for formulating claims to rights beyond national belonging. This elaboration of individual rights in the postwar era has laid the foundation upon which more expansive claims and rights are advanced. The definition of individual rights as an abstract, universal category, as opposed to being attached to an absolute status of national citizenship, has licensed a variety of interests (environmentalists, regional movements, indigenous groups, as well as immigrants) to make further claims on the state (see Chapter 39, in this volume).

A complementary development is the emergence of multi-level polities. The gradual unfolding of the EU, for example, suggests that political authority is increasingly dispersed among local, national and transnational political institutions. The diffusion and sharing of sovereignty, in turn, enables new actors, facilitates competition over resources and makes possible new organizational strategies for practising citizenship rights. The existence of multi-level polities creates new opportunities for mobilizing and advancing demands within and beyond national boundaries.

These developments have significant implications for the notions of identity and rights, on the one hand, and the organization and practice of citizenship, on the other. In today's Europe, conventional conceptions of citizenship are no longer adequate to understand the dynamics of rights and membership. Citizenship, as a nationally delimited construct, is a poor predictor of the distribution of rights and privileges; and claims-making and participation are not axiomatically concomitant with the national order of things.

In the following sections, I focus on two key aspects of the changing models of citizenship: the decoupling of rights and identity, and the expansion of claims-making and mobilization. Here, I expand on what I called 'post-national citizenship' elsewhere (Soysal 1994). I then consider the analytical purview of this construct in relation to other theoretical positions that also seek to address the postwar transformations of the nation-state and citizenship.

Rights and Identity

The postwar elaboration of human rights as a global principle, in national and international institutions but also in scientific and popular discourses, legitimates the rights of persons beyond national collectivities. This authoritative discourse of individual rights has been instrumental in the formalization and expansion of many citizenship rights to those who were previously excluded or marginalized in society: women, children, gays and lesbians, religious and linguistic minorities, as well as immigrants. Particularly in the case of immigrants, the extension of various membership rights has significantly blurred the conventional dichotomy between national citizens and aliens.

The erosion of legal and institutional distinctions between nationals and aliens attests to a change in models of citizenship across two phases of immigration in the twentieth century. The model of national citizenship, anchored in territorialized notions of cultural belonging, was dominant during the massive migrations at the turn of the century, when immigrants were either expected to be moulded into national citizens (as in the case of European immigrants to the United States) or categorically excluded from the polity (as in the case of the indentured Chinese labourers in the United States). The postwar immigration experience reflects a time when national citizenship has lost ground to new forms of citizenship, which derive their legitimacy from deterritorialized notions of persons' rights, and thus are no longer unequivocally anchored in national collectivities. These post-national forms can be explicated in the membership of the long-term non-citizen immigrants in Western countries, who hold various rights and privileges without a formal nationality status; in the increasing instances of dual citizenship, which breaches the traditional notions of political membership and loyalty in a single state; in EU citizenship, which represents a multi-tiered form of membership; and in sub-national citizenship in culturally or administratively autonomous regions of Europe (such as the Basque country, Catalonia and Scotland). The membership rights of non-citizen immigrants generally consist of full civil rights, social rights (education and many of the welfare benefits), and some political rights (including local voting rights in some countries). In the emerging European system, certain groups of individuals are more privileged than others – dual citizens and nationals of EU countries have more rights than (non-European) resident immigrants and political refugees; they in turn have more rights than temporary residents and those immigrants who do not hold a legal resident status (see also Morris 2002). Thus, what is increasingly in place is a multiplicity of membership forms, which occasions exclusions and inclusions that no longer coincide with the bounds of the nation(al).

Paradoxically, as the source and legitimacy of rights increasingly shift to the transnational level, identities in the main remain particularistic and locally defined and organized. The same global rules and institutional frameworks that celebrate personhood and human rights at the same time naturalize collective identities around national and ethno-religious particularism by legitimating the right to 'one's own culture' and identity. Through massive decolonizations in the postwar period and the subsequent work of the international organizations such as the United Nations, the United Nations Educational, Scientific and Cultural Organization (UNESCO) and the Council of Europe, the universal right to 'one's own culture' has gained increasing legitimacy, and collective identity has been redefined as a category of human rights. In the process, what we normally regard as unique characteristics of collectivities (culture, language and standard ethnic traits) have become variants of the universal core of humanness or selfhood. Once institutionalized as a right, identities occupy a vital place in individual and collective actors' narratives and strategies. In turn, identities proliferate and become more and more expressive, authorizing ethnic nationalism and particularistic group claims of various sorts. Accordingly, even when former nation-states are dissolving (for example, the Soviet Union and Yugoslavia), the 'emerging' units aspire to become a territorial state with self-determination and the world political community grants them this right. In national and world polities, identity emerges as a pervasive discourse of participation and is enacted as a symbolic (and organizational) tool for creating group solidarities and mobilizing claims.

Thus, while rights acquire a more universalistic form and are divorced from national belonging, at the same time identities become particularistic and expressive. This decoupling of rights and identity is one of the most elemental characteristics of post-national citizenship. Individuals obtain rights and protection, and thus membership, within states that are not 'their own'. An immigrant in Germany, for instance, need not have a 'primordial' attachment of a cultural and historical kind to German-ness in order to attain social, economic and political rights. Their rights derive from universalizing discourses and structures celebrating the individual and human rights as world-level organizing principles. The idea of the nation, on the other hand, persists as an intense metaphor of identity and at times an idiom of war. It is still the source of a pronounced distinctiveness but divests from its grip on citizenship rights.

Claims-making and Mobilization: The Practice of Citizenship

With the postwar reconfigurations in citizenship, along with dissociation of rights and identity, the old categories that attach individuals to national welfare systems and distributory mechanisms become blurred. The postwar reification of personhood and individual rights expands the boundaries of political community by legitimating individuals' claims beyond their membership status in a particular nation-state. This inevitably changes the nature and locus of struggles for social equality and rights. New forms of mobilizing and advancing claims emerge, beyond the frame of national citizenship.

Two features of these emerging forms are crucial. First, while collective groups increasingly rally around claims for particularistic identities, they connect their claims to transnationally institutionalized discourses and agendas. Immigrant groups in Europe advance claims for group-specific provisions and emphasize their group identities. Their claims, however, are not simply grounded in the particularities of religious or ethnic narratives. On the contrary, they appeal to the universalistic principles and dominant discourses of equality, emancipation and individual rights.

When immigrant associations advocate the educational rights and needs of immigrant children in school, they employ a discourse that appropriates the rights of the individual as its central themes. They invoke the international instruments and conventions on human rights to frame their position. They forward demands about mother-tongue instruction, Islamic *foulard* or *halal* food by asserting the 'natural' rights of individuals to their own cultures, rather than drawing upon religious teachings and traditions. For instance, the issue of wearing the Islamic *foulard* in school, which erupted into a national crisis in France in the early 1990s, was not only a topical contention over immigrant integration or French *laicism* but entered into the public arena as a matter of rights of individuals (see Feldblum 1993; Kastoryano 2002; Kepel 1997). During the debates, the head of the Great Mosque of Paris (one of the highest authorities for the Muslim community) declared the rules preventing wearing scarves in school to be discriminatory on the grounds of individual rights. His emphasis was on personal rights, rather than religious traditions or duties: 'If a girl asks to have her hair covered, I believe it is her most basic right' (*Washington Post*, October 23, 1989). As epitomized in this case, immigrants advance claims for difference that are affirmed by universalistic and homogenizing ideologies of human rights. By doing so, they appropriate host-country discourses, participate in the host-country public spaces and exercise civic projects as they amplify and practise difference.

The second feature of the new forms of claims-making is that the organizational strategies employed by collective groups acquire a transnational and sub-national character, along with national ones. Their participation extends beyond the confines of a unitary national community, covers multiple localities and transnationally connects public spheres. In the case of immigrant groups, for example, we find political parties, mosque organizations and community associations that operate at local levels but also assume transnational forms by bridging diverse public spaces. An example of this is the Alevite groups (a sub-sect of Islam), organized in both Turkey and Germany. Based on their experience in, and borrowing models from, the German education system, they have raised demands for the recognition of denominational schools in Turkey, which do not have a legal standing in the Turkish educational system. In a similar vein, Turkish immigrant groups have pushed for their local voting rights in settlement countries, while at the same time put pressure on the Turkish government to facilitate their rights to vote in Turkish national elections. As such, they envision their participation in diverse civic spaces, for example in both Berlin and Turkey. The Mexican and Central American immigrant communities in the United

States have made similar claims, demanding dual citizenship and dual voting rights in their countries of origin and residence. The governments of Mexico, Columbia and the Dominican Republic have indeed passed legislation allowing dual nationality.

All of this implies that the public spheres within which immigrants act, mobilize, and advance claims have broadened. In pursuing their claims, the mobilization of immigrant groups entails multiple states and political agencies, and they target trans- and sub-national institutions, as much as the national ones. For example, the much-debated Islamic *foulard* issue was not simply a matter confined to the discretion of a local school board but has traversed the realms of local, national and transnational jurisdictions – from local educational authorities to the European Court of Human Rights.

While immigrant groups further particularistic claims and solidarities, paradoxically, they appeal to the universalistic principles of human rights and connect to a diverse set of public spheres. As such, their mobilization is not simply a reinvention of cultural particularism. Drawing upon universalistic repertoires of making claims, they participate in and contribute to the reification of the host society and global discourses.

Such experience of immigrant communities in Europe indicates a deviation from the earlier forms of claims-making and participation in the public sphere. Much of the decolonization and civil rights movements of the 1960s and the first women's movements were attempts to redefine individuals as part of the national collectivity. Similarly, labour movements were historically linked to the shaping of a national citizenry. It is no coincidence that the welfare state developed as part of the national project, attaching labour movements to nations (as in Bismarckian Germany). However, the emerging forms of collective participation and claims-making in Europe are less and less nationally defined citizenship projects. Individuals and collective groups set their agenda for realization of rights through particularistic identities that are embedded in, and driven by, universalistic discourses of human rights. This shift in focus from national collectivity to particularistic claims does not necessarily imply disengagement from public spheres. Neither does it mean the disintegration of civic arenas. On the contrary, it evinces new forms of mobilization through which individuals enact and practise their citizenship.

These new forms of claims-making and participation, which discursively and organizationally go beyond nationally demarcated parameters, highlight the other aspect of post-national citizenship. Post-national citizenship is not just an assortment of legal rights and privileges or a legal status attached to a person, as implied in Marshallian definitions of citizenship. It signifies a set of practices through which individuals and groups activate their membership within and without the nation-state. Individuals and collectivities interact with, and partake in, multiple public spheres, and hence alter the locus of participation and set the stage for new mobilizations.

The Value of 'Individuality' as the Underlying Principle of Citizenship

How does post-national citizenship fare against the current landscape of European policy, particularly in the field of immigration? The 2000s mark a new policy orientation in Europe that prompted some observers to comment on the 'return' of the nation-centred citizenship projects (see, for example, essays in Joppke and Morawska 2003). 'Selective migration' and 'integration' constitute the core facets of this new orientation.

The creation of a common immigration policy framework has preoccupied the EU agendas since the 1990s. The precepts of this framework, which were finally formalized in the 1999 Tampere meeting, strongly prioritize 'integration' and 'social cohesion', while facilitating the mobility of skilled labour within and without the EU (European Council 1999). In the following decade, in accordance with the common policy framework, most European countries set further limitations on unskilled labour migration (including family reunification), while welcoming students, scientists, specialist professionals and entrepreneurs. Several countries (notably, Austria, Denmark, France, Germany, the Netherlands and the UK) have also introduced legislation, making integration a prerequisite for long-term residency and naturalization. In certain cases, access to social benefits is linked to participation in integration and language classes, and non-compliance can accrue sanctions. Most symbolic of all, citizenship and integration tests are compulsory on the route to naturalization. Once considered a US idiosyncrasy, citizenship tests and oath-taking are now touted as indispensable steps towards integration throughout Europe.

Given the heightened preoccupation with the immigration–security nexus (not only in the context of 'terrorism' but also urban riots) in the first decade of the twenty-first century, the urgency assigned to social cohesion in European policy circles is not surprising. Integration and selective migration also proffer a convenient language to reclaim 'national boundaries' in a climate where electoral opinion is adversarial to immigration. However, such immediate political imperatives fall short of explaining the underlying logic of the new policy agenda. For that, I maintain that we need to move beyond the much-exercised 'nation talk'.

Indeed, despite the symbolic command they profess, the current citizenship and integration tests do not reveal anything distinctive about the particularities of the nation (bar the questions about ordinary symbols such as the flag or national anthem) or a distinct philosophy of integration. A systematic review of their content finds that the largest thematic category addresses the notions of individual rights and democracy (Michalowski 2009; see also Joppke 2008). The history questions are in the main geared towards capturing the present day of the country and Europe. The questions to appraise values are primarily related to the rights of the individual, such as civic freedoms, and the rights of the underprivileged sections of society, such as women and the disabled. Knowledge of democratic institutions and legal structure occupies a prominent place, in anticipation of a rights-bearing individual fluent in a world of tax offices, schools, courts and labour markets. The British test, 'Life in the UK: A Journey to Citizenship', poses a series of questions about how to conduct daily life in the country (e.g., 'what is the number to call in an emergency?'). The German citizenship test, along with questions such as 'which religion marked German and European culture?' (Christianity) and 'what is the German traditional activity for Easter?' (painting eggs), includes questions on the rights of individuals within the Basic Law and broader human rights conventions, the significance of social market economy, marital rights of women and parental decision making on schooling.

Integration, as conveyed in these tests, is not a nation-centred project. In its place, integration acquires the purpose of achieving social cohesion driven by active, participatory and productive individuals. The thrust is put on individual immigrants' own effort and responsibility to take part productively in the rights and institutions offered in the system.

As such, rather than a reversal, the new European immigration agenda is a continuum of the broader trends that underscore the transformation of citizenship in the postwar era. Along with immigration, the primacy of the individual is implicated in a number of related European policy areas. Most notably, in welfare policy, the new Social Project, whose architecture was sealed with the Lisbon Strategy in 2000, has shifted the emphasis away from 'a passive providing state' to 'self-activity, responsibility and mobilization' among citizens (Taylor-Gooby 2008). Accordingly, a plethora of policy instruments provision investment in individuals' capacities – skill training and improvement programmes, job insertion and apprenticeship schemes, and lifelong learning towards enhanced employability and self-realization, among others. In education, as part of strategies to boost human capital, raising standards in Maths, Language and Science subjects has become a staple of national curricular reforms. Civics or citizenship teaching in schools now projects 'cosmopolitan' individuals, globally aware and adaptive, with emphasis on developing children's capabilities as effective, engaged and responsible young persons (Soysal and Szakacs 2010; Soysal and Wong 2007).

What underlies all these European policy reforms is the trust in the value of individuality and its transformative capacity, which increasingly organizes the logic of the 'good citizen' and 'good society'. Sanctified as a collective good, individuality, on the one hand, elicits the recognition of universal qualities (as opposed to ascriptive ones, such as race, gender and class) and enhancement of universal freedoms and rights. This is what made possible the expansion of the boundaries of citizenship in the postwar Europe. On the other, the same tenet also nourishes the idea of individuality as a form of capital. Realizing self-potential becomes a right and a responsibility, and forms expectations about the self and others. Individuals are all expected to invest in themselves and their abilities. Being productive, creative and active defines a higher form of life. Immigrants, along with other vulnerable sections of the society (ethnic minorities, youth and women), are disadvantaged by this push. As 'outsiders', they have the added burden of proving the potential and worth of their individuality.

Reinforced by the authoritative backing of expert professionals and international organizations, economic and political liberalization now pretty much drive the policy reforms worldwide (Simmons, Dobbin and Garrett 2006). It is the uneasy tension between the realization of transformative capacities of individuality and maintenance of social justice – the tension between the two forms of liberalization – that occasions new forms of exclusions. Post-national citizenship highlights these emerging fault lines, which no longer simply cut across national lines but beyond.

Coda: Delimiting the Contours of Post-national Citizenship

In concluding, I address three major confusions that the discussions of post-national citizenship seem to raise. In so doing, my intention is to differentiate post-national citizenship from other theoretical constructs that are also deployed to account for the shifts in the national order of things. I also intend to re-articulate its theoretical expanse in depicting the new topography of rights and membership and the contemporary dynamics of exclusion and inclusion.

First, post-national citizenship does not refer to an identity or a unitary legal status. It is an analytical concept to narrate the changes in the very institutions of rights and identity, which locate citizenship and its practice in increasingly transnational discourses and multiple public spheres. It does not mark the emergence of a legal status or identity at the world level, ascribed by a single, unified political and judicial structure. If anything, post-national citizenship projects variability of membership forms and identities (as opposed to the unitary mode of national citizenship) that remain constructed within historically shaped institutional parameters while appropriating transnationally legitimated scripts (see also Gupta and Ferguson 1992; Malkki 1995).

Thus, it is an oversight to attribute post-national citizenship simply to supranational legal and judicial processes (see Jacobson and Ruffer 2003). Likewise, it is unproductive to associate post-national citizenship with 'transnational communities' – a theoretical formulation that presumptively accepts the formation of tightly bounded communities and solidarities (on the basis of common cultural and ethnic references) between places of origin and arrival (see Basch, Glick Schiller and Szanton Blanc 1994; Portes, Guarnizo and Landolt 1999; Levitt 2001; Vertovec 2004). Such interactions might be intensified by advances in international transportation and communication technologies, but post-national citizenship does not imply the necessary advent of transnational solidarities or communal bonds, or the formation of 'diasporic' identities and interests (Soysal 2000). Rather, it emphasizes the multi-connectedness of public spheres and the increasingly universalistic conceptions and discourses of rights, which are no longer limited by national constellations.

Second, post-national citizenship does not imply the 'withering of the nation-state' or the declining purpose of the state. The same transnational frameworks that celebrate human rights, and thus foster post-national citizenship, equally reify the nation-state's agency and sovereignty. The transnational normative and institutional domain does not necessarily host a harmonious and coherent rule system. It accommodates a heterogeneous set of principles often with conflicting outcomes and effects. Inasmuch as they are contradictory, the principles of human rights and nation-state sovereignty are equally part of the same transnational discourse and institutional terrain. Thus, as the source and legitimacy of rights increasingly move to the transnational level, rights and membership of individuals remain organized within nation-states. The nation-state continues to be the repository of cultures of nationhood and institutions through which rights and membership policies are implemented. This is what leads to the incongruity between the legitimation and organization of post-national citizenship, which has paradoxical implications for the exercise of citizenship rights. Nation-states and their boundaries persist as reasserted by sovereignty narratives, restrictive immigration policies and differentiated access schemes, while universalistic personhood rights transcend the same boundaries, giving rise to new models and understandings of membership.

Hence, post-national citizenship is not a sign of a linear procession from national to transnational. That is, we cannot (should not) postulate post-national citizenship as a stage within the much-assumed dichotomy of national and transnational, and the expected transition between the two. Post-national citizenship confirms that in postwar Europe the national no longer has primacy but it coexists with the transnational, mutually reinforcing and reconfiguring each other. The transnational factors into the nationally defined spaces and institutions, and the local and national, are re-articulated within the transnational. This position resonates with Saskia Sassen's (2006) illuminating conceptualization of global processes as multiple scaling. In that, specific elements of the global manifest themselves within what has been historically constituted as national, and 'transboundary formations' globally link national processes and actors — as exemplified in the cross-border networks of activists carrying out local struggles for human rights and environment; the deployment of international instruments such as human rights in national courts; or the adoption and implementation of policies essential for the functioning of global markets at the national scale.

Lastly, post-national citizenship is not in itself a normative prescription and should not be superfluously conflated with theoretical positions such as cosmopolitanism that profess a moral commitment to the transformative capabilities of universal values (Habermas 2003; but see Beck and Grande 2007 for a more critical view). Nor does post-national citizenship presume public spheres free of conflict or devoid of exclusions. That is to say, on the one hand, post-national citizenship reveals an ongoing process of definition and redefinition of rights and participation. On the other, it productively brings to the fore the fact that there are no longer absolute and clear-cut patterns of exclusion and inclusion that simply coincide with the bounds of the national (see also Brysk and Shafir 2004). In today's Europe, formal nationality status itself is not the main indicator of inclusion and exclusion. Rights, membership and participation are increasingly matters beyond the vocabulary of national citizenship. Under the rubric of post-national citizenship, inclusions and exclusions shape simultaneously and at varying levels – local, national and European.

The increasingly expansive definition of rights may appear as a contradiction in the face of attempts to deregulate the welfare state and eliminate policy categories based on the collective (such as affirmative action and welfare provisions). However, the co-presence of post-national citizenship with the breakdown of the social project is no coincidence. Both trends derive from the global dominance of the ideologies and institutions of liberal individualism. While these ideologies contribute to the dismantling of the welfare state project, at the same time, they enable various groups in advancing identity-based claims justified on the basis of individual rights. Thus, the same transnational processes that lead to marginalization and exclusions also create grounds for, and spaces of, claims-making and mobilization and facilitate the expansion of rights.

However, the new spaces of citizenship and claims-making are not necessarily free of conflict. By emphasizing the hegemony of discourses and strategies of human or personhood rights, which resolutely underlines post-national citizenship, one should not take a naive position and assume that individuals and groups effortlessly attain rights, or that they readily bond together and arrive at agreeable positions. Post-national rights are results of struggles, negotiations and arbitrations by actors at local, national and transnational levels and are contingent upon issues of distribution and equity. Like any form of rights, they are subject to retraction and negation. Rather than denying the certitude of conflict and contestation for rights, post-national citizenship as a category and practice draws attention to the multi-layered and diverse forms that they take and new arenas in which they are enacted.

Our dominant theories and conceptualizations have yet to catch up with the changes in the institutions of citizenship, rights and identity. They have yet to respond to the challenge posed by emergent actors, border-crossings and non-conventional mobilizations. Post-national citizenship is an attempt to capture and incorporate these changes by assigning transnational institutions and discourses a more predominant analytical role than it is usually granted in prevailing studies. Otherwise, we will continue to have models that do not work, anomalies in existing paradigms and incongruities between official rhetoric and institutional actualities.

Further Reading

Gupta, A. and Ferguson, J. 1992: Beyond 'culture': space, identity, and the politics of difference. *Cultural Anthropology* 7: 6–23.

Hobsbawm, E. 1990: *Nations and Nationalism since 1780: Programme, Myth, Reality.* Cambridge: Cambridge University Press.

Sassen, S. 2006: *Territory, Authority, Rights: From Medieval to Global Assemblages.* Princeton, NJ: Princeton University Press.

Shafir, G.I. (ed.) 1998: *The Citizenship Debate: A Reader.* Minneapolis: University of Minnesota Press.

Soysal, Y.N. 1994: *Limits of Citizenship: Migrants and Postnational Membership in Europe.* Chicago: University of Chicago Press.

Part IV

Democracy and Democratization

A. Social Movements
B. Structures of Participation

35

Protest and Political Process

David S. Meyer

To understand social protest movements, it is necessary to look at how politics and the influence of the state permeate areas of life not usually considered political. Social movements are characterized in the following ways: they address the state to adjudicate disputes and make binding decisions; they challenge cultural codes and transform participants' everyday lives; as well as conventional, they also use non-conventional political means; they are not unitary actors but are composed of a multiplicity of organizations, groups and individuals. Social movements are also related to the political process in that they rise and decline according to conditions created by the state. States themselves are constrained by their relationship to other states and global politics and economics. Social movements take different forms according to whether the state is repressive or liberal democratic. Critical to their emergence is the construction of political opportunities on the part of state elites. Meyer concludes with an analysis of the effects of social movements in three distinct but interdependent areas: public policy, culture and the lives of participants.

A woman seeking an abortion at a Planned Parenthood clinic anywhere in the United States these days is likely to walk past 'street counsellors' who will plead with her not to 'murder her unborn child'. Brandishing graphic pictures of aborted foetuses, they will scream and threaten her, with damnation if not violence. These protesters want not only to stop each woman they encounter from having an abortion, but also to encourage government to make it more difficult for women to get legal abortions. Their allies often choose alternative tactics, ranging from lobbying legislators to shooting doctors. Government regulates not only access to abortion, but also the distance from the clinic entrance that protesters must stay. The politics of protest outside mainstream political institutions is thus tightly tied to politics and policy inside

The Wiley-Blackwell Companion to Political Sociology, First Edition. Edited by Edwin Amenta, Kate Nash, and Alan Scott.
© 2012 Blackwell Publishing Ltd. Published 2012 by Blackwell Publishing Ltd.

political institutions. We can understand the politics of protest only by analysing its relationship to the more routine actions within mainstream politics.

Although social movements like the anti-abortion movement continue to challenge day-to-day routine politics, they have in themselves become somewhat routine. Much of the activity falls into conventional categories, but a great deal of protest politics slips beneath the radar of social science (for reviews, see Meyer 2007; Meyer and Tarrow 1998). Fuller understanding of the sources and impacts of social protest movements requires considering factors frequently missing from conventional political analysis. We need to recognize broader sources and arenas of politics, different and additional sources of political power, and a wider range of significant actors. Politics and the influence of the state permeate areas of social life not generally considered political. The sources of political power are not simply those recognized in constitutions, laws or academic studies of voting or public opinion. And influence is to be found not only in policies and laws, but also in the ways people live their lives.

I begin by describing the social movement, distinguishing it from other social and political phenomena. Protest politics, I argue, are the product of people trying to come to terms with circumstances they view as unacceptable by employing ostensibly non-political means to political ends. This does not happen spontaneously; rather, it is the result of organizing and mobilization efforts by committed activists. I then consider the circumstances under which social movements emerge and the general dynamics of their development. I discuss the ways in which the prospects for mobilizing people into particular movement activities are directly related to both mainstream politics and the structure of opportunities offered within a state. Importantly, neither opportunities nor mobilization efforts are bounded by national boundaries, and I examine how increased political and economic globalization influences the prospects for social movement mobilization. Next, I examine the multiple impacts of social movements on state and society. I conclude with a discussion of the impact that understanding social movements and protest politics generally can have on contemporary political analysis.

Protest Politics and Social Movements

Like military planners and political pundits, social movement analysts are generally fighting and defining the last war, leading to distorted views of the contemporary phenomena. A very brief and schematic review of the development of scholarship can lead us to a more comprehensive evaluation of movements. Analysts of social movements considering protest politics in the 1950s, with the memory of Nazism painfully fresh, wrote with fascism in mind, and thus defined movements as dysfunctional, irrational and exceptionally dangerous (e.g., Kornhauser 1959). They contrasted movements with less disruptive and more routine interest-group politics, which they saw as representatives of citizen concerns in healthier and more pluralist polities. The implication was that social movements were an alternative to 'real' politics, and potentially very dangerous. Effective political institutions would allow citizens to exercise influence in more moderate ways; unruly protest would be unnecessary.

If political openness and the wide distribution of resources were to quell or pre-empt protest, the movements of the 1960s in exactly the most open and democratic polities provided a shock to social science. Empirical studies of student activists found that they were more likely than their less active colleagues to be politically oriented, socially engaged and psychologically well adapted (Kenniston 1968). Policy-oriented analysts recognized that social unrest led to concessions from government (Piven and Cloward 1971), and re-conceptualized protest strategies as rational efforts by those poorly positioned to make claims on government through conventional means. For those left outside the pluralist arena, protest was a 'political resource' (Lipsky 1968; McCarthy and Zald 1977); protest augmented rather than supplanted conventional strategies of influence.

But protest is also more than this. Protest serves as a vehicle not only for expressing political claims, but also for building communities, forging connections among people and constructing a sense of self. Social movements develop, in embryo, the world in which they want to live, creating in microcosm the larger political structures they envision (or 'prefigurative politics', see Breines 1982). Protest movements include both efforts to transform society and the politics of transforming one's more immediate community and one's self. The world outside the social movement involves political claims, representation and institutional politics; the world inside involves the production of identity and meaning. These are complementary rather than conflicting aspects of the reality of social protest. Let me suggest four consistent elements that distinguish social movements from other social and political phenomena.

First, *social movements make claims on the state* or some other authority seen to have the capacity to redress activist concerns. The development of the nation-state itself, Tarrow has pointed out, made possible the development of the modern social movement (Tilly 1978; Tarrow 1998). The state has the capacity to process claims, adjudicate disputes and make decisions binding on losers. But states are not completely autonomous actors or insular contexts for political action. Movements may also seek to enlist or provoke other social or political institutions, both below and above the level of the nation-state, to augment their influence on the state. Nonetheless, the state remains the focal point of social movement claims and activities. In the case of the Greensboro sit-in movement, for example, protesters engaged local business directly, but also sought to mobilize portions of the federal government on their behalf. Anti-abortion protesters target local landlords who rent to women's health clinics, but also seek to mobilize support from more risk-adverse allies.

Second, *social movements challenge cultural codes and transform the lives of their participants*. Protest is about more than the claims expressed on placards. Women who march though parks *en masse* at midnight, for example, are not simply urging local governments to improve police protection, but asserting power and confidence for themselves, 'taking back the night'. Such a march can succeed even if political leaders do not respond with policy reforms. The permeability of the state to dissident claims affects how directly activists target it.

For this reason, Vaclav Havel (1985), facing circumstances that made direct challenge to the communist state of Czechoslovakia exceedingly difficult, implored his allies to 'live in truth', to carve out a sphere of human activity autonomous from state-sponsored social institutions, seeking some transcendent vision of justice and humanity, as an end in itself, and as a means of exercising leverage on the state. Havel offered that this could entail, initially, refusing to mouth the slogans of workers' rule that decorated daily life. Havel's notion was that by such living, often through almost silent protest, dissidents could carve out a public space autonomous from the state, in which they could build civil society.

Third, *social movements use means additional to those offered and accepted by mainstream politics*. Movements may engage in conventional political activities, such as lobbying, running electoral campaigns and conducting public education campaigns. They will also, however, employ non-conventional means of proffering their claims in visible challenges. Such activities can include demonstrations, boycotts, pickets, civil disobedience and political violence. Although conventional political analyses treat these tactics as epiphenomena, apart from the more important (and more conventional) political expressions, contemporary protest politics mandate that we look at a broader definition of what comprises politics, beginning with choices individuals make in their personal lives and human interactions.

Of course, individual states draw the boundaries of what comprises acceptable political conduct differently. Peace and democracy activists in the former East Germany expressed their concerns by wearing patches depicting a statue of a workman banging swords into ploughshares. Employing the symbol of a statue given to East Germany by the Soviet Union represented a politics of irony more than confrontation; nonetheless, the government banned the symbol. Activists then identified themselves and provoked opposition by sporting blank patches (Tismaneanu 1989; Meyer and Marullo 1992). The important point here about movements is that challengers pick tactics that place them at the edges of political legitimacy. They are defined by their dynamic interaction with mainstream politics.

Even as states draw the boundaries of what comprises legitimate political activity differently, it's important to recognize that political and cultural constraints weigh differently on different actors. An obvious example: throughout history men have enjoyed a broader range of political options than women, and available space for organizing and mobilizing varies by gender across national contexts. States also often afford differential tolerance for political action based on race and ethnic background, religious affiliation, class and occupation. In essence, what different constituencies can do to create disruption, and how much tolerance they face, varies greatly.

Fourth, *movements are comprised of a diverse field of organizations and actors working in pursuit of the same general goals* rather than unitary actors. The boundaries marking a social movement from society in general are fluid; formal organizations, subtle tendencies and critical dissidents rise and fall rapidly. Allied groups cooperate (generally) in pursuit of political goals and compete (frequently) for support from other citizens and for recognition as legitimate representatives of the movement.

Competitive tension between organizations can make movements more effective. The Greensboro students who started a national civil rights sit-in campaign were not affiliated with the major civil rights organizations of the day, although they were certainly influenced by established organizations, particularly the National Association for the Advancement of Colored People (NAACP) and the Southern Christian Leadership Council (SCLC). Ella Baker, who had been instrumental in creating the SCLC after the successful bus boycott in Montgomery, persuaded the SCLC to sponsor a national conference to create a new student-based organization, the Student Nonviolent Coordinating Committee (SNCC) (Sitkoff 1981). Baker, who was frustrated by the dominance of SCLC by a small group of ministers, shepherded SNCC's creation, and its initial vision of itself as a movement organization committed to grassroots activity.

Forming a new organization is a way to engage a neglected constituency, give voice to new claims and emphases, and support different tactics. In this case, SNCC was explicitly targeted towards youth generally, and students in particular; it emphasized voting rights and engaged in community campaigns and direct action. SNCC gave the older civil rights organizations a radical edge that made the movement as a whole more volatile and less predictable, establishing a greater presence in American political life in the 1960s.

Similarly, Randall Terry, an American vehemently opposed to abortion, founded Operation Rescue when he grew frustrated with what he saw as the relative invisibility and passivity of the anti-abortion movement. Operation Rescue's non-violent and confrontational politics at abortion clinics invigorated less confrontational organizations, and also mobilized an abortion rights opposition. For a time, its efforts reduced the amount of anti-abortion violence (Meyer and Staggenborg 1996).

Movements are transient and volatile political phenomena that are about more than the expressed claims they explicitly express. Social movements attempt to change public policy, political coalitions and how people live their lives. Sometimes they succeed – to some degree. But movements are inherently unstable; they give way to more routinized and institutionalized political forms that incorporate, ignore or normalize social movement claims (Meyer and Tarrow 1998). The processes by which this takes place reflect the peculiar political location of movements, at the edges of mainstream legitimacy.

Movement Organization and Mobilization

Although protest often appears sudden and spontaneous, it rarely is. The work of staging and coordinating a sustained social movement campaign is costly, in terms of activist time, and often based on other resources, including external support. But the organizational infrastructure of a social movement varies across contexts, depending on the prevalent forms of social and political organization. In wealthier countries, social movements are organized, in part, by formal and relatively permanent specialist organizations that forge alliances with mainstream institutional actors, including elected officials and bureaucrats, professional associations and a variety of institutions in civil society. As a result, contemporary social movements are generally coalition affairs, whose boundaries and composition change from issue to issue. Importantly, these coalitions often have wings inside and outside state institutions.

The organizations that give rise to social movements often survive the peaks of social movement activism, and work to sustain both themselves as organizations and their political campaigns. The organizations themselves provide a resource for subsequent waves of mobilization, sometimes over generations. The long-lived organizations perform a variety of tasks to aid the cause, including research on the issue they care about, public education, and lobbying efforts for reform. In effect, between episodes of dramatic social movement activism, organizations continue the struggle, albeit less visibly. Their efforts during ostensibly quiet periods influence the shape of dramatic periods of activism in the future.

Organizations link activists to each other, often across issues. Organizations also serve as holders of political legitimacy, formal organizational resources (e.g., office space, mailing lists and informal political contacts) that facilitate political activism. Those who would launch new political campaigns soon understand the wisdom of starting by organizing the organized. Enlisting established groups in an incipient effort provides important access to activists, institutional allies and mass media.

Organizers recruit activists both directly and through intermediaries. Perhaps most importantly, activists depend upon mass media to project information about their cause and their activities to a broader audience. In recent years, however, the growth of new media has afforded organizers additional routes to attention. Using websites, for example, organizations can project their own ideas unmediated – and unedited – by media gatekeepers. Using social networking sites, organizers can both percolate ideas and promote actions far more efficiently than formerly. At the same time, how effectively the new media reach beyond already established activist networks to mobilize new participants remains to be seen. Scholars are only beginning to confront the ramifications of the new media on social movement organizations (SMOs). To be sure, the social and political context is critical.

The Trajectory of Social Protest

If movements are indeed transient phenomena, then it is important to look at the circumstances under which they arise, how they develop in interaction with mainstream politics, the ways they fade and the residue or impact they leave. Why do people *sometimes* choose to challenge long-standing policies, such as segregation in the United States, or social injustices such as discrimination, or conditions such as Soviet domination of Eastern Europe? Four freshmen who sat up late one January night in Greensboro decided the time had come to do something, but why did the time arrive in 1960, not 10 years earlier or later?

The range of contestable issues and available tactics at any time is shaped by the experiences of the constituencies mobilized and audiences targeted, and particularly by the degree of tolerance the state offers. In repressive regimes that restrict political participation severely, the decision to engage in activism often involves embracing an identity of 'dissident' laden with real risks. In the Czechoslovakia of 1968–1989, circulating *samizdat* literature, attending house meetings, refusing to join the Communist Party, or signing a charter of human rights were all high-risk political strategies. The repressive state made activities taken for granted in liberal polities both political and risky.

In contrast, choosing to participate in liberal polities necessitates decisions about how to participate and with whom. When the state offers readily accessible, relatively low-cost and essentially no-risk means of participation – such as voting or political campaigning – to choose protest movement activity is not obviously 'natural'. People resorting to non-conventional or movement activities should occur only when they believe that more conventional routes to influence are either not available or not effective. People choose to participate in a social movement not only for instrumental political influence but also to cultivate and fulfil some sense of their own identity.

Finally, there is the critical issue of choosing which claims to make and issues to engage. Paradoxically, this may be somewhat simpler in more repressive or closed polities: when conventional means of political access are restricted, virtually all demands for political change first necessitate pressing for political openness. Again, during the Cold War, dissidents across the former Eastern Europe, despite their divisions on fundamental issues, united behind the basic principles of democratic participation.

In contrast, in open polities it is possible to engage on a broad spectrum of political issues. Organizers press their special claims, trying to link them to potential activists' concerns. Issue activists try to launch new campaigns, but only periodically do their entreaties reach responsive audiences in the political mainstream and threaten to alter the normal conduct of politics. Although it is easiest analytically to focus on their efforts, attributing success or failure to the tactics or rhetoric of appeals for mobilization, this is fundamentally mistaken. External political realities alter the risks or costs that citizens are willing to bear in making decisions about whether to engage in political activism and what issues are viable for substantial challenges. It makes sense to be more concerned about nuclear war, for example, when the president of the United States suggests that it may be inevitable and survivable, and increases spending on nuclear weapons; it also makes sense to distrust the more conventional styles of politics that produced such a president (Meyer 1990). Similarly, it seems more reasonable to organize for women's rights when the state establishes a commission on women, formally prohibits discrimination and suggests that it may play a role in combating it (Costain 1992). Activists are not ineluctably linked to one set of issues. American activists concerned with social justice may protest against nuclear testing in 1962, for voting rights in 1964, against the war in Vietnam in 1967 and for an Equal Rights Amendment in 1972 without dramatically altering their perception of self or justice. Rather, they will be responding to the most urgent, or the most promising, issues that appear before them. In this way, the issues that activists mobilize around are those the state sets out as challenges and opportunities.

The important point is that movements arise within a particular constellation of social and political factors. Movements do not decline because they run out of gas, recognize their failures, or because adherents get bored and move on to something else (contrary to, e.g., Downs 1972). Rather, protest movements decline when the state effects some kind of new arrangement with at least some activists or sponsors. Such arrangements can include repression, incorporating new claims or constituencies in mainstream institutions, and policy reform. Protest campaigns dissipate when activists no longer believe that a movement strategy is possible, necessary or potentially effective. Repression inhibits the perception of possibility. In contrast, when established political institutions such as parties and interest groups take up some of the claims of challenging social movements, the perception that extra-institutional activity is necessary erodes.

Globalization and Transnational Activism

Most of the research on social movements focuses on struggles directed against a state or some other sub-national authority. More than ever, however, states themselves are embedded in larger political and economic systems that affect the grievances and resources available to activists, as well as the capacity of the state to respond to or repress social movements. The notion of human rights, for example, implies universal standards that transcend national boundaries. Supranational bodies articulate such standards, providing activists within a state both rhetorical resources and, potentially, access to external resources for mobilization. The same may be said for transnational communities bounded by ethnicity or religion.

It's useful to think of the institutional structure of a polity as being nested in a larger set of institutions, more or less tightly, with the boundaries of the state being more or less permeable to the infusion of resources, both material and ideational, from outside the polity. Local activists can try to combat what they view as oppressive local or national governments to mobilize outside attention and pressure, effecting what Margaret Keck and Kathryn Sikkink have termed the 'boomerang' effect. By figuratively throwing claims beyond their ostensible target, activists can (a) exert pressure on their target and (b) mobilize resources, including activists, to work on their behalf.

Activists can use the rhetoric and symbols of supranational or transnational regimes to legitimate and explain their own efforts. American civil rights activists, for example, who challenged oppressive state governments, did so while quoting Christian prayers and Constitutional doctrine, affirming their ties to powerful allies outside or above their antagonists, and sometimes mobilizing their efforts. Responses to such entreaties are often long in arriving, but sometimes they do arrive.

Thus, human rights activists in what used to be Eastern Europe explicitly referenced the standards of the Helsinki Accords, a human rights accord signed by the United States and the Soviet Union. Charter 77, for example, explicitly called upon the Soviet Union and allied governments to live up to the language of Helsinki, an Agreement their leaders had signed. Eastern activists cooperated with both governments and social movements in the West, whose attention sometimes offered an element of political protection, and more frequently signalled encouragement. The often underground networks they sustained formed the basis of effective mobilization much later, during the revolutions of 1989.

Similarly, and even more dramatically, anti-apartheid activists in South Africa made appeals that extended well beyond Africa for states to boycott the apartheid state. The economic boycott, in conjunction with a meaningful and isolating social stigma, exerted substantial pressure on the government, promoting reforms, and ultimately a negotiated end to apartheid. In effect, activists mobilized external allies, who pressured their opponents, and external resources, which sustained their efforts.

Activists have found common cause with activist allies in other states for hundreds of years, dating back, at least, to the abolitionist campaigns that ultimately ended slavery in Europe and the United States. The feminist and peace movements have also forged transnational alliances that sometimes coordinated campaigns against practices and policies common in many states. In the contemporary era, campaigners against corporate globalization have operated across national borders, coordinating the dates of large protests and claims, and even travelling across those national borders to meet and to stage political actions. They have also established more or less permanent institutions, such as the World Social Forum, which serve as clearinghouses and coordinators of SMOs globally. The growth and spread of new communications technologies, most notably the Internet, have facilitated the building of activist communities across national boundaries. In this way, the contemporary social movement, while still mostly targeting the state, is not bound by state borders, a reality that scholars are beginning to address.

Constructing Political Opportunity

Regardless of the objective conditions of context, political alignments, potential participation or public policy, movements don't emerge unless substantial numbers of people are invested with feelings of both urgency and efficacy. The job of the organizer is to persuade significant numbers of people that the issues they care about are indeed *urgent*, that alternatives are *possible*, and that the constituencies they seek to mobilize can in fact be invested with *agency* (Gamson and Meyer 1996).

But organizers do not construct these interpretations in a vacuum, nor do potential activists interpret each new appeal solely on its own terms. Both operate in a larger political environment, a crucible in which their values are honed. Critical to the successful emergence of protest movements is a positive feedback loop through which well-positioned elites reinforce both an alternative position on issues and the choice of protest as a strategy. In the case of civil rights in the United States, for example, the Supreme Court's 1954 decision, *Brown v. Board of Education*, legitimated criticism of segregation and offered the promise of federal government intervention as a powerful ally against Southern state and local governments. The decision suggested new possibilities for social organization.

Organizers recognize, then, that in order first to promote and then to sustain activism, they need to build and reinforce not only a shared understanding of a social problem but also a sense of community. The sources of community and the struggles for change differ from context to context and movement to movement. Successful labour organizers in Poland built unions around the shared experiences of their members, both at the workplace and at home, addressing the range of concerns in both spheres. East German dissidents organized in the Protestant Church, while the intellectuals in Czechoslovakia who spearheaded the revolution of 1989 found political space in the now-famous Magic Lantern theatre. The first step in launching any effective political campaign is searching out and filling available free spaces, nurturing in embryo the social values that activists want to see expressed in the larger society. Even in a repressive state with an underdeveloped civil society, social movement mobilization is the activity of the organized, *en bloc*, rather than a mystical melding of atomized individuals.

The Effects of Social Protest Movements

Social movements challenge current public policies, and sometimes they also alter governing alliances and public policy. This is not, however, the end of their influence. Movement activists aspire to change not only specific policies but also broad cultural and institutional structures; they therefore can affect far more than their explicitly articulated targets. Movements change the lives of those who participate in them in ways that can radically reconstruct subsequent politics, including subsequent social protest movements. Movements build communities of struggle – communities that can sustain themselves and also change in unanticipated ways. We can see the influence of protest movements in three distinct but interdependent areas: public policy, culture and participants (Meyer and Whittier 1994). Each of these is important not just for its impact on the larger society, but also for its direct and indirect effects on other social movements:

- *Policy*: Movements generally organize and mobilize around specific policy demands ranging from passing a civil rights ordinance to ending a war. Activists also seek to represent their concerns and their claimed constituencies within mainstream political institutions, to speak for those who protest. Public policy includes symbolic and substantive components, and policy-makers can make symbolic concessions to try to avoid granting the aggrieved group's substantive demands or giving it new power. In domestic policy, elected officials can offer combinations of rhetorical concessions or attacks, in conjunction with symbolic policy changes, to respond to or pre-empt political challenges (Edelman 1971). Visible appointments to high-level positions, rhetorical flourishes and symbolic policy changes may quiet, at least momentarily, a challenging movement demanding substantive reforms. Both symbolic and substantive concessions in response to pressure from one social movement change the context in which other challengers operate. They open or close avenues of influence, augment or diminish the pressure a movement can bring to bear, or raise or lower the costs of mobilization. Thus, movements can alter the structure of political opportunities they and others face in the future.
- *Culture*: Social movements struggle on a broad cultural plane where state policy is only one parameter (Fantasia 1988; Whittier 1995). Movements must draw from mainstream public discourse and symbols to recruit new activists and advance their claims, yet they must also transform those symbols in order to create the environment they seek. Symbols, meanings and practices forged in the cauldron of social protest often outlive the movements that created them. The familiar peace symbol, for example, designed to support the British Campaign for Nuclear Disarmament in the 1950s, migrated to the United States during its anti-war movement, back to Europe in the 1980s, and to Asia as a rallying point for pro-democracy movements in the 1990s.

    Indeed, in the absence of concrete policy successes, movements are likely to find culture a more accessible venue in which to work, building support for subsequent challenges on matters of policy. In the late 1970s and 1980s, Eastern European dissidents chose explicitly 'anti-political' strategies of participation, in a deliberate attempt to create a 'civil society', that is, a set of social networks and relationships independent of the state. Publication of *samizdat* literature, production of underground theatre and appropriating Western rock music to indigenous political purposes were all important political work for democratic dissidents. This battle, in the least promising of circumstances, proved to be critical in precipitating and shaping the end of the Cold War.
- *Participants*: Finally, social movements influence the people who participate in them. As the Greensboro veterans noted, taking responsibility for changing the segregated South changed their lives forever. People who participate in move-

ments step into history as actors, not simply as victims, and this transformation is not easily reversible. Movement activists forge new identities in struggle, identities that carry on beyond the scope of a particular campaign or movement. Someone who has forged an identity in the struggle of collective action and exercised political power through membership in a community of struggle will not readily submit to being acted upon by distant authorities in the future.

Activists come to see themselves as members of a group that is differentiated from outsiders. They interpret their experiences in political terms, and politicize their actions in both movement contexts and everyday life. Collective identities constructed during periods of peak mobilization endure even after protest dies down. One-time movement participants continue to see themselves as progressive activists even as organized collective action decreases, and they make personal and political decisions in light of this identity. Veterans of Freedom Summer, for example, became leading organizers in the peace and student movements of the 1960s, the feminist and anti-nuclear movements of the 1980s, and beyond (McAdam 1988). By changing the way individuals live, movements affect longer-term changes in the society.

In summary, movements can influence not only the terrain upon which subsequent challengers struggle, but also the resources available to challengers and the general atmosphere surrounding the struggle. In changing policy and the policy-making process, movements can alter the structure of political opportunity that new challengers face. By producing changes in culture, movements can change the values and symbols used by both mainstream and dissident actors. They can expand the tactical repertoire available to new movements. By changing participants' lives, movements alter the personnel available for subsequent challenges.

Further Reading

Keck, M.E. and Sikkink, K. 1998: *Activists beyond Borders*. Ithaca, NY: Cornell University Press, 1998.

McAdam, D. 1982: *Political Process and the Development of Black Insurgency*. Chicago: University of Chicago Press.

McAdam, D., McCarthy, J.D. and Zald, M.N. (eds) 1996: *Comparative Perspectives on Social Movements: Political Opportunities, Mobilizing Structures, and Cultural Framings*. Cambridge: Cambridge University Press.

Meyer, D.S. 2007: *The Politics of Protest: Social Movements in America*. New York: Oxford University Press.

Meyer, D.S. and Tarrow, S. (eds.) 1998: *The Social Movement Society*. Lanham, MD: Rowman & Littlefield.

Piven, F.F. and Cloward, R.A. 1979: *Poor People's Movements*. New York: Vintage.

Tarrow, S. 1998: *Power in Movement*, 2nd edn. Cambridge: Cambridge University Press.

Tarrow, S. 2005: *The New Transnational Activism*. Cambridge: Cambridge University Press.

Tilly, C. 1978: *From Mobilization to Revolution*. Reading, MA: Addison Wesley Longman.

36

Global Social Movements and Transnational Advocacy

Valentine M. Moghadam

Globalization remains a contested subject for scholars, policy-makers and activists. Its enthusiasts stress the promises of free trade, deregulation and flexibility while its detractors emphasize the problems of inequalities, unfair trade relations and militarism. Meanwhile, activists across countries have mobilized against the adverse effects of globalization and have created transnational advocacy networks. This suggests a connection between globalization and global social movements and raises a number of questions. Are there distinct forms of collective action that may be identified and associated with the age of globalization? What are the modalities of transnational advocacy and to what extent have they been effective? What is the role of the state and the interstate system in shaping movement activity and transnational advocacy? These questions are addressed in part through reference to three of the more visible transnational/global social movements: feminism, Islamism and global justice.

Contemporary globalization is marked by a distinct set of economic policies (neoliberal capitalism and integrated markets), the worldwide dissemination of cultural products (largely from the West), and a political-military project of domination (spearheaded by the United States). As such, it has engendered competition and contestation – even among its agents and supporters – and grievances and resistance from its detractors. A key characteristic of the present era is the proliferation of networks of activists within global social movements. With the spectacular spread of information and communication technologies (ICTs), non-state actors are able to transcend territorial borders to frame claims, mobilize supporters and coordinate activities.

The Wiley-Blackwell Companion to Political Sociology, First Edition. Edited by Edwin Amenta, Kate Nash, and Alan Scott.
© 2012 Blackwell Publishing Ltd. Published 2012 by Blackwell Publishing Ltd.

In turn, global social movements reflect and contribute to the expansion of what has been termed *global civil society* or the *transnational public sphere*. Here, social movements, advocacy networks, militant opposition groups, diverse publics, and media networks interact outside the control of states and markets and offer different conceptions of 'the good society'. An ongoing debate pertains to whether global civil society should be viewed in normative terms; whether it should be acknowledged that not all participating networks, representations and discourses are emancipatory; and whether it may be more useful to refer to multiple and sometimes overlapping transnational public spheres. Examining Islamist movements along with the feminist and global justice movements illustrates the salience of the debate.

Globalization: Economic, Cultural, and Political Dimensions

While globalization proponents emphasize the presumed benefits of free trade and liberalized markets (though the financial crisis of 2007–2009 called this rosy view into question), left-wing critics view globalization as a class project or as 'the new imperialism' (Harvey 2003; Bello 2000). For some, it is a historic stage in the maturation of capitalism; the reorganization of world production through new technologies and organizational innovations has given rise to a transnational capitalist class and the making of a transnational state apparatus (Sklair 2001; Robinson 2004). For others, globalization is another word for the processes that they have always referred to as 'world-systemic': integration into the economic zones of core, periphery and semi-periphery, with their attendant hierarchies of states, and forms of resistance known as anti-systemic movements. The capitalist world economy has experienced cyclical processes and secular trends for hundreds of years, with various 'waves of globalization' (Chase-Dunn 1998).

Trade unionists, transnational feminist networks (TFNs) and global justice activists, including the recent Occupy Wall Street protestors, decry the social costs of globalization, such as unemployment, job insecurity and growing inequalities. They propose the establishment of core labour standards, fair trade, democratization of global economic management and a tax on speculative financial flows (the Tobin tax). For such critics, globalization should be vigorously opposed by organized movements starting at the grassroots, local and community levels, and reaching across borders. Some prefer 'deglobalization' and a return to local democracy, while other call for 'another world', or a more people-oriented globalization (*altérmondialisation*), or implementation of Keynesianism on a world scale to create a kind of global social democracy.

Political globalization refers to the growing power of institutions of global governance such as the World Bank, the International Monetary Fund (IMF) and the World Trade Organization (WTO). But it also refers to the spread and influence of international non-governmental organizations (INGOs), social movement organizations and transnational advocacy networks operating across borders and constituting a kind of global civil society for the promotion of democracy and rights.

Another debate over globalization concerns the extent to which the sovereignty of nation-states and the autonomy of national economies have been weakened by globalization. Early analyses tended to overemphasize the purported end of the Westphalian system of state sovereignty, as if weaker states in the world-system had

not always been vulnerable to the intervention of the powerful, and as if all states in
the world-system now faced equally diminished capacity. Some (Castells, Urry, Beck,
early Sassen; see discussion in Moghadam 2009, ch. 2) went so far as to argue that fixed
and strong state systems had been replaced by networks and flows (see discussion in
Moghadam 2009: ch. 2). An alternative perspective, provided by world-system theory,
would recognize differences in state capacity vis-à-vis global markets and institutions of
global governance across the core, periphery and semi-periphery. By the same token,
transnational social movements would be expected to have different resources and to
encounter different state responses across economic zones and indeed across different
types of states (i.e., democratic vs. authoritarian states in the semi-periphery).

Globalization is also viewed in terms of 'world culture' through the internationalization of standards and norms, increasing modes of organization, the emergence of
multiple and overlapping identities, and the presence of hybrid sites such as world
cities, free trade zones, offshore banking facilities, border zones and ethnic mélange
neighbourhoods (Pieterse 2004). Such socio-cultural processes are said to permit
transnational interactions, connections and mobilizations. The dark side is that
cultural diffusion has hardened some oppositional identities, taking the form of
reactive movements. Fundamentalisms and communalisms, for example, seek to
recuperate traditional patterns, including patriarchal gender relations, in reaction
to the 'Westernizing' trends of globalization. Benjamin Barber used the term 'jihad' as
shorthand to describe religious fundamentalism, disintegrative tribalism, ethnic
nationalisms and similar kinds of identity politics carried out by local peoples 'to
sustain solidarity and tradition against the nation-state's legalistic and pluralistic
abstractions as well as against the new commercial imperialism of McWorld' (Barber
2001: 232). Instead of advocating for democratic institutions and human rights, jihad
is likely to resort to violent means to protest global injustice and to implement its own,
narrow view of 'the good society'.

From Social Movements to Transnational Advocacy and Action

Theoretical frameworks explaining transnational social movements and advocacy
include those that focus on macro-level theorizing (e.g., world polity and world-
system theories) and those that emphasize middle-range dynamics – specifically, social
movement analysis, which will be the focus of the discussion that follows. Indeed, the
social movement paradigm is well established in political sociology.

A social movement is constituted by mobilized groups engaged in sustained
contentious interactions with power-holders, usually state authorities. Scholars have
long shown that the roots of social protest, organizing and movement-building are
located in broad processes of social change that destabilize existing power relations
and increase the leverage of challenging groups. Sidney Tarrow has noted that social
movements emerged in the eighteenth century from 'structural changes that were
associated with capitalism' such as 'new forms of association, regular communication
linking center and periphery, and the spread of print and literacy' (cited in Keck and
Sikkink 1998: 37). In a Marxian sense, social movements (like revolutions) are
associated with the contradictions of modernity and capitalism, which produce both
oppressive structures and opportunities for agency and mobilization. But scholars

have also analysed more proximate factors, and this has led to explanatory frame-works such as rational-choice-based resource mobilization, new social movements and political process theorizing. There is now an appreciation of the interconnection of political, organizational and cultural processes in social movements, with scholars arguing that the three factors play roles of varying analytic importance over the course of the movement (McAdam, McCarthy and Zald 1996). In addition to studying the role of political opportunities, mobilizing structures and cultural frames, scholars examine cycles and waves of protest, and 'collective action repertoires' such as boycotts, strikes, barricades, marches and mass petitioning.

All movements have some structure, but not all movements have major formal organizations that dominate and direct movement activity. According to Luther Gerlach, social movements are 'segmentary, polycentric, and reticulate' (SPR). Illustrating his SPR thesis by way of the environmental movement, he showed that social movements have many, sometimes competing, organizations and groups (segmentary); they have multiple and sometimes competing leaders (polycentric); and they are loose networks that link to each other (reticulate). Despite the segments, however, there is a shared opposition and ideology. In the environmental movement that he described, for example, *social movement organizations* (SMOs) ranged from the very radical and decentralized Earth First! to Greenpeace and to Germany's Greens (who later evolved into the Green Party). Gerlach argued that the SPR nature of SMOs allows them to be flexible, adaptive, and to resonate with larger constituencies through different tactics (for example, direct action versus lobbying and legal strategies). It also 'promotes striving, innovation, and entrepreneurial experimenta-tion in generating and implementing socio-cultural change' (Gerlach 1999: 95). This argument is relevant to other movements, too, including the global Islamist, feminist and justice movements. The type of mobilizing structures found in global social movements includes not only formal organizations but more fluid networks – and in the case of the Islamist movement, cells that act independently of any larger or more formal organization.

The role of emotions has been observed as both an impetus for transnational social movement participation and a tool in recruitment and advocacy efforts. Commitment, zeal, moral outrage, ethics – these are aspects of social movement building and participation that scholars oriented towards rational choice theorizing have neglected (Goodwin, Jasper and Polletta 2001). No-one who examines Islamist movements can deny that there are strong emotional undercurrents and motivations among partici-pants. When Muslim-owned media such as al-Jazeera and al-Arabiyya dwell on bombings in Afghanistan, Iraq and Palestine, this can be regarded as a movement event that is also an emotion-producing ritual. The presence of emotions such as humil-iation, anger and frustration has been widely noted in connection with Muslim militants, by observers as well as by Islamists themselves.

Similarly, emotions play a role in the feminist and global justice movements. Violence against women is addressed analytically by feminists but it is often con-fronted in emotive terms. Global justice activists frequently articulate their opposition to neoliberal capitalism and the international financial institutions in moral terms. Social movement actors do not simply engage in cool-headed cost–benefit calcula-tions, but also express strong feelings about injustices. Nor are these expressions limited to anger, alienation and moral outrage. At anti-globalization protests and demonstrations there is always satire, parody, music, puppetry – indeed, often a festival-like atmosphere. Joy, anger, commitment, solidarity – in short, emotions are as much aspects of the (global) social movement experience as are the 'entrepreneurial' dimensions posited by resource-mobilization theory.

While the broad parameters of social movement theorizing remain relevant, they have been modified to account for both non-Western and transnational movements. In the 1980s, theorizing focused on movements within single societies, typically in the mature democracies of Europe and the United States. Theorists of 'new social movements' posited the centrality of postindustrial values and norms in the emergence of animal rights, environmental, gay and feminist movements. Indeed, feminist movements tended to be presented as localized and identity-focused. As globalization proceeded in the 1990s, researchers took note of cross-border mobilizations on the part of what came to be known as transnational advocacy networks (Keck and Sikkink 1998), transnational social movements (Smith, Chatfield and Pagnucco 1997) and global social movements (O'Brien et al. 2000). By the turn of the new century, it was clear that economic justice issues had not disappeared.

The UN conferences of the 1990s were important to the growth of global social movements and their organizations/networks in at least two ways. First, they provided a forum for the discussion of global issues by governments and non-governmental actors, a physical space for networking and mobilizing, and an opportunity to create or expand transnational activist networks. Second, international declarations and treaties on development, human rights, environmental protection and so on could be used to 'frame' local grievances and campaigns. For political sociologists, it became increasingly clear that the analytical point of departure would have to take account of the transnational, and that local–global linkages would have to be theorized.

Women had been organizing and mobilizing across borders in 'transnational feminist networks' since at least the mid-1980s; their grievances pertained to the effects of economic restructuring, patriarchal fundamentalisms and violence against women (Moghadam 2005). Like environmental activists, they took their cause to intergovernmental organizations and took part in the United Nations (UN) world conferences. Middle East specialists, including the feminist scholars among them, wrote of the spread of Islamist movements in the region and noted the diffusion of the discourses and norms of a politicized Islam in other regions, including among immigrant groups in Europe. The attacks of 11 September 2001 broadened the scope of the study of Islamist movements beyond the purview of area specialists. Mainstream social scientists became interested in analysing militant Islam and the 'war on terror', while the 2003 invasion of Iraq by the United States and Britain produced numerous studies on war, 'empire' and the new imperialism. At the same time, new transnational political spaces had opened up, in the form of the World Social Forum (WSF) and the regional forums. The new century saw the Global Justice Movement (GJM) meeting regularly in Porto Alegre, Brazil – as well as Mumbai, Nairobi and other venues – to protest neoliberal globalization and the wars in Afghanistan and Iraq, and to offer alternatives.

A new body of literature emerged, therefore, taking these novel departures into consideration. In the new century, a consensus emerged that the response to globalizing economic, political and cultural developments had taken the form of transnational collective action, including the emergence of global social movements and advocacy networks focused on human rights, the environment and economic justice (della Porta and Tarrow 2005; della Porta *et al.* 2006; Santos 2006; Smith 2009; Moghadam 2009). While scholars acknowledged that transnational social movements were not historically unprecedented but dated back to the late eighteenth century, it was clear that the scope of transnationalization and the scale of international ties among activists had increased dramatically in the period of late capitalism, or economic globalization. What is more, while social movement theory – especially in its resource mobilization form – had emphasized the importance of organizations, the network form – with its flexibility and fluidity – appeared to be most conducive to an era of globalization and the form most characteristic of transnational social movements.

Other observations were that 'old values' such as religious solidarities could motivate transnational activism. Such actions could be peaceful and within legal boundaries, or they could be extremist in nature. The spread of Islamist movements, for example, raised questions about the 'secularization thesis' associated with Weberian sociology and modernization theory; it also showed that religious movements could be politicized, could constitute a transnational network and could be militant. Certainly the emergence of the al-Qaeda network in the late 1990s suggested that globalization facilitates the formation of loosely organized, deterritorialized transnational groups, including those motivated by religiously inflected ideologies.

Tarrow defines global or transnational social movements as 'socially mobilized groups with constituents in at least two states, engaged in sustained contentious interactions with power-holders in at least one state other than their own, or against an international institution, or a multinational economic actor' (Tarrow 2005: 214). Global social movements are often comprised of domestically based organizations or transnational networks, in a web of intersecting networks that are fluid and non-hierarchical but also consist of a number of more prominent, vocal and visible organizations.

What is it that transnational social movements do? The pioneering study on transnational advocacy networks by Margaret Keck and Kathryn Sikkink focused on the research, lobbying and advocacy work of such networks, along with their interaction with intergovernmental organizations. Chadwick Alger (in Smith *et al.* 1997: 262) observed that transnational social movements created and activated global networks to mobilize pressure outside states; participated in multilateral and inter-governmental political arenas; acted and agitated within states; and enhanced public awareness and participation. In the process, such mobilizations, interactions and transnational advocacy contributed to the making of a transnational public sphere (Guidry, Kennedy and Zald 2000: 3).

A defining feature of transnational activists is their ability to shift their activities among levels and across borders, coordinating with groups outside their own country. This has been made possible by one of the 'gifts' of globalization – the new information and computer technologies, mobile phones, the Internet, and to a lesser extent, satellite television – which has led to the expansion of 'cyber-activism'. Tech-savvy transnational networks have set up extensive, interactive and increasingly sophisticated multimedia Web sites, where one can find state-ments, research reports and manifestoes, as well as discussion forums, chat rooms, tutorials and digital libraries. Such Web sites, many of which are linked to each other, create or support communities of activists while also providing them with resources. For even more rapid communication and coordination, activists turn to instant messaging, social networking sites, YouTube and other modalities. Recourse to such technologies to connect with the world appears to be widespread in the global South and especially in authoritarian countries that limit democratic mobilizations. This was vividly demonstrated by the Iranian 'Green Protests' in the summer of 2009 and afterwards, and the protests in Tunisia and Egypt in early 2011, which led to the collapse of governments in the two countries. The Iranian protests, along with police repression, were captured live through mobile phones, sent immediately to social network sites and disseminated throughout the world. This reality elucidates the notion of 'time-space compression' and shows that social movements can operate simultaneously in domestic and global spaces. Through instant messaging, YouTube, Facebook, Twitter and so on, the new media technologies allow for rapid communication and dissemination, often frustrating state attempts to keep dissidence and repression under cover.

Islamism, Feminism, and Global Justice

Early theorists of transnational advocacy networks focused on ideational and ethical motivations for the emergence of the human rights, environmental and solidarity movements. However, the 1997–1998 mobilization against the Multilateral Agreement on Investment and the 'Battle of Seattle' in late 1999 confirmed that movement interest in class, inequality and economic issues had returned. Subsequently, the economic crises of 2007–2009 starkly demonstrated the capacity of integrated global financial markets to wreak havoc on domestic businesses and communities, and the crises were met by the (re-)emergence of public debates and studies questioning the viability of capitalism. The worldwide expansion of militant Islamist movements also confirmed that the new world order included violent networks as well as INGOs dedicated to lobbying and advocacy. Today, scholarship on global social movements addresses questions of opportunities and resources for movement-building and advocacy, the place of violence in social movements and transnational networks, the relationship between transnational social movements and the building of democracy, and the salience of gender in movement dynamics. The research is informed by a variety of theoretical frameworks, including Marxist, world polity, world-system, feminist and social movements.

Beginning with macro-level and historical features, Islamist, feminist and global justice movements of today seek political change and socio-cultural transformations but operate within the constraints of a global capitalist order, an interstate system and patriarchal cultures. They also have historical antecedents in the eighteenth, nineteenth and early twentieth centuries. The GJM can be linked back to transnational movements of workers, socialists, communists, progressives and anarchists during an economic period that Karl Polanyi (2001 [1944]) called the 'great transformation'. Although the GJM consists of numerous movements, networks and organizations that are quite autonomous, it has an overall affinity with traditional left-wing politics. Many of the older activists and intellectuals were once affiliated with left-wing organizations or solidarity movements; many of the younger activists are involved in labour and economic justice causes; and the writings of Karl Marx are well known to many activists. Human rights groups also abound in the GJM, and some scholars have found similarities between their moral discourse, tactics and strategies and those of the much earlier anti-slavery movement in the United States and Britain (e.g., Keck and Sikkink 1998: ch. 2).

The Islamist movements that burst onto the international scene in the late 1970s and spread in the 1980s were rooted in eighteenth-, nineteenth- and early twentieth-century revival movements (e.g., Salafists, Wahabists, Mahdists), which in turn claimed to be following the path taken by the Prophet Muhammad in the seventh century AD (Moaddel 2005). Other sources of inspiration and guidance are the writings of Abul Ala Mawdudi (who founded the Jamiat-e Islami in India in 1941), and the Egyptians Rashid Rida, Hasan al-Banna (who founded the Muslim Brotherhood in 1929) and Seyyid Qutb, all of whom took issue with modernity as it was proceeding in their countries and called for a return to strict implementation of *Sharia* law. Seyyid Qutb's 1948–1950 stay in the United States and his experience in Egyptian prisons convinced him that the Jahiliyya – the so-called age of darkness that characterized pre-Islamic Arabia – had returned and needed to be combated. Today's Islamists use this term to describe the state of the world and justify their aggressive tactics. From Ibn Taymiyyah they adopted the duty to wage *jihad* against apostates and unbelievers (Esposito 2002: 45–46). The violence of militant Islamists is rejected, however, by liberal Islamists or ordinary Muslims across the world.

The global women's movement has roots in first-wave feminism, with its focus on suffrage and justice for women, and in second-wave feminism, with its demands for equality and cultural change. Scholars have identified liberal, socialist and militant strands in both waves. First-wave feminism brought about international women's organizations around abolition, women's suffrage, trafficking in women, anti-militarism and labour legislation for working women and mothers. In promoting women's rights, maternity legislation and an end to child labour, they engaged with intergovernmental bodies such as the League of Nations and the International Labour Organization.

The early twentieth century also saw the emergence of an international socialist women's movement. In 1900 the Socialist International passed the first pro-woman suffrage resolution, and suffrage became a demand of socialist parties in 1907. Within the Second International, the women's organizations of France, Germany and Russia mobilized thousands of working-class as well as middle-class women for socialism and women's emancipation. In Asian countries, as Kumari Jayawardena showed, many of the women's movements and organizations that emerged were associated with socialist or nationalist movements. Although feminists and leftists have not always agreed on priorities or strategies, there has been a long-standing affinity that helps to explain the involvement of feminists in the GJM today.

The historical roots of global Islamism, feminism and justice help legitimize and sustain the movements. Each, however, focuses on contemporary problems, inequalities and injustices to mobilize for social and political change. Islamist activism has been motivated by corrupt, authoritarian or pro-Western regimes in their own Muslim-majority countries; by solidarity with their confrères in Palestine, Iraq and Afghanistan; and by opposition to secularizing and westernizing tendencies. Many Islamist movements are focused on national-level problems and have national-level goals (for example, Palestinian Hamas and Lebanese Hezbollah) even while they may be in close contact with other Islamist movements and governments. The transnational Islamist movement consists of groups and networks ranging from moderate to extremist, using methods that range from parliamentarism to spectacular violence. This reality confirms that like globalization itself, global social movements are complex and contradictory. That is, globalization has produced life-affirming non-violent social movements but also deadly rebellions, martyrdom operations and transnational networks of violent extremists.

In contrast to militant Islamist movements, the global feminist and justice movements espouse economic, political and cultural change brought about through peaceful and democratic means. Transnational feminist activism is motivated by concern for women's human rights in an era of neoliberal globalization, militarism, war and patriarchal fundamentalisms. TFNs – the principal mobilizing structure of global feminism – consist of women from two or more countries who mobilize for research, lobbying, advocacy and civil disobedience to protest gender injustice and promote women's human rights, equality and peace. The GJM consists of loosely organized mobilized groups that protest the downside of globalization and call for economic and social justice. A key institution is the WSF, a gathering place for the numerous transnational networks and nationally based advocacy groups that have grown exponentially since the mid-1990s. Initially hosted by the Brazilian Workers' Party and the landless peasant movement, the WSF was created as a forum for the participation and supporters of grassroots movements across the globe, and a counterpart to forums of representatives of governments, political parties and corporations. In particular, the WSF is the opposite of, and alternative to, the World Economic Forum, a grouping of business and political elites that meets annually in Davos, Switzerland.

These three transnational social movements are interconnected, inasmuch as feminists and moderate Islamists have taken part in the WSF; and the GJM includes individuals and groups active in TFNs. All three movements are counter-hegemonic in that they are opposed to globalization's hegemonic tendencies of neoliberalism, expansion and war. Each movement itself is global, inasmuch as it targets states and international institutions, and is a coalition of local, grassroots groups as well as transborder networks. All three make extensive use of information technologies to connect with members, reach out to supporters, recruit followers, raise awareness, mobilize financial resources and promote their vision. But there are differences. For most Islamists, the solution to current problems is the widespread application of Islamic laws and norms; global justice activists present a variety of alternatives to neoliberalism, from deglobalization to cosmopolitan social democracy; transnational feminists insist on the application of international conventions on women's human rights. (See Table 36.1.)

Studying Global Social Movements

If the study of globalization includes poring over international data sets to discern capital flows, economic growth and patterns of political governance, the study of transnational social movements requires a mix of methods, of which observation, interviews, Web site analyses and participant observation are typical. In studying

Table 36.1 Social movement features of global feminist, Islamist and justice movements

	Opportunities and resources	Mobilizing structures and SMOs	Frames
Feminist	Socio-demographics: education and employment UN Decade for Women (1976–1985) and 1990s UN conferences Resources: women's organizations, donor agencies, European foundations	DAWN, WIDE, WLUML, WEDO, WILPF, Madre, WLP, Code Pink, etc.	Women's rights are human rights; end feminization of poverty; end violence against women; empowerment; gender justice; gender mainstreaming
Islamist parliamentarian extremist	Resources from Muslim states (IRI, Saudi Arabia, Libya); publicity and support via Arab media US-sponsored Afghan war, 1980–1992; resources from Muslim states (Taliban, Saudi Arabia, Sudan); personal wealth; publicity via al-Jazeera	Hamas, Hezbollah, Muslim Brotherhood Al-Qaeda and affiliates	Islam is the solution; establish Sharia law; justice for Palestine 'Crusaders' out of Muslim lands; liberate Palestine, Afghanistan, Iraq; jihad against 'near enemy' and 'far enemy'; global Caliphate
Global justice	UN conferences of 1990s; PT government of Brazil; occasional support from EU and social democratic governments; rise of left-wing governments in Latin America	Third World Network; ENDA; Focus on the Global South; Oxfam; Jubilee 2000; World Social Forum	Against neoliberal globalization; for biodiversity and cultural diversity (*altermondialisation*); economic justice; end third-world debt; make poverty history; environmental protection; human rights; anti-war; *another world is possible*

Islamist movements, for example, scholars have visited offices and other institutions, conducted interviews (sometimes in prisons), utilized memoirs by former Islamists and used hyperlink and content analysis methodology to analyse extremist groups' Web sites. The study of TFNs requires attendance at feminist conferences; observations at protest events or UN conferences; reading of TFN Web sites and publications; and interviews with key figures. Scholars of the GJM attend the WSF, conduct surveys and in-depth interviews, and closely follow the writings and publications of scholar-activists and other GJM leaders. Quantitative analyses using large-N data sets from international yearbooks have produced a 'mapping' of the growth, density and geographic distribution of global social movements.

Some researchers have tried to empirically test the relationship between globalization – whether measured by growing inequalities or by state integration in the world polity – and the rise and spread of global contentious politics and of transnational social movements. Jackie Smith and Dawn Wiest (2005) found a positive relationship between state integration into the world polity and civil society integration into transnational networks or global civil society. Others have looked at the relationship between world culture or economic globalization, on the one hand, and less salutary forms of global contentious politics, including violent militancy, on the other (Lizardo 2006; Wiest 2007). The new century also saw studies on the WSF as an institution of the GJM and as a site for the building of global democracy (Santos 2006; della Porta 2007; Smith and Karides 2008; Smith and Smythe 2010). Research proliferated on women's and transnational feminist movements, and on the status of feminism within the GJM (Moghadam 2005; Eschle and Maiguashca 2009). Islamist movements became the subject of numerous studies, though these are predominantly located within either area studies or the new field of 'terrorism studies', with only a limited scholarship using social-movement concepts (Wictorowicz 2004).

Another area of research pertains to the relationship of transnational social movements and advocacy networks to state systems. The state's economic capacity may have waned as a result of neoliberalism, and global social movements often criticize hegemonic institutions of global governance such as the World Bank, the IMF and the WTO. Nonetheless, both the state and the interstate system remain relevant to the study of global social movements. Among other reasons, the nature of the state and the absence or presence of elite allies and coalitions with state entities can be critical to a movement's formation and growth. In some cases, states have provided protest groups with needed leverage for their collective action. For example, the GJM found an ally in the Brazilian government. In particular, the Workers' Party and the city of Porto Alegre were crucial to the making of the WSF, as Boaventura Santos has explained. In the past, Islamist movements received funding and moral support from the United States, Saudi Arabia, Pakistan and other state entities. In the 1990s, TFNs received financial support from various European Union government agencies or from the European Commission. The feminist movement in Morocco found an ally in the progressive coalition government of Prime Minister Yousefi and in the new king, which led to the reform of the highly patriarchal family law in 2004. In contrast, the Iranian feminist campaign for equality has faced state hostility and repression, though it has the backing of TFNs (Moghadam and Gheytanchi, 2010).

Global Social Movements and Global Civil Society

In their study of the GJM, Mario Pianta and Raffaele Marchetti define global civil society is 'the sphere of cross-border relationships and activities carried out by collective actors – social movements, networks, and civil society organizations – that are independent from governments and private firms and operate outside the international reach of states and markets'. Global social movements are 'cross-border, sustained, and collective social mobilizations on global issues, ...' (in Della Porta 2007: 30–31). But are all such mobilizations part of global civil society?

Many scholars have viewed social movements and civil society through a progressive lens, defining them in terms of rights, democratic action, politics from below and human emancipation. However, the rise of non-state and anti-corporate movements, organizations and networks that appear to eschew values of equality, democracy and human rights has called such a view into question. What of a network such as al-Qaeda? Or the cells created by disaffected young Muslim men in Europe that planned and executed terrorist bombings? Or neo-Nazi groups in Europe? Mary Kaldor and the other editors of the *Global Civil Society Yearbook* have therefore concluded that 'the normative content [of global civil society] is too contested to be able to form the basis for any operationalization of the concept' (Anheier, Glasius and Kaldor 2001: 21). Conversely, Rupert Taylor (2004) takes a strong position in favour of the normative content, and offers a subjective as well as objective analysis of global civil society. There is little to be gained analytically, he argues, in including any and all non-state actors in the definition of (global) civil society. This is also the position of the transnational feminist network Women Living Under Muslim Laws, which has issued statements decrying women's human rights violations by non-state actors and has published a manual on the subject (see Moghadam 2005, 2009).

Globalization in its economic, political and cultural aspects has engendered grievances and opposition, leading to non-state organizing and collective action. It also has provided the means for rapid cross-border communication, coordination and action – whether for human rights, environmental protection, women's rights, global democracy or Islamic laws and norms. Within each global social movement there may be various frames and methods to achieve goals. Certainly the SPR nature of social movements guarantees the presence of different tendencies, including radical, militant or even terrorist wings. Not all forms of transnational activism, therefore, may be viewed as emancipatory or transformative. As for the capacity of (democratic) global social movements to change the course of globalization, only time – and of course sustained mobilizations – will tell.

Further Readings

Boli, J. and Thomas, G. 1997: World culture in the world polity: a century of international NGOs. *American Sociological Review* 62(2): 171–190.

Chase-Dunn, C. and Gills, B. 2005: Waves of globalization and resistance in the capitalist world system: social movements and critical globalization studies. In R. Appelbaum and W. Robinson (eds) *Critical Globalization Studies*. London: Routledge.

Gautney, H., Dahbour, O., Dawson, A. and Smith, N. (eds) 2009: *Democracy, States, and the Struggle for Global Justice*. New York: Routledge.

Gillan, K., Pickerill, J. and Webster, F. 2008: *Anti-War Activism: New Media and Protest in the Information Age*. London: Palgrave Macmillan.

Moghadam, V. 2009: *Globalization and Social Movements: Islamism, Feminism, and the Global Justice Movement*. Lanham, MD: Rowman & Littlefield.

Pianta, M. and Marchetti, R. 2007: The global justice movements: the transnational dimension. In D. Della Porta (ed.) *The Global Justice Movement*. Boulder, CO: Paradigm.

37

Global Governance
and Environmental Politics

Brenda Holzinger and Gabriela Kütting

Keeping both structures and agency in view, this chapter examines the literature on global governance and environmental politics. As a concept, 'global governance' is derived from that of 'regimes'. Environmental regimes are seen as the main institutions leading to environmental preservation and improvement. The chapter also considers the way in which activists work through transnational economic, social and cultural networks to achieve their aims. The discourse of environmental politics has widened to consider public and private governance, including non-state and business actors, yet still falls short in issues such as global equity. It shows what achievements can be made through global governance mechanisms, but also indicates the shortcomings of any solutions to global environmental problems that only use governance as a remedial mechanism.

The term 'global governance' emerged in the mid-1990s as the popular name for describing the contemporary structure of international relations. It evolved within the context of the most recent era of political and economic globalization in response to a rapidly expanding playing field where states were increasingly joined by a variety of transnational actors in the policy-making arena. This shift from 'international' to 'global' is important because it signalled not only a change in the economic and political structure of world politics, but also, simultaneously, an expansion of power that allowed new actors to enter and shape the political arena. The 1992 Rio Earth Summit, the first truly global conference, was also a significant sign because it reflected the globalization of an environmental consciousness that understood the world as an integrated ecosystem.

The Wiley-Blackwell Companion to Political Sociology, First Edition. Edited by Edwin Amenta, Kate Nash, and Alan Scott.
© 2012 Blackwell Publishing Ltd. Published 2012 by Blackwell Publishing Ltd.

The Structural Dimension of Global Environmental Governance

The global character of environmental degradation can largely be linked to the rise of the fossil fuel economy and the decreasing distance of time and space in the relations between different parts of the globe (Daly 1996). Historically, environmental issues were considered local concerns solely within the state's realm, but beginning in the late 1960s and early 1970s, an understanding of the global concept of 'one earth' as an interconnected ecosystem independent of political boundaries began to emerge (Conca, Alberty and Dabelko 1995). On the one hand, the doomsday feeling of *one* planet reaching its limits was reinforced by the first photographs of the planet from outer space in 1968. These images illuminated the global rather than state-based nature of ecosystems at a time when the Club of Rome pointed out the limits for growth of existing consumptive patterns in industrialized countries (Meadows 1972). On the other hand, seminal pieces of literature such as Rachel Carson's *Silent Spring*, Paul Ehrlich's *The Population Bomb* and Garrett Hardin's works about the tragedy of the commons and the lifeboat ethic (whose messages have been subject to violent criticism since) influenced the way environmental thought became a political priority in international politics from the 1970s onwards. Like James Lovelock's *The Ages of Gaia*, these texts influenced the study of international relations and environmental politics with their holistic, and consequently global, view of ecological and social interaction.

Political economy analysis evolved as the academic home for students of international relations who wished to push beyond the theoretical confines of the state-centric realists to comprehend how political forces and economic interactions shape political structures and outcomes. Traditionally, the study of political economy goes back to the beginnings of modern capitalism and the social relations that evolved in this period, which then developed and changed throughout modernity (Gill 1997; Hoogvelt 1997). Although the relationship between environmental degradation and a global economy was made relatively early in the environmental thought literature, the environment as a guiding principle has not formed part of mainstream political economy analysis within international relations theory. Instead, it entered the field through radical political, historical and ecological scholarship, as well as through some types of ecological economic analysis (Merchant 1992; Daly 1996; Eckersley 1995; Dryzek 1997). These approaches usually define the rise of modern capitalism as the point in history when society became increasingly alienated from its physical environment and perceived itself instead to be mastering or harnessing it – a process that became more intense as modern capitalism became more sophisticated. Essentially, the rise of modern capitalism, the Enlightenment, Newtonian science and the industrial revolution acted in concert to bring about a change in society–environment relations as humans in the core economies saw themselves as increasingly *controlling* nature rather than either relying upon it or being dominated by it (Merchant 1992). This in turn led to a perception of decreasing dependency on the environment, which, consequently, resulted in environmental neglect and exploitation through a simple failure to understand ecological processes and their significance for life on the planet. Perhaps the best way to explain how economic organization affects the environment is with the idea of Daly's steady-state economy (1992). He describes two visions of the economy, that of standard economics and that of the steady-state economy:

For standard economics ... the economy is an isolated system in which exchange value circulates between firms and households. Nothing enters from the environment, nothing exits to the environment. It does not matter how big the economy is relative to its environment. For all practical purposes an isolated system has no environment. For steady-state economics, the preanalytic vision is that the economy is an open subsystem of a finite and non-growing ecosystem (the environment). The economy lives by importing low-entropy matter-energy (raw materials) – and exporting high-entropy matter-energy (waste). Any subsystem of a finite non-growing system must itself at some point also become non-growing. (1992 xiii)

The implication of the steady-state economy approach is that it is physically impossible to continue extracting resources and creating waste while simultaneously expecting continued, unlimited economic growth. In addition, society's current economic organization disregards the first two laws of thermodynamics which determine the existence of energy on the planet. The first law states that the amount of existing energy and matter is constant and unchangeable. The second law of thermodynamics argues that the state and quality of existing energy can change. In industrial society existing energy gets transformed into 'waste', a form of energy that cannot be reused, thus in effect diminishing the amount of energy available.

In addition to this physical side of environmental change, ecological economics writers such as Martinez-Alier (2002) and Daly argue that conventional economics neglects the moral side of environmental exploitation, because it is too fixated on markets and efficiency rather than on connections. These ideas connect directly to contemporary debates in the environmental justice literature (Martinez-Alier 2002). They also resonate strongly in the human rights literature, particularly with fourth-world studies that use a holistic framework in which indigenous rights are preconditioned upon environmental, economic, political and cultural respect (Anaya 2009). The argument about moral issues as economic externalities combines well with the ecological world-systems theory literature, which also focuses on global structures and their relationship with environmental degradation (Hornborg 1998; Chew 2001 1998; Goldfrank, Goodman and Szasz 1999).

The main argumentative thrust of world-systems analysis suggests that the rise and fall of world civilizations can be traced to environmental degradation, and particularly deforestation, as a main contributory factor in the decline of empires or large powers. Thus, the nature of capitalism can be understood through the social relations of production, labour and the environment. Ponting, in his environmental history of the world, advances a similar argument, although not couched in theoretical terms (1991). These are views of history that integrate an environmental or ecological perspective into predominantly social-historical accounts. The main argument of Sing Chew's thesis, for example, is that both the rise and fall of trading relations and different phases in world history can be analysed from an historical materialist perspective as done by Wallerstein, or alternatively, from a focus on the social relations of production (Frank 1998; Gill 1997).

These approaches, however, neglect the relationship between environmental preservation, natural resource depletion and the material basis of production. In fact, the demise of most empires or large powers also coincides with a decline in the natural resource base through over-exploitation or another form of exhaustion.

Forensic research, documented through carbon testing, suggests that even the two historical periods of dark ages are linked to the depletion of the natural resource base (Chew 2001). Although it has some flaws, the world-systems approach is a significant framework because it integrates the environment into political economy in a holistic manner that incorporates social with environmental analysis. However, it is also important to remember that although environmental degradation has always existed under systems of mass production, *modern* capitalism is a qualitatively different phase of this problem, and environmental degradation under *globalization* is qualitatively different again.

Global Environmental Governance, Agency and the State

The changing role and nature of actors in the international system is usually identified as the most important dimension of political globalization for international relations because it marks the expanding institutionalization of the international system, the increasingly global participation in these institutions, and the inclusion of non-state actors. In the area of political globalization, this does not necessarily mean that any intergovernmental or transnational organization needs to operate globally, but rather that new processes and agency, and structural developments, have a global impact. To quote Prakash and Hart:

> Ipso facto, globalization refers to processes that potentially encompass the whole globe. The process does not have to have actually encompassed the whole globe to be associated with the phenomenon of globalization but there has to be at least a potential for its omnipresence. Thus, one should be able to identify the degree to which a particular globalization process has actually attained globality. (1998: 3)

A large part of the academic debate about global governance focuses on the changing role of the state in the international system, its potential replacement by other actors and the decline of sovereignty (Baker; 2002). In the words of Lipschutz:

> One of the central issues facing human civilisation at the end of the 20th century is governance: who rules? Whose rules? What rules? What kind of rules? At what level? In what form? Who decides? On what basis? Many of the problems that give rise to questions such as these are transnational and transboundary in nature, with the result that the notion of global 'management' has acquired increasing currency in some circles. This is especially true given that economic globalization seems to point toward a single integrated world economy in which the sovereign state appears to be losing much of its authority and control over domestic and foreign affairs. (1999: 259)

Although the debate about the loss of state sovereignty is one of the cornerstones of political globalization studies, from a critical global political economy perspective the frame of a transfer of power or political division of labour yields a richer analysis (Mittelman 2000).

While it is certainly possible to argue that states are losing power to other actors, states remain the founders and funders of those institutions which are supposed to challenge the power of the state. Thus, it is necessary to talk about two different states—the Northern, developed state and the Southern, developing state. The Northern states are generally the world's wealthiest and include those that are advanced in terms of development, industrialization, democratic participation, social welfare, education and human rights. The Southern states, on the other hand, are often extremely poor and lack a functioning middle class. They are also often partially developed or even underdeveloped (with development arrayed along a continuum from developing to extremely underdeveloped) with either very young or newly commencing industrialization processes. Southern states can also often be characterized by corruption, an absence of meaningful democratic participation, human rights violations and a lack of social welfare and education resources that would allow a middle class to emerge. Rather than declining, it seems the power of the Northern state is actually fortified through global economic governance institutions, which, at the end of the day, represent its interests. Consequently, it is actually the power of the developing-country state that is being either undermined by global governance or prevented from evolving in the first place because most developing countries have never been in a position of structural power. Therefore, it could be argued that global economic institutions are a form of structural power in Lukes' terms rather than evidence of the decline of the power of the state (Lukes 1974).

The global politico-economic framework legitimized by states and international institutions provides a formidable system for the efficient transfer of resources from the periphery to the core (Cox 1996; Mittelman 2000; Saurin 1996b). Any environmental governance efforts are subordinated to this goal and do not generally form part of political economy analyses of globalization practices. Instead, global environmental governance is analysed through the institutional literature (Bernstein 2001; Young 2000 2002). Despite the increasing environmental rhetoric in the form of the sustainable development discourse (Redclift 1987 – despite its age still one of the best books on the subject), there has been no real attempt to confront squarely the strained nature of environment–society relations. Consequently, with a few notable exceptions, there has been no valid effort to accommodate environmental imperatives with social needs (Lipschutz 1999; Gillespie 2001; Saurin 1996a).

Regimes and the Environment

The system of international environmental politics that emerged after the first United Nations Conference on the Human Environment in 1972 is one based entirely on voluntary agreements among states that manifest in many forms, including, for example, international institutions, conventions, declarations, protocols and principles of decision making (Young 2000, Biermann 2006). However, because there is no enforcement mechanism in the international realm where the state reigns supreme, the legitimacy of all global environmental agreements rests solely on compliance achieved through the less tangible, non-legal and usually unwritten avenues of 'soft power' (Nye 2004). Examples of soft power include shared norms and expectations, the desire of some states to be viewed as credible actors, the wish of other states to demonstrate their capacity and reliability, and, when necessary, even simple peer pressure (Keohane 2005; Nye 2004; Krasner 1983). These interactions occur within frameworks called *regimes*, which are generally defined as 'institutions possessing norms, decision rules, and procedures which facilitate a convergence of expectations' (Krasner 1983). The regime perspective provides a theoretical framework that allows an understanding of how social and environmental issues can be managed globally through complex constellations of law, institutions, rights, rules, principles of decision making, norms and expectations (Young 2000).

Regime theory was first introduced by John Ruggie in the mid-1970s and it gained significant popularity by the 1980s as cooperation among states grew (Krasner 1983). By the mid-1990s, however, the literature contained many solid critiques. For example, some scholars have argued that regime theory must be embedded within a larger historical and normative context (Stevis 2006; Lipschutz 2001), while others critique it as still too state-centric (Stokke 2000). Many who focus on regimes argue for more attention to regime effectiveness and political process (Stokke 2000; Vogler 2003; Peterson 2000; Kütting 2004). Additionally, regime theory has been charged with bias in favour of the already powerful actors, silencing the weaker voices, perpetuating the status quo, failing to consider social power relationships, not grappling effectively with market forces, an inability to force the participation of hegemonic powers that do not wish to participate (Lipschutz 2001), and a lack of appreciation for the subjective nature of scientific assumptions (Paterson 1995). Lucy Ford argues that another serious weakness in the regime literature is its minimal attention to social grassroots movements as potentially radical agents of change (Ford 2003). Finally, regime theory also fails to adequately address questions of power, morality, fairness or justice, whether the context is within societies, across societies or between generations.

Despite these shortcomings, some scholars have invested their efforts in revising regime theory (Vogler 2003; Haas 1989). Traditionally, regimes and the analytical approaches used for their study have been state-centric, but recently the understanding of regimes has expanded significantly so that it now includes not only institutions, but also informal political networks and elements of civil society. As Olav Schram Stokke writes, '... regime analysis is gradually taking a more inclusive approach in dealing with both the focus and mechanisms of governance, hence moving closer to the study of global governance' (2000: 35). However, John Vogler argues that it could be important to reinvigorate a regime focus to global governance that would approach institutions through a social-constructivist lens. This analytical model, according to Vogler, might be 'more capable of comprehending the kind of normative changes that are required to make global governance for sustainability a reality' (2003: 37). It is also possible to argue that globalization is the new global regime if globalization is understood as the reorganization of the state from within the ongoing dynamics of capital accumulation and the unequal distribution of its benefits and consequences. As such, the globalization regime has brought about changes in travel and information technology that has made it possible to significantly widen the scope of participants in the international political process.

Global Governance, Civil Society and the Environment

Increasing disappointment with state-sponsored policies and international organizations has led to the rise of new participants in the form of transnational protest movements and non-governmental actors (including corporations) in civil society. These civil society actors have created additional and alternative forms of global governance that have become part of the global network of regulations, norms and ethics (Wapner 1995; Ford 2003; Hess 2009). This phenomenon is particularly true for global environmental governance where non-governmental organizations (NGOs) are ever more important participants in international environmental institutions, an arena traditionally limited to states (Breitmeier, Young and Zürn 2006). Environmental NGOs have gained more influence on states as well as public policy by working within and across societies themselves (Wapner 1995). Wapner argues that these organizations are political actors in their own right and that transnational activist societal efforts should be seen through the concept of 'world civic politics'. The extraordinary level of non-state actor participation in the 1992 Rio Earth Summit is viewed by many as the ultimate expression of the importance of global civil society. More importantly, growing out of this summit, the Climate Change Convention institutionalized many non-state actors as integral parts of the global environmental governance process.

Lucy Ford cautions, however, that non-state actors participating in more formal parts of the global environmental governance process become *deradicalized* as they become institutionalized, which in turn undermines their potential role as agents of social and political change (2003). This is extremely important because contemporary scholars derive much of their understanding about global civil society through Antonio Gramsci's work, which translated traditional Marxist assumptions about the political significance of social struggle into a call for increased mobilization through trade unions and social networks (Cox 1999). Hegel is the originator of the term 'civil society' with his attempts to distinguish activist governance from instrumentalities of state rule, but Gramsci elevated the concept above and beyond ordinary political actors, which is why his perspective has been newly invigorated in attempts to understand global governance and the changing nature of state power. For Gramsci, the seeds of counter-hegemony lie within civil society because it occupies a unique and powerful political space above the individual and below the state. But he also believed that scholars are a significant part of the counter-hegemonic project because they are the agents of necessary changes in global consciousness (Cox 1999). Unfortunately, as some have pointed out, scholars within international relations and international environmental politics have often been reactive rather than proactive with respect to furthering our understanding of the current global environmental government framework and how it must be improved to adequately protect against continued environmental degradation (Stevis 2006).

Global Environmental Governance

Today's activists do not target their efforts directly at the state, but work instead through transnational economic, social and cultural networks to achieve their aims, which often include educating and empowering local communities. The concept here is that groups of people engage in forms of association with the intention of pursuing 'great aims in common'. For example, there is empirical evidence of a relatively dense network of international action by green groups and a substantial resource transfer from green groups in the OECD countries to those in the developing countries (Rohrschneider and Dalton 2002). These resource transfers demonstrate the power of global civil society actors to forge links between the local and the global, and consequently contribute to the changing structure of global environmental governance. In some cases, civil society actors help shape international governance, but sometimes transnational governance exists as an additional layer that makes the relationship between structure and agency murkier (Keck & Sikkink 1998; Princen 1994). In the environmental realm, this governance is institutionalized in the form of hundreds of international environmental agreements and voluntary arrangements, covering all sorts of regional and global issues ranging from the Climate Change Convention to forest stewardship councils. Although these multitudes of issue-based regimes are the focus of environmental study within the context of international relations and global politics, none of the available frameworks are adequately able to resolve the increasing number of normative issues deeply embedded in this structure.

Recent debates in Copenhagen about global climate change reveal the huge and growing North–South divide. Whether the issue is a cap and trade carbon emission control system or reducing the effects of degradation and deforestation, it is clear that a very high level of resentment exists among the developing states as well as a widely held expectation that the developed nations should foot the entire climate change bill. In fact, it could be argued effectively that the essence of the matter is not environmental governance per se, but rather it is the relationship between economic and environmental governance, which lacks environmental provisions in the economic sphere and gives precedence to economic institutions and regulations over environmental ones (Conca 2000; Gillespie 2001; Jeong 2001). This status quo determines that environmental governance will remain forever a sideshow of limited environmental effectiveness despite the contrary suggestion of most of the mainstream global environmental politics literature. Similarly, despite the inclusion of global civil society, Kyoto and the Climate Change Convention appear ineffective for international environmental protection because these agreements do not take the environment as their starting point even though their focus is global climate change. Ultimately, therefore, these agreements are fairly marginal to global environmental governance from an eco-centric perspective (Kütting 2000).

There are a number of global governance organizations that are closely related to global environmental governance. These include the environmental institutions of the UN as well as non-environmental organizations such as the World Trade Organization (WTO), the International Monetary Fund (IMF) and the World Bank, which have a strong impact on environmental governance through their economic, trade, investment and development policies (Clapp 2001; Dauvergne 2001). Global economic and political governance, which structurally determines environmental governance, leads to the marginalization of ecological considerations and a lack of understanding of environment–society relations. This means that global governance policies are formulated in the absence of an understanding of social dependence on ecological foundations. Thus, the absence of environmental priorities in the WTO is more indicative of global environmental governance than is the drafting of international environmental agreements that are negotiated within the constraints of this global-institutional economic framework. Likewise, the structural adjustment policies of the World Bank and IMF, which do not actually represent changes in structure, send a strong environmental message through the subordinate role they apportion to environmental considerations. Although the World Bank has put environmental policy high on its agenda, this has been done within a sustainable development framework that assumes unlimited growth and denies the basic realities of environmental equity and resource access (Williams 2001; Miller 1995).

In the global political economy, equity and social justice as an issue can be found in the formation of what Mittelman (2000) calls the global division of labour and power, and in Robert Paehlke's discussion on democracy, equity and the environment (2003). Under neoliberal forms of labour and power organization, equity and social justice are not concepts that are explicitly included in the definition of the main principles of this ideology. Neoliberal institutions such as the World Bank or the IMF are committed to the alleviation of poverty and environmental degradation. However, there is an unspoken assumption that this can be done without structural change. This is important because the use of the term structural adjustment policies reveals that institutions like the World Bank and the IMF often want to appear to be agents of change when they are simply institutionalizing the status quo under the guise of a project or a loan. In fact, social justice and equity are quite deliberately not a major issue in neoliberal circles because of the importance of the competition principle. It could well be argued that an excessive pursuit of equity or social justice would be perceived as a hindrance to the balancing force of competition, and thus the compatibility between these aims would be called into question.

Some scholars call for a consumption-based analytical orientation as the remedy to current theoretical inabilities to address issues of social and environmental justice (Kütting 2004). Such a framework would allow exploration of the historical, cultural, sociological and economic roots of global consumption patterns, and, at the same time, provide clear policy guidelines to government actors, empower the individual citizen and create opportunities for mass action (Maniates 2001). Global commodity chain analysis, based loosely on world-systems theory, is comprised of labour and production process networks whose end result is a finished commodity – usually a consumer good (Wallerstein 1995). This model emphasizes some of the previously identified normative dimensions of consumption and environmental degradation that have been largely ignored by traditional economic and political analyses. Because it uses the commodity as a starting point and places it within the larger social context, global commodity chain analysis is able to comprehend and link relationships between different production processes and actors that are spatially and temporally displaced from one another. Furthermore, this analytical perspective has a strong historical dimension that allows the exploration of important core–periphery issues, as well as a robust transnational nature that allows significant insights into the larger picture of global economic restructuring (Kütting 2004).

The lens of consumption also illuminates a serious defect in the underlying premise of global development that is institutionalized in the UN Millennium Development Goals. The basic assumption that the current standard of living enjoyed by the richest 20% of the world can be extended globally is fundamentally flawed because it is grounded in a continually expanding consumer-based economy, which in turn depends upon the production of a constantly increasing stockpile of goods. Escalating the production of goods requires a continually increasing percentage of ever-dwindling natural resources, which in turn emits more and more greenhouse gases into the atmosphere. The only way to reverse this process is to fundamentally alter global patterns of consumption, but it is the subject of immense disagreement between the developed and developing worlds. This seemingly irreconcilable difference would not be a hurdle in a system of global environmental governance that places the environment as the highest priority and bases all policy choices on ecological principles. However, even the consumption framework must be embedded within an eco-holistic framework if it is to achieve the ultimate goal of sustainably integrating humans and the natural environment.

Conclusion

This chapter has discussed the various dimensions of the relationship between globalization and environment. Environmental degradation can be understood as a structural issue which is directly related to the emergence of a global economy. Here, both the structural origins as well as the consequences of environmental degradation are global in reach. Environmental degradation can also be studied from an agency perspective where the increasingly global nature of the environmental phenomenon manifests itself through the rise of transnational activity in the form of the rise of new actors, new forms of political and economic governance and also an increasing awareness of the involvement of the individual citizen in this process – as part of civil society but also as consumer. These linkages between structure and agency, between local and global and between the social, political and economic reveal the limitations of global political and economic governance when it comes to social and environmental justice, and also shows that the socio-cultural, the economic and the ecological/environmental dimensions are intrinsically linked.

Further Reading

Kütting, G. and Lipschutz, R. (eds.) 2009: *Environmental Governance: Power and Knowledge In a Local-Global World*. London: Routledge.

Lipschutz, R. 2003: *Global Environmental Politics: Power, Perspectives and Practice*. Washington DC: CQ Press.

Young, O., Schroeder, H. and King, L. (eds.) 2008: *Institutions and Environmental Change*. Cambridge, MA: MIT Press.

38

Rural Social Movements

Marc Edelman

Rural social movements are highly diverse across space and time and also include widely varying class, cultural and occupational groups. They often manifest both class and identity dimensions and cannot be described as either 'old' or 'new' social movements. This chapter focuses mainly on contemporary movements of the rural poor, particularly in the global South, but it also briefly examines as historical antecedents anti-colonial peasant wars and early-twentieth-century transnational agrarian movements. The global crisis of food and agriculture that began in the late 1970s provides the backdrop for new types of peasant and farmer mobilizations. Organized agriculturalists, generally more than organized labour, presented coherent, sustained opposition to neoliberal globalization. By the late 1980s, transnational agrarian movements emerged as important actors in global civil society. Vía Campesina, with member organizations in over 60 countries, has become a particularly dynamic movement and a fount of innovative ideas and experiments in socially and economically sustainable rural development. Vía Campesina's campaigns against market-led agrarian reform, for food sovereignty and for a United Nations (UN) convention on peasants' rights are discussed in detail. The most recent, post-2007 food crisis – characterized by rising commodity prices and intensified investment in farmland for export crops, biofuel stocks and speculative gain – has exacerbated agrarian conflicts in many regions of the global South and given new urgency to questions of rural development and social justice.

Contemporary rural social movements – like rural populations themselves – defy easy characterization. Smallholders, pastoralists, tenant farmers, sharecroppers, squatters, fisher folk, forest dwellers, indigenous peoples, landless labourers, large landowners and agro-industrial entrepreneurs are among the groups that have sought to defend their interests through organized campaigns and struggles. Conflicts and coalitions between these sectors, as well as with urban groups and non-governmental

The Wiley-Blackwell Companion to Political Sociology, First Edition. Edited by Edwin Amenta, Kate Nash, and Alan Scott.
© 2012 Blackwell Publishing Ltd. Published 2012 by Blackwell Publishing Ltd.

organizations (NGOs), mark the constantly shifting terrain of rural politics. In some countries, large and small farmers have united to press governments for price supports, market access, credit and extension services, while in others large landowners routinely hire gunmen to assassinate squatters and peasant activists. Large, national-level militant organizations shape agrarian outcomes in some places, such as Brazil and South Africa, while elsewhere small cooperatives and associations either steer clear of politics or seek redress only for local grievances. Some groups of small and medium-size agricultural producers enthusiastically embrace alliances with organizations of the landless, even as others reject such ties as potential threats to their status as employers and property owners.

Peasant and farmer organizations that lobby or employ pressure tactics are found virtually everywhere, including in developed countries where only a small portion of the economically active population works in agriculture. Farmers' unions in France, the United States and Canada, for example, wield substantial political influence. In less developed countries, such as Ecuador and Bolivia, peasant and indigenous movements helped to topple national governments in the early twenty-first century. Even under highly repressive regimes, such as in China and Burma, peasants have managed to organize at the local and sometimes the regional level. While the Chinese government actively suppresses independent peasant movements, rural unrest and 'rightful resistance' are widespread, with 'runaway villages' sometimes taking up arms against corrupt officials (O'Brien and Li 2006). These and similar conflicts have brought major administrative reforms, including reductions in the taxes agriculturalists pay to local governments. In Burma, peasant insurgencies among ethnic minorities constitute one of the more significant challenges to the military regime.

Transnational agrarian movements, which link national and regional peasant and farmer organizations, play an increasingly prominent role in global civil society and in debates about contentious issues such as global trade policy, genetically modified organisms (GMOs), agrarian reform, food sovereignty, environmental crises, and the human rights of activists and the rural poor. There are important world regions – such as China, Burma and much of the former Soviet Union – where the purportedly 'global' transnational agrarian organizations have little or no presence and where widespread land conflicts pit repressive regimes against movements that are usually forced to remain informal and ephemeral. Transnational agrarian movements nonetheless constitute one of the most creative and vocal forces on the international scene that advocate and work for an environmentally and socially sustainable transformation of the countryside.

The Rural Crises

In the past three decades, the rural world has experienced extraordinarily dramatic transformations. The farm crisis that began in the late 1970s was an agrarian 'perfect storm': prices for fossil-fuel-based fertilizers and pesticides skyrocketed, interest rates spiked, monetary policies intended to slow inflation undermined state capacity, and the breakdown of the Bretton Woods system of capital controls and fixed exchange rates and then the 1986 initiation of the General Agreement on Tariffs and Trade (GATT) Uruguay Round led to a rapid expansion and liberalization of global agricultural trade.

Grain producers, in particular, previously insulated within their national economies, now faced heightened competition from abroad, although in the European Union (EU), the United States and Japan farmers continued to benefit from high levels of tariff protection. Mergers among giant agribusinesses accelerated, giving a handful of corporations growing dominance of input sales, post-harvest processing and export trade, and allowing them to garner a rising share of the value added between field and dinner plate. In Latin America, and in much of Africa, the debt crisis of the early 1980s brought neoliberal reforms that often had a devastating impact on small agricultural producers. Ironically, in the global South, the neoliberal 'state reforms' of the 1980s and after, encouraged by the international financial institutions, meant dismantling the commodities purchasing boards and the complex system of subsidies for inputs, machinery, fuel, water and credit that none other than the World Bank had helped to set up in country after country in the 1950s and 1960s in order to make capital-intensive, 'green revolution' agriculture possible in conditions of poverty.

The advent of the World Trade Organization (WTO) in the mid-1990s – along with several important bi- and multilateral free trade agreements, such as NAFTA – heightened pressures on agricultural producers and particularly on those with insufficient access to capital, technology and land. Surpluses produced with subsidies in the United States and the EU were 'dumped' in the global South or donated as 'food aid', undermining local markets and ruining farmers. New forms of export-oriented, chemical-intensive contract farming for winter vegetables, cut flowers and other crops incorporated some better-off peasant producers in Africa and Latin America, but often at the cost of deepening subordination to corporate sponsors, worsening nutritional and health status, and reduced biodiversity. A variety of environmental problems also contributed to destabilizing rural livelihoods, from agrochemical contamination of soil and water, to deforestation, erosion and quickening climate change (IAASTD 2009).

These complex, interrelated rural crises spurred an exodus from the countryside as displaced rural people flocked to towns and cities or migrated abroad in search of work. In the mid-1990s, the World Bank reported that for the first time in history less than half the world's labour force (49%) worked in agriculture. Urbanization, the rise of service economies in the Global North and expanding industrialization in much of the global South tended to diminish the clout of rural areas and rural interests in national politics. Even with the expansion of export-oriented contract farming and other new agribusinesses, few governments in the global South viewed agriculture any more as a key engine of development. Many peasants in Africa, Latin America, Asia and elsewhere abandoned farming altogether and became shock troops for warlords in predatory resource or drug wars, as in Liberia and Colombia, or perpetrators of genocides, as in Rwanda and the Balkans (and earlier in Cambodia). Paradoxically perhaps, given this diminished profile, there are more peasants today than ever before in history, even if they constitute a smaller proportion of the overall human population (Van der Ploeg 2008: xiv)

Peasant and Farmer Movements since the 1980s

In the 1960s and 1970s social scientists commonly distinguished between *farmers*, who were commercially oriented and employed wage labour and advanced technology, and *peasants*, who were said to be subsistence-oriented and who used family labour and rudimentary technology. More recently, an important intervention by Jan Douwe Van der Ploeg argues that the 'peasant condition' or 'principle' consists of various interrelated elements that permit survival in a hostile environment, including a 'self-controlled resource base', 'co-production' or interaction between humans and nature, cooperative relations that allow peasants to distance themselves from monetary relations and market exchange, and an ongoing 'struggle for autonomy' or 'room for maneuver' that reduces dependency and aligns farming 'with the interests and prospects of the . . . producers' (Van der Ploeg 2008: 32). Nonetheless, Van der Ploeg acknowledges that many developed-country farmers, especially in Western Europe, increasingly adopt aspects of the 'peasant condition' in order to assure survival. The distinction between peasant and farmer ideal types also has proven problematical as the rural poor adopt modern technology, as agriculturalists in developed and less developed countries collaborate around issues of common concern, as rural people migrate to cities (and sometimes back to the countryside), and as peasants and farmers themselves stress their commonalities and minimize their differences. In many languages the terms equivalent to 'peasant' – the Spanish *campesino* or the French *paysan*, for example – are more inclusive, signifying simply 'country people' and including many farmers.

More than any other social type, the peasant is a synecdoche for the past, for backwardness and stasis, obstinacy and underdevelopment. The lexicons of every major language are replete with disparaging terms for the uncouth rural poor. Among social scientists and planners, orthodox Marxists and conservative free marketers alike have long predicted and hoped for the disappearance of the peasantry. Yet as late as the 1970s, many social scientists and policy-makers also considered peasants key historical protagonists and some celebrated or even romanticized their resistance to imperialism and colonialism. Early-twentieth-century peasant insurgencies against elites and colonial powers sometimes attracted thousands or even millions of supporters. The Mexican and Chinese revolutions and, in the post-Second World War era, the Vietnam War and anti-colonial struggles in Africa brought massive social upheavals and reshaped global geopolitics. The agrarian dimension and peasant social base of these movements led to wide-ranging land reforms (Wolf 1969). In countries where violence did not occur or was minimal, peasant activists and some sectors of the dominant groups shared the perception that timely rural reforms could avert major conflicts or revolutions and also worked to organize and implement change. But by the 1980s rapid urbanization in the global South, along with lessened reliance on agriculture and growing pluriactivity among rural households, increasingly led social scientists and policy-makers to neglect both rural development and what was once called 'the agrarian question', that is, the ways in which the incorporation of agrarian social classes into capitalism shaped political-economic outcomes.

Peasant and farmer organizations nonetheless have been more active, tenacious and outspoken than organized labour in resisting the neoliberal 'reforms' of the 1980s and after. In country after country, trade unions were hard hit by deindustrialization and public-sector retrenchment. In newly industrializing countries – notably in China but also in much of Central America – political repression, pro-business labour laws, cutthroat competition and a huge reserve army of impoverished rural migrants stymied efforts to organize the urban working classes. Peasants and farmers, however, faced with intensifying attacks on their livelihoods, were able to draw on age-old protest repertoires and resistance tactics — land occupations, road blockades, cooperative labour exchanges, village assemblies — to mobilize and in some cases check or reverse the free-market onslaught. As peasant and farmer organizations in different countries and world regions established cross-border alliances in the late 1980s and 1990s, they increasingly borrowed protest repertoires from counterparts abroad, evolved new and often theatrical protest forms, and mounted pressure campaigns against the supranational governance institutions, such as the WTO, the World Bank and the International Monetary Fund (IMF), which they viewed as the managers of the process of elite-led neoliberal globalization.

The Origins of Transnational Agrarian Movements

Transnational agrarian movements are neither a new phenomenon nor are they simply an outcome of recent revolutions in communications technology, the emergence of supranational governance institutions or a weakening of the contemporary state system under globalization. Transnational peasant and farmer organizations have existed since the turn of the twentieth century. In the aftermath of the First World War, for example, agrarian political parties came to power in Bulgaria and Yugoslavia and had major influence in Czechoslovakia, Poland, Romania, Hungary, Austria and the Netherlands. In the early 1920s, several of these parties created an alliance known as the 'Green International' or International Agrarian Bureau, which was headquartered in Prague. The Green International's main adversaries were oligarchic large landowners' groups and the communists, who generally disdained the agrarian movements' 'petty bourgeois' aspirations for small property and improved access to bank credit and other resources. At its height, in 1929, the Green International included 17 member parties in Central and Eastern Europe, but it declined rapidly during the world economic crisis of the 1930s, as fascist parties came to power and decimated several of the key agrarian parties. In 1923, partly in response to the rising profile of the agrarian parties, the Moscow-based Communist International set up a 'Red Peasant International' or 'Krestintern' (a conjunction of the Russian '*Krest'yianskii Internatsional*' or Peasant International). The Krestintern sought alliances with the agrarian parties, as well as with China's Kuomintang Nationalists, but enjoyed little success. By the end of the decade, as Stalin consolidated his hold on the Soviet Union and increasingly turned against the peasantry, the Krestintern was essentially moribund.

Several other early transnational agrarian movements were (and are) politically centrist or conservative in orientation. The Associated Country Women of the World (ACWW) was founded in 1933 and today claims a membership of nine million in 365 participating organizations in 70 countries. ACWW emphasizes empowering rural women through education, skills training and income generation and disaster relief projects. It generally eschews political advocacy and draws members mainly from Anglophone countries or the English-speaking middle classes elsewhere. The International Federation of Agricultural Producers (IFAP) formed in 1946 and includes many national associations of large agriculturalists and some peasant and small farmer organizations. IFAP has worked closely throughout its history with the UN Food and Agriculture Organization (FAO). While it long emphasized technical and policy measures to boost productivity, in recent years it has begun to focus on issues of long-term sustainability and the role that farmers might play in resolving the crises of environmental degradation, rising commodity prices (since 2006) and global climate change. In late 2010 IFAP experienced an internal crisis that led several regional farmers' coalitions to weaken or sever their ties to the international federation.

In the aftermath of the 1980s farm crisis, new types of transnational agrarian movements emerged alongside and in opposition to the existing mainstream organizations such as ACWW and IFAP. In Europe the European Farmers Coordination (usually abbreviated CPE for its name in French, Coordination Paysanne Européenne), founded in 1986, united organizations in over a dozen countries that sought to reform the EU's Common Agricultural Policy and to keep agriculture out of the General Agreement on Tariffs and Trade (which became the World Trade Organization or WTO in 1995). In Central America, similarly, peasant organizations joined forces to participate in the regional integration process initiated in the early 1990s, following the conclusion of the civil wars in El Salvador and Nicaragua. In the rest of Latin America, peasant, indigenous and Afro-descendant movements that staged protests against the 1992 Columbian Quincentenary celebrations contributed to forming the Coordinadora Latinoamericana de Organizaciones del Campo (CLOC, Latin American Coordination of Peasant Organizations).

Vía Campesina, a Transnational Agrarian Movement

In 1993, representatives of the national organizations in the European and Latin American regional coalitions, together with groups from Canada, the Philippines, India and elsewhere, met in Belgium and founded a transnational movement called Vía Campesina. The name means 'Peasant Road', invoking an aspiration for a peasant-centred development model, though the organization is always referred to by its Spanish name. Vía Campesina currently links over one hundred organizations of small- and medium-sized agricultural producers, landless, rural women, indigenous people and agricultural workers in over 60 countries in the Americas, Europe, Asia and Africa. The membership is diverse and includes landless peasants in Brazil, small dairy farmers in Europe, well-off farmers in South India, wheat producers in Canada and land-poor peasants in Mexico. The main issues of concern to Vía Campesina include global trade rules, intellectual property and genetically modified organisms, the survival of family farms, sustainable alternatives to corporate-controlled industrial agriculture, agrarian reform, the human rights of peasant activists, and 'food sovereignty', which it defines as the right to protect national production and to shield domestic markets from the dumping of low-priced agricultural imports. Vía Campesina and its component sub-national, national and regional organizations have participated in numerous militant and theatrical protest actions against the WTO, the World Bank and the IMF, summit meetings of G-8 governments, and large agribusiness corporations such as Monsanto, Cargill and Syngenta. The movement has also been a prominent participant in global civil society gatherings, such as the World Social Forums.

For its first three years, Vía Campesina's structure was based on an International Coordinating Committee (ICC), with representatives of organizations from different regions, each of which was responsible for overseeing activities in their respective areas of the world. Many communications activities were initially centred in the offices of the Canadian National Farmers Union in Saskatoon and the European Farmers Coordination in Brussels. In 1996, an International Operational Secretariat was established to oversee the entire network and complement the work of the ICC. Because of the Central Americans' extensive experience in cross-border organizing, responsibility for the Secretariat was entrusted to the Honduran member coalition and its coordinator Rafael Alegría. In 2004 the headquarters moved to the Jakarta office of the Federation of Indonesian Peasants and Henry Saragih became Vía Campesina coordinator.

Much of the Vía Campesina's organizing is carried out by its constituent groups, often with funds from European and Canadian non-governmental organizations (NGOs). The Vía Campesina itself has a small staff and a modest budget. Despite its reliance for funding on developed-country NGOs, Vía Campesina has frequently criticized the claims of some NGOs to represent or to advocate on behalf of the rural poor and has argued that this type of advocacy is best carried out by the peasant organizations themselves. Vía Campesina has, however, formed strategic alliances with organizations such as the International Planning Committee for Food Sovereignty, the German-based Food First Information and Action Network (FIAN) and the Land Research Action Network (LRAN), an international team of activist researchers sponsored by research centres based in Brazil, Mexico, the United States and Thailand. These alliances have permitted Vía Campesina access to state-of-the-art information and analysis on issues such as global trade negotiations, the World Bank's market-oriented land reform programme, the implications of genetically modified crops and discussions about rights-based approaches to development in the UN.

Although Vía Campesina claims to be a 'global' or 'world' movement, its geographical coverage is uneven. Probably the largest single-member movement is the Brazilian Landless Movement (MST, Movimento dos Trabalhadores Rurais Sem Terra). In Brazil, the MST is now so closely identified with Vía Campesina that many Brazilians have the impression that Vía Campesina is a Brazilian and not an international organization. Vía Campesina supporters typically sport green kerchiefs and baseball caps at public events, a practice adopted from the MST, whose members often wear matching caps and red tee-shirts. The MST practice of beginning meetings and other activities with a '*mistica*' or improvised ritual incorporating song, theatre or poetry has also become emblematic of Vía Campesina events.

Many other Vía Campesina member movements, however, are quite small and in several countries, including France and the United States, the largest peasant and farmer organizations are affiliated with the more conservative International Federation of Agricultural Producers (IFAP) and not with Vía Campesina. Vía Campesina has no presence in China or in a number of other countries, such as Burma and most of the former Soviet republics, where repressive regimes have blocked peasants from organizing. It has a large number of member organizations in Latin America and Europe and only a handful in Africa and the Middle East. In Francophone Africa many peasant organizations are affiliated with ROPPA (Réseau des Organizations Paysannes et de Producteurs de l'Afrique de l'Ouest, Network of Peasants' and Producers'

Organizations of West Africa), an alliance with similar aims to Vía Campesina but which has remained outside it. A number of other transnational agrarian coalitions, such as MIJARC (International Movement of Catholic Agricultural and Rural Youth), have warm relations with Vía Campesina but also remain outside it.

Most of the Asian Vía Campesina members have only joined since 2004. The Korean Peasant League has demonstrated a capacity for mobilizing thousands of supporters for international protests, as occurred at the 2005 WTO Ministerial Conference in Hong Kong, when hundreds of Korean protestors donned orange life vests and plunged into the harbour in an effort to bypass a police cordon and swim to the meeting. Many Korean rural activists also participated in the 2003 anti-WTO demonstrations in Cancún, Mexico, and one, Lee Kyang Hae, who was holding a sign that said 'WTO kills farmers', stabbed himself to death as a protest during a large march. Even though Lee belonged to a non-Vía Campesina organization (the Korean Advanced Farmers Federation), Vía Campesina commemorates 10 September, the anniversary of Lee's death, as an 'international day of struggle against the WTO'. Member organizations of Vía Campesina also frequently stage protests on 17 April, 'the international day of peasant struggle', which commemorates the 1996 massacre by hired gunmen of 19 peasants involved in a land occupation in Eldorado dos Carajás, Brazil. The killing occurred while a Vía Campesina international conference was taking place in Tlaxcala, Mexico, which contributed to giving the event immediate international resonance. Subsequent Vía Campesina conferences have been held in 2000 in Bangalore, India, in 2004 in São Paulo, Brazil, and in 2008 in Mozambique.

Vía Campesina has come to have a high profile in global civil society. The protest actions it has taken, along with its allies, have arguably contributed to slowing global trade negotiations. Vía Campesina supporters participated in the 1999 'Battle of Seattle' actions that contributed to derailing the WTO ministerial meeting. They have also been a significant presence at subsequent protests against WTO ministerial meetings in Cancún, Hong Kong and Geneva. Vía Campesina organizations have maintained that the WTO's Agreement on Agriculture (AoA) ought to be scrapped, since food is a necessity and thus not like any other commodity, and the model of farming that the AoA encourages facilitated the penetration of transnational capital in agriculture and had deleterious impacts on small producers, human health and the environment. They call for taking agriculture 'out of the WTO', but apart from occasional suggestions that the UNCTAD (United Nations Conference on Trade and Development), the International Labour Organization (ILO) or the FAO be charged with regulating global agricultural trade, they have put forth few concrete alternative proposals.

By the early 1990s, agrarian reform had largely dropped off the development agenda in most of the world as free-market policies became the order of the day and many earlier reforms were labelled 'failures' when beneficiaries either abandoned their plots or sold them to large-scale producers. In Latin America, in particular, diverse reform programmes had been thwarted by elite intransigence, by privatization measures and 'counter-reforms' or by the failure to provide the complementary resources – credit, titling, irrigation, technical assistance and training, and transport, processing and marketing facilities – required for the success of peasant enterprises. At the 1996 FAO World Food Summit peasant organizations, citing spreading land invasions by peasants in Brazil, Malawi and Zimbabwe, pressured insistently to once again give agrarian reform a central place in rural development policy-making. In 1999, the Vía Campesina and the German-based Food First Information and Action Network (FIAN) launched a Global Campaign on Agrarian Reform intended to take advantage of this growing momentum and to counter the World Bank's attempts to promote 'market-assisted land reform' programmes, in which public- and private-sector credits are made available to beneficiaries who individually negotiate land purchases with willing sellers (Rosset, Patel and Courville 2006). Vía Campesina and FIAN believe that the World Bank approach will not solve the problem of access to land for the poorest farmers or for those in places where property ownership is highly skewed and the supply of land is inelastic. In early 2001, the World Bank's Director of Rural Development responded to the pressure by changing the programme's name from 'market-assisted' to 'community-managed' and by suggesting that the Bank's approach was complementary 'and not a substitute' for laws enabling governments to expropriate land for distribution to peasants. When commodity prices spiked in 2008, setting off a wave of speculation in farmland that some termed a 'global land grab' (GRAIN 2008), the market-based approach to more equitable land distribution appeared all the more inadequate.

Another Vía Campesina campaign – for 'food sovereignty' – was launched in 1996 and grew out of the organization's critique of both the neoliberal restructuring of agriculture and the FAO's technical, quantitative definition of 'food security' (Wittman, Desmarais and Wiebe 2010). According to the FAO, 'food security exists when all people, at all times, have physical and economic access to sufficient, safe and nutritious food that meets their dietary needs and food preferences'. This was, according to its critics, an approach that was completely compatible with input-intensive, large-scale industrial agriculture and globalized agricultural trade. As Vía Campesina and its allies point out, the FAO food security approach says nothing about how the food is produced, and at what social and environmental cost, or about the rights of peasants to continue producing food or of peoples to make decisions about the foods that they consume. This critique was developed and refined in several international conferences during the early and mid-2000s. The 'food sovereignty' proposal generated considerable resonance with a wide variety of agrarian, environmentalist and human rights organizations, attracting a larger number of allies than any other Vía Campesina initiative. The International Planning Committee for Food Sovereignty (IPC), for example, is a coalition of some 800 NGOs and transnational organizations of peasants and small farmers, fisher folk, pastoralists, indigenous peoples and agricultural workers. IPC was a product of the discontent of many civil society groups following the 1996 FAO World Food Summit. 'Food sovereignty', according to IPC and Vía Campesina, 'is the right of peoples to healthy and culturally appropriate food produced through ecologically sound and sustainable methods, and their right to define their own food and agriculture systems. It puts the aspirations and needs of those who produce, distribute and consume food at the heart of food systems and policies rather than the demands of markets and corporations . . .. [It] prioritises local and national economies and markets and empowers peasant and family farmer-driven agriculture, artisanal-fishing, pastoralist-led grazing, and food production, distribution and consumption based on environmental, social and economic sustainability . . .. It ensures that the rights to use and manage lands, territories, waters, seeds, livestock and biodiversity are in the hands of those of us who produce food. Food sovereignty implies new social relations free of oppression and inequality between men and women, peoples, racial groups, social and economic classes and generations.'

As even backers of the food sovereignty framework acknowledge, the concept's working definition is fraught with ambiguities and contradictions. The reference to 'those who produce, distribute and consume food', for example, could be read as including the same transnational corporations that are denounced in the second half of the sentence. Similarly, empowering 'peasant and family farmer-driven agriculture' could conceivably *disempower* farm workers. The intentional use of rights-based language in the food sovereignty discussion is one effort to address these tensions, as well as to stake out a position in the broader debates between proponents of rights-based and market-based approaches to development. Food sovereignty advocates point out that demanding a *right* to shape food policy is in contrast with the *privilege* that is now exercised by a handful of developed-country policy-makers and giant corporations. Framing democratic control of the food system as a right implies that it must be respected, protected and fulfilled, like other rights guaranteed under international law.

Vía Campesina's effort to have the UN adopt a Declaration and eventually an 'International Convention on the Rights of Peasants' is another ambitious effort to employ rights-based concepts to advance a pro-peasant agenda in international arenas (Edelman and James 2011). The initiative emerged from a 2000 Workshop on Peasants' Rights in North Sumatra, Indonesia, a 2001 conference on agrarian reform in Jakarta, and a 2002 Vía Campesina conference in Jakarta, which published the first draft text of a proposed Declaration. Championed by Asian – especially Indonesian – Vía Campesina member organizations, the idea was quickly adopted by the broader, transnational coalition. The campaign developed in collaboration with two NGOs, first the Geneva-based Centre Europe-Tiers Monde (CETIM) and later the Heidelberg-based Food First Information and Action Network (FIAN). Its activities have included sending human rights fact-finding missions to more than a dozen countries, the publication of three annual compendiums on 'peasant rights violations' and lobbying at the UN General Assembly, the UN Human Rights Council and other UN agencies.

Vía Campesina's peasants' rights initiative is characterized by some deliberate slippage between calls for a declaration and for a binding convention. In general, non-binding declarations have attracted broader support among UN member states and, while they have sometimes led to binding conventions, these have tended to be significantly more contentious and to require long processes of ratification by signatory states. Non-binding declarations have, on the other hand, sometimes become part of customary international law or 'soft' law, an objective that is clearly a desirable intermediate goal for Vía Campesina. In many respects the strategy takes inspiration from the campaign of indigenous peoples' organizations that culminated in the 2007 UN Declaration on the Rights of Indigenous Peoples. The latter effort marked the first time that the negotiations preceding adoption of a human rights declaration or convention included, in addition to state actors, civil society representatives of the rights-bearing group that was the subject of the proposed international instrument.

The first draft of Vía Campesina's Peasants' Rights Declaration, published in 2002 in stilted English and somewhat more polished French and Spanish, detailed a bundle of rights, many of which were already part of existing UN Conventions. In 2007 Via Campesina adopted a draft with more lucid language and various conceptual refinements. Many of the rights enumerated in the draft Peasants' Rights Declaration are already part of existing international instruments. Among these are the rights of 'peasant women and men' to freedom of association and expression, physical integrity, personal security, health, food, and water for consumption and irrigation, as well as freedom from political persecution and from discrimination 'based on their economic, social and cultural status'. Other rights enumerated in the draft Declaration, however, are indicative of an effort to push existing norms beyond their current bounds, such as claims of a 'right to reject' intellectual property of crop genetic material or demands for participation in international economic policy-making processes. The authors of the draft Declaration sought to achieve these objectives in part through asserting that peasants, like indigenous peoples, were a vulnerable group, with culturally specific characteristics and practices that deserved international recognition and protection.

In 2009 and 2010, Vía Campesina representatives addressed the UN General Assembly and the UN Human Rights Council (UNHRC) on the need for a peasants' rights convention. In February 2010 the UNHRC Advisory Committee submitted its report on 'discrimination in the context of the right to food' that included as an appendix the entire text of Vía Campesina's draft Peasants' Rights Declaration. In effect, the draft Peasants' Rights Declaration's perspective on the right to food is being incorporated directly into the UN agenda as a result of years of civil society pressure within the FAO, the UNHRC and other agencies, the very significant presence of peasants among those in need of food, and the approach of the 2015 target date for the Millennium Development Goals. Notably absent from the discussion so far, however, are elements of the draft Peasants' Rights Declaration that demand rights to conserve and exchange or sell traditional seed varieties, to intervene in markets and set prices, to participate in economic decision-making at the international and national levels, and 'to reject interventions that can destroy local agricultural values'.

The Worsening Food Crisis

The world food crisis since 2007, marked by rising prices for petroleum-based products and agricultural commodities, presented peasant and farmer organizations with new and difficult challenges. Accustomed for decades to declining prices for the main internationally traded agricultural commodities, peasant and farmer organizations in many countries had centred their actions around demands for stopping developed-country dumping of subsidized grain, implementing supply management mechanisms and securing market access for poor farmers. The sudden post-2007 price rises, which provoked food riots in dozens of countries, did not usually result in a bonanza for agricultural producers, since input costs also rose drastically and, in many countries, the public-sector extension agencies that served small farmers and the state commodities boards that purchased crops had been undermined or abolished as part of pro-market reforms in the 1980s and 1990s. The new situation of rising prices negatively impacted peasants who were net consumers of food and also often pitted rural producers against urban residents and national governments that sought to tax or otherwise limit exports in an effort to keep food costs low for consumers. In developed countries and in the larger exporting countries in the global South farmers had to devote more of their energy to understanding and investing in complex markets for agricultural futures and options, leaving them less time for actual production-related tasks. In some cases, notably Argentina, these new conditions fostered previously unthinkable alliances between wealthy and poor agriculturalists' organizations. In many places, however, highly volatile agricultural markets and rising production costs led to new waves of farm foreclosures and heightened processes of rural–urban migration.

The food price spikes were inseparably bound up with two interrelated sources of pressure on the peasant land base. In order to guarantee their national food supplies, sovereign wealth funds and private capital from wealthy food-deficit nations, particularly but not only in the Persian Gulf region, increasingly invested in agricultural lands in the global South, hoping to produce and export basic foodstuffs (GRAIN 2008). At the same time, rising petroleum prices generated interest in biofuels, which increasingly competed with food crops for arable land and contributed to further driving up food prices. As the finance and real-estate bubbles burst in the United States and Western Europe, capital shifted into farmland in Africa, South Asia and South America, kindling new agrarian conflicts and reframing debates over rural development and social justice.

Concluding Remarks

The rural upheavals of recent decades are not easily pigeonholed in a tired taxonomy of 'identity-' versus 'class-based' organizations, or 'new' or 'old' social movements. The discourse of the transnational agrarian movements, and of Vía Campesina in particular, is replete with references to 'people of the land' and 'local communities' and its 'mistica' rituals reinforce a powerful subjective sense of belonging among its adherents. While all of this is suggestive of a certain kind of shared identity, the very success of Vía Campesina has also entailed growing internal tensions, including differences between organizations that represent affluent farmers and poor agricultural labourers or the landless, as well as conflicts over alliances, funding sources, vetting new members, and strategies and tactics. Some organizations that joined Vía Campesina in its early days have blocked other groups in their regions that they perceive as rivals from joining. In a few cases, national organizations have withdrawn from international work in order to rededicate themselves to national-level lobbying and pressure campaigns. At the same time, the transnational agrarian movements' embrace of environmentalism and claims to group rights signal a persistent and deeply rooted identity dimension in their politics. Class-based conflicts continue to wrack the rural world, particularly in land struggles and employer–employee conflicts, but growing migration and pluriactivity – 'the new rurality', as some scholars call it – also undermine class and even peasant identities. In the early twenty-first century the movements of the rural poor have nonetheless, to the surprise of many, emerged as a laboratory that is richly productive of transformational and emancipatory ideas and experiments.

As French farm activist José Bové once asked, what if the peasant world, supposedly so archaic and conservative, turned out to be the incarnation of true modernity?

Further Reading

Borras, S.M., Jr., Edelman, M. and Kay, C. (eds.) 2008: *Transnational Agrarian Movements Confronting Globalization*. Oxford: Wiley-Blackwell.

Bryceson, D., Kay, C. and Mooij, J. (eds.) 2000: *Disappearing Peasantries? Land and Labor in Africa, Asia and Latin America*. London: Immediate Technology Publications.

Desmarais, A.A. 2007: *La Vía Campesina: Globalization and the Power of Peasants*. Halifax, NS: Fernwood Publishing.

Holt-Giménez, E. 2006: *Campesino a campesino: Voices From Latin America's Farmer to Farmer Movement for Sustainable Agriculture*. Oakland: Food First Books.

McKeon, N., Watts, M. and Wolford, W. 2004: *Peasant Associations In Theory and Practice*. Geneva: UN Research Institute for Social Development.

Moyo, S. and Yeros, P. (eds.) 2005: *Reclaiming the land: The Resurgence of Rural Movements in Africa, Asia, and Latin America*. London: Zed Books.

Rosset, P.M. 2006: *Food is Different: Why we Must Get the WTO Out of Agriculture*. London: Zed Books.

Wolford, W. 2010. *This Land Is Ours Now: Social Mobilization and The Meanings Of Land in Brazil*. Durham, NC: Duke University Press.

39

Towards a Political Sociology of Human Rights

KATE NASH

The study of human rights is now expanding in sociology, despite disciplinary blind spots. Here Nash outlines the implications of studying human rights in relation to globalization and state transformation, the limits of legalization, and questions of solidarity and subjectivity. The 'human rights field' links micro-social interactions to macro-institutional structures, conflicts over particular human rights cases to state formation, and to the social and cultural relationships in which they are embedded.

Why are sociologists increasingly interested in human rights? In fact, until quite recently discussion of the topic turned on why sociologists have historically *neglected* the study of rights. One of the main reasons is undoubtedly the now familiar problem of 'methodological nationalism', the way in which sociologists have tended to equate 'society' as the object of their study with the territory of nation-states in a way that precludes understanding of social relations and interdependencies across borders (see Beck and Sznaider 2006; Sznaider and Levy 2006). It is not really surprising, then, that 'globalization' leads to interesting questions concerning the uses and effects of human rights. Other reasons given for the lack of sociologists' interest include disciplinary tendencies towards cultural relativism combined with a suspicion of the individualism of rights. Studies of citizenship, focused on institutions and collectivism, have not faced the same difficulties. Although citizenship and human rights are entwined (see, for example, Soysal 1994; Somers 2008; Nash 2009a), human rights are less concrete, less obviously tied to the nation-state, and to legal facts of membership and territoriality, than citizenship rights. They seem, therefore, to raise difficult questions of universality, morality and ontology that sociology, formed in terms of value-neutrality

The Wiley-Blackwell Companion to Political Sociology, First Edition. Edited by Edwin Amenta, Kate Nash, and Alan Scott.
© 2012 Blackwell Publishing Ltd. Published 2012 by Blackwell Publishing Ltd.

and relativism, is ill-equipped to address (Turner 1993; Morris 2006; Somers and Roberts 2008).

In one of the earliest and most widely read discussions of human rights, Bryan Turner argued that, in order to get beyond relativism and value-neutral positivism, sociologists would do well to take the vulnerability of the human body as providing a universal necessity for human rights (Turner 1993, 2006). Similarly, Blau and Moncada argue that sociologists should embrace the moral project of the human rights movement, becoming as committed to their realization as any other activists (Blau and Moncada 2005). In my view, moral commitment is unnecessary and undesirable for the development of the sociology of human rights. Foundational claims certainly do not seem to be needed to motivate the majority of human rights activists. The expansion of human rights since the end of the Cold War is due to geopolitical contingencies rather than the achievement of solid ontological foundations. Most importantly, however, the expansion of human rights in conditions of uneven and unequal development is far from coherent and throws up 'tragic dilemmas' that cannot be solved within a human rights framework. 'Humanitarian intervention' is only the most dramatic example: where states are involved in, or do not prevent, ongoing and massive violence towards vulnerable people within their jurisdiction, is military intervention by more powerful states ever desirable, given that it will always be undertaken for, at best, a mixture of strategic and moral reasons? What we need in order to understand the post-Cold War expansion of human rights are theories and methodologies that enable critical distance on how they are being used and institutionalized in a range of different, even contradictory ways.

The sociological suspicion of human rights as individualist is not easily overcome. It is justified in that human rights are predominantly, though not exclusively, individual rights. The Universal Declaration of Human Rights (UDHR), supplemented by the International Covenant on Civil and Political Rights (ICCPR) and the International Covenant on Economic, Social and Cultural Rights (ICESCR), is the basis of human rights practice today. Especially in the West, it is civil rights that have set the human rights agenda, with an emphasis on freedom of speech and association, and the prevention of wrongful imprisonment, torture and murder by the state. In fact, it is still often argued that only civil rights can really be treated as rights at all (e.g., Ignatieff 2001). It is difficult, then, for non-governmental organizations (NGOs) and developing states to put entitlements to social, economic and public goods on the agendas of inter-governmental organizations (IGOs) such as the World Bank and the G-20, and of the most effective bodies of the United Nations (UN), notably the Security Council.

Nevertheless, as sociologists we should understand that even individual rights are inherently social. In standard terms civil rights are called 'negative rights' because they enable the clear identification of specific obligations on the part of specific agents to *stop* state repression. Legal judgment may clearly identify and rectify violations of civil rights. In contrast, social, economic and cultural rights are called 'positive rights', requiring open-ended obligations on the part of states to provide resources and benefits that cannot be as clearly specified, or as easily achieved given limited capacities. From a sociological point of view, however, the distinction between negative and positive rights is misleading. This is not because social, economic and cultural rights are intrinsically more valuable than civil rights, even if without the basic means of subsistence, freedoms of speech, protest and mobilization are worth nothing. It is rather that *all* human rights are social. If we consider classic civil rights to personal freedom, for example, they actually require massive investment and organization: the police force must be trained not to respond immediately to perceived wrongdoing or disturbances with violence; conditions of imprisonment and police questioning must be closely monitored to prevent inappropriate techniques of extracting 'the truth'; those who cannot afford legal representation must nevertheless enjoy equality with others in a fair trial; and so on. These conditions are extremely difficult to achieve: in practice, human rights require social institutions to promote and monitor their ongoing exercise, and at least minimal agreement on their meaning and value. This is no less true of civil rights to individual freedom than it is of social rights to education or health care. Indeed, as we have seen recently in the imprisonment of terrorist suspects in Europe and 'unlawful combatants' in the United States, securing rights requires constant vigilance by well-funded, professional and highly motivated human rights organizations even in wealthy and reasonably well-functioning liberal democracies.

Once we understand human rights as social constructions rather than as moral absolutes or as legal entitlements (the latter being the most common way of seeing them in an area of study that is dominated by legal experts), it is clear that sociologists have an important role in investigating the specific historical, cultural and geopolitical conditions that make it possible to secure respect for human rights in practice. Human rights are social in that they are constructed and sustained in ongoing practices that orient and organize intentions and actions. Although they may be claimed by individuals, it is only through collective meanings and institutions that they can be effective. In addition, sociologists may be interested in the often unintended effects of the institutionalization of human rights on other aspects of social life. Once we understand human rights in this way, it is clear that every branch of sociology actually concerns the study of human rights! However, there are a number of areas in which sociologists are now working directly on questions of human rights.

Human Rights, Globalization and State Transformation

Human rights are globalizing. This may seem a strange thing to say: human rights are universal – they are supposed to apply to all individuals as human beings. Surely, then, they are *necessarily* global? Although universal in form, however, it is clear that human rights are far from universal in practice. Human rights are now globalizing in that there is increasing emphasis on making them really work, and this calls conventional state borders into question.

However, human rights are globalizing in quite a particular way in relation to the state in comparison with other cross-border flows of globalization. Far from bypassing or weakening states, demands for human rights must engage state actors. Although rights attach to individuals, it is states that sign and ratify international human rights agreements. The vast majority of states have now committed themselves to precise and detailed international human rights agreements which human rights activists then use to try to hold them to account. Human rights claims are ultimately directed to states as the only forms of social organization with the resources and legitimacy to properly guarantee human rights. Paradoxically, it is also only state actors (and occasionally those who are complicit with them, like multinational corporations in US tort law), who are technically in breach of international human rights law (Meckled-Garcia and Cali 2006). Globalization thus *adds* to states' responsibilities to reform and monitor their own organization to stop and to prevent human rights violations.

This picture is complicated, however, as the reform of state responsibilities in relation to both citizens and non-citizens through human rights agreements leads to the intense politicization of state sovereignty. The legal convention of sovereignty constructs states as independent. It is linked to democracy in that sovereignty ensures that it is the will of the people that prevails within a particular jurisdiction; there should be no outside interference that overrides or interferes with the successful performance of that will. The history of sovereignty is complex, and significantly different for different states. Established in principle in the Treaty of Westphalia in 1648, sovereignty was extended to European colonies only as they freed themselves from imperialism in the twentieth century. Crucially too, sovereignty is in tension with principles of human rights established by the UDHR. In fact, the UDHR was created at the high point of the ideal of sovereignty: it is independent states that agree to uphold and respect universal human rights. At the same time, however, the UDHR asserts that the rights of individuals *within* states must be respected, encoding quite a different political understanding of international relations. Human rights law, sometimes called 'cosmopolitan law' when it effectively reaches inside states, puts state sovereignty into question (as we will see below in the example of Roper *vs*. Simmons). In principle the tension between sovereignty and human rights can be dissolved if states are all genuinely oriented towards enacting identical interpretations of human rights agreements. In practice, sovereignty, while far from obsolete, is often highly contentious in affairs concerning human rights (Sznaider and Levy 2006; see discussion in Nash 2009b: 71–78).

The globalization of human rights strains the legal convention of sovereignty, albeit differently along existing geopolitical fault lines: it is harder to bring pressure to bear on large, economically and militarily powerful states than on smaller ones, which continue to be enmeshed in post-colonial economic and military relations. On occasion, as in the NATO air strikes on Kosovo most strikingly, but also in the current war in Iraq, arguments that the protection of human rights requires military intervention have provided a justification for simply overriding state sovereignty (Habermas 2002; Cushman 2005). In the case of humanitarian intervention in Libya in 2011 (unlike the earlier cases), it was legally sanctioned by the UN. Humanitarian intervention is extremely contentious. It is, however, very difficult to get states to actually put in place structures and procedures to prevent or deal with human rights abuses, even when they have signed and ratified international agreements. According to 'world polity' theorists, signing and ratifying human rights treaties is part of a world culture that has become pervasive since the Second World War, in which experts and professionals advise nation-states about their responsibilities and true purposes. The result is formal 'isomorphism', or structural similarity between states in terms of constitutions and appropriate legal models for the control of populations and territory, which does not necessarily result in actual changes in repressive state action (Meyer *et al*. 1997; Meyer 1999; Boli and Thomas 1997) (see Schofer *et al*., Chapter 6, in this volume). Indeed, Hafner-Burton and Tsuisui found from statistical analysis that ratification of international agreements may actually be accompanied by *worsening* human rights abuses. It is only, they argue, when states are linked into global civil society, when international non-governmental organizations (INGOs) put pressure on elites to comply with human rights norms, that they begin to be effective (Hafner-Burton and Tsutsui 2005). In fact, effective pressure does not just come from civil society actors, but also from other states (we look at these processes in more detail below).

The way state actors 'learn' to comply with human rights agreements is leading to state transformation, sometimes in unexpected ways. Complex arrangements to regulate and monitor ever more detailed and specific regulations concerning human rights involve negotiations between states, IGOs (like the UN) and NGOs over the details of human rights abuses, and how international agreements are to be interpreted and administered. Such arrangements are leading to states increasingly becoming 'disaggregated' across borders, as government regulators, judges and legislators network with their counterparts from other states and with officials from IGOs to share information, harmonize regulation and develop ways of enforcing international law (Slaughter 2004; see also Held 1995b). Saskia Sassen argues that managing human rights is contributing to the way in which the work of national legislatures and judiciaries is now caught up in processes of globalization that 're-orient particular components of institutions and specific practices ... towards global logics and away from historically shaped national logics' (Sassen 2006: 2). She argues that the national state is being 'hollowed out' – becoming denationalized as state elites increasingly address domestic concerns through international networks and organizations.

Agreeing and managing human rights standards is of course just one aspect of the denationalization of the state, which is far more evident with regard to economic restructuring through financial deregulation, international trade agreements, rules governing multinational companies and so on (Sassen 2006; see also Jessop 1997). However, as a number of sociologists have suggested, the development of human rights may be especially important in a context in which states are also denationalizing with respect to citizenship: legal and illegal migration in conditions that make it easier than ever to maintain links with 'home', long-term residency of non-citizens and increasing rates of dual citizenship all make for uncoupling 'nation' from 'state' (even if they are accompanied by ever more draconian controls over people crossing state borders) (Sassen 2006; Nash 2009a; Schuster 2003) (see Moghadam, Chapter 36, in this volume). Human rights are certainly relevant to citizens. This is especially the case in Europe with its highly developed legal system for guaranteeing rights across state borders, and Margaret Somers suggests that claims for human rights may become more significant in the United States too as the poorest people, those who cannot gain a livelihood in the market, effectively no longer enjoy citizenship rights to basic resources (Somers 2008). But non-citizens are very often in a position where human rights are the only tools available to them to try to gain a degree of material security and freedom in the states in which they arrive, live, work and raise families. The paradigm case here is 'denizens', long-term residents without citizenship who have been able to gain social and economic rights through the use of international human rights law (Soysal 1994; Jacobsen 1996; cf. Bosniak 2006 on the United States). The other main group that has recourse to human rights is asylum-seekers and refugees (Bogusz *et al.* 2004; Morris 2010).

The most dramatic examples of state denationalization through human rights involve the use of customary international law in national courts, which confirm and extend its status *as* law while binding the national state in the particular case in question. In such cases we can see how human rights can be 'intermestic' in practice, both international and domestic at the same time (Nash 2009b: 14). Customary international law is defined as established state practice, which states understand to be followed from a 'sense of legal obligation' (Steiner and Alston 2000: 70). States do not have to have signed or ratified particular conventions to be found in breach of customary international law. Such legal cases are invariably extremely controversial, especially where it appears that the legislature or the executive is bypassed or overridden by the judiciary. International human rights law may, on occasion, alter the balance of power between different branches of the state. A good example is the case of Roper *vs*. Simmons in which the US Supreme Court decided that capital punishment for juveniles, allowed under US law (by a special reservation from the ICCPR that created worldwide scandal), was counter to 'evolving standards of decency'. The court report explicitly stated that it was no longer acceptable because no other state in the world now publicly endorsed juvenile capital punishment (Roper *v* Simmons, US, 551. 2005). The way in which the court drew on customary international law created widespread debate, with dissenting judges and others arguing that it is fundamentally undemocratic to do so: courts should decide what *is* the law, not what it *should* be, and law banning juvenile capital punishment was not passed by elected representatives of the American people. At the same time that states appear to be increasingly bound by detailed human rights constraining limits of state action in relation to individuals, the contestation of state sovereignty, linked to ideals of democracy as popular sovereignty, becomes ever more acute in mobilizations *against* the extension of human rights.

Human Rights Organizations, Legalization and the Limits of Law

If human rights are ultimately secured only through states, what is also crucial is the pressure that political and legal advocacy organizations put on governments and the judiciary to uphold international human rights agreements to which states have committed themselves. Just as states are being 'stretched' through the globalization of human rights, so human rights organizations, even those that operate *within* states, are now invariably linked into global networks. Indeed, such organizations may survive only because of the way they are supported across national borders. Commonly, domestic human rights organizations bypass their own repressive states and search out international allies – INGOs and/or representatives of state actors that are powerfully positioned in IGOs – bringing pressure to bear on state elites from above and below. It is argued that where such campaigns are successful, which may take many years, eventually state elites alter their behaviour to comply with international human rights norms (Keck and Sikkink 1998; Risse, Ropp and Sikkink 1999). In many cases, of course, human rights organizations are not successful and state elites continue either to deny, ignore, or, occasionally, to offer justifications for the human rights violations for which they are responsible, while ordinary people are also often willing to ignore what they know to be happening (Cohen 2001; Hafner-Burton 2007).

Why do organizations have such difficulty in successfully bringing pressure to bear on states, even when they have signed up to international agreements that ostensibly commit them to accepting responsibility for guaranteeing human rights? There is no doubt that law is important to securing human rights, but it is clearly not enough. One reason is that human rights law itself is ambivalent. Although it is predominantly concerned with protecting the civil rights of the individual, international human rights law was nevertheless crafted by state elites for whom protecting the very existence of the state itself is an important consideration. We see this very clearly in the fact that the traditional state prerogative to suspend law in times of national emergency is explicitly enabled in international human rights law. This means that, under certain conditions, states may legally detain individuals without proper procedures just at the point at which 'suspicious individuals', often members of racialized ethnic minorities, are likely to be the victims of a state supported by a majority fearful for its safety (Agamben 2005; Rajagopal 2003: 176–182). The terrorist suspects who are still being held under 'control orders' in the UK, legally now, without ever having been tried and without even having seen the evidence against them, is one example of what is possible once a state of emergency is in place. Another is the Indian Armed Forces (Special Powers) Act which has legally permitted police and military to use a range of methods, including lethal force against gatherings of more than five people in 'disturbed areas' like Kashmir since 1958, and which is closely linked to human rights violations, including extrajudicial executions, torture and rape. Even where the law appears to be absolutely clear in prohibiting certain state actions and even in states which are apparently well regulated by the rule of law, responsibility for human rights can quite easily be evaded by professional legal obfuscation. In Guantánamo Bay, for example, detainees were incarcerated without recourse to fair trials from 2001 until 2008, when after lengthy and hugely elaborate legal proceedings the US Supreme Court finally ruled that their cases should be tried in civilian courts. Many trials are still pending in 2011.

The law is important, then, to respect for human rights, but even when the law is established and there are reasonably well-functioning institutions to put it into practice, it is far from enough. The law itself does not stand outside or above social life: what the law means depends on how it is socially constructed and on how actors are able to win the authority to definitively pronounce on its meaning. One aspect of the limits of law that has been rather little discussed in the sociology of human rights is differences in state formation and the administration of law. Post-colonial theorists like Partha Chatterjee, for example, have suggested that in most states in the world there is little chance of people gaining human rights in practice, even if they have them on paper. Where states are embedded in 'cellular societies' based on 'moral communities' of kinship, caste or religion, states do not have the capacities to control populations and administer law bureaucratically. Chatterjee argues that in 'political society', as distinct from the 'civil society' of the wealthy, the poorest people are gaining *de facto* rights, not as individuals through impartial procedures of law and bureaucracy but using 'fixers', well-connected, influential people linked to political parties who coordinate with state officials, using the democratic power of numbers and political mobilization in the name of 'moral community'. In such cases, a strict line between legality and illegality would actually work to the detriment of those most vulnerable to violence and exploitation (Chatterjee 2004). More conceptual and empirical research is needed to unpack differences in state formation that work against the bureaucratic procedures assumed by advocates of legalizing human rights (see Nash 2011).

In short, law is itself social; whether and how law is codified and administered is a factor in how well human rights ideals are realized in any particular case, but it is just one factor amongst others. The codification of human rights in international law is important insofar as it enables concrete and specific demands for justice. But the sociology of human rights displaces law as the main focus of research into human rights. Our interest is at least as much on the limits of law *as such*, and not just on what makes the law effective in specific cases.

Subjectivity and Solidarity

A shorthand way of summing up the extra-legal conditions that are necessary for the realization of human rights that is especially current in policy circles is 'human rights culture'. This term covers a sense that what is needed to realize human rights is more than a bureaucratic state governed by the (international) rule of law; more even than well-organized and well-funded human rights organizations that are able to bring it to account. What is needed is a change in 'hearts and minds', recognition of the value and importance of human rights throughout society, from state officials to TV viewers, voters and taxpayers. Committing human rights abuses must become unthinkable. At the very least there must be outrage when such abuses become public. Unless people feel real concern to respect and uphold human rights, if opportunities to cut corners, bypass regulation or to express hatred for those who are vulnerable are widely condoned, law that genuinely discourages abuses will either not be made, or it will quite simply be ineffective. 'Human rights culture' represents, therefore, a sense that human rights do not just concern structures and organizations: inter-subjective understandings of what human rights are and why they are valuable are also crucial to their realization.

A sociological debate that is relevant to the possibility of 'human rights culture' concerns the extent to which human rights are contributing to a new sense of cosmopolitan membership in world society. We have already noted that there are some occasions on which human rights law has real effects within states that have been historically configured as national, and we have also looked at some of the controversy that accompanies such occasions. Sociologists debate whether such uses of human rights are contributing to individuals disengaging from the nation. Is identifying as a member of 'humanity', a human being amongst others, becoming more common as an experience? And if so, how is this experience linked to national identity? Does it replace or displace it? With what effects?

Kurasawa's (2007) study of practices that address injustices in global civil society – of bearing witness, forgiveness, foresight and aid – suggests that they may be producing new forms of unity and solidarity, piecemeal and from the 'bottom up'. On the other hand, other sociologists fear that because of the emphasis of human rights on individuals, they are rather more likely to exacerbate the individualizing effects of neoliberalism, and to undermine still further experiences of solidarity, constructed as national solidarity, on which policies of redistribution through the welfare state have depended (Bauman 1999; Turner 2002; Beck 2006). It is surely the case that, for the most part, those who practise 'cosmopolitan virtues' of disengagement from the nation are likely to be privileged, 'frequent flyer cosmopolitans' (Calhoun 2003).

My research on 'human rights culture' suggests that nationalism is being reworked, even revivified, in political struggles over human rights. I compared contestations over the authority to define human rights between state actors in the judiciary and government, professionals involved in NGOs, and media representations of human rights in the United States and UK. I found that in the most controversial cases the 'imagined community' of the nation, far from becoming outdated as a result of creative uses of human rights, is an important dimension of the conflicts over resources, both material and moral, which they produce (Nash 2009b). It is only really human rights activists who now understand human rights as already having established global citizenship in which individuals enjoy rights as human beings, and who identify as members of a global political community in which obligations to respect rights are clearly specified and binding. For the most part, human rights issues are framed in terms of the interests and values of the nation, especially by politicians and in the media, but also quite frequently by lawyers, judges and sometimes even members of nationally based human rights organizations. Such national framings of human rights are, of course, generally conservative, seeking to preserve sovereignty in international relations and the privileges of national citizenship at home. Unexpectedly, however, arguments intended to demonstrate that a state should uphold and extend international human rights law may also be couched in nationalist terms. Such arguments were made, for example, in the Pinochet case, especially in the liberal media. It was argued there that the UK government should extradite General Pinochet to stand trial in Spain for the murder, disappearances and torture for which he was responsible in Chile in the 1970s (even though he had been granted an amnesty by an elected Chilean government), because as a well-ordered, outward-looking state, Britain should take the lead in a global human rights regime to make impunity for such crimes impossible. Although the sentiments that motivate what I call 'cosmopolitan nationalism' – the construction of certain national states as having a global mission to further human rights – are undoubtedly honourable, such formulations come uncomfortably close to imperialism. In the controversies I studied, then, 'pure' cosmopolitanism, identification with humanity, was rare: national identities were being reworked, sometimes in quite unexpected ways to justify treating human beings as legal and not just moral equals, regardless of citizenship status, and even in some cases regardless of citizenship status or of residence within the state.

Human Rights Are Political

My aim in this chapter has been to show the relevance of sociology to the study of human rights. But what I have actually been arguing for is a *political* sociology of human rights. Human rights are political both in the narrower and the broader sense of the term. As I have repeatedly emphasized in this chapter, they are political in the narrow sense in that they invariably concern states, both as violators and, paradoxically, as guarantors of human rights. But human rights are also political in the broader sense of the term, involving the contestation of existing power relations and the articulation of new political visions. In this respect, what is sometimes referred to as 'the politics of politics', the remaking of the state is crucial. If human rights are socially constructed, the task of sociologists is to understand how particular definitions of human rights become established. Who decides what human rights are and should be and who has which entitlements? Conflicts over definitions may be ended temporarily, if not finally resolved, through authoritative definitions that decide the limits and scope of how they are to be administered. The actual administration of law and policy, however, itself involves practices in which definitions of human rights are contested, defined and redefined. The 'human rights field' links micro-social interactions to macro-institutional structures, conflicts over particular human rights cases to fundamental changes in state formation and in the social relationships in which states are embedded.

Finally, there is also a good general argument, beyond considerations of how to do sociology, to be made for treating human rights as inherently political. It is only where human rights are treated as one set of political tools among others in campaigns to bring about a more peaceful and just world that they stand a chance of being effective. Where human rights are treated as moral 'trumps', which admit of no discussion or compromise over their limits in a particular case, they can lead rather to an intensification of disputes, as well as to the pre-emption of democracy by an international elite of lawyers, judges and advocacy organizations (Ignatieff 2001). It is by carefully considering different cases to find out when and how human rights are effective and when they fail, not by taking a moral stance, nor by contenting ourselves with studying positive law, that sociologists may contribute to their realization.

Further Reading

Ignatieff, M. 2001: *Human Rights as Politics and Idolatry*. Princeton, NJ: Princeton University Press.

Morris, L. (ed.) 2006: *Rights: Sociological Perspectives*. London: Routledge.

Nash, K. 2009: *The Cultural Politics of Human Rights*. Cambridge: Cambridge University Press.

Somers, M. 2008: *Genealogies of Citizenship: Markets, Statelessness, and the Right to Have Rights*. Cambridge: Cambridge University Press.

Turner, B. 2006: *Vulnerability and Human Rights*. University Park: Pennsylvania University Press.

40

Democratization

Dietrich Rueschemeyer

Historically, democratization is a fairly recent phenomenon – the Greek city-states
notwithstanding. It became important only after the rise of the modern state and the
emergence of capitalism, which changed the power distribution in modern societies
and 'mobilized' populations through vast increases in urbanization, communication
and transportation. Recent studies of democratization have focused on causal analysis. Rational choice modelling, comparative institutional history and reinvestigations of specific democratization processes in Europe are different – fundamentally
complementary – approaches. Trying to assess the quality of really existing democracies raises complex questions of what is possible, what is desirable, and how changes
in constitutional process come about.

Democratization refers to developments approaching and deepening democracy.
Conventionally defined by civil rights (especially freedoms of expression and association), regular elections with comprehensive suffrage and the government's responsibility to the elected representatives, democracies vary greatly in their distance from
the implicit ideal of collective decision making that is equally responsive to the
preferences of all citizens.

The study of democratization has moved in the past generation towards a tighter
theoretical analysis of the relevant causal conditions. These new approaches will be
the first major concern of this overview. Their discussion will be preceded by sketches
of earlier ideas about factors advancing or undermining democracy, which formed the
background to the current explanatory attempts. The final section examines the
problems of deepening democracy. This raises issues that inevitably involve normative
as well as factual judgements.

The Wiley-Blackwell Companion to Political Sociology, First Edition. Edited by Edwin Amenta,
Kate Nash, and Alan Scott.
© 2012 Blackwell Publishing Ltd. Published 2012 by Blackwell Publishing Ltd.

Earlier Ideas about What Advances Democratization

The study of democratization is closely linked to actual developments in the history of constitutional arrangements. Thus Aristotle's ideas took off from comparative observations of Greek city-states. The long history of large-scale agrarian political systems gave little evidence of far-reaching moves towards democracy. Capitalist commercialization and industrialization put the issue firmly on the political as well as the intellectual agenda; today's discussions are still influenced by ideas of John Stuart Mill, Alexis de Tocqueville and Karl Marx. The breakdowns of democracy in Europe between the World Wars raised important questions about the staying power of democracy and, more surprisingly, about the possibility that totalitarian rule and democratic politics may have certain causal conditions in common.

The most important background to current theories of democracy was laid by the response of social science to the proliferation of 'new nations' as a consequence of decolonization after the Second World War. The early dominant perspective, 'modernization theory', essentially applied the understanding of nineteenth-century social science of how Europe was transformed by the rise of capitalism and the ascent of the modern state to the conditions and the future of 'developing countries'. It was a broad, makeshift portrayal of agrarian social formations turning into industrial societies, a picture not based on detailed knowledge of diverse conditions and trajectories in different parts of the global 'South'. Apparently supported by substantial correlations between indicators of economic development and of democratic forms of government, modernization theory's central weakness was that it did not focus on identifying the main causal mechanisms and the social actors driving that transformation forward. Increasing levels of economic development, spreading education, proliferating means of communication, decline of tradition as well as other developments were linked to democratization; but the nature of these links remained vague, and some argued simply that growing economic and societal complexity called for a pluralist political system. On the role of pro-democratic social actors and their interests, several of the earlier theories were remembered as offering plausible candidates ranging from Aristotle on the middle class to Marx on the bourgeoisie (and later in history on the working class), while others – echoing de Tocqueville – saw a diverse and lively civil society as decisive.

The wave of democratic transitions in South America and Southern Europe, which preceded the fall of European communism, was the subject of excellent studies of political change (see O'Donnell and Schmitter 1986 and the other volumes in the collection of *Transitions from Authoritarian Rule*). But these studies did not overcome the diffuseness of causal analysis in modernization theory. If anything, the new studies added to the proliferation of potentially relevant conditions. Focusing on the shorter-term processes of transition, they introduced such factors as transitional coalitions of the old and the new or uncertainties about the consequences of concessions and compromises; and they raised unresolved questions about the conditions of consolidation of democracy.

Recent Research Focused on Causal Analysis

During the past two decades a new set of analyses aimed at a sharper theoretical understanding of the conditions promoting and obstructing democracy. These attempts agree remarkably on the fundamental causal constellations. The advance of democracy and its obstruction are basically determined by the power balance among pro-democratic and anti-democratic collective interests. These interests are predominantly but not exclusively material interests, concerned with maintaining or changing unequal distributions. Extreme inequalities in advantage and power rule out democracy. Lesser degrees of inequality open possibilities for struggles about democratization. If the emergence and stabilization of democratic forms of rule are a function of the power balance among opposed interests, democracy will inevitably represent a compromise-equilibrium among the contending forces, though one variously reinforced by democratic institutions as a form of credible commitment. This equilibrium was early understood as deriving from the balance between the costs of toleration and the costs of repression and, by extension, between the costs of insurgence and the costs of resignation in the calculation of the contending groups (Dahl 1971: 14–16).

Studies adopting this approach explain substantial and long-term change in constitutional form by changing constellations of interest and advantage, by threat perceptions and the costs of repression and insurgence, and by changing power resources of the contending parties. The latter are inherently distributed unevenly. Various elites can mobilize coercive power, administrative efficiency, control over capital, as well as leverage over cultural hegemony for protecting their interests. For 'the many' the main chance of gaining countervailing power lies in overcoming the collective action problem via organization.

Within this emerging consensus about the explanation of democratization we can distinguish several divergent but potentially complementary tendencies. The most radical and radically simplifying approach begins with modelling the micro-foundations of contests about political constitution along the lines of rational-choice theory (Boix 2003; Acemoglu and Robinson 2006). Democratization as well as its absence and its reverses are then essentially results of the inequalities and struggles between the haves and the have-nots. Starting from similar premises, other analyses (e.g., Rueschemeyer, Stephens and Stephens 1992, but also works by Collier and Luebbert) give greater weight to the complexities of class formation, of historically shaped relations among groups and classes, and of institutional structures as these emerge in comparative historical analysis. Finally there are a number of attempts (e.g., works in progress by Ertman, Weyland and Ziblatt as well as Tilly 2004, 2007), which engage in historical research in order to identify overlooked causal conditions and sequences of democratization and obverse developments. Significantly, dichotomous contrasts of democracy vs. non-democracy are here replaced by movements towards and away from democracy. This introduces a link to the analysis of deepening existing democratic rule, which will be considered in the concluding section.

Rational choice modelling of the forces shaping constitutional forms builds on a long tradition of rationalist reflections on how individual preferences are aggregated in democratic and authoritarian political systems. Beginning with a conflict between poor and rich, which is then complicated by introducing a middle category, these works come to important conclusions about the chances of democratization under conditions of contrasting degrees of economic inequality and on the effects of capital mobility, which reduces the chance of expropriation. Boix offers a short, preliminary summary of what he sees as the determinants of constitutional outcomes: 'the extent of inequality, the degree of capital mobility, the political resources of the classes or sectors involved in the struggle to determine the constitutional framework of the country, and, in part, uncertainty of political conditions' (2003: 130).

Formalizing these relations improves the logical clarity of the claims developed. This brings certain arguments into particularly sharp relief – for instance about the role of credible commitments in making negotiation and compromise feasible or about institutions as powerful tools for the stabilization of commitments. Formally stating that degree of inequality, mobility of resources vs. local boundedness and chances of political self-organization have critical consequences for the balance of power in a struggle over constitutional form is an important advance. But unless we can identify critical thresholds in these factors, develop substantive ideas about what accounts for change in them and estimate the perceptions and interpretations of historical actors, we have a set of clearly stated relevant factors, but possibly little notion of when to expect successful repression, material concessions without yielding political power, initiatives towards democratization and effective transitions towards democracy. What is at first sight a fully developed theory capable of explanation and prediction may have to be more realistically assessed as a focused 'theory frame', a construct that clearly defines a problem and identifies the most relevant causal conditions with evidence and argument, but is not in a position to make definitive predictions and explanations on the basis of sufficiently identified conditions. An interesting combination of a rational choice model and close attention to the perceptions and interpretations of historical actors is Gerard Alexander's analysis of *The Sources of Democratic Consolidation* (2002) in Western Europe. He sees consolidation emerging when the political right realizes that its interests are safe within democracy, safe enough to give up on coercive means of repression.

This is more explicitly acknowledged in the second variant of explanatory research indicated above. Thus, in *Capitalist Development and Democracy* (Rueschemeyer *et al.* 1992) we self-consciously constructed a focused theory frame that treated democracy as a matter of power, which reflects the balance of power within society, the balance of power between state and self-organized society, and the impact of the balance of international power on the country in question. The analysis then focused on changes in the empowerment of excluded groups – not only, but very importantly of the working class. Capitalist development increased the chances of collective organization of excluded groups by way of advances in transportation and communication and urbanization. And it weakened the power of large landholders. Within this theory frame, *Capitalist Development and Democracy* offered an explanation of democratization and breakdowns of democracy in forty-odd countries. The hypotheses used in explanation were largely inspired by the frame, though additional mechanisms were also considered. In the concluding assessment, the theory frame was modified and specified but largely affirmed.

Closely related to the distinction between theory frame and historical explanation is the fact that this second mode of explanatory research on democratization is not content with such a-historical categorizations as 'the rich', 'the poor' and an abstract 'middle'. It gives greater attention to historically shaped, typically institutionally embedded, and often cross-nationally variable conditions and social formations that are of critical importance for democratization and its reverse. Among these are:

- the chances of collective self-organization of subordinate and excluded groups;
- inter-organizational relations that can strengthen pro-democratic forces but alternatively can also amplify the power of anti-democratic forces (a reminder

that a simple measure of the strength of 'civil society' is not a reliable predictor of democratization);

- intergroup relations that foster or inhibit the formation and specific delineations of larger solidarities and that give a historically variable shape to such social configurations as self-employed middle class, employed white-collar groups, blue-collar working class, or managerial and capital-owning bourgeoisie;
- relations among classes and class fragments that predispose them for coalitions with other classes or incline them towards distance and rejection;
- relations between the state apparatus and different groups and class fragments that make for differential access, political support and material gain.

Such plainly relevant but irritatingly variable constellations cannot be dismissed as negligible detail, because there is powerful evidence that they are causally relevant for democratization and breakdowns of democracy. Furthermore, some findings suggest that motivational premises centred exclusively on material gain and loss may have to be supplemented by the consideration of status and honour, as is commonly done in work on class formation inspired by the work of Weber.

Yet the first two approaches of the new explanatory thrust in research on democratization can be strongly complementary. Inquiries into historically and institutionally grounded variations across countries that are relevant for democracy can benefit from implicit and explicit modelling of overriding factors. Weberian analyses have often shown us how building a pure type on extreme assumptions can sharpen our view for significant deviations from the ideal model. In turn, there is a good chance that comparative work on what seems at first just a random variation on a dominant theme can lead to solid specification and thus bring a theory frame closer to a fully developed theory.

Much the same can also be said of the third tendency within the new push for explanatory analysis of democratization. There are first several projects that venture more deeply into the historical processes of democratization and de-democratization in Europe. Yet they are as much inspired by the search for theoretically plausible explanation as the other two approaches just discussed. In fact, two of them were prefaced by critical examinations of the theoretical literature on democratization (Ertman 1998; Ziblatt 2006).

Thomas Ertman has long been engaged in a project *Taming the Leviathan: Building Democratic Nation-States in 19th and 20th Century Western Europe*. In the first results of this work he examines longitudinally the effects of political parties and voluntary associations on the chances of democratization and breakdowns of democracy in 12 European countries (e.g., 2010). Reviving concerns of Eckstein, Lijphart and Rokkan, he gives central place to the interactions among religious affiliation, party appeal and associational patterns. This allows him to explain why associational density was related to radically divergent outcomes – to fascism and national socialism in Italy and Germany, but to persistent democracy in eight other European countries. A critical role is played by strong conservative parties that let themselves be exposed to electoral competition.

Daniel Ziblatt has set out on an ambitious research project that pursues similar goals. Ziblatt is looking more closely at partial transitions towards democracy in the broad phase of European democratization, comparing especially developments in

Britain and in Germany (e.g., 2009). Organized political parties help make democracy safe for incumbent interests, reducing the threat of democracy and turning the long-run unfolding of institutions that constitute democracy into a more settled process.

Kurt Weyland (2009) focuses in a number of published and unpublished papers on diffusion of constitutional change, contrasting the high frequency of diffusion after the revolutions of the long nineteenth century, which however had greatly divergent results, with a much slower rate of diffusion but greater rates of successful democratization towards the end of the nineteenth and the beginning of the twentieth centuries. He sees the major explanation for this double contrast in the larger role of parties and other politically relevant organizations. They introduced more caution as well as successful action into the broad process. That all three of these reconsiderations of democratization in Europe point to the significant role of parties recalls that Rueschemeyer *et al.* (1992) noted in the concluding revision of their theory frame that 'political parties emerged as a crucial mediating mechanism' (p. 287) and should be given a more distinctive role in the conceptual model.

The late Charles Tilly (2004, 2007) has offered us a broad theoretical exploration that complements such analytically oriented historical research and may be interpreted as a congenial framework. It builds on a lifetime of work on state formation, contention, inequality, and trust relations; but it results specifically from a shift in Tilly's analytic strategy from the comparative historical analysis of large-scale phenomena to the identification of specific causal mechanisms. Such universal causal links, if repeatedly identified in different historical circumstances, can in varied combinations account for historical processes at hand.

He defines democratization not as the attainment of a defined system of rule called democracy but as any 'increase in conformity between state behavior and citizens' expressed demands'. This conformity is specified in different dimensions that roughly correspond to the elements of conventional compound definitions of democracy – of civil liberties as well as of broad, equalized and binding consultation of the citizenry by the state. Three master hypotheses about advancing democratization (and by implication its reverse) point to complex transformations: first, the dissolution of trust networks outside public politics and their integration into the realm of public politics; second, the insulation of public politics from inequalities grounded in social categories that shape life chances, categories such as gender, race, religion and stark versions of class; and third, the reduction of autonomous centres of power whether within or outside the state. For each of these broad hypotheses Tilly offers many specific hypotheses. They open up many ideas to which results of the searching reinvestigations of democratization, say in Europe, can be linked.

Two of Tilly's master hypotheses leave us with an intriguing puzzle. The reduction of autonomous power centres and the integration of trust networks into public politics may well support not only democratization but also, alternatively, fascist and totalitarian politics as well. This insight, articulated in Dahrendorf's (1967) assessment of democracy in Germany and adumbrated earlier in theories of 'mass society', is just briefly acknowledged. What differentiates these outcomes from each other remains to be explored. This is clearly decisive for our understanding of what happened in twentieth-century Europe.

Tilly comes to empirical generalizations that in large part conform to the thrust of earlier models and theory frames but also raise important new questions. These include:

- Democratization is best understood as a matter of conflict.
- It is often initiated by pressure from below.
- Developments of de-democratization tend to be faster than democratizing changes.
- Both democratization and de-democratization often occur in the same time periods.

Tilly is extremely sceptical about a fundamental assumption of the starker modelling approaches – that the contending forces in struggles about constitutional form pursue clear long-term goals on the basis of rationally assessed information and expectations. This raises the complex issues of agency and structure in explaining change and its directions. Yet Tilly probably goes too far in his scepticism. True, clear-cut goals will often be fudged because of complications in the self-organization of large collectives, because of linkages among diverse collectives with divergent central interests, because matters of status and honour may compete with material interests in the formulation of collective goals, and because of the inherent difficulties of anticipating both changing opportunities and long-term consequences of constitutional change. However, large collectives, if sufficiently coordinated and organized, have through their leadership longer time horizons than individuals, informal groups and inchoate movements. They are likely to return again and again to similar-interest constellations and develop collective goals based on renewed assessments and insights. After all, what is at stake are structured inequalities in class, status and power, issues that affect in most complex societies the central life interests of the opposed constituencies. Clearly a rational action model writ large for broad collectivities simplifies things radically; but it may still be a useful guide to the modal thrust of many collective participants in constitutional struggles.

Tilly's late work on democratization has the potential of linking the most strongly theory-oriented recent work to the renewed historical investigations that pay close attention to partial advances and reversals of democratization and yet view them in a larger longitudinal and comparative context. Ultimately, all three of the tendencies in recent work discussed here can complement and stimulate each other. Keeping them in dialogue holds the best promise for substantial advances in our understanding of democracy and democratization.

Questions about the Quality of Democracy

At the end of the twentieth century democracy became vastly more common. Huntington (1991) discussed this as the 'third wave' of democratization. Furthermore, Przeworski and Limongi (1997) offered the – not unquestioned – finding that democracies in countries with incomes above a certain level (GNP/cap of 6000 USD at purchasing power parities in 1985) do not slide back to authoritarian constitutional forms, that they are in effect consolidated. Yet at the same time a number of observers have pointed out that late-democratizing countries often show serious and increasing flaws in their actual operations (O'Donnell 1999). These – apparently contradictory – developments have reopened older questions about the quality of democracy (Diamond and Morlino 2005).

Here is a large and diverse field of issues, only a few of which will be discussed here. The far left has long denounced regime forms conventionally labelled democracy – as well as virtually all really existing democracies – as inherently deficient: they are merely formal and do not create even a semblance of real power sharing. Softer versions of these critiques persisted when the majority of socialist parties with a voluntary following became social democratic in character. To be content with the conventional criteria of democracy – civil rights (especially freedoms of expression and association); regular elections with comprehensive suffrage; and the government's responsibility to the elected representatives – means indeed that the powerful political effects of inequality in economic resources, social and cultural power, as well as social status are neglected. Every person is treated *as if* he or she had an equal or near-equal voice in politics, a patently fictitious premise. Given the profound symbolic power of the equal right to vote, this raised the question of whether and how democracies can make popular participation in collective decision making more real. Other critics called for more intense and broader participation in government, because this would enhance the quality of collective as well as personal life (MacPherson 1977). Or they claimed that democratization had also to be extended to forms of social life other than the sphere of politics proper – to employment relations, for instance, or to school and family life. Finally, social welfare provisions across the whole population have been considered the mark of real rather than formal democracy.

The broad moral appeal of the idea of democracy makes it tempting to bring other policy patterns under the umbrella of deepening democracy. To avoid this, a number of distinctions will be helpful. We must clearly define and justify what is meant by making democracy more real or deepening it. Once that is achieved, empirical arguments can point to conditions and means of making democracy more real, to factors instrumental for but not identical with democracy. For instance, making family and school life less authoritarian may give educational support to political democracy, even though we may want to reserve the main normative argument to the political sphere.

Any conception of deepening democracy also has to contend with important value choices, since democracy involves different dimensions that can come into conflict with each other. Thus, democratic government should be effective as well as supportive of broad power sharing. Almost all democratic nation-states treat this trade-off between efficiency and equality by robustly opting for representative instead of direct democracy and by leaving much of the preparation and the implementation of legislation to administrative bodies. Another tension between different value dimensions of democracy has been the object of much greater ideological conflict – the tension between liberty and equality. Some have argued that advancing political equality and the reduction of social and economic inequality that it requires are fundamentally at odds with the liberty of individuals and groups. However, comparison of different democracies tells us that liberty and equality can travel far together, further than the arguments of – for instance – Hayek in *The Road to Serfdom* (2007 [1944]) allowed.

In both instances we observe how empirical evidence is intricately intertwined with value choice. The robust option for representative democracy and an effective administrative state apparatus reflects not only the strength of efficiency values but also largely unquestioned empirical premises about the coordination problems of radical democracy in large nation-states. Scepticism about claims that liberty and equality are in conflict is not in the first place due to stronger or weaker options for one or the other value; rather it is based on empirical comparisons of personal and group liberties in democratic countries with greatly different supports for political, social and economic equality. We will encounter similarly diverse forms of interplay between value choice and empirical evidence in the following.

Some Reflections on Deepening and Subverting Democracy

Steps of deepening democracy – and, not infrequently, of subverting it – have been commonplace in the long history of approaches to forms of democracy defined by the triad of comprehensive suffrage, civil rights and responsibility of the state. And these guaranties of formal democracy need nurturing and defence even after it is first achieved. If in the nineteenth century curtailing the suffrage was a mainstay of keeping democracy at bay, in the twentieth keeping the state apparatus responsive to elected representatives and institutionalizing civil rights and the rule of law have become perhaps more critical to maintaining democratic rule than free and comprehensive elections.

The following reflections on deepening democracy begin therefore with comments on developments in the three defining dimensions of democracy as commonly understood. This will be followed by a discussion of how political equality can be advanced beyond formal democracy. In the first set of comments, disagreement on values is reduced to a minimum because the strong normative appeal of the idea of democracy itself creates a presumption for implementing the defining triad of characteristics. Normative disagreement is much more visible when it comes to extending political equality more substantially.

Democracies with apparently comprehensive suffrage do not thereby give an equal chance to different groups to express their interests through voting. Improvements of access to voting participation – through abolishing fees, literacy tests and property qualifications as well as through easing participation by convenient registration and holiday voting – may be opposed for partisan reasons; but few important values stand in the way of creating a somewhat more level playing field for different political interests with these simple measures.

Yet if we return to the underlying question of an equal chance for expressing one's interests politically, that is, if we consider seriously reducing political inequality as well as the social and economic inequalities that undergird it, we move into much more controversial territory. One might think that constraining the flow of money into election campaigns would be a fairly uncontroversial goal. And it has non-partisan support in many countries. In the United States, too, it did lead to bipartisan legislation; but this was overruled by a narrow majority of the Supreme Court. A simple and plausible proposition opens the view on deeper disagreements: if we find that upper-middle-class voting participation is in many countries higher than the participation of working-class and poor citizens, this seems primarily due to the greater chances of higher-class interests to win out in politics, even though numbers would not be on their side. To remedy this pattern would require transformations that are likely to be massively opposed for reasons of interest as well as democratic principle.

Civil rights (and especially the freedoms of speech and organization), secured through effective rule of law and also through significant support in civil society, are taken for granted in most mature democracies, though in times of crisis this protection can weaken significantly (as it did in the McCarthy period, under the impact of 9/11, and in some responses to the financial crisis of 2008/2009). Historically, the rights to free speech and especially the right to free coalition had to be secured against much harsher opposition. And in many less well-established democracies, free speech and freedom to organize are much more weakly established.

The responsiveness of the state to elected representatives and to the policy directions expressed in elections has weakened greatly in the course of the twentieth century and beyond. This now may well be the weakest point in the triad of formal guarantees of democracy, even though this weakness is not commonly recognized. The main causes are increasingly intricate problems of policy design, growing international and security problems, and the overwhelming advantages of the state in knowledge and administrative capacity. The current financial crisis illustrates the complexity of issues, the influence of narrow interests on state action, and the disconnect between opinion in society and a realistic understanding of how the crisis came about, what can be done to mitigate it and how to guard against a recurrence. The greatest responsibility to cope with these issues – both in normal times and in times of crisis – falls on the press, which at present finds itself in a period of troubled transformation. Countries with strong parties and other policy-related organizations such as unions and think tanks have an advantage over others with less organizational density in the political sphere.

Beyond improvements and defences against deterioration in the elementary characteristics of democracy there is the wide field of deepening democracy by transcending its conventional forms. Looking for ways of moving closer to political equality for all citizens leaves out many other themes, but it is central to the ideal of collective decision making that is equally responsive to the preferences of all citizens.

Democracy, even in its most formal incarnation, requires that the sphere of politics is to some extent separate and insulated from the system of inequality in society. Where political power is fused with control over the economy, great social power and the highest social status, as it was in feudalism, democracy is inconceivable. This fundamental proposition implies two corollaries about political equality in formally democratic countries: while minor reductions of political inequality can be achieved within the political sphere itself, more substantial reductions have to contain the spillover of social power, economic resources and social status into the arena of politics, and even greater change requires that social inequalities in class, status and power have to be reduced themselves. Since social inequalities can never be fully eradicated, an emancipation of politics from social and economic inequality can only be approached by partial steps, and even these partial steps will be opposed by powerful interests. Whichever reductions can be realized depends on the power balance in society; that is, it depends in principle on the same factors that made formal democracy possible.

Scanning the power resources available to different forces in complex societies, a reasonable assessment of the main power concentrations that would have to be contained and possibly reduced include the following:

- the state apparatus with the expertise, tax-based funding, organizational capacity and, ultimately, coercion at its disposal;
- capital ownership which has great power over marketing, investment and employment as well as persuasive social and political influence unless it is subject to near-perfect competition, which is rarely the case;
- high-income earners who have disproportionate political influence despite the best efforts to prevent earning advantage from seeping into politics;
- high social status which gives incumbents an unequal measure of trust and political voice that is hard to counteract because status is inherently based to a large extent on spontaneous consent;
- and finally 'cultural hegemony' or the dominant influence on the development and diffusion of culture, which is inherently reserved for limited positions in society and thus profoundly unequal, even though it is in most rich and complex societies internally pluralistic.

These concentrations of power are self-reinforcing and become the foundations of overwhelming inequality, unless they are powerfully checked. The power resources of 'the few' can be counterbalanced to some extent by strong collective organization of the less advantaged. Collective organization in parties, unions and other politically relevant voluntary associations is the single most important power resource of subordinate groups and classes. If well developed, they can make full use of the numerical advantage of 'the many' by mobilizing their constituencies; they can even diminish the income advantage of the well-to-do with many small contributions; they can lobby for the interests they represent between elections; and they can protect their followers against dominant cultural influences by advancing their own views and critiquing views at odds with them.

If the interests of the many are successfully represented in a democratic context over a long period, public policy is likely to improve public education as well as protections against illness, unemployment and poverty. In combination with effective collective organization, such policies turn the members of subordinate classes into better-informed citizens who will participate in politics with more competence and greater self-respect. This is evident from cross-national studies of citizens' participation in voting and other political activities. The overall level of such participation is higher and class differences in participation are virtually absent in countries with the strongest social policies. In short, welfare state policies provide the basis of a resilient and deepened democracy. If pursued in a democratic context, they do not advance equality at the expense of liberty.

The bottom lines of these reflections on deepening democracy are simple. However desirable in principle – and in many countries there is little disagreement on this – processes of deepening democracy do not come about by themselves. They depend, much as the attainment of conventional democracy, on the relevant balances of power. Consequently, there are substantial differences in the depth of the democratic process even among countries with similar social structures and economies. Yet formal democracy does provide an opening for struggles to go beyond the defining triad of its characteristics. And democratic struggles for more political equality can avoid violent confrontation and damage to the other main value dimensions of democracy.

Further Reading

Acemoglu, D. and Robinson, J.A. 2006: *Economic Origins of Dictatorship and Democracy*. Cambridge: Cambridge University Press.

Dahl, R.A. 1971: *Polyarchy: Participation and Opposition*. New Haven, CT: Yale University Press.

Huntington, S. 1991: *The Third Wave: Democratization in the Late Twentieth Century*. Norman: University of Oklahoma Press.

Rueschemeyer, D., Stephens, E.H. and Stephens, J.D. 1992: *Capitalist Development and Democracy*. Cambridge: Polity Press, and Chicago, IL: Chicago University Press.

Ziblatt, D. 2006: How did Europe democratize? *World Politics 58*(2): 311–338.

41

Feminism and Democracy

JUDITH SQUIRES

Feminism has been, and continues to be, an important source of democratic innovation. Second-wave women's movement activism revitalized theories of democracy by asserting the importance of participatory democracy and eroding the boundaries of the public and the private. Global feminist campaigns to increase the levels of female representation within national parliaments have generated new mechanisms for securing fair representation in practice, including gender quotas, and have led to innovative theories of representation, such as the idea of the 'politics of presence'. The emergence of women's policy agencies, which interact with women's civil society organizations and female parliamentarians to bring women's interests into the policy agenda, has created interest in extra-parliamentary representative practices and new theoretical interest in representative claims-making. Meanwhile the way in which feminist non-government organizations (NGOs) now pursue gender equality via new modes of bureaucratic governance is creating new practices, and theories, of democratic governance. Finally, the transnational networking among feminist actors, facilitated by the preparations for the four United Nations women's conferences, underpins emerging notions of cosmopolitan democracy.

The two traditions of democracy and feminism share many common preoccupations, but have had a complex, and at times fraught, association. The democratic tradition long predates feminism: only in the nineteenth century did democrats begin to take seriously the issue of women's democratic rights. The feminist tradition on the other hand has been characterized by its commitment to revitalizing democratic theory and practice, initially via women's movement activism beyond the state and more recently by democratic innovation within the state.

The Wiley-Blackwell Companion to Political Sociology, First Edition. Edited by Edwin Amenta, Kate Nash, and Alan Scott.
© 2012 Blackwell Publishing Ltd. Published 2012 by Blackwell Publishing Ltd.

Both the theory and practice of democracy are subject to continual experimentation and innovation, frequently driven by a commitment to democratic participation and political equality. Much of the recent literature on democratic innovation has focused on issues of identity and difference in the context of the perceived exclusion of minority groups, attempting to rethink democracy as more inclusive of oppressed groups (Kymlicka 1995; Taylor 1994), and on the extension of democratic practices beyond the nation-state in the context of the perceived diminishing capacity of states to influence their own destinies, attempting to rethink democracy both above and below the level of the nation-state (Held 2010). Feminism has informed both the theory and practice of democratic innovation in key ways: feminist campaigns for increased female representation have informed some of the best thinking about democratic inclusion (Benhabib 1996; Phillips 1995; Young 1990b, 2000), while feminist transnational democratic practices have informed some of the best thinking about democracy beyond the state (Eschle 2001; Ackerly and Okin 1999).

Participatory Democracy: The Women's Movement

Nineteenth-century feminists in Western liberal democracies initially campaigned for the right to vote and to stand in elections, concentrating on formal equality before the law. Yet, the failure of these formal rights to generate the increased equality of outcome that many had anticipated led to a growing scepticism amongst political activists about formal representative democracy and an active exploration of more participatory forms of democracy. The Women's Movement actively experimented with democratic practices during the 1970s, attempting to develop new forms of democratic inclusion for women. During the peak of the second-wave movements there were a large number of protest strategies adopted, including spontaneous action and well-organized campaigns of sit-ins, marches and demonstrations, such as the 'Reclaim the Night' actions in England and West Germany in 1977, and in Italy in 1978. All these forms of political protest were 'movement events', working outside the formal mechanisms of procedural politics. The women's movement aspired to be open to all, non-hierarchical and informal, with many women organizing outside of state structures in such things as women's peace movements and ecology movements (Millett 1970; Mies and Shiva 1993; Morgan 1970). Issues of participatory democracy became central, with great attention paid to organizational practice (Pateman 1970). Such experiments influenced the practices of the Left, as documented by Sheila Rowbotham, Lynne Segal and Hilary Wainwright in *Beyond the Fragments* (1979).

However, for many women the experiences of the radical participatory democracy of the women's movement became paradoxical (Phillips 1991). The emphasis on participation was too demanding for those who were juggling many other demands on their time, and the lack of representative structures raised serious questions of accountability. The absence of formal structures often worked to create an insularity that left many women feeling excluded and silenced. By the 1980s many feminists became again more centrally concerned with the importance of mainstream politics, working to increase the numbers of women present within parties and legislatures, and to pursue policies in the interests of women.

Representative Democracy: Women in Parliament

By the end of the 1980s the focus of democratic theorists' attention had turned back to the institutions of parliamentary democracy. The events in Eastern Europe focused attention on the importance of democratic elections and representative government. Meanwhile the social movements in the West had lost much of their energy and enthusiasm for active participation. Both the democratic and feminist traditions turned their attention to liberal democracy, with its focus on individual rights, periodic elections and representative government (Phillips 1991: 13). For some participatory democrats this turn to representative government was perceived to be something of a capitulation to pragmatism. Yet, the goal of equal representation within national parliaments has proved to be more practically challenging and theoretically interesting than many had predicted.

The Universal Declaration of Human Rights affirms that everyone has the right to take part in the government of his or her country, and the UN Beijing Platform for Action states:

> Achieving the goal of equal participation of women and men in [d]ecision-making will provide a balance that more accurately reflects the composition of society and is needed in order to strengthen democracy and promote its proper functioning . . . Without the active participation of women and the incorporation of women's perspectives at all levels of decision-making, the goals of equality, development and peace cannot be achieved.
>
> United Nations (1995: 181)

It therefore calls on governments to:

> [c]ommit themselves to establishing the goal of gender balance in governmental bodies and committees, as well as in public administrative entities, and in the judiciary, including, *inter alia*, setting specific targets and implementing measures to substantially increase the number of women with a view to achieving equal representation of women and men, if necessary through positive action, in all governmental and public administration positions.
>
> United Nations (1995:190)

Similarly, the Charter of Rome states that the 'equal participation of women and men in decision-making processes is our major goal at European level', and in its Recommendation of 2 December 1996 the Council of the European Union calls on the member states to develop suitable measures and strategies to correct the under-representation of women in decision-making positions. It is therefore now widely acknowledged that women are under-represented politically around the world, and that this under-representation is problematic.

Since women first gained the right to stand for election the percentage of women in national parliaments has risen steadily, from 3% in 1945 to 11.6% in 1995, to 19.1% in 2010. The rate of change in women's electoral success has not been as great as many people had expected, suggesting that factors other than direct legal restrictions matter. The level of female representation varies significantly across states: Rwanda, Sweden, South Africa, Cuba, Iceland, the Netherlands and Finland all have more than 40% of women in their national parliament. By contrast, a significant number of countries, including Kenya, Hungary, Turkey, Brazil, Kuwait and Georgia, still have less than 10%. There are a range of cultural and economic factors that have been shown to affect the level of women's representation internationally, ranging from the level of secularism and the length of time that women have had the vote, to rates of female participation in paid employment and levels of state provision of child-care. Yet political factors, such as party ideology, electoral system and candidate-selection rules, are clearly crucial. Internationally, higher levels of female representation have generally been secured within parties on the left, under proportional electoral systems, and where selection rules require that women be selected (Norris 1993:312). The significance of party selection rules in particular has focused attention on the use of gender quotas as a key mechanism for increasing the political representation of women.

Gender quotas have now been introduced in over 100 countries globally. So rapid has been the recent uptake of quota policies in relation to women's candidate selection that commentators suggest that 'quota fever' has affected the world (Dahlerup 1998). There are two main types of gender quota: party and legislative. Party quotas are measures that are adopted voluntarily by political parties to aim for a certain proportion of female candidates (usually 25–50%). These measures govern either the composition of party lists (in countries with proportional representation electoral systems) or the selection of candidates (in countries with plurality systems). Legislative quotas are mandatory provisions (enacted through reforms to electoral laws of constitutions) that apply to all parties. Party quotas were first adopted by social democratic parties in Western Europe in the 1970s, whereas legislative quotas first appeared in the 1990s, largely in developing and post-conflict countries in Latin America and Africa, respectively. Although it is possible to achieve high levels of women's representation without quotas (as in Denmark and Finland), the adoption of quotas has led to dramatic increases in the percentage of women in parliament in countries as diverse as Rwanda, Sweden, Argentina and Nepal. The implementation of party quotas has helped increase women's representation to 41% in the Netherlands and 40% in Norway, and the use of legislative quotas has increased women's representation to 39% in both Costa Rica and Argentina (www.quotaproject.org).

Advocates of gender quotas have frequently argued that women have interests that are best represented by women. Yet as Lovenduski notes, 'that understanding has been fiercely contested by feminists, their sympathizers and their opponents in a continuing and sometimes acrimonious debate' (Lovenduski and Norris 1996: 1). To assess whether women are an 'interest group' and, if so, what interests they have, Sapiro claims that one needs to consider both women's 'objective situation' and their consciousness of their own interests (Sapiro 1998: 164). This is politically significant because, contrary to the Burkean notion of paternalistic representation of the interests of others, political systems are, Sapiro suggests, not likely to represent previously under-represented groups 'until those groups develop a sense of their own interests and place demands upon the system.' (Sapiro 1998: 167) Moreover, if the interests in question are not clear and pre-formed, but are still in the process of being uncovered via processes of consciousness-raising, it will then be more difficult to distinguish between the represented and the representative. In these circumstances women would seem to be best placed to advocate the interests of women.

However, others have argued against casting women as simply another interest group among many. Diamond and Hartsock, for instance, refute the idea that fairness requires that women promote their interests within the existing political system equally with all other such interest groups (1998). This, they claim, underplays the distinctive and radical challenge posed by the recognition of women's experiences and political ambitions, which cannot simply be integrated into the system. The inclusion of questions of reproduction and sexuality into the political process will transform the very concept of the political, eroding the public/private distinction and, presumably (though they do not state this directly), undermining the current system of representative democracy in favour of a more participatory one. Nonetheless, within the confines of the current representative system they are clear that 'only women can "act for" women in identifying "invisible" problems affecting the lives of large numbers of women' (Diamond and Hartsock 1998: 198).

The feminist turn back to parliamentary democracy has generated a rich seam of theoretical work on representative practices, in which contemporary feminist theorists have suggested that there are theoretically coherent grounds for presuming a relationship between the numbers of women elected to political office and the passage of legislation beneficial to women as a group. In her influential work Anne Phillips attempts to synthesize the interest-based and identity-based approaches in a 'politics of presence'. Ideas-based approaches focus on the responsiveness of representatives to those they are representing: as long as they are responsive, it matters little who the representatives are (Phillips 1995: 6). A politics of presence, on the other hand, focuses on the messengers as well, requiring that the overly cerebral concentration on beliefs and interests be extended to recognize the political significance of the identity of the representatives. The gender (and any other social identity deemed politically significant) of the representative is therefore 'an important part of what makes them representative ...' (Phillips 1995: 13). Similarly, Iris Young's 'politics of difference' aimed to address the 'unrepresentative' nature of existing electoral and legislative processes by proposing that a certain number of seats in the legislature be reserved for the members of marginalized groups that have suffered oppression, and who need guaranteed representation in order that their distinct voice can be heard (Young 1990: 184). These theoretical contributions defend the idea that disadvantaged groups gain advantages from descriptive representation because it enhances their substantive representation (Mansbridge 2003).

The practice of representation has also been subject to intense scrutiny within the more empirical 'women and politics' literature (Celis et al. 2008). The object of concern for these scholars has been the representation of women's substantive interests, which generally seek to document the presence of female bodies, then measure the prevalence of women's policy concerns, and interrogate the thorny question of the relation between these two (Mateo Diaz 2005: 189). This preoccupation with the 'who' and 'what' of representation has tended to generate a theoretical frame which assumes a static relation of substitution between the bodies and minds of the representatives and those of their constituents. Although the theoretical work of democratic theorists such as Young had rejected the 'logic of identity', whereby representatives are assumed to be present for their constituents and act as they would act (Young 2000: 127), this logic underpins many of the more empirical studies of women in parliament. As Childs and Krook note, the contention that women representatives seek the substantive representation of women is too often simply 'read' off from their bodies in a manner that is both essentialist and reductive (Childs and Krook 2008). For example, feminist political scientists have frequently made appeal to the notion of 'critical mass' to suggest that higher levels of descriptive representation (more women in parliaments) will generate better levels of substantive representation (greater legislative attention to women's issues).

Constitutive Representation: How the Substantive Representation of Women Occurs

Recent feminist scholarship has begun to reclaim the more relational focus of the theoretical articulations of the politics of difference, and explore *how* the substantive representation of women occurs. Deliberative theories of representation have recently emerged within feminist democratic theory, depicting the 'represented' in a more active light, authorizing, communicating, evaluating. Representation here becomes a form of participation. In Young's account, for example, representation is a cycle of anticipation and recollection between constituents and representative, and its analysis entails 'taking temporality seriously' (Young 2000: 129). The moment of authorization (via election) needs to be supplemented by a moment of accountability that entails more than simply re-authorizing via re-election. 'All existing representative democracies could be improved by additional procedures and fora through which citizens discuss with one another and with representatives their evaluation of policies representatives have supported' (Young 2000: 132). From this perspective greater 'listening and connectedness' is required, for representation is cast as a deliberative systemic process. Similarly, Mansbridge suggests that the traditional model of 'representation as promising' needs to be supplemented by a further model of representation as 'anticipatory' (Mansbridge 2003: 515). She argues that the appropriate normative criteria for judging this form of representation are systemic, in contrast to the dyadic criteria appropriate for representation by promising, and deliberative rather than aggregative. This approach is more deliberative because it requires communication between the represented and representative and depicts the represented as 'educable' by representatives, the media, opposition candidates and others who all seek to offer 'explanations' of the representatives' votes (Mansbridge 2003). This turns our attention to communication – the pursuit of knowledge about the representatives' decisions, their rationale and implications. Here representation comes to be viewed as communication or deliberation and the bifurcation between participation and representation is eroded. These recent theoretical developments provide important tools in terms of interrogating the way in which representation unfolds. Political theorists have focused their attention on articulating more deliberative models of representation, attempting to revive representative theories from the critics of deliberative and direct democrats by giving it a more communicative edge (Young 2000; Mansbridge 2003). The interest in deliberative representation reflects a growing disenchantment with aggregative politics and focuses attention on anticipation and education, exploring ways in which communicative practices might render representatives more accountable.

In addition to this development, the concept of the 'constitutive representation of gender' has been developed (Squires 2007b) to create conceptual space for the claim

that female politicians engage in representative claims-making (Saward 2010), constructing the group that they claim to represent and articulating their interests in ways
that are both enabling and constraining (Bacchi 1999). These accounts of representation also focus on representative practices, emphasizing the ways in which representation is a creative process, constituting rather than simply depicting what is seen.
For instance, the Instituto de la Mujer, the state department for women established in
Spain in 1982, used its location within the state to represent women as equal to men by
creating a 'model of Spanish womanhood' capable of taking up the opportunities of
the market (Mohammad 2005: 249). Those capable of the necessary transformation
to fit this model are brought to the fore, while those who are not are relegated to the
periphery. In this way the ideal of gender equality prescribes a particular model of
womanhood and valorizes it over others. Understanding representation as a constitutive practice turns attention away from gender as fixed categories, to the ongoing
gendering of policy and institutions (Eveline and Bacchi 2005: 502). This constitutive
theory of representation alters the nature of the relation between representative and
represented, focusing on the power relations that mutually constitute both.

Expansive Democracy: State Feminism

Meanwhile, a second development is extending our understanding of democratic
representation in another direction. An interest in extra-parliamentary representation
coincides with the emergence of complex forms of 'governance' that appear to
challenge the model of representative government with its 'simple, serial flows of
power between the represented and their representatives' (Judge 1999). Gender
scholars clearly draw our attention to the growing complexity of representative
practices in the context of multi-level governance, arguing that national representation
institutions have ceased to be the exclusive sites where the interests of women are being
represented. Given that state reconfiguration has rendered the policy-making process
more complex with the involvement of many different actors at different levels of
governance, a broadened version of representation is needed which takes into account
government performance, the institutionalized voice of women and the challenges of
accountability (Mackay 2008). Similarly, Celis *et al.* suggest that 'the focus on policy
change formulated and approved by members of parliament limits substantive
representation to one set of actors and a single site of political representation' (Celis
et al. 2008: 99). The need to address extra-parliamentary forms of representation has
focused attention on women's policy agencies, generating explorations of the impact
of women's civil society organizations and femocrats on the policy agenda (Stetson and
Mazur 1995; Outshoorn and Kantola 2007; Squires 2007a).

   In the 1980s and 1990s women's issues were introduced onto the agendas of diverse
social and political groups and institutions, and as feminist activists entered into trade
unions, political parties and state bureaucracies the women's movement increasingly
engaged with these institutions and feminist attention expanded to incorporate these
areas (Banaszak *et al.* 2003: 21). Gradually feminist activism adopted a more state-
oriented stance, and the form of political engagement adopted by gender-equality
advocates shifted from separatist autonomous groups to greater engagement with the
state (Chappell 2000a, 2002a, 2002b; Kantola 2006).

The emergence of these agencies as one of the central mechanisms for realizing women's substantive political representation created what is often called 'state feminism' and women working within women's policy agencies have come to be referred to as 'femocrats', a term coined in Australia and New Zealand in the 1980s (Franzway, Court and Connell 1989: 133). These femocrats are argued to have the potential to act as important agents for women's increased representation by facilitating the creation of a 'triangle of empowerment' between women in elected office, women's movements and appointed officials within the policy agencies (Vargas and Wieringa 1998). The first women's policy agencies emerged following the United Nations World Conference on Women in Mexico City in 1975, which recommended that governments establish agencies dedicated to promoting gender equality and improving the status and conditions of women. The need for state-based institutions charged formally with furthering women's status and gender equality has been mentioned systematically at every women's conference since and has figured prominently in UN official policy directives (Mazur 2005: 2).

Following the lead given by the 1975 United Nations Conference on Women, policy agencies were actively promoted by transnational women's groups and widely adopted by national governments throughout the late 1970s and 1980s (Chappell 2002b). By the mid-1980s 127 states had created women's policy agencies (Mazur 2005: 2). The trend to establish such agencies continued throughout the 1990s, with 165 countries operating women's policy agencies of some form by 2004. This represented a dramatic response to the 1975 recommendation, and has been widely viewed by gender-equality advocates as a significant indicator of success. Yet the emergence of these agencies also marked a 'bureaucratization of feminism', about which many feminists retain a lingering suspicion, given the women's movement's earlier tendency to focus on informal political activism. Both the feminist embrace of bureaucratization and the state embrace of women's policy concerns were as swift as they were surprising. As True and Mintrom note: 'This rapid global diffusion of a state-level bureaucratic innovation is unprecedented in the post-war era' (True and Mintrom 2001: 30).

The emergence of women's policy agencies marked a sea change in feminist political relations with the state, given that the women's movement in the 1970s and 1980s had frequently been expressly hostile to the state and repudiated formal political engagement in favour of autonomous movement activism. While early second-wave feminists focused on extending the boundaries of the 'political' by exploring heterogeneous political processes rather than formal political institutions, the apparent receptiveness of many liberal democratic states to demands for women's increased participation led many feminists to believe that engagement with the state should not be viewed entirely cynically as inevitably entailing co-option. However, not all feminists supported this goal. Within advanced industrial democracies socialist feminists lobbied throughout the 1970s and 1980s within political parties for the inclusion of women's demands in their policy agendas, while radical feminists placed women's issues high on the political agenda via social movement activism. It was liberal feminists in particular who embraced the idea that women's policy agencies might pursue the interests of women within the state. The women's movement in all its diverse manifestations remained ambivalent about the desirability of women's policy agencies, which seemed to signify an alignment between feminist demands and a liberal pluralist view of the state, in which women are understood to constitute a potentially unitary group whose interests can be extended through the state (Franzway *et al.* 1989: 140). The bureaucratization of feminism was therefore viewed from the outset as both a significant achievement and a source of concern: providing greater access to decision making, but potentially entailing co-option and depoliticization. Sensitive to these tensions, many liberal and socialist feminists nonetheless decided to push for the increased representation of women's affairs in decision-making, aiming to gain access to policy-making power structures (Franzway *et al.* 1989). While this has at times been viewed as a capitulation to reformist politics in developed countries, women's movement demands for women's policy agencies within developing countries have usually been framed by wider demands for regime change and democratization, with women's entry into the state being represented as a means of securing greater transparency and good governance (Alvarez 1999; Baldez 2002).

There is debate as to whether women's policy agencies perform a representative function. Weldon suggests that women's policy agencies and women's movements together are more effective than large numbers of women in the legislature at securing policy action, whereas Anne-Marie Goetz argues that 'it is muddled thinking' to expect women's policy agencies to be accountable to women's movements, for they are directly accountable, like all other bureaucratic units, to the elected government (Goetz 2005: 6). She suggests that to hold policy agencies directly accountable to the women's movement is to expect women's policy agencies to perform a 'representative function even though the staff and leadership of these agencies are not directly elected' (Goetz 2005: 6). How one might determine what is to count as a democratically acceptable mechanism of authorization and accountability once we step beyond the parliamentary process is one of the central issues currently confronting feminist democratic theory.

More recently, the fragmentation of the women's movement and restructuring of the state both have profound implications for the ability of women's policy agencies to represent women and women's issues within state bureaucracies. The representative function of women's policy agencies is challenged given that both the constituency which they aim to represent and the institution that they hope to influence have been rendered more complex than early models of state feminism anticipated (Outshoorn and Kantola 2007). Throughout the 1980s and 1990s the state has 'reshaped, relocated and rearticulated its formal powers and policy responsibilities' (Banaszak *et al.* 2003: 4). Though the process of state reconfiguration has been highly differentiated, Banaszak *et al.* outline four key features, which they label uploading, downloading, lateral loading and off-loading. Uploading describes the process of state authority shifting up to supranational organizations such as the EU, whereby individual member states have transferred formal decision-making competences in specific policy areas to the regional body. Downloading, by contrast, describes the process of state authority shifting down to sub-state bodies such as the newly established Scottish Parliament. These two processes represent a 'vertical reconfiguration' of the state (Banaszak *et al.* 2003: 4). Horizontal reconfiguration of the state also occurs in the form of lateral loading, whereby power shifts across state spheres, from elected bodies to the courts or executive agencies of government. Off-loading describes the process by which traditional state responsibilities shift to civil society organizations, including the market, family and community. Traditional neo-corporatist arrangements, which gave privileged state access to some industries and trade unions, have been replaced by 'partnerships' that provide new political opportunities to a diverse range of groups.

These reconfiguration processes are crucial for women's movements insofar as they provide both negative and positive opportunities that differ fundamentally from the state context that women's movements faced in the 1960s and early 1970s. Firstly, downloading state powers in the form of devolution has given some feminists opportunities for engaging in constitutional design, helping to shape new state structures in the making (Mackay 2008), and augmenting the recent focus on the representative and administrative branches of the state with an increased interest in the constitutional (Waylen 2008). Secondly, uploading state powers to regional and international bodies has increased women's opportunities to use supra-state institutions to put pressure on the state to increase women's representation, encouraging the development of transnational NGO activism. Thirdly, off-loading state powers to civil society organizations, which leads to the use of 'partnerships' in policy-making and implementation, gives feminist NGOs new responsibilities and powers (Newman 2001).

Various forms of state off-loading have empowered certain feminist NGOs, further fragmenting the women's movement by creating a growing disjuncture between those groups that work with the state and those that do not. But, perhaps more significantly still, some forms of off-loading threaten to replace the problematic – but democratic – process of group representation with a more bureaucratic process in which the technical pursuit of 'gender equality' becomes disentangled from the political process of defining its nature. For example, states seeking gender advice and knowledge increasingly contract NGOs to provide research on indicators of gender inequality, or evaluate the effectiveness of policy outcomes. With the growth in new public management (introducing private-sector techniques of governance into the public sector) there has been a notable tendency to devalue in-house policy expertise in favour of contracting out. Feminist NGOs are therefore increasingly involved in gender policy assessments, project execution and social services delivery (Alvarez 1999: 182): 'the perfect sites to channel international funds now seeking alternatives to the state', feminist organizations become 'entangled with the development apparatus and neoliberal policies, and even financially dependent on them for this subsistence' (Mendoza 2002: 308). In this way NGOs have become professionalized technical experts, in a contractual relationship to the state, rather than autonomous organizations advocating political change.

Although much of the financial support for NGOs in the developing countries comes from private donors and bilateral and multilateral agencies keen to promote a thriving civil society, the criteria for determining which NGOs will be consulted rarely entails considerations relating to their ability to mediate with civil society constituencies, usually focusing on more technical criteria, and privileging those NGOs deemed politically trustworthy (Alvarez 1999: 193, 198). These processes have given the NGOs better access to state policy-making, but also increased their distance from more movement-oriented activities. Given that their role as gender experts frequently entails advising on or carrying out government women's programmes, the boundary between the policy community and appointed officials is blurred and the space for contestatory politics is lost to more technical endeavours. While many of the actors in these NGOs initially negotiated both technical expertise and critical advocacy roles, their involvement in the former has increasingly been bought at the expense of the latter.

Cosmopolitan Democracy: Transnational Activism

One cannot understand the creation of women's policy agencies by nearly every democratic state around the globe within the space of just three decades without reference to the transnational networking among feminist actors, facilitated by the preparations for the four UN women's conferences. These conferences, held in Mexico City (1975), Copenhagen (1980), Nairobi (1985) and Beijing (1995), brought thousands of women together from around the world (True 2003: 377), fostering a rapid increase in the number of women's international non-governmental organizations (INGOs) and facilitating the development of new gender-equality policy networks. The activities of women's transnational social movements, coupled with the work of the UN's own women's policy agencies, the Commission on the Status of Women (CSW) and the Division of the Advancement of Women (DAW), have secured the global creation of women's policy agencies on a state level. The key achievement here was the ability of women's transnational social movements to secure a commitment to the creation of women's policy agencies as an international norm associated with good governance.

In addition to the turn to the state, the informal local organizational structures of 1970s feminism were gradually augmented by activism beyond the borders of nation-states, making strategic use of global communication technologies and the United Nations women's world conferences to network on an international level (Mendoza 2002: 296). Feminists pursuing gender-equality goals have made extensive use of transnational links, using the support of international organizations and other (often more powerful) states to put pressure on their own government, in what is known as the 'boomerang effect' (Keck and Sikkink 1998). International treaty commitments have been widely deployed by transnational and local activists to pressurize national governments to conform to international norms by improving national institutional support for the advancement of women. As Walby notes, 'Feminist political activists have been important players in the construction of a newly globalized world' (Walby 2002: 549). Feminists have also used transnational networks to learn from local struggles elsewhere in the world and to benefit from the organizational support offered by transnational feminist activists. Egalitarian activists have used non-governmental forums to share ideas and expertise, thereby developing a transnational leadership cadre that promotes international learning among gender-equality activists. These developments facilitate the creation of new spaces and institutions in which egalitarian aspirations can be affirmed, and so offers new political opportunities that feminists have been quick to exploit. As a result of these developments, state feminism and transnational feminism have emerged as important complements to the social movement feminism that characterized the 1970s. The women's movement has pursued its goals by using intergovernmental institutions and transnational conferences to put pressure on national governments to introduce legislative changes and institutional reforms. While the diversification in the sites and modes of engagement led inevitably to the fragmentation of the movement, causing many commentators to suggest that feminism is in abeyance, the gains secured at the state and transnational levels suggest that this development should not be understood as a decline in feminist activism, but rather as a change in the repertoire and form that it takes.

Conclusion

The debates outlined above show the extent to which feminist theory is closely connected to practice. In other branches of democratic theory there is a growing perception that normative political theory needs to rethink its mode of operation, and engage more directly in empirical enquiry if it is to remain truly relevant to the challenges that we now face. It has been argued that there is a 'dismal disconnection between theoretical Endeavour and empirical investigation' (Stears 2005: 326). The historically close connection between feminist scholarship and activism, the commitment to normative goals and political change, and the attention paid by feminists to the epistemic issues surrounding empirical inquiry, knowledge production and expertise all work to ensure that this is not the case in relation to feminist democratic analysis.

The emphasis of early second-wave feminism on informal grassroots democratic practices has done much to draw attention, in both theory and practice, to the limitations of defining politics too narrowly and locating democratic practice within the formal institutions only. The democratization of everyday life has come to be seen as a central requirement for the realization of active democratic participation for all. The more recent turn within feminist theory towards consideration about the mechanisms for realizing full participation within the formal institutions of politics is now focusing attention on the equally significant issue of democratization of the representative system itself. These two developments combined highlight the democratic significance of ensuring the active participation of all social groups in the various decision-making bodies of the polity. The current reflections on mechanisms of fair representation invigorate existing democratic theory and suggest new, more inclusive, forms of democratic practice.

Further Reading

Outshoorn J. and Kantola, J. (eds) 2007: *Changing State Feminism*. Basingstoke: Palgrave.
Phillips, A. 1991: *Engendering Democracy*. Cambridge: Polity Press.
Squires, J. 2007: *The New Politics of Gender Equality*. Basingstoke: Palgrave.
Young, I. 2000: *Inclusion and Democracy*. Oxford: Oxford University Press.

42

Democracy and Capitalism in the Wake of the Financial Crisis

Colin Crouch

There have now been two successive policy regimes since the Second World War that have temporarily succeeded in reconciling the uncertainties and instabilities of a capitalist economy with democracy's need for stability for people's lives and capitalism's own need for confident mass consumers. The first of these was the system of public demand management generally known as Keynesianism. The second was not, as has often been thought, a neoliberal turn to pure markets, but a system of markets alongside extensive housing and other debt among low- and medium-income people linked to unregulated derivatives markets. It was a form of privatized Keynesianism. This combination reconciled capitalism's problem, but in a way that eventually proved unsustainable. After its collapse there is debate over what will succeed it. Most likely is an attempt to re-create it on a basis of corporate social responsibility – a theme that is also more generally reshaping the relationship of business to democratic politics.

Following the fall of communism at the end of the twentieth century it became common to equate capitalism with democracy (Fukuyama 1992). The equation was strengthened by a growing preference of governments in the United States for the regimes they supported in Latin America and to a lesser extent the Arab world to submit themselves to periodic re-election. The spread of markets, giving consumers freedom of choice in the market, seemed to go alongside the spread of voting procedures giving citizens choice in the polity. Further, because dictatorships involved 'big government', democracy was considered to produce polities within which citizens would ask governments to do less and, by implication, markets to do more.

The Wiley-Blackwell Companion to Political Sociology, First Edition. Edited by Edwin Amenta, Kate Nash, and Alan Scott.
© 2012 Blackwell Publishing Ltd. Published 2012 by Blackwell Publishing Ltd.

This was a very different perspective from that of capitalist thinkers of the nineteenth century, for whom there was a fundamental distinction between liberalism and democracy. By liberalism they understood a polity of free and open debate, with government strictly answerable to an electorate of citizens, but with citizenship limited to men owning property above some specified level. North (1990) has shown how it was precisely political regimes based on such restricted citizenship that had produced the legal basis of market capitalism in the eighteenth century. In fact, the property-owning elite of that period had come from an even more restricted land-owning oligarchy than envisaged by nineteenth-century thinkers. As North points out, the rules of the market depend primarily on the protection of property rights. In the first instance this protection was against the king or other sovereign political power, which had to be persuaded not to interfere with property rights or restrict trade by granting monopolies (Wensley 2009). But equally, and during the course of the nineteenth century increasingly, property owners sought defence from interference in their rights by the propertyless masses. Democracy was the potential enemy of the capitalist economy. As political movements representing the industrial working class gravitated towards Marxist ideas, these fears became very real. Often property owners decided that, if forced to choose between an anti-liberal regime that would still defend property rights and a liberalism that was sliding towards democracy, they would prefer the former. During the 1920s and 1930s this led many to make a further compromise, preferring the demotic anti-liberalism of fascism and Nazism, antithesis though that was to nineteenth-century liberalism, to a democracy that increasingly seemed to imply Bolshevism.

These elites could not see how mass prosperity could be achieved quickly enough to satisfy the demands of a literally hungry populace before the anger of that populace would have dismantled property rights. The more optimistic, such as the British, saw hope in a gradual simultaneous expansion of both property ownership and citizenship, the former being aided by the growing wages and stability of skilled manual workers, the increasing ranks of office workers, and phenomena like the building society movement that spread residential property ownership. But the problem was not only that workers were poor and lacked property. Their lives were also deeply insecure, as the growing market economy was subject to wide fluctuations. Early social policy, starting in Germany and gradually spreading to France, the Austrian empire, Britain and elsewhere, tried to put a basic floor under this insecurity, but its ambitions and therefore its achievements were limited.

A more substantive answer to the poverty problem came in the early twentieth century from the mass production system of manufacture associated initially with the Ford Motor Company in the United States. Technology and work organization could enhance the productivity of low-skilled workers, enabling goods to be produced more cheaply and workers' wages to rise, so that they could afford more goods. The mass consumer and mass producer arrived together. It is significant that the breakthrough occurred in the large country that came closest to a basic idea of democracy (albeit on a racial basis) during that period. Democracy as well as technology contributed to construction of the model. However, as the Wall Street crash of 1929, coming just a few years after the launch of the Fordist model, showed, the issue of insecurity remained just as great. The problem of reconciling the instability of the market with consumer-voters' need for stability remained unresolved. In much of Europe tendencies towards both communism and fascism were strengthened.

By the end of the Second World War it was clear to elites throughout the then industrializing world that the attempt to defend property from democracy through fascism had been a disaster. Capitalism and democracy would have to be interdependent, at least in those parts of the world where popular movements could not be easily resisted. The virtuous spiral of US Fordist model of mass production technology linked to rising wages and therefore to rising mass consumption and more demand for mass-produced goods was part of the answer. The more extensive approach to social policy of the kind emerging in the Scandinavian and British welfare states addressed the problem of insecurity (see Hort and Therborn, Chapter 32, in this volume). Confident, secure working-class consumers, far from being a threat to capitalism, could enable an expansion of markets and profits on an unprecedented scale. Capitalism and democracy became interdependent. But capitalism was now becoming dependent on workers becoming confident consumers, willing to spend, while labour markets needed workers to work flexibly, accepting occasional unemployment and periods of declining incomes. The level of living at which social policy could sustain purchasing power would be below that needed to sustain an expanding, consumption-driven economy.

According to neoclassical theory the problem should be a minimal one: if markets are genuinely free, adaptation to shocks is rapid. Further, the only shocks are exogenous ones, since the constant, microscopic adjustment to endogenous changes that takes places in pure markets prevents anything like a 'shock' from developing. There were several reasons why the problem could not be resolved that way. First, markets in the postwar economy did not start from a position of 'purity'. Even if it is true that there are no endogenous shocks in a pure market, the process of achieving a pure market from a starting point in a highly impure one includes plenty of shocks. Second, while it might be assumed that the fully informed, rationally calculating actors envisaged by economic theory might appropriately discount past shocks when planning future expenditure, there are strong reasons to believe that ordinary consumers do not act that way. Their knowledge of likely futures is highly defective; their capacity to take financial risks is very low. Their most likely guide to the future is likely to be their experience of the past, and they will err on the side of risk aversion when making their judgements. The adult generations of the postwar period, with their experience of two world wars and a major world slump, were likely to be particularly risk averse.

Various approaches emerged to solving this dilemma, but one became dominant: that known as Keynesian demand management, after the British economist John Maynard Keynes. In times of recession, when confidence was low, governments would go into debt in order to stimulate the economy with their own spending. In times of inflation, when demand was excessive, they would reduce their spending, pay off their debts and reduce aggregate demand. The model implied large state budgets, to ensure that changes within them would have an adequate macro-economic effect. The new, growing welfare state provided that.

While Keynesian policies were adopted in only a few countries, they had important international effects, mainly because of the dominance of the US economy. It was US consumers, and to some extent those in the other Keynesian countries, who bought the exports of Germany and other countries with weaker domestic markets. In addition, the vast injections of Marshall Aid from the United States which benefited nearly all of non-communist Europe, and the similar assistance extended to Japan, meant that public spending – in this case another country's public spending – further stimulated these economies and maintained the security of working people's lives. Germany's own formal economic policy stance depended on balanced budgets, an autonomous central bank and a high priority on avoiding inflation. But during this period the German economy depended for its stability, not on pure markets, but on a general Keynesian environment.

The Keynesian model protected ordinary people from the rapid fluctuations of the market that had brought instability to their lives, smoothing the trade cycle and enabling them gradually to become confident mass consumers of the products of a therefore equally confident mass production industry. Unemployment was reduced to very low levels. The welfare state not only provided instruments of demand management for governments, but also brought real services in areas of major importance to people outside the framework of the market: more stability. Arm's-length demand management plus the welfare state protected the rest of the capitalist economy from both major shocks to confidence and attacks from hostile forces, while the lives of working people were protected from the vagaries of the market. It was a true social compromise. As conservative critics pointed out from the start, there was always likely to be a ratchet effect in the mechanism: it was easy for governments to increase spending in a recession, bringing lower unemployment, more public services and more money in people's pockets. It would be far more difficult at times of boom in a democracy to reverse these trends. This was the seed of destruction at the heart of the model. Keynesian economies were highly vulnerable to the inflationary shocks unleashed by the general rise in commodity prices during the 1970s, particularly the oil price rises of 1973 and 1978 (Crouch 1993: ch. 7). The wave of inflation that then affected the advanced countries of the West, though nothing like what had been experienced in Germany in the 1920s, or in various parts of Latin America and Africa more recently, more or less destroyed the model – though with different responses depending on different experiences with the Keynesian model itself.

On to Privatized Keynesianism

An intellectual challenge to Keynesianism had long been ready. The advocates of a return to 'real' markets had never ceased to be active, and a range of policies was in readiness. The key objective was to have governments withdraw from accepting overall responsibility for the economy. While for the purposes of this chapter we are concentrating on demand management, Keynesianism had become emblematic of a far wider range of policies of regulation, welfare provision and subsidy. Combined with Fordist production systems, the model now appears to characterize a particular historical period and a stage in the development of capitalism, or a distinctive accumulation regime (Boyer 2004a, 2004b, 2005). Seen from one perspective (Giddens 1998) it was suited to a mass industrial working class producing standardized goods and accepting standardized government and welfare services. But that class was now declining in size and importance as employment in advanced economies became increasingly concentrated in services. The period when political stability depended on a coincidence between the interests of the industrial working class in the global northwest and capitalism was coming to an end, quite apart from the inflationary crisis. But the crisis provided the historical moment for transition to a new economic model. Within a decade or so, such ideas as the absolute priority of near-zero inflation at whatever cost in terms of unemployment, the withdrawal of state assistance to firms and industries in difficulties, the priority of competition, the predominance of a shareholder maximization as opposed to a multiple stakeholder model of the corporation, the deregulation of markets and the liberalization of global capital flows had become orthodoxy. Where governments in countries with weak economies were unwilling to accept them, they were imposed as conditions for assistance from or membership of such international bodies as the International Monetary Fund (IMF), the World Bank, the Organization for Economic Co-operation and Development (OECD) or the European Union. When the Soviet Union collapsed in 1989, the more westerly of its former allies were brought within the scope of the new model through the assistance offered by these international organizations.

A further change that had taken place in the meantime was the declining autonomy of the nation-state. The postwar political economy had been founded on the basis of governments that could exercise considerable discretion in how they managed their economies. By the 1980s the process generally known as globalization, both a producer and a product of the deregulation of financial markets, had eroded much of that autonomy. The only actors capable of rapid action at global level were transnational corporations (TNCs), which preferred their own private regulation to that by governments. This both advanced and even rendered necessary the new model – even though tensions remained and remain unresolved as to how market-dominant oligopolistic corporations could be consistent with the concept of regulation by near-perfect markets.

Just as a class – that of industrial workers – can be seen as the bearers of the Keynesian model, the class of finance capitalists, geographically grounded primarily in the United States and the UK but extending across the globe, embodied the new one. Whereas the tight labour markets and regulated capitalism of the Keynesian period had seen a gradual reduction in inequalities of wealth in all advanced countries, the following period was to see a reversal of these trends (OECD 2009), with the highest rewards going to those working in financial institutions.

However, in democratic countries capitalism remained dependent on mass con-sumption. If labour markets and workers' incomes were to become increasingly flexible, the old puzzle of capitalism's paradoxical need for confident consumers but insecure workers would return. Two developments came together to rescue the neoliberal model from the instability that would otherwise have been its fate: the growth of credit markets for poor and middle-income people, and of derivatives and futures markets among the very wealthy. This combination produced a model of privatized Keynesianism (Bellofiore and Halevi 2009; Crouch 2008, 2009) that occurred initially by chance, a real case of market entrepreneurship, but which gradually became a matter for public policy so important as to threaten the entire neoliberal project. Instead of governments taking on debt to stimulate the economy, individuals did so. In addition to the housing market there was an extraordinary growth in opportunities for bank loans and credit cards.

This explains the great puzzle of the period: how did moderately paid American workers in particular, who have little legal security against instant dismissal from their jobs, and salaries that might remain static for several years, maintain consumer confidence, when continental European workers with more or less secure jobs and annually rising incomes were bringing their economies to a halt by their unwillingness to spend? US, British and, in particular, Irish (Hay 2008) house prices were rising every year; the proportion of the value of the house on which a loan could be raised was also rising until it reached more than 100%; credit-card possibilities were growing. With some exceptions, European property values remained stable. Mortgage, credit-card and other debt held by people in the bottom 40% of the income distribution reached considerably higher levels in the Anglo-American economies than in typical continental European ones, though mortgage debt was also high in the Scandinavian countries, especially Denmark (Crouch 2011a). Bohle (2009) also describes how Austrian and Swedish banks brought unsecured mortgages to, respectively, Hungary and Latvia, making possible short-lived consumption-led booms.

Neoliberal anti-inflationary policy bears down on the prices of goods and services that lose their value as they are consumed. Producers of food, material goods and services like restaurants or health centres confront an environment hostile to rises in their prices. This is not the case with assets, non-consumables that keep their value after purchase: real property, financial holdings, and many art objects. A rise in their price is simultaneously a rise in their value, and does not contribute to inflation. Assets, and earnings based on assets, have not been the objects of neoliberal counter-inflation policy. Therefore, anything that could be switched from earnings derived from the sale of normal goods and services to an asset base did very well. This applied to proportions of salaries paid as share options and to spending funded by extended mortgages based on property values rather than by salaries and wages. Eventually governments, especially British ones, began to incorporate privatized Keynesianism into their public policy thinking, though the phrase did not occur to them. While a reduction in the price of oil would be seen as good news (because it reduced inflationary pressure), a reduction in the price of houses would be seen as a disaster (as it would undermine confidence in debt), and government would be expected to act through fiscal or other measures to get house prices rising again.

Most of this housing and consumer debt was necessarily unsecured; that was the only way in which privatized Keynesianism could have the same countercyclical stimulant effect as the original variety. Prudential borrowing against specified collateral would not have helped the moderate-income groups who had to keep spending despite the insecurity of their labour market positions. The possibility of prolonged, widespread unsecured debt was in turn made possible through innovations that had taken place in financial markets, innovations that for a long time had seemed to be an excellent example of how, left to themselves, market actors find creative solutions. Through markets in derivatives and futures the great finance houses learned how to trade in risk. They found they could buy and sell risky holdings provided only that purchasers were confident that they could find further purchasers in turn; and that depended on the same confidence. Provided markets were free from regulation and capable of extensive reach, these trades enabled a very widespread sharing of risk, which made it possible for people to invest in many ventures that would otherwise have seemed unwise. Meanwhile, the liberation of global finance markets brought funds located in ever more extended parts of the world to share the burdens of risk bearing.

An inability to share risks widely had been at the heart of the economic collapses of 1929 and the 1870s. In the 1940s it had seemed that only state action could solve this problem for the market. But now, absolutely in tune with neoliberal ideology and expectations, there was a market solution. And, through the links of these new risk markets to ordinary consumers via extended mortgages and credit-card debt, the dependence of the capitalist system on rising wages, a welfare state and government demand management that had seemed essential for mass consumer confidence had been abolished. The bases of prosperity shifted from the social democratic formula of working classes supported by government intervention to the neoliberal conservative one of banks, stock exchanges and financial markets. This fundamental political shift was more profound than anything that could be produced by alternations between nominally social democratic and neoliberal conservative parties in government as the result of democratic elections.

After Privatized Keynesianism: The Responsible Corporation?

But, just as the Keynesian period lasted 30 years from the mid-1940s to the mid-1970s, so the new model underwent a crisis almost exactly 30 years further on. All theories of market economics depend on the assumption that market actors are perfectly informed, but privatized Keynesianism encouraged stock traders to develop forms of knowledge that encouraged self-destructive decisions. Bad debts were funding bad debts, and so on in an exponentially growing mountain. (For good accounts of this process, see Froud *et al.* 2004; Wolf 2008). While in principle the values of assets traded in secondary markets are based on the original monetary values of the assets being purchased, in practice they became totally detached from them. Discovering exactly what was contained in a bundle of mortgage and other debts that had been purchased would take time, and time was a highly expensive resource when earnings depended heavily on the velocity with which one could make transactions. Further, risks were being so widely shared that it seemed that little was at stake in any individual transaction. No-one had an incentive to take note of the values that assets might possess in the 'real' economy. In an additional twist, information technology (IT), which was supposed to have made it so much easier for market traders to gain information on a global basis, intensified the premium being placed on ignorance. By making transactions so much faster to implement, IT raised the opportunity cost of any detailed searches for complex information, like the composition of a bundle of risks that one was deciding to acquire in a rapidly changing market.

Eventually the ratings agencies, the market's own solution to certifying the quality of financial institutions and indeed national economies, seem to have followed the same path. Aware that the traders in the markets who were using the ratings were not interested in substantive knowledge about some 'real' value of assets, they also followed the judgement of the secondary markets themselves about the trading value of assets, making a mechanism used for verification dependent for its own information on the activities that they were verifying. Another major step took place when, through the centrality of US stock exchanges, the accounting principles of most major trading countries in the world were pressured into following Anglophone approaches to accountancy. These privileged the interests of financial market operators over those of protecting creditors (Botzem and Quack 2006).

Not surprisingly, therefore, when the secondary markets collapsed no-one had any idea of exactly how much money had been lost or where it had gone. If the only information that counts is totally reflexive and cannot be validated outside of itself, then information cannot play the role that the market needs it to play. But for so many years no-one holding power within or over the system paid any attention this, despite the strong warning that had been sounded only a few years before when the dot.com bubble burst. Here too, asset values had become totally based on an almost infinite regress of expectations of value, gradually losing all touch with what the actual products of Internet-based firms might be.

Some people became extremely wealthy in the process, but this does not mean that they were parasites; very many people benefited from the growing purchasing power that this system generated. Once privatized Keynesianism had become a model of general economic importance, it became a kind of collective good, however nested in private actions it was. Necessary to it was behaviour by banks that has to be defined as irresponsible, as it involved their not carrying out checks and accountancy practices that they were in principle assumed to do. Therefore *that very irresponsibility became a collective good*. There has been considerable discussion of the serious moral hazards involved in governments coming to the aid of banks that have suffered from this irresponsibility; but there is a far wider moral hazard involved in this complicity of virtually whole societies in the irresponsible practices in the first place.

What Next?

And so a second regime to reconcile democracy and stable mass consumption with the market economy ended. Both Keynesianism and its privatized mutant each lasted 30 years. Given the rapidly changing character of capitalist economies, and the absence of any ultimate solution to their need to combine flexible labour and confident consumer, that probably counts as considerable durability. But the question arises: How are capitalism and democracy to be reconciled now? Also, how will the enormous moral hazard established by governments' recognition of financial irresponsibility as a collective good now be managed?

Economic prosperity continues to depend on supplies of capital through efficient markets far more than it previously depended on the industrial workers of the Western world. A difference of geographical reach is part of the explanation. The decline of the Western industrial working class does not mean a decline in that class globally. More people are engaged in manufacturing activities today than ever before; but they are divided into national, or at best world regional, lumps with very different histories, cultures, levels of living, organized interests, and trajectories. Finance capital does not come in such parcels but more like a liquid or gas, capable of changing shape and flowing across jurisdictions and regions. We remain dependent on both labour and capital, but the former is subject to *divide et imperia*, the latter is not – unless we see a major return to economic nationalism and limitations on capital movements that will lead to the break-up of the major corporations that dominate the global economy and probable major economic decline.

The most likely new model is one that in fact depends increasingly on those corporations; the logic of globalization that imparted an important role to TNCs has not disappeared with the financial system (Crouch 2011b). There has always been a tension at the centre of neoliberalism: is it about markets or about giant firms? They are far from being the same: the more that a sector is dominated by giant firms, the less it resembles the pure market that in principle lies behind nearly most of today's public policy. There may well be intense competition among giant firms, but it is not the competition of the pure market. This is supposed to be characterized by very large numbers of actors, such that each remains incapable of having an effect on prices by its own actions, and certainly incapable of wielding political influence. In the pure market everyone is a price taker; no-one a price maker. Neoliberalism, while it uses the rhetoric of consumer sovereignty and rule by choice expressed through the market, is underpinned by a model of the market economy that is capable of accommodating monopoly power.

While the neoliberal epoch was just beginning in the mid-1970s, economists and lawyers at the University of Chicago, the main centre for the generation of neoliberal ideology, were preparing a new doctrine of competition and monopoly that was soon to influence the US courts, undermining the old principles of anti-trust legislation that had been at the heart of US and, more recently, European competition law (Amato 1997; Cucinotta, Pardolesi and Van Den Bergh 2002).

It was not necessary, the doctrine argued, for there to be actual competition for customer welfare to be maximized. Sometimes a monopoly, by its very domination of the market, can offer customers a better deal than a number of competing firms (Bork 1978; Posner 2001). This is not the place to examine the merits of this argument in detail. It is necessary only to understand that neoliberalism does not share the difficulty that neoclassical economics has within market domination and monopoly capitalism. The recent banking crisis has seen governments supporting, and gaining the support of competition authorities for, mergers and acquisitions that considerably reduce competition and choice. This remains consistent with dominant interpretations of neoliberalism, which are in reality more concerned with the firm than with the market.

Governments are being presented with a dilemma: on the one hand, they face public demands for increased regulation of banks' conduct in the wake of the crisis. On the other, they want them to return to that conduct, as low- and medium-wage workers in insecure neoliberal labour markets will not be able to sustain the consumption levels that the economy needs unless they have access to unsecured credit. There will be a gradual slip away from the initially tough, post-crisis regulatory stance towards a negotiated, voluntary regulatory system policed by banks themselves in informal relations with government. This will be made easier by the fact that the crisis reduced the number of major players, firms with easy access to governments and often shaped by governments themselves as they negotiated mergers during the course of the 2008 rescue packages. Governments that acquired banks in the bout of unforeseen and temporary nationalization that followed the October 2008 collapse will re-privatize them by levering them into the hands of a small number of leading existing firms deemed responsible enough to run them in good order. We should therefore anticipate a shift from unregulated privatized Keynesianism to self-regulated privatized Keynesianism.

The financial sector will here be following a general trend within modern economies that again reframes the relationship between capitalism and democracy. Sharing neoliberal prejudices against government as such, worried at the impact of regulation on growth and believing in the superiority of corporate directors over themselves in making judgements, politicians are coming increasingly to rely on corporate social responsibility (CSR) for the achievement of several policy goals.

Many serious political observers take little interest in CSR, seeing it as a public relations gimmick or a device for pre-empting demands for government regulation. But firms are increasingly claiming that they can address very serious issues through their CSR strategies: pollution control, environment-friendly sourcing, the treatment of labour in global supply chains, even the spread of HIV-AIDS in Africa resulting from the operations of global logistics firms. This activity has to be distinguished from corporate philanthropy, in which firms use some of their profits to fund 'good causes' unrelated to their business activities. Under CSR they claim to tackle negative consequences flowing directly from these activities but which do not enter into their normal market calculations – what economists call 'externalities'. This is starting to be taken seriously as a socio-political phenomenon (Campbell 2007; Crouch 2006; Néron 2010; Sabel, Fung and Karkainen 1999; Vogel 2008). Some observers even speak of firms as citizens or as administrators of citizenship rights (Crane, Matten and Moon 2008). The United Nations has launched its own CSR project, called The Global Compact (Rasche and Kell 2010; Ruggie 2007, 2009).

Banks asserting that they can guarantee responsible behaviour in secondary markets constitute an addition to the list of the scope of CSR. In affirming that they can take on these challenges, corporations dispense with their normal defence in a market economy: 'We are only here to make a profit; we operate only within the market; it is not our job, but that of government, to take account of wider social concerns.' Instead they claim that they can make a better job of looking after social concerns than government. Although the Chicago defenders of the giant firm mentioned above did not have this in mind at all, it is a logical consequence of the change in economic thinking that they launched, which sees the giant corporation rather than the perfect market as the epitome of capitalism.

While it is beyond our scope here to track it in detail, this set of changes can be set alongside another: the growing tendency for governments to contract the delivery of public services to private firms. In theory, government departments are here the principals and the firms only the agents in a contract relationship, a distinction that represents the difference between policy-making and policy implementation. However, in any complex contract the agent influences the ideas of the principal, as the former acquires knowledge of the tasks and develops its own preferences. It is doubtful that any complex contract could be delivered efficiently and knowledgeably if the principal–agent distinction were perfectly respected. But in the case of the privatized contracting out of public services this has an important political implication. Contracting firms become, in part, public policy-makers.

Through both extended CSR and public service contracting, modern 'Chicago' giant corporations have ceased to be pure market participants and have become political actors, ending the sharp separation between governments and private firms that has long been considered fundamental to the liberal market economy. These developments have radical implications for the relationship between capitalism and democracy. Capitalism is becoming less and less legitimated in terms of the market, freedom of choice and an absence of government involvement. Rather, there is a public policy partnership between government and firms, or even autonomous actions by firms commended by governments.

But there is then an interesting twist, as this process represents a considerable enhancement of current trends towards a displacement of oppositional political activity from parties to civil society organizations and social movements. Governments of all parties have to make similar deals with corporations, fearing equally and irrespectively of their ideological preferences for their country's ability to attract liquid capital if they are too demanding of them, and so differences among parties on core economic policies shrink. Party politics, and therefore formal democracy as we understand it, still has much with which to concern itself: the relative share of public spending; questions of multiculturalism; security. But it vacates the former heartland of basic economic strategy. This space is then occupied by a range of civil society activist groups – environmentalists, defenders of workers' rights, general opponents of large concentrations of power – critical of corporate behaviour. It is already the case that for nearly every major corporation there is a Web site revealing details of its conduct, assessing its fulfilment of its social responsibility claims. More directly threatening to firms is the danger that behaviour on their part that is seen as irresponsible will be viewed negatively by customers; shopping can even become a form of political action (Hertz 2001).

This new politics has the major advantage that it will not be so trapped at the nation-state level as party politics; many of these groups are transnational (Spini 2006). From a democratic perspective it is, however, an unsatisfactory politics, as it lacks the formal citizenship egalitarianism of electoral democracy, while retaining many of the bad habits of parties. Activist groups – or citizens' initiatives to give them their more useful German name (*Bürgerinitiativen*) – are just as capable as are parties of seeking attention with exaggerated claims or (in contrast) developing friendly relations with corporations in exchange for various resources. The struggle between them and the corporations is also highly unequal. The new social movements and civil society organizations, important as they will be to twenty-first-century politics, do not constitute a rising new class that stands for a general social interest. They are not a functional interest; they are not deeply rooted within the social structure. The dominant interests of contemporary society remain the great corporations, particularly those in the financial sector. Any contender for their place as the dominant group within advanced capitalism will have to offer an equivalent centrality. In the absence of that occurring, plurality, liberalism and political vibrancy in general, though not democracy as such, in contemporary society will depend on these citizens' initiatives.

Acknowledgement

This chapter draws heavily on my 2009 article: Privatised Keynesianism: An Unacknowledged Policy Regime. *The British Journal of Politics and International Relations* 11: 382–399.

Further Reading

Davis, G.F. 2009: *Managed by the Markets: How Finance Reshaped America*. Oxford: Oxford University Press.

Finlayson, A. 2009: Financialisation, financial literacy and asset-based welfare. *British Journal of Politics and International Relations* 11(3): 400–421.

Harvey, D. 2005: *A Brief History of Neoliberalism*. Oxford: Oxford University Press.

Medema, S.G. 2009: *The Hesitant Hand: Taming Self Interest in the History of Economic Ideas*. Princeton, NJ: Princeton University Press.

Mellahi, K., Morrell, K. and Wood, G. 2010: *The Ethical Business*. London: Palgrave.

References

Aapola, S., Gonick, M. and Harris, A. 2005: *Young Femininity: Girlhood, Power and Social Change*. Basingstoke: Macmillan.

Abbott, A. 1992: From causes to events: notes on narrative positivism. *Sociological Methods and Research* 20: 428–455.

Abercrombie, N. and Turner, B.S. 1978: The dominant ideology thesis. *British Journal of Sociology* 29: 149–170.

Abrams, S. 2010: *Where Everyone Knows Your Name: A Socio-Rational Logic of Political Participation in Advanced Industrial Democracies*. PhD Dissertation, Harvard University Department of Government.

Abu-Lughod, L. 1990: The romance of resistance: tracing transformations of power through Bedouin women. *American Ethnologist* 17 (1): 41–55.

Acemoglu, D. and Robinson, J.A. 2006: *Economic Origins of Dictatorship and Democracy*. Cambridge: Cambridge University Press.

Acker, J. 1989: The problem with patriarchy. *Sociology* 23 (2): 235–240.

Ackerly, B. and Okin, S.M. 1999: Feminist social criticism and the international or movement for women's rights as human rights. In I. Shapiro and C. Hacker-Cordón (eds) *Democracy's Edge*. Cambridge: Cambridge University Press.

Adams, J.F., Samuel Merrill III and Grofman, B. 2005: *A Unified Theory of Party Competition. A Cross-National Analysis Integrating Spatial and Behavioral Factors*. Cambridge: Cambridge University Press.

Adams, J., Clemens, E.S. and Orloff, A. (eds) 2005: *Remaking Modernity: Politics, History, and Sociology*. Durham, NC: Duke University Press.

Adkins, L. 1999: Community and economy: a retraditionalization of gender? *Theory, Culture and Society* 16 (1): 119–139.

Adorno, T.W. 1991: *The Culture Industry: Selected Essays on Mass Culture*. London: Routledge.

Agamben, G. 1998: *Homo Sacer. Sovereign Power and Bare Life*. Stanford, CA: Stanford University Press.

Agamben, G. 2005: *State of Exception*. Chicago, Il.: University of Chicago Press.

Ahmed, S. 1997: 'It's a sun-tan, isn't it?' Autobiography as an identificatory practice. In H.S. Mirza (ed.) *Black British Feminism. A Reader*. London: Routledge.

The Wiley-Blackwell Companion to Political Sociology, First Edition. Edited by Edwin Amenta, Kate Nash, and Alan Scott.
© 2012 Blackwell Publishing Ltd. Published 2012 by Blackwell Publishing Ltd.

Ahrne, G. 1996: Civil society and civil organizations. *Organization* 3 (1): 109–210.

Aidukaite, J. (ed.) 2009: *Poverty, Urbanity and Social Policy: Central and Eastern Europe Compared*. New York: Nova Science.

Alber, J. 1982: *Vom Armenhaus zum Wohlfahrtstaat*. Frankfurt am Main: Campus Verlag.

Alcoff, L.M. 1999a: Philosophy and racial identity. In M. Bulmer and J. Solomos (eds) *Ethnic and Racial Studies Today*. London: Routledge.

Alcoff, L.M. 1999b: Towards a phenomenology of racial embodiment. *Radical Philosophy* 95: 15–26.

Aldrich, J. 1995: *Why Parties?* Chicago, IL: Chicago University Press.

Alesina, A. and Glaeser, E. 2004: *Fighting Poverty in Europe and the United States*. New York: Cambridge University Press.

Alexander, G. 2002: *The Sources of Democratic Consolidation*. Ithaca, NY: Cornell University Press.

Alexander, J.C. 1988: *Durkheimian Sociology: Cultural Studies*. Cambridge: Cambridge University Press.

Alexander, J.C. 1982: *Theoretical Logic in Sociology*, Vol. 2: *The Antinomies of Classical Thought: Marx and Durkheim*. Berkeley: University of California Press.

Alexander, J.C. 2000: Theorising the good society: hermeneutics, normative and empirical discourses. *Canadian Journal of Sociology* 25 (3): 271–309.

Alexander, J.C. 2006: *The Civil Sphere*. New York: Oxford University Press.

Alexander, J.C. 2010: *The Performance of Politics: Obama's Victory and the Democratic Struggle for Power*. New York: Oxford University Press.

Almond, G. and Verba, S. 1963: *The Civic Culture, Political Attitudes and Democracy in Five Nations*. Princeton, NJ: Princeton University Press.

Alpert, H. 1961 [1939]: *Emile Durkheim and His Sociology*. New York: Russell and Russell.

Alvarez, S. 1999: Advocating feminism: the Latin American NGO boom. *International Feminist Journal of Politics* 1 (2): 181–209.

Amato, G. 1997: *Antitrust and the Bounds of Power*. Oxford: Hart.

Amenta, E. 1991: Making the most of a case study: theories of the welfare state and the American experience. *International Journal of Comparative Sociology* 32: 172–194.

Amenta, E. 1998: *Bold Relief: Institutional Politics and the Origins of Modern American Social Policy*. Princeton, NJ: Princeton University Press.

Amenta, E. 2003: What we know about the development of social policy: comparative and historical research in comparative and historical perspective. In D. Rueschemeyer and J. Mahoney (eds) *Comparative Historical Analysis in the Social Sciences*. New York: Cambridge University Press.

Amenta, E. 2005: State-centered and political institutionalist theory: retrospect and prospect. In T. Janoski, R. Alford, A. Hicks and Schwartz, M. (eds) *Handbook of Political Sociology: States, Civil Societies, and Globalization*. New York: Cambridge University Press.

Amenta, E. Caren, N. and Olasky, S.J. 2005: Age for leisure? Political mediation and the impact of the Pension Movement on old-age policy. *American Sociological Review* 70: 516–538.

Amenta, E. 2006: *When Movements Matter: The Townsend Plan and the Rise of Social Security*. Princeton, NJ: Princeton University Press.

Amenta, E. 2009: Making the most of an historical case study: configuration, sequence, casing, and the US old-age pension movement. In C.C. Ragin and D. Byrne (eds) *The Handbook of Case-Oriented Methods*. Thousand Oaks, CA: Sage.

Amenta, E. and Ramsey, K.M. 2010: Institutional theory. In K.T. Leicht and J. C. Jenkins (eds) *The Handbook of Politics: State and Civil Society in Global Perspective*. New York: Springer.

Amiraux, V. 2011: The challenge to Muslims' integration into the European Union: social troubles, political issues and legal questions around a racialization process. In S. Akbarzadeh (ed.) *Handbook of Political Islam*. London: Routledge.

Ammerman, N. (ed.) 2007: *Everyday Religion: Observing Modern Religious Lives*. Oxford: Oxford University Press.

Amoore, L. and De Goede, M. 2008: *Risk and the War on Terror*. London and New York: Routledge.

Anaya, S.J. 2009: *International Human Rights and Indigenous Peoples*. New York: Aspen.

Anderson, B. 1983: *Imagined Communities*. London: Verso.

Anderson, B. 1991: *Imagined Communities*, rev. edn. London: Verso.

Anderson, L.S. 2003: Constructing policy networks: social assistance reform in the Czech Republic. *International Journal of Public Administration* 26: 635–663.

Anderson, P. 1974a: *Lineages of the Absolutist State*. London: New Left Books.

Anderson, P. 1974b: *Passages from Antiquity to Feudalism*. London: New Left Books.

Andreas, P. 2009: *Border Games: Policing the U.S.–Mexico Divide,* 2nd edn. Ithaca, NY: Cornell University Press.

Andrejevic, M. 2003: *Reality TV: The Work of Being Watched*. Lanham, MD: Rowman & Littlefield.

Andvig, J.C. and Moene, K.O. 1990: How corruption may corrupt. *Journal of Economic Behaviour and Organization* 13 (1): 63–76.

Andvig, J.C., Fjeldstad. O., Amundsen, I., Sissener, T. *et al.* 2000: *Research on Corruption. A Policy Oriented Study*. Final Report commissioned by NORAD. CMI and NUPI: Bergen and Oslo, Norway.

Ang, L. 1996: *Living Room Wars: Re-Thinking Media Audiences for a Postmodern World*. London: Routledge.

Anheier, H., Glasius, M. and Kaldor, M. (eds) 2001: *The Global Civil Society Yearbook*. Oxford: Oxford University Press.

Aoki, M. 2001: *Toward a Comparative Institutional Analysis*. Cambridge, MA: MIT Press.

Appadurai, A. 2006: *Fear of Small Numbers: An Essay on the Geography of Anger*. Durham, NC: Duke University Press.

Aquinas, T. 1959: *Selected Political Writings*, ed. A.P. D'Entreves. Oxford: Blackwell.

Aradau, C. and van Munster, R. 2007: Governing terrorism through risk: taking precautions (un)knowing the future. *European Journal of International Relations* 13 (1): 89–115.

Arato, A. 1981: Civil society against the state: Poland 1980–81. *Telos* Spring 47: 23–47.

Archibugi, D. (ed.) 2003: *Debating Cosmopolitics*. London: Verso.

Archibugi, D. 2008: *The Global Commonwealth of Citizens. Toward Cosmopolitan Democracy*. Princeton, NJ: Princeton University Press.

Arendt, H. 1991: *On Revolution*. Harmondsworth: Penguin.

Aries, P. 1978: *The Hour of our Death*. Harmondsworth: Penguin.

Aristotle 1988: *The Politics*. Cambridge: Cambridge University Press.

Aron, R. 1964: *German Sociology*, trans. M. and T.B. Bottomore. Glençoe, II.: The Free Press.

Arzheimer, K. 2009: Contextual factors and the extreme right vote in Western Europe, 1980–2002. *American Journal of Political Science* 53 (2): 259–275.

Asad, T. 2003: *Formations of the Secular: Christianity, Islam, Modernity*. Stanford, CA: Stanford University Press.

Asad, T., Brown, W., Butler, J. and Mahmood, S. 2009: *Is Critique Secular? Blasphemy, Injury, and Free Speech*. The Townsend Paper in The Humanities UC Berkeley. Berkeley: University of California Press.

Ashenden, S. and Owen, D. (eds) 1999: *Foucault Contra Habermas: Recasting the Dialogue Between Genealogy and Critical Theory*. London: Sage.

Ashford, S. and Timms, N. 1992: The unchurching of Europe. In S. Ashford and N. Timms (eds) *What Europe Thinks*. Aldershot: Ashgate.

Atkinson, W. 2010: *Class, Individualisation and Late Modernity: In Search Of the Reflexive Worker*. Basingstoke: Palgrave.

Bacchi, C. 1999: *Women, Policy and Politics: The Construction of Policy Problems*. London: Sage.

Bachrach, P. and Baratz, M.S. 1963: Decisions and nondecisions: an analytical framework. *American Political Science Review* 57 (3): 632–642. Reprinted in A. Scott, K. Nash and M. A. Smith (eds) *New Critical Writings in Political Sociology*, Vol. One: *Power, State and Inequality*. Farnham: Ashgate, 2009.

Bachrach, P. and Baratz, M.S. 1975: Power and its two faces revisited: reply to Geoffrey Debnam. *American Political Science Review* 69 (3): 900–904.

Badie, B. 1999: *Un monde sans souveraineté, les états entre ruse et responsabilité*. Paris: Fayard.

Badie, B. and Birnbaum, P. 1982: *Sociologie de l'Etat*, Paris: Hachette.

Bagdikian, B.H. 1992: *The Media Monopoly*, 4th edn. Boston: Beacon.

Baker, D. and LeTendre, G. 2005: *National Differences, Global Similarities: World Culture and the Future of Schooling*. Stanford, CA: Stanford University Press.

Baker, G. 2002: Problems in the theorisation of global civil society. *Political Studies* 50 (5): 928–943.

Baldassarri, D. and Berman, P. 2007: Dynamics of political polarization. *American Sociological Review*, 72: 784–811.

Baldassarri, D. and Gelman, A. 2008: Partisans without constraint: political polarization and trends in American public opinion. *American Journal of Sociology* 114 (2): 408–446.

Baldez, L. 2002: *Why Women Protest: Women's Movements in Chile*. Cambridge: Cambridge University Press.

Baldwin, P. 1990: *The Politics of Social Solidarity – the Class Basis of the European Welfare State 1875–1975*. Cambridge: Cambridge University Press.

Baldwin, P. 2005: Beyond weak and strong: rethinking the state in comparative policy history. *Journal of Policy History* 17: 12–33.

Balibar, E. 1991: The nation form: history and ideology. In E. Balibar and I. Wallerstein (eds) *Race, Nation, Class. Ambiguous Identities*. London: Verso.

Balibar, E. 1995: *The Philosophy of Marx*. London: Verso.

Ball, S. 2003: *Class Strategies and the Education Market*. London: Falmer.

Balzacq, T., Tugba, B., Bigo, D., Guittet E.P. *et al.* 2009: Security practices. In R.A. Denemark (ed.) *The International Studies Encyclopedia*. Oxford: Wiley-Blackwell/ISA. DOI: 10.1111/b.9781444336597.2010.x.

Banaszak, L.A., Beckwith, K. and Rucht, D. 2003: When power relocates: interactive changes in women's movements and states. In L.A. Banaszak, K. Beckwith and D. Rucht (eds) *Women's Movements Facing the Reconfigured State*. New York: Cambridge University Press.

Banaszak, L., Beckwith, K. and Rucht, D. (eds) 2003: *Women's Movements Facing the Reconfigured State*. Cambridge: Cambridge University Press.

Bandelow, N.C., Schumann, D. and Widmaier, U. 2000: European governance by the emergence of a new type of package deals. *German Policy Studies* 1: 8–38.

Banfield, E.C 1958: *The Moral Basis of a Backward Society*. Glencoe, IL: The Free Press.

Banfield, E.C. 1975: Corruption as a feature of governmental organization. *Journal of Law and Economics* 18 (3): 587–605.

Banton, M. 1997: *Ethnic and Racial Consciousness*, 2nd edn. London: Longman.

Barbalet, J.M. 1988: *Citizenship: Rights, Struggle and Class Inequality*. Minneapolis: University of Minnesota Press.

Barber, B. 1996: *Jihad vs. McWorld: Terrorism's Challenge to Democracy*. New York: Ballantine Books.

Barkawi, T. 2005: *Globalization and War*. Lanham, MD: Rowman & Littlefield.

Barker, F. 1984: *The Tremulous Private Body. Essays in Subjection*. London: Methuen.

Barker, R.S. 2001: *Legitimating Identities: The Self-Presentation of Rulers and Subjects*. Cambridge: Cambridge University Press.

Barker, V. 2006: The politics of punishing: building a state governance theory of American imprisonment variation. *Punishment and Society* 8: 5–32.

Barker, V. 2009: *The Politics of Imprisonment*. Oxford: Oxford University Press.

Barrett, D. and Kurzman, C. 2004: Globalizing social movement theory: the case of eugenics. *Theory and Society* 33: 487–527.

Barrow, C.W. 1993: *Critical Theories of the State: Marxist, neo-Marxist, post-Marxist*. Madison: University of Wisconsin Press.

Barry, A., Osborne, T. and Rose, N. (eds) 1996: *Foucault and Political Reason: Liberalism, Neo-liberalism and Rationalities of Government*. Chicago, IL: University of Chicago Press.

Barry, B.M. 1970: *Sociologists, Economists and Democracy*. Basingstoke: Macmillan.

Barry, B.M. 2001: *Culture and Equality. An Egalitarian Critique of Multiculturalism*. Cambridge: Polity Press.

Bartels, L. 2008: *Unequal Democracy*. New York: Russell Sage Foundation.

Barth, F. 1969: *Ethnic Groups and Boundaries. The Social Organization of Culture and Difference*. Oslo: Universitetsforlaget.

Barth, F. 1994: Enduring and emerging issues in the analysis of ethnicity. In H. Vermeulen and C. Govers (eds) *The Anthropology of Ethnicity: Beyond 'Ethnic Groups and Boundaries'*. Amsterdam: het Spinhuis.

Bartolini, S. and Mair, P. 1990: *Identity, Competition and Electoral Availability: The Stabilisation of European Electorates, 1885–1985*. New York: Cambridge University Press.

Barzel, Y. 2002: *A Theory of the State: Economic Rights, Legal Rights, and the Scope of the State*. Cambridge: Cambridge University Press.

Basch, L., Glick Schiller, N. and Szanton Blanc, C. 1994: *Nations Unbound: Transnational Projects, Postcolonial Predicaments, and Deterritorialized Nation-States*. Langhorne, PA: Gordon and Breach.

Bataille, G. 1985: *Visions of Excess*. Manchester: Manchester University Press.

Baudrillard, J. 1998: *The Consumer Society*. London: Sage.

Bauman, Z. 1999: *In Search of Politics*. Cambridge: Polity Press.

Baumgartner, F.R. and Jones, B.D. 1993: *Agendas and Instability in American Politics*. Chicago, IL: University of Chicago Press.

Baumgartner, F.R. and Leech, B.L. 1998: *Basic Interests: The Importance of Groups in Politics and in Political Science*. Princeton, NJ: Princeton University Press.

Baumgartner, F.R. and Leech, B.L. 2001: Interest niches and policy bandwagons: patterns of interest group involvement in national politics. *Journal of Politics* 63: 1191–1213.

Baumgartner, F.R., Gray, V. and Lowery, D. 2009: Congressional influence on state lobbying activity. *Political Research Quarterly* 62: 552–567.

Beaman, L. 2008: Defining religion: the promise and the peril of legal interpretation. In R. Moon (ed.) *Law and Religious Pluralism in Canada*. Vancouver: University of British Columbia Press.

Beck, U. 1992: *Risk Society*. London: Sage.

Beck, U. 2003: The silence of words: on terror and war. *Security Dialogue* 34 (3): 255–267.

Beck, U. 2005: *The Cosmopolitan Vision*. Cambridge: Polity Press.

Beck, U. 2006: *Power in the Global Age*, Cambridge: Polity Press.

Beck, U. 2007: Beyond class and nation: reframing social inequalities in a globalizing world. *British Journal of Sociology* 58: 679–705.

Beck, U. and Grande, E. 2007: *Cosmopolitan Europe*. Cambridge: Polity Press.

Beck, U. and Sznaider, N. 2006: Unpacking cosmopolitanism for the social sciences: a research agenda. *The British Journal of Sociology* 57 (1): 1–23.

Becker, G. 1964: *Human Capital*. New York: National Bureau of Economic Research, Columbia University Press.

Becker, G. 1968: Crime and punishment. An economic approach. *Journal of Political Economy* 76 (2): 169–217.

Beckett, K. 1997: *Making Crime Pay: Law and Order in Contemporary American Politics*. New York: Oxford University Press.

Beckett, K. and Herbert, S. 2008: Dealing with disorder: social control in the post industrial city. *Theoretical Criminology* 12: 5–30.

Beckett, K. and Herbert, S. 2009: *Banished: The Transformation of Urban Social Control*. Oxford: Oxford University Press.

Beckett, K. and Sasson, T. 2000: *The Politics of Injustice: Crime and Punishment in America*. Newbury Park, CA: Pine Forge Press.

Beckett, K. and Western, B. 2001: Governing social marginality: welfare, incarceration, and the transformation of state policy. In D. Garland (ed.) *Mass Imprisonment: Social Causes and Consequences*. London: Sage Publications.

Beckett, K., Nyrop, K. and Pfingst, L. 2006: Race, drugs, and policing: understanding disparities in drug delivery arrests. *Criminology* 44: 105–137.

Beckford, J. 1989: *Religion in Advanced Industrial Society*. London: Unwin Hyman.

Beckford, J. and Demerath, N.J. (eds) 2007: *The Sage Handbook of the Sociology of Religion*. London: Sage.

Beckford, J. and Wallis, J. (eds) 2007: *Theorising Religion: Classical and Contemporary Debates*. Aldershot: Ashgate.

Beetham, D. 1989: Max Weber and liberal political theory. *Archives Européennes de Sociologie* 30: 311–323.

Beetham, D. 1991a: *The Legitimation of Power*. Basingstoke: Macmillan.

Beetham, D. 1991b: *Max Weber and the Theory of Modern Politics*, 2nd edn. Cambridge: Polity Press.

Beetham, D. and Lord, C.J. 1998: *Legitimacy and the European Union*. Harlow and New York: Addison Wesley Longman.

Beisel, N. 1997: *Imperiled Innocents: Anthony Comstock and Family Reproduction in Victorian America*. Princeton, NJ: Princeton University Press.

Béland, D. 2005: Ideas and social policy: an institutionalist perspective. *Social Policy and Administration* 39: 1–18.

Béland, D. 2007: Ideas and institutional change in social security: conversion, layering, and policy drift. *Social Science Quarterly* 88: 20–38.

Béland, D. 2010: Reconsidering policy feedback: how policies affect politics. *Administration & Society* 42: 568–590.

Bell, R. 1985: *Holy Anorexia*. Chicago, IL: University of Chicago Press.

Bellah, R.N. 1959: Durkheim and history. *American Sociological Review* 24: 447–465.

Bellah, R.N. 1970: Civil religion in America. In R.N. Bellah *Beyond Belief*. New York: Harper and Row.

Bellah, R.N. 1980: Introduction. In R.N. Bellah and P. Hammond (eds) *Varieties of Civil Religion*. San Francisco, CA: Harper and Row.

Bellah, R.N. 1991: *Beyond Belief: Essays on religion in a post-traditional world*. Berkeley, CA: University of California Press.

Bello, W. 2000: Building an iron cage. In S. Anderson (ed.) *Views from the South: The Effects of Globalization and the WTO on Third World Countries*. Chicago, IL: FoodFirst and the International Forum on Globalization.

Bellofiore, R. and Halevi, J. 2009: Deconstructing Labour. A Marxian-Kaleckian perspective on what is 'new' in contemporary capitalism and economics. In C. Gnos and L-P. Rochon (eds) *Employment, Growth and Development. A Post-Keynesian Approach*. Cheltenham: Edward Elgar.

Bender, C. 2003: *Heaven's Kitchen: Living Religion at God's Love We Deliver*. Chicago, IL: Chicago University Press.

Benford, R.D. and Snow, D.A. 2000: Framing processes and social movements: an overview and assessment. *Annual Review of Sociology* 26: 611–639.

Benhabib, S. (ed.) 1996: *Democracy and Difference: Contesting the Boundaries of the Political*. Princeton, NJ: Princeton University Press.

Benhabib, S. 2002: *The Claims of Culture*. Princeton, NJ: Princeton University Press.

Benhabib, S. 2004: *The Rights of Others*. Cambridge: Cambridge University Press.

Bennett, A. 2008: Process tracing: a Bayesian perspective. In H.E. Brady and D. Collier (eds) *The Oxford Handbook of Political Methodology*. Oxford: Oxford University Press.

Bennett, A. and Elman, C. 2006: Qualitative research: recent developments in case study methods. *Annual Review of Political Science* 9: 455–476.

Bennett, C.J. 1991: What is policy convergence and what causes it? *British Journal of Political Science* 21: 215–233.

Bennett, T., Emmison, M. and Frow, J. (1999) *Accounting for Tastes: Australian Everyday Cultures*. Cambridge: Cambridge University Press.

Bennett, T., Savage, M., Silva, E.B., Warde, A. *et al.* 2009: *Culture, Class, Distinction*. London: Routledge.

Bensel, R.F. 1991: *Yankee Leviathan: The Origins of Central State Authority in America, 1859–1877*. Cambridge: Cambridge University Press.

Benson, B.L. 1990: *The Enterprise of Law. Justice without the State*. San Francisco: Pacific Research Institute for Public Policy.

Benson, B.L. and Baden, J. 1985: The political economy of governmental corruption: the logic of underground government. *Journal of Legal Studies* 14 (2): 391–410.

Benson, R. and Saguy, A. 2005: Constructing social problems in an age of globalization: a French-American comparison. *American Sociological Review* 70: 233–259.

Berezin, M. 2009: *Illiberal Politics in Neoliberal Times: Culture, Security and Populism in the New Europe*. New York: Cambridge University Press.

Berger, P.L. and Luckmann, T. 1966: *The Social Construction of Reality: A Treatise in the Sociology of Knowledge*. Garden City, NY: Anchor.

Berkovitch, N. and Gordon, N. 2008: The political economy of transnational regimes: the case of human rights. *International Studies Quarterly* 52: 881–904.

Berle, A.A. and Means, G.C. 1932: *The Modern Corporation and Private Property*. Basingstoke: Macmillan.

Berman, H.J. 1983: *Law and Revolution the Formation of the Western Legal Tradition*. Cambridge: Harvard University Press.

Bernard, M. 1996: Civil society after the first transition. *Communist and Post-Communist Studies* 29 (3): 309–333.

Bernstein, S. 2001: *The Compromise of Liberal Environmentalism*. New York: Columbia University Press.

Berry, J.M. 1994: An agenda for research on interest groups. In W. Crotty, M.A. Schwartz and J. C. Green (eds) *Representing Interests and Interest Group Representation*. Lanham, MD: University Press of America.

Betsill, M.M., Hochstetler, K. and Stevis, D. (eds) 2006: *International Environmental Politics*. New York: Palgrave Macmillan.

Beveridge, W. 2000 [1942]: *Social Insurance and Allied Services [The Beveridge Report]*. In R. Goodin and D. Mitchell (eds) *The Foundations of the Welfare State*, vol. II. Cheltenham: Elgar.

Bevir, M. and Rhodes, R.A.W. 2010: *The State as Cultural Practice*. Oxford: Oxford University Press.

Beyer, P. (ed.) 1993: *Religion and Globalization*. London: Sage.

Beyer, P. 2001: *Religion in the Process of Globalization. Würzburg*: Ergon Verlag.

Beyers, J. and Kerremans, B. 2007: Critical resource dependencies and the Europeanization of domestic interest groups. *Journal of European Public Policy* 14: 460–481.

Beyers, J., Eising, R. and Maloney, W. 2008: Researching interest group politics in Europe and elsewhere: much we study, little we know? *West European Politics* 31: 1103–1128.

Bezes, P. 2009: *Réinventer l'État: les réformes de l'administration française 1962–2008*. Paris: PUF.

Bhabha, H.K. (ed.) 1990: *Nation and Narration*. London: Routledge.

Bhabha, H.K. 1994a: Frontlines/borderposts. In A. Bammer (ed.) *Displacements. Cultural Identities in Question*. Bloomington: Indiana University Press.

Bhabha, H.K. 1994b: *The Location of Culture*. London: Routledge.

Bhargava, R. 2010: *The Promise of India's Secular Democracy*. New Delhi: Oxford University Press.

Biermann, F. 2006: *A World Environment Organization*. Aldershot: Ashgate.

Bigo, D., Bonelli, L. and Deltombe, T. 2008: *Au nom du 11 septembre: Les démocraties à l'épreuve de l'antiterrorisme*. Paris: La Découverte.

Bigo, D. 1996: *Polices en réseaux. L'expérience européenne*. Paris: Presses de Sciences Po.

Bigo, D. 2006: Globalized-in-security: the field and the Ban-Opticon. In *Traces: A Multilingual Series of Cultural Theory*. Hong Kong: University of Hong Kong Press.

Bigo, D. and Tsoukala, A. 2008: *Terror, Insecurity and Liberty. Illiberal Practices of Liberal Regimes after 9/11*. New York: Routledge.

Bigo, D., Carrera, S., Guild, E. and Walker, R.J.B. 2010: *Europe's 21st Century Challenge: Delivering Liberty and Security*. Aldershot: Ashgate.

Billig, M. 1995: *Banal Nationalism*. London: Sage.

Binderkrantz, A. 2005: Interest group strategies: navigating between privileged access and strategies of pressure. *Political Studies* 53: 694–715.

Birch, A.H. 1959: *Small Town Politics*. Oxford: Oxford University Press.

Black, D. 2004: The geometry of terrorism. *Sociological Theory* 22 (1): 14–25.

Black, J. 2000: *War: Past, Present, and Future*. Stroud: Sutton.

Black, J. 2004: *Rethinking Military History*. London: Routledge.

Blakeley, G. and Bryson, V. (eds) 2007: *The Impact of Feminism on Political Concepts and Debates*. Manchester: Manchester University Press.

Blau, J. and Moncada, A. 2005: *Human Rights beyond the Liberal Vision*. Lanham, MD: Rowman & Littlefield.

Bleich, E. 2003: *Race Politics in Britain and France: Ideas and Policymaking since the 1960's*. New York: Cambridge University Press.

Block, F. 1987: *Revising State Theory: Essays in Politics and Postindustrialism*. Philadelphia, PA: Temple University Press.

Bloemraad, I. 2006: Becoming a citizen in the United States and Canada: structured mobilization and immigrant political incorporation. *Social Forces* 85: 667–695.

Bloemraad, I., Korteweg, A. and Yurdakul, G. 2008: Citizenship and immigration: multiculturalism, assimilation, and challenges to the nation-state. *Annual Review of Sociology* 34: 153–179.

Bloom, M. 2005: *Dying to Kill: The Allure of Suicide Terror*. New York: Columbia University Press.

Blumer, H. 1958: Race prejudices as a sense of group position. *Pacific Sociological Review* 1: 3–7.

Bobbio, N. 1989: *Democracy and Dictatorship: The Nature and Limits of State Power*. Cambridge: Polity Press.

Bobo, L.D. 2001: Race, interests and beliefs about affirmative action: unanswered questions and new directions. In J.D. Skrentny (ed.) *Color Lines: Affirmative Action, Immigration and Civil Rights Options for America*. Chicago, IL: University of Chicago Press.

Bobo, L.D. and Gilliam, F.D. Jr. 1990: Race, sociopolitical participation and black empowerment. *American Political Science Review* 84: 377–393.

Bobo, L.D. and Tuan, M. 2006: *Prejudice in Politics: Group Position, Public Opinion, and the Wisconsin Treaty Rights Dispute*. Cambridge, MA: Harvard University Press.

Bogusz, B., Cholewindski, R., Cygan, A. and Szyzczak, E. (eds) 2004: *Irregular Migration and Human Rights: Theoretical, European and International Perspectives* Leiden: Martinus Nijhof.

Bohle, D. 2009: East European capitalism: what went wrong? *Intervention. European Journal of Economics and Economic Policies* 6 (1): 32–43.

Boix, C. 2003: *Democracy and Redistribution*. Cambridge: Cambridge University Press.

Boli, J. 1987: World polity sources of expanding state authority and organization, 1870–1970. In G. Thomas, J. Mayer, F. Ramirez and J. Boli (eds) *Institutional Structure: Constituting State, Society, and the Individual*. Beverly Hills: Sage.

Boli, J. 2005: Contemporary developments in world culture. *International Journal of Contemporary Sociology* 46 (5/6): 383–404.

Boli, J. and Thomas, G. 1997: World culture in the world polity: a century of international NGOs. *American Sociological Review* 62 (2): 171–190.

Boli, J. and Thomas, G.M. (eds) 1999: *Constructing World Culture: International Organizations since 1875*. Stanford, CA: Stanford University.

Boli, J. and Thomas, G.M. 1999: INGOs and the organization of world culture. In J. Boli and G.M. Thomas (eds) *Constructing World Culture: International Nongovernmental Organizations Since 1875*. Stanford, CA: Stanford University Press.

Bollen, K. 1989: *Structural Equations with Latent Variables*. New York: Wiley-Interscience.

Bonastia, C. 2006: *Knocking on the Door: The Federal Government's Attempt to Desegregate the Suburbs*. Princeton, NJ: Princeton University Press.

Bonditti, P. 2001: L'organisation de la lutte anti-terroriste aux Etats-Unis. *Cultures & Conflits* 44 (2): 65–76.

Bonilla-Silva, E. 2003: *Racism without Racists: Color-blind Racism and the Persistence of Racial Inequality in the United States*. Lanham, MD: Rowman & Littlefield.

Booth, J. 1985: *The End and the Beginning: The Nicaraguan Revolution*, 2nd edn. Boulder, CO: Westview Press.

Bordo, S. 1993: *Unbearable Weight. Feminism, Western Culture and the Body*. Berkeley: University of California Press.

Bordo, S. 1999: *The Male Body. A New Look at Men in Public and Private*. New York: Farrar, Strauss and Giroux.

Bork, R.H. 1978: *The Antitrust Paradox: A Policy At War With Itself*. New York: The Free Press.

Bornschier, S. 2010: *Cleavage Politics and the Populist Right: The New Cultural Politics in Western Europe*. Philadelphia, PA: Temple University Press.

Borradori, G., Habermas, J. and Derrida, J. 2003: *Philosophy in a Time of Terror: Dialogues with Jürgen Habermas and Jacques Derrida*. Chicago, IL: University of Chicago Press.

Borras, S.M., Jr., Edelman, M. and Kay, C. (eds) 2008: *Transnational Agrarian Movements Confronting Globalization*. Oxford: Wiley-Blackwell.

Börzel, T.A. 1998: Organizing Babylon: on the different conceptions of policy networks. *Public Administration* 76: 253–273.

Bosniak, L. 2006: *The Citizen and the Alien: Dilemmas of Contemporary Membership*. Princeton, NJ: Princeton University Press.

Boswell, T. and Brown, C. 1999: The scope of general theory: methods for linking deductive and inductive comparative history. *Sociological Methods and Research* 28: 154–185.

Bottero, W. 2005: *Class*. Cambridge: Polity Press.

Botzem, S. and Quack, S. 2006: Contested rules and shifting boundaries: international standard-setting in accounting. In M.L. Djelic and K. Sahlin-Andersson (eds) *Transnational Governance: Institutional Dynamics of Regulation*. Cambridge: Cambridge University Press.

Boudon, R. 1982: *The Unintended Consequences of Social Action*. Basingstoke: Macmillan.

Bourdieu, P. 1977a: Remarques provisoires sur la perception sociale du corps. *Actes de la recherche en sciences sociales* 14: 51–54.

Bourdieu, P. 1977b: *Outline of a Theory of Practice*. Cambridge: Cambridge University Press.

Bourdieu, P. 1980a: *Le sens pratique*. Paris: Minuit.

Bourdieu, P. 1980b: Le capital social. Notes provisoires. *Actes de la Recherche en Sciences Sociales* 3: 2–3.

Bourdieu, P. 1986: *Distinction,* London: Routledge.

Bourdieu, P. 1990: *The Logic of Practice*. Stanford, CA: Stanford University Press.

Bourdieu, P. 1996: *The State Nobility: Elite Schools In the Field of Power*. Cambridge: Cambridge University Press.

Bourdieu, P. 1997: *Excitable Speech. A Politics of the Performative*. London: Routledge.

Bourdieu, P. 1998: *La domination masculine*. Paris: Seuil.

Bourdieu, P. 1999: Rethinking the state: genesis and structure of the bureaucratic field. In G. Steinmetz (ed.) *Culture: State-Formation after the Cultural Turn*. Ithaca, NY: Cornell University Press.

Bourdieu, P. 1993: *Bodies that Matter: The Discursive Limits of Sex*. London: Routledge.

Bousquet, A. 2009: *The Scientific Way of Warfare: Order and Chaos on the Battlefields of Modernity*. New York: Columbia University Press.

Boyer, R. 2004a: *The Future of Economic Growth*. Cheltenham: Edward Elgar.

Boyer, R. 2004b: New growth regimes, but still institutional diversity. *Socio-Economic Review* 2 (1): 1–32.

Boyer, R. 2005: From shareholder value to CEO power: the paradox of the 1990s. *Competition & Change* 9 (1): 7–47.

Boyle, E.H. 2002: *Female Genital Cutting: Cultural Conflict in the Global Community*. Baltimore, MD: Johns Hopkins University.

Boyle, E.H., McMorris, B.J. and Gomez, M. 2002: Local conformity to international norms: the case of female genital cutting. *International Sociology* 17: 5–33.

Bradley, D., Huber, E., Moller, S., Nielsen, F. *et al.* 2003: Distribution and redistribution in postindustrial democracies. *World Politics* 55: 193–228.

Bradley, K. 2000: The incorporation of women into higher education: paradoxical outcomes? *Sociology of Education* 73: 1–18.

Brady, H.E. and Collier, D. (eds) 2004: *Rethinking Social Inquiry: Diverse Tools, Shared Standards*. Lanham: Rowman & Littlefield.

Braman, D. 2004: *Doing Time on the Outside*. Ann Arbor: University of Michigan Press.

Breiner, P. 1996: *Max Weber and Democratic Politics*. Ithaca, NY: Cornell University Press.

Breiner, P. 2004a: Translating Max Weber exile attempts to forge a new political science. *European Journal of Political Theory* 3 (2): 133–149.

Breiner, P. 2004b: 'Unnatural selection': Max Weber's concept of *Auslese* and his criticism of the reduction of political conflict to economics. *International Relations* 18 (3): 289–307.

Breines, W. 1982: *Community and Organization in the New Left 1962–1968: The Great Refusal*. New York: Praeger.

Breitmeier, H, Young, O. and Zürn, M. 2006: *Analyzing International Environmental Regimes*. Cambridge, MA: MIT Press.

Brenner, N. and Theodore, N. 2002: Cities and the geographies of 'actually existing neoliberaism'. In N. Brenner and N. Theodore (eds) *Spaces of Neoliberalism – Urban Restructuring in North America and Western Europe*. Oxford: Blackwell.

Brenner, N. 2004: *New State Spaces*. Oxford: Oxford University Press.

Breuer, S. 1991: *Max Webers Herrschaftssoziologie*. Frankfurt am Main: Campus Verlag.

Breuer, S. 1998: The concept of democracy in Weber's political sociology. In R. Schroeder (ed.) *Max Weber, Democracy and Modernization*. New York: St. Martin's Press.

Breuilly, J. 1982: *Nationalism and the State*. Manchester: Manchester University Press.

Breuilly, J. 1996: Approaches to nationalism. In G. Balakrishnan and B. Anderson (eds) *Mapping the Nation*. London: Verso.

Bridges, G.S. and Steen, S. 1998: Racial disparities in official assessments of juvenile offenders: attributional stereotypes as mediating mechanisms. *American Sociological Review* 63: 554–570.

Brook, B. 1999: *Feminist Perspectives on the Body*. Harlow: Addison Wesley Longman.

Brooks, C. 2006: Voters, satisficing, and public policymaking: recent directions in the study of electoral politics. *Annual Review of Sociology* 32: 191–211.

Brooks, C. and Manza, J. 2007: *Why Welfare States Persist*. Chicago, IL: University of Chicago Press.

Brown, B. and Jolivette, G. 2005: *Three Strikes: The Impact After More than a Decade*. Sacramento: Legislative Analysts' Office.

Brown, G.W. and Held, D. 2010: *The Cosmopolitanism Reader*. Cambridge: Polity Press.

Brown, W. 2009: Introduction. In T. Asad, W. Briwn, J. Butler, S. Mahmood *Is Critique Secular? Blasphemy, Injury, and Free Speech*. Berkeley, CA: The Townsend Centre for the Humanities.

Brown, W.P. 2005: *Edgework: Critical Essays on Knowledge and Politics*. Princeton, NJ: Princeton University Press.

Browne, W.P. 1998: *Groups, Interests, and U.S. Public Policy*. Washington, DC: Georgetown University Press.

Brubaker, R. 2009: Ethnicity, race, and nationalism. *Annual Review of Sociology* 35: 21–42.

Brubaker, R., Loveman, M. and Stamatov, P. 2004: Ethnicity as cognition. *Theory and Society* 33 (1): 31–64.

Bruce, M. 1968: *The Coming of the Welfare State*, 4th edn. London: Batsford.

Bruce, S. 1999: *Choice and Religion: A Critique of Rational Choice Theory*. Oxford: Oxford University Press.

Brunn, H.H. 2007: *Science, Values and Politics in Max Weber's Methodology*. Aldershot: Ashgate.

Bryant, C.G.A. 1995: Civic nation, civil society, civil religion. In J.A. Hall (ed.) *Civil Society. Theory, History, Comparison*. Cambridge: Polity Press.

Bryce, J. 1921: *Modern Democracies*, vol. II. New York: Macmillan.

Bryceson, D., Kay, C. and Mooij, J. (eds) 2000: *Disappearing Peasantries? Land and Labor in Africa, Asia and Latin America*. London: Immediate Technology Publications.

Brysk, A. and Shafir, G. (eds) 2004: *People Out of Place: Globalization, Human Rights and the Citizenship Gap*. New York: Routledge.

Bryson, V. 2007: *Gender and the Politics of Time*. Cambridge: Policy Press.

Bubeck, D. 1995: *A Feminist Approach to Citizenship*. Florence: European University Institute.

Budge, I. and Farlie, D. 1983: *Explaining and Predicting Elections. Issue Effects and Party Strategies in Twenty-Three Democracies*. London: Allen & Unwin.

Budgeon, S. 2001: Emergent feminist (?) identities: young women and the practice of micro-politics. *European Journal of Women's Studies* 8 (1): 7–28.

Bull, B. 2008: Policy networks and business participation in free trade negotiations in Chile. *Journal of Latin American Studies* 40 (2): 195–224.

Bull, H. 1977: *The Anarchical Society. A Study of Order in World Politics*. New York: Columbia University Press.

Bulmer, M. (ed.) 1974: *Working Class Images of Society*. London: Routledge and Kegan Paul.

Burchell, G., Gordon, C. and Miller, P. (eds) 1991: *The Foucault Effect. Studies in Governmentality*. Chicago, IL: University of Chicago Press.

Bureau of Justice Statistics 2009: Justice expenditure and employment extracts, 2006. NCJ 224394.

Burke, P. 1992: *The Fabrication of Louis XIV*. New Haven, CT: Yale University Press.

Burkett, P. 1999: *Marx and Nature. A Red and Green Perspective*. New York: St Martin's Press.

Burkitt, I. 1999: *Bodies of Thought. Embodiment, Identity and Modernity*. London: Sage.

Burleigh, M. and Wipperman, W. 1991: *The Racial State, 1933–1945*. Cambridge: Cambridge University Press.

Burnham, J. 1941: *The Managerial Revolution*. New York: John Day.

Burrows, R. and Gane, N. 2007: Geodemographics, software, and class. *Sociology*, 40 (5): 793–812.

Burstein, P. 1991: Policy domains: organization, culture, and policy outcomes. *Annual Review of Sociology* 17: 327–350.

Burstein, P. 1998: Interest organizations, political parties and the study of democratic policies. In A. Costain and A. McFarland (eds) *Social Movements and American Political Institutions*. Lanham, MD: Rowman & Littlefield.

Butler, D. and Stokes, D. 1971: *Political Change in Britain*. Harmondsworth: Penguin.

Butler, J. 1990: *Gender Trouble. Feminism and the Subversion of Identity*. London: Routledge.

Butler, J. 1993: *Bodies That Matter: On the Discursive Limits of Sex*. New York: Routledge.

Butler, J. 1997: *Excitable Speech. A Politics of the Performative*. London: Routledge.

Butler, J. 2000: Competing universalities. In J. Butler, E. Laclau and S. Žižek *Contingency, Hegemony, Universality: Contemporary Dialogues on the Left*. London: Verso.

Butler, T. and Watt, P. 2008: *Understanding Social Inequality*. London: Sage.

Cadot, O. 1987: Corruption as a gamble. *Journal of Public Economics* 33 (2): 223–244.

Cairns, D. and Richards, S. 1988: *Writing Ireland: Colonialism, Nationalism and Culture.* Manchester: Manchester University Press.

Calhoun, C. 2003: The class consciousness of frequent travellers: towards a critique of actually existing cosmopolitanism. In D. Archibugi (ed.) *Debating Cosmopolitics.* London: Verso.

Calhoun, C. 2007: *Nations Matter. Culture, History, and the Cosmopolitan Dream.* London: Routledge.

Campbell, A., Converse, P., Miller, W. and Stokes, D. 1960: *The American Voter.* New York: Wiley.

Campbell, J.L. 1998: Institutional analysis and the role of ideas in political economy. *Theory and Society* 27: 377–409.

Campbell, J.L. 2002: Ideas, politics, and public policy. *Annual Review of Sociology* 28: 21–38.

Campbell, J.L. 2004: *Institutional Change and Globalization.* Princeton, NJ: Princeton University Press.

Campbell, J.L. 2007: Why would corporations behave in socially responsible ways? An institutional theory of corporate social responsibility. *Academy of Management Review* 32 (3): 946–967.

Canovan, M. 2000: Patriotism is not enough. In C. McKinnon and I. Hampsher-Monk (eds) *The Demands of Citizenship.* London: Continuum.

Carey, J.M. and Shugart, M.S. 1995: Incentives to cultivate a personal vote: a rank ordering of electoral formulas. *Electoral Studies* 14 (4): 417–439.

Carey, S, Gibney, M. and Poe, S. 2010: *The Politics of Human Rights: the Quest for Dignity.* Cambridge: Cambridge University Press.

Carpenter, D.P. 2001: *The Forging of Bureaucratic Autonomy.* Princeton, NJ: Princeton University Press.

Carrera, S. and Guild, E. 2004: *Security versus Justice.* Aldershot: Ashgate.

Carroll, P. 2009: Articulating theories of states and state formation. *Journal of Historical Sociology* 22: 553–603.

Carson, R. 1958: *Silent Spring.* Harmondsworth: Penguin.

Carter, E. 2005: *The Extreme Right in Western Europe.* Manchester: Manchester University Press.

Carter, E., Donald, J. and Squires, J. (eds) 1993: *Space and Place: Theories of Identity and Location.* London: Lawrence & Wishart.

Cartier-Bresson, J. 1997: La corruption dans les pays capitalistes Tardifs. In Jean Cartier-Bresson (ed.) *Pratiques et controle de la corruption.* Paris, Montchrestien.

Casanova, J. 1994: *Public Religions in the Modern World.* Chicago, IL: Chicago University Press.

CASE Collective 2006: Critical approaches to security in Europe: A networked manifesto. *Security Dialogue* 37 (4): 443–487.

Cassese, S. and Wright. V. (eds.) 1996: *The Restructuring of the State.* London, Frances Pinter.

Castel, R. 2009: *La montée des incertitudes. Travail, protections, statut de l'individu.* Paris: Seuil.

Castells, M. 2000: *The Rise of the Network Society.* Oxford: Blackwell.

Castells, M. 2009: *Communication Power.* Oxford: Oxford University Press.

Castoriadis, C. 1987: *The Imaginary Institution of Society.* Oxford: Oxford University Press.

CCCS 1982: *The Empire Strikes Back: Race and Racism in 70s Britain.* London: Hutchinson in association with the Centre for Contemporary Cultural Studies.

Celis, K., Childs, S., Kantola, J. and Krook, M. 2008: Rethinking women's substantive representation. *Representation* 44 (2): 99–110.

Chambliss, W. 1999: *Power, Politics and Crime*. Boulder, CO: Westview Press.

Chan, T.W. and Goldthorpe, J.H. 2007: Social status and cultural consumption: music in England. *European Sociological Review* 23 (1): 1–19.

Chappell, L. 2000: Interacting with the state: feminist strategies and political opportunities. *International Feminist Journal of Politics* 2 (2): 244–275.

Chappell, L. 2002a: The femocrat strategy: expanding the repertoire of feminist activists. *Parliamentary Affairs* 55 (1): 85–98.

Chappell, L. 2002b: *Gendering Government: Feminist Engagement with the State in Australia and Canada*. Vancouver: UBC Press.

Chase-Dunn, C. 1998: *Global Formation: Structures of the World Economy*, 2nd edn. Lanham, MD: Rowman & Littlefield.

Chase-Dunn, C. and Gills, B. 2005: Waves of globalization and resistance in the capitalist world system: social movements and critical globalization studies. In R. Appelbaum and W. Robinson (eds) *Critical Globalization Studies*. London and New York: Routledge.

Chase, C. 1998: Hermaphodites with attitude: mapping the emergence of intersex political activism. *GLQ* 4: 189–211.

Chatterjee, P. 2004: *The Politics of the Governed: Reflections on Popular Politics in Most of the World*. New York: Columbia University Press.

Chaves, M. 1994: Secularization as declining religious authority. *Social Forces* 72(3): 749–774.

Chen, A.S. and Weir, M. 2009: The long shadow of the past: risk pooling and the political development of health care reform in the States. *Journal of Health Politics, Policy, and Law* 34 (5): 679–716.

Chernilo, D. 2006: Social theory's methodological nationalism. Myth and reality. *European Journal of Social Theory* 9 (1): 5–22.

Chew, S. C. 1998: *World Ecological Degradation; Accumulation, Urbanization and Deforestation 3000 BC–AD 2000*. Walnut Creek, CA: Altamira.

Chew, S. 2001: *World Ecological Degradation. Accumulation, Urbanization and Deforestation 3000 BC–AD 2000*. Walnut Creek, CA: AltaMira.

Childs, S. and Krook, M. 2008: Critical mass theory and women's political representation. *Political Studies*, 56 (3): 725–736.

Chong, D. and Druckman, J.N. 2007: Framing theory. *Annual Review of Political Science* 10: 103–126.

Cladis, M. 1992: *A Communitarian Defense of Liberalism: Emile Durkheim and Contemporary Social Theory*. Stanford, CA: Stanford University Press.

Clapp, J. 2001: *Toxic exports, the Transfer of Hazardous Wastes from Rich to Poor Countries*. New York: Cornell University Press.

Clark, I. 2005: *Legitimacy in International Society*. Oxford: Oxford University Press.

Clark, J.C.D 1990: National identity. State formation and patriotism: the role of history in the public mind. *History Workshop Journal* 29: 95–102.

Clark, R. 1984: *The Basque Insurgents: ETA, 1952–1980*. Madison, WI: University of Wisconsin Press.

Clarke, P. 2009: Introduction. towards a more organic understanding of religion within a global framework. In P. Clarke (ed.) *The Oxford Handbook of Sociology of Religion*. Oxford: Oxford University Press.

Claverie, E. 2003: *Les guerres de la Vierge. Anthropologie des apparitions*. Paris: Gallimard.

Clear, T. 2007: *Imprisoning Communities*. New York: Oxford University Press.

Clemens, E.S. and Cook, J.M. 1999: Politics and institutionalism: explaining durability and change. *Annual Review of Sociology* 25: 441–466.

Cockburn, C. 2007: *From Where We Stand: War, Women's Activism and Feminist Analysis*. London: Zed Books.

Coen, D. and Thatcher, M. 2008: Network governance and multi-level delegation: European networks of regulatory agencies. *Journal of Public Policy* 28: 49–71.

Cohen, A.P. 1985: *The Symbolic Construction of Community*. London: Routledge.

Cohen, J. and Arato, A. 1992: *Civil Society and Political Theory*. Cambridge, MA: MIT Press.

Cohen, S. 1972: *Folk Devils and Moral Panics: The Creation of Mods and Rockers*. London: MacGibbon and Kee.

Cohen, S. 2001: *States of Denial: Knowing about Atrocities and Suffering*. Cambridge: Polity Press.

Coicaud, J-M. 2002: *Legitimacy and Politics: A Contribution to the Study of Political Right and Political Responsibility*. Cambridge: Cambridge University Press.

Coker, C. 2002: *Waging War without Warriors*. Boulder, CO: Lynne Rienner.

Cole, W.M. 2005: Sovereignty relinquished? Explaining commitment to the international human rights covenants, 1966–1999. *American Sociological Review* 70: 472–495.

Cole, W.M. 2006: When all else fails: international adjudication of human rights abuse claims, 1976–1999. *Social Forces* 84: 1909–1935.

Coleman, J.S. 1988: Social capital in the creation of human capital. *American Journal of Sociology* 94: 95–120.

Coleman, J.S. 1990: *Foundations of Social Theory*. Cambridge, MA: The Belknap Press of Harvard University Press.

Coleman, J.S. 1994: A rational choice perspective on economic sociology. In N.J. Smelser and R. Swedberg (eds) *The Handbook of Economic Sociology*. Princeton, NJ: Princeton University Press.

Collins, R. 1975: *Conflict Sociology: Toward an Explanatory Science*. New York: Academic Press, 1975.

Collins, R. 1986: Imperialism and legitimacy: Weber's theory of politics. In R. Collins *Weberian Sociological Theory*. Cambridge: Cambridge University Press.

Collins, R. 1998: Democratization in a world historical perspective. In R. Schroeder (ed.) *Max Weber's Idea of Democracy and Modernization*. New York: St Martin's Press.

Comfort, M.L. 2008: *Doing Time Together: Love and Family in the Shadow of the Prison*. Chicago, IL: University of Chicago Press.

Conca, K, Alberty, M. and Dabelko, G. (eds) 1995: *Green Planet Blues*. Boulder, CO: Westview Press.

Conca, K. 2000: The WTO and the undermining of global environmental governance. *Review of International Political Economy*, 7 (3): 484–494.

Condorcet, M.J.A. 1976 [1794]: Sketch for the historical picture of the progress of the human mind. In *Selected Writings*, ed. K.M. Baker. Indianapolis: Bobbes-Merrill.

Connell, R.W. 2005: Change among gatekeepers: men, masculinities and gender equality in the global arena. *Signs* 30 (3): 1801–1825.

Connolly, W.E. 1991: *Identity/Difference*. Ithaca, NY: Cornell University Press.

Connolly, W.E. 1995: *The Ethos of Pluralization*. Minneapolis: University of Minnesota Press.

Connor, W. 1978: A nation is a nation, is a state, is an ethnic group, is a... *Ethnic and Racial Studies* 1 (4): 379–388.

Connor, W. 1994: *Ethnonationalism: The Quest for Understanding*. Princeton, NJ: Princeton University Press.

Coole, D. 2005: Rethinking agency: a phenomenological approach to embodiment and agentic capacities. *Political Studies* 53: 124–142.

Cooter, R., Harrison, M. and Sturdy, S. (eds) 1998: *War, Medicine and Modernity*. Stroud: Sutton.

Cornelius, W.A. and Tsuda, T. 2004: Controlling immigration: the limits of government intervention. In W.A. Cornelius, T. Tsuda, P.L. Martin and J.F. Hollifield (eds) *Controlling Immigration: A Global Perspective*. Stanford, CA: Stanford University Press.

Cornell, S.E. and Hartmann, D. 1998: *Ethnicity and Race: Making identities in a Changing World*. Thousand Oaks, CA: Pine Forge Press.

Costain, A.N. 1992: *Inviting Women's Rebellion*. Baltimore, MD: Johns Hopkins University.

Côté, P. and Richardson, J. 2001: Disciplined litigation, vigilante litigation, and deformation. Dramatic organization change in Jehovah's Witnesses. *Journal for the Scientific Study of Religion* 40: 11–26.

Cotterell, R. (ed.) 2010: *Emile Durkheim: Justice, Morality and Politics*. Aldershot: Ashgate.

Cox, G. 1997: *Making Votes Count. Strategic Coordination in the World's Electoral Systems*. New York: Cambridge University Press.

Cox, R. 1996: *Approaches to World Order*. Cambridge: Cambridge University Press.

Cox, R. 1997: A perspective on globalisation. In J.H. Mittelman (ed.) *Globalisation, Critical Reflections*. London: Lynne Rienner.

Cox, R. 1999: Civil society at the turn of the millennium: prospects for an alternative world order. *Review of International Studies* 25 (1): 3–28.

Cramer, C. 2006: *Civil War is not a Stupid Thing: Accounting for Violence in Developing Countries*. London: Hurst.

Crane, A., Matten, D. and Moon, J. 2008: *Corporations and Citizenship*. Cambridge: Cambridge University Press.

Crenshaw, K. 1991: Mapping the margins: intersectionality, identity politics and violence against women of color. *Stanford Law Review* 43 (6): 1241–1299.

Crenshaw, M. 1981: The causes of terrorism. *Comparative Politics* 13 (4): 379–399.

Crewe, I. 1974: Introduction: studying elites in Britain. In I. Crewe (ed.) *British Political Sociology Yearbook*, Vol. 1: *Elites in Western Democracies*. London: Croom Helm.

Crompton, R. 2008: *Class and Stratification*. Cambridge: Polity Press.

Crompton, R. and Jones, G. 1984: *A White Collar Proletariat: Gender and Deskilling In Clerical Work*. Basingstoke: Macmillan.

Crossley, N. 2001: *The Social Body. Habit, Identity and Desire*. London: Sage.

Crouch, C. 1977: *The Politics of Industrial Relations*. Manchester: Manchester University Press.

Crouch, C. 1993: *Industrial Relations and European State Traditions*. Oxford: Oxford University Press.

Crouch, C. 2006: Modelling the firm in its market and organizational environment: methodologies for studying corporate social responsibility. *Organization Studies* 27 (10): 1533–1551.

Crouch, C. 2008: What will follow the demise of privatized Keynesianism? *The Political Quarterly* 79 (4): 476–487.

Crouch, C. 2009: Privatized Keynesianism: an unacknowledged policy regime. *The British Journal of Politics and International Relations* 11: 382–399.

Crouch, C. 2011a forthcoming: Employment, consumption, debt and European industrial relations systems. *Industrial Relations*.

Crouch, C. 2011b: *The Strange Non-Death of Neoliberalism*. Cambridge: Polity Press.

Crouch, C. and Streeck, W. (eds) 1997: *Political Economy of Modern Capitalism*. London: Sage.

Crowley. T (ed.) 1991: *Proper English? Readings in Language, History and Cultural Identity*. London: Routledge.

Cruikshank, B. 1999: *The Will to Empower: Democratic Citizens and Other Subjects*. Ithaca, NY: Cornell University Press.

Cucinotta, A., Pardolesi, R. and Van Den Bergh, R. (eds) 2002: *Post-Chicago Developments in Antitrust Law*. Cheltenham: Edward Elgar.

Cushman, T. 2005: *A Matter of Principle: Humanitarian Arguments for War in Iraq*. Berkeley: University of California Press.

D'Andrade, R. 1995: *The Development of Cognitive Anthropology*. New York: Cambridge University Press.

Dahl, R.A. 1957: The concept of power. *Behavioral Scientist* 2 (3): 201–215. Reprinted in J. Scott (ed.) *Power*, 3 vols. London: Routledge, 1994.

Dahl, R.A. 1961: *Who Governs?* New Haven, CT: Yale University Press.

Dahl, R.A. 1998: *On Democracy*. New Haven, CT: Yale University Press.

Dahl, R.A.1971: *Polyarchy: Participation and Opposition*. New Haven, CT: Yale University Press.

Dahlerup, D. 1998: Using quotas to increase women's political representation. In A. Karam (ed.) *Women in Parliament beyond Numbers*. Stockholm: IDEA.

Dahrendorf, R. 1967: *Society and Democracy in Germany*. Garden City, NY: Doubleday.

Dal Lago, A. and Palidda, S. 2010: *Conflict, Security and the Reshaping of Society; The Civilization of War*. New York: Routledge.

Dalton, R.J. 1996: Comparative politics: micro-behavioral perspectives. In R.E. Goodin (ed.) *A New Handbook of Political Science*, pp. 336–352. New York: Oxford University Press.

Dalton, R.J. 2003: *Democratic Challenges, Democratic Choices*. Oxford: Oxford University Press.

Dalton, R.J. and Wattenberg, M. (eds) 2000: *Parties Without Partisans: Political Change in Advanced Industrial Democracies*. Oxford: Oxford University Press.

Dalton, S. 2008: Beyond intellectual blackmail: Foucault and Habermas on reason, truth, and Enlightenment. *E-Logos. Electronic Journal for Philosophy*. http://nb.vse.cz/kfil/elogos/history/dalton08.pdf (accessed 12 April 2011).

Daly, H. 1992: *Steady State Economics*. Washington, DC: Island Press.

Daly, H. 1996: *Beyond Growth – The Economics of Sustainable Development*. Boston, MA: Beacon Press.

Dandeker, C. 1990: *Surveillance, Power and Modernity: Bureaucracy and Discipline from 1700 to the Present Day*. Cambridge: Polity Press.

Dauvergne, P. 2001: *Loggers and Degradation in the Asia-Pacific*. Cambridge: Cambridge University Press.

Davie, G. 1994: *Religion in Britain since 1945: Believing without Belonging*. Oxford: Blackwell.

Davie, G. 2002: *Europe, the Exceptional Case. Parameters of Faith in the Modern World*. London: Darton, Longman and Todd.

Davie, G. 2007: *The Sociology of Religion*. London: Sage.

Davies, G. and Derthick, M. 1997: Race and social welfare policy: the Social Security Act of 1935. *Political Science Quarterly* 112 (2): 217–235.

Davis, A., Gardner B.B. and Gardner M.R. 1941: *Deep South*. Chicago, IL: Chicago University Press.

Davis, F.J. 1991: *Who Is Black? One Nation's Definition*. University Park: Pennsylvania State University Press.

Davis, G.F. 2009: *Managed by the Markets: How Finance Reshaped America*. Oxford: Oxford University Press.

Davis, K. 1995: *Reshaping the Female Body: The Dilemma of Cosmetic Surgery*. London: Routledge.

Davis, K. 2007: *The Making of Our Bodies, Ourselves: How Feminism Travels Across Borders*. Durham, NC: Duke University Press.

Davis, K. 2008: Intersectionality as buzzword: a sociology of science perspective on what makes a feminist theory successful. *Feminist Theory* 9 (1): 67–85.

Davis, S. 1987: *Apartheid's Rebels: Inside South Africa's Hidden War*. New Haven, CT: Yale University Press.

Dayan, D. and Katz, E. 1992: *Media Events: The Live Broadcasting of History*. Cambridge, MA: Harvard University Press.

De Nooy, W., Mrvar, A. and Batagelj, V. 2005: *Exploratory Social Network Analysis with Pajek*. New York: Cambridge University Press.

De Sousa Santos, B. 2006: *The Rise of the Global Left: The World Social Forum and Beyond*. London: Zed Books.

Dean, J. 1996: *Solidarity of Strangers*. Berkeley: University of California Press.

Dean, J. 2010: *Rethinking Contemporary Feminist Politics*. Basingstoke: Palgrave Macmillan.

Dean, M. 1999: *Governmentality: Power and Rule in Modern Society*. London: Sage.

Dean, M. and Hindess, B. (eds) 1998: *Governing Australia: Studies in Contemporary Rationalities of Government*. Melbourne: Cambridge University Press.

Dearing, J.W. and Rogers, E.M. 1996: *Agenda-Setting*. Thousand Oaks, CA: Sage.

Defert, D. 1991 Popular Life' and insurance technology. In G. Burchell, C. Gordon and P. Miller (eds.) *The Foucault Effect*. Chicago, IL: University of Chicago Press.

Delanty, G. 2001: Cosmopolitanism and violence – the limits of global civil society. *European Journal of Social Theory* 4 (1): 41–52.

della Porta, D. (ed.) 2007: *The Global Justice Movement: Cross-National and Transnational Perspectives*. Boulder, CO: Paradigm.

della Porta, D. 1992: *Lo scambio occulto*. Bologna: Il Mulino.

della Porta, D. and Tarrow, S. (eds) 2005: *Transnational Protest and Global Activism*. Lanham, MD: Rowman & Littlefield.

della Porta, D. and Vannucci, A. 1999: *Corrupt Exchanges. Actors, Resources, and Mechanisms of Political Corruption*. New York: Aldine de Gruyter.

della Porta, D. and Vannucci, A. 2005a: The governance mechanisms of corrupt transactions. In J. Lambsdorff, M. Taube and M. Schramm (eds) *The New Institutional Economics of Corruption*. London: Routledge.

della Porta, D. and Vannucci, A. 2005b: The moral (and immoral) costs of corruption. *Politische Vierteljahresschrift*, Sonderheft 35: *Dimensionen politischer Korruption*, ed. Ulrich von Alemann: 109–134.

della Porta, D. and Vannucci, A. 2010: *The Governance of Corruption*. Burlington, VT: Ashgate.

della Porta, D. and Y. Mény (eds) 1996: *Democracy and Corruption in Europe*. London: Pinter.

della Porta, D., Andretta, M., Mosca, L. and Reiter, H. 2006: *Globalization from Below: Transnational Activists and Protest Networks*. Minneapolis: University of Minnesota Press.

Demerath, N.J. 2007: Secularization and sacralization deconstructed and reconstructed. In J. Beckford and N. J. Demerath (eds.) *The Sage Handbook of the Sociology of Religion*.

Deng, F., Kimaro, S., Lyons, T., Rothchild, D. *et al.* 1996: *Sovereignty as Responsibility: Conflict Management in Africa.* Washington: Brookings Institution Press.

Dershowitz, A.M. 2007: *Preemption: A Knife that Cuts Both Ways.* New York: W.W. Norton & Co.

Desai, M. 2005: Transnationalism: the face of feminist politics post-Beijing. *International Social Science Journal* 57 (2): 319–330.

Desmarais, A.A. 2007: *La Vía Campesina: Globalization and the Power of Peasants.* Halifax, NS: Fernwood.

Desrosière, A. 1998: *The Politics of Large Numbers.* Cambridge, MA: Harvard University Press.

Deutsch, K. 1966: *Nationalism and Social Communication.* Cambridge, MA: MIT Press.

Diamond, I. and Hartsock, N. 1998: Beyond interests in politics: a comment on Virginia Sapiro's 'When are women's interests interesting?' In A. Phillips (ed.) *Feminism and Politics.* Oxford: Oxford University Press.

Diamond, L. and Morlino, L. 2004: The quality of democracy. An overview. *Journal of Democracy* 15 (4): 20–31.

Dick, P.K. 2002: *The Minority Report.* New York: Citadel Press.

Dietz, M. 1985: Citizenship with a feminist face: the problem with maternal thinking. *Political Theory* 13 (1): 19–37.

Dietz, M. 1987: Context is all: feminism and theories of citizenship. *Daedulus*, 116 (4): 1–24.

Dikötter, F. 1994: *Discourse of Race in Modern China.* Stanford, CA: Stanford University Press.

Dillon, M. 2007: Governing terror: the state of emergency of biopolitical emergence. *International Political Sociology* 1 (1): 7–28.

Dillon, M. and Reid, J. 2001: Global liberal governance: biopolitics, security and war. *Millennium: Journal of International Studies* 30 (1): 41–66.

DiMaggio, P.J. 1997: Culture and cognition. *Annual Review of Sociology* 23: 263–287.

DiMaggio, P.J. and Powell, W.W. 1983: The iron cage revisited: institutional isomorphism and collective rationality in organizational fields. *American Sociological Review* 48: 147–160.

Dion, D. 1998: Evidence and inference in the comparative case study. *Comparative Politics* 30: 127–145.

Dobbin, F.R. 1993: The social construction of the great depression: industrial policy during the 1930s in the United States, Britain, and France. *Theory and Society* 22: 1–56.

Dobbin, F.R. 1994: *Forging Industrial Policy: The United States, Britain, and France in the Railway Age.* New York: Cambridge University Press.

Dobbin, F.R. 2009: *Inventing Equal Opportunity.* Princeton, NJ: Princeton University Press.

Dobbin, F.R., Simmons, B. and Garrett, G. 2007: The global diffusion of public policies: social construction, coercion, competition, or learning? *Annual Review of Sociology* 33: 449–472.

Domhoff, G.W. 1967: *Who Rules America?* Englewood Cliffs, NJ: Prentice Hall.

Domhoff, G.W. 1971: *The Higher Circles: The Governing Class in America.* New York: Vintage Books.

Domhoff, G.W. 1979: *The Powers That Be: Processes of Ruling Class Domination in America.* New York: Vintage.

Domhoff, G.W. 1998: *Who Rules America? Power and Politics in the Year 2000.* Mountain View, CA: Mayfield.

Domhoff, G.W. 2009: *Who Rules America? Challenges to Corporate and Class Dominance*, 6th edn. Philadelphia, PA: McGraw-Hill.

Donnelly, J. 1989: *Universal Human Rights in Theory and Practice*. Ithaca, NY: Cornell University Press.

Donzelot, J. and Gordon, C. 2008: Governing liberal societies – the Foucault effect in the English-speaking world. *Foucault Studies* 5: 48–62.

Douglas, M. 1966: *Purity and Danger*. London: Routledge.

Dowding, K. 1995: Model or metaphor? A critical review of the policy network approach. *Political Studies* 43: 136–158.

Dowding, K. 1996: *Power*. Buckingham: Open University Press.

Downes, A. 2008: *Targeting Civilians in War*. Ithaca, NY: Cornell University Press.

Downing, B.M. 1992: *The Military Revolution and Political Change: Origins of Democracy and Autocracy in Early Modern Europe*. Princeton, NJ: Princeton University Press.

Downs, A. 1957: *An Economic Theory of Democracy*. New York: Harper and Row.

Downs, A. 1972: Up and down with ecology: the issue attention cycle. *Public Interest* 28: 38–50.

Droogers, A. 2009: Defining religion. A social science approach. In P. Clarke (ed.) *The Oxford Handbook of Sociology of Religion*. Oxford: Oxford University Press.

Drori, G.S. 2007: Institutionalism and globalization Studies. In R. Greenwood, C. Oliver, R. Suddaby and K. Sahlin-Andersson (eds) *Handbook of Organizational Institutionalism*. London: Sage.

Drori, G.S., Meyer, J.W. and Hwang, H. (eds) 2006: *Globalization and Organization: World Society and Organizational Change*. New York: Oxford University.

Drori, G.S., Meyer, J.W. Ramirez, F.O. and Schofer, E. 2003: *Science in the Modern World Polity: Institutionalization and Globalization*. Stanford, CA: Stanford University.

Dryzek, J. 1997: *The Politics of the Earth, Environmental Discourses*. Oxford: Oxford University Press.

du Gay, P. and Scott, A. 2010: State transformation or regime shift. Addressing some confusions in the theory and sociology of the state. *Sociologica* 2. DOI: 10.2383/32707.

Dudziak, M. 2000: *Cold War Civil Rights*. Princeton, NJ: Princeton University Press.

Duffield, M. 2001: *Global Governance and the New Wars: The Merging of Development and Security*. London: Zed Books.

Dür, A. 2008a: Interest groups in the European Union: how powerful are they? *West European Politics* 31: 1212–1230.

Dür, A. 2008b: Measuring interest group influence in the EU: a note on methodology. *European Union Politics* 9: 559–576.

Dür, A. and De Bièvre, D. 2007a: The question of interest group influence. *Journal of Public Policy* 27: 1–12.

Dür, A. and De Bièvre, D. 2007b: Inclusion without influence? NGOs in European Trade policy. *Journal of Public Policy* 27: 79–101.

Duran P. 2009: Légitimité, droit et action publique. *Année Sociologique* 59: 323–344.

Durkheim, E. 1957: *Professional Ethics and Civic Morals*, trans. C. Brookfield. London: Routledge.

Durkheim, E. 1958 [1928]: *Socialism and Saint-Simon*, ed. E. Goundner, trans. C. Sattler. Yellow Springs, OH: Antioch Press.

Durkheim, E. 1961 [1925]: *Moral Education*, trans. E.K. Wilson and H. Schnurer. New York: The Free Press.

Durkheim, E. 1969 [1898]: Individualism and the intellectuals. *Political Studies* 17: 14–30.

Durkheim, E. 1977 [1938]: *The Evolution of Educational Thought*, trans. P. Collins. London: Routledge.

Durkheim, E. 1984 [1893]: *The Division of Labor in Society*, trans. W.D. Halls. Basingstoke: Macmillan.

Durkheim, E. 1995 [1912]: *The Elementary Forms of the Religious Life*, trans. K.E. Fields. New York: The Free Press.

Durkheim, E. 2009 [1917]: The politics of the future. *Durkheimian Studies* 15: 3–6.

Durkheim. E. 1987: *Selected Writings*, ed. A. Giddens. Cambridge: Cambridge University Press.

Duverger, M. 1954: *Political Parties*. London: Methuen.

Dworkin, A. 1981: *Pornography: Men Possessing Women*. London: The Women's Press.

Eade, J. 1996: Ethnicity and the politics of cultural difference: an agenda for the 1990s? In T. Ranger, Y. Samad and O. Stuart (eds) *Culture, Identity and Politics. Ethnic Minorities in Britain*. Aldershot: Avebury.

Eagleton, T. 1991: *Ideology: An Introduction*. London: Verso.

Eckersley, R. 1995: *Markets, the State and the Environment*. London: Routledge.

Edelman, L. 1992: Legal ambiguity and symbolic structures: organizational mediation of law. *American Journal of Sociology* 97 (6): 1531–1576.

Edelman, M. 1964: *The Symbolic Uses of Politics*. Urbana: University of Illinois Press.

Edelman, M. 1971: *Politics as Symbolic Action*. Chicago, IL: Markham.

Edelman, M. and James, C. 2011: Peasants' rights and the UN system: Quixotic struggle? Or emancipatory idea whose time has come? *Journal of Peasant Studies* 38 (1): 1–30.

Edwards, M. 2004: *Civil Society* Cambridge: Polity Press.

Ehlers, S., Schiraldi, V. and Zeidenberg, J. 2004: *Still Striking Out: Ten Years of California's Three Strikes*. Washington, DC: Justice Policy Institute.

Ehrlich, P. 1968: *The Population Bomb*. New York: Ballantine Books.

Eisenstadt, S. N. 1973: *Tradition, Change, and Modernity*. New York: Wiley, 1973.

Eisenstadt, S. 2000: Multiple modernities. *Daedalus*. 129 (1): 1–29.

Eising, R. 2004: Multilevel governance and business interests in the European Union. *Governance* 17: 211–245.

Elff, M. 2007: Social structure and electoral behavior in comparative perspective: The decline of social cleavages in Western Europe revisited. *Perspectives on Politics* 5 (2): 277–294.

Elff, M. 2009: Social divisions, party positions, and electoral behavior. *Electoral Studies* 28 (2): 297–308.

Elias, N. 1987: *The Loneliness of the Dying*. Oxford: Blackwell.

Elias, N. 1991 [1939]: *The Civilizing Process. Oxford: Blackwell*.

Elias, N. and Dunning. E. 1986: *Quest for Excitement: Sport and Leisure in the Civilizing Process*. Oxford: Blackwell.

Ellickson, R.C. 1991: *Order without Law: How Neighbors Settle Disputes*. Cambridge, MA: Harvard University Press.

Elliott, J. H. 1985: Power and propaganda in the Spain of Philip IV. In S. Wilentz (ed.) *Rites of Power: Symbolism, Ritual, and Politics since the Middle Ages*. Philadelphia, PA: University of Pennsylvania Press.

Elshtain, J.B. 1981: *Public Man, Private Woman*. Oxford: Martin Robertson.

Elster, J. 1989: *The Cement of Society. A Study of Social Order*. Cambridge: Cambridge University Press.

Ely, J. 1992: The politics of 'civil society.' *Telos*, 93: 173–191.

Emirbayer, M. 1996: Useful Durkheim. *Sociological Theory* 14 (2): 109–130.

English, R. 2003: *Armed Struggle: The History of the IRA*. Oxford: Oxford University Press.

Epstein, J. and Straub, K. 1991: *Body Guards: The Cultural Politics of Gender Ambiguity*. London: Routledge.

Erel, U. 2009: *Migrant Women Transforming Citizenship*. Farnham: Ashgate.

Eriksen, T.H. 1993: *Ethnicity and Nationalism. Anthropological Perspectives*. London: Pluto.

Erikson, R., MacKeun, M. and Stimson, J. 2002: *The Macropolity*. New York: Cambridge University Press.

512 REFERENCES

Ertman, T. 1997: *Birth of the Leviathan: Building States and Regimes in Medieval and Early Modern Europe*. Cambridge: Cambridge University Press.

Ertman, T. 1998: Democracy and dictatorship in interwar Western Europe revisited. *World Politics* 50: 475–505.

Ertman, T. 2010: The Great Reform Act of 1832 and British democratization. *Comparative Political Studies* 43: 1000–1023.

Eschle, C. 2001: *Global Democracy, Social Movements and Feminism*. Boulder, CO: Westview Press.

Eschle, C. and Maiguashca, B. 2009: *Making Feminist Sense of the Global Justice Movement*. Lanham, MD: Rowman & Littlefield.

Esping-Andersen, G. (ed.) 1996: *Welfare States in Transition*. London: Sage.

Esping-Andersen, G. 1990: *The Three Worlds of Welfare Capitalism*. Cambridge: Polity Press.

Esping-Andersen, G. 2009: *The Incomplete Evolution*. Cambridge: Polity Press.

Esposito, J. 2002: *Unholy War: Terror in the Name of Islam*. Oxford: Oxford University Press.

Etzioni, A. 1995: *The Spirit of Community – Rights. Responsibilities and the Communitarian Agenda*. London: Fontana Press.

Etzioni, A. 2007: *Security First: For a Muscular, Moral Foreign Policy*. New Haven, CT: Yale University Press.

European Council 15 and 16 October 1999: Presidency Conclusions. http://www.europarl. europa.eu/summits/tam_en.htm (accessed 9 April 2011).

Evans, G. (ed.) 1999: *The End of Class Politics?* Oxford: Oxford University Press.

Evans, G. 2010: Models, measures and mechanisms: an agenda for progress in cleavage research. *West European Politics* 33: 634–647.

Evans, G. and Tilley, J. 2011: How parties shape class politics: explaining the decline of the class basis of party support. *British Journal of Political Science* 41: in press.

Evans, G. and Whitefield, S. 1993: Identifying the bases of party competition in Eastern Europe. *British Journal of Political Science* 23 (4): 521–548.

Evans, P.B., Rueschemeyer, D. and Skocpol, T. (eds) 1985: *Bringing the State Back In*. New York: Cambridge University Press.

Eveline, J. and C. Bacchi. 2005: What are we mainstreaming when we mainstream gender? *International Feminist Journal of Politics* 7 (4): 496–512.

Fanon, F. 1967: *Black Skin, White Masks*. New York: Grove Press.

Fantasia, R. 1988: *Cultures of Solidarity*. Berkeley: University of California.

Farhang, S. 2010: *The Litigation State*. Princeton, NJ: Princeton University Press.

Farnam, T.W. and Eggen, D. 2010. Interest-group spending for midterm up fivefold from 2006. *Washington Post* October 4. www.washingtonpost .com (accessed 6 October 2010).

Farquhar, D. 1996: *The Other Machine. Discourse and Reproductive Technologies*. London: Routledge.

Farrington, D.P., Langan, P.A. and Tonry, M. 2004: Cross-national studies in crime and justice. Bureau of Justice Statistics, NCJ200988.

Fassin, D. and Fassin, E. 2006: *De la Question Sociale à la Question Raciale?* Paris, France: La Découverte.

Faucher-King, F. and Le Galès, P. 2010: *The New Labour Experiment*. Stanford, CA: Stanford University Press.

Favazza, A. 1996: *Bodies Under Siege: Self-Mutilation and Body Modification in Culture and Psychiatry*. Baltimore, MD: Johns Hopkins University Press.

Favre, P. 2005: *Comprendre le monde pour le changer, épistémologie du fait politique*. Paris: Presses de Sciences Po.

Feeley, M.M. and Simon, J. 1992: The new penology: notes on the emerging strategy of corrections and its implications. *Criminology* 30: 449–474.

Fehér, F. and Heller, A. 1986: *Eastern Left–Western Left*. Cambridge: Polity Press.

Fehér, M. Daddaff, R. and Tazi, N. 1989: *Fragments for a History of the Human Body*, 3 vols. New York: Zone.

Feinstein, L. and Slaughter, A-M. 2004: A duty to prevent. *Foreign Affairs* January/February: 136–150.

Feldblum, M. 1993: Paradoxes of ethnic politics: the case of Franco-Maghrebis in France. *Ethnic and Racial Studies* 16 (5): 2–74.

Ferguson, A. 1966 [1767]: *An Essay on the History of Civil Society*. Edinburgh: Edinburgh University Press.

Ferguson, K. E. 1984: *The Feminist Case Against Bureaucracy*. Philadelphia, PA: Temple University Press.

Ferguson, J. 1990: *The Anti-Politics Machine: Development, Depoliticization, and Bureaucratic Power in Lesotho*. Cambridge: Cambridge University Press.

Fernando, M. 2010: Reconfiguring freedom: Muslim piety and the limits of secular law and public discourse in France. *American ethnologist* 37 (1): 19–35.

Ferree, M.M. and Tripp, A.M. (eds) 2006: *Global Feminism: Transnational Women's Activism, Organizing and Human Rights*. New York: New York University Press.

Fine, R. 2007: *Cosmopolitanism* London: Routledge.

Finlayson, A. 1998a: The discourse of nation and the discourse of sexuality. In T. Carver and V. Mottier (eds) *The Politics of Sexuality*. London: Routledge.

Finlayson, A. 1998b: Ideology discourse and nationalism. *Journal of Political Ideologies* 31: 99–118.

Finlayson, A. 2003: *Making Sense of New Labour*. London: Lawrence and Wishart.

Finlayson, A. 2009: Financialisation, financial literacy and asset-based welfare. *British Journal of Politics & International Relations* 11 (3): 400–421.

Finnemore, M. 1996: Norms, culture, and world politics: insights from sociology's institutionalism. *International Organization* 50: 325–347.

Flap, H.D. and De Graaf, N.D. 1986: Social capital and the attained occupational status. *The Netherlands' Journal of Sociology* 22: 145–161.

Fligstein, N. 2008: *Euroclash*. Oxford: Oxford University Press.

Fligstein, N. and Sweet, A.S. 2002: Constructing polities and markets: an institutionalist account of European integration. *American Journal of Sociology* 107: 1206–1243.

Flora P. (ed.) 1986–1987: *Growth to Limits – The West European Welfare State since World War II*, vols. I, II and IV. New York: Walther de Gruyter.

Foley, M. and Edwards, B. 1996: The paradox of civil society. *Journal of Democracy* 7 (3): 38–52.

Ford, L. 2003: Challenging global environmental governance: social movement agency and global civil society. *Global Environmental Politics* 3 (2): 120–134.

Foster, H. and Hagan J. 2007: Incarceration and intergenerational social exclusion. *Social Problems* 54: 399–433.

Foucault, M. 1975: *The Birth of the Clinic*. London: Tavistock.

Foucault, M. 1977: *Discipline and Punish: The Birth of the Prison*. Harmondsworth: Penguin.

Foucault, M. 1978: *The History of Sexuality*, vol. 1. Harmondsworth: Penguin.

Foucault, M. 1979: Social Security. In D. L. Kritzman (ed.) *M. Foucault: Politics, Philosophy and Culture, Interviews and Other Writings 1977–1984*. London: Routledge.

Foucault, M. 1980: *Power/Knowledge: Selected Interviews and Other Writings, 1972–1977*. New York: Pantheon.

Foucault, M. 1981: Omnes et Singulatim: towards a criticism of 'political reason'. In S. McMurrin (ed.) *The Tanner Lectures on Human Values, II*. Salt Lake City: University of Utah Press.

Foucault, M. 1982: The subject and power. In H. L. Dreyfus and P. Rabinow (eds) *Michel Foucault: Beyond Structuralism and Hermeneutics*. Brighton: Harvester.

Foucault, M. 1985: *The Use of Pleasure*. Harmondsworth: Penguin.

Foucault, M. 1988a: The ethic of care for the self as a practice of freedom. In J. Bernauer and D. Rasmussen (eds) *The Final Foucault*. Cambridge, MA: MIT Press.

Foucault, M. 1988b: Social security. In D.L. Kritzman (ed.) *Michel Foucault: Politics, Philosophy and Culture, Interviews and Other Writings 1977–1984*. London: Routledge.

Foucault, M. 1991: Governmentality. In G. Burchell, C. Gordon and P. Miller (eds) *The Foucault Effect*. Chicago, IL: University of Chicago Press.

Foucault, M. 2008: *The Birth of Biopolitics: Lectures at the College de France, 1978–1979*, ed. M. Senellart. London: Palgrave Macmillan.

Foucault, M. 2009: *Security, Territory, Population: Lectures at the Collège De France, 1977–1978*. New York: Picador.

Foucault, M. 1980: *Herculin Barbin: Being the Recently Discovered Memoirs of a Nineteenth Century Hermaphrodite*. New York: Pantheon.

Fourcade-Gourinchas, M. and Babb, S.L. 2002: The rebirth of the liberal creed: paths to neoliberalism in four countries. *American Journal of Sociology* 108: 533–579.

Frank, A.G. 1998: *ReOrient: Global Economy in the Asian Age*. Berkeley: University of California Press.

Frank, D.J. and Meyer, J.W. 2002: The profusion of individual roles and identities in the postwar period. *Sociological Theory* 20: 86–105.

Frank, D.J, Hironaka, A. and Schofer, E. 2000: The nation state and the natural environment over the twentieth century. *American Sociological Review* 65: 96–116.

Frank, D.J. 1997: Science, nature, and the globalization of the environment, 1870–1990. *Social Forces* 76: 409–437.

Frank, D.J. and Gabler, J. 2006: *Reconstructing the University: Worldwide Shifts in Academia in the Twentieth Century*. Stanford: Stanford University Press.

Frank, D.J. and McEneaney, E. 1999: The individualization of society and the liberalization of state policies on same-sex sexual relations, 1984–1995. *Social Forces* 77: 911–944.

Frank, D.J., Hardinge, T. and Wosick-Correa, K. 2009: The global dimensions of rape-law reform: a cross-national study of policy outcomes. *American Sociological Review* 74: 272–290.

Frank, D.J., Longhofer, W. and Schofer, E. 2007: World society, NGOs, and environmental policy reform in Asia. *International Journal of Comparative Sociology* 48: 275–295.

Franklin, M. (ed.) 2004: *Voter Turnout and the Dynamics of Electoral Competition in Established Democracies since 1945*. Cambridge: Cambridge University Press.

Franklin, M. 2010: Cleavage research: a critical appraisal. *West European Politics* 33: 648–658.

Franzway, S., Court, D. and Connell, R.W. 1989: *Staking a Claim: Feminism, Bureaucracy and the State*. Cambridge: Polity Press.

Fraser, N. 1989a: Foucault on modern power: empirical insights and normative confusions. In N. Fraser *Unruly Practices: Power, Discourse and Gender in Contemporary Social Theory*. Cambridge: Polity Press.

Fraser, N. 1989b: *Unruly Practices: Power, Discourse and Gender in Contemporary Social Theory*. Cambridge: Polity Press.

Fraser, N. and Gordon, L. 1992: Contract versus charity: why is there no social citizenship in the United States? *Socialist Review* 22: 45–67.

Freeman, R. 2004: What, me vote? In Kathryn Neckerman (ed.) *Social Inequality*. New York: Russell Sage Foundation.

Freud, S. 1976 [1930]: *Civilization and Its Discontents*. London: Hogarth Press.

Frost, M. 1998: Migrants, civil society and sovereign states: investigating an ethical hierarchy. *Political studies* XLVI, 5: 871–885.

Froud, J., Johal, S., Papazian, V. and Williams, K. 2004: The temptation of Houston: a case study of financialisation. *Critical Perspectives On Accounting* 15 (6/7): 885–909.

Frymer, P. 1999: *Uneasy Alliances: Race and Party Politics in America*. Princeton, NJ: Princeton University Press.

Fukuyama, F. 1992: *The End of History and the Last Man*. London: Hamish Hamilton.

Fukuyama, F. 1995: *Trust: the Social Virtues and the Creation of Prosperity*. New York: The Free Press.

Galaskiewicz, J. 1979: *Exchange Networks and Community Politics*. Beverly Hills, CA: Sage.

Gamble, A. 1993: *The Free Market and the Strong State*, 2nd edn. Basingstoke: Palgrave.

Gamson, W.A. 1992: *Talking Politics*. New York: Cambridge University Press.

Gamson, W.A. and Meyer, D.S. 1996: Framing political opportunity. In D. McAdam, J.D. McCarthy and M.N. Zald (eds) *Comparative Perspectives on Social Movements: Opportunities, Mobilizing Structures, and Cultural Framings*. Cambridge: Cambridge University.

Gamson, W.A. and Modigliani, A. 1989: Media discourse and public opinion on nuclear power: a constructionist approach. *American Journal of Sociology* 95: 1–37.

Gane, M. (ed.) 1992: *The Radical Sociology of Durkheim and Mauss*. London: Routledge.

Gareau, F. 2004: *State Terrorism and the United States: From Counterinsurgency to the War on Terrorism*. Atlanta: Clarity Press.

Garfinkel, H. 1954 (1967): Passing and the managed achievement of sex status in an 'intersexed' person. In H. Garfinkel *Studies in Ethnomethodology*. Englewood Cliffs: Prentice Hall, 1967.

Garfinkel, I., Rainwater, L. and Smeeding, T. 2010: *Wealth and Welfare States: Is America a Laggard or Leader?* New York: Oxford University Press.

Garland, D. 1990: *Punishment and Modern Society: A Study in Social Theory*. Chicago, IL: University of Chicago Press.

Garland, D. 1996: The limits of the sovereign state: strategies of crime control in contemporary society. *British Journal of Criminology* 36: 445–471.

Garland, D. 2001: *The Culture of Control: Crime and Social Control in Contemporary Society*. Chicago, IL: University of Chicago Press.

Gat, A. 2006: *War in Human Civilization*. Oxford: Oxford University Press.

Gautney, H., Dahbour, O., Dawson, A. and Smith, N. (eds) 2009: *Democracy, States, and the Struggle for Global Justice*. New York: Routledge.

Geddes, A. 2003: *The Politics of Migration and Immigration in Europe*. Thousand Oaks, CA: Sage Publications.

Geddes, B. 1990: How the cases you choose affect the answers you get: selection bias in comparative politics. In James A. Stimson (ed.) *Political Analysis*. Ann Arbor: University of Michigan Press.

Geertz, C. 1973: *The Interpretation of Cultures*. New York: Basic Books.

Geertz, C. 1983: Centers, kings, and charisma: reflections on the symbolics of power. In *Local Knowledge*. New York: Basic Books.

Gellner, E. 1983: *Nations and Nationalism*. Oxford: Blackwell.

Gellner, E. 1994: *Conditions of Liberty, Civil Society and its Rivals*. Harmondsworth: Penguin.

Gellner, E. 1995: The importance of being modular. In J. A. Hall (ed.) *Civil Society. Theory, History, Comparison*. Cambridge: Polity Press.

Gellner, E. 2006: *Nations and Nationalism*, 2nd edn, introduction by John Breuilly. Oxford: Blackwell.

Genz, S. 2006: Third Way/ve: the politics of postfeminism. *Feminist Theory* 7 (3): 333–353.

George, A.L. and Bennett, A. 2005: *Case Studies and Theory Development in the Social Sciences*. Cambridge, MA: MIT Press.

Gerges, F. 2009: *The Far Enemy: Why Jihad Went Global*, 2nd edn. Cambridge: Cambridge University Press.

Gerlach, L. 1999: The structure of social movements: environmental activism and its opponents. In J. Freeman and V. Johnson (eds) *Waves of Protest: Social Movements Since the Sixties*. Lanham, MD: Rowman & Littlefield.

Gerteis, J. 2007: *Class and the Color Line: Interracial Class Coalition in the Knights of Labor and the Populist Movement*. Durham, NC: Duke University Press.

Ghaziani, A. and Ventresca, M. 2005: Keywords and cultural change: frame analysis of business model public talk, 1975–2000. *Sociological Forum* 20 4: 523–559.

Giddens, A. 1973a: Elites in the British class structure. *Sociological Review* 20: 345–372. Reprinted in J. Scott (ed.) *Power*, 3 vols. London: Routledge, 1994.

Giddens, A. 1973b: *The Class Structure of the Advanced Societies*. London: Hutchinson.

Giddens, A. 1984: *The Constitution of Society*. Cambridge: Polity Press.

Giddens, A. 1985: *The Nation-State and Violence*. London: Polity Press.

Giddens, A. 1991: *Modernity and Self Identity*. Cambridge: Polity Press.

Giddens, A. 1998: *The Third Way: The Renewal of Social Democracy*. Cambridge: Polity Press.

Gill, R. 2007: *Gender and the Media*. Cambridge: Polity Press.

Gill, S. and Mittelman, J. (eds) 1997: *Innovation and Transformation in International Studies*. Cambridge: Cambridge University Press.

Gillan, K, Pickerill, J. and Webster, F. 2008: *Anti-War Activism: New Media and Protest in the Information Age*. London: Palgrave Macmillan.

Gilleard, C. and Higgs, P. 2000: *Culture and Aging: Self, Citizen and the Body*. London: Prentice-Hall.

Gillespie, A. 2001: *The Illusion of Progress*. London: Earthscan.

Gillespie, M. 2002: Dynamics of diasporas: South Asian media and transnational cultural politics. In G. Sald and T. Tufte (eds) *Global Encounters: Media and Cultural Transformation*. Luton: University of Luton Press.

Gilley, B. 2009: *The Right to Rule: How States Win and Lose Legitimacy*. New York: Columbia University Press.

Gilman, S.L. 2009: *Fat. A Cultural History of Obesity*. Cambridge: Polity Press.

Gilmore, R.W. 2007: *Golden Gulag: Prisons, Surplus, Crisis and Opposition in Globalizing California*. Berkeley: University of California Press.

Gilroy, P. 1987: *There Ain't No Black in the Union Jack*. London: Hutchinson.

Gitlin, T. 1978: Media sociology: the dominant paradigm. *Theory and Society* 6: 205–253.

Glasman, M. 1994: The great deformation: Polanyi, Poland and the terrors of planned spontaneity. *New Left Review* 204: 59–86.

Glaze, L.E. and Bonczar, T.P. 2009: Probation and parole in the United States, 2008. Bureau of Justice Statistics, NCJ 228230.

Glazer, N. and D. P. Moynihan (eds) 1975: *Ethnicity. Theory and Experience*. London: Harvard University Press.

Glenn, E.N. 2002: *Unequal Freedom: How Race and Gender Shaped American Citizenship and Labor*. Cambridge, MA: Harvard University Press.

Glynos, J. and Howarth, D. 2007: *Logics of Critical Explanation in Social and Political Theory*. London: Routledge.

Goertz, G. and Mahoney, J. 2009: Scope in case-study research. In David Byrne and Charles C. Ragin (eds) *The Sage Handbook of Case-Based Methods*. Thousand Oaks: Sage.

Goetz, A-M. 2005: Advocacy administration in the context of economic and political Liberalisation. Paper presented to the UN Division for the Advancement of Women meeting on National Machinery, 29 November–2 December, Rome. http://www.un.org/womenwatch/daw/egm/nationalm2004/documents.html (accessed 9 April 2011).

Goffman, E. 1963a: *Stigma*. Englewood Cliffs: Prentice-Hall.

Goffman, E. 1963b: *Behavior in Public Places. Notes on the Social Organization of Gatherings*. New York: The Free Press.

Goffman, E. 1967: *Interaction Rituals. Essays on Face-to-Face Behavior*. New York: Pantheon Books.

Goffman, E. 1974: *Frame Analysis: An Essay on the Organization of Experience*. London: Harper and Row.

Goffman, E. 1979: *Gender Advertisements*. Basingstoke: Macmillan.

Goldberg, E. 1996: Thinking about how democracy works. *Politics and Society* 24: 7–18.

Goldfrank, W, Goodman, D. and Szasz, A. (eds) 1999: *Ecology and the World System*. London: Greenwood Press.

Goldman, M. 2005: *Imperial Nature: The World Bank and Struggles for Social Justice in the Age of Globalization*. New Haven, CT: Yale University Press.

Goldstein, J. and Keohane, R.O. 1993: Ideas and foreign policy: an analytical framework. In J. Goldstein and R.O. Keohane (eds) *Ideas and Foreign Policy: Beliefs, Institutions, and Political Change*. Ithaca, NY: Cornell University Press.

Goldstein, W. (ed.) 2006: *Marx, Critical Theory, and Religion. A Critique of Rational Choice*. Leiden: Brill.

Goldstone, J.A. 2003: Comparative historical analysis and knowledge accumulation in the study of revolutions. In J. Mahoney and D. Rueschemeyer (eds) *Comparative Historical Analysis in the Social Sciences*. Cambridge: Cambridge University Press.

Goldthorpe, J.H. 1980: *Social Mobility and the Class Structure in Modern Britain*. Oxford: Clarendon.

Goldthorpe, J.H. 1999: Modeling the pattern of class voting in British elections, 1964–1992. In G. Evans (ed.) *The End of Class Politics? Class Voting in Comparative Context*. Oxford: Oxford University Press.

Gooding-Williams, R. 1998: Race, multiculturalism and democracy. *Constellations* 5 (1): 18–41.

Goodwin, J. 2001: *No Other Way Out: States and Revolutionary Movements, 1945–1991*. New York: Cambridge University Press.

Goodwin, J. 2006: A theory of categorical terrorism. *Social Forces* 84 (4): 2027–2046.

Goodwin, J., Jasper, J. and Polletta, F, (eds), 2001: *Passionate Politics: Emotions and Social Movements*. Chicago, IL: University of Chicago Press.

Gordon, J. 2010: *Invisible War: The United States and the Iraq Sanctions*. Cambridge, MA: Harvard University Press.

Gordon, L. 1994: *Pitied but not Entitled: Single Mothers and the History of Welfare, 1890–1935*. Cambridge, MA: Harvard University Press.

Gorski, P.S. 2003: *The Disciplinary Revolution: Calvinism and the Rise of the State in Early Modern Europe*. Chicago, IL: University of Chicago Press.

Gottschalk, M. 2006: *The Prison and the Gallows: The Politics of Mass Incarceration in America*. London: Cambridge University Press.

Gough, I. 2004: Welfare regimes in developments contexts. In I. Gough and G. Wood with A. Barrientos, P. Bevan *et al. Insecurity and Welfare Regimes in Asia, Africa and Latin America: Social Policy in Development Contexts*. Cambridge: Cambridge University Press.

Gough, I. and Therborn, G. 2010: The global future of the welfare states. In F.G. Castles, S. Leibfried, J. Lewis, H. Obinger *et al.* (eds) *The Oxford Handbook of the Welfare State*. Oxford: Oxford University Press.

Gough, I. and Wood, G. with Barrientos, A., Bevan, P. *et al.* 2004: *Insecurity and Welfare Regimes in Asia, Africa and Latin America: Social Policy in Development Contexts*. Cambridge: Cambridge University Press.

Gould, D.B. 2009: *Moving Politics: Emotion and ACT-UP's Fight against AIDS*. Chicago, IL: University of Chicago Press.

Graham, H.D. 1990: *The Civil Rights Era: Origins and Development of National Policy, 1960–1972*. New York: Oxford University Press.

GRAIN 2008: *Seized: The 2008 Landgrab For Food and Financial Security*. October. http://www.grain.org/briefings_files/landgrab-2008-en.pdf (accessed 9 April 2011).

Gramsci, A. 1971: *Selections from the Prison Notebooks*. London: Lawrence & Wishart.

Granovetter, M. 1985: Economic action, social structure, and embeddedness. *American Journal of Sociology* 83: 1420–1443.

Grant, W. 2001: Pressure politics: from 'insider' politics to direct action? *Parliamentary Affairs* 54: 337–348.

Gray, V. and Lowery, D. 1996: *The Population Ecology of Interest Representation*. Ann Arbor: University of Michigan Press.

Greenaway, J., Salter, B. and Hart, S. 2007: How policy networks can damage democratic health: a case study in the government of governance. *Public Administration* 85: 717–738.

Greenberg, D.F. and West, V. 2001: State prison populations and their growth, 1971–1991. *Criminology* 39: 615–654.

Greenberg, S.B. 1980: *Race and State in Capitalist Development*. New Haven, CT: Yale University Press.

Greenfeld, L. 1992: *Nationalism. Five Roads to Modernity*. Cambridge, MA: Harvard University Press.

Greenwood, J. 2003: *Interest Representation in the European Union*. Basingstoke: Palgrave Macmillan.

Grenfell, M. 2008a (ed.): *Pierre Bourdieu: Key Concepts*. Durham: Acumen.

Grenfell, M. 2008b: Interest. In M. Grenfell (ed.) *Pierre Bourdieu: Key Concepts*. Durham: Acumen.

Griffin, L. 1992: Temporality, events, and explanation in historical sociology: an introduction. *Sociological Methods & Research* 20 (4): 403–427.

Grimm, D. 2009: Conflicts between general laws and religious norms. *Cardozo Law Review* 30 (6): 2369–2382.

Grofman, B. 2004: Downs and two-party convergence. *Annual Review of Politics*, 7: 25–46.

Grossman, E. 2004: Bringing politics back in: rethinking the role of economic interest groups in European integration. *Journal of European Public Policy* 11: 637–454.

Grossman, H. 2007: Marx, classical economics, and the problem of dynamics. *International Journal of Political Economy* 36 (2): 6–83.

Grossmann, M. 2006: Environmental advocacy in Washington: a comparison with other interest groups. *Environmental Politics* 15: 628–638.

Grossmann, M. 2009: Just another interest group? The organized representation of ethnic groups in American national politics. *National Political Science Review* 11: 291–307.

Grossmann, M. and Dominguez, C.B.K. 2009: Party coalitions and interest group networks. *American Politics Research* 37: 767–800.

Gründger, F. 1994: Beveridge meets Bismarck: echo, effects, and evaluation of the Beveridge Report in Germany. In J. Hills, J. Ditch and H. Glenmerster (eds) *Beveridge and Social Security*. Oxford: Clarendon Press.

Guidry, J, Kennedy, M. and Zald, M. 2000: Globalizations and social movements. In J. Guidry, M. Kennedy and M. Zald (eds) *Globalizations and Social Movements: Culture, Power and the Transnational Public Sphere*. Ann Arbor: University of Michigan Press.

Guittet, E., Perier, M. and Bigo, D. 2005: Suspicion et exception. *Cultures et Conflits* 58 (2): 53–101.

Gupta, A. and Ferguson, J. 1992: Beyond 'culture': space, identity, and the politics of difference. *Cultural Anthropology* 7: 6–23.

Gusfield, J.R. 1963: *Symbolic Crusade: Status Politics and the American Temperance Movement*. Urbana: University of Illinois Press.

Guttsman. W.L. 1963: *The British Political Elite*. London: MacGibbon and Kee.

Haas, P.M. 1989: Do regimes matter? Epistemic communities and Mediterranean pollution control. *International Organization*, 43 (3): 377–403.

Haas, P.M. 1992: Introduction: epistemic communities and international policy coordination. *International Organization* 46: 1–35.

Habermas, J. 1976: *Legitimation Crisis*. Cambridge: Polity Press.

Habermas, J. 1987: *The Theory of Communicative Action, Lifeworld and System: A Critique of Functionalist Reason*, vol. 2. Cambridge: Polity Press.

Habermas, J. 1989: *The Structural Transformation of the Public Sphere*. Cambridge: Polity Press.

Habermas, J. 1992: Citizenship and national identity: some reflections on the future of Europe. *Praxis International* 12 (1): 1–19.

Habermas, J. 1996: The European nation-state — its achievements and its limits. On the past and future of sovereignty and citizenship. In G. Balakrishnan (ed.) *Mapping the Nation*. London: Verso.

Habermas, J. 2001: *The Postnational Constellation: Political Essays*. Cambridge: Polity Press.

Habermas, J. 2002: Bestiality and humanity: a war between legality and morality *Constellations* 6 (3): 263–272.

Habermas, J. 2003: *The Future of Human Nature*. Cambridge: Polity Press.

Hacker, J. and Pierson, P. 2010: *Winner-Take-All Politics*. New York: Simon & Shuster.

Hacker, J.S. 2002: *The Divided Welfare State*. New York: Cambridge University Press.

Hafner-Burton, E. and Tsutsui, K. 2005: Human rights in a globalizing world: the paradox of empty promises. *American Journal of Sociology* 110 (5): 1373–1411.

Hafner-Burton, E. and Tsutusi, K. 2007: Justice lost! The failure of international human rights law to matter where needed most. *Journal of Peace Research*, 44 (4): 407–425.

Hagan, J. and Palloni, A. 1990: The social reproduction of a criminal class in working class London, circa 1950–1980. *American Journal of Sociology* 96: 265–299.

Haggard, S. and Kaufmann, R.R. 2008: *Development, Democracy and Welfare States: Latin America, East Asia and Eastern Europe*. Princeton, NJ: Princeton University Press.

Hahm, D.E. 2000: Kings and constitutions: Hellenistic theories. In C. Rowe and M. Schofield (eds) *The Cambridge History of Greek and Roman Political Thought*. Cambridge: Cambridge University Press.

Hahn, T. 2001: The difference the Middle Ages makes: color and race before the modern world. *Journal of Medieval and Early Modern Studies* 31 (1): 1–38.

Hajnal, Z. 2006: *Changing White Attitudes toward Black Political Leadership*. New York: Cambridge University Press.

Hall, J.A. (ed.) 1995: *Civil Society: Theory, History, Comparison*. Cambridge: Polity Press.

Hall, J.A. 1985: *Powers and Liberties*. Berkeley: University of California Press.

Hall, P.A. 1993: Policy paradigms, social learning, and the state: the case of economic policy making in Britain. *Comparative Politics* 25: 275–296.

Hall, P.A. and Soskice, D. (eds) 2001: *Varieties of Capitalism*. Oxford: Oxford University Press.

Hall, P.A. and Taylor, R.C.R. 1996: Political Science and the Three Institutionalisms. *Political Studies* 44: 936–957.

Hall, S. 1978: *Policing the Crisis: Mugging, the State, and Law and Order*. Basingstoke: Macmillan.

Hall, S. 1996: Politics of identity. In T. Ranger, Y. Samad and O. Stuart (eds) *Culture, Identity and Politics. Ethnic Minorities in Britain*. Aldershot: Avebury.

Hall, S. 2003 [1989]: New ethnicities. In L.M. Alcroff and E. Mendieta (eds) *Identities: Race Class, Gender and Difference*. Oxford: Blackwell.

Hall, S. 1992: The question of cultural identity. In S. Hall, D. Held and T. McGrew (eds.) *Modernity and its Futures*. Cambridge: Polity.

Hall, S. and Gieben, B. (eds) 1992: *Formations of Modernity*. Cambridge: Polity Press in association with the Open University.

Hall, S. and Jefferson, T. (eds) 1976: *Resistance Through Rituals: Youth Subcultures in Post-War Britain*. New York: Harper Collins.

Hallett, T. and Ventresca, M.J. 2006: Inhabited institutions: social interaction and organizational form in Gouldner's patterns of industrial bureaucracy. *Theory and Society* 35: 213–236.

Halman, L. and Pettersson, T. 2003: Religion and social capital revisited. In Halman L. and Riis, O. (eds) *Religion in Secularizing Societies: The Europeans' Religion At the End of the XXth Century*. Leiden: Brill.

Halpin, D. and Jordan, G. 2009: Interpreting environments: interest group response to population ecology pressures. *British Journal of Political Science* 39: 243–265.

Halsey, A.H., Heath, A.F. and Ridge, J. 1980: *Origins and Destinations*. Oxford: Clarendon Press.

Hammond, P. and Machacek, D. 2009: Religion and the state. In P. Clarke (ed.) *The Oxford Handbook of the Sociology of Religion*. Oxford: Oxford University Press.

Hann, C.M. 1995: Philosophers' models on the Carpathian Lowlands. In J.A. Hall (ed.) *Civil Society. Theory, History, Comparison*. Cambridge: Polity Press.

Haraway, D.J. 1991: *Simians, Cyborg and Women. The Reinvention of Nature*. London: Free Association.

Hardin, G. 1968: The tragedy of the commons. *Science*, 162 (3859): 1243–1248.

Hardin, G. 1974: Living on a lifeboat. *BioScience*, 23 (10): 561–568.

Hargreaves, A. 1995: *Immigration, Race and Ethnicity in Contemporary France*. New York: Routledge.

Haritaworn, J. 2010: Wounded subjects: sexual exceptionalism and the moral panic on 'migrants homophobia' in Germany. In E.G. Rodriguez, M. Boatca and S. Costa (eds) *Decolonizing European Sociology. Transdisciplinary Approaches*. Farnham: Ashgate.

Harris, E. 2009: *Nationalism. Theories and Cases*. Edinburgh: Edinburgh University Press.

Harrop, M. 1986: The press and post-war elections. In I. Crewe and M. Harrop (eds) *Political Communications: The General Election Campaign of 1983*. Cambridge: Cambridge University Press.

Harvey, D. 1982: *The Limits to Capital*. Oxford: Blackwell.

Harvey, D. 1994: *The Condition of Post-Modernity*. Oxford: Blackwell.

Harvey, D. 2003: *The New Imperialism*. Oxford: Oxford University Press.

Harvey, D. 2005: *A Brief History of Neoliberalism*. Oxford: Oxford University Press.

Harvey, J. and Sparks, R. 1991: The politics of the body in the context of modernity. *Quest* 43: 164–189.

Haslam, M. (ed.) 1986: *Psycho-legal Aspects of Sexual Problems*. Burgess Hill Shering.

Hatzfeld, H. l971: *Du paupérisme à la sécurité sociale*. Paris: Armand Colin.

Havel, V. 1985: The power of the powerless. In Havel *et al. The Power of the Powerless*. Armonk, NY: M.E. Sharpe.

Havel, V. 1988: Anti-political politics. In J. Keane (ed.) *Civil Society and the State: New European Perspectives*. London: Verso.

Hay, C. 2008: Good inflation, bad inflation: the housing boom, economic growth and the disaggregation of inflationary preferences in the UK and Ireland. *The British Journal of Politics and International Relations* 11: 461–478.

Hayek, F. von 2007 [1944]: *The Road to Serfdom*. Chicago, IL: University of Chicago Press.

Health Commission 2009: *Investigation into Mid Staffordshire NHS Foundation Trust*. London: Healthcare Commission.

Hearn, J. 2001: Men, fathers and the state: national and global relations. In B. Hobson (ed.) *Making Men into Fathers*. Cambridge: Cambridge University Press.

Heater, D. 1990: *Citizenship*. London: Longman.

Heath, A., Jowell, R. and Curtice, J. 1991: *Understanding Political Change: The British Voter, 1964–87*. London: Pergamon.

Heath, A., Jowell, R., and Curtice, J. 2001: *The Rise of New Labour: Party Policies and Voter Choices*. Oxford: Oxford University Press.

Heath, A.F., Curtice, J. and Jowell, R. 1985: *How Britain Votes*, London: Pergamon.

Hechter, M. 1986: Rational choice theory and the study of race and ethnic relations. In J. Rex and D. Mason (eds) *Theories of Race and Ethnic Relations*. Cambridge: Cambridge University Press.

Hechter, M. 2000: *Containing Nationalism*. Oxford: Oxford University Press.

Hegel, G.F.W. 1967 [1821]: *Philosophy of Right*. Oxford: Oxford University Press.

Heidenheimer, A.J., Johnston M. and LeVine V.T. (eds) 1989: *Political Corruption: A Handbook*. New Brunswick: Transaction Publishers.

Heimer, K. and Kruttschnitt, C. 2005: *Gender and Crime*. New York: NYU Press.

Heinz, J.P., Laumann, E.O., Nelson, R.L. and Salisbury, R.H. 1993: *The Hollow Core: Private Interests in National Policymaking*. Cambridge, MA: Harvard University Press.

Held, D. 1995a: *The Problem of Autonomy and the Global Order*. Cambridge: Polity Press.

Held, D. 1995b: *Democracy and the Global Order: From the Modern State to Cosmopolitan Governance*. Cambridge: Polity Press.

Held, D. 2010: *Cosmopolitanism: Ideals and Realities*. Cambridge: Polity Press.

Helgerson, R. 1992: *Forms of Nationhood: The Elizabethan Writing of England*. Chicago, IL: University of Chicago Press.

Heller, A. 1982: Phases of legitimation in Soviet-type societies. In T.H. Rigby and F. Féher (eds) *Political Legitimation in Communist States*. Basingstoke: Macmillan.

Hemmings, C. 2005: Telling feminist stories. *Feminist Theory* 6 (2): 115–139.

Hendin, H. 1997: *Seduced by Death. Doctors, Patients and the Dutch Cure*. New York: Norton.

Hendrix, C.S. 2010: Measuring state capacity: theoretical and empirical implications for the study of civil conflict. *Journal of Peace Research* 47: 273–285.

Henley, N.M. 1977: *Body Politics: Power, Sex and Non Verbal Communication*. Englewood Cliffs, NJ: Prentice Hall.

Herbert, D. 2003: *Religion and Civil Society*. Aldershot: Ashgate.

Herman, E. and O'Sullivan, G. 1989: *The Terrorism Industry: The Experts and Institutions That Shape Our View of Terror*. New York: Pantheon.

Herman, E.S. and McChesney, R.W. 1997: *The Global Media: The New Missionaries of Corporate Capitalism*. London: Cassell.

Hernes, H. 1987: *Welfare State and Woman Power: Essays in State Feminism*. London: Norwegian University Press.

Hertz, N. 2001: Better to shop than vote? *Business Ethics: A European Review* 10: 190–193.

Hervieu-Léger, D. 2000: *Religion as a Chain of Memory*. Cambridge: Polity Press.

Hess, D. 2009: *Localist Movements in a Global Economy*. Cambridge, MA: MIT Press.

Hewitt, C. 1974: Policy-making in post-war Britain: a national level test of elitist and pluralist hypotheses. *British Journal of Political Science* 4 (2): 187–216. Reprinted in J. Scott (ed.) *Power*, 3 vols. London: Routledge, 1994.

Heywood, P. (ed.) 1997: *Political Corruption*. Oxford: Blackwell.

Hibou, B. (ed.) 2004: *Privatising the State*. London: Hurst & Co.

Hicks, A. 1999: *Social Democracy and Welfare Capitalism: A Century of Income Security Politics*. Ithaca, NY: Cornell University Press.

Higson, A. 1995: *Waving the Flag: Constructing a National Cinema in Britain*. Oxford: Clarendon Press.

Hill, P. 2004: *Black Sexual Politics. African American, Gender and the New Racism*. New York: Routledge.

Himmelfarb, G. 2000: The demoralization of society: what's wrong with the civil society. In D. E. Eberly (ed.) *The Essential Civil Society Reader: The Classic Essays*. Lanham, MD: Rowman & Littlefield.

Hindess, B. 1996: *Discourses of Power: From Hobbes to Foucault*. Oxford: Blackwell.

Hindess, B. 2004: Citizenship for all. *Citizenship Studies* 8 (3): 305–315.

Hindess, B. 2009: A tale of origins and disparity. *Cultural Economy* 2 (1/2): 213–217.

Hinich, M.J. and Munger, M.C. 1996: *Ideology and the Theory of Political Choice*. Ann Arbor: University of Michigan Press.

Hintze, O. 1970, Staatsverfassungs und Heeresverfassung. In O. Hintze *Staat und Verfassung*. Goettingen: Vandenhoeck und Ruprecht.

Hironaka, A. 2000: The globalization of environmental protection: the case of environmental impact assessment. *International Journal of Comparative Sociology* 43: 65–78.

Hironaka, A. 2005: *Neverending Wars: The International Community, Weak States, and the Perpetuation of Civil War*. Cambridge, MA: Harvard University Press.

Hironaka, A. 2010: *Tokens of Power: Changing Military Interests*. Irvine, CA: Unpublished book manuscript.

Hirschmann, N.J. 1996: Rethinking obligation for feminism. In N.J. Hirschmann and C. Stegano (eds) *Revisioning the Political*. Boulder, CO: Westway Press.

Hjellbrekke, J., Roux, B.L., Korsnes, O., Lebaron, F. *et al.* 2007: The Norwegian Field of Power Anno 2000. *European Societies*, 9 (2): 245–273.

Hobbes, T. 1994 [1660]: *Leviathan*. London: Everyman.

Hobsbawm, E. 1990: *Nations and Nationalism since 1780: Programme, Myth, Reality*. Cambridge: Cambridge University Press.

Hobsbawm, E. and Ranger, T. (eds) 1992: *The Invention of Tradition*. Cambridge: Cambridge University Press.

Hobson, B. and Lister, R. 2002: Citizenship. In B. Hobson, J. Lewis and B. Siim (eds) *Contested Concepts in Gender and Social Politics*. Cheltenham: Edward Elgar.

Hochschild, A.R. 2003: *The Commercialization of Intimate Life: Notes From Home and Work*. San Francisco and Los Angeles: University of California Press.

Hochschild, J. and Weaver, V. 2007: The skin color paradox and the American racial order. *Social Forces* 86 (2): 1–28.

Hoffman, J. 1995: *Beyond the State*. Oxford: Blackwell.

Holland, S. 1995: Descartes goes to Hollywood: Mind, body and gender in contemporary cyborg cinema. *Body and Society* 1 (3/4): 157–174.

Holloway, J. and Piciotto, S. (eds) 1978: *State and Capital: a Marxist Debate*. London: Arnold.

Holmes, M. 2002: Rethinking the meaning and management of intersexuality. *Sexualities* 5 (2) 159–180.

Holt-Giménez, E. 2006: *Campesino a campesino: Voices From Latin America's Farmer to Farmer Movement for Sustainable Agriculture*. Oakland, CA: Food First Books.

Hood, C. 1998: *The Art of the State*, Oxford: Oxford University Press.

Hoogvelt, A. 1997: *Globalisation and the Postcolonial World*. Basingstoke: Macmillan.

hooks. b. 1982: *Black Looks. Race and Representation*. Toronto: Between the Lines.

Horkheimer, M. and Adorno, T.W. 1972: *Dialectic of Enlightenment*. New York: Seabury.

Hornborg, A. 1998: Ecosystems and world systems: accumulation as an ecological process. *Journal of World-Systems Research*, 4 (2): 169–177.

Horowitz, D.L. 2000 [1985]: *Ethnic Groups in Conflict*. Berkeley: University of California Press.

Hout, M. and Greely, A. 2006: *The Truth about Evangelical Protestants*. Chicago, IL: University of Chicago Press.

Houtman, D., Achterberg, P. and Derks. A. 2008: *Farewell to the Leftist Working Class*. New Brunswick, NJ: Transaction Publishers.

Howard, M. 1961: *The Franco-Prussian War: The German Invasion of France, 1870–1871*. London: Rupert Hart-Davis.

Howard, M. 1976: *War in European History*. Oxford: Oxford University Press.

Howarth, D. 1997: Complexities of identity/difference: black consciousness ideology in South Africa. *Journal of Political Ideologies* 2 (1): 51–78.

Huber, E. and Stephens, J. 2001: *Development and Crisis of the Welfare State*. Chicago, IL: University of Chicago Press.

Hübinger, G. 2009: Max Weber's 'sociology of the state' and the science of politics in Germany. *Max Weber Studies* 9 (1/2): 17–32.

Huckfeldt, R. and Sprague, J. 1995: *Citizens, Politics and Social Communication: Information and Influence in an Election Campaign*. Cambridge: Cambridge University Press.

Hume, D. 1987 [1742]: *Essays: Moral, Political and Literary*. Indianapolis: Liberty Fund.

Hunter, F. 1953: *Community Power Structure*. Chapel Hill: University of North Carolina Press.

Huntington, S.P. 1968: *Political Order in Changing Society*. New Haven, CT: Yale University Press.

Huntington, S.P. 1991: *The Third Wave: Democratization in the Late Twentieth Century*. Norman: University of Oklahoma Press.

Huntington, S.P. 2004: *Who Are We? The Challenges to America's Identity*. New York: Simon & Schuster.

Husted, B.W. 1994: Honor among thieves: a transaction-cost interpretation of corruption in Third World Countries. *Business Ethics Quarterly* 4 (1): 17–27.

Hutchinson, J. 1987: *The Dynamics of Cultural Nationalism: The Gaelic Revival and the Creation of the Irish Nation State*. London: Allen & Unwin.

Hutchinson, J. and A.D. Smith 1996: Introduction. In J. Hutchinson and A.D. Smith (eds) *Ethnicity*. Oxford: Oxford University Press.

Hutchinson, J. and Smith, A.D. (eds) 1994: *Nationalism: A Reader*. Oxford: Oxford University Press.

Huysmans, J, Dobson, A. and Prokhovnik, R. 2006: *The Politics of Protection: Sites of Insecurity and Political Agency*. New York: Routledge.

IAASTD 2009: *Agriculture at a Crossroads: Global Report*. Washington, DC: International Assessment of Agricultural Knowledge, Science and Technology for Development & Island Press. http://www.agassessment.org/reports/IAASTD/EN/Agriculture%20at%20a% 20Crossroads_Global%20Report%20 (English).pdf (accessed 9 April 2011).

Ignatieff, M. 2001: *Human Rights as Politics and Idolatry*. Princeton, NJ: Princeton University Press.

Ignatieff, M. 2004: *The Lesser Evil: Political Ethics in an Age of Terror*. Edinburgh: Edinburgh University Press.

Immergut, E.M. 1998: The theoretical core of the new institutionalism. *Politics & Society* 26: 5–34.

Inglehart, R. 1990: *Culture Shift in Advanced Industrial Society*. Princeton, NJ: Princeton University Press.

Inglehart, R. 1997: *Modernization and Post-Modernization*. Princeton, NJ: Princeton University Press.

Inglehart, R. and Norris, P. 2003: *Rising Tide: Gender Equality and Cultural Change Around the World*. Cambridge: Cambridge University Press.

Innis, H.A. 1950: *Empire and Communications*. Oxford: Oxford University Press.

Isaac, J.C. 1987: *Power and Marxist Theory: A Realist Approach*. Ithaca, NY: Cornell University Press.

Isin, E.F. and Turner, B.S. 2002: Citizenship studies: an introduction. In E.F. Isin and B.S. Turner (eds) *Handbook of Citizenship Studies*. London: Sage.

Iversen, T. 1994: Political leadership and representation in West European democracies. A test of three models of voting. *American Journal of Political Science* 38 (1): 45–74.

Iyengar, S. and McGrady, J.A. 2007: *Media Politics: A Citizen's Guide*. New York: W.W. Norton.

Jacobs, D. and Helms, R. 1996: Towards a political model of incarceration: a time-series examination of multiple explanations for prison admission rates. *American Journal of Sociology* 102: 323–357.

Jacobs, D. and Carmichael, J.T. 2001: The politics of punishment across time and space: a pooled time-series analysis of imprisonment rates. *Social Forces* 80: 61–91.

Jacobs, D. and Helms, R.E. 1996: Toward a political model of incarceration: a time-series examination of multiple explanations for prison admission rates. *American Journal of Sociology* 102: 323–357.

Jacobs, D. and Helms, R.E. 2001: Towards a political sociology of punishment: politics and changes in the incarcerated population. *Social Science Research* 30: 171–194.

Jacobs, J. 1961: *The Death and Life of Great American Cities*. New York: Vintage Books.

Jacobs, L. and King, D. (eds) 2009: *The Unsustainable American State*, New York: Oxford University Press.

Jacobsen, D. 1996: *Rights Across Borders: Immigration and the Decline of Citizenship*. Baltimore, MD: John Hopkins University.

Jacobson, D. and Ruffer, G.B. 2003: Courts across borders: the implications of judicial agency for human rights and democracy. *Human Rights Quarterly* 25: 74–92.

Jamieson, K.H. 1984: *Packaging the Presidency: A History and Criticism of Presidential Campaign Advertising*. New York: Oxford University Press.

Jamieson, K.H. 1988: *Eloquence in an Electronic Age: The Transformation of Political Speechmaking*. New York: Oxford University Press.

Jay, M. 1992: *Force Fields: Between Intellectual History and Cultural Critique*. London: Routledge.

Jenkins, R. 1992: *Pierre Bourdieu*. London: Routledge.

Jenkins, R. 1997: *Rethinking Ethnicity: Arguments and Explorations*. London: Sage.

Jeong, H. (eds) 2001: *Global Environmental Policies*. New York: Palgrave.

Jepperson, R.L. and Meyer, J.W. 2011: Multiple levels of analysis and the limits of methodological individualisms. *Sociological Theory* 29 (1): 54: 73.

Jepperson, R.L. 1991: Institutions, institutional effects, and institutionalism. In W.W. Powell and P.J. DiMaggio (eds) *The New Institutionalism in Organizational Analysis*. Chicago, IL: University of Chicago Press.

Jepperson, R.L. 2002: The development and application of sociological neoinstitutionalism. In J. Berger & M. Zelditch, Jr. (eds) *New Directions in Contemporary Sociological Theory*. Lanham, MD: Rowman & Littlefield.

Jepperson, R.L., Wendt, A. and Katzenstein, P.J. 1996: Norms, identity, and culture in national security. In P.J. Katzenstein (ed.) *The Culture of National Security*. New York: Columbia University.

Jessop, B. 1982: *The Capitalist State: Marxist Theories and Methods*. Oxford: Martin Robertson.

Jessop, B. 1990: *State Theory: Putting Capitalist States in their Place*. Cambridge: Polity.

Jessop, B. 1997: Capitalism and its future: remarks on regulation, government and governance. *Review of International Political Economy* 4 (3): 561–581.

Jessop, B. 1999: Globalization and the national state. Draft: published by the Department of Sociology, Lancaster University. http://www.lancaster.ac.uk/sociology/soc012rj.html (accessed 9 April 2011).

Jessop, B. 2002: *The Future of the Capitalist State*. Cambridge: Polity Press.

Jessop, B. 2006: State and state-building. In R. Rhodes, S. Binder and B. Rockman (eds) *The Oxford Handbook of Political Institutions*. Oxford: Oxford University Press.

Jessop, B. 2007: *State Power: A Strategic-Relational Approach*. Cambridge: Polity Press.

Jessop, B., Brenner, N. and Jones, M.R. 2008: Theorizing sociospatiality. *Environment and Planning D: Society and Space* 26 (3): 389–401.

Joas, H. 2009: The sacredness of the person. *Theory* (Newsletter of the International Sociological Association Research Group 16), Autumn/Winter: 2–3.

Joas, H. and Knobl, W. 2009: *Social Theory: Twenty Introductory Lectures*. Cambridge: Cambridge University Press.

Johnson, K.S. 2007: *Governing the American State*. Princeton, NJ: Princeton University Press.

Johnston, H. and Klandermans, B. (eds) 1995: *Social Movements and Culture*. Minneapolis: University of Minnesota Press.

Johnston, M. 2005: *Syndromes of Corruption: Wealth, Power, and Democracy*. Cambridge: Cambridge University Press.

Jones, K.B. 1988: Towards the revision of politics. In K.B. Jones and A.G. Jónasdóttir (eds) *The Political Interests of Gender*. London: Sage.

Jones, K.B. 1990: Citizenship in a woman-friendly polity. *Signs* 15 (4): 781–812.

Jonker, G. and Amiraux V. (eds) 2006: *Politics of Visibility. Young Muslims in European Public Spaces*. Bielefeld: Transcript Verlag.

Joppke, C. 1999: *Immigration and the Nation-State: The United States, Germany and Great Britain*. New York: Oxford University Press.

Joppke, C. 2009: *Veil: Mirror of Identity*. Cambridge: Polity.

Joppke, C. and Morawska, E. (eds) 2003: *Toward Assimilation and Citizenship: Immigrants in Liberal Nation-States*. London: Palgrave Macmillan.

Joppke, Christian, 2008: Immigration and the identity of citizenship: the paradox of universalism. *Citizenship Studies* 12 (6): 533–546.

Jordan, G. and Maloney, W.A. 2007: *Democracy and Interest Groups*. Basingstoke: Palgrave Macmillan.

Jordan. T. 1995: Collective bodies: raving and the politics of Gilles Deleuze and Felix Guattari. *Body and Society* 1 (1): 125–144.

Jouvenel, B. de 1962: *On Power: Its Nature and the History of Its Growth*. Boston, MA: Beacon Press.

Judge, D. 1999: *Representation: Theory and Practice*. London: Routledge.

Juteau, D. 1996: Theorising ethnicity and ethnic communalisms at the margins: from Quebec to the world system. *Nations and Nationalism* 2 (1): 45–66.

Kabeer, N. 2005: Introduction. The search for inclusive citizenship. In N. Kabeer (ed.) *Inclusive Citizenship*. London & New York: Zed Books.

Kaldor, M. 1993: Yugoslavia and the new nationalism. *New Left Review* 197: 96–112.

Kaldor, M. 1999: *New and Old Wars: Organized Violence in a Global Era*. Cambridge: Polity Press.

Kaldor, M. 2000: *Global Insecurity*. London: Continuum.

Kane, A. 1991: Cultural analysis in historical sociology: the analytic and concrete forms of the autonomy of culture. *Sociological Theory* 9: 53–69.

Kantola, J. 2006: *Feminists Theorize the State*. Basingstoke: MacMillan.

Kastoryano, R. 2002: *Negotiating Identities. States and Immigrants in France and Germany*. Princeton, NJ: Princeton University Press.

Katz, E. and Lazarsfeld, P.F. 1955: *Personal Influence: The Part Played by People in the Flow of Mass Communications*. Glencoe, IL: The Free Press.

Katz, R. and Mair, P. 1995: Changing models of party organization and party democracy: the emergence of the cartel party. *Party Politics* 1 (1): 5–28.

Katz, R. and Mair, P. 2009: The cartel party thesis: a restatement. *Perspectives on Politics* 7 (4): 753–766.

Katznelson, I. 1997: Structure and configuration in comparative politics. In M.I. Lichbach and A.S. Zuckerman (eds) *Comparative Politics: Rationality, Culture, and Structure*. New York: Cambridge University Press.

Katznelson, I. 2005: *When Affirmative Action was White: The Untold History of Racial Inequality in America*. New York: W.W. Norton.

Kaup, K.P. 2002: Regionalism versus ethnicnationalism. *The China Quarterly*, 172: 863–884.

Kawata, J. (ed.) 2006: *Comparing Political Corruption and Clientelism*. Burlington, VT: Ashgate.

Keal, P. 2003: *European Conquest and the Rights of Indigenous Peoples*. Cambridge: Cambridge University Press.

Keane, J. (ed.) 1988: *Civil Society: New European Perspectives*. London: Verso.

Keating, M. 2001: *Nations against the State. The New Politics of Nationalism in Quebec, Catalonia and Scotland*, 2nd edn. Basingstoke: Palgrave.

Keck, M. and Sikkink, K. 1998: *Activists beyond Borders: Advocacy Networks in International Politics*. Ithaca, NY: Cornell University Press.

Kedar, O. 2005: When moderate voters prefer extreme parties: policy balancing in parliamentary elections. *American Political Science Review*, 99 (2): 185–200.

Kedar, O. 2009: *Voting for Policy, Not Parties. How Voters Compensate for Power Sharing*. Cambridge: Cambridge University Press.

Keeley, L. 1996: *War before Civilization*. Oxford: Oxford University Press.

Kellner, D. 2002: Theorizing globalization. *Sociological Theory* 20 (3): 285–305.

Kelly, N. 2009: *The Politics of Income Inequality*. Cambridge: Cambridge University Press.

Kenis, P. and Schneider, V. 1991: Policy networks and policy analysis: scrutinizing a new analytical toolbox. In B. Marin and R. Mayntz (eds) *Policy Networks: Empirical Evidence and Theoretical Considerations*. Frankfurt am Main: Campus Verlag.

Kenniston, K. 1968: *Young Radicals*. New York: Harcourt, Brace, and World.

Kenny, M. 2003: Communitarianism. In Alan Finlayson (ed.) *Contemporary Political Theory: A Reader and Guide*. Edinburgh: Edinburgh University Press.

Kenworthy, L. 2004: *Egalitarian Capitalism*. New York: Russell Sage Foundation.

Keohane, R.O. 2005: *After Hegemony: Cooperation and Discord in the World Political Economy*. Princeton, NJ: Princeton University Press.

Keohane, R.O. and Nye, J.S. 1977: *Power and Interdependence: World Politics in Transition*. Boston, MA: Little, Brown.

Kepel, G. 1997: *Allah in the West: Islamic Movements in America and Europe*. Palo Alto: Stanford University Press.

Kersbergen, K.van and Manow, P. 2009: *Religion, Class Coalitions, and Welfare States*. Cambridge: Cambridge University Press.

Kershaw, P. 2006: Care*fair*: choice, duty and the distribution of care. *Social Politics*, 13 (3): 341–371.

Kershaw, P., Pulkingham, J. and Fuller, S. 2008: Expanding the subject: violence, care and (in) active citizenship. *Social Politics* 15 (2): 182–206.

Kertzer, D.I. 1988: *Ritual, Politics, and Power*. New Haven, CT: Yale University Press.

Kim, Nadia. 2008: *Imperial Citizens: Koreans and Race from Seoul to LA*. Stanford, CA: Stanford University Press.

Kim, Y.S., Jang Y.S. and Hwang, H. 2002: Structural expansion and the cost of global isomorphism: a cross-national study of ministerial structure, 1950–1990. *International Sociology* 17: 481–503.

Kind, D.R. 1999: *In the Name of Liberalism: Illiberal Social Policy in the USA and Britain*. New York: Oxford University Press.

Kinder, D.R. and Sanders, L.M. 1996: *Divided by Color: Racial Politics and Democratic Ideals*. Chicago, IL: University of Chicago Press.

King, D. 2000: *Making Americans: Immigration, Race, and the Origins of the Diverse Democracy*. Cambridge, MA: Harvard University Press.

King, D. and Hansen, R. 1999: Experts at work: state autonomy, social learning and eugenic sterilization in 1930s Britain. *British Journal of Political Science* 29: 77–107.

King, D. and Lieberman, R. 2009: Ironics of the American state. *World Politics* 61: 547–588.

King, D. and Smith, R. 2005: Racial orders in American political development. *American Political Science Review* 99 (1): 75–92.

King, G., Keohane, R.O. and Verba, S. 1994: *Designing Social Inquiry: Scientific Inference in Qualitative Research*. Princeton, NJ: Princeton University Press.

Kingdon, J.W. 1995: *Agendas, Alternatives, and Public Policies*, 2nd edn. New York: Harper Collins.

Kirchheimer, O. 1966: The transformation of the Western European party system. In J. LaPalombara and M. Weiner (eds) *Political Parties and Political Development*. Princeton, NJ: Princeton University Press.

Kisby, B. 2007: Analysing policy networks: towards an ideational approach. *Policy Studies* 28: 71–90.

Kiser, E. and Hechter, M. 1998: The debate on historical sociology: rational choice theory and its critics. *American Journal of Sociology* 104 (3): 785–816.

Kitschelt, H. 1989a: *The Logics of Party Formation*. Ithaca, NY: Cornell University Press.

Kitschelt, H. 1989b: The internal politics of parties: the law of curvilinear disparity revisited. *Political Studies* 37 (3): 400–421.

Kitschelt, H. 1992: The formation of party systems in East Central Europe. *Politics and Society* 20 (1): 7–50.

Kitschelt, H. 1994: *The Transformation of European Social Democracy*. Cambridge: Cambridge University Press.

Kitschelt, H. (in collaboration with A.J. McGann) 1995: *The Radical Right in Western Europe: A Comparative Analysis*. Ann Arbor: Michigan University Press.

Kitschelt, H. 2000: Linkages between citizens and politicians in democratic polities. *Comparative Political Studies* 33 (6/7): 845–879.

Kitschelt, H. and Wilkinson, S. 2007: Introduction. In H. Kitschelt and S. Wilkinson (eds) *Patrons, Clients and Policies*. Cambridge: Cambridge University Press.

Kitschelt, H., Hawkins, K., Luna, J.P., Rosas, G. *et al.* 2010: *Latin American Party Systems*. Cambridge: Cambridge University Press.

Kitschelt, H., Mansfeldova, Z., Markowski, R. and Toka, G. 1999: *Post-Communist Party Systems: Competition, Representation, and Inter-Party Cooperation*. Cambridge: Cambridge University Press.

Klapper, J.T. 1960: *The Effects of Mass Communication*. Glencoe, IL: The Free Press.

Klitgaard, R. 1988: *Controlling Corruption*. Berkeley: University of California Press.

Klitgaard, R., MacLean-Abaroa, R. and Parris H.L. 2000: *Corrupt Cities: A Practical Guide to Cure and Prevention*. Washington, DC: The World Bank.

Knijn, T. and Kremer, M. 1997: Gender and the caring dimension of welfare states: toward inclusive citizenship. *Social Politics* 4 (3): 328–361.

Knoke, D. 1986: Associations and interest groups. *Annual Review of Sociology* 12: 1–21.

Knoke, D. 1994: *Political Networks*. Cambridge: Cambridge University Press.

Knoke, D. 1998: The organizational state: origins and prospects. *Research in Political Sociology* 8: 147–163.

Knoke, D. 2001: *Changing Organizations: Business Networks in the New Political Economy*. Boulder, CO: Westview Press.

Knoke, D. 2004: The sociopolitical construction of national policy domains. In C.H.C.A. Henning and C. Melbeck (eds) *Interdisziplinäre Sozialforschung: Theorie und empirische Anwendungen*. Frankfurt am Main: Campus Verlag.

Knoke, D. 2011: Policy networks. In J. Scott and P. Carrington (eds) *Sage Handbook of Social Network Analysis*. Thousand Oaks, CA: Sage.

Knoke, D., Pappi, F., Broadbent, J. and Tsujinaka, J. 1996: *Comparing Policy Networks: Labor Politics in the US, Germany and Japan*. New York: Cambridge University Press.

Kohl, J. 1985: *Staatsausgaben in Westuropa*. Frankfurt am Main/New York: Campus Verlag.

Kohlmorgen, L., Hein, W. and Bartsch, S. 2007: Networks and governance: transnational networks as a basis for emancipatory politics in global society? *Peripherie* 27 (105–106): 8–34.

Konrad, G. 1984: *Antipolitics*. London: Harcourt Brace Jovanovich.

Kooiman, J. 2003: *Governing as Governance*. London: Sage.

Kornhauser, W. 1959: *The Politics of Mass Society*. Glencoe, IL: The Free Press.

Korpi, W. 1983: *The Democratic Class Struggle*. London: Routledge.

Korpi, W. 2003: Welfare-state regress in Western Europe: politics, institutions, globalization, and Europeanization. *Annual Review of Sociology* 29: 589–609.

Korpi, W. and Palme, J. 2003: New politics and class politics in the context of austerity and globalization: welfare state regress in18 countries, 1975–95. *American Political Science Review* 97 (3): 425–446.

Krasner, Stephen A. 1983: *International Regimes*. New York: Cornell University Press.

Kricsi, H. 2004: Political Context and Opportunity. In D.A. Snow, S.A. Soule and H. Kriesi (eds) *The Blackwell Companion to Social Movements*. Oxford: Blackwell.

Kriesi, H., Adam, S. and Jochum, M. 2006: Comparative analysis of policy networks in Western Europe. *Journal of European Public Policy* 13: 341–361.

Krook, M.L. 2008: Campaigns for candidate gender quotas: a new global women's movement. In S. Grey and M. Sawer (eds) *Women's Movements: Flourishing or in Abeyance?* London: Routledge.

Krucken, G. and Drori, G.S. (eds) 2009: *World Society: The Writings of John W. Meyer*. Oxford: Oxford University Press.

Kruttschnitt, C. and Gartner, R. 2005: *Marking Time in the Golden State*. Cambridge: Cambridge University Press.

Kumar, K. 1993: Civil society: an inquiry into the usefulness of an historical term. *British Journal of Sociology* 44 (3): 375–395.

Kumar, K. 2006: English and French national identity: comparisons and contrasts. *Nations and Nationalism* 12 (3): 413–432.

Kumar, K. 2010: Nation-states as empires, empires as nation-states: two principles, one practice? *Theory and Society* 39: 119–143.

Kurasawa, F. 2004: A cosmopolitanism from below: alternative globalization and the creation of a solidarity without bounds. *European Journal of Sociology* 45 (2): 233–255.

Kurasawa, F. 2007: *The Work of Global Justice: Human Rights as Practices*. Cambridge: Cambridge University Press.

Kütting, G. 2000: *Environment, Society and International Relations*. London: Routledge.

Kütting, G. 2004: *Globalization and Environment, Greening Global Political Economy*. New York: SUNY Press.

Kütting, G. and Lipschutz, R. (eds.) 2009: *Environmental Governance: Power and Knowledge in a Local-Global World*. London: Routledge.

Kwon, H-J. 2005: *Transforming the Developmental Welfare State in East Asia*. London: Palgrave.

Kymlicka, W. 1995: *Multicultural Citizenship*. Oxford: Oxford University Press.

Kymlicka, W. and Norman, W. 1994: Return of the citizen: a survey of recent work on citizenship theory. *Ethics* 104: 352–381.

La Noue, G.R. and Sullivan, J.C. 2001: Deconstructing affirmative action categories. In J.D. Skrentny (ed.) *Color Lines: Affirmative Action, Immigration and Civil Rights Options for America*. Chicago, IL: University of Chicago Press.

Laborde, C. 2000: *Pluralist Thought and the State in Britain and France, 1900–25*. Basingstoke: Macmillan.

Lachmann, R. 2010: *State and Power*. Cambridge: Polity Press.

Laclau, E. 1996: *Emancipation(s)*. London: Verso.

Laclau, E. 2007: *On Populist Reason*. London: Verso.

Laitin, D.D. 1995: The civic culture at thirty. *American Political Science Review* 89: 168–173.

Lambsdorff, J. G. 2007: *Institutional Economics of Corruption and Reform*. Cambridge: Cambridge University Press.

Lamont, M 1992: *Money, Morals, and Manners*. Princeton, NJ: Princeton University Press.

Lamont, M. and Thévenot, L. (eds) 2000: *Rethinking Comparative Historical Sociology: Repertoires of Evaluation in France and the United States*. New York: Cambridge University Press.

Lange, P. 2007: Commenting on comments: investigating responses to antagonism on YouTube. Paper presented at Society for Applied Anthropology Conference, Tampa, Florida, 31 March.

Lange, P. 2008a: (Mis)Conceptions about YouTube. In G. Lovink and S. Niederer (eds) *Responses to YouTube*. Institute of Network Cultures, Amsterdam: International Communication Association.

Lange, P. 2008b: Publicly private and privately public: social networking on YouTube. *Journal of Computer-Mediated Communication* 13: 361–380.

Laqueur, T. 1990: *Making Sex. Body and Gender from the Greeks to Freud*. Harvard: Harvard University Press.

Larner, W. and Walters, W. (eds) 2004: *Global Governmentality. Governing International Spaces*. London: Routledge.

Lasch, C. 1979: *The Culture of Narcissism*. New York: Norton.

Lash, S. and Urry, J. 1987: *The End of Organized Capitalism*. Cambridge: Polity Press.

Lassman, P. and Speirs, R. (eds) 1994: *Weber: Political Writings*. Cambridge: Cambridge University Press.

Latour, B. 2005: *Reassembling the Social: an Introduction to Actor-Network-Theory*. Oxford: Oxford University Press.

Laumann, E.O. and Knoke, D. 1987: *The Organizational State: A Perspective on the Social Organization of National Energy and Health Policy Domains*. Madison, WI: University of Wisconsin Press.

Laumann, E.O. and Pappi, F.U. 1976: *Networks of Collective Action: A Perspective on Community Influence Systems*. New York: Academic Press.

Laumann, E.O., Galaskiewicz, J. and Marsden, P.V. 1978: Community structure as interorganizational linkages. *Annual Review* of Sociology 4: 455–484.

Laurie, Alison 1967: *Imaginary Friends*. New York: Owl Publishing Company.

Lavdas, K.A., Papadakis, N.E. and Gidarakou, M. 2006: Policies and networks in the construction of the European higher education area. *Higher Education Management and Policy* 18: 129–139.

Laver, M. 2005: Policy and the dynamics of party competition. *American Political Science Review* 99 (2): 263–282.

Lawler, S. 2000: *Mothering the Self*. London, Routledge.

Lawrence, B. (ed.) 2005: *Messages to the World: The Statements of Osama bin Laden*. London: Verso.

Lawrence, S. and Travis, J. 2004: The new landscape of imprisonment: mapping America's prison expansion. Washington, DC: Urban Institute Justice Policy Center.

Lazarsfeld, P. F., Berelson, B. and Gaudet, H. 1948: *The People's Choice*. New York: Columbia University Press.

Le Galès, P. and Scott, A. 2010: A British bureaucratic revolution? Autonomy without control or 'freer actors more rules'. English Annual selection, *Revue Française de Sociologie* 51: 119–146.

Lebaron, Frederic 2000: Economists and the economic order: the field of economists and the field of power in France. *European Societies* 3 (1): 91–110.

Leca, J. 1992: Questions on citizenship. In C. Mouffe (ed.) *Dimensions of a Radical Democracy*. London: Verso.

Lechner, F.J. and Boli, J. 2005: *World Culture: Origins and Consequences*. Oxford: Blackwell.

Lee, J. and F.D. Bean 2010: *The Diversity Paradox: Immigration and the Color Line in 21st Century America*. New York: Russell Sage Foundation.

Lee, T. 2002: *Mobilizing Public Opinion: Black Insurgency and Racial Attitudes in the Civil Rights Era*. Chicago, IL: University of Chicago Press.

Leff, N. 1964: Economic development through bureaucratic corruption. *American Behavioral Scientist* 8 (2): 8–14.

Lefort, C. 1986: *The Political Forms of Modern Society: Bureaucracy, Democracy, Totalitarianism*. Cambridge: Polity Press.

Lehmann, D. 2002: Religion and globalization. In L. Woodhead, P. Fletcher, H. Kawanami and D. Smith (eds) *Religions in the Modern World*. London: Routledge.

Lehmbruch, G. 1989: Institutional linkages and policy networks in the federal system of West Germany. *Publius* 19 (4): 221–235.

Leibfried, S. and Mau, S. (eds) (2008): *Welfare States: Construction, Deconstruction, Reconstruction*, 3 vols. Cheltenham: Edward Elgar.

Leibfried, S. and Zürn, M. (eds) 2007: *Transforming the Golden-Age Nation State?* Basingstoke: Palgrave.

Levi-Strauss, C. 1963: *Structural Anthropology*. New York: Basic Books.

Levi, M. 2002: The state of the study of the state. In I. Katznelson and H. Milner (eds.) *The State of the Discipline*. New York: Norton/APSA.

Levine, E. 2008: Remaking *Charlie's Angels*: the construction of post-feminist hegemony. *Feminist Media Studies* 8 (4): 375–389.

Levitt, J. 2010: Confronting the impact of citizens united. *Yale Law & Policy Review* 29 (1): 217–232.

Levitt, P. 2001: *The Transnational Villagers*. Berkeley: University of California Press.

Lewis, J. 1992: Gender and the development of welfare regimes. *Journal of European Social Policy* 2 (3): 159–173.

Lewis, R. and Rolley, K. 1997: (Ad)dressing the dyke: lesbian looks and lesbian looking. In M. Nava, A. Blake, I. MacRury and B. Richards (eds) *Buy this Book*. London: Routledge.

Lichterman, P. 2005: *Elusive Togetherness*. Princeton, NJ: Princeton University Press.

Lie, J. 2004a: *Modern Peoplehood*. Cambridge, MA: Harvard University Press.

Lie, J. 2004b: *Multi-Ethnic Japan*. Cambridge, MA: Harvard University Press.

Lieberman R.C. 1998: *Shifting the Color Line: Race and the American Welfare State*. Cambridge, MA: Harvard University Press.

Lieberman, R.C. 2009: Civil rights and the democratization trap: the public-private nexus and the building of American democracy. In D. King, R.C. Lieberman and G. Ritter (eds) *Democratization in America*. Baltimore, MD: Johns Hopkins University Press.

Lien, D.D. 1986: A note on competitive bribery games. *Economic Letters*, 22 (4): 337–431.

Lijphart, A. 1977: *Democracy in Plural Societies*. New Haven, CT: Yale University Press.

Lijphart, A. 1997: Unequal participation: democracy's unresolved dilemma. *The American Political Sciences Review* 19(1): 1–14.

Lindert, P. H. 2004: *Growing Public. Social Spending and Economic Growth*, 2 vols. Cambridge: Cambridge University Press.

Lipiètz, A. 1997: The post-Fordist world: labour relations, international hierarchy and global ecology. *Review of International Political Economy*, 4 (1): 1–41.

Lipjhart, A. 1979: Religious vs. linguistic vs. class voting. *American Political Science Review* 73: 442–458.

Lipjhart, A. 1997: Unequal participation: democracy's unresolved dilemma. *American Political Science Review* 91: 1–14.

Lipjhart, A. 1999: *Patterns of Democracy: Government Forms and Performance in 36 Countries*. New Haven, CT: Yale University Press.

Lipschutz, R, Mayer, J. 1996: *Global civil society and global environmental governance*. New York: SUNY Press.

Lipschutz, R. 1999: Approaches to global governance theory. In M. Hewson and T. Sinclair (eds) *From Local Knowledge and Practice to Global Environmental Governance*. New York: SUNY press.

Lipschutz, R. 2001: Environmental history, political economy and change: frameworks and tools for research and analysis. *Global Environmental Politics* 1 (3): 72–91.

Lipschutz, R. 2003: *Global Environmental Politics: Power, Perspectives and Practice*. Washington, DC: CQ Press.

Lipset, S.M. 1960: *Political Man*. New York: Anchor Books.

Lipset, S.M. 1963: *The First New Nation: The United States in Historical and Comparative Perspective*. New York: Basic Books.

Lipset, S.M. 1981 [1960]: *Political Man*, expanded edn. Baltimore, MD: Johns Hopkins University Press.

Lipset, S.M. 1983: *Political Man*, 2nd edn. London: Heinemann.

Lipset, S.M. 1996: *American Exceptionalism: A Double-edged Sword*. New York: Norton.

Lipset, S.M. and Rokkan, S. 1967: Cleavage structures, party systems, and voter alignments. An introduction. In S.M. Lipset and S. Rokkan (eds) *Party Systems and Voter Alignments. Cross-National Perspectives*. New York: The Free Press.

Lipsky, M. 1968: Protest as a political resource. *American Political Science Review* 62, 1144–1158.

Lipton, Eric. 2010: A G.O.P. leader tightly bound to lobbyists. *New York Times* September 11. www.nytimes.com (accessed 5 October 2010).

Lister, R. 2003: *Citizenship: Feminist Perspectives*, 2nd edn. Basingstoke and New York: Palgrave.

Lister, R. 2007: Citizenship. In G. Blakeley and V. Bryson (eds) *The Impact of Feminism on Political Concepts and Debates*. Manchester: Manchester University Press.

Lister, R. 2009: Citizenship, civil society and conflict: a gendered perspective. In P. Baert, S. Koniordos, G. Procacci and C. Ruzza (eds) *Citizenship, Civil Society and Conflict*. London and New York: Routledge.

Lister, R. Williams, F., Anttonon, A, Bussemaker, J. *et al.* 2007: *Gendering Citizenship in Western Europe*. Cambridge: Policy Press.

Liu, D. and Boyle, E.H. 2001: Making the case: the women's convention and gender discrimination in Japan. *International Journal of Comparative Sociology* 42: 389–404.

Lizardo, O. 2006: The effect of economic and cultural globalization on anti-U.S. transnational terrorism 1971–2000. *Journal of World-Systems Research* 7 (1): 144–186.

Lloyd-George, D. 2000 [1908]: Old Age Pension Bill. Order for second reading. In R. Goodin and D. Mitchell (eds) *The Foundations of the Welfare State*, vol. II. Cheltenham: Elgar.

Lock, M. 2002: *Twice Dead. Organ Transplant and the Reinvention of Death*. Berkeley: California University Press.

Locke, J. 1980 [1681–1683]: *Second Treatise on Civil Government*, ed. C.B. Macpherson. Indianapolis, IN: Hackett.

Lockwood, D. 1957: *The Black Coated Worker*. London: Allen & Unwin.

Lockwood, D. 1966: Sources of variation in working class images of society. *Sociological Review* 14 (3): 244–267.

Lockwood, D. 1995: 'Foreword' to T. Butler and M. Savage *Social Change and the Middle Classes*. London: UCL Press.

Logan, J. R. Molotch, H. L. 1987: *Urban Fortunes: The Political Economy of Place*. Berkeley, CA: University of California Press.

Lomax, B. 1997: The strange death of civil society in Hungary. *Journal of Communist Studies and Transition Studies* 13 (1): 41–63.

Longhofer, W. and Schofer, E. 2010: National and global origins of environmental association. *American Sociological Review* 74 (4): 505–533.

Lotke, E. and Wagner, P. 2003: Prisoners of the census: electoral and financial consequences of counting prisoners where they go, not where they come from. *Pace Law Review* 24: 587–607.

Lounsbury, M., Ventresca, M.J. and Hirsch, P. 2003: Social movements, field frames, and industry emergence. *Socio-Economic Review* 1: 71–104.

Loury, G. 1977: A dynamic theory of racial income differences. In P.A. Wallace and A. Le Mund (eds) *Women Minorities and Employment Discrimination*, Lexington, MA: Lexington Books.

Loury, G. 1987: Why should we care about group inequality? *Social Philosophy and Policy* 5: 249–271.

Lovelock, J. 1988: *The Ages of Gaia: A Biography of our Living Earth*. Oxford: Oxford University Press.

Loveman, M. 2005: The modern state and the primitive accumulation of state power. *American Journal of Sociology* 110: 1651–1683.

Lovenduski, J. 2005: *Feminising Politics*. Cambridge: Polity Press.

Lovenduski, J. 2007: Unfinished business: equality policy and the changing context of state feminism in Great Britain. In J. Outshoorn and J. Kantola (eds) *Changing State Feminism*. Basingstoke: Palgrave MacMillan.

Lovenduski, J. and Norris, P. (eds) 1996: *Women in Politics*. Oxford: Oxford University Press.

Lowi, T.J. 1964: American business, public policy, case studies and political theory. *World Politics* 16: 677–715.

Luckmann, T. 1967: *The Invisible Religion: The Problem of Religion in Modern Society*. London: Macmillan.

Luhmann, N. 1982: *The Differentiation of Society*. New York: Colombia University Press.

Luhmann, N. 1984: *Soziale Systeme. Grundriß einer allgemeinen Theorie*. Frankfurt am Main: Suhrkamp.

Lui, F.T. 1986: A dynamic model of corruption deterrence. *Journal of Public Economics*, 31 (2): 215–236.

Luker, K. 1984: *Abortion and the Politics of Motherhood*. Berkeley: University of California Press.

Lukes, S. 1974: *Power: A Radical View*. Basingstoke: Macmillan.

Lukes, S. 1975: *Emile Durkheim: His Life and Work*. Harmondsworth: Penguin.

Lustick, I. 1996: History, historiography, and political science: historical records and selection bias. *American Political Science Review* 90: 605–618.

Luzi, S., Hamouda, M.A., Sigrist, F. and Tauchnitz, E. 2008: Water policy networks in Egypt and Ethiopia. *Journal of Environment and Development* 17: 238–268.

Lynch, M.P. 2010: *Sunbelt Justice: Arizona and the Transformation of American Punishment*. Stanford, CA: Stanford Law Books.

Maarek, P.J. 1993: *Political Marketing and Communication*. Luton: Luton University Press.

Mabbett, I. (ed.) 1985: *Patterns of Kingship and Authority in Traditional Asia*. London: Croom Helm.

Mackay, F. 2008: 'Thick' conceptions of substantive representation: women, gender and political institutions. *Representation* 44 (2): 125–139.

Mackenzie, C. and Stoljar, N. 2000: Introduction: autonomy refigured. In C. Mackenzie and N. Stoljar (eds) *Relational Autonomy: Feminist Perspectives on Autonomy, Agency and the Social Self*. New York: Oxford University Press.

MacKenzie, D. 2006: *An Engine, Not a Camera: How Financial Models Shape Markets*. Cambridge, MA: MIT Press.

MacKinnon, C. 1989: *Toward a Feminist Theory of the State*. Cambridge: Harvard University Press.

Macpherson, C. B. 1977: *The Life and Times of Liberal Democracy*. Oxford: Oxford University Press.

Mahmood, S. 2005: *Politics of Piety: The Islamic Revival and the Feminist Subject*. Princeton, NJ: Princeton University Press.

Mahoney, C. 2008: *Brussels versus the Beltway: Advocacy in the United States and the European Union*. Washington, DC: Georgetown University Press.

Mahoney, C. and Baumgartner, F.R. 2008: Converging perspectives on interest group research in Europe and America. *West European Politics* 31: 1253–1273.

Mahoney, J. and Schensul, D. 2006: Historical context and path dependence. In R.E. Goodin and C. Tilly (eds) *The Oxford Handbook of Contextual Political Analysis*. New York: Oxford University Press.

Mahoney, J. 2000: Path dependence in historical sociology. *Theory and Society* 104 (4): 1154–1196.

Mahoney, J. 2003: Knowledge accumulation in comparative historical research: the case of democracy and authoritarianism. In D. Rueschemeyer and J. Mahoney (eds) *Comparative Historical Analysis in the Social Sciences*. New York: Cambridge University Press.

Mahoney, J. 2010a. After KKV: the new methodology of qualitative research. *World Politics* 62: 120–147.

Mahoney, J. 2010b. *Colonialism and Postcolonial Development: Spanish America in Comparative Perspective*. Cambridge: Cambridge University Press.

Mahoney, J. and Terrie, P.L. 2009: The proper relationship of comparative-historical analysis to statistical analysis: subordination, integration, or separation? In C. C. Ragin and D. Byrne (eds) *The Handbook of Case-Oriented Methods*. Thousand Oaks, CA: Sage.

Mair, P. 1997: *Party System Change. Approaches and Interpretations*. Oxford: Oxford University Press.

Malkki, L.H. 1995: *Purity and Exile: Violence, Memory, and National Cosmology among Hutu Refugees in Tanzania*. Chicago, IL: University of Chicago Press.

Maltese, J. A. 1994: *Spin Control: The White House Office of Communications and the Management of Presidential News*, 2nd edn. Chapel Hill: University of North Carolina Press.

Mancini, S. 2009: The power of symbols and symbols as power. *Cardozo Law Review* 30 (6): 2629–2668.

Maniates, M. 2001: Individualization: plant a tree, buy a bike, save the world. *Global Environmental Politics*, 1 (3): 53–71.

Mann, M. 1984: Capitalism and militarism. In M. Shaw (ed.) *War, State and Society*. Basingstoke: Macmillan.

Mann, M. 1986 [1984]: The autonomous power of the state: its origins, mechanisms and results. In J.A. Hall (ed.) *States in History*. Oxford: Blackwell.

Mann, M. 1986: *The Sources of Social Power*, Vol. 1: *A History of Power from the Beginning to AD 1760*. Cambridge: Cambridge University Press.

Mann, M. 1988: *States, War and Capitalism: Studies in Political Sociology*. Oxford: Blackwell.

Mann, M. 1993: *The Sources of Social Power*, Vol. 2: *The Rise of Classes and Nation States, 1760–1914*. Cambridge: Cambridge University Press.

Mann, M. 2005: *The Dark Side of Democracy. Explaining Ethnic Cleansing*. Cambridge: Cambridge University Press.

Mann, M.1984: The autonomous power of the state: its origins, mechanisms and results. *Archives Européennes de Sociologie* 25: 185–212.

Mansbridge, J. 2003: Rethinking representation. *American Political Science Review* 97 (4): 515–528.

Manza, J. and Brooks, C. 1999: *Social Cleavages and Political Change*. New York: Oxford University Press.

Manza, J. and Wright, N. 2003: Religion and political behavior. In M. Dillon (ed.) *Handbook of the Sociology of Religion*. New York: Cambridge University Press, pp. 297–314.

Manza, J. and Uggen, C. 2006: *Locked Out: Felon Disenfranchisement and American Democracy*. New York: Oxford University Press.

Manza, J. and Wright, N. 2003: Religion and political behavior. In M. Dillon (ed.) *Handbook of the Sociology of Religion*. Cambridge: Cambridge University Press.

Manza, J., Brooks, C. and Sauder, M. 2004: Money, participation, and votes: social cleavages and electoral politics. In T. Janoski, R. Alford, A. Hicks and M.A. Schwarz (eds) *The Handbook of Political Sociology*. New York: Cambridge University Press.

March, J.G. and Johan P. Olsen. 1984: The new institutionalism: organizational factors in political life. *American Political Science Review* 78: 734–749.

Marcuse. H. 1969: *Eros and Civilization*. New York: Sphere Books.

Marin, B. and Mayntz, R. (eds) 1991: *Policy Networks: Empirical Evidence and Theoretical Considerations*. Boulder, CO: Westview Press.

Marinetto, M. 2007: *Social Theory, the State and Modern Society*. Milton Keynes: Open University Press/McGraw-Hill.

Markoff, J. 1996: *Waves of Democracy*. Thousand Oaks, CA: Pine Forge Press.

Marsh, D. 1998: *Comparing Policy Networks*. Buckingham: Open University Press.

Marsh, D. and Rhodes. R.A.W. (eds) 1992: *Policy Networks in British Government*. Oxford: Clarendon Press.

Marsh, D. and Smith, M. 2000: Understanding policy networks: towards a dialectical approach. *Political Studies* 48 (4): 4–21.

Marshall, T.H. 1950: *Citizenship and Social Class and other Essays*. Cambridge: Cambridge University Press.

Martin, J.L. 2003: What is field theory? *American Journal of Sociology* 109: 1–49.

Martinez-Alier, J. 2002: *The Environmentalism of the Poor: A Study of Ecological Conflicts and Valuation*. Cheltenham: Edward Elgar.

Martínez-Torres, M.E. and Rosset, P.M. 2010: La Vía Campesina: the birth and evolution of a transnational social movement. *Journal of Peasant Studies* 37 (1): 149–175.

Marx, A.W. 1998: *Making Race and Nation: A Comparison of South Africa, the United States, and Brazil*. New York: Cambridge University Press.

Marx, K. 1973 [1871]: The civil war in France. In D. Fernbach (ed.) *Karl Marx: The First International and After*. Harmondsworth: Penguin.

Marx, K. 1978 [1847]: *The Poverty of Philosophy*. Peking: Foreign Languages Press.

Marx, K. and Engels, F. 1845–1846: The German Ideology. In *Marx–Engels Collected Works*, vol. 5. London: Lawrence & Wishart, 1976.

Marx, K. and Engels, F. 1848: *The Manifesto of the Communist Party*.

Marx, K. 1976 [1867]: *Capital*, vol. 1, trans. B. Fowkes. Harmondsworth: Penguin.

Marx, K. 1981 [1844]: *Economic and Philosophic Manuscripts*. London: Lawrence & Wishart.

Mason, D. 1999: The continuing significance of race? Teaching ethnic and racial studies in sociology. In M. Bulmer and J. Solomos (eds) *Ethnic and Racial Studies Today*. London: Routledge.

Massoglia, M. 2008a: Incarceration, health, and racial health disparities. *Law and Society Review* 42: 275–306.

Massoglia, M. 2008b: Incarceration as exposure: the prison, infectious disease, and other stress-related illnesses. *Journal of Health and Social Behavior* 49: 56–71.

Massoglia, M. and Schnittker, J. 2009: No real release. *Contexts* 8: 38–42.

Mateo Diaz, M. 2005: *Representing Women? Female Legislators in West European Parliaments*. Oxford: ECPR.

Mauss, M. 1973 [1936]: Techniques of the body. *Economy and Society* 2: 70–87.

May, J.D. 1973: Opinion structure of political parties: the special law of curvilinear disparity. *Political Studies* 21 (2): 135–151.

Mayer, J. 2010: Covert operations: the billionaire brothers who are waging a war against Obama. *New Yorker* August 30. www.newyorker.com (accessed 5 October 2010).

Mayntz, R. 1993: Governing failures and the problem of governability. In J. Kooiman (ed.) *Modern Governance*, London: Sage.

Mazur, A. 2005: The impact of women's participation of leadership on policy outcomes: a focus on women's policy machineries. Paper presented at the United Nations Expert Group Meeting on Equal Participation of Women and Men in Decision-Making Processes, 24–27 October.

McAdam, D. 1982: *Political Process and the Development of Black Insurgency, 1930–1970*. Chicago, IL: University of Chicago Press.

McAdam, D. 1988: *Freedom Summer*. New York: Oxford University Press.

McAdam, D., McCarthy, J.D. and Zald, M.N. (eds) 1996: *Comparative Perspectives on Social Movements: Political Opportunities, Mobilizing Structures, and Cultural Framings*. Cambridge: Cambridge University Press.

McAdam, Doug. 1982: *Political Process and the Development of Black Insurgency*. Chicago, IL: University of Chicago Press.

McCammon, H.J., Muse, C.S., Newman, H.D. and Terrell, T.M. 2007: Movement framing and discursive opportunity structures: the political successes of US women's jury movements. *American Sociological Review* 72: 725–749.

McCarthy, J.D. and Zald M.N. 1977: Resource mobilization and social movements: a partial theory. *American Sociological Review* 82: 1212–1241.

McCarthy, T. 1992: The critique of impure reason: Foucault and the Frankfurt School. In T.E. Wartenberg (ed.) *Rethinking Power*. Albany: State University of New York Press.

McCombs, M.E. and Shaw, D.L. 1972: The agenda-setting function of mass media. *Public Opinion Quarterly*, 36, 176–187.

McCombs, M.E. 2004: *Setting the Agenda: The Mass Media and Public Opinion*. Cambridge: Polity Press.

McFarland, A.S. 2007: Neopluralism. *Annual Review of Sociology* 10: 45–66.

McGarry, R.H. and B. O'Leary (eds) 1993: *The Politics of Ethnic Conflict Regulation*. London: Routledge.

McGuinniss, J. 1970: *The Selling of the President, 1968*. London: Andre Deutsch.

McKeon, N., Watts, M. and Wolford, W. 2004: *Peasant Associations in Theory and Practice*. Geneva: UN Research Institute for Social Development.

McNeill, W. 1982: *The Pursuit of Power: Technology, Armed Force, and Society since A.D. 1000*. Chicago, IL: University of Chicago Press.

McNeill, W. 1995: *Keeping Together in Time: Dance and Drill in Human History*. Cambridge, MA: Harvard University.

McRobbie, A. 2009: *The Aftermath of Feminism: Gender, Culture and Social Change*. London: Sage.

Meadows, D. 1972: *The Limits to Growth: A Report on the Club of Rome's Project on the Predicament of Mankind*. Washington, DC: Island Press.

Meckled-Garcia, S. and Cali, B. 2006: Human rights *legalized* – defining, interpreting, and implementing an ideal. In S. Meckled-Garcia and B. Cali (eds) *The Legalization of Human Rights: Multidisciplinary Perspectives on Human Rights Law*. London: Routledge.

Medema, S.G. 2009: *The Hesitant Hand: Taming Self Interest in the History of Economic Ideas*. Princeton, NJ: Princeton University Press.

Mellahi, K., Morrell, K. and Wood, G. 2010: *The Ethical Business*. London: Palgrave.

Melossi, D. 1985: Punishment and social action: changing vocabularies of punitive motive within a political business cycle. *Current Perspectives in Social Theory* 6: 169–197.

Melucci, A. 1996: *Challenging Codes: Collective Action in the Information Age*. New York: Cambridge University Press.

Mendez, M-L. 2008: Middle class identities in a neoliberal age: tensions between contested authenticities. *The Sociological Review*, 56 (2): 220–237.

Mendoza, B. 2002: Transnational feminisms in question. *Feminist Theory* 3 (3): 295–314.

Mennell, S. 1995: Civilisation and decivilisation, civil society and violence. *Irish Journal of Sociology* 5: 1–21.

Merchant, C. 1992: *Radical Ecology: The Search for a Livable world*. London: Routledge.

Merrill, Samuel, III and Grofman, B. 1999: *A Unified Theory of Voting: Directional and Proximity Spatial Models*. Cambridge: Cambridge University Press.

Merton, R.K. 1972: The latent functions of the machine. In M.S. Bruce (ed.) *Urban Bosses. Machines and Progressive Reformers*. Lexington, DC: Heat.

Meyer, D.S. 1990: *A Winter of Discontent: The Nuclear Freeze and American Politics*. New York: Praeger.

Meyer, D.S. 2000: Social movements: creating communities of change. In M.A. Tetreault and R.L. Teske (eds) *Feminist Approaches to Social Movements, Community, and Power*. Columbia, South Carolina: University of South Carolina Press.

Meyer, D.S. 2007: *The Politics of Protest: Social Movements in America*. New York: Oxford University Press.

Meyer, D.S. and Marullo, S. 1992: Grassroots mobilization and international politics: peace protest and the end of the Cold War. *Research in Social Movements, Conflict, and Change* 14: 99–140.

Meyer, D.S. and Staggenborg, S. 1996: Movements, countermovements, and the structure of political opportunity. *American Journal of Sociology* 101: 1628–1660.

Meyer, D.S. and Tarrow, S. (eds) 1998: *The Social Movement Society*. Lanham, MD: Rowman & Littlefield.

Meyer, D.S. and Whittier, N. 1994: Social movement spillover. *Social Problems* 41 (2): 277–298.

Meyer, J, Boli, J, Thomas, G. and Ramirez, F. 1997: World society and the nation-sate. *American Journal of Sociology* 103 (1): 144–181.

Meyer, J.W. 1989: Conceptions of Christendom: notes on the distinctiveness of the West. In M. Kohn (ed.) *Cross-National Research in Sociology*. Newbury Park, CA: Sage.

Meyer, J.W. 1999: The changing cultural content of the nation-state: a world society perspective. In G. Steinmetz (ed.) *State/Culture: State-Formation after the Cultural Turn*. Ithaca, NY: Cornell University Press.

Meyer, J.W. 2000: Globalization. Sources and effects on states and societies. *International Sociology* 15: 233–248.

Meyer, J.W. 2009: Reflections: institutional theory and world society. In G. Krucken and G.S. Drori (eds) *World Society: The Writings of John W. Meyer*. Oxford: Oxford University.

Meyer, J.W. and Rowan, B. 1977: Institutionalized organizations: formal structure as myth and ceremony. *American Journal of Sociology* 83: 340–363.

Meyer, J.W., Boli, J., Thomas, G.M. and Ramirez, F.O. 1997: World society and the nation-state. *American Journal of Sociology* 103: 144–181.

Meyer, J.W., Frank, D.J., Hironaka, A., Schofer, E. *et al.* 1997: The structuring of a world environmental regime, 1870–1990. *International Organization* 5: 623–651.

Meyer, J.W., Ramirez, F.O. and Soysal, Y. 1992: World expansion and mass education, 1870–1980. *Sociology of Education* 65: 128–149.

Michalowitz, I. 2007: What determines influence? Assessing conditions for decision-making influence of interest groups in the EU. *Journal of European Public Policy* 14: 132–151.

Michalowski, I. 2009: Citizenship tests in five countries. An expression of political liberalism? *WZB Discussion Paper*. Berlin: Wissenschaftszentrum Berlin für Sozialforschung.

Michels, R. 1962 [1911]: *Political Parties*. New York: The Free Press.

Michnik, A. 2001: Confessions of a converted dissident. *Eurozine*. http://www.eurozine.com/articles/2001-12-28-michnik-en.html (accessed 9 April 2011).

Middlemas, K. 1980: *Politics in Industrial Society: The Experience of the British System since 1911*. London: Deutsch.

Midgley, J. and Tang, K.L. (eds) 2010: *Social Policy and Poverty in East Asia. The Role of Social Security*. New York: Routledge.

Mies, M. and Shiva, V. 1993: *Ecofeminism*. Halifax, NS: Fernwood.

Migdal, J. 2001: *State in Society,* Cambridge: Cambridge University Press.

Migdal, J. 2009: Studying the state. In M.I. Lichbach and A.S. Zuckerman (eds) *Comparative Politics. Rationality, Culture and Structure*, 2nd edn. Cambridge: Cambridge University Press.

Miliband, R. 1969: *The State in Capitalist Society*. London: Weidenfeld & Nicolson.

Mill, J.S. 1967: *Essays on Government, Jurisprudence, Liberty of the Press and Law of Nations*. New York: Kelly.

Mill, J.S. 1972: *Utilitarianism, On Liberty and Considerations on Representative Government*. London: Dent.

Mill, J.S. 1977 [1865]: Considerations on representative government. In J. M. Robson (ed.) *Collected Works of John Stuart Mill*. Toronto: University of Toronto Press.

Miller, D. 2000: *Citizenship and National Identity*. Cambridge: Polity Press.

Miller, E.A and Banaszak-Holl, J. 2005: Cognitive and normative determinants of state policymaking behavior: lessons from the sociological institutionalism. *Publius* 35 (2): 191–216.

Miller, M. 1995: *The Third World in Global Environmental Politics*. Colorado: Lynne Rienner.

Miller, P. and Rose, N. 2008: *Governing the Present*. Cambridge: Polity Press.

Miller, T. 1993: *The Well-Tempered Self: Citizenship, Culture, and the Post-Modern Subject*. London: John Hopkins University Press.

Miller, W. L. 1991: *Media and Voters: The Audience, Content, and Influence of Press and Television at the 1987 General Election*. Oxford: Oxford University Press.

Millett, K. 1970: *Sexual Politics*. New York: Doubleday Books.

Mills, C.W. 1956: *The Power Elite*. New York: Oxford University Press.

Mintz, B. and Schwartz, M. 1985: *The Power Structure of American Business*. Chicago, IL: Chicago University Press.

Misztal, B. 1996: *Trust in Modern Societies: The Search for the Bases of Social Order*. Cambridge: Polity Press.

Mittelman, J. 1997: *Globalisation, Critical Reflections*. London: Lynne Rienner.

Mittelman, J. 2000: *The Globalization Syndrome*. Princeton, NJ: Princeton University Press.

Mizruchi, M. S. 1982: *The American Corporate Network, 1900–1974*. London: Sage.

Moaddel, M. 2005: *Islamic Modernism, Nationalism, and Fundamentalism: Episode and Discourse*. Chicago, IL: University of Chicago Press.

Moghadam, V.M. 2005: *Globalizing Women: Transnational Feminist Networks*. Baltimore, MD: The Johns Hopkins University Press.

Moghadam, V.M. 2009: *Globalization and Social Movements: Islamism, Feminism, and the Global Justice Movement*. Lanham, MD: Rowman & Littlefield.

Moghadam, V.M. and Gheytanchi, E. 2010: Political opportunities and strategic movements: comparing feminist campaigns in Iran and Morocco. *Mobilization* 15 (3): 267–288.

Mohammad, R. 2005: The Cinderella complex – narrating Spanish women's history, the home and visions of equality: developing new margins. *Transactions of the Institute of British Geographers* 30 (2): 248–261.

Mohanty, C.T. 2003: *Feminism Without Borders: Decolonizing Theory, Practicing Solidarity*. Durham, NC: Duke University Press.

Mohmood, S. (2009) Religion reason and secular affect: an incommensurable divide? *Critical Inquiry* 35 (4): 386–362.

Mommsen, W. 1974: *The Age of Bureaucracy Perspectives on the Political Sociology of Max Weber*. New York: Harper & Row.

Mommsen, W. 1990. *Max Weber and German Politics, 1890–1920*. Chicago: University of Chicago Press.

Montesquieu, C. de S. 1949 [1748]: *The Spirit of the Laws*. London: Collier-Macmillan.

Montpetit, E. 2005: A policy network explanation of biotechnology policy differences between the United States and Canada. *Journal of Public Policy* 25: 339–366.

Moore, B. Jr. 1966: *Social Origins of Dictatorship and Democracy*. Harmondsworth: Penguin.

Moore, S.W. 1957: *The Critique of Capitalist Democracy*. New York: Paine-Whitman.

Moran, M. 2003: *The British Regulatory State*. Oxford: Oxford University Press.

Morgan, K.J. and Prasad, M. 2009: The origins of tax systems: a French-American comparison. *American Journal of Sociology* 114: 1350–1394.

Morgan, R. 1970: *Sisterhood is Powerful*. London: Random House.

Morris, J. 2005: *Citizenship and Disabled People*. London: Disability Rights Commission.

Morris, L. (ed.) 2006: *Rights: Sociological Perspectives*. London: Routledge.

Morris, L. 2002: *Managing Migration: Civic Stratification and Migrants' Rights*. New York: Routledge.

Morris, L. 2006: Sociology and rights – an emergent field. In L. Morris (ed.) *Rights: Sociological Perspectives*. London: Routledge.

Morris, L. 2010: *Asylum, Welfare and the Cosmopolitan Ideal: A Sociology of Rights*. London: Routledge.

Moskos, C, Williams, J. and Segal, D. (eds) 2000: *The Postmodern Military: Armed Forces after the Cold War*. Oxford: Oxford University Press.

Mouffe, C. 1992: Feminism, citizenship and radical democratic politics. In J. Butler and J.W. Scott (eds) *Feminists Theorize the Political*. New York: Routledge.

Moyo, S. and Yeros, P. (eds) 2005: *Reclaiming the land: The Resurgence of Rural Movements in Africa, Asia, and Latin America*. London: Zed Books.

Moyser, G. and Wagstaffe, M. 1987: Studying elites: theoretical and methodological issues. In G. Moyser and M. Wagstaffe (eds) *Research methods in Elite Studies*. London: Allen & Unwin.

Moyser, G. and Wagstaffe, M. (ed.) 1987: *Research Methods in Elite Studies*. London: Allen & Unwin.

Mullaney, T. 2010: *Coming to Terms with the Nation: Ethnic Classification in Modern China*. Berkeley: University of California Press.

Müller, O. 2008: Religion in central and eastern Europe. Was there a re-awakening after the breakdown of communism? In Pollack, D. and Olson D. (eds): *The Role of Religion in Modern Societies*. New York: Routledge.

Murray, J. and Farrington, D.P. 2008: Parental imprisonment: long-lasting effects on boys' internalizing problems through the life-course. *Developmental Psychopathology* 20: 273–290.

Mutz, D. 2006: *Hearing the Other Side: Deliberative Versus Participatory Democracy*. New York: Cambridge University Press.

Myrdal, A. and Myrdal, G. 1934: *Kris i befolkningsfrågan*. Stockholm: Bonners.

Myles, J. and Pierson, Paul, 2001: The comparative political economy of pension reform. In P. Pierson (ed.): *The New Politics of the Welfare State*. Oxford: Oxford University Press.

Nadelmann, E. 1993: *Cops across Borders: The Internationalization of U.S. Criminal Law Enforcement*. University Park: Pennsylvania State University Press.

Nairn, T. 1981: *The Break-Up of Britain. Crisis and Neo-Nationalism*. London: Verso.

Nash, J. C. 2008: Re-thinking Intersectionality. *Feminist Review* 89: 1–15.

Nash, K. 2000 (ed.): *Readings in Contemporary Political Sociology*, Oxford: Blackwell.

Nash, K. 2002: A movement moves . . . is there a women's movement in England today? *European Journal of Women's Studies* 9 (3): 311–328.

Nash, K. 2003: Cosmopolitan political community: why does it feel so right? *Constellations* 10 (4): 506–518.

Nash, K. 2009a: Between citizenship and human rights. *Sociology* 43 (6): 1–17.

Nash, K. 2009b: *The Cultural Politics of Human Rights*. Cambridge: Cambridge University Press.

Nash, K. 2010: *Contemporary Political Sociology: Globalization, Politics, and Power*. Oxford: Wiley-Blackwell.

Nash, K. (2011): States of human rights. *Sociologica* 1/201, doi: 10.2383/34620.

Neal, A 2009: *Exceptionalism and the Politics of Counter-Terrorism: Liberty, Security and the War on Terror*. New York: Routledge.

Negrine, R. 2008: *The Transformation of Political Communication: Continuities and Changes in Media and Politics*. Basingstoke: Palgrave Macmillan.

Nelkin, D. and Lindee, M.S. 1995: The mediated gene. In J. Terry and J. Urla (eds.) *Deviant Bodies*. Bloomington, IN: Indiana University Press.

Néron, P. -Y. 2010: Business and the polis: what does it mean to see corporations as political actors? *Journal of Business Ethics* 94 (3): 333–352.

Neuman, I. and Sending, O.J. 2010: *Governing the Global Polity: Practice, Mentality, Rationality*. Ann Arbor: University of Michigan Press.

Newman, J. 2001: *Modernising Governance*. London: Sage.

Ngai, M.M. 2004: *Impossible subjects: Illegal aliens and the Making of Modern America*. Princeton, NJ: Princeton University Press.

Nieuwbeerta, P., Brooks, C. and Manza, J. 2006: Cleavage-based voting in cross-national perspective: evidence from six countries.' *Social Science Research* 35: 88–128.

Nisbet, R.A. 1965: *Emile Durkheim*. Englewood Cliffs, NJ: Prentice-Hall.

Nisbet, R.A. 1966: *The Sociological Tradition*. New York: Basic Books.

Nixon, S. 2003 *Advertising Cultures*. London: Sage.

Nobles, M. 2000: *Shades of Citizenship: Race and the Census in Modern Politics*. Stanford, CA: Stanford University Press.

Norris, P. 1993: Comparative legislative recruitment. In J. Lovenduski and P Norris (eds) *Gender and Party Politics*. London: Sage.

Norris, P. 2004: *Electoral Engineering: Voting Rules and Political Behavior*. New York: Cambridge University Press.

Norris, P. and Inglehart, R. 2004: *Sacred and Secular: Religion and Politics Worldwide*. New York: Cambridge University Press.

North, D.C. 1990: *Institutions, Institutional Change, and Economic Performance*. Cambridge: Cambridge University Press.

Norval, A.J. 1993: Minoritarian politics and the pluralisation of democracy. *Acta Philosophica* XIV(2): 121–140.

Norval, A.J. 1996: *Deconstructing Apartheid Discourse*. London: Verso.

Norval, A.J. 1999: Hybridization: the im/purity of the political. In J. Edkins, N. Persram and V. Pin-Fat (eds) *Sovereignty and Subjectivity*. London: Lynne Rienner.

Novas, C. and Rose, N. 2000: Genetic risk and the birth of the somatic individual. *Economy and Society* 29: 485–513.

Nownes, A.J. 2004: The population ecology of interest group formation: mobilizing gay and lesbian rights interest groups in the Unites States, 1950–98. *British Journal of Political Science* 34: 49–67.

Nownes, A.J. and Lipinski, D. 2005: The population ecology of interest group death: gay and lesbian rights interest groups in the Unites States, 1945–98. *British Journal of Political Science* 35: 303–319.

Nye, J. S. 1967: Corruption and political development. A cost–benefit analysis. *American Political Science Review* 61 (2): 417–427.

Nye, J.S. Jr. 2004: *Soft Power: The Means to Success in World Politics*. New York: Public Affairs.

O'Brien, K.J. and Lianjiang Li. 2006: *Rightful Resistance in Rural China*. Cambridge: Cambridge University Press.

O'Brien, R, Goetz, A-M, Scholte, J. and Williams, M. 2000: *Contesting Global Governance: Multilateral Economic Institutions and Global Social Movements*. Cambridge: Cambridge University Press.

O'Donnell, G. 1999: *Counterpoints. Selected Essays on Authoritarianism and Democratization*. Notre Dame, IN: Notre Dame University Press.

O'Donnell, G. and Schmitter, P.C. 1986: *Transitions from Authoritarian Rule: Tentative Conclusions about Uncertain Democracies*. Baltimore, MD: John Hopkins University Press.

O'Shaughnessy, N.J. 1990: *The Phenomenon of Political Marketing*. Houndmills, Basingstoke: Macmillan.

OECD 1985: *Social Expenditure, 1960–1980*: Paris: OECD.

OECD 2009: *Income Distribution and Poverty*. http://www.oecd.org/els/social/inequality (accessed 9 April 2011).

Offe, C. 1984: *Contradictions of the Welfare State*. London: Hutchinson.

Offe, C. and Preuß, U. 1991: Democratic institutions and moral resources. In D. Held (ed.) *Political Theory Today*. Cambridge: Polity Press.

Okin, S.M. 1989: *Justice, Gender and the Family*. New York: Basic Books.

Okin, S.M. 1991: Gender, the public and the private. In D. Held (ed.) *Political Theory Today*. Cambridge: Polity Press.

Oldfield, A. 1990: *Citizenship and Community, Civic Republicanism and the Modern World*. London: Routledge.

Olivier, M. and Kuhnle, S. (eds) 2008: *Norms and Institutional Design – Social Security in Norway and South Africa*. Johannesburg: Sun Press.

Omi, M. and Winant, H. 1994: *Racial Formation in the United States: From the 1960s to the 1990s*. New York: Routledge.

Ordeshook, P.C. 1997: The spatial analysis of elections and committees: four decades of research. In D.C. Mueller (ed.) *Perspectives on Public Choice. A Handbook*. Cambridge: Cambridge University Press.

Orloff, A. 1999: Motherhood, work, and welfare in the United States, Britain, Canada, and Australia. In G. Steinmetz (ed.) *State/Culture: State-Formation after the Cultural Turn*. Ithaca, NY: Cornell University Press.

Orloff, A.S. 1993: Gender and the social rights of citizenship: the comparative analysis of gender relations and welfare states. *American Sociological Review* 58: 303–328.

Orren, K. and Skowronek, S. 2002: The study of American political development. In I. Katznelson and H. V. Milner (eds) *Political Science: The State of the Discipline*. New York: W.W. Norton.

Orton, J.D. and Weick, K.E. 1990: Loosely coupled systems: a reconceptualization. *Academy of Management Review* 15: 203–223.

Ostrom, E. 1994: Constituting social capital and collective action. *Journal of Theoretical Politics* 6 (4): 527–562.

Outshoorn J. and Kantola, J. (eds) 2007: *Changing State Feminism*. Basingstoke: Palgrave.

Outshoorn, J. and Kantola, J. 2007: Changing state feminism. In J. Outshoorn and J. Kantola (eds) *Changing State Feminism*. Basingstoke: Palgrave MacMillan.

Owens, B. 2001: *Lifting the Fog of War*. Baltimore, MD: Johns Hopkins University Press.

Ozkirimli, U. 2010: *Theories of Nationalism. A Critical Introduction*, 2nd edn. Basingstoke: Palgrave Macmillan.

Padamsee, T. 2009: Culture in connection: re-contextualizing ideational processes in the analysis of policy development. *Social Politics* Winter: 413–445.

Padilla, F.M. 1985: *Latino Ethnic Consciousness: The Case of Mexican Americans and Puerto Ricans in Chicago*. Notre Dame, IN: University of Notre Dame Press.

Paehlke, R. 2003: *Democracy's Dilemma – Environment, Social Equity and the Global Economy*. Cambridge, MA: MIT Press.

Page, J. 2004: Eliminating the enemy: the import of denying prisoners access to higher education in Clinton's America. *Punishment and Society* 6: 357–378.

Pager, D. 2003: The mark of a criminal record. *American Journal of Sociology* 108: 937–975.

Pager, D. 2007: *Marked: Race, Crime, and Finding Work in an Era of Mass Incarceration*. Chicago, IL: University of Chicago Press.

Panebianco, A. 1988: *Political Parties. Organization and Power*. Cambridge: Cambridge University Press.

Papadopoulos, A.G. and Liarikos, C. 2007: Dissecting changing rural development policy networks: the case of Greece. *Environment and Planning C: Government and Policy* 25: 291–313.

Papastergiadis, N. 1997: Tracing hybridity in theory. In. P. Werbner and T. Modood (eds) *Debating Cultural Hybridity: Multi-Cultural Identities and the Politics of Anti-Racism.* London: Zed Books.

Pape, R. 2005: *Dying to Win: The Strategic Logic of Suicide Terrorism.* New York: Random House.

Pape, R. 2005: *Dying to Win: The Strategic Logic of Suicide Terrorism.* New York: Random House.

Paredes, S.V. 2008: Policy networks and organizational change in Mexican forestry policy. *Gestion y Politica Publica* 17: 101–144.

Parke, R.D. and Clarke-Stewart, K.A. 2003: The effects of parental incarceration on children: perspectives, promises, and policies. In J. Travis and M. Waul (eds) *Prisoners Once Removed.* Washington, DC: Urban Institute Press.

Parker, A., Russo, M., Sommer, D. and Yeager, P. (eds) 1992: *Nationalisms and Sexualities.* London: Routledge.

Parker, G. 1996: *The Military Revolution: Military Innovation and the Rise of the West, 1500–1800.* Cambridge: Cambridge University Press.

Parsons, T. 1937: *The Structure of Social Action.* New York: The Free Press.

Parsons, T. and Shils, E.A. (eds) 1951: *Toward a General Theory of Action: Theoretical Foundations for the Social Sciences.* New York: Harper Torchbooks.

Pascall, G. 1993: Citizenship – a feminist analysis. In G. Drover and P. Kerans (eds) *New Approaches to Welfare Theory.* Aldershot: Edward Elgar.

Pateman, C. 1970: *Participation and Democratic Theory.* Cambridge University Press: Cambridge.

Pateman, C. 1988: *The Sexual Contract.* Cambridge: Polity Press.

Pateman, C. 1989: *The Disorder of Women.* Cambridge: Polity Press.

Pateman, C. 1992: Equality, difference and subordination: the politics of motherhood and women's citizenship. In G. Bock and S. James (eds) *Beyond Equality & Difference.* London: Routledge.

Patomäki, H. and Pursianen, C., 1999: Western models and the Russian idea: beyond 'inside/outside' in discourses on civil society. *Millennium* 28 (1): 53–77.

Patterson, M. 1995: Radicalising regimes? Ecology and the critique of IR theory. In J. MacMillan and A. Linklater (eds.) *New Directions in International Relations.* London: Pinter.

Pearce, F. 1989: *The Radical Durkheim.* London: Unwin Hyman.

Pederson, S. 1990: Gender, welfare and citizenship in Britain during the Great War. *The American Historical Review* 95 (4): 983–1006.

Pedriana, N. 1997: Political culture wars 1960s style: equal employment opportunity – affirmative action and the Philadelphia Plan. *American Journal of Sociology* 103: 633–691.

Pedriana, N. and Stryker, R. 2004: The strength of a weak agency: enforcement of Title VII of the Civil Rights Act and the expansion of state capacity, 1965–1971. *American Journal of Sociology* 110: 709–760.

Pelczynski, Z.A. 1988: Solidarity and the rebirth of civil society in Poland 1976–81. In J. Keane (ed.) *Civil Society and the State: New European Perspectives.* London: Verso.

Perrson, T. and Tabolini, G. 2004: *The Economic Effects of Constitutions.* Cambridge, MA: MIT Press.

Peters, B.G. 1997: Can't row, shouldn't steer: what's a government to do? *Public Policy Administration* 12 (2): 51–61.

Petersen, R.A. 1992: Understanding audience segmentation: from elite and mass to omnivore' and univore. *Poetics,* 21: 243–258.

Peterson, M.J. 2000: International organizations and the implementation of environmental regimes. In O. Young (ed.) *Global Governance, II*. Cambridge, MA: MIT Press.

Peterson, R.A. and Anand, N. 2004: The production of culture perspective. *Annual Review of Sociology* 30: 311–334.

Peterson, R.A. and R.M. Kern 1996: Changing highbrow taste: from snob to omnivore. *American Sociological Review* 61: 900–907.

Pettit, B. and Western, B. 2004: Mass imprisonment and the life course: race and class inequality in U.S. incarceration. *American Sociological Review* 69: 151–169.

Pew Center on the States. 2008: *One in 100: Behind Bars in America 2008*. Washington, DC: The Pew Charitable Trust.

Pew Global Attitudes Survey 2010: *Widespread Support for Banning Full Islamic Veil in Western Europe*, 8 July. Washington, DC: Pew Research Centre Publications.

Phillips, A. (ed.) 1998: *Feminism and Politics*. Oxford: Oxford University Press.

Phillips, A. 1991: *Engendering Democracy*. Cambridge: Polity Press.

Phillips, A. 1993: *Democracy and Difference*. Cambridge: Polity Press.

Phillips, A. 1995: *The Politics of Presence*. Oxford: Clarendon Press.

Pianta, M. and Marchetti, R. 2007: The global justice movements: the transnational dimension. In D. della Porta (ed.) *The Global Justice Movement*. Boulder CO: Paradigm Publishers.

Pierson, P. 1994: *Dismantling the Welfare State: Reagan, Thatcher and the Politics of Retrenchment*. Cambridge: Cambridge University Press.

Pierson, P. 2000: Increasing returns, path dependence, and the study of politics. *American Political Science Review* 94 (2): 251–267.

Pierson, P. 2003: Big, slow-moving, and . . . invisible: macrosocial processes in the study of comparative politics. In D. Rueschemeyer and J. Mahoney (eds) *Comparative Historical Analysis in the Social Sciences*. New York: Cambridge University Press.

Pierson, P. and Skocpol, T. 2002: Historical institutionalism in contemporary political science. In I. Katznelson and H.V. Milner (eds) *Political Science: The State of the Discipline*. New York: W.W. Norton.

Pieterse, J. 2004: *Globalization and Culture: Global Mélange*. Lanham, MD: Rowman & Littlefield.

Pincoffs, E.L. 1966: *The Rationale of Legal Punishment*. New York: Humanities Press.

Piven, F.F. and Cloward, R.A. 1971: *Regulating the Poor*. New York: Pantheon.

Piven, F.F. and Cloward, R.A. 1979: *Poor People's Movements*. New York: Vintage.

Pizzorno, A., 1992: La corruzione nel sistema politico. In D. della Porta (ed.) *Lo scambio occult*. Bologna: Il Mulino.

Plato 2001: *The Republic*, ed. G.R.F. Ferrari. Cambridge: Cambridge University Press.

Poggi, G. 1977: The constitutional state of the nineteenth century: an elementary conceptual portrait. *Sociology* 11: 311–332. Reprinted in A. Scott, K. Nash and M.A. Smith (eds) *New Critical Writings in Political Sociology*, Vol. One: *Power, State and Inequality*. Farnham: Ashgate, 2009.

Poggi, G. 1990: *The State: Its Nature, Development and Prospects*. Cambridge: Polity Press.

Polanyi, K. 2001 [1944]: *The Great Transformation*. Boston, MA: Beacon Press.

Pollack, D. and Olson D. 2008: *The Role of Religion in Modern Societies*. New York: Routledge.

Polletta, F. 2006: *It Was like a Fever: Storytelling in Protest and Politics*. Chicago, IL: University of Chicago Press.

Polsby, N.W. 1980: *Community Power and Political Theory*, 2nd edn. New Haven, CT: Yale University Press.

Ponting, C. 1991: *A Green History of the World*. Harmondsworth: Penguin.

Porter, B. 1994: *War and the Rise of the State: The Military Foundations of Modern Politics*. New York: The Free Press.

Porter, M. 1995: *Trust In Numbers: The Pursuit of Objectivity In Science and Public Life*, Princeton, NJ: Princeton University Press.

Porter, R. 1991: History of the body. In P. Burke (ed.) *Perspectives on Historical Writing*. Cambridge: Polity Press.

Portes, A. 1998: Social capital: its origins and applications in modern sociology. *Annual Review of Sociology* 24: 1–24.

Portes, A., Guarnizo, L.E. and Landolt, P. 1999: The study of transnationalism: pitfalls and promise of an emergent research field. *Ethnic and Racial Studies* 22: 217–237.

Posner, R. A. 2001: *Anti-Trust Law*, 2nd edn. Chicago, IL: University of Chicago Press.

Postone, M. 1993: *Time, Labour, and Domination*. Cambridge: Cambridge University Press.

Poulantzas, N. 1978: *State, Power, Socialism*. London: Verso.

Powell, G. 2000: *Elections as Instruments of Democracy*. New Haven, CT: Yale University Press.

Prakash, A. and Hart, J.A. (eds) 1998: *Globalisation and Governance*. London: Routledge.

Pressman, J. and Wildavsky, A. 1973: *Implementation*. Berkeley: University of California Press.

Prieur, A., Rosenlund, L. and Skjott-Larsen, J. 2008: Cultural capital today: a case study from Denmark. *Poetics*, 36: 45–71.

Princen, T. 2001: Consumption and its externalities: where economy meets ecology. *Global Environmental Politics*, 1 (3): 11–30.

Princen, T. and Finger, M. (eds) 1994: *Environmental NGOs in World Politics*. London: Routledge.

Przeworski, A. 1985: *Capitalism and Social Democracy*. Cambridge: Cambridge University Press.

Przeworski, A. and Limongi, F. 1997: Modernization: theories and facts. *World Politics* 49 (2): 155–183.

Przeworski, A. and Sprague, J. 1986: *Paper Stones*. Chicago, IL: University of Chicago Press.

Przeworski, A. and Teune, H. 1970: *The Logic of Comparative Social Inquiry*. New York: Wiley-Interscience.

Puar, J. 2007: *Terrorist Assemblages: Homonationalism in Queer Times*. Durham, NC: Duke University Press.

Puri, J. 2006: Stakes and states: sexual discourses from New Delhi. *Feminist Review* 83: 139–148.

Putnam, R.D. 1973: *The Beliefs of Politicians: Ideology, Conflict and Democracy in Britain and Italy*. New Haven, CT: Yale University Press.

Putnam, R.D. 1993: *Making Democracy Work: Civic Traditions in Modern Italy*. Princeton, NJ: Princeton University Press.

Putnam, R.D. 1995: Bowling alone: America's declining social capital. *Journal of Democracy* 6: 65–78.

Putnam, R.D. 1996: The strange disappearance of civic America. *American Prospect* 24: 34–48.

Putnam, R. D. 2000: *Bowling Alone. The Collapse and Revival of American Community*. New York: Simon and Schuster.

Rabinowitz, G. and McDonald, S.E. 1989: A directional theory of issue voting. *American Political Science Review* 83 (1): 93–121.

Ragin, C.C. 1987: *The Comparative Method: Moving Beyond Qualitative and Quantitative Strategies*. Berkeley: University of California Press.

Ragin, C.C. 2000: *Fuzzy-Set Social Science*. Chicago, IL: University of Chicago Press.

Ragin, C.C. 2006: Set relations in social research: evaluating their consistency and coverage. *Political Analysis* 14: 291–310.

Ragin, C.C. 2008: *Redesigning Social Inquiry: Fuzzy Sets and Beyond*. Chicago, IL: University of Chicago Press.

Ragin, C.C. and Amoroso, L. 2010: *Constructing Social Research: The Unity and Diversity of Method*, 2nd edn. Thousand Oaks, CA: Pine Forge Press.

Ragin, C.C. and Becker, H.S. (eds) 1992: *What Is a Case? Exploring the Foundations of Social Inquiry*. New York: Cambridge University Press.

Ragin, C.C. and Rihoux, B. 2004: Qualitative comparative analysis (QCA): state of the art and prospects. *Qualitative Methods* 2: 3–13.

Ragin, C.C. and Schneider, G.A. 2010: Case oriented theory building and theory testing. In M. Williams and P. Vogt (eds) *The Sage Handbook of Methodological Innovations*. London: Sage.

Rai, M. 2006: *7/7: The London Bombings, Islam and the Iraq War*. London: Pluto Press.

Rajagopal, B. 2003: *International Law from Below: Development, Social Movements, and Third World Resistance*. Cambridge: Cambridge University Press.

Rajaram, P. 2004: The irregular migrant as homo sacer: migration and detention in Australia, Malaysia, and Thailand. *International Migration* 42 (1): 33–64.

Ramirez, F.O. and Wotipka, C.M. 2001: Slowly but surely? The global expansion of women's participation in science and engineering fields of study, 1972–92. *Sociology of Education* 74: 231–251.

Ramirez, F.O., Soysal, Y. and Shanahan, S. 1997: The changing logic of political citizenship: cross-national acquisition of women's suffrage rights, 1890–1990. *American Sociological Review* 62: 735–745.

Rasche, A. and Kell, G. 2010: *The UN Global Compact: Achievements, Trends and Challenges*. Cambridge: Cambridge University Press.

Ray, L.J. 1993: *Rethinking Critical Theory: Emancipation in an Age of Global Social Movements*. London: Sage.

Ray, L.J. 1996: *Social Theory and the Crisis of State Socialism*. Cheltenham: Edward Elgar.

Ray, L.J. 2009: At the end of the postcommunist transformation? Normalization or Imagining Utopia? *European Journal of Social Theory* 12 (3): 321–336.

Reay, D. 1998: *Class War: Mothers' Involvement in Children's Schooling*. London: UCL.

Redclift, M. 1987: *Sustainable Development, Exploring the Contradictions*. London: Routledge.

Redclift, M. 1996: *Wasted; Counting the Coast of Global Consumption*. London: Earthscan.

Redclift, M. and Benton, T. (eds) 1994: *Social Theory and the Global Environment*. London: Routledge.

Reeves, K. 1997: *Voting Hopes or FEARS? White Voters, Black Candidates and Racial Politics in America*. New York: Oxford University Press.

Reilly, P.R. 1991: *The Surgical Solution*. Baltimore, MD: Johns Hopkins University Press.

Renan, E. 1990: What is a nation? In H. Bhaba (ed.) *Nation and Narration*. London: Routledge.

Reskin, B. 1998: *The Realities of Affirmative Action in Employment*. Washington, DC: American Sociological Association.

Rheingold, H. 2000: *The Virtual Community: Homesteading on the Electronic Frontier*. Cambridge, MA: MIT Press.

Rhodes, R.A.W. 1990 Policy networks: a British perspective. *Journal of Theoretical Politics* 2: 293–317.

Richardson, D. 2000: Constructing sexual citizenship. *Critical Social Policy* 20 (1): 105–135.

Richardson, J. 2009: Religion and the law. An interactionist view. In P. Clarke (ed.) *The Oxford Handbook of the Sociology of Religion.* Oxford: Oxford University Press.

Rieger, E. and Leibfried, S. 2003: *Limits to Globalization. Welfare States and the World Economy.* Cambridge: Polity Press.

Riesebrodt, M. 2008: Theses on a theory of religion. *International Political Anthropology* 1 (1): 25–41.

Rihoux, B. and Ragin, C.C. (eds) 2009: *Configurational Comparative Methods: Qualitative Comparative Analysis (QCA) and Related Techniques.* Thousand Oaks, CA: Sage.

Riley, D. 2005: Civic associations and authoritarian regimes in interwar Europe: Italy and Spain in comparative perspective. *American Sociological Review* 70: 288–310.

Rimlinger, G.V. 1971: *Welfare Policy and Industrialization in Europe, America, and Russia.* New York: John Wiley & Sons.

Risse, T., Ropp, S. and Sikkink, K. 1999: *The Power of Human Rights: Institutional Norms and Domestic Change.* Cambridge: Cambridge University Press.

Ritter, G. 1979: *The Corrupting Influence of Power.* Westport. CT: Hyperion Press.

Robbers, G. (ed.) 2005: *State and Church in the European Union.* Baden-Baden: Nomos.

Roberts, S. M. 2004: Gendered globalization. In L.A. Staeheli, E. Kofman and L.J. Peake (eds) *Mapping Women, Mapping Politics: Feminist Perspectives on Political Geography.* New York: Routledge.

Robinson, W. 2004: *A Theory of Global Capitalism.* Baltimore, MD: The Johns Hopkins University Press.

Rödel, U., Frankenberg, G. and Dubiel, H. 1989: *Die demokratische Frage.* Frankfurt am Main: Suhrkamp.

Rohrschneider, R. and Dalton, R.J. 2002: A global network? Transnational cooperation among environmental groups. *Journal of Politics,* 64 (2): 510–534.

Rohrschneider, R. and Whitefield, S. 2009: Understanding cleavages in political party systems. issue positions and issue salience in 13 postcommunist democracies. *Comparative Political Studies* 42 (2): 280–313.

Rorty, R. 1980: *Philosophy and the Mirror of Nature.* Oxford: Blackwell.

Rosas, A. 1985: State sovereignty and human rights: towards a global constitutional project. In D. Beetham (ed.) *Politics and Human Rights,* Oxford: Blackwell.

Rose Ackerman, S. 1978: *Corruption. A Study in Political Economy.* New York: Academic Press.

Rose-Ackerman, S. 1999: *Corruption and Government: Causes, Consequences, and Reform.* Cambridge: Cambridge University Press.

Rose, A. M. 1967: *The Power Structure: Political Process in American Society.* New York: Oxford University Press.

Rose, N. and Miller, P. 1992: Political power beyond the state: problematics of government. *British Journal of Sociology* 43 (2): 173–205.

Rose, N. 1999: *Powers of Freedom: Reframing Political Thought.* Cambridge: Cambridge University Press.

Roshwald, A. 2006: *The Endurance of Nationalism: Ancient Roots and Modern Dilemmas.* Cambridge: Cambridge University Press.

Rosset, P.M. 2006: *Food is Different: Why We Must Get the WTO out of Agriculture.* London: Zed Books.

Rosset, P.M., Patel, R. and Courville, M. (eds) 2006: *Promised Land: Competing Visions of Agrarian Reform.* Oakland, CA: Food First Books.

Rothman, D.J. 2002: *Conscience and Convenience*. Hawthorne, NY: Aldine De Gruyter.

Rothstein, B. 1998: *Just Institutions Matters: The Moral and Political Logic of the Welfare State*. Cambridge: Cambridge University Press.

Rousseau, J-J. 1963 [1762]: *The Social Contract and Discourses*. London: Dent.

Rowbotham, S., Segal, L. and Wainwright, H. 1979: *Beyond the Fragments: Feminism and the Making of Socialism*. Merlin Press: London.

Roy, O. 2010: *Holy Ignorance: When Religion and Culture Part Ways*. New York: Columbia/ Hurst.

Ruddick, S. 1989: *Maternal Thinking: Towards a Politics of Peace*. London: Women's Press.

Rueda, D. 2008: *Social Democracy Inside Out: Partisanship and Labor Market Policy in Advanced Industrialized Democracies*. New York: Oxford University Press.

Rueschemeyer, D. 2003: Can one or a few cases yield theoretical gains? In J. Mahoney and D. Rueschemeyer (eds) *Comparative Historical Analysis in the Social Sciences*. Cambridge: Cambridge University Press.

Rueschemeyer, D., Stephens, E.H. and Stephens, J.D. 1992: *Capitalist Development and Democracy*. Chicago, IL: Chicago University Press.

Ruggie, J.G. 2007: 'Business and human rights: the evolving international agenda', *American Journal of International Law*, 101 (4): 819–840.

Ruggie, J.G. 2009: *Business and human rights: towards operationalizing the 'protect, respect and remedy' framework*. United Nations Human Rights Council, Eleventh Session, New York, 22 April.

Rusche, G. and Kirchheimer, O. 1939: *Punishment and Social Structure*. New York: Columbia University Press.

Rutenberg, J. 2010: With another $1 million dollar donation, Murdoch expands his political sphere. *New York Times*, October 1. www.nytimes.com (accessed 5 October 2010).

Sabatier, P.A. and Jenkins-Smith, H.C. 1999: The advocacy coalition framework: an assessment. In P.A. Sabatier (ed.) *Theories of the Policy Process*. Boulder, CO: Westview Press.

Sabel, C., Fung, A. and Karkainen, B. 1999: Beyond backyard environmentalism *Boston Review*, 24 (5). http://bostonreview.net/BR24.5/sabel.html (accessed 9 April 2011).

Sabol, W.J., West, H.C. and Cooper, M. 2009: *Prisoners in 2008*. Bureau of Justice Statistics, NCJ 228417.

Sachs, W. 2000: *Planet Dialectics, Explorations in Environment and Development*. Basingstoke: Palgrave.

Sachs, W., Loske, R. and Linz, M. 1998: *Greening the North, a Post-industrial Blueprint for Ecology and Equity*. London: Zed Books.

Salecl, R. 1993: National identity and socialist moral majority. In E. Carter, J. Donald and J. Squires (eds) *Space and Place: Theories of Identity and Location*. London: Lawrence & Wishart.

Sampson, A. 1962: *The Anatomy of Britain*. London: Hodder and Stoughton.

Samuels, D. and Shugart, M.S. 2010: *Presidents, Parties, and Prime Ministers How the Separation of Powers Affects Party Organization and Behavior*. Cambridge: Cambridge University Press.

Sandefur, R.L. and Laumann, E.O. 1998: A paradigm for social capital. *Rationality and Society* 10 (4): 481–501.

Sani, G. and Sartori, G. 1983: Polarization, fragmentation and competition in western democracies. In H. Daalder and P. Mair (eds) *Western European Party Systems: Continuity and Change*. Beverly Hills: Sage.

Sapiro, V. 1998: When are interests interesting? In A. Phillips (ed.) *Feminism and Politics*. Oxford: Oxford University Press.161–193.

Sartori, G. 1970: Concept misformation in comparative politics. *American Political Science Review* 64 (4): 1033–1041.

Sarvasy, W. 1992: Beyond the difference versus equality policy debate: postsuffrage feminism, citizenship and the quest for a feminist welfare state. *Signs* 17 (2): 329–362.

Sassatelli, R. 2007: *Consumer Culture. History, Theory and Politics*: London: Sage.

Sassatelli, R. 2010: *Fitness Culture. Gyms and the Commercialisation of Discipline and Fun*. Basingstoke: Palgrave.

Sassen, S. 2006: *Territory, Authority, Rights: From Medieval to Global Assemblages*. Princeton, NJ: Princeton University Press.

Saurin, Julian. 1996a: International relations, social ecology and the globalisation of environmental change. In M. Imber and J. Vogler (eds) *The Environment and International Relations*. London: Routledge.

Saurin, Julian. 1996b: Globalisation, poverty and the promise of modernity. *Millennium*, 25 (3): 657–680.

Sautman, B. 1994: Anti-black racism in post-Mao China. *The China Quarterly* 138: 413–437.

Savage, M. 2000: *Class Analysis and Social Transformation*. Milton Keynes: Open University Press.

Savage, M. 2008: Culture, class and classification. In T. Bennett and J. Frow (eds) *The Sage Handbook of Cultural Analysis*. London: Sage.

Savage, M. 2010: *Identities and Social Change in Britain since 1940: The Politics of Method*. Oxford: Clarendon.

Savage, M. 2011: The lost urban sociology of Pierre Bourdieu. In G. Bridge and S. Watson (eds) *A Companion to the City*. Oxford: Wiley-Blackwell.

Savage, M. and Williams, K. 2008: *Remembering Elites*. Oxford: Wiley-Blackwell.

Savage, M., Bagnall, G. and Longhurst, B.J. 2005: *Globalisation and Belonging*. London, Sage.

Savage, M., Barlow, J., Dickens, P. and Fielding, A.J. 1992: *Property, Bureaucracy and Culture: Middle Class Formation in Contemporary Britain*. London: Routledge.

Savelsberg, J.J. 1994: Knowledge, domination, and criminal punishment. *American Journal of Sociology* 99: 911–943.

Saward, M. 2010: *The Representative Claim*. Oxford: Oxford University Press.

Scammell, M. 1995: *Designer Politics: How Elections are Won*. Basingstoke: Macmillan.

Scarrow, S.E. 2000: Parties without members? Party organization in a changing electoral environment. In R.J. Dalton and M.P. Wattenberg (eds) *Parties Without Partisans: Political Change in Advanced Industrial Democracies*. Oxford: Oxford University Press.

Schattschneider, E.E. 1960: *The Semi-Sovereign People*. New York: Holt, Rinehart and Winston.

Schermerhorn, R.A. 1978: *Comparative Ethnic Relations: A Framework for Theory and Research*. Chicago, IL: University of Chicago press.

Scherrer, A. 2009: *G8 against Transnational Organized Crime*. Aldershot: Ashgate.

Scheuerman, W.E. 2004: *Liberal Democracy and the Social Acceleration of Time*. Baltimore, MD: Johns Hopkins University Press.

Schlesinger, J.A. 1984: On the theory of party organization. *Journal of Politics* 46 (2): 369–400.

Schnapper, D. 1994: *La communauté des citoyens: sur l'idée moderne de nation*. Paris: Gallimard.

Schneiberg, M. and Clemens, E. 2006: The typical tools for the job: research strategies in institutional analysis. *Sociological Theory* 3: 195–227.

Schneider, G.A. 2008: *Interest organizations, policy change, and the prison boom: towards a social movements perspective on incarceration growth*. Unpublished manuscript.

Schneider, M. 1996: Sacredness. Status and bodily violation. *Body and Society* 2 (4): 75–92.

Schneider, V. 1992: The structure of policy networks: a comparison of the 'chemical control' and 'telecommunications' policy domains in Germany. *European Journal of Political Research* 21: 91–130.

Schneider, V., Dang-Nguyen, G. and Werle, R. 1994: Corporate actor networks in European policy-making: harmonizing telecommunications policy. *Journal of Common Market Studies* 32: 473–498.

Schneider, V.1986: Exchange networks in the development of policy: regulation of chemicals in the OECD, EEC, and the Federal Republic of Germany. *Journal für Sozialforschung* 26: 383–416.

Schnittker, J. and John, A. 2007: Enduring stigma: the long-term effects of incarceration on health. *Journal of Health and Social Behavior* 48: 115–130.

Schofer, E. 2003: The Global Institutionalization of Geological Science, 1800–1990. *American Sociological Review* 68: 730–759.

Schofer, E. and Hironaka, A. 2005: World society and environmental protection outcomes. *Social Forces* 84: 25–47.

Schofer, E. and Meyer, J.W. 2005: The worldwide expansion of higher education in the twentieth century. *American Sociological Review* 70: 898–920.

Schofield, N. 1997: Multiparty electoral politics. In D.C. Mueller (ed.) *Perspectives on Public Choice. A Handbook*. Cambridge: Cambridge University Press.

Scholte, J. A. 1993: *International Relations of Social Change*. Milton Keynes: Open University Press.

Scholte, J.A. 2000: *Globalization, a critical introduction*. Basingstoke: Palgrave.

Scholz, J.T. and Wang C-L. 2006: Cooptation or transformation? Local policy networks and federal regulatory enforcement. *American Journal of Political Science* 50: 81–97.

Schroeder, R. 1998: From Weber's political sociology to contemporary liberal democracy. In R. Schroeder (ed.) *Max Weber's Idea of Democracy and Modernization*. New York: St Martin's Press.

Schuster, L. 2003: *The Use and Abuse of Political Asylum*. London: Frank Cass.

Schuurman, F. (eds) 2001: *Globalization and development studies*. London: Sage.

Schwartz, H. 2000: *States versus Markets*, 2nd edn. Basingstoke: Macmillan.

Scott, A. 2000: Capitalism, Weber and democracy. *Max Weber Studies* 1 (1): 33–55.

Scott, J. (ed.) 1990: *The Sociology of Elites*, 3 vols. Cheltenham: Edward Elgar.

Scott, J. (ed.) 1994: *Power*, 3 vols. London: Routledge.

Scott, J. 1982: *The Upper Classes: Property and Privilege in Britain*. Basingstoke: Macmillan.

Scott, J. 1990: *A Matter of Record: Documentary Sources in Social Research*. Cambridge: Polity Press.

Scott, J. 1991a: Networks of corporate power: a comparative assessment. *Annual Review of Sociology* 17: 181–203.

Scott, J. 1991b: *Social Network Analysis*. London: Sage.

Scott, J. 1991c: *Who Rules Britain?* Cambridge: Polity Press.

Scott, J. 1997: *Corporate Business and Capitalist Classes*. Oxford: Oxford University Press.

Scott, J. 2001: *Power*. Cambridge: Polity Press.

Scott, J. and Griff, C. 1984: *Directors of Industry*. Cambridge: Polity Press.

Scott, J.C. 1990: *Domination and the Arts of Resistance*. New Haven, CT: Yale University Press.

Scott, J.C.1998: *Seeing Like a State*. New Haven, CT: Yale University Press.

Scutt, J.A. (ed.) 1990: *The Baby Machine*. London: Green Print.

Seaton, J. 1999: Why do we think the Serbs do it? The new 'ethnic' wars and the media. *Political Quarterly* 70 (4): 254–270.

Segal, L. (2007) *Slow Motion. Changing Masculinities, Changing Men*, 3rd edn. Basingstoke: Palgrave.

Seidman, G. 2001: Guerrillas in their midst: armed struggle in the South African anti-apartheid movement. *Mobilization: An International Quarterly* 6 (2): 111–127.

Seligman, A. 1993: The fragile ethical vision of civil society. In B.S. Turner (ed.) *Citizenship and Social Theory*. London: Sage.

Seligman, A. 1995: Animadversions upon civil society and civic virtue in the last decade of the twentieth century. In J. A. Hall (ed.) *Civil Society*. Cambridge: Polity Press.

Senechal de la Roche, R. 1996: Collective violence as social control. *Sociological Forum* 11 (1): 97–128.

Sennett, R. 1999: *The Corrosion of Character: The Personal Consequences of Work in the New Capitalism*. New York: Norton.

Seol, D-H. and Skrentny, J.D. 2009a. Ethnic return migration and hierarchical nationhood: Korean Chinese foreign workers in South Korea. *Ethnicities* 9 (2): 147–174.

Seol, D-H. and Skrentny, J.D. 2009b. Why is there so little migrant settlement in East Asia? *International Migration Review*. 43 (3): 578–620.

Sevenhuijsen, S. 1998: *Citizenship and the Ethics of Care*. London and New York: Routledge.

Sewell, W.H., Jr. 1992: A theory of structure: duality, agency, and transformation. *American Journal of Sociology* 98: 1–29.

Sewell, W.H., Jr. 2006: *Logics of History*. Chicago, IL: University of Chicago Press.

Shafir, G.I. (ed.) 1998: *The Citizenship Debate: A Reader*. Minneapolis: University of Minnesota Press.

Shafir, G.I. 1998: Introduction: the evolving tradition of citizenship. In G. Shafir (ed.) *The Citizenship Debate: A Reader*. Minneapolis: University of Minnesota Press.

Shakespeare, T. 1998: Choices and rights: Eugenics, genetics and disability equality. *Disability and Society* 13 (5): 665–681.

Shapiro, J.P 1993: *No Pity: People with Disabilities Forging a New Civil Right Movement*. New York: Times Books.

Shaw, M. 1988: *Dialectics of War*. London: Pluto.

Shaw, M. 1991: *Post-Military Society: Militarism, Demilitarisation and War at the End of the Twentieth Century*. Cambridge: Polity Press.

Shear, M.D. 2010: Chamber of commerce vows to 'ramp up' political activity. *New York Times*, October 12. www.nytimes.com (accessed 13 October 2010).

Shefter, M. 1978: Party and patronage: Germany, England, and Italy. *Politics and Society* 7 (4): 403–451.

Shilling, C. 2008: *Changing Bodies. Habit, Crisis and Creativity*. London: Sage.

Shils, E. 1957: Primordial, personal, sacred and civil ties. *British Journal of Sociology* 7: 130–145.

Shils, E. 1975: Center and periphery. In E. Shills *The Constitution of Society*. Chicago, IL: University of Chicago Press.

Shleifer, A. and Vishny, R.W. 1993: Corruption. *The Quarterly Journal of Economics* 108 (3). 599–617.

Shonfield, A. 1965: *Modern Capitalism*. Oxford: Oxford University Press.

Siim, B. 2000: *Gender and Citizenship*, Cambridge: Cambridge University Press.

Sikkink, K. 1998: Transnational politics, international relations theory, and human rights. *PS: Political Science and Politics* 31: 516–523.

Silva, E.B. and Warde, A. (eds) 2010: *Cultural Analysis and Bourdieu's Legacy*. London, Routledge.

Simmel, G. 1997 [1908]: Sociology of senses. In D. Frisby and M. Featherstone (eds) *Simmel on Culture*. London: Routledge.

Simmons, B.A., Dobbin, F. and Garrett, G. 2006: The international diffusion of liberalism. *International Organization* 60: 781–810.

Simon, J. 1993: *Poor Discipline: Parole and the Social Control of the Underclass, 1890–1990*. Chicago, IL: University of Chicago Press.

Simon, J. 2007: *Governing Through Crime: How the War on Crime Transformed American Democracy and Created a Culture of Fear*. New York: Oxford University Press.

Singer, P. 2003: *Corporate Warriors: The Rise of the Privatized Military Industry*. Ithaca, NY: Cornell University Press.

Sitkoff, H. 1981: *The Struggle for Black Equality 1954–1980*. New York: Hill and Wang.

Sivan, E. 1989: The Islamic resurgence: civil society strikes back. *Journal of Contemporary History* 25 (2/3): 353–362.

Skeggs, B. 1997: *Formations of Class and Gender*. London: Sage.

Skeggs, B. 2004: *Class, Self, Culture*. London: Routledge.

Skeggs, B. 2005: The Making of class and gender through visualizing moral subject formation. *Sociology* 39 (5): 965–982.

Skerry, P. 2000: *Counting on the Census? Race, Group Identity, and the Evasion of Politics*. Washington, DC: Brookings Institution.

Skinner, Q. 2009: A genealogy of the modern state. *Proceedings of the British Academy* 162: 325–370.

Sklair, L. (eds) 1994: *Capitalism and Development*. London, Routledge.

Sklair, L. 2001: *The Transnational Capitalist Class*. Oxford: Blackwell.

Sklair, L. 2002: *Globalization, Capitalism and its alternatives*. Oxford: Oxford University Press.

Skocpol, T. 1979: *States and Social Revolutions: A Comparative Analysis of France, Russia, and China*. New York: Cambridge University Press.

Skocpol, T. 1985: Bringing the state back in: strategies of analysis in current research. In P.B. Evans, D. Rueschemeyer and T. Skocpol (eds) *Bringing the State Back In*. New York: Cambridge University Press.

Skocpol, T. 1992: *Protecting Soldiers and Mothers*. Cambridge, MA: Harvard University Press.

Skocpol, T. 1995: *Social Policy in the United States: Future Possibilities in Historical Perspective*. Princeton, NJ: Princeton University Press.

Skogstad, G. 2003: Legitimacy and/or policy effectiveness? Network governance and GMO regulation in the European Union. *Journal of European Public Policy* 10: 321–338.

Skowronek, S. 2009: Taking stock. In L. Jacobs and D. King (eds) *The Ungovernable American State*. Oxford: Oxford University Press.

Skowronek, S. and Glassman, M. (eds) 2007: *Formative Acts, American Politics in the Making*. Philadelphia: University of Pennsylvania Press.

Skrentny, J.D. 1996: *The Ironies of Affirmative Action: Politics, Culture and Justice in America*. Chicago, IL: University of Chicago Press.

Skrentny, J.D. 2002: *The Minority Rights Revolution*. Cambridge, MA: Harvard University Press.

Skrentny, J.D. 2006: Policy-elite perceptions and social movement success: understanding variations in group inclusion in affirmative action. *American Journal of Sociology* 111 (6): 1762–1815.

Slater, D. 1998: Trading sexpics on IRC: embodiment and authenticity on the internet. *Body and Society* 4 (4): 90–118.

Slaughter, A-M. 2004: *A New World Order*. Princeton, NJ: Princeton University Press.

Smelser, N.J. 1976: *Comparative Methods in the Social Sciences*. Englewood Cliffs, NJ: Prentice Hall.

Smilde, D. and May, M. 2010: *The Emerging Strong Program in the Sociology of Religion*. New York: SSRC Working Papers.

Smith, A-M. 1995: A symptomology of an authoritarian discourse. In Carter J. Donald and J. Squires (eds) *Cultural Remix: Theories of Politics and the Popular*. London: Lawrence & Wishart.

Smith, A. 1976 [1776]: *An Inquiry into the Nature and Causes of the Wealth of Nations*, ed. R.H. Campbell and A.S. Skinner. Oxford: Clarendon Press.

Smith, A.D. 1981: *The Ethnic Revival in the Modern World*. Cambridge: Cambridge University Press.

Smith, A.D. 1986: *The Ethnic Origins of Nations*. Oxford: Blackwell.

Smith, A.D. 1991: *National Identity*. Harmondsworth: Penguin.

Smith, A.D. 1995: *Nations and Nationalism in a Global Era*. Cambridge: Polity Press.

Smith, A.D. 1998: *Nationalism and Modernism. A Critical Survey Of Recent Theories Of Nations and Nationalism*. London: Routledge.

Smith, A.D. 2004: *The Antiquity of Nations*. Cambridge: Polity Press.

Smith, C. 1996: *Disruptive Religion. The Force of Faith in Social Movement Activism*. New York: Routledge.

Smith, J, Chatfield, C. and Pagnucco, R. (eds) 1997: *Transnational Social Movements and Global Politics*. Syracuse: Syracuse University Press.

Smith, J. 1998: Global civil society? Transnational social movement organizations and social capital. *American Behavioral Scientist* 42 (1): 93–107.

Smith, J. 2002: Briding global dives? Strategic framing and solidarity in transnational social movement organizations. *International Sociology* 17: 505–528.

Smith, J. 2009: *Social Movements for Global Democracy*. Baltimore, MD: Johns Hopkins University Press.

Smith, J. and Johnston, H. (eds) 2002: *Globalization and Resistance: Transnational Dimensions of Social Movements*. Lanham, MD: Rowman & Littlefield.

Smith, J. and Karides, M. 2008: *Global Democracy and the World Social Forum*. Boulder, CO: Paradigm.

Smith, J. and Wiest, D. 2005: The uneven geography of global civil society: national and global influences on transnational association. *Social Forces* 84: 621–651.

Smith, P. 1998: Fascism, communism and democracy as variations on a common theme. In J.C. Alexander (ed.) *Real Civil Societies*. London: Sage.

Smith, P. 2001: *Cultural Theory: An Introduction*. Oxford: Blackwell.

Smith, P.J. and Smythe, E. 2010: (In)fertile ground? Social forum activism in its regional and local dimension. *Journal of World-System Research* XVI (1): 6–28.

Sniderman, P.M. and Carmines, E.G. 1997: *Reaching Beyond Race*. Cambridge, MA: Harvard University Press.

Sniderman, P.M. and Piazza, T. 1993: *The Scar of Race*. Cambridge, MA: Harvard University Press.

Snow, D.E., Rochford, B., Worden, S. and Benford, R. 1986: Frame alignment processes, mobilization and movement participation. *American Sociological Review* 51: 464–481.

Snowden Jr, F.M. 1995: Europe's oldest chapter in the history of black–white relations. In B.J. Bowser (ed.) *Racism and Anti-Racism in World Perspective*. Thousand Oaks, CA: Sage.

Snyder, M. 2006: Unlikely godmother: the UN and the global women's movement. In M.M. Ferree and A.M. Tripp (eds) *Global Feminism: Transnational Women's Activism, Organizing and Human Rights*. New York: New York University Press.

Solomos, J. and Back, L. 1996: *Racism and Society*. Houndsmills, Basingstoke: Macmillan.

Somers, M.R. 1993: Citizenship and the place of the public sphere: law, community, and political culture in the transition to democracy. *American Sociological Review* 58: 587–620.

Somers, M.R. 1999: The privatization of citizenship: how to unthink a knowledge culture. In V.E. Bonnell and L. Hunt (eds) *Beyond the Cultural Turn: New Directions in the Study of Society and Culture*. Berkeley, CA: University of California Press.

Somers, M.R. 2008: *Genealogies of Citizenship: Markets, Statelessness, and the Right to Have Rights*. Cambridge: Cambridge University Press.

Somers, M.R. and Block, F. 2005: From poverty to perversity: ideas, markets, and institutions over 200 years of welfare debate. *American Sociological Review* 70: 260–287.

Somers, M.R. and Roberts, C. 2008: Toward a new sociology of rights: a genealogy of buried bodies of citizenship and human rights. *Annual Review of Law and Social Sciences* 4: 385–425.

Sontag, S. 1988: *AIDS and its Metaphors*. New York: Ferrar, Straus and Giroux.

Soysal, Y. 1994: *Limits of Citizenship Migrations and Postnational Citizenship in Europe*. Chicago, IL: Chicago University Press.

Soysal, Y. 2000: Citizenship and identity: living diasporas in post-war Europe? *Ethnic and Racial Studies* 23: 1–15.

Soysal, Y. and Szakacs, S. 2010: Reconceptualizing the Republic: diversity and education in France, 1945–2008 *Journal of Interdisciplinary History* 44: 97–115.

Soysal, Y. and Wong, S.Y. 2007: Educating future citizens in Europe and Asia. In A. Benavot and C. Braslavsky (eds) *School Knowledge in Comparative and Historical Perspective: Changing Curricula in Primary and Secondary Education*. New York: Springer.

Spini, D. 2006: *La società postnazionale*. Rome: Meltemi.

Spivak, G. 2002: Ethics and politics in Tagore, Coetzee, and certain scenes of teaching. *Diacritics* 32 (3/4): 17–31.

Spruyt, H. 2009: War, trade and state formation. In R.E. Goodin (ed.) *The Oxford Handbook of Political Science*. Oxford: Oxford University Press.

Squires, J. 2007a: *The New Politics of Gender Equality*. Basingstoke: Palgrave.

Squires, J. 2007b: The constitutive representation of gender. *Representation*, 44 (2): 187–204.

Staeheli, L.A., Kofman, E. and Peake, L.J. (eds) 2004: *Mapping Women, Mapping Politics: Feminist Perspectives on Political Geography*. New York: Routledge.

Stark, R. and Finke R. 2000: *Acts of Faith: Explaining the Human Side of Religion*. Berkeley: University of California Press.

Stawbridge, S. 1982: Althusser's theory of ideology and Durkheim's account of religion. *Sociological Review* 30 (1): 125–140.

Stears, M. 2005: The vocation of political theory: principles, empirical inquiry and the politics of opportunity. *European Journal of Political Theory* 4 (4): 325–350.

Steel, D. 2004: Social mechanisms and causal inference. *Philosophy of the Social Sciences* 34: 55–78.

Steensland, B. 2008a: Why do policy frames change? Actor-idea coevolution in debates over welfare reform. *Social Forces* 86: 1027–1054.

Steensland, B. 2008b: *The Failed Welfare Revolution: America's Struggle over Guaranteed Income Policy*. Princeton, NJ: Princeton University Press.

Steffensmeier, D.J., Ulmer, J.T. and Kramer, J.H. 1998: The interaction of race, gender, and age in criminal sentencing: the punishment of being young, black, and male. *Criminology* 36: 763–798.

Steinberg, D. L. 1997: *Bodies in Glass: Genetics, Eugenics, Embryo Ethics*. Manchester: Manchester University Press.

Steiner, H. and Alston, P. (eds) 2000: *International Human Rights in Context: Law, Politics, Morals*, 2nd edn. Oxford: Oxford University Press.

Steinmetz, G. (ed.) 1999: *State/Culture: State-Formation after the Cultural Turn*. Ithaca, NY: Cornell University Press.

Steinmetz, G. 1992: Reflections on the role of social narratives in working-class formation: narrative theory in the social sciences. *Social Science History* 16: 489–516.

Steinmetz, G. 1999: Introduction: culture and the state. In G. Steinmetz (ed.) *State/Culture: State-Formation after the Cultural Turn*. Ithaca, NY: Cornell University Press.

Steinmetz, G. 2007: *The Devil's Handwriting: Precoloniality and the German Colonial State in Qindao, Samoa, and Southwest Africa*. Chicago, IL: University of Chicago Press.

Steinmetz, G. 2008: The colonial state as social field: ethnographic capital and native policy in the German overseas empire before 1914. *American Sociological Review* 73: 589–612.

Steinmo, S. 1993: *Taxation and Democracy: Swedish, British and American Approaches to Financing the Modern State*. New Haven, CT: Duke University Press.

Steinmo, S., Thelen, K. and Longstreth F. (eds) 1992: *Structuring Politics: Historical Institutionalism in Comparative Analysis*. Cambridge: Cambridge University Press.

Stetson, D. M. and Mazur, A. (eds) 1995: *Comparative State Feminism*. Thousand Oaks, CA: Sage.

Stevis, D. 2006: The trajectory of the study of international environmental politics. In M.M. Betsill, K. Hochstetler and D. Stevis (eds) *International Environmental Politics*. New York: Palgrave Macmillan.

Stinchcombe, A.L. 1968: *Constructing Social Theories*. New York: Harcourt, Brace and World.

Stinchcombe, A.L. 1997: On the virtues of the old institutionalism. *Annual Review of Sociology* 23: 1–18.

Stokes, S. 2005: Perverse accountability. A formal model of machine politics with evidence from Argentina. *American Political Science Review* 99 (2): 315–327.

Stokke, O.S. 2000: Regimes as Governance Systems. In O. Young (ed.) *Global Governance, II*. Cambridge, MA: MIT Press.

Stokman, F., Ziegler, R. and Scott, J. (eds) 1985: *Networks of Corporate Power*. Cambridge: Polity Press.

Stoler, A.L. 1995: *Race and the Education of Desire: Foucault's History of Sexuality and the Colonial Order of Things*. Durham, NC: Duke University Press.

Stone, D.A. 1989: Causal stories and the formation of policy agendas. *Political Science Quarterly* 104: 281–300.

Storey, H. 1995: Human rights and the new Europe. In D. Beetham (ed.) *Politics and Human Rights*. Oxford: Blackwell.

Strang, D. 1990: From dependency to sovereignty: an event-history analysis of decolonization 1970–1987. *American Sociological Review* 55: 846–860.

Strang, D. and Macy, M.W. 2001: In search of excellence: fads, success stories, and adaptive emulation. *American Journal of Sociology* 107: 147–182.

Strang, D. and Meyer, J.W. 1993: The institutional conditions for diffusion. *Theory and Society* 22: 487–511.

Strang, D. and Soule, S.A. 1998: Diffusion in organizations and social movements: from hybrid corn to poison pills. *Annual Review of Sociology* 24: 265–290.

Strange, S. 1996: *The Retreat of the State*. Cambridge: Cambridge University Press.

Strawbridge, S. 1982: Althusser's theory of ideology and Durkheim's account of religion: an examination of some striking parallels. *Sociological Review* 30 (1): 125–140.

Strayer, J.R. 1970: *On the Medieval Origins of the Modern State*. Princeton, NJ: Princeton University Press.

Streeck, W. 2010: The fiscal crisis continues: From liberalization to consolidation. *Comparative European Politics* 8: 505–514.

Streeck, W. and Thelen, K. 2005: Introduction: institutional change in advanced political economies. In W. Streeck and K. Thelen (eds) *Institutional Change in Advanced Political Economies*. Oxford: Oxford University Press.

Strolovitch, D.Z. 2007: *Affirmative Advocacy: Race, Class, and Gender in Interest Group Politics*. Chicago, IL: University of Chicago Press.

Stryker, R. 1990: Science, class, and the welfare state: a class-centered functional account. *American Journal of Sociology* 96: 684–726.

Suárez, D.F. 2008: Rewriting citizenship? Civic education in Costa Rica and Argentina. *Comparative Education Review* 44: 485–503.

Sugrue, T.J. 2008: *Sweet Land of Liberty: The Forgotten Struggle for Civil Rights in the North*. New York: Random House.

Sutton, J.R. 2000: Imprisonment and social classification in five common-law democracies, 1955–1985. *American Journal of Sociology* 106: 350–386.

Svallfors, S (ed.) 2007: Introduction. In S. Savallfors (ed.) *The Political Sociology of the Welfare State: Institutions, Social Cleavages and Orientations*. Stanford, CA: Stanford University Press.

Swank, D. 2002: *Global Capital, Political Institutions, and Policy Change in the Developed Welfare States*. New York: Cambridge University Press.

Swartz, D. 1998: *Culture and Power: Sociology of Pierre Bourdieu*. Chicago, University of Chicago Press.

Swenson, P.A. 2002: *Capitalists against Markets: The Making of Labor Markets and Welfare States in the United States and Sweden*. Oxford: Oxford University Press.

Swidler, A. 2001: *Talk of Love: How Culture Matters*. Chicago, IL: University of Chicago Press.

Sznaider, N. and Levy, D. 2006: Sovereignty transformed: a sociology of human rights. *The British Journal of Sociology* 57 (4): 657–676.

Sztompka, P. 1993: *The Sociology of Social Change*. Oxford: Blackwell.

Tamás, G.M 1994: A disquisition on civil-society. *Social Research* 61 (2): 205–222.

Tarrow, S. 1996: Making social science work across space and time. A critical reflection on Robert Putnam's *Making Democracy Work*. *American Political Science Review* 90: 389–397.

Tarrow, S. 1998: *Power in Movement*, 2nd edn. Cambridge: Cambridge University Press.

Tarrow, S. 2005: *The New Transnational Activism*. Cambridge: Cambridge University Press.

Tasker, Y. and Negra, D. 2007: Introduction: feminist politics and post-feminist culture. In Y. Tasker and D. Negra (eds) *Interrogating Post-Feminism: Gender and the Politics of Popular Culture*. Durham, NC: Duke University Press.

Tastsoglou, E. and Dobrowolsky, A. (eds) 2006: *Women, Migration and Citizenship*, Aldershot and Burlington VT: Ashgate.

Tate, K.T. 2004: *Black Face in the Mirror: African Americans and Their Representatives in the US Congress*. Princeton, NJ: Princeton University Press.

Tate, K.T. 2010: *What's Going On? Political Incorporation and the Transformation of Black Public Opinion*. Washington, DC: Georgetown University Press.

Taylor, C. 1994: The politics of recognition. In A. Gutmann (ed.) *Multiculturalism*. Princeton, NJ: Princeton University Press.

Taylor, C. 2007: *A Secular Age*. Cambridge: Belknap.

Taylor, R. (ed.). 2004: *Creating a Better World: Interpreting Global Civil Society*. Bloomfield, CT: Kumarian Press.

Taylor, R. 1999: Political science encounters 'race' and 'ethnicity'. In M. Bulmer and J. Solomos (eds) *Ethnic and Racial Studies Today*. London: Routledge.

Taylor, V., Kimport, K., van Dyke, N. and Anderson, E.A. 2009: Culture and mobilization: tactical repertoires, same-sex weddings, and the impact on gay activism. *American Sociological Review* 74: 865–890.

Taylor-Gooby, P. 2008: The new welfare state settlement in Europe. *European Societies* 10 (1): 3–24.

Teles, S.M. 2001: Positive action or affirmative action? The persistence of Britain's antidiscrimination regime. In J.D. Skrentny (ed.) *Color Lines: Affirmative Action, Immigration and Civil Rights Options for America*. Chicago, IL: University of Chicago Press.

Terry, J. and Urla. J. (eds) 1995: *Deviant Bodies*. Bloomington: Indiana University Press.

Thatcher, M. 1998: The development of policy network analysis. From modest origins to overarching frameworks *Journal of Theoretical Politics* 10: 389–411.

Thatcher, M. 2007: *Internationalization and Economic Institutions: Comparing the European Experience*. Oxford: Oxford University Press.

Thelen, K. 1999: Historical institutionalism in comparative politics. *Annual Review of Political Science* 2: 369–404.

Thelen, K. 2003: How institutionalism evolves: insights from comparative historical analysis. In J. Mahoney and J. Rueschemeyer (eds) *Comparative Historical Analysis in the Social Sciences*. New York: Cambridge University Press.

Therborn, G. 2006: Meanings, mechanisms, patterns, and forces: an introduction. In G. Therborn (ed.) *Inequalities of the World*. London: Verso.

Thompson, E.P. 1966: *The Making of the English Working Class*. London, Gollancz.

Thompson, J.B. 1995: *The Media and Modernity: A Social Theory of the Media*. Cambridge: Polity Press.

Thompson, J.B. 1997: Scandal and social theory. In J. Lull and S. Hinerman (eds) *Media Scandals: Morality and Desire in the Popular Culture Marketplace*. Cambridge: Polity Press.

Thompson, J.B. 2000: *Political Scandal*. Cambridge: Polity Press.

Thompson, J.B. 2005: The new visibility. *Theory, Culture and Society* 22 (6): 31–51.

Thompson, K. 1986: *Beliefs and Ideologies*. London: Tavistock.

Thompson, K. 2002: *Emile Durkheim*, 2nd edn. London: Routledge.

Thompson, K. 2004: Durkheimian cultural sociology and cultural studies. *Thesis Eleven* 79: 16–24.

Thomson, J. 1996: *Mercenaries, Pirates and Sovereigns: State-building and Extraterritorial Violence in Early Modern Europe*. Princeton, NJ: Princeton University Press.

Thomson, P. 2008: Field. In Grenfell (ed.) *Pierre Bourdieu: Key Concepts*. Durham: Acumen.

Tilly, C. (ed.) 1975: *The Formation of National States in Western Europe*. Princeton, NJ: Princeton University Press.

Tilly, C. 1978: *From Mobilization to Revolution*. Reading, MA: Addison Wesley Longman.

Tilly, C. 1981: Useless Durkheim. In *As Sociology Meets History*. New York: Academic Press.

Tilly, C. 1985: War making and state making as organized crime. In P. Evans, D. Rueschemeyer and T. Skocpol (eds) *Bringing the State Back In*. Cambridge: Cambridge University Press.

Tilly, C. 2004: *Contention and Democracy in Europe, 1650–2000*. Cambridge: Cambridge University Press.

Tilly, C. 2007: *Democracy*. Cambridge: Cambridge University Press.

Tilly, C.1992: *Coercion, Capital, and European states* AD *990–1992*. Oxford: Blackwell.

Tilly, C. 2010: Cities, states and trust networks, chapter one of *Cities and States in World History. Theory and Society* 39: 265–280.

Tismaneanu, V. 1989: Nascent civil society in the German Democratic Republic. *Problems of Communism* 38: 91–111.

Tocqueville, A. 1946 [1835]: *Democracy in America*. Oxford: Oxford University Press.

Toke, D. and Marsh, D. 2003: Policy networks and the GM crops issue: assessing the utility of a dialectical model of policy networks. *Public Administration* 81: 229–251.

Tomz, M. and van Houweling R. 2008: Candidate positioning and voter choice. *American Political Science Review* 102 (3): 303–318.

Tomz, M. and van Houweling, R. 2009: The electoral implications of candidate uncertainty. *American Political Science Review* 103 (1): 83–98.

Tönnies, F. 1974 [1887]: *Community and Association*. London: Routledge.

Tonry, M. 1996: *Malign Neglect: Race, Crime, and Punishment in America*. New York: Oxford University Press.

Tonry, M. 2004: *Thinking About Crime: Sense and Sensibility in American Penal Culture*. New York: Oxford University Press.

Tonry, M. 2009: Explanations of American punishment policies: a national history. *Punishment & Society* 11: 377–394.

Travis, J. 2005: *But They All Come Back: Facing The Challenges Of Prisoner Reentry*. Washington, DC: Urban Institute Press.

Triandafyllidou, A. 2001: *Immigrants and National Identity in Europe*. New York: Routledge.

Trigilia, C. 1998: *Sociologia economica. Stato, mercato e società nel capitalismo moderno*. Bologna: Il Mulino.

Tripp, A.M. 2006: The evolution of transnational feminisms: consensus, conflict, and new dynamics. Global feminism. In M.M. Ferree and A.M. Tripp (eds) *Global Feminism: Transnational Women's Activism, Organizing and Human Rights*. New York: New York University Press.

True, J. 2003: Mainstreaming gender in global public policy. *International Feminist Journal of Politics* 5 (3): 368–396.

True, J. and M. Mintrom 2001: Transnational networks and policy diffusion: the case of gender Mainstreaming. *International Studies Quarterly* 45 (1): 27–57.

Truman, D.B. 1951: *The Governmental Process: Political Interests and Public Opinion*. New York: Alfred A. Knopf.

Tsuda, T. 2003: *Strangers in the Ethnic Homeland: Japanese Brazilian Return Migration in Transnational Perspective*. New York: Columbia University Press.

Tsutsui, K. 2004: Global Civil Society and Ethnic Social Movements in the Contemporary World. *Sociological Forum* 19: 63–88.

Tsutsui, K. 2006: Redressing past human rights violations: global dimensions of contemporary social movements. *Social Forces* 85: 331–354.

Tsutsui, K. and Shin, H-J. 2008: Global norms, local activism and social movement outcomes: global human rights and resident Koreans in Japan. *Social Problems* 55: 391–418.

Turk, A. 1982: Social dynamics of terrorism. *Annals of the American Academy of Political and Social Science* 436 (1): 119–128.

Turner B.S. (ed.) 1993: *Citizenship and Social Theory*. London: Sage.

Turner, B.S. 1989: Outline of a theory of citizenship. *Sociology* 24: 89–217.

Turner, B.S. 1993: Outline of a theory of human rights. *Sociology* 27: 489–512.

Turner, B.S. 1996: *The Body and Society*, 2nd edn. London: Sage.

Turner, B.S. 2002: Cosmopolitan virtue, globalization and patriotism. *Theory, Culture and Society* 19 (1/2): 45–63.

Turner, B.S. 2006: *Vulnerability and Human Rights*. University Park: Pennsylvania University Press.

Tyler, I. 2008: Chav mum, chav scum: class disgust in contemporary Britain. *Feminist Media Studies* 8 (1): 17–34.

Uggen, C. and Manza, J. 2002: Democratic contraction? The political consequences of felon disenfranchisement in the United States. *American Sociological Review* 67: 777–803.

Uggen, C. Manza, J. and Thompson, M. 2006: Citizenship, democracy, and the civic reintegration of criminal offenders. *The Annals of the American Academy of Political and Social Science* 605: 281–310.

Uggen, C. van Brakle, M. and McLaughlin, H. 2009: Punishment and social exclusion: national differences in prisoner disenfranchisement. In A. Ewald and B. Rottinghaus *Criminal Disenfranchisement in an International Perspective*. Cambridge: Cambridge University Press.

United Nations. 1995: *Platform for Action and the Beijing Declaration*. New York.

Urry, J. 2003: *Sociology Beyond Societies*. London: Routledge.

Vail, L. 1993: *The Creation of Tribalism in Southern Africa*. London: James Curry.

Vajda, M. 1988: East-Central European Perspectives. In J. Keane (ed.) *Civil Society and the State: New European Perspectives*. London: Verso.

Valverde, M. 1996: 'Despotism' and ethical liberal governance. *Economy and Society* 25 (3): 357–372.

Valverde, M. 1998: *Diseases of the Will: Alcohol and the Dilemmas of Freedom*. Cambridge: Cambridge University Press.

van Creveld, M. 1989: *Technology and War: From 2000 B.C. to the Present*. New York: The Free Press.

van Creveld, M. 1991: *The Transformation of War*. New York: The Free Press.

van den Berghe, P.L. 1981: *The Ethnic Phenomenon*. New York: Elsevier Press.

van den Berghe, P.L. 1986: Ethnicity and the sociobiology debate. In J. Rex and D. Mason (eds) *Theories of Race and Ethnic Relations*. Cambridge: Cambridge University Press.

van der Brug, W., Fennema, M. and Tillie, J. 2005: Why some anti-immigrant parties fail and others succeed. A two-step model of aggregate electoral support. *Comparative Political Studies* 38: 537–573.

van der Ploeg, J.D. 2008: *The New Peasantries: Struggles for Autonomy and Sustainability in an Era of Empire and Globalization*. London: Earthscan.

Vannucci, A. 1997: *Il mercato della corruzione*. Milan: Società Aperta.

Vargas, V. and Wieringa S. 1998: Triangles of empowerment: processes and actors in the making of public policy. In G. Lycklama, A. Nijeholt, V. Vargas and S. Wieringa (eds) *Women's Movement and Public Policy in Europe, Latin America and the Caribbean*. New York: Garland.

Vertovec, S. 2004: Migrant transnationalism and modes of transformation. *International Migration Review* 38: 970–1001.

Vidich, A.J. and Bensman, J. 1968: *Small Town in Mass Society*. Princeton, NJ: Princeton University Press.

Voet, R. 1998: *Feminism and Citizenship*. London: Sage.

Vogel, D. 2008: Private global business regulation. *Annual Review of Political Science* 11: 261–282.

Vogel, U. 1988: Under permanent guardianship: women's condition under modern civil law. In K. B. Jones and A. G. Jónasdóttir (eds) *The Political Interests of Gender*. London: Sage.

Vogel, U. 1994: Marriage and the boundaries of citizenship. In B. van Steenbergen (ed.) *The Condition of Citizenship*. London: Sage.

Vogler, J. 2003: Taking institutions seriously: how regime analysis can be relevant to multilevel environmental governance. *Global Environmental Politics* 3 (2): 25–39.

Voyce M. 2006: Shopping malls in Australia: the end of public space and the rise of 'consumerist citizenship'? *Journal of Sociology* 42 (3): 269–228.

Vu, T. 2010: Studying the state through state formation. *World Politics* 62: 148–175.

Wacquant, L. 2001: Deadly symbiosis: when ghetto and prison meet and mesh. *Punishment & Society* 3: 95–133.

Wagner-Pacifici, R. and Schwartz, B. 1991: The Vietnam Veterans Memorial: commemorating a difficult past. *American Journal of Sociology* 97: 376–420.

Wakefield, S. 2007: *The Consequences of Incarceration for Parents and Children*. PhD thesis, University of Minnesota.

Wakefield, S. and Uggen, C. 2010: Incarceration and stratification. *Annual Review of Sociology* 36: 387–406.

Walby, S. 1994: Is citizenship gendered? *Sociology* 28 (2): 379–395.

Walby, S. 2002: Feminism in a global era. *Economy and Society* 31 (4): 533–557.

Wald, K. and Wilcox, C. 2006: Getting religion: has political science rediscovered the faith factor. *American Political Science Review* 100 (4): 523–529.

Waldfogel, J. 1994: The effect of criminal conviction on income and the trust 'reposed in the workmen.' *Journal of Human Resources* 29: 62–81.

Walker, H.A. and Cohen, B.P. 1985: Scope statements: imperatives for evaluating theory. *American Sociological Review* 50: 288–301.

Walker, J.L. Jr. 1991: *Mobilizing Interest Groups in America: Patrons, Professionals, and Social Movements*. Ann Arbor: University of Michigan Press.

Walker, R.B.J. 1994: Social Movements/World Politics. *Millennium* 23 (3): 669–700.

Walker, R.B.J. 2010: *After the Globe, Before the World*. New York: Routledge.

Walkerdine, V., Lucey, H. and Melody, J. 2002: *Growing up Girl: Psychsocial Explorations of Gender and Class*. Basingstoke: Palgrave.

Wallerstein, I. 1986: *Africa and the Modern World*, Trenton, NJ: Africa World Press.

Wallerstein, I. 1995: *After Liberalism*. New York: The New Press.

Wallman, S. 1978: The boundaries of race: processes of ethnicity in England. *Man*, 13: 200–217.

Walmsley, R. 2009: *World Prison Population List*, 8th edn. London: Home Office Research, Development and Statistics Directorate.

Walters, N. 2010: *Living Dolls. The Return of Sexism*. London: Virago Press.

Walton, J. 1966: Substance and artifact: the current status of research on community power structure. *American Journal of Sociology*, 71 (4): 430–438.

Walzer, M. 2004: *Arguing About War*. New Haven, CT: Yale University Press.

Wapner, P. 1995: Politics beyond the state: environmental activism and world civic politics. *World Politics*, 47 (3): 311–340.

Wapner, P. 2002: World Summit on Sustainable Development: toward a post Jo'Burg environmentalism. *Global Environmental Politics*, 3 (1): 1–10.

Warner, S.R. 1993: Work in progress toward a new paradigm for the sociological study of religion in the United States. *American Journal of Sociology* 98 (5): 1044–1093.

Warner, W.L. 1936: American class and caste. *American Journal of Sociology*. 42: 234–237.

Warner, W.L. 1949: *Social Class in America*. San Francisco: Harper and Row.

Wartenberg, T.E. (ed.) 1992: *Rethinking Power*. Albany: State University of New York Press.

Wasserman, S. and Faust, K. 1994: *Social Network Analysis: Methods and Applications*. New York: Cambridge University Press.

Waylen, G. 2008: Women's substantive representation: lessons from transitions to democracy. *Parliamentary Affairs*, 61 (3): 518–534.

Weaver, R. K. 2010: Paths and forks or chutes and ladders: negative feedbacks and policy regime change. *Journal of Public Policy*, 30, 137–162.

Weber, M. 1918a [1994]: Parliament and government in Germany under a new political order. In P. Lassman and R. Speirs (eds) *Weber: Political Writings*. Cambridge: Cambridge University Press.

Weber, M. 1918b [1994]: Socialism. In P. Lassman and R. Speirs (eds) *Weber: Political Writings*. Cambridge: Cambridge University Press.

Weber, M. 1919 [1994]: The profession and vocation of politics. In P. Lassman and R. Speirs (eds) *Weber: Political Writings*. Cambridge: Cambridge University Press.

Weber, M. 1948: *From Max Weber: Essays in Sociology*, ed. H.H. Gerth and C. Wright Mills. London: Routledge.

Weber, M. 1949a [1917]: The meaning of 'ethical neutrality' in sociology and economics. In E. Shils and H. Finch (eds) *The Methodology of the Social Sciences*. New York: The Free Press.

Weber M. 1949b [1904]: 'Objectivity' in Social Science and Social Policy. In E. Shils and H. Finch (eds) *The Methodology of the Social Sciences*. New York: The Free Press.

Weber, M. 1978 [1922]: *Economy and Society. An Outline of Interpretative Sociology*, ed. G. Roth and C. Wittich, 2 vols. Berkeley: University of California Press.

Weber, M. 1989 [1919]: Science as a vocation. In P. Lassman and I. Velody (eds) *Max Weber's Science as a Vocation*. London: Unwin Hyman.

Weber, M. 2002 [1920]: *The Protestant Ethic and the Spirit of Capitalism*, trans. S. Kalberg. Oxford: Blackwell.

Wedeen, L. 1999: *Ambiguities of Domination: Politics, Rhetoric, and Symbols in Contemporary Syria*. Chicago, IL: University of Chicago Press.

Weeden, K. and Grusky, D. 2005: The case for a new class map. *American Journal of Sociology* 111: 141–212.

Weininger, E. 2005: Foundations of Pierre Bourdieu's class analysis. In E.O. Wright (ed.) *Approaches to Class Analysis*. Cambridge: Cambridge University Press.

Weir, M. 1992: *Politics and Jobs: The Boundaries of Employment Policy in the United States* Princeton, NJ: Princeton University Press.

Weiss, L. 1998: *The Myth of the Powerless State*. Cambridge: Polity Press.

Weitz, R. (ed.) 1998: *The Politics of Women's Bodies. Sexuality, Appearance and Behaviour*. Oxford: Oxford University Press.

Wensley, R. 2009: Market ideology, globalization and neoliberalism. In P. Maclaran. M. Saren, B. Stern and M. Tadajewski (eds) *The Handbook of Marketing Theory*. London: Sage.

Wessels, B. 2004: Contestation potential of interest groups in the EU: emergence, structure, and political alliances. In Gary Marks and Marco Steenbergen *European Integration and Political Conflict: Citizens, Parties, Groups*. Cambridge: Cambridge University Press.

Western, B. 1997: *Between Class and Market*. Princeton, NJ: Princeton University Press.

Western, B. 2002: The impact of incarceration on wage mobility and inequality. *American Sociological Review* 67: 526–546.

Western, B. 2006: *Punishment and Inequality in America*. New York: Russell Sage Foundation.

Western, B. and Beckett, K. 1999: How unregulated is the US labor market? The penal system as a labor market institution. *American Journal of Sociology* 104: 1030–1060.

Western, B. and Wildeman, C. 2009: Punishment, inequality, and the future of mass incarceration. *Kansas Law Review* 57: 851–877.

Westholm, A. 1997: Distance versus direction: the illusory defeat of the proximity theory of electoral choice. *American Political Science Review* 91 (4): 865–884.

Weyland, K. 2007: The diffusion of revolution: '1848' in Europe and America. *International Organization* 63, 3: 391–423.

Whelehan, I. 2000: *Overloaded: Popular Culture and the Future of Feminism*. London: The Women's Press.

White, S., Gill, G. and Slider D. 1993: *The Politics of Transition: Shaping a post-Soviet Future*. Cambridge: Cambridge University Press.

Whittier, N. 1995: *Feminist Generations: The Persistence of the Radical Women's Movement*. Philadelphia, PA: Temple University Press.

Whyte, J. 1990: *Interpreting Northern Ireland*. Oxford: Clarendon Press.

Wictorowicz, Q. (ed.). 2004: *Islamic Activism*. Bloomington: Indiana University Press.

Wiest, D. 2007: A story of two transnationalisms: global salafi, jihad and transnational human rights mobilization in the Middle East and North Africa. *Mobilization* 12 (2): 137–160.

Wiktorowicz, Q. (ed.) 2004: *Islamic Activism. A Social Movement Theory Approach*. Bloomington: Indiana University Press.

Wiktorowicz, Q. and Kaltner, J. 2003: Killing in the name of Islam: Al-Qaeda's justification for September 11. *Middle East Policy* 10 (2): 76–92.

Wildavsky, A.1964: *Leadership in a Small Town*. Totowa, NJ: Bedminster Press.

Wildeman, C. 2009: Parental imprisonment, the prison boom, and the concentration of childhood advantage. *Demography* 46: 265–280.

Wildeman, C. 2010: Paternal incarceration and children's physically aggressive behaviors: evidence from the fragile families and child wellbeing study. *Social Forces* 89: 285–310.

Wilensky, H. 1975: *The Welfare State and Equality*. Berkeley: University of California Press.

Wilkinson, R. and Pickett, K. 2009: *The Spirit Level*. Harmondsworth: Penguin.

Williams, K.M. 2008: *Mark One or More: Civil Rights in Multiracial America*. Ann Arbor, MI: University of Michigan Press.

Williams, M. 2001: In search of global standards: the political economy of trade and the environment. In D. Stevis and V. Assetto (eds) *The International Political Economy of the Environment – Critical Perspectives*. 12th International Political Economy Yearbook. Colorado: Lynne Rienner.

Williams, M. 2003: Words, images, enemies: securitization and international politics. *International Studies Quarterly*, 47 (4): 511–532.

Williams, P. 2008: *Security Studies: An Introduction*. New York: Routledge.

Willis, P. 1977: *Learning to Labour: How Working Class Kids Get Working Class Jobs*. New York: Columbia University Press.

Wilson, K. 2007: Agency. In G. Blakeley and V. Bryson (eds) *The Impact of Feminism on Political Concepts and Debates.* Manchester: Manchester University Press.

Witte, J.M., Reinicke, W.H. and Benner, T. 2000: Beyond multilateralism: global public policy networks. *Internationale Politik und Gesellschaft* 2: 176–188.

Wittman, H., Desmarais, A.A. and Wiebe, N. (eds) 2010: *Food Sovereignty: Reconnecting Food, Nature and Community.* Halifax: Fernwood Publishing.

Wolf, E.R. 1969: *Peasant Wars of the Twentieth Century.* New York: Harper & Row.

Wolf, M. 2008: *Fixing Global Finance.* Baltimore, MD: John Hopkins University Press.

Wolford, W. 2010: *This Land Is Ours Now: Social Mobilization and The Meanings Of Land in Brazil.* Durham, NC: Duke University Press.

Wolin, S. 1996: Fugitive democracy. In S. Benhabib (ed.) *Democracy and Difference.* Princeton, NJ: Princeton University Press.

Wolpe, H. 1988: *Race, Class and the Apartheid State.* London: James Curry.

Woodcock, M. (1998): Social capital and economic development: towards a theoretical synthesis and policy framework. *Theory and Society* 27 (2): 151–208.

World Bank 1994: *Averting the Old Age Crisis. Policies to Protect the Old and Promote Growth.* Washington, DC: World Bank.

Wouters, C. 1986: Formalization and informalization: changing tension balances in civilizing process. *Theory, Culture and Society* 3 (2): 1–18.

Wright, E.O. 1985: *Classes.* London: Verso.

Wright, P. 1985: *On Living in an Old Country.* London: Verso.

Wuthnow, R. 1985: State Structures and Ideological Outcomes. *American Sociological Review* 50: 799–821.

Yackee, J.W. and Yackee, S.W. 2006: A bias towards business? Assessing interest group influence on the U.S. bureaucracy. *Journal of Politics* 68: 128–139.

Yeatman, A. 1993: *Post-modern Revisionings of the Political.* London: Routledge.

Young, I. 2000: *Inclusion and Democracy.* Oxford: Oxford University Press.

Young, I.M 1990a: *Throwing like a Girl and Other Essay in Feminist Philosophy and Social Theory.* Bloominghton: University of Indiana Press.

Young, I.M. 1990b: *Justice and the Politics of Difference.* Princeton, NJ: Princeton University Press.

Young, O. (ed.) 2000: *Global Governance,* 2nd edn. Cambridge, MA: MIT Press.

Young, O. 2002: *The Institutional Dimensions of Environmental Change.* Cambridge, MA: MIT Press.

Young, O., Schroeder, H. and King, L. (eds.) 2008: *Institutions and Environmental Change.* Cambridge, MA: MIT Press.

Yuval-Davis, N. 1997: *Gender and Nation.* London: Sage.

Yuval-Davis, N. 2006: Human/women's rights and feminist transversal politics. In M.M. Ferree and A.M. Tripp (eds) *Global Feminism: Transnational Women's Activism, Organizing and Human Rights.* New York: New York University Press.

Zerilli, L. 2005: *Feminism and the Abyss of Freedom.* Chicago, IL: University of Chicago Press.

Zerubavel, E. 1997: *Social Mindscapes: An Invitation to Cognitive Sociology.* Cambridge, MA: Harvard University Press.

Ziblatt, D. 2006a: *Structuring the State,* Princeton, NJ: Princeton University Press.

Ziblatt, D. 2006b: How did Europe democratize? *World Politics* 58 (2): 311–338.

Ziblatt, D. 2009: Shaping democratic practice and the causes of electoral fraud: the case of nineteenth-century Germany. *American Political Science Review* 103 (1): 1–21.

Ziliak, J.P. 2009: Introduction. In J.P. Ziliak (ed.) *Welfare Reform and Its Long-Term Consequences for America's Poor*. Cambridge: Cambridge University Press.

Zimring, F.E. and Hawkins, G.J. 1991: *The Scale of Imprisonment*. Chicago, IL: University of Chicago Press.

Žižek, S. 1989: *The Sublime Object of Ideology*. London: Verso.

Žižek, S. 2002: *Welcome to the Desert of the Real*. London: Verso.

Zolberg, A. 1999: Matters of state. In C. Hirschman, P. Kasinitz and J. DeWind (eds) *The Handbook of International Migration: The American Experience*. New York: Russell Sage Foundation.

Zuckerman, A (ed.) 2006: *The Social Logic of Politics*. Philadelphia, PA: Temple University Press.

Index

The Wiley-Blackwell Companion to Political Sociology, First Edition. Edited by Edwin Amenta,
Kate Nash, and Alan Scott.
© 2012 Blackwell Publishing Ltd. Published 2012 by Blackwell Publishing Ltd.